HISTORICAL DICTIONARY

The historical dictionaries present essential information on a broad range of subjects, including American and world history, art, business, cities, countries, cultures, customs, film, global conflicts, international relations, literature, music, philosophy, religion, sports, and theater. Written by experts, all contain highly informative introductory essays of the topic and detailed chronologies that, in some cases, cover vast historical time periods but still manage to heavily feature more recent events.

Brief A–Z entries describe the main people, events, politics, social issues, institutions, and policies that make the topic unique, and entries are cross-referenced for ease of browsing. Extensive bibliographies are divided into several general subject areas, providing excellent access points for students, researchers, and anyone wanting to know more. Additionally, maps, photographs, and appendixes of supplemental information aid high school and college students doing term papers or introductory research projects. In short, the historical dictionaries are the perfect starting point for anyone looking to research in these fields.

HISTORICAL DICTIONARIES OF SPORTS

Jon Woronoff, Series Editor

Competitive Swimming, by John Lohn, 2010.
Basketball, by John Grasso, 2011.
Golf, by Bill Mallon and Randon Jerris, 2011.
Figure Skating, by James R. Hines, 2011.
The Olympic Movement, Fourth Edition, by Bill Mallon and Jeroen Heijmans, 2011.
Tennis, by John Grasso, 2011.
Soccer, by Tom Dunmore, 2011.
Cycling, by Jeroen Heijmans and Bill Mallon, 2011.
Skiing, by E. John B. Allen, 2012.
Track and Field, by Peter Matthews, 2012.
Baseball, by Lyle Spatz, 2013.
Ice Hockey, by Laurel Zeisler, 2013.
Football, by John Grasso, 2013.

Historical Dictionary of Football

John Grasso

The Scarecrow Press, Inc.
Lanham • Toronto • Plymouth, UK
2013

Published by Scarecrow Press, Inc.
A wholly owned subsidiary of The Rowman & Littlefield Publishing Group, Inc.
4501 Forbes Boulevard, Suite 200, Lanham, Maryland 20706
www.rowman.com

10 Thornbury Road, Plymouth PL6 7PP, United Kingdom

Copyright © 2013 by John Grasso

All rights reserved. No part of this book may be reproduced in any form or by any electronic or mechanical means, including information storage and retrieval systems, without written permission from the publisher, except by a reviewer who may quote passages in a review.

British Library Cataloguing in Publication Information Available

Library of Congress Cataloging-in-Publication Data

Grasso, John.
 Historical dictionary of football / John Grasso.
  pages cm. — (Historical dictionaries of sports)
 Includes bibliographical references.
 ISBN 978-0-8108-7856-3 (cloth : alk. paper) — ISBN 978-0-8108-7857-0 (ebook) 1. Football—United States—Dictionaries. I. Title.
 GV948.85.G73 2013
 796.3303—dc23
                                                              2013001762

∞™ The paper used in this publication meets the minimum requirements of American National Standard for Information Sciences—Permanence of Paper for Printed Library Materials, ANSI/NISO Z39.48-1992. Printed in the United States of America

Contents

Editor's Foreword *Jon Woronoff*		vii
Reader's Note		ix
Preface		xi
Acronyms and Abbreviations		xiii
Chronology		xvii
Introduction		1
THE DICTIONARY		25
Appendixes		
A	Pro Football Hall of Fame Inductees	445
B	Canadian Football Hall of Fame Inductees	453
C	Super Bowl Champions	461
D	National Football League Champions	465
E	American Football League Champions	467
F	All-America Football Conference Champions	469
G	Grey Cup Champions	471
H	World Bowl Champions	477
I	International National Football League Games	479
J	Foreign-Born National Football League Players	483
K	Bowl Championship Series National Champions	495
L	College Champions	497
M	Rose Bowl Champions	505
N	Heisman Trophy Winners	509

O	National Collegiate Athletic Association Football Bowl Subdivision	513
P	Football Films	519
Bibliography		523
About the Author		559

Editor's Foreword

In most cases, sports unite nations in the sense that people play the same sports around the world. This certainly applies to all forms of athletics, and to tennis, golf, basketball, and gradually baseball. But in the case of football, the world is strangely divided, with mainly North Americans playing what is often called American football, while Europeans, Asians, Africans, and even Latin Americans are playing soccer, which, to compound the problem, is often also called football or something closely resembling that term. Admittedly, American football—or football for short, in this volume at least—is making inroads in other parts of the world, or it is at least familiar in one way or another to people in nonplaying countries. So this book actually has two possible publics, North Americans who know the game and want more details, especially records, and "others" who also need some basic tutoring in what the game is all about. By the way, although the word *playing* was used above, the vast majority of those who follow the sport do not actually play it, although they may have done so when they were younger, but watch it in the stadium or on television.

Historical Dictionary of Football does an exceptionally good job of presenting the sport to both publics. The introduction traces the birth and development of football; its gradual, if halting, spread abroad; the formation of rules and regulations; and particularly the emergence of major teams, leagues, and players. This information is examined more closely in the dictionary section, where the primary focus is on the teams and players, literally hundreds of them, and also the various rules and regulations, the different positions within the team, the plays and stratagems and other technical aspects, the leagues, and some of the figures who have made notable contributions to the sport. A list of acronyms and abbreviations assists readers in negotiating both the book and other literature on the subject. The impressive chronology demonstrates just how long football has been around and how it has progressed throughout the years. Numerous appendixes give detailed statistics on Hall of Fame inductees, league and bowl champions, and Heisman Trophy winners, just to name a few. The bibliography provides both general reading and works on specific teams or players with titles both for adults and juveniles.

This volume was written by John Grasso, someone who is becoming increasingly familiar to our readers. Grasso has already written *Historical Dictionary of Basketball* and *Historical Dictionary of Tennis*, and he is working on a similar volume on boxing. Aside from these works, he has written numerous articles on basketball and boxing in particular, which are mentioned in the author's note; however, as he says, his interest in sports is eclectic and wide ranging, and he was been following football since he was a kid, playing touch football and following the New York Giants and New York Jets. Throughout the years, he has attended numerous games both at the college and professional levels. Although this is his first book on football, he has considerable background as a researcher and is a member of the Professional Football Researchers Association.

Jon Woronoff
Series Editor

Reader's Note

One complication of a book about football is that while the season used to take place in the fall months with a postseason game on 1 January, the season now extends well into January and occasionally February. As such, the Super Bowl for the 2011 season is played in 2012. In speaking of the 2011 Super Bowl champion, it is unclear whether it is meant to be the winner of the game played in 2011 or the winner of the Super Bowl following the 2011 season (actually played in 2012). The NFL attempts to avoid this dilemma by assigning roman numerals to their Super Bowls, but to tell the reader that the Tampa Bay Buccaneers won Super Bowl XXXVII is not as informative as saying they won the 2003 Super Bowl. I have tried to use that convention throughout the book, that is, the year that the game was played rather than the season it represented.

When a team's record is cited as xx–xx–xx, it refers to the number of games won, lost, and tied; if listed as just xx–xx, then it is only games won and lost.

Such American football accolades as All-American, Most Valuable Player, and even national collegiate champion have been bestowed by several organizations and, as such, while noteworthy, do not carry the same weight as in other sports. Consequently, space requirements do not always permit recognizing each individual honor gained by players in the dictionary section.

College statistics are not exceptionally reliable, and there are often discrepancies both in terms of individual statistics and even a school's historical won-lost-tied record. This is especially true in recent years, as a school may have some of their game results vacated due to various recruiting infractions, and the vacated results are often reported differently in various sources. Another factor causing record discrepancies is that in the early part of the 20th century, some schools played rugby rather than football. The rivalry between California and Stanford is one such example. Some sources list the overall results between the two schools as 57–46–11 for Stanford, while others have the series at 52–43–10. The former result includes rugby games played between the two schools from 1906 to 1914.

The source used for this book for college statistics has been primarily the College Football Data Warehouse (www.cfbdatawarehouse.com).

To facilitate the rapid and efficient location of information and make this book as useful a reference tool as possible, extensive cross-references have been provided in the dictionary section. Within individual entries, terms that have their own entries are in **boldface** the first time they appear. Related terms that do not appear in the text are indicated in the *See also*. *See* refers to other entries that deal with the same topic.

Preface

It is impossible in a book of this size to cover all aspects of a sport that has been played for nearly 150 years. I have tried to include a fair representation of both amateur (collegiate) and professional players, coaches, teams, and executives from all eras. As can be seen by the list of individuals inducted into the Pro Football Hall of Fame (appendix A) and Canadian Football Hall of Fame (appendix B), there are many contributors to the sport who are omitted from this volume. Space limitations have restricted entries to brief sketches, and readers interested in additional details are advised to make use of the extensive bibliography. It is hoped that the information contained within this resource will provide the neophyte with a general introduction and that some of the anecdotal details will be of interest to the reader with a broader background.

I'd like to thank Dorothy A. Grasso for condoning my reclusive hobbies for more than 40 years; Steve Grasso, manufacturing engineer and Corvette and motocross racer; and Dr. Laurel Zeisler, speech therapist and ice hockey expert. All have provided their continuing encouragement and support. I'd also like to thank Rob Zeisler for attending a college football game with me, even though he would have rather been anywhere else; James Hernandez, Charlotte Valley soccer star; Trinity Grasso, international clarinetist; Lindsey Zeisler, percussionist and Egyptologist; and Dorothy Rose Zeisler, artist and trumpeter, for putting up with a silly grandpa. Thanks are also extended to Dr. Bill Mallon, orthopedic surgeon and Olympic Games expert, for getting me involved with this project and suggesting a few entries for the dictionary, including Johnny Chung, about whom I had completely forgotten; Tony Bijkerk, secretary general of the International Society of Olympic Historians, for information on Dutch books on American football; and Jon Woronoff, editor, for helping to bring this work to fruition.

This book is dedicated to my best friend, Stuart Demsker. I have known Stu since kindergarten, and he has been my companion for almost every football game I have witnessed in person. He has been a loyal New York Jets' season-ticket holder for more than 40 years, and I have been his guest nearly every year for a Jets' home game. For the past 20 years, we have also attempted to see a college football game at a different venue each year. Our football experiences have included Grambling versus Morgan State at Yankee Stadium, the Brooklyn Dodgers Continental Football League team at Randall's Island, most of the venerable Ivy League stadiums, and small colleges the likes of Wilkes, Hamilton, and C. W. Post, as well as such major schools as Syracuse and Virginia Tech. Stu's wife, Adele, is also worthy of mention, as she has put up with Stu's sports watching activities for 40 years without complaint and always has a nice hot meal ready when we return from a game.

Acronyms and Abbreviations

GENERAL

AAFC	All-America Football Conference
ABC	American Broadcasting Company
ACC	Atlantic Coast Conference
ACL	anterior cruciate ligament
AFAF	Asian Federation of American Football
AFC	American Football Conference
AFL	American Football League
APFA	American Professional Football Association
ASU	Arizona State University
BC	Boston College
BCS	Bowl Championship Series
BYU	Brigham Young University
CAA	Colonial Athletic Association
CBS	Columbia Broadcasting System
CFC	Canadian Football Council
CFL	Canadian Football League, Continental Football League
CRFU	Canadian Rugby Football Union
CRU	Canadian Rugby Union
DAC	Downtown Athletic Club
EFAF	European Federation of American Football
ESPN	Entertainment and Sports Programming Network
FBS	Football Bowl Subdivision
FCS	Football Championship Subdivision
FG	field goal
FSU	Florida State University
HBCU	historically black colleges and universities
IAAUS	Intercollegiate Athletic Association of the United States
IFAF	International Federation of American Football
IOC	International Olympic Committee
IRFU	Interprovincial Rugby Football Union
IWFL	Independent Women's Football League

LCF	Ligue Canadienne de Football
LSU	Louisiana State University
MEAC	Mid-Eastern Athletic Conference
MLB	Major League Baseball
MMA	mixed martial arts
MNF	*Monday Night Football*
MSU	Michigan State University
MVP	Most Valuable Player
MVSU	Mississippi Valley State University
NAFL	National American Football League
NAIA	National Association of Intercollegiate Athletics
NAIB	National Association of Intercollegiate Basketball
NASCAR	National Association for Stock Car Auto Racing
NBA	National Basketball Association
NBC	National Broadcasting Company
NCAA	National Collegiate Athletic Association
NCCAA	National Christian College Athletic Association
NFC	National Football Conference
NFHS	National Federation of State High School Associations
NFL	National Football League
NFLPA	National Football League Players Association
NHRA	National Hot Rod Association
NJCAA	National Junior College Athletic Association
NWFL	National Women's Football League
NYU	New York University
OFAF	Oceania Federation of American Football
OG	Olympic Games
ORFU	Ontario Rugby Football Union
OSU	Ohio State University
PAFAF	Pan American Federation of American Football
PAT	point after touchdown (conversion)
PFRA	Professional Football Researchers Association
PP&K	punt, pass, and kick
SDSU	San Diego State University
SEC	Southeastern Conference
SMU	Southern Methodist University
SUNY	State University of New York
SWAC	Southwestern Athletic Conference
SWC	Southwest Conference
TAMU	Texas A&M University
TCU	Texas Christian University
UCLA	University of California, Los Angeles

UFL	United Football League
USC	University of Southern California
USF	University of San Francisco
USFL	United States Football League
UTEP	University of Texas, El Paso
VMI	Virginia Military Institute
VPI	Virginia Polytechnic Institute (Virginia Tech)
WAC	Western Athletic Conference
WFA	Women's Football Alliance
WFL	World Football League
WIFU	Western Interprovincial Football Union
WLAF	World League of American Football
WSFL	Women's Spring Football League

COUNTRIES

AUS	Australia
CAN	Canada
ENG	England
ESP	Spain
GER	Germany
IRL	Ireland
JPN	Japan
MEX	Mexico
SWE	Sweden

POSITIONS

B	back
C	center
CB	cornerback
DB	defensive back
DE	defensive end
DL	defensive lineman
DT	defensive tackle
E	end
F	fullback
FB	fullback
FL	flanker
FS	free safety

G	guard
H	halfback
HB	halfback
K	kicker
LB	linebacker
LS	long snapper
MG	middle guard
ML	middle linebacker
NT	nose tackle
OL	offensive lineman
P	punter
PK	placekicker
Q	quarterback
QB	quarterback
R	running back
RB	running back
S	safety
SE	split end
SL	strong side linebacker
SS	strong safety
T	tackle
TB	tailback
TE	tight end
WB	wingback
WL	weak side linebacker
WR	wide receiver

Chronology

1861 Toronto, Ontario, Canada, 9 November: The first documented Canadian football game is played.

1869 New Brunswick, New Jersey, 6 November: A ball game is played between the College of New Jersey (now known as Princeton University) and Rutgers College (now Rutgers University) with 25 players to a side. It is considered by historians to be the first intercollegiate football game, although it bears little resemblance to the modern-day game. Rutgers wins six goals to four.

1873 New York, New York, 20 October: Representatives from Columbia University, Princeton University, Rutgers College, and Yale University meet and draft the first set of football rules.

1876 Springfield, Massachusetts, 23 November: The Intercollegiate Football Association is formed by representatives of Columbia University, Harvard University, and Princeton University. A representative from Yale University is also present at the meeting, which defines a set of football rules based on the Rugby Football Union rules.

1882 At a rules meeting, the system of downs is implemented. A team that does not gain five yards in three downs (or loses 10 yards in three downs) must give up the ball to their opponents.

1883 Canada, 6 January: The Ontario Rugby Football Union is formed.

1888 Amherst, Massachusetts: The first African American college football player, William H. Lewis, plays for Amherst College. After graduating from Amherst in 1892, Lewis transfers to Harvard Law School and plays football for Harvard University. Lewis goes on to become U.S. assistant attorney general in 1910.

1889 Caspar Whitney selects the first All-American college football team. It was published in *This Week's Sports* magazine. Of the 11 players selected, five are from Princeton, three from Yale, and three from Harvard. Included on that team are Amos Alonzo Stagg and William "Pudge" Heffelfinger of Yale.

1890 Pasadena, California, 1 January: The first Tournament of Roses Parade is held. Twelve years later, a college football game (later known as the Rose Bowl) is first held in conjunction with the parade. **West Point, New York, 29 November:** The first football game between the United States Military Academy (Army) and the United States Naval Academy (Navy) is played. Navy wins, 24–0.

1892 Pittsburgh, Pennsylvania, 12 November: Pudge Heffelfinger is paid $500, plus $25 in expenses, to play a game for the Allegheny Athletic Association against the Pittsburgh Athletic Club and becomes the first professional football player. He scores the game's only touchdown, and Allegheny wins, 4–0.

1896 Chicago, Illinois, 8 February: The presidents of the University of Chicago, the University of Illinois, the University of Michigan, the University of Minnesota, Northwestern University, Purdue University, and the University of Wisconsin meet to discuss intercollegiate athletics and found the Intercollegiate Conference of Faculty Representatives, more commonly known as the Western Conference. After more schools join, it is renamed the Big Ten Conference.

1901 Chicago, Illinois, 28 November: The University of Michigan concludes their game season with a 50–0 victory over the University of Iowa. Michigan's totals for the season are 10 victories, 506 points scored, and zero points scored against. They are invited to play a postseason game against Stanford University on New Year's Day.

1902 Pasadena, California, 1 January: The Tournament East–West football game is played at Tournament Park. The University of Michigan defeats Stanford University, 49–0. The game is played in conjunction with the Tournament of Roses Parade and is considered to be the first Rose Bowl, even though it was not then known by that name. **Elmira, New York, 21 November:** The Philadelphia Athletics professional football team defeats the Kanaweola Athletic Club, 39–0, in the first professional football game played at night. **New York, New York, 29 December:** Syracuse Athletic Club defeats New York, 5–0, at Madison Square Garden in the first indoor professional game. Three nights later, they defeat the Orange Athletic Club, 36–0, to win a tournament billed as the "World Series of Football."

1903 Indianapolis, Indiana, 31 October: A train en route to Indianapolis for the Purdue–Indiana football game crashes and kills 17 people, including 14 members of the Purdue football team. Among the survivors is Purdue player and future governor of Indiana Harry G. Leslie, who, after being thought dead and taken to the morgue, is revived.

1905 Washington, D.C., 9 October: President Theodore Roosevelt invites university representatives Dr. Edward H. Nichols (team physician) and head coach William T. Reid of Harvard, head coach Arthur Hildebrand and John B. Fine (athletic committee head) of Princeton, and Walter Camp (athletic head) and head coach John Owsley of Yale University to a luncheon at the White House, along with Secretary of State Elihu Root, to discuss football and possible methods for eliminating its brutality. It is hoped by the president that with the cooperation of the athletic advisors, the rules may be amended to eliminate the brutality that makes the game objectionable to many people. **Chicago, Illinois, 30 November:** The University of Chicago defeats the University of Michigan, 2–0, ending Michigan's 56-game winning streak. During that time, Michigan outscored their opponents 2,821 to 40.

1906 New York, New York, 31 March: In response to President Theodore Roosevelt's request to enact reforms to better control the sport of football, 62 schools become charter members of the Intercollegiate Athletic Association of the United States (IAAUS). In 1910, the organization's name is changed to the National Collegiate Athletic Association (NCAA).

1908 Washington, Pennsylvania, 19 September: Washington & Jefferson College defeats Denison University and becomes the first college whose players wear numbers on their uniforms.

1909 Toronto, Ontario, Canada, 4 December: The University of Toronto Varsity Blues defeat the Toronto Parkdale Canoe Club, 26–6, in an amateur rugby contest to win a trophy commissioned by the Canadian governor general, Albert Henry George Grey, the 4th Earl Grey. The trophy becomes known as the Grey Cup and is now awarded to the champion of the Canadian Football League.

1911 Cambridge, Massachusetts, 11 November: The Carlisle Indian School, led by Jim Thorpe under coach Glenn "Pop" Warner, defeats Harvard University, 18–15. Harvard had been national collegiate champions the previous year.

1912 New York, New York, 3 February: The football rules committee announces a series of major rules changes. The three most significant ones are as follows: a touchdown is now worth six points rather than the previous five; four downs are permitted to gain 10 yards instead of three downs; the field is shortened from 110 yards to 100 yards.

1916 Pasadena, California, 1 January: The first game known as the "Rose Bowl" is played at Tournament Park. The State College of Washington (now known as Washington State University) defeats Brown University,

14–0. **Atlanta, Georgia, 7 October:** Georgia Tech defeats Cumberland College, 222–0, in the most one-sided football game in history. **Kankakee, Illinois, 14 October:** St. Viator College defeats Lane Technical Institute, 205–0. Leo Schlick of St. Viator scores exactly 100 points in the game on 12 touchdowns and 28 of 29 extra points.

1917 Annapolis, Maryland, 6 October: West Virginia University defeats the Naval Academy, 7–0. This is the first game that a college team coached by Gil Dobie has lost.

1920 Canton, Ohio, 20 August: At a meeting attended by representatives of four Ohio-based professional football clubs, the Akron Pros, Canton Bulldogs, Cleveland Indians, and Dayton Triangles, the American Professional Football Conference is formed. **Canton, Ohio, 17 September:** At a subsequent meeting that includes representatives of two teams from Indiana (the Hammond Pros and Muncie Flyers), three teams from Illinois (the Rock Island Independents, Decatur Staleys, and Racine Cardinals [based in Chicago]), and the Rochester Jeffersons (based in New York), the 10-team league is renamed the American Professional Football Association (APFA), and Jim Thorpe is named league president. **Rock Island, Illinois, 25 September:** The Rock Island Independents defeat the St. Paul Ideals, 48–0, in the first game of the newly formed APFA. Rock Island's victory counts toward the APFA's final standings even though St. Paul is not a league member.

1921 Pittsburgh, Pennsylvania, 8 October: The University of Pittsburgh defeats the University of West Virginia, 21–13, in their traditional rivalry game known as the "Backyard Brawl." The game is broadcast on KDKA radio and is the first college football game to be broadcast. **Boston, Massachusetts, 29 October:** Centre College, a school of only 300 students, defeats Harvard University, 6–0. Harvard had been national champions in 1919 and 1920, and this upset victory by Centre's Praying Colonels is later rated the number one sports upset of the first half of the 20th century by the Associated Press in 1950.

1922 Milwaukee, Wisconsin, 30 September: The Oorang Indians of Marion, Ohio, play their first National Football League (NFL) game against the Milwaukee Badgers and are defeated, 13–2. The Indians, led by Jim Thorpe, are composed entirely of Native Americans on a team organized by Airedale dog breeder Walter Lingo, primarily to promote his Oorang Kennels of LaRue, Ohio.

1924 New York, New York, 18 October: In describing the results of the Notre Dame upset of Army at the Polo Grounds, sportswriter Grantland Rice refers to the Notre Dame backfield as the "Four Horsemen." **Champaign,**

Illinois, 18 October: In the first game played at the University of Illinois' new Memorial Stadium, Harold "Red" Grange of Illinois returns the opening kickoff 95 yards for a touchdown. He then runs for touchdowns of 67, 56, and 44 yards in the first quarter. By the end of the game he had run for five touchdowns; passed for one touchdown; and compiled 212 yards rushing, 64 yards passing, and 126 yards on kickoff returns. Illinois defeats Michigan, 39–14, and stops Michigan's 20-game winning streak. **Billings, Montana, 1 November:** Forrest "Frosty" Peters of the Montana State College freshman team dropkicks 17 field goals in a game in 25 attempts against Billings Polytechnic Institute. Montana State wins the game, 64–0. Peters transfers to the University of Illinois after his freshman year and later plays briefly in the NFL.

1925   Pasadena, California, 1 January: Elmer Layden scores three touchdowns, two on long interception returns, to lead Notre Dame to a 27–10 victory over previously undefeated Stanford and win the national collegiate championship. **Chicago, Illinois, 23 November:** Famed collegian Red Grange signs with the Chicago Bears of the NFL to play the remaining games of the season for $2,000 per game plus a percentage of the gate receipts. **Chicago, Illinois, 26 November:** Grange's presence on the Bears attracts a crowd estimated at 40,000 to Chicago's Wrigley Field (then known as Cubs' Park), the largest attendance for a professional football game to that date. **New York, New York, 6 December:** Grange's appearance in New York draws an estimated 70,000 fans to the Polo Grounds and saves the season for the New York Giants' owners.

1928   Bronx, New York, 10 November: Notre Dame upsets Army, 12–6, after Notre Dame coach Knute Rockne inspires his team with a halftime speech to win the game for the "Gipper," former Notre Dame star player George Gipp, who died in 1920.

1929   Pasadena, California, 1 January: In the second quarter of the Rose Bowl, center Roy Riegels of the University of California picks up a fumble but runs the wrong way. Chased by a teammate and Georgia Tech players, he is tackled on his own one-yard line. On the ensuing play, California attempts a punt, but it is blocked through their own end zone for a two-point safety. Both teams later score touchdowns, but Georgia Tech wins the game by a score of 8–7. **Providence, Rhode Island, 10 November:** The Providence Steam Roller is defeated by the Frankford Yellow Jackets. This is the fourth NFL game for Providence in six days. They lose three and tie one. **Chicago, Illinois, 28 November:** Ernie Nevers of the Chicago Cardinals scores all 40 of his team's points in a defeat of the Chicago Bears. He runs for a record six touchdowns (still the NFL record) and kicks four extra points. **New York, 29**

November: Long Island University defeats Brooklyn College, 22–11, to win the New York Metropolitan Conference championship in a game played under the Pop Warner experimental scoring system. Under these rules, the point after a touchdown is eliminated, touchdowns count for six points, and first downs are worth one point. Another modification to the rule eliminates the second-half kickoff and places the ball at the spot where the first half ended.

1931   Chase County, Kansas, 31 March: Notre Dame coach Knute Rockne is killed in an airplane crash en route to Los Angeles.

1932   Los Angeles, California, 8 August 1932: An American football game is played as a demonstration sport at the Olympic Games. An all-star game between seniors from three West Coast colleges (California, Stanford, and the University of Southern California) and three East Coast colleges (Harvard, Yale, and Princeton) is played, with the West Coast team winning, 7–6. **Chicago, Illinois, 18 December:** After the Portsmouth Spartans and Chicago Bears finish the regular season in a tie for first place, a tiebreaking playoff game is scheduled. Due to extreme weather conditions, the game is moved indoors to Chicago Stadium. The game is played on an 80-yard field with other special rules in place and is won by the Bears, 9–0. As a result of the popular success of the game, an annual postseason playoff game is scheduled for the following season.

1933   Chicago, Illinois, 17 December: The Chicago Bears defeat the New York Giants at Wrigley Field, 23–13, in the league's first postseason championship game.

1934   Chicago, Illinois, 31 August: The first College All-Star game is played at Soldier Field before a crowd of 79,432 and ends in a scoreless tie. The game, a creation of Chicago sportswriter Arch Ward, is played to benefit Chicago-area charities and matches the previous season's NFL champions, the Chicago Bears, against an all-star team of graduated college seniors. **New York, New York, 9 December:** The New York Giants defeat the Chicago Bears, 30–13, on an icy field at the Polo Grounds. Trailing 13–3, the Giants don sneakers borrowed from a local college in the second half and, with the added traction, score 27 points in the final quarter to win.

1935   El Paso, Texas, 1 January: The first Sun Bowl is played. A team of El Paso All-Stars defeats a team from Ranger College, 25–21. **Miami, Florida, 1 January:** The first Orange Bowl is played. Bucknell University defeats the University of Miami (Florida), 26–0, before 5,134 fans at Miami Field. **New Orleans, Louisiana, 1 January:** The first Sugar Bowl takes place at Tulane Stadium. Tulane University defeats Temple University, 20–14. **New York, New York, 9 December:** The Downtown Athletic Club (DAC) presents a trophy to halfback Jay Berwanger of the University of Chicago as the best college football player east of the Mississippi River. The award, known as the Downtown Athletic Club Trophy, is renamed the Heisman Memorial Trophy in 1936, after the death of John Heisman, athletic director of the DAC.

1936 Philadelphia, Pennsylvania, 8 February: The NFL holds its first draft of college players at the Ritz-Carlton Hotel. With the first overall selection, the Philadelphia Eagles pick Heisman Trophy winner Jay Berwanger, who declines their contract offer and opts to enter the business world.

1937 Dallas, Texas, 1 January: The initial Cotton Bowl game is played. Texas Christian University defeats Marquette University, 16–6, before 17,000 fans. **Havana, Cuba, 1 January:** Auburn and Villanova tie, 7–7, in a game billed as the Bacardi Bowl. The game is almost canceled when it is discovered that Cuban dictator Fulgencio Batista's photograph is not included in the game program. After it is added, the game is permitted to be played.

1939 Los Angeles, California, 15 January: At Wrigley Field, the NFL plays its first All-Star Game. The NFL champion New York Giants defeat a team of league all-stars, 13–10.

1940 Hanover, New Hampshire, 16 November: Due to an error by the officials, Cornell University receives a fifth down with nine seconds remaining in the game and uses it to score a touchdown, giving them a 7–3 victory over Dartmouth College and extending their winning streak to 19 consecutive games. Afterward, a review of the films of the game discloses the mistake. Cornell sends a telegram acknowledging their defeat and offers the victory to Dartmouth. **Washington, D.C., 8 December:** The Chicago Bears defeat the Washington Redskins, 73–0, in the NFL championship game. Through 2012, no NFL team has ever scored more points in either a regular-season or playoff game.

1941 Clementon, New Jersey, 4 January: At a meeting of the NCAA Football Rules Committee, unlimited substitution is permitted at any time during the game. Previously, the same player could not be substituted twice within the same quarter, and most players played both offense and defense as a result. **7 December:** The NFL plays its regular schedule, with games in New York, Chicago, and Philadelphia. During the games, announcements are made in the stadiums requesting all military personnel to immediately report to their units. Fans remain unaware that Pearl Harbor has been bombed until the games conclude.

1942 Durham, North Carolina, 1 January: Less than one month after the bombing of Pearl Harbor, the U.S. government prohibits large public gatherings on the West Coast and forbids the playing of the annual Rose Bowl at the 100,000-seat venue in Pasadena, California. The game is relocated to Durham and is played before an estimated crowd of 56,000 fans.

1943 Chicago, Illinois, 19 June: At a meeting of NFL owners, it is decided to allow the Philadelphia Eagles and Pittsburgh Steelers to merge for the 1943 season, since both teams were shorthanded due to the war. The team would be based in Philadelphia, with Philadelphia coach Earle "Greasy" Neale and Pittsburgh coach Walt Kiesling becoming co-coaches. **Washington, D.C., 15 November:** Sammy Baugh of the Washington Redskins sets an NFL record by intercepting four Detroit Lions passes. Baugh also throws four touchdown passes himself as Washington defeats Detroit, 42–20.

1944 Chicago, Illinois, 4 June: Arch Ward, a sportswriter for the *Chicago Tribune*, organizes the All-America Football Conference (AAFC), a professional league in direct competition with the NFL. The AAFC begins play during the 1946 season.

1945 Cleveland, Ohio, 16 December: In the first quarter of the NFL championship game, Washington Redskins quarterback Sammy Baugh attempts to pass from his own end zone and the pass hits the goalpost. The result of the play is a safety, which becomes the margin of defeat as the Cleveland Rams win, 15–14. The NFL later changes the rule so that future errant passes that hit the crossbar are just considered incomplete passes.

1946 New York, New York, 12 January: De Benneville "Bert" Bell, president and part owner of the Pittsburgh Steelers, is chosen as NFL commissioner, replacing Elmer Layden, who was fired the previous day. **Cleveland, Ohio, 6 September:** The Cleveland Browns defeat the Miami Seahawks, 44–0, before 60,135 fans at Municipal Stadium in the opening game in the AAFC.

1948 Philadelphia, Pennsylvania, 19 December: The Philadelphia Eagles defeat the Chicago Cardinals, 7–0, in a driving snowstorm to win the NFL championship. Steve Van Buren's five-yard run for a touchdown in the fourth quarter is the game's only score.

1949 Philadelphia, Pennsylvania, 9 December: The AAFC and NFL merge, forming the National American Football League (NAFL). The new league contains 13 teams, 10 from the former NFL, plus the Cleveland Browns, Baltimore Colts, and San Francisco 49ers from the AAFC. Three months later, the NAFL reverts to the old name of the National Football League.

1950 Ottawa, Ontario, Canada, 12 August: The New York Giants of the NFL play a preseason exhibition game against the Canadian football team the Ottawa Rough Riders. The first half is played under Canadian rules and the second half using NFL rules. This is the first game of any kind played by the NFL outside of the United States. **Philadelphia, Pennsylvania, 16 September:** In a Super Bowl of sorts, the AAFC champion Cleveland Browns defeat the NFL champion Philadelphia Eagles, 35–10, in the first game of the regular season after the Browns and two other AAFC teams have been merged into the NFL. **Columbus, Ohio, 25 November:** In a game played in near-blizzard conditions, Michigan wins a Rose Bowl berth by defeating Ohio State, 9–3, despite not gaining a first down or completing a forward pass. Two blocked punts, one recovered in the end zone for a touchdown and the other blocked out of the end zone for a safety, are the game's only scores.

1951 Los Angeles, California, 28 September: Quarterback Norm Van Brocklin of the Los Angeles Rams passes for a record 554 yards in a 54–14 victory over the New York Yanks (still the NFL record as of the 2012 season). **New Brunswick, New Jersey, 3 November:** The College Football Hall of Fame is established; 32 players and 21 coaches are named to its inaugural class, which is announced at the Rutgers–Fordham football game. A campaign to raise funds for a permanent home for the Hall is begun, but it is not until 1978 that a permanent site is created.

1952 Dallas, Texas, 19 January: Giles Miller purchases the New York Yanks franchise and establishes an NFL team in Dallas. After seven games with minimal attendance, Miller returns the team to the league and it plays its last five games as a road team.

1953 Baltimore, Maryland, 7 September: In the first game ever played by the new Baltimore Colts franchise, defensive back Bert Rechichar of the Colts kicks a record 56-yard field goal in his first field-goal attempt in the NFL. He also returns a pass interception for a touchdown.

1954 Dallas, Texas, 1 January: In the Cotton Bowl, Dicky Moegle of Rice Institute is tackled by Tommy Lewis of the University of Alabama while running down the sideline for a potential touchdown. Lewis was not in the game at the time but standing near his team's bench helmetless.

1955 Portland, Oregon, 29 August: In a preseason exhibition game, under experimental rules, the Los Angeles Rams defeat the New York Giants, 23–17, in overtime. The Rams win the toss for possession to start the overtime and march 70 yards, with Paul "Tank" Younger rushing for the final two yards and the game-winning touchdown.

1956 Winnipeg, Manitoba, Canada, 22 January: The Canadian Football Council is formed, combining the two major leagues of Canadian football, the Western Interprovincial Football Union and the Interprovincial Rugby Football Union (also known as the Big Four). This new organization eventually leads to interleague play in 1958 as the Canadian Football League (CFL). **Chilliwack, British Columbia, Canada, 9 December:** Gordon Sturtridge, Mel Becket, Ray Syrnyk, and Mario DeMarco, all members of the CFL Saskatchewan Roughriders, are killed in a plane crash while returning from the league's All-Star Game in Vancouver.

1957 San Francisco, California, 27 October: Tony Morabito, owner of the San Francisco 49ers, dies of a heart attack during the 49ers game against the Chicago Bears at Kezar Stadium. The 49ers are apprised of the fact at halftime and rally from a 17–7 deficit to win, 21–17. **Norman, Oklahoma, 16 November:** Notre Dame University defeats the University of Oklahoma, 7–0, ending Oklahoma's record winning streak at 47 games. The defeat takes place on Statehood Day in Oklahoma, the 50th anniversary of Oklahoma's entering the Union.

1958 Fort Lauderdale, Florida, 12 January: The NCAA Football Rules Committee passes a new rule allowing for two points on a conversion after a touchdown if the ball is run or passed over the goal line from the three-yard line. The one-point conversion for a placekick or dropkick through the uprights remains in effect. This is the first change to a scoring rule since 1912. **Winnipeg, Manitoba, Canada, 19 January:** The Canadian Football Council is renamed the Canadian Football League. **New York, New York, 28 December:** The Baltimore Colts defeat the New York Giants, 23–17, on a one-yard run by Alan Ameche at 8:15 of overtime. This is the first NFL non-exhibition game to go into overtime and is described by some as the "greatest game ever played."

1959 Los Angeles, California, 23 March: The Los Angeles Rams of the NFL trade nine players to the Chicago Cardinals for only one player, Ollie Matson, the star running back. Neither team improves significantly as a result of the unusual trade. **Philadelphia, Pennsylvania, 11 October:** NFL commissioner Bert Bell suffers a heart attack and dies while watching the Philadelphia Eagles–Pittsburgh Steelers NFL game.

1960 Boston, Massachusetts, 9 September: The Denver Broncos defeat the Boston Patriots, 13–9, at Nickerson Field in the first game of the American Football League (AFL). Gino Cappelletti of Boston scores the league's first points with a 35-yard field goal in the first quarter. **Houston, Texas, 9**

October: Howard Glenn of the Titans of New York suffers a broken neck in a game against the Houston Oilers and succumbs later that day. **Toledo, Ohio, 29 October:** A plane carrying the California Polytechnic State University football team crashes during takeoff at Toledo Express Airport. Twenty-two of the 48 people onboard are killed, including 16 members of the football team.

1961 Miami, Florida, 7 January: The Detroit Lions defeat the Cleveland Browns, 17–16, in a game matching the NFL's second-place teams. The game, officially called the Bert Bell Benefit Bowl (but more popularly known as the Playoff Bowl or Runner-Up Bowl), is played annually through 1970.

1962 Toronto, Ontario, Canada, 1–2 December: The Grey Cup is suspended with 9:29 left in the fourth quarter as fog makes the field unplayable. The fog began in the second quarter, and, by the fourth quarter, fans could not see the action on the field, receivers could not see the quarterback, and punt returners could not see the ball in the air. The game is resumed the following day, and Winnipeg defeats Hamilton, 28–27, for the championship of the CFL. **Houston, Texas, 23 December:** The Houston Oilers defeat the Dallas Texans in the AFL championship game on a 25-yard field goal by Tommy Brooker at 2:54 of the second 15-minute overtime period. This is the first professional game to go to two overtimes.

1963 Canton, Ohio, 7 September: The Pro Football Hall of Fame is established in Canton, Ohio. The 17-member inaugural class consists of players Sammy Baugh, Earl "Dutch" Clark, Harold "Red" Grange, Mel Hein, Wilbur "Pete" Henry, Robert "Cal" Hubbard, Don Hutson, John "Blood" McNally, Bronko Nagurski, Ernie Nevers, and Jim Thorpe, while coaches George Halas and Earl "Curly" Lambeau and contributors Bert Bell, Joe Carr, Tim Mara, and George Preston Marshall are also inducted. **Washington, D.C., 24 November:** After conferring with White House press secretary Pierre Salinger, NFL commissioner Alvin "Pete" Rozelle decides that the league will play all scheduled football games on Sunday, 25 November, just two days after President John F. Kennedy's assassination. Rozelle later says that it was the worst mistake he made in his career. **Philadelphia, Pennsylvania, 7 December:** Instant replay is used for the first time in televising a football game. Although technical problems prevent it from being used earlier in the game, Army's final touchdown run by quarterback Rollie Stichweh in the fourth quarter is replayed, causing fans watching on television to be confused and think that Army had scored again. The game had been postponed from its original 24 November scheduled date due to the assassination of President John F. Kennedy.

1964 Rensselaer, Indiana, 27 July: Chicago Bears' running back Willie Galimore and split end John "Bo" Farrington are killed in an automobile accident. **Buffalo, New York, 13 September:** In an AFL game, Pete Gogolak kicks two field goals and four extra points in the Buffalo Bills' 34–17 win over the Kansas City Chiefs. Gogolak is the first player to kick soccer-style using the side of his foot rather than his toe. His success prompts other teams to employ former soccer players as their placekickers. **San Francisco, California, 25 October:** Minnesota Vikings' defensive end Jim Marshall picks up a fumble, runs 66 yards with the ball to the end zone, and throws the ball out of the end zone in celebration of what he thinks is a touchdown. Unfortunately, he gets twisted around after recovering the ball and runs the wrong way, and the result is a safety against the Vikings. Despite the gaffe, the Vikings win, 27–22.

1965 Miami Beach, Florida, 2 January: After his University of Alabama team loses to the University of Texas in the Orange Bowl, 21–17, Joe Namath signs a contract with the New York Jets of the AFL for a reported $427,000. This action serves to escalate the war between the AFL and NFL. **Chicago, Illinois, 12 December:** Rookie running back Gale Sayers of the Chicago Bears ties an NFL record by scoring six touchdowns in the Bears' 61–20 defeat of the San Francisco 49ers.

1966 New York, New York, 8 June: The NFL and AFL agree on the terms of a future merger between the two leagues. The leagues will operate as separate entities through 1969, but a postseason championship game between each league's champion will be held beginning in January 1967. A common draft will be held in March 1967, effectively ending the bidding war for college players. **Washington, D.C., 27 November:** The Washington Redskins defeat the New York Giants, 72–41. The 113 total points is the most scored in an NFL game. Washington kicks a field goal with seven seconds left to set the regular-season record of 72 points. Giants' kicker Pete Gogolak kicks five of six extra points and misses two field-goal attempts. His brother, Charlie, playing for the Redskins, kicks nine of 10 extra points and one field goal.

1967 Los Angeles, California, 16 January: The Green Bay Packers of the NFL defeat the Kansas City Chiefs of the AFL, 35–10, before 61,946 fans in the 93,000-seat Los Angeles Coliseum in the first AFL–NFL world championship game. The game, later known as the Super Bowl, is televised by both the CBS and NBC television networks, each with a separate announcing staff. **Washington, D.C., 12 June:** The U.S. Supreme Court rules in favor of plaintiff Wally Butts, former University of Georgia head football coach, in his suit against Curtis Publishing Company, publishers of the *Saturday Eve-*

ning Post. Butts sued for libel after the *Post* ran an article alleging that he and University of Alabama head coach Paul "Bear" Bryant had conspired to fix games. **Green Bay, Wisconsin, 31 December:** The Green Bay Packers defeat the Dallas Cowboys, 21–17, on a quarterback sneak by Bart Starr behind Jerry Kramer's block with 16 seconds remaining to win the NFL championship. The weather conditions are possibly the worst ever for a professional football game, with the temperature holding at -15 degrees Fahrenheit and a windchill factor of -48 degrees Fahrenheit. Several players are subsequently treated for frostbite.

1968 Oakland, California, 17 November: NBC breaks away from the New York Jets–Oakland Raiders AFL game with the Jets leading, 32–29, with one minute to play to present a filmed presentation of the Johanna Spyri children's classic *Heidi*. The Raiders score two touchdowns in the final minute and defeat the Jets, 43–32. Football viewers flood the NBC switchboards with protests, resulting in television networks' decision to telecast future games in their entirety, regardless of the length of game.

1969 Miami, Florida, 12 January: The New York Jets become the first AFL team to win the Super Bowl with their 16–7 upset victory of the NFL's Baltimore Colts. **Denver, Colorado, 21 September:** Steve O'Neal of the New York Jets is credited with a 98-yard punt in a game against the Denver Broncos. With the ball on the Jets' one-yard line, O'Neal punts from his end zone. The ball lands over the head of Denver's receiver and rolls to the Denver one-yard line, where it is downed by the Jets. **New Brunswick, New Jersey, 26 September:** The U.S. Postal Service issues a six-cent stamp commemorating 100 years of intercollegiate football.

1970 Orlando, Florida, 15 August: Pat Palinkas becomes the first woman to appear in a professional football game when she is the placekick holder for her husband, Steve Palinkas, for the Orlando Panthers in an Atlantic Coast Football League preseason game. **Los Angeles, California, 18 September:** The NFL completes its merger with the AFL, and the first game of the new 26-team league is played. The Los Angeles Rams defeat the St. Louis Cardinals, 34–13, in a rare Friday night game. **Cleveland, Ohio, 21 September:** *Monday Night Football* debuts on the ABC television network. Keith Jackson, Don Meredith, and Howard Cosell announce the game at Cleveland Stadium between the Cleveland Browns and New York Jets. The Browns win, 31–21. **Silver Plume, Colorado, 2 October:** A twin-engined propliner airplane carrying part of the Wichita State University football team crashes into a mountain en route to Logan, Utah, for a scheduled game with Utah State. Of the 36 passengers and crew of four, 31 die. **New Orleans, Louisiana, 8**

November: Tom Dempsey kicks a 63-yard field goal on the final play of the game to give the New Orleans Saints a 19–17 victory over the Detroit Lions. This is the longest field goal in NFL history, breaking the previous record by seven yards. **Ceredo, West Virginia, 14 November:** A chartered airplane carrying 37 members of the Marshall University football team, eight Marshall coaches, and 25 football fans crashes while landing at Tri-State Airport. All 75 passengers, including the four-person flight crew and an employee of the airline, are killed.

1971 Detroit, Michigan, 24 October: Wide receiver Chuck Hughes of the Detroit Lions suffers a fatal heart attack in a game against the Chicago Bears at Tiger Stadium. **Chicago, Illinois, 31 October:** Dallas Cowboys' coach Tom Landry, with two top-caliber quarterbacks on his team, Craig Morton and Roger Staubach, alternates them on nearly every play. The experiment fails, as the Cowboys lose to the Chicago Bears, 23–19, despite gaining 481 yards of offense and 26 first downs to the 194 yards and seven first downs tallied by the Bears.

1972 Hamilton, Ontario, Canada, 28 November: The Canadian Football Hall of Fame opens. **Pittsburgh, Pennsylvania, 23 December:** In the American Football Conference (AFC) Divisional Playoff game with no timeouts left, 22 seconds remaining in the game, Pittsburgh losing, 7–6, and the ball on the Oakland Raiders' 40-yard line, Pittsburgh quarterback Terry Bradshaw's pass is deflected and caught at the shoe tops by Pittsburgh running back Franco Harris, who continues running with it and scores the winning touchdown. The play is later dubbed the "Immaculate Reception" by sportswriter Myron Cope.

1973 Los Angeles, California, 14 January: The Miami Dolphins defeat the Washington Redskins, 14–7, in the Super Bowl to cap an undefeated season with their 17th consecutive victory. The Dolphins are the first NFL team to finish 14–0 in the regular season.

1974 New York, New York, 25 April: The NFL announces several major rule changes for the 1974 season. Among them are moving the goalposts back 10 yards from the goal line to the end line at the back of the end zone, moving kickoffs back from the 40-yard line to the 35-yard line, missed field-goal attempts beyond the 20-yard line being spotted at the line of scrimmage instead of the 20-yard line, and a 15-minute sudden-death overtime period being played when regular-season games are tied after the 60 minutes of regulation time. **Philadelphia, Pennsylvania, 10 July:** The Philadelphia Bell defeat the Portland Storm, 33–8, in one of five inaugural games in the new World Football League. They draw a crowd of 55,534, the highest attendance of the five games. Other games are played in Birmingham, Alabama; Memphis, Tennessee; Chicago, Illinois; and Orlando, Florida. **Denver, Colorado, 22 September:** The Denver Broncos and Pittsburgh Steelers play the first regular-season overtime game in NFL history. Although the game is tied, 35–35, at the end of regulation time, neither team scores in the sudden-death 15-minute overtime period, and the final result is a tie.

1976 Chicago, Illinois, 23 July: The annual College All-Star Game, matching the NFL against college seniors, is temporarily halted with 1:22 remaining in the third quarter due to lightning. When the fans become unruly and tear down the goalposts, NFL commissioner Pete Rozelle terminates the game. The following year, the annual game is discontinued. **Tokyo, Japan, 16 August:** The NFL plays an exhibition game outside of North America for the first time. The St. Louis Cardinals defeat the San Diego Chargers, 20–10. **Tampa, Florida, 12 December:** The Tampa Bay Buccaneers are defeated by the New England Patriots, 31–14. Tampa Bay, an expansion team, finishes their first NFL season winless with a record of 0–14, the first NFL team to lose that many games in one season.

1978 East Rutherford, New Jersey, 19 November: With the New York Giants leading the Philadelphia Eagles, 17–12, and 31 seconds remaining in the game, Giants quarterback Joe Pisarcik, after taking the snap from center instead of kneeling down and effectively ending the game, attempts to hand off to running back Larry Csonka but instead fumbles the ball. Philadelphia defender Herman Edwards catches the fumble in midair and returns it 26 yards for a game-winning touchdown. **Jacksonville, Florida, 29 December:** Near the end of the Gator Bowl, with Clemson leading Ohio State, 17–15, frustrated Ohio State coach Woody Hayes punches an opposing player who had just intercepted an Ohio State pass. Hayes is fired the next day, bringing his 33-year coaching career (28 years at Ohio State) to an end.

1979 Dallas, Texas, 1 January: In a game played in unusually cold conditions for Texas, Notre Dame defeats Houston, 35–34, in the Cotton Bowl after trailing 34–12 after three quarters. Notre Dame's quarterback, Joe Theismann, suffering from the flu, is revitalized by a bowl of chicken soup during halftime and responds by leading the Irish to score 23 points in the final quarter.

1980 Miami, Florida, 20 December: In a meaningless season-ending game between the Miami Dolphins and New York Jets, NBC television producer Don Ohlmeyer attempts a television first—an announcerless game. The only audio that was broadcast was the public address system at the Orange Bowl, which the Jets won, 24–17. Extensive use of graphics, a novelty for the time, helped keep the television audience abreast of the game.

1982 New York, New York, 21 September: The NFL Players Association goes on strike against the NFL. No games are played for 57 days, and the NFL season is shortened from 16 to nine games, but the playoffs are expanded to include the top eight teams from each conference. **Berkeley, California, 20 November 1982:** With four seconds left to play and Stanford University leading the University of California, 20–19, in a traditional rivalry game known as the "The Big Game," California receives the kickoff and keeps lateraling the ball while advancing toward the goal line. Midway through the play, the Stanford marching band starts to come onto the field, thinking the game is over. After five laterals, Kevin Moen, of California, runs through the band and scores the winning touchdown as time expires. This has become known as "The Play."

1983 Los Angeles, California, 6 March: The United States Football League (USFL) plays its first games. The Los Angeles Express defeat the New Jersey Generals, 20–15, in a nationally televised game. Other games are played in Tampa, Florida; Tempe, Arizona; Washington, D.C.; and Denver, Colorado.

1984 Owings Mills, Maryland, 29 March: Baltimore Colts' owner Robert Irsay hires a dozen Mayflower moving vans to move the Colts equipment in the middle of the night from their training complex outside of Baltimore to Indianapolis, Indiana. **Los Angeles, California, 30 June:** The Los Angeles Express of the USFL defeats the Michigan Panthers, 27–21, in three overtimes, the longest professional football game in history. The game ends at 3:33 of the third overtime, when Mel Gray runs 24 yards for a touchdown. **Anaheim, California, 30 September:** The Los Angeles Rams defeat the New York Giants, 33–12. The Rams score a record three safeties—all in the third quarter—on two blocked punts out of the end zone and a quarterback sack. **Anaheim, California, 7 December:** Eric Dickerson of the Los Angeles Rams rushes for 215 yards against the Houston Oilers to bring his season total to 2,007 yards, setting a new NFL record for rushing yardage in one season. He rushes for 98 additional yards the following week for a season total of 2,105 yards.

1986 London, England, 3 August: The first American Bowl is played. The Chicago Bears defeat the Dallas Cowboys, 17–6, at Wembley Stadium in an NFL preseason game.

1987 New York, New York, 22 September: The NFL Players Association again goes on strike against the NFL. The NFL cancels the following week's games but then plays the next three weeks using replacement players, although the strike is ended on 15 October.

1989 Tokyo, Japan, 5 August: The Los Angeles Rams defeat the San Francisco 49ers in the first American Bowl played in Asia. **El Segundo, California, 3 October:** Art Shell is named head coach of the Los Angeles Raiders. Shell becomes the first black NFL head coach since 1921, when Fritz Pollard was player-coach of the Akron Pros.

1991 Frankfurt, Germany, 23 March: The London Monarchs defeat the Frankfurt Galaxy, 24–11, before 23,619 fans as the World League of American Football begins play with six teams in the United States, one in Canada, and three in Europe (Barcelona, Spain; London, England; and Frankfurt, Germany).

1993 Buffalo, New York, 3 January: In a first-round AFC playoff game, the Buffalo Bills trail the Houston Oilers by 32 points, 35–3, in the third quarter. The Bills then score 28 points in that quarter and seven more in the fourth quarter, while Houston is held to only three points in the fourth quarter. Regulation time ends with the score tied 38-all. The Bills then score a field goal in overtime for the largest comeback in NFL history. **Hamilton, Ontario, Canada, 23 February:** The CFL expands by adding a U.S.-based team for the first time in its history, the Sacramento (California) Gold Miners, who begin play later that year. **Rosemont, Illinois, 26 October:** The NFL awards an expansion franchise to a management group from Charlotte, North Carolina. The team, named the Carolina Panthers, will begin play in the 1995 season. **Rosemont, Illinois, 30 November:** The NFL awards an expansion franchise to a Jacksonville, Florida, group headed by Wayne Weaver. The Jacksonville Jaguars will also begin play in 1995.

1994 Orlando, Florida, 22 March: The NFL adopts the two-point conversion rule. **Los Angeles, California, 12 June:** Former Buffalo Bills running back O. J. Simpson is charged with the murder of his wife, Nicole Brown, and her friend, Ronald Goldman. Five days later, after failing to turn himself into the authorities, he is captured after a televised low-speed auto chase on a Los Angeles freeway. **Mexico City, Mexico, 15 August:** The largest crowd in NFL history, 112,376 fans, attends the preseason American Bowl between the Houston Oilers and Dallas Cowboys at Estadio Azteca, won by Houston, 6–0.

1995 Los Angeles, California, 3 October: O. J. Simpson is found not guilty of murder and is exonerated. Two years later, in a civil trial, he is found guilty of "wrongful death" and ordered to pay $33.5 million in damages. **Cleveland, Ohio, 7 November:** Cleveland Browns' owner Art Modell announces plans to move the Browns to Baltimore, Maryland, for the 1996 season.

1996 Kansas City, Missouri, 15 February: The NCAA votes to require all Division I-A games that end in a tie to play an overtime period to determine a winner. Unlike the NFL's sudden-death overtime, the NCAA overtime will place the ball on the 25-yard line, and each team will have four downs to attempt to score, alternating possessions until one team outscores their opponent.

1997 Canton, Ohio, 25 July: The U.S. Postal Service issues a new commemorative sheet of stamps featuring football coaches Vince Lombardi, Glenn "Pop" Warner, Paul "Bear" Bryant, and George Halas.

1998 Oklahoma City, Oklahoma, 26 September: Prairie View A&M University ends their 80-game losing streak with a victory over Langston University, 14–12. Their last victory had been on 28 October 1989. Prairie View ensures their victory by stopping a two-point conversion attempt with 34 seconds left in the game.

1999 Tempe, Arizona, 5 January: The University of Tennessee defeats Florida State University, 23–16, at the Fiesta Bowl to win the new Bowl Championship Series national championship. **Phoenix, Arizona, 17 March:** The NFL adds an instant replay rule, allowing coaches to challenge certain calls on the field and require the referee to review it via instant replay. **Swarthmore, Pennsylvania, 4 September:** In a game billed as "Somebody Has to Win," Swarthmore College defeats Oberlin College, 42–6, ending the nation's longest losing streak at 28 games. Oberlin, who entered the game with a losing streak of 19 games, continues to lose for the next two seasons before breaking their losing streak at 44 with a victory over Kenyon, 53–22, on 20 October 2001. **Atlanta, Georgia, 5 October:** Houston businessman Bob McNair pays a record $700 million to acquire an NFL expansion franchise in Houston. The team does not begin play until the 2002 season. **Fort Worth, Texas, 20 November:** LaDainian Tomlinson of Texas Christian University sets the NCAA record with 406 yards rushing in one game on 43 carries. He gains 287 yards in the second half, also a NCAA record, and scores six touchdowns, as Texas Christian defeats the University of Texas at El Paso, 52–24.

2001 Las Vegas, Nevada, 3 February: The XFL begins play, with the Las Vegas Outlaws defeating the New York/New Jersey Hitmen, 19–0, at Sam Boyd Stadium. The league survives one season and disbands on 10 May. **New York, New York, September 13:** NFL commissioner Paul Tagliabue announces that the coming week's schedule of NFL games will be postponed due to the September 11 terrorist attacks. The postponed games are played the week after the regular season is scheduled to end, and, consequently, the Super Bowl is played in February for the first time.

2002 New Orleans, Louisiana, 3 February: Adam Vinatieri kicks a 48-yard field goal with seven seconds remaining in the game to give the New England Patriots a 20–17 victory over the St. Louis Rams in the Super Bowl. This is the first Super Bowl to be decided on the final play of the game.

2003 Phoenix, Arizona, 23 November: Jeff Wilkins of the St. Louis Rams kicks a 29-yard field goal with no time remaining at the end of the first half, then kicks a 24-yard field goal with no time remaining at the end of regulation time to send the game into overtime, and then kicks the game-winning field goal after 10:22 of the sudden-death overtime period to give the Rams a 30–27 victory over the Arizona Cardinals.

2004 Houston, Texas, 1 February: Adam Vinatieri's 41-yard field goal with four seconds remaining in the game gives the New England Patriots a 32–29 victory over the Carolina Panthers in one of the most exciting Super Bowl games in NFL history.

2005 Mexico City, Mexico, 2 October: The Arizona Cardinals defeat the San Francisco 49ers, 31–14, in the first regular-season NFL game played outside the United States.

2006 Foxboro, Massachusetts, 1 January: On his last play in his final NFL game, Doug Flutie dropkicks an extra point. This is the first successful dropkick in the NFL since 1941. **Northbrook, Illinois, 8 August:** At a meeting of NFL owners, Roger S. Goodell is selected as the commissioner of the NFL, replacing Paul Tagliabue, who retires effective 1 September. **Evanston, Illinois, 21 October:** The Michigan State Spartans trail the Northwestern Wildcats, 38–3, with 9:54 left in the third quarter. Michigan State scores 14 points in that quarter and 24 more points in the fourth quarter to achieve the biggest comeback in NCAA history and win the game, 41–38.

2007 Houston, Texas, 21 October: Rob Bironas of the Tennessee Titans kicks a record eight field goals without a miss, including the winning one as time expires, to defeat the Houston Texans, 38–36. **Minneapolis, Minnesota, 4 November:** Antonio Cromartie of the San Diego Chargers returns a missed field goal 109 yards for a touchdown as the Minnesota Vikings defeat the Chargers, 35–17. This is the longest run in NFL history. In the same game, the Vikings' Adrian Peterson establishes another NFL record by rushing for 296 yards (253 in the second half) on 30 carries with three touchdowns. **East Rutherford, New Jersey, 29 December:** The New England Patriots defeat the New York Giants, 38–35, and become the first NFL team to finish the regular season at 16–0. Five weeks later, the Giants defeat the Patriots in the Super Bowl, 17–14, ending the Patriots' undefeated season.

2008 Green Bay, Wisconsin, 28 December: The Detroit Lions are defeated by the Green Bay Packers, 31–21. The Lions conclude the NFL season with a record of zero wins and 16 losses, the first NFL team to do so.

2009 Arlington, Texas, 20 September: An NFL attendance record is set at the new Cowboys Stadium, as 105,121 fans gather to see the New York Giants defeat the Dallas Cowboys, 33–31.

2010 Stockholm, Sweden, 26 June–3 July: The first International Federation of American Football women's tournament is held. Six teams enter, and the United States wins easily, winning all three games and outscoring their opposition, 201–0. **Bloomington, Minnesota, 12 December:** A heavy snowstorm initially causes the New York Giants–Minnesota Vikings game to be postponed from Sunday, 12 December, to Monday. The roof of the Vikings' home field, the Metrodome, collapses early Sunday morning, and the game is played on Monday in Detroit. **Philadelphia, Pennsylvania, 26 December:** Another heavy blizzard causes the Vikings–Philadelphia Eagles Sunday night game to be postponed to Tuesday, 28 December. This is the first NFL game to be played on a Tuesday since 1946.

2011 Phoenix, Arizona, 12 August: The Jacksonville Sharks defeat the Arizona Rattlers in ArenaBowl XXIV, 73–70. The Sharks' quarterback, 40-year-old Aaron Garcia, completes a pass with two seconds remaining for the win. **University Park, Pennsylvania, 29 October:** In an unusual October blizzard, Penn State University defeats the University of Illinois, 10–7, on a touchdown in the last two minutes of the game to give Coach Joe Paterno his 409th career victory, surpassing Eddie Robinson as the all-time leader in coaching victories for major college football. Two weeks later, Paterno is fired by Penn State for failure to report an assistant coach's alleged deviant sexual activities with young boys. Less than three months later, Paterno is dead from cancer.

2012 Orlando, Florida, 9 March: The Arena Football League begins its 25th season amidst chaos as the players strike and the nationally televised opening game between the Orlando Predators and Pittsburgh Power is played by replacement players using special rules. **New York, New York, 21 March:** NFL Commissioner Roger Goodell suspends New Orleans Saints head coach, Sean Payton, for the entire 2012 season for Payton's knowledge of a "bounty system" that rewarded Saints defensive players for deliberately injuring their opponents. **Indianapolis, Indiana, 23 July:** The NCAA rules that all Penn State victories from 1998 to 2011 are vacated and fines Penn State $60 million as a result of conviction of Penn State assistant coach Jerry Sandusky for pedophilia. **Green Bay, Wisconsin, 9 September:** David Akers of San Francisco ties the NFL record with a 63-yard field goal in the second quarter to help the 49ers defeat the Packers, 30–22. The game is officiated by replacement officials as the regular NFL officials are on strike. **New Orleans, Louisiana, 9 September:** The Washington Redskins score exactly 10 points in each quarter (the first time in NFL history) and defeat the New Orleans Saints, 40–32. **Norfolk, Virginia, 22 September:** Taylor Heinicke of Old Dominion University completes 55 of 79 passes for a NCAA Division I record of 730 yards to lead his team to a 64–61 victory over the University of New Hampshire. **Seattle, Washington, 24 September:** The Seattle Seahawks defeat the Green Bay Packers on a last-second Hail Mary pass to the end zone that is erroneously ruled a catch by the replacement officials. The controversial ending results in the NFL quickly reaching an agreement with the striking officials two days later. **New Orleans, Louisiana, 7 October:** Drew Brees throws a touchdown pass in his 48th consecutive game breaking Johnny Unitas' record set in 1959. Brees continues his streak for six more games before being shut out on 29 November by the Atlanta Falcons.

2013 New Orleans, Louisiana, 3 February: In one of the most unusual Super Bowl games, the San Francisco 49ers nearly come back from a 28–6 third quarter deficit but lose to the Baltimore Ravens, 34–31. The game is delayed for 34 minutes shortly after the start of the second half by a power outage that blacked out most of the lights at the Louisiana Superdome.

Introduction

Gridiron football, American football, or just plain football, is the most popular sport in the United States in the 21st century. Although attempts have been made to develop the sport outside North America, it is still predominantly a North American sport, with similar games (but significant rules differences) played in the United States and Canada.

FOOTBALL'S BEGINNINGS

Unlike the sport of basketball, which was invented by a physical education instructor (Dr. James Naismith) and had a clearly defined set of rules from its beginning in 1891, the sport of American football evolved from various outdoor ball-kicking games. It began as a variant of rugby. Rugby itself was developed as a variant of soccer (the sport known throughout most of the world as "football"). Rugby had its origin at the Rugby School in Rugby, Warwickshire, England, about 85 miles northwest of London.

The game known as rugby reportedly began in 1823, when William Webb Ellis, a student at the Rugby School, while playing soccer at the school, caught the ball, and, because it was nearing the game's five o'clock curfew, ran with the ball toward the goal to reach the goal before the clock struck five. This was in strict violation of the rules and has since been commemorated by a plaque on the school's wall that reads as follows: "This Stone Commemorates the Exploit of William Webb Ellis Who With a Fine Disregard of the Rules of Football, as Played in His Time, First Took the Ball in His Arms and Ran With It, Thus Originating the Distinctive Feature of the Rugby Game. A.D. 1823."

From then onward, there were two forms of football, the traditional one (soccer), in which the ball is kicked, and the new Rugby one, in which the ball is carried. The two games and variations of them were played in the United States in the first half of the 19th century, and, on 6 November 1869, teams from the College of New Jersey (now known as Princeton University) and Rutgers College (now Rutgers University) met at Rutgers field in New Brunswick, New Jersey, and played a game with 25 players on each side. This game was a cross between rugby and soccer, and it has been considered by historians to be the first game of American football. The first team to score six goals was the winner, and Rutgers prevailed, six goals to four.

During the next few years, other schools began to play similar games, but each had its own set of rules. In 1873, representatives from four colleges—Yale, Columbia, Princeton, and Rutgers—met in New York City and created the first set of intercollegiate football rules in the United States. In 1876, a subsequent meeting in Springfield, Massachusetts, formed the Intercollegiate Football Association, and the rules were somewhat modified. From 1876 to 1894, this organization met at least annually, and the rules continued to be modified.

Walter Camp of Yale University was one of the main innovators in the formation of rules and strategy in the early game. In 1882, the concept of downs was created. Prior to 1882, a team could retain possession indefinitely if it did not attempt to score a field goal. If the game's result was a tie, the previous year's winner would retain the trophy, thus the use of the "block tactic," in which a team would attempt to retain possession and play for a tie game. The new rule read as follows: "If in three consecutive fairs and downs a team shall not have advanced the ball five yards nor lost 10 yards, they shall surrender the ball to their opponents in the spot of the last down." (The word *fair* referred to inbounding the ball to begin play.)

The following year, a numerical scoring system, which awarded points to the various types of scores, was introduced. A safety was worth one point, a touchdown two points, a goal from a try four points, and a goal from the field five points. (After a touchdown was scored, a team would be allowed a "try" for a goal.) Prior to the numerical scoring system, the various scores were weighed, but that often led to disputes.

The scoring system was modified in 1884, raising the value of a touchdown to four points and a safety to two points and lowering the goal from try to two points. In 1898, the touchdown was raised to five points and goal from try lowered to one point. In 1904, the field goal was lowered to four points, and, in 1909, it was lowered once more to three points. It was not until 1912 that the modern system of scoring—touchdown six points, field goal three points, safety two points, and successful try following a touchdown one point—was adopted. This scoring system has remained in place through the 21st century with just a slight modification allowing for a two-point try. In the game's first two decades, little publicity was given to individual players, but this would change beginning in 1889.

EARLY DEVELOPMENT

In 1889, Caspar Whitney selected the first All-American college football team for a periodical known as *This Week's Sports*. All-American teams became an annual event, and, after the periodical folded in 1891, *Harper's Weekly* listed them. Walter Camp succeeded Whitney as team selector and continued to select All-American teams until his death in 1925. Various other publications have also selected All-American teams, and this practice continues in the 21st century.

The game continued to grow, and, although the best teams were still in the eastern part of the country, the game spread and was played at colleges and universities throughout the rest of the United States. The 1889 All-American team was comprised of ends Amos Alonzo Stagg from Yale and Arthur Cumnock from Harvard; tackles Hector Cowan from Princeton and Charles Gill from Yale; guards William "Pudge" Heffelfinger from Yale and John Cranston from Harvard; center William George from Princeton; quarterback Edgar Allan Poe from Princeton (a distant relative of the famed author); halfbacks Roscoe Channing from Princeton and James Lee from Harvard; and fullback Knowlton "Snake" Ames from Princeton. Other notable football players of the 1890s included end Frank Hinkey from Yale; tackle John H. Outland from the University of Pennsylvania (for whom the Outland Trophy is named); guard T. Truxton Hare from the University of Pennsylvania; fullback Pat O'Dea from the University of Wisconsin, Madison (an Australian famed for his dropkicking ability); and end Arthur Poe from Yale (Edgar Allan Poe's brother).

On 1 January 1902, a football game was played in conjunction with the annual Tournament of Roses Parade in Pasadena, California. It matched the University of Michigan against the local team of Stanford University in a contest known as the Tournament East–West football game. Michigan, possibly the best collegiate team in the country that season, had won all 10 of their previous games, outscoring their opponents 501–0. Included in that total was a 128–0 victory over Buffalo and an 89–0 defeat of Beloit. Michigan easily defeated Stanford, 49–0, in a game that is considered to be the first postseason bowl game and the forerunner of the Rose Bowl. Michigan continued their dominance, and, from 1901 to 1905, under coach Fielding "Hurry-Up" Yost, they compiled a record of 55–1–1 and outscored their opponents 2,821–42. They were undefeated in 56 straight games before losing the last game of the 1905 season, 2–0, to the University of Chicago. Michigan's teams were referred to as "point a minute."

During the first decade of the 20th century, a small school in Pennsylvania made its mark in football history. The Carlisle Indian School in Carlisle, Pennsylvania, began fielding football teams in 1893. These teams consisted solely of the Native Americans who attended the school. Beginning in 1899, under coach Glenn "Pop" Warner, Carlisle played some of the better schools, including Harvard, Yale, Columbia, the University of Pennsylvania, and the University of Chicago. From 1907 to 1913, Carlisle had a combined record of 69–15–4. For several of those years, Carlisle's star was Jim Thorpe, who, in 1950, was voted as the Greatest Athlete of the first half of the century by the Associated Press.

In the early 20th century, college football faced a severe challenge, which was remedied by President Theodore Roosevelt. The game had become increasingly brutal, with players suffering severe injuries and even death. In 1905, 18 players died from injuries suffered in football games. A movement was begun to ban the sport, and Charles Eliot, the president of Harvard University, was one of its leaders. At the White House on 9 October 1905, President Roosevelt met with two athletic advisors from each Harvard, Yale, and Princeton Universities to discuss possible methods for modifying the rules to eliminate the brutality. On 31 March 1906, the Intercollegiate Athletic Association of the United States (later renamed the National Collegiate Athletic Association [NCAA]) was founded with 62 charter members. Also at that meeting, several rules changes were enacted, including leveling additional penalties for various types of rough play, requiring 10 yards to be gained for a first down rather than five, and legalizing the forward pass.

Among the most prominent players from 1900 to 1919 were Michigan's star halfback, Willie Heston; tackle Hamilton Fish of Harvard (later a U.S. congressman); end John Reed Kilpatrick of Yale (later a brigadier general in the U.S. Army and head of Madison Square Garden); back Walter Eckersall (later a sportswriter for the *Chicago Tribune* and football referee); and ends Tom Shevlin of Yale and Paul Robeson of Rutgers.

THE EARLY PROFESSIONALS

The popularity of football was such that many athletic associations fielded teams and competed against other such organizations. As was the custom of the times, the teams often competed for side bets. Teams attempted to get the best players in the area to play for them, and it was not unusual for athletic associations to pay a player's expenses to get an outstanding player to represent them in a game. The first recorded instance of a player receiving more than expense money occurred on 12 November 1892, when the Allegheny Athletic Association of Pittsburgh, Pennsylvania, paid William "Pudge" Heffelfinger, a former college star at Yale, $500 plus $25 expenses to play for them in a game against the Pittsburgh Athletic Club. The investment paid off, as he scored the game's only touchdown, giving Allegheny a 4–0 victory. Former Princeton end Ben "Sport" Donnelly was hired by Allegheny the following week for $250. Other teams in the Ohio-Pennsylvania area began paying players, and, by 1897, the Latrobe Athletic Association (in Latrobe, Pennsylvania, 40 miles southeast of Pittsburgh) used only professional players.

An organization known as the National Football League was created in 1902, with three teams from Pennsylvania, the Philadelphia Phillies, Philadelphia Athletics, and Pittsburgh Stars. The teams were comprised of numerous professional baseball players and Connie Mack, manager of the Philadelphia Athletics baseball team. Among the members on that team were George "Rube" Waddell, star baseball pitcher, who played fullback, and New York Giants star pitcher Christy Mathewson, who was a fullback and punter for the Pittsburgh Stars. The league only lasted one season, and the Stars were declared league champions by virtue of a Thanksgiving Day victory over the Athletics.

A tournament billed as the "World Series of Football" was played indoors at New York's Madison Square Garden from 29 December 1902 to 1 January 1903. Five teams took part, the Syracuse Athletic Club, Knickerbocker Athletic Club, Warlow (or Warslow) Athletic Club (also known as the Whitestone Indians), Orange (New Jersey) Athletic Club, and a team comprised of members of the Philadelphia Athletics and Philadelphia Phillies football teams but called the "New York" team. The event's promoter, Tom O'Rourke, manager of Madison Square Garden, called the team "New York" in the hopes that a "local" team would draw more fans. Syracuse defeated New York, 5–0, the first night; the Knickerbockers defeated Warlow, 11–6, on the second night; Syracuse defeated the Knickerbockers, 36–0, on the third night; and Syracuse won the tournament by defeating Orange on the fourth night, also by a score of 36–0.

Professional football continued to grow, and, during the first decade of the 20th century, the state of Ohio developed quite a following for the sport, with teams in Akron, Canton, Cincinnati, Cleveland, Columbus, Dayton, Elyria, Massillon, Shelby, Toledo, and Youngstown. Seven Nesser brothers played for the Columbus Panhandles, and Jim Thorpe was Canton's leading attraction. The Ohio League began in 1902 and lasted until 1919. Upstate New York also had a New York Pro Football League during much of that time, with teams in Buffalo, Rochester, Syracuse, and Tonawanda, among others.

Among the most prominent early professional players in addition to Jim Thorpe and the Nesser brothers were Lawson Fiscus, John Brallier, Ed Abbaticchio (also a Major League Baseball player), and Charles Barney. The first black professional players included Charles Follis of Shelby, Charles "Doc" Baker of Akron, Henry McDonald of Rochester, Gideon "Charlie" Smith of Canton, Robert "Rube" Marshall of Rock Island, and Fritz Pollard of Akron. Other important individuals of the early pro years included David Berry, manager of the Latrobe Athletic Association, and Philadelphia baseball owners Ben Shibe and John Rogers, who also sponsored football teams.

COLLEGE FOOTBALL DURING THE 1920S: THE GOLDEN AGE OF SPORT

The 1920s have been called the "Golden Age of Sport." During that decade, sportswriters made heroes out of the best players in the major sports leagues. These figures included Babe Ruth in baseball, Jack Dempsey in boxing, Bobby Jones in golf, Bill Tilden in tennis, and Red Grange in football, all who were idolized much more than previous sportsmen. College football thrived during that era. During the 1920s, even though the professionals played football on Sundays, colleges played on Saturdays and were followed much more closely than the pros. Most colleges had football teams and large fan followings. Several of the major schools even played games at large stadiums, and schools like the University of Notre Dame would play in Chicago or New York against such rivals as the United States Military Academy (Army) or United States Naval Academy (Navy). The annual Army–Navy game was held in Philadelphia, New York, or Chicago.

Under coach Knute Rockne, Notre Dame became America's most popular team. From 1918 to 1930, his Fighting Irish teams compiled a won-lost-tied record of 105–12–5, and they were national champions in 1919, 1920, 1924, 1927, 1929, and 1930. From 1919 to 1924, their record was 55–3–1. The Notre Dame backfield of quarterback Harry Stuhldreyer, halfbacks Jim Crowley and Don Miller, and fullback Elmer Layden was immortalized by sportswriter Grantland Rice. In describing the Notre Dame–Army game of 18 October 1924, he wrote: "Outlined against a blue-gray October sky, the Four Horsemen rode again. In dramatic lore their names are Death, Destruction, Pestilence, and Famine. But those are aliases. Their real names are Stuhldreyer, Crowley, Miller, and Layden." Notre Dame's publicist capitalized on this article and billed their backfield as the "Four Horsemen" in reference to a popular Rudolph Valentino movie of that era, *The Four Horsemen of the Apocalypse*. In Notre Dame's final game of the 1924 season, they were matched against Stanford University in the Rose Bowl on 1 January 1925. Both teams were undefeated entering the game. Stanford featured fullback Ernie Nevers, and Notre Dame had the Four Horsemen. Notre Dame prevailed, 27–10, even though Nevers gained 114 yards, intercepted a pass, and punted for a 42.0-yard average.

Another collegiate football hero of the 1920s was Harold "Red" Grange. On the same date as the Notre Dame–Army game in 1924, the University of Illinois played their first home game at their new Memorial Stadium in Champaign, Illinois, against the University of Michigan. Entering the game, Michigan had a 20-game winning streak. Grange had one of the greatest days ever for a collegiate football player. He returned the opening kickoff 95 yards for a touchdown. He then ran for touchdowns of 67, 56, and 44 yards in the first quarter. With the limited substitution rules in effect in that era, he did not play in the second quarter. In the third quarter, he ran for a 12-yard touchdown. He completed his day by throwing a pass in the fourth quarter for one more touchdown. By the end of the game he had run for five touchdowns; passed for one touchdown; and compiled 212 yards rushing, 64 yards passing, and 126 yards on kickoff returns. Illinois defeated Michigan, 39–14, ending Michigan's undefeated streak.

In addition to Grange, Nevers, and the Four Horsemen, there were several other talented collegiate players of the 1920s. These included ends Bennie Oosterbaan of Michigan and Vic Hanson of Syracuse; tackles Bronko Nagurski of Minnesota and Fred "Duke" Slater of Iowa (one of the few black college players of the era); and backs Benny Friedman of Michigan, Ken Strong of New York University, and George "The Gipper" Gipp of Notre Dame.

PROFESSIONAL FOOTBALL OF THE 1920S: THE BEGINNINGS OF THE NATIONAL FOOTBALL LEAGUE

On 20 August 1920, a meeting occurred in Canton, Ohio, at a Hupmobile automobile dealership that led to the creation of one of the most important sporting enterprises in world history. The auto dealership was owned by Ralph Hay, who was also the owner of the Canton Bulldogs professional football team. Also at that historic meeting were representatives of three other Ohio-based professional football clubs: the Akron Pros, Cleveland Indians, and Dayton Triangles. Frank Nied and Art Ranney represented Akron, Jimmy O'Donnell and Stan Cofall represented Cleveland, and Carl Storck represented Dayton. The meeting resulted in the formation of the American Professional Football Conference, and Hay was elected league secretary. Hay then contacted other important professional midwestern football teams and invited them to a subsequent meeting at the dealership on 17 September 1920.

At that meeting, representatives of two teams from Indiana (the Hammond Pros and Muncie Flyers), three teams from Illinois (the Rock Island Independents, Decatur Staleys, and Racine Cardinals [based in Chicago]), and the Rochester Jeffersons (based in New York) met. The organization of 10 teams was renamed the American Professional Football Association (APFA), and Jim Thorpe was named league president. Hay had been offered the league presidency but felt that Thorpe's name would better help build the league's following. Later that year, four additional teams were added, the Buffalo All-Americans, Detroit Heralds, Columbus Panhandles, and Chicago Tigers.

The league did not play a balanced schedule, and only games played against league members counted in the league standings. At the season's end, the Akron Pros were declared league champions, with a record of eight wins, no losses, and three ties. The Decatur Staleys were second, at 10–1–2, and the Buffalo All-Americans were third, at 9–1–1.

In 1921, Columbus owner Joe Carr was named league president. The league expanded its membership to 21 teams and now stretched from Minneapolis to New York City, although seven of the teams only played four or fewer league games. The Green Bay Packers entered the league in 1921, and 90 years later they are still in the league. The league championship was disputed, with both Buffalo and Chicago claiming it. The All-Americans finished the 1921 season on 27 November, with a record of 8–0–2, and claimed the league title. For some unknown reason, they agreed to play two additional games as exhibitions. They defeated Akron in Buffalo on 3 December, and then traveled overnight to play the Staleys which had relocated from Decatur to Chicago in 1921, the next day. They were defeated by the Staleys, who then claimed the league title. The league's executive committee voted for the Staleys, who were named league champions.

In 1922, Carr moved the league's headquarters to Columbus, renamed the league the National Football League (NFL), improved the league's organization by drafting a league constitution, developed franchise membership criteria, created the concept of team's territorial rights, and generally helped make the league a viable entity. The 1922 NFL had 18 teams, including one of the most unusual teams in professional sports history, the Oorang Indians.

The Oorang Indians were owned by Walter Lingo, a breeder of Airedale dogs and owner of the Oorang Kennels. Lingo was a friend of Jim Thorpe, a Sac and Fox Indian and one of the greatest athletes of all time. Lingo purchased an NFL franchise for $100 and used it as a basis for advertising his Airedales. The team, based in LaRue, Ohio, a town with a population of fewer than than 1,000, was a traveling team with all games played on the road. Thorpe was player-coach and recruited only Native Americans for the team, which featured players from nine different Indian tribes. Halftime shows featured the Airedales performing tricks and the Indians performing dances and tomahawk-throwing exhibitions. Football was secondary to Airedale promotion. As a result, the team won only three of nine games in 1922, and one of 11 games in 1923. The novelty wore off after two seasons, and Lingo dissolved the team.

The NFL continued to survive, with 20 teams in 1923, 18 in 1924, and 20 in 1925. That year, the New York Giants became league members. That same year, famed collegian Harold "Red" Grange joined the Chicago Bears for the last five games of the season. The games in which he played broke attendance records, and, on 6 December 1925, an estimated 70,000 fans attended the Bears–Giants game at the Polo Grounds, the largest crowd by far for a professional football game to that point. Grange's popularity was such that his agent, Charles C. "C. C." Pyle, attempted to form his own team, the New York Yankees, with Grange as the star, to play in the NFL in 1926. When the league declined to offer them an NFL franchise, Pyle and Grange formed their own league, the American Football League (AFL), in direct competition with the NFL. Even though Grange starred for the New York Yankees of the AFL in 1926, the other teams did not draw well, and the league failed after just one season. The 22-team NFL continued to do well in 1926, even without Grange.

The New York Yankees, featuring Grange, were accepted into the NFL in 1927. The league competed with just 12 teams that year. By 1928, it was down to just 10 teams. The league fluctuated between 10 and 12 teams for the next few years, but, by 1932, the depth of the Depression, it had only eight teams. That season ended in an unusual way. The Chicago Bears had a record of 6–1–6. The Portsmouth Spartans had a record of 6–1–4. The Green Bay Packers had a record of 10–3–1. Even though the Packers won more games than any other NFL team, the league championship was determined by won-lost percentage. Tie games were disregarded in calculating that percentage, so the Bears and Spartans were considered to be tied for the league title. A tiebreaking playoff game was scheduled.

Due to extreme weather conditions, the game was moved indoors to Chicago Stadium and was played on an 80-yard field with other special rules in place. The Bears won, 9–0, and, as a result of the popularity of the game, the following season the 10-team league was divided in half, and the winners of the East Division met the winners of the West Division in a postseason game billed as the NFL Championship Game.

COLLEGE FOOTBALL DURING THE 1930S: RISE OF THE BOWL GAMES

College football continued its popularity in the 1930s. The annual postseason Rose Bowl game, played on New Year's Day, had proven to be quite popular, and, as a result, four other warm-climate cities began holding similar events. On 1 January 1935, the Sun Bowl, in El Paso, Texas, was played for the first time. That same day, in Miami, Florida, the Orange Bowl was played, and in New Orleans, Louisiana, the Sugar Bowl was held. In Dallas, Texas, on

New Year's Day 1937, the Cotton Bowl was originated. Although some of collegiate football's best teams and players were active during the 1930s and the sport retained its popularity, the legendary status accorded to teams and players of the 1920s was absent during the 1930s.

One of the collegiate football highlights of the 1930s was the 1932 Colgate University team, which, under coach Andy Kerr, won all nine of their games and did not allow a single point to be scored against them. They were described in the press of that era as "undefeated, untied, unscored upon, and uninvited," although the only postseason game that year was the Rose Bowl. The Rose Bowl invited the University of Pittsburgh, which also was undefeated but had played two scoreless ties and defeated Notre Dame, Army, and Stanford.

Following the 1935 college football season, the Downtown Athletic Club (DAC) of New York presented an award to the most outstanding player in college football. This award was simply known as the Downtown Athletic Club Trophy, and it was presented to halfback Jay Berwanger of the University of Chicago. In 1936, following the death of the DAC's athletic director, John Heisman, the award was renamed the John Heisman Memorial Trophy.

The 1939 University of Tennessee team also was undefeated, untied, and unscored upon. After being invited to the Rose Bowl, their streak came to an end, as the University of Southern California not only scored against them but defeated them, 14–0.

Under coach Jim Crowley (one of Notre Dame's famed "Four Horsemen"), Fordham University had excellent teams during the middle of the decade. The front line of their 1936 team was given the nickname the "Seven Blocks of Granite" by team publicist Tim Cohane (a future nationally acclaimed sportswriter). One of the "Seven Blocks" was Vincent Lombardi, who would later become a renowned NFL coach.

PROFESSIONAL FOOTBALL OF THE 1930S: THE NFL CHAMPIONSHIP GAME

During the 1930s, the NFL began to stabilize. In 1933, the 10-team league had changed to a two-division organization, with the division winners meeting in a postseason NFL Championship Game. From 1933 until 1943, when World War II impacted the league, the NFL had nine or 10 teams each season with minimal franchise changes. The 1933 NFL had teams in New York, Brooklyn, Boston, Philadelphia, and Pittsburgh in the East Division, and Chicago (the Bears and Cardinals), Portsmouth, Green Bay, and Cincinnati in the West Division. By 1942, Boston had relocated to Washington, Portsmouth had moved to Detroit, and Cleveland replaced Cincinnati.

The league's strength was confined to four teams, with only the Green Bay Packers or Chicago Bears representing the West Division from 1933 to 1942, and only the Washington Redskins or New York Giants representing the East Division during that time. The 1940 NFL Championship Game between the Bears and Redskins was an anomaly, as Chicago inexplicably defeated Washington, 73–0, in the most one-sided game in NFL history.

The NFL survived another competitive threat when a new American Football League began play in 1936, but it lasted only two seasons. Another unrelated American Football League started in 1940 and played in 1941, but the league curtailed operations after the outbreak of World War II and never resumed following the war.

Among the innovations of the NFL during the 1930s was the creation of an annual draft of college seniors. This idea of Philadelphia Eagles' owner Bert Bell (later NFL commissioner) proved to be one of the best features of the league and enabled the weaker teams to be able to successfully compete.

COLLEGE FOOTBALL IN THE 1940S: WARTIME AND UNLIMITED SUBSTITUTION

The war impacted college sports in several ways. Since the annual New Year's Day Rose Bowl, held in Pasadena, California, in 1942, occurred less than one month after Pearl Harbor, the U.S. government was wary of a large group of fans attending a game on the West Coast. The game was consequently relocated to Durham, North Carolina, home of Duke University, which was defeated by the University of Oregon, 20–16.

As students were drafted for the war, many colleges suspended fielding football teams during the wartime years. In an attempt to ease the burden of finding skilled players, the NCAA eliminated the restrictive substitution rules and permitted unlimited substitution, a rule that was in effect until 1954. Many service training facilities fielded teams, and some of the best football was played by the Great Lakes Naval Training Center team, the North Carolina Pre-Flight School team, and the Randolph Field team. An Associated Press poll of the top 20 teams in 1944 included 10 service teams, as well as the United States Military Academy (Army) and United States Naval Academy (Navy). During the war years, Army, which usually fielded competitive college teams, had the nation's top team from 1944 to 1946. During that time, the team boasted an undefeated record of 27–0–1.

After the war, interest in sports increased. As a result, the years from 1946 to 1949 saw a multitude of postseason college bowl games added. Many were not held for more than one or two seasons, and such games as the Alamo

Bowl, Aloha Bowl, Angel Bowl, Bean Bowl, Cajun Bowl, Camellia Bowl, Cattle Bowl, Corn Bowl, Delta Bowl, Dixie Bowl, Fish Bowl, Fruit Bowl, Hoosier Bowl, Ice Bowl, Iodine Bowl, Kickapoo Bowl, Olympian Bowl, Optimist Bowl, Paper Bowl, Pecan Bowl, Raisin Bowl, Salad Bowl, Tobacco Bowl, and Turkey Bowl were played for the first and, in many cases, the last time. Others like the Tangerine Bowl (1946–1982), Cigar Bowl (1947–1954), Gator Bowl (1946–2011), Potato Bowl (1948–1967), and Refrigerator Bowl (1948–1956) originated during that period but lasted quite a bit longer.

Among the top college players of the 1940s were quarterbacks Angelo Bertelli and Johnny Lujack of Notre Dame; halfbacks Felix "Doc" Blanchard ("Mr. Inside") of Army, Glenn Davis ("Mr. Outside") of Army, Tom Harmon of the University of Michigan, and Jackie Jensen of the University of California (later a Major League Baseball player); ends Bill Swiacki of Columbia and Leon Hart of Notre Dame; centers Chuck Bednarik of the University of Pennsylvania and Clayton Tonnemaker of the University of Minnesota; tackles Dewitt "Tex" Coulter of Army and Leo Nomellini of the University of Minnesota; and guards Alex Agase of Purdue and the University of Illinois and Chuck Taylor of Stanford.

PROFESSIONAL FOOTBALL DURING THE 1940S: WARTIME AND INTEGRATION

On 7 December 1941, a day that "will live in infamy," in the words of President Franklin Delano Roosevelt, the NFL played its regular schedule, with games in New York, Chicago, and Philadelphia. Although the fans in attendance were unaware of the bombing of Pearl Harbor, they knew that something unusual had happened, since throughout the games announcements were made in the stadiums requesting that all military personnel immediately report to their units. The NFL did not suspend activity, and, the following week, the Chicago Bears and Green Bay Packers met in a tiebreaker game to determine the West Division championship. On 21 December, the Bears met the New York Giants in the NFL Championship Game.

As with other professional team sports like baseball and basketball, the U.S. government did not prohibit them from being played during World War II, but the leagues themselves were required to adjust to the severe manpower shortage. In 1942, the NFL was able to continue operation with the same 10 teams that played in 1941, and an 11-game schedule was played. The following year, 1943, was a different story, as only eight teams were able to field squads. The Cleveland Rams suspended operations for that season, and the Philadelphia Eagles and Pittsburgh Steelers merged. That team was popularly known as the "Steagles." Of the 24 players on the Steagles who played in five or more games, 15 were classified 4-F due to assorted ailments, six others had a 3-A classification as fathers, and three others were classified 1-A and were serving in the military and playing when they could get passes to do so. By the time the war ended in 1945, 638 former NFL players had served in the military, and 355 of them were commissioned officers. Two New York Giants, Al Blozis and Jack Lummus, were killed during the war, as were 19 other men who had played in the NFL at one time or another.

The 1944 NFL season saw the Rams return to action, and a new team, the Boston Yanks, was added to the league. The Eagles and Steelers also were able to field complete teams, but, to have a balanced 10-team league, the Steelers combined with the Chicago Cardinals and played as Card-Pitt. By 1945, the war had ended, and the league had most of its servicemen back.

In 1946, a new problem arose for the NFL. A competitor, the All-America Football Conference (AAFC), began play. The new eight-team AAFC had teams in Brooklyn, New York, Miami, Buffalo, Cleveland, San Francisco, Los Angeles, and Chicago. The NFL also had teams in New York, Chicago, and Los Angeles. One of the AAFC's problems was a lack of competition within the league, as the Cleveland Browns completely dominated the scene, won the championship each year, and had a combined record of 47–4–3 for their four years in the league. Although the competition impacted the NFL somewhat, it was the AAFC that suffered more, and it folded in 1950, with three AAFC teams being allowed to join the NFL.

The other significant change in professional football of the 1940s was the reintroduction of black players. During the first decade of the NFL, there were several black players who contributed significantly to the game, including Fritz Pollard, who was a coach of the Akron Pros, and Fred "Duke" Slater, who played in the NFL from 1922 to 1931. After 1933, black players were unofficially banned, and although there were quite a few good black collegiate players, including future baseball Hall of Famer Jackie Robinson, none were signed by NFL teams. From its inception, the AAFC signed blacks, including two of the best players on the Cleveland Browns, running back Marion Motley and lineman Bill Willis. In 1946, the Los Angeles Rams of the NFL also signed halfback Kenny Washington and end Woody Strode. From that time onward, the NFL integrated seamlessly, and, as in professional basketball, the proportion of black players gradually increased to the point where, in the 21st century, the overwhelming majority of players are of African American heritage.

COLLEGE FOOTBALL IN THE 1950S: THE UNIVERSITY OF OKLAHOMA

College football continued to be popular in the 1950s, and the dominant team of the decade was the University of Oklahoma. Under head coach Charles "Bud" Wilkinson, they were voted as the national collegiate champion in 1950, 1953, 1955, 1956, and 1957, and, from 10 October 1953 until 16 November 1957, Oklahoma won a record 47 consecutive games. Other strong college teams of the 1950s included Georgia Tech, Michigan State, and the University of Tennessee.

Many of the postseason bowl games that were initiated during the postwar years were discontinued, and, for most of the 1950s, the New Year's Day bowl games were the four major ones—Rose, Orange, Cotton, and Sugar—and the three lesser ones—Gator, Tangerine, and Sun.

In 1954, for financial reasons, the NCAA abolished the unlimited substitution rules that had been in effect since the start of World War II. In 1958, another major rules change helped differentiate the college game from the professional one. The NCAA Rules Committee passed a new rule allowing for two points on a conversion after a touchdown if the ball was run or passed over the goal line from the three-yard line. The one-point conversion for a placekick or dropkick through the uprights remained in effect.

As professional football became a more viable career, most of the top collegiate football players of the 1950s played in the NFL after graduation. A few who did not included halfback Pete Dawkins, Heisman Trophy winner from Army whose career was spent in the U.S. Army, where he attained the rank of brigadier general; end Ron Beagle, Maxwell Award winner from Navy who served in the U.S. Marines and then entered the business world; and Bill Carpenter, who at Army was known as the "lonely end," since he did not join their huddle and was positioned as a flanker, 20 yards from the line of scrimmage. Carpenter also fulfilled his military commitment and served in Vietnam, where he won multiple decorations (including the Distinguished Service Cross) for his combat bravery and achieved the rank of lieutenant general.

PROFESSIONAL FOOTBALL DURING THE 1950S: PRO FOOTBALL'S GREATEST GAME

Professional football in the 1950s began with the Cleveland Browns and ended with the Baltimore Colts and New York Giants. In 1950, the NFL expanded by three teams and removed its competition at the same time. The

AAFC, competitor to the NFL from 1946 to 1949, folded, and the NFL added two of the AAFC's best teams, the Cleveland Browns and San Francisco 49ers, and one of its worst, the Baltimore Colts. The Colts survived the 1950 season but folded in 1951.

The Cleveland Browns, winners of the AAFC championship all four seasons, continued their dominance of professional football by reaching the NFL Championship Game each year from 1950 to 1955, and winning it in 1950, 1954, and 1955. Their opposition during those six years was either the Detroit Lions or Los Angeles Rams, the Rams in 1950, 1951, and 1955, and the Lions in 1952, 1953, and 1954.

During the latter half of the decade, the Giants became the team to beat and were NFL champions in 1956 and runners-up in 1958 and 1959. The Giants' opponents in 1958 were the Baltimore Colts—not the former AAFC team that died in 1951, but a new version that could actually trace its heritage to the league's origin. The Colts began as a new team with new owners in 1953, but the franchise's history, through a series of relocations, ownership changes, and team name changes, can actually be traced back to the Dayton Triangles, one of the original teams that founded the APFA (the NFL's predecessor) in 1920.

The 1958 NFL Championship Game between the Giants and these new Colts was the first NFL Championship Game to be tied at the end of regulation time and require a sudden-death overtime period to decide it. The game has been called the "greatest game ever played" (although there have been many other games that can challenge that claim). It did, however, greatly increase the league's popularity.

One reason for the NFL's rise in popularity can be traced to television. In 1950, the Los Angeles Rams became the first NFL team to televise all its games, both home and away. Other teams followed, and the sport's fan base increased due to the added exposure. The 1958 NFL Championship Game was televised nationally, and its exciting ending, coupled with the fact that one of its participants was the nation's largest city, helped to improve the NFL's favorability. By the end of the 1950s, the NFL was approaching America's unofficial "national pastime" as the country's favorite spectator sport.

COLLEGE FOOTBALL IN THE 1960S: THE UNIVERSITY OF ALABAMA

The University of Alabama dominated 1960s college football. Under coach Paul "Bear" Bryant, they were voted national champions in 1961, 1964, 1965, and 1966. Notre Dame, Ohio State, Michigan State, the University of

Southern California, and the University of Texas were also among the nation's top teams.

In 1965, the rules were changed to allow unlimited substitution, and teams developed two platoons, offensive and defensive. As professional football became a lucrative career, most of the top collegiate football players played professionally upon graduation. Among the few who did not was Ernie Davis, star running back for Syracuse University and the first black Heisman Trophy winner, who was headed for the NFL after being drafted by the Washington Redskins and traded to the Cleveland Browns. Davis was stricken with leukemia prior to the start of the Browns training camp, and he never played in the NFL, succumbing to the disease the following year. Quarterback Jake Gibbs, who led the University of Mississippi to the national championship in 1960, passed up an NFL career to play professional baseball with the New York Yankees. Guard Mike McKeever, who, along with his twin brother, Marlin McKeever, became the first twins to be named All-Americans, suffered a head injury during his senior year that terminated his chances for a pro football career.

PROFESSIONAL FOOTBALL DURING THE 1960S: THE AMERICAN FOOTBALL LEAGUE, FOURTH EDITION

The big news in professional football in the 1960s was the birth of the American Football League (AFL) in 1960. This was the fourth major professional league with that name but by far the most successful. It was formally established on 14 August 1959, with play beginning in the 1960 season, and the league came about when Lamar Hunt, son of millionaire oilman H. L. Hunt, attempted to purchase an NFL franchise but was rebuffed. Several other wealthy businessmen were also attempting to get NFL franchises at that time and were also unsuccessful.

They decided to form their own league in direct competition with the NFL. On 14 August 1959, the league was formally established, with franchises given to Dallas (Lamar Hunt), New York (sportscaster Harry Wismer), Houston (Kenneth S. "Bud" Adams, another wealthy Texas oilman), Denver (Bob Howsam), Los Angeles (Barron Hilton, hotel magnate) and Minneapolis–St. Paul (Max Winter). Later that year, Buffalo (Ralph Wilson) and Boston (Billy Sullivan) received franchises. World War II hero and former South Dakota governor Joe Foss was selected as the league commissioner. After the Minneapolis group was able to join the NFL, they dropped out of the AFL and were replaced by Oakland (owned by real estate developer Chet Soda) in January 1960.

A five-year television contract for roughly $10 million was signed in June. The eight teams that began the season were the Boston Patriots, Buffalo Bills, Houston Oilers, and the Titans of New York in the East Division, and the Dallas Texans, Denver Broncos, Los Angeles Chargers, and Oakland Raiders in the West Division. The league began play on 9 September 1960, and teams played a 14-game schedule with an AFL championship game on 1 January 1961, which was won by the Houston Oilers over the Los Angeles Chargers. Although most of the teams lost money, the fact that most were owned by wealthy businessmen enabled the league to stay afloat. In 1961, the Chargers, unable to compete successfully with the NFL's Los Angeles Rams, relocated to San Diego.

The league's turning point occurred in 1964, when a new television contract for $36 million was signed. This enabled teams to entice college graduates to join the AFL, and Joe Namath, college star at the University of Alabama, was signed for an unprecedented $427,000. Other top players also received huge contracts, and a bidding war with the NFL ensued.

On 8 June 1966, the NFL and AFL signed a merger agreement that provided for a common draft of college players, an annual AFL–NFL World Championship Game to be initially played in January 1967, and a merger into one league beginning with the 1970 season. The AFL–NFL World Championship Game later became known as the Super Bowl.

The first two of these games were one-sided victories for the Green Bay Packers of the NFL, but the third annual AFL–NFL World Championship Game, played on 12 January 1969, proved that the AFL was not the lesser league, as the New York Jets, behind quarterback Joe Namath, defeated the NFL's Baltimore Colts, 16–7. The AFL put the icing on the cake with a 23–7 victory by the Kansas City Chiefs over the Minnesota Vikings on 11 January 1970, in the last AFL–NFL World Championship Game played before the leagues completed their merger and competed as one league in 1970.

COLLEGE FOOTBALL IN THE 1970S: TRAGEDY

The decade of the 1970s began tragically, when two plane crashes within one month killed 14 members of the Wichita State University football team (and 17 others) and 37 members of the Marshall University football team (and 38 others).

In 1972, the NCAA allowed freshmen to compete in football. They had previously not been allowed to play on varsity teams (except for a brief period during World War II), although some schools fielded freshman teams that competed against other schools' freshman teams in limited schedules.

In 1973, the NCAA created a three-division structure that, with a few minor modifications and name changes, still exists in the 21st century.

The University of Alabama, Ohio State University, the University of Oklahoma, the University of Nebraska, and the University of Southern California had the most powerful teams during the decade, with Alabama being recognized as national champion in 1973, 1975, 1977, 1978, and 1979. Archie Griffin of Ohio State became the first and only player to win the Heisman Trophy twice (a record that still stands as of 2012).

Several illustrious coaches retired during the decade, including College Football Hall of Famers Frank Broyles (1957–1976 at Arkansas, 144–58–5 won-lost-tied record), Hugh Duffy Daugherty (1954–1972 at Michigan State, 109–69–5), Bob Devaney (1962–1972 at Nebraska, 101–20–2). Woody Hayes (1951–1978 at Ohio State, 205–61–10), Frank Kush (1958–1979 at Arizona State, 173–57–1), John McKay (1960–1975 at Southern California, 127–40–8), Ara Parseghian (1964–1974 at Notre Dame, 95–17–4), Tommy Prothro (1955–1964 at Oregon State, 1965–1970 at UCLA, combined 104–55–5), Darrell Royal (1955–1976 at Texas, 167–47–5), and Ben Schwartzwalder (1949–1973 at Syracuse, 153–91–3).

PROFESSIONAL FOOTBALL IN THE 1970S: MERGER, SUPER BOWL, AND *MONDAY NIGHT FOOTBALL*

The year 1970 was a monumental one for professional football. During that season, the merger between the AFL and NFL was completed, and one 26-team league was formed. The league was divided into two conferences, American and National, and each conference was divided into three divisions. After the regular season ended, a three-week playoff series was played. The three division winners plus the team with the next best record in each conference participated in the tournament, with the two surviving teams meeting in the league's championship game, the Super Bowl.

One of the league's greatest triumphs was the success of an innovation proposed by NFL commissioner Alvin "Pete" Rozelle. It began in 1970 as an experiment by the ABC television network and quickly became an American institution. Rozelle was looking to expand television coverage during the 1960s and decided to experiment with night football. Although the NFL had played a few Saturday night games during the early 1950s, the league had not yet achieved the extensive fan interest that it would later find during the decade, and the games did not achieve high ratings.

As the NFL fan base greatly increased during the 1960s, Rozelle wanted to try again. Although the networks were initially unreceptive of the idea of preempting their regular family television programming in the evening, Rozelle convinced ABC (then the least-watched and lowest-rated network) to televise a weekly game on Monday nights. Once the agreement was made, ABC producer Roone Arledge decided to try a different slant on the broadcast and emphasize its entertainment value. With that in mind, he hired Howard Cosell, a lawyer whose style of broadcasting was argumentative and controversial. Along with Cosell, Arledge attempted to hire an established football play-by-play announcer, and, since his first two choices, Vince Scully and Curt Gowdy, were unavailable, he settled for Keith Jackson, an experienced and capable announcer. Arledge then sought a color analyst and tried to hire Frank Gifford, a former New York Giants NFL player who had been working as a football color analyst in New York, but he was also unavailable. Gifford suggested Don Meredith, a recently retired former Dallas Cowboys quarterback who had come across quite well when interviewed by Gifford following the Cowboys loss in the infamous Ice Bowl game that Meredith had quarterbacked.

The first *Monday Night Football* game took place on 21 September 1970, in a game between the New York Jets (the defending NFL champions) and Cleveland Browns in Cleveland. The interplay between the pompous, opinionated Cosell and the laid back, humorous Meredith turned out to be much more entertaining than expected, and the event soon became must-see watching for a large portion of America's males.

The following year, Gifford became available, and he replaced Jackson as the play-by-play reporter, even though he had previously only been a color analyst. The team of Gifford, Meredith, and Cosell had exceptional chemistry, and the show became a success.

COLLEGE FOOTBALL FROM 1980 TO THE 21ST CENTURY

Bowl Games and More Bowl Games but Still No Undisputed National Champion

The major change in college football during the last two decades of the 20th century was the proliferation of postseason bowl games. In 1935, when the first Orange Bowl and Sugar Bowl were played on 1 January, they joined the Rose Bowl as the only three bowl games played by major colleges. Three other bowl games featuring lesser schools were also played that postseason.

In 1949, when postwar sports activity was at its height, there were nine bowl games featuring major colleges and 22 bowl games featuring lesser colleges. Most of those 31 games were not played for more than a few years, and, by 1959, there were only eight major bowls and seven minor ones being held. This figure stayed relatively constant for the next 20 years, although one or two bowls were added each year. By 1980, the figures stood at 15 major and eight minor bowls. By the year 2000, with the advent of cable television and many more television networks looking for sports programming during the holidays, there were 31 bowl games, with most of them involving major colleges. In 2011, there were 40 bowl games.

What makes this plethora frustrating for the football fan, however, is that bowl sponsors change from year to year. Invitations to compete are offered to teams that the sponsors feel will draw the most attention to their game. The continuity that was once a feature of the bowl system, where the Rose Bowl was contested between the Pacific Coast Conference champion and the Big Ten Conference champion, the Orange Bowl featured the Big Eight Conference champion, and the Cotton Bowl had the Southwest Conference champion, has been lost.

Many of the current bowl games have sponsors' names attached to the title of the game. In some of these bowls, the sponsors first modified the original name by adding their name and then after a few years dropped the original name and only used their name. One such example is the Peach Bowl, which became the Chick-fil-A Peach Bowl, and which is now simply the Chick-fil-A Bowl. Others change from year to year depending on the current sponsor. The annual game played in Orlando, Florida, that began in 1946 as the Tangerine Bowl evolved to its present title, the Capital One Bowl. Another postseason game first played in Orlando in 1990 usurped the Tangerine Bowl name at first but has since been known as the Blockbuster Bowl; Carquest Bowl; MicronPC Bowl; MicronPC.com Bowl; Visit Florida Tangerine Bowl; Mazda Tangerine Bowl; and, its 2011 title, the Champs Sports Bowl. Apparently, as long as it is more college football, fans and sponsors do not care what it is called.

Throughout the more than 100 years of college football, one of the sport's major shortcomings has been the lack of a definitive national champion. Beginning in the 1920s, various media organizations, including the Helms Athletic Foundation, United Press International, the Associated Press, and, in recent years, *USA Today*, have annually selected one champion, usually by polling sportswriters and/or coaches. More often than not (as illustrated in appendix L), more than one school receives that honor, as different organizations have conflicting viewpoints.

An attempt to remedy this practice occurred during the 1990s. In 1992, a Bowl Coalition was formed consisting of five conferences, the University of Notre Dame (an independent nonconference school), and six bowl games. A complex formula was developed to determine which winner of one of the bowl games would be considered national champion. But the coalition was short lived, lasting only three years, and one of the major problems was the exclusion of teams from the Big Ten and Pacific-10 conferences, since they had a contractual agreement to meet in the Rose Bowl, which was not part of the Bowl Coalition.

In 1995, the Bowl Coalition was replaced by the Bowl Alliance, with a modified structure, but it, too, did not include the Big Ten and Pac-10 conferences. In 1998, those two conferences agreed to participate, and the Rose Bowl was added to the list of participating bowls. The NCAA classified its member schools as Division I Football Bowl Subdivision and Division I Football Championship Subdivision teams. The latter teams have lesser football programs than the former but do play a tournament after the regular season is concluded, and a definitive champion is crowned. A complicated system is still employed to select the participating teams in the Football Bowl Subdivision.

A Bowl Championship Series National Championship Game is played, with the site varying amongst several bowl venues. The American Football Coaches Association is contractually bound to vote the winner of this game as national champion, but since no final tournament is played, there still occasionally remains controversy as to which team is the best in the nation. It seems inevitable that a final collegiate tournament will someday happen, but it would require a substantial change in the current bowl structure.

PROFESSIONAL FOOTBALL FROM 1980 TO THE 21ST CENTURY

Competition and Labor Problems

The major events in professional football during the last three decades of the 20th century involved competition and labor strife. After the merger of the AFL and NFL in 1970, it would have appeared that the league could relax and reap the benefits of its united front, but, as usual in American society, a successful enterprise brings competition. In 1974, this occurred with the birth of the innovative World Football League (WFL), which, despite its international-sounding name, was limited to 11 teams in the continental United States and one in Hawaii. The WFL did manage to entice several NFL stars to join, notably Miami Dolphins Larry Csonka, Paul Warfield, and Jim Kiick; however, the league folded in 1975, before its second season could be completed, but several of its innovations were later adopted by the NFL.

These changes included kickoffs being taken from the 30-yard line instead of the 40-yard line; goalposts being moved to the back of the end zone instead of on the goal line; some penalties being reduced to 10 yards instead of 15; missed field goals now being returned to the line of scrimmage instead of the 20-yard line; and bump-and-run pass coverage being prohibited once the receiver is more than three yards downfield. Other innovations that have not yet been added by the NFL, although they are part of Canadian football, include the disallowance of fair catches on punts, the allowance of backs to be in forward motion prior to the snap of the ball, and the permittance of receivers to have only one foot in bounds for a catch to be considered legal. Two innovations that have not been adopted by either the Canadian Football League or NFL are overtime being changed to a 15-minute non-sudden-death period, during which touchdowns are worth seven points, as well as the addition of an "action point" try following a touchdown, where the ball is placed on the five-yard line and must be run or passed over the goal line for an additional point.

Shortly after the WFL folded, the NFL expanded and, in 1976, added teams in Tampa, Florida (Tampa Bay Buccaneers), and Seattle, Washington (Seattle Seahawks). In 1978, the NFL extended its regular season to 16 games and expanded its playoff structure from an eight-team, three-week series to a 10-team, four-week series.

Another competitive threat occurred in 1983, with the creation of the United States Football League (USFL). Their games were played in the spring and summer months, thus avoiding head-to-head scheduling conflicts, but they strongly competed with the NFL for signing collegians. The USFL lasted three seasons and then sued the NFL for antitrust violation. They surprisingly won the suit but were awarded only one dollar in nominal damages, effectively ending their life.

The other major concern of the NFL during the 1980s was labor problems. Although the NFL Players Association (NFLPA) was established in 1956, it was not until 1968 that a collective bargaining agreement was reached with the NFL. A players' strike, countered by an NFL lockout, took place on 3 July 1968, but by 14 July it had ended. Another lockout/strike happened in July 1970. Four years later, another strike was called. This one lasted from 1 July 1974 until 10 August 1974. In 1982, a major labor disruption occurred. Two weeks into the season, the NFLPA struck on 21 September. Games for the next several weeks were cancelled until an agreement was reached on 16 November. Teams played just nine of their scheduled 16 games, and the playoffs were modified so that 16 teams played a postseason tournament rather than the 10 teams that normally took part.

The 1987 season featured another strike, which began on 22 September, two weeks after the season began. This time, after cancelling the games on the weekend of 27 September, the NFL played the following three weeks using replacement players. During these volatile years, a series of suits and countersuits also took place. The NFLPA also decertified and recertified, but, in 1993, a stabilization occurred and a new collective bargaining agreement was reached. This was successfully renewed five times, until 2010, and another labor dispute occurred in 2011. This time it was in the form of a lockout, which did not end until 4 August 2011. The new collective bargaining agreement lasts until 2021, hopefully bringing stability in the NFL for some time.

GROWTH OF THE INTERNATIONAL GAME

For most of the 19th and 20th centuries, the sport of American football (and its Canadian version) was played almost exclusively in North America. In the 1970s, however, the NFL saw the potential for developing a worldwide market and began playing games overseas. The league played its first game outside North America on 16 August 1976, when the St. Louis Cardinals met the San Diego Chargers in a preseason exhibition game in Tokyo, Japan. Two years later, Mexico City saw its first NFL action, when the New Orleans Saints and Philadelphia Eagles met there during the preseason. In 1983, the NFL played its first game in London, England, and followed it by playing there four more times during the decade.

In 1986, the league played its first American Bowl, a preseason game played outside the United States. From 1986 to 2005, there were 79 American Bowl games played in London, England; Tokyo and Osaka, Japan; Montreal, Toronto, and Vancouver, Canada; Berlin, Germany; Barcelona, Spain; Mexico City and Monterrey, Mexico; Dublin, Ireland; and Sydney, Australia.

In 2005, the NFL played its first regular-season game in Mexico City and drew a record 103,467 fans, the largest NFL attendance in history. (The attendance record was surpassed in 2009, when the Dallas Cowboys opened Cowboys Stadium and drew 105,121 fans). Since 2007, the league has played an annual regular-season game in London, England, and the Buffalo Bills have moved one of their home games to Toronto, Canada, each season from 2008 to 2012.

The NFL also began a quasi-international league in 1991 called the World League of American Football (WLAF). It began with 10 teams—three in Europe (London, England; Barcelona, Spain; and Frankfurt, Germany), one in Canada (Montreal), and six in the United States (New York/New Jersey, Orlando, Raleigh-Durham, Birmingham, San Antonio, and Sacramento). A 10-game season was played during the spring months, and the season culminated with the World Bowl game. After the second year, the league suspended activity for two years, but it resumed play in 1995 as a strictly European league. It featured teams in Amsterdam, Netherlands; Edinburgh, Scotland; and Dusseldorf, Germany. These are in addition to the other three European teams. In 1998, the league was renamed NFL Europe (later changed to NFL Europa in 2007). NFL Europe lasted through the 2007 season but was only popular in Germany. By the 2007 season, five of the six teams in the league were based there. The NFL continued its overseas marketing by scheduling annual regular-season games in England.

In 2012, a new experiment began known as the Elite Football League of India. The venture is being backed by several prominent American investors, including former NFL players Mike Ditka, Michael Irvin, and Ron Jaworski. Brandon Chillar, one of only four NFL players of Indian descent, is also an investor. The initial season saw eight teams representing cities in India, Pakistan, and Sri Lanka play a total of 26 games. Time will tell whether football can be successfully staged in a country where field hockey and cricket are the major sports.

In the nearly 150 years that the sport of American football has been played, it has grown from an activity played by a handful of college men on a Saturday afternoon to one of America's largest businesses, employing thousands. It is followed closely by most of the citizens of the United States and still gaining followers around the world.

A

ADDERLEY, HERBERT ALLEN "HERB." B. 8 June 1939, Philadelphia, Pennsylvania. Herb Adderley attended Northeast High School in Philadelphia, where he starred in baseball, basketball, and **football**. After graduating in 1957, he enrolled at **Michigan State University**. Adderley was selected by the **Green Bay Packers** in the first round of the 1961 **National Football League (NFL) Draft** as the 12th selection overall, and also by the Titans of New York in the **American Football League** Draft in the second round as the 13th overall pick. He signed with Green Bay. Although he played **halfback** in college, Green Bay had sufficient strength in that position, and, after a few games, he was converted to **cornerback**, where he played the rest of his professional career. Six feet tall and 205 pounds, Adderley also served as a kick **returner** from 1961 to 1965. He played from 1961 to 1969 for the Packers and from 1970 to 1972 for the **Dallas Cowboys**.

In his 12-year NFL career, Adderley recorded 48 **interceptions** and nine **touchdowns** (two as a kick returner) in 164 regular-season games. In eight postseason games, he scored a touchdown in 1967 in the Super Bowl on a 60-yard interception return. In postseason play, he returned eight kicks for a 20.1 yard average and intercepted five passes.

Adderley was selected for the **Pro Bowl** five times, from 1963 to 1967. He played on NFL championship teams with the Packers in 1961, 1962, 1965, 1966, and 1967, as well as two with the Cowboys, in 1971 and 1972. He played in four of the first six **Super Bowls**, winning in 1967 and 1968 with the Packers, losing in 1971 with the Cowboys, and winning with them in 1972.

Adderley was traded to the Los Angeles Rams in 1973, but he chose to retire. In retirement, he has worked as a broadcaster and an **assistant coach** for Temple University, as well as an assistant coach for the Philadelphia Bell in the **World Football League**. Adderley was inducted into the **Pro Football Hall of Fame** in 1981.

AIKMAN, TROY KENNETH. B. 21 November 1966, West Covina, California. Troy Aikman was raised in Cerritos, California. At the age of 12, he moved with his family to Henryetta, Oklahoma, where he attended Henryetta

High School. Aikman starred in both baseball and **football** and was offered a contract by the New York Mets after he graduated from high school but elected to enroll at the **University of Oklahoma** instead. After breaking his ankle during his sophomore year and losing his starting **quarterback** position, he transferred to the **University of California, Los Angeles**, for the 1986 football season. As a transfer student, Aikman was ineligible for the team that year but played in 1987 and 1988. He led the Bruins to a 20–4 record in those two years, including two bowl victories.

At six feet, four inches tall and 220 pounds, Aikman was the ideal size for a professional quarterback, and he was chosen as the first overall selection in the 1989 **National Football League (NFL) Draft** by the **Dallas Cowboys**. He was the Cowboys' starting quarterback from 1989 to 2000; led them to **Super Bowl** victories in 1993, 1994, and 1996; and was the Super Bowl Most Valuable Player in 1993. Aikman was also selected for six **Pro Bowls**. In his 12-year NFL career, he started and played in 165 regular-season games and had a won-lost record of 94–61. He completed 2,898 **passes** in 4,715 attempts for 32,942 yards, with 165 passes for **touchdowns**. Aikman also ran for nine touchdowns. In postseason play, he appeared in 16 games, 15 as the starting quarterback, and had a record of 11–4 in those games. He completed 320 of 502 passes for 3,849 yards and 23 touchdowns. He also ran 32 times for 87 yards and one touchdown.

Aikman was inducted into the **Pro Football Hall of Fame** in 2006 and the **College Football Hall of Fame** in 2008, and he has worked as a television commentator since his retirement from active play. He and former Cowboys' quarterback **Roger Staubach** formed Hall of Fame Racing in 2003, and, from 2005 to 2009, they were coowners of a NASCAR team.

ALABAMA, UNIVERSITY OF. The University of Alabama is located in Tuscaloosa, Alabama. Their **football** program began in 1892, and, since then, through 2012, Crimson Tide teams have compiled a record of 793–299–40. In addition, they have competed in 60 postseason **bowl games** with a record of 34–22–3 and one game won but vacated due to recruiting infractions. They have been selected as national collegiate champions in 19 different seasons. Home games since 1929 are played at Bryant-Denny Stadium. Its seating capacity in 1929 was 12,000, but it has been expanded throughout the years and is now one of the world's largest outdoor arenas, with a seating capacity of 101,821. Since 1932, Alabama football teams have competed in the **Southeastern Conference** of the **National Collegiate Athletic Association**. Their main rival is **Auburn University**. The teams have met annually since 1948 in a contest known as the Iron Bowl.

Alabama's most successful **coach** was **Paul "Bear" Bryant**. He was their head coach from 1958 to 1982 and, beginning in 1959, led them to 24 consecutive postseason bowl games. Bryant was inducted into the **College Football Hall of Fame** in 1986. Other Alabama coaches who have been elected to that Hall are Wallace Wade (Alabama coach from 1923 to 1930), Frank Thomas (1931–1946), and Gene Stallings (1990–1996).

Alabama alumni in the College Football Hall of Fame include **quarterbacks** Harry Gilmer, Allison "Pooley" Hubert, and Riley Smith; **halfbacks** Johnny Mack Brown, Millard "Dixie" Howell, and Johnny Musso; **fullback** Johnny Cain; **ends Don Hutson** and Ozzie Newsome; offensive **linemen** John Hannah, Frank Howard, Vaughn Mancha, Billy Neighbors, Fred Sington, and Don Whitmire; defensive **tackle** Marty Lyons; and **linebackers** Cornelius Bennett, Lee Roy Jordan, and Woodrow Lowe. In 2009, **running back** Mark Ingram became the first Alabama player to win the **Heisman Trophy**.

Through 2012, there have been 275 **professional football** players who have attended Alabama, 263 in the **National Football League**, six in the **American Football League**, and six in the **All-America Football Conference**. They include **Pro Football Hall of Famers** John Hannah, Don Hutson, **Joe Namath**, Ozzie Newsome, **Bart Starr**, Dwight Stephenson, and Derrick Thomas. Other Alabama alumni who played professional football include Shaun Alexander, Bob Baumhower, Cornelius Bennett, Howard Cross, Cornelius Griffin, Charley Hannah, Lee Roy Jordan, E. J. Junior, Chris Mohr, Mike Pitts, Jeff Rutledge, Ken Stabler, and Deshea Townsend.

ALBERT, FRANK CULLEN "FRANKIE." B. 27 January 1920, Chicago, Illinois. D. 5 September 2002, Palo Alto, California. Frankie Albert attended Glendale High School in Glendale, California, and **Stanford University**. A five-foot, 10-inch, 165-pound, left-handed **quarterback**, he led Stanford to a victory over the **University of Nebraska** in the **Rose Bowl** on 1 January 1941, resulting in an undefeated season, with a record of 10–0. Under **Coach** Clark Shaughnessy, he was one of the first **T formation** quarterbacks.

Albert was selected by the **Chicago Bears** in the 1942 **National Football League (NFL) Draft**, but, due to World War II, he did not play **professional football** until 1945. He played for the Los Angeles Bulldogs in the minor league Pacific Coast Football League that year. The following year, he played for the **San Francisco 49ers** in the newly formed **All-America Football Conference (AAFC)**. Albert led the 49ers to second-place finishes in four straight seasons from 1946 to 1949. In 1950, the 49ers became members of the NFL, as the AAFC and NFL merged. Albert remained with the 49ers through the 1952 season. He concluded his professional playing career with one season in Canada in 1953, where, in 14 games for the **Calgary Stampeders**, he completed 104 of 225 **passes** for 1,568 yards and 12 **touchdowns** and carried the ball 53 times for -26 yards **rushing** and two touchdowns.

In his six-year combined AAFC/NFL career, Albert played in 90 games, completed 831 passes in 1,564 attempts for 10,795 yards and 115 touchdowns, ran 329 times for 1,272 yards and 27 touchdowns, and **punted** 299 times for a 43.0-yard average. He also attempted five **conversions** but was only successful once. In his first two seasons, he was occasionally used as a punt and kick **returner**, averaged 19.4 yards in five **kickoff** returns, and returned one punt for six yards. He appeared in only two postseason games in 1949 and completed 17 passes in 41 attempts for 204 yards and two touchdowns. He also ran 14 times for 92 yards and no touchdowns in those two games.

Albert later coached the 49ers for three years, from 1956 to 1958. In 1957, his 49ers finished in second place in the Western Division, losing a **playoff** to the **Detroit Lions**. In 1956, he was selected to the **College Football Hall of Fame**.

ALL-AMERICA FOOTBALL CONFERENCE (AAFC). The All-America Football Conference (AAFC) was a **professional football** league that existed in competition with the **National Football League (NFL)** from 1946 to 1949. Its founder was Chicago sportswriter Arch Ward, who gathered a number of wealthy businessmen to form the league. Such major-league **stadiums** as Yankee Stadium, **Los Angeles Memorial Coliseum**, and Cleveland's Municipal Stadium were among the venues employed by the league.

The AAFC began in 1946, with the **New York Yankees, Brooklyn Dodgers**, Buffalo Bisons, and **Miami Seahawks** in the Eastern Division, and the **Cleveland Browns, Los Angeles Dons, San Francisco 49ers**, and Chicago Rockets in the Western Division. In 1947, the **Baltimore Colts** replaced the Seahawks, and the Bisons were renamed the Bills. The 1949 season saw the Rockets renamed the Hornets and the Yankees and Dodgers merge into the **Brooklyn–New York Yankees**, as a seven-team league resulted. The Browns, **coached** by **Paul Brown** and featuring stars **Otto Graham**, Marion Motley, and **Lou Groza**, won the league championship in each of the AAFC's four seasons. In 1950, three teams from the AAFC (Cleveland Browns, Baltimore Colts, and San Francisco 49ers) were absorbed into the NFL, and the remaining five AAFC teams were disbanded. *See also* APPENDIX F (for a list of league champions).

ALL-AMERICAN. An All-American is a scholastic player selected as being among the best for a season in American sport. The term was originated in the 1890s by sportswriters Caspar Whitney and **Walter Camp**, who selected collegiate "All-American **football** teams" beginning in 1889. Basketball's earliest All-American teams were named following the 1928–1929 season.

ALLEN, GEORGE HERBERT. B. 29 August 1918, Detroit, Michigan. D. 31 December 1990, Palos Verdes Estates, California. George Allen attended Lake Shore High School in St. Clair Shores, Michigan, where he was on the track team and played **football** and basketball. He continued his education at Alma College and then enlisted in the U.S. Navy, where he was an officer trainee at Marquette University. After his military commitment ended, he attended Eastern Michigan University and majored in education. He then earned a master's degree in physical education from the **University of Michigan** in 1947.

Allen began his football **coaching** career at Morningside College in 1948. He coached there until 1951, and at Whittier College from 1951 to 1956. In 1957, he was hired by the Los Angeles Rams of the **National Football League (NFL)** as an **assistant coach**. He was an assistant with the **Chicago Bears** from 1958 to 1965 and, in 1966, was given his first head coaching opportunity with the Rams. Allen coached them from 1966 to 1970, and the **Washington Redskins** from 1971 to 1977. He led the Rams to the NFL Western Conference championship game in 1967 and 1969, but they were defeated both times. As the Redskins' coach, he took them to the 1972 **Super Bowl**, where they lost to the **Miami Dolphins**. Allen was hired by the Rams in 1978, but his strict discipline caused conflicts with some of the Rams' players and he was fired prior to the start of the season. In 12 years as an NFL coach, his teams had a combined record of 116–47–5 in regular-season play and 2–7 in the postseason.

Allen went on to do some television work as a football commentator before returning as head coach in the new **United States Football League (USFL)** in 1983 and 1984, leading the Arizona Wranglers to the USFL championship game in 1984. He was out of football for several years and then returned as head coach of Long Beach State University in 1990. That job, however, might have indirectly resulted in his death. After the season-ending game, won by Long Beach State in November, his players dumped a bucket of ice water on him (as was the tradition in football at that time). He became ill shortly afterward and died on 31 December 1990.

In Allen's 14 years of coaching **professional football**, his teams never had a losing record. He was inducted into the **Pro Football Hall of Fame** as a coach in 2002. His son, George, served as U.S. senator and governor of Virginia.

ALLEN, MARCUS LEMARR. B. 26 March 1960, San Diego, California. Marcus Allen attended Abraham Lincoln High School in San Diego, California. In high school, he played both **quarterback** on **offense** and **safety** on **defense**. The six-foot, two-inch, 210-pound Allen was converted to a **running back** when he played for the **University of Southern California (USC)** from 1978 to 1981. He won the **Heisman Trophy** in 1981, his senior year. That same year, he became the first college player to **rush** for more than 2,000 yards in one season, and he gained a total of 2,342 yards in 12 games. In four years at USC, the Trojans had a record of 40–6–2 and were national collegiate champions in 1978 and **conference** champions in 1978 and 1979.

Allen was selected by the Los Angeles Raiders in the first round of the 1982 **National Football League (NFL) Draft** as the 10th overall selection. He played for the Raiders from 1982 to 1992, and for the **Kansas City Chiefs** from 1993 to 1996. He was named the NFL's Offensive Rookie of the Year following the 1982 season. He starred for the Raiders in the 1984 **Super Bowl** and was named the game's Most Valuable Player after **running** for a then-record 191 yards, catching two **passes** for an additional 18 yards, and scoring two **touchdowns** (one of them on a 74-yard touchdown run).

In his 16-year NFL career, in 222 regular-season games, Allen carried the ball 3,022 times for 12,243 yards and 123 touchdowns. He also caught 587 passes for 5,411 yards and 21 touchdowns. On **option plays**, he passed the ball 27 times, with 12 completions for 282 yards and six touchdowns. In 1983, Allen also recovered a teammate's **fumble** in the **end zone** for an additional touchdown. In the postseason, he appeared in 16 games, ran 267 times for 1,347 yards and 11 touchdowns, and caught 53 passes for 530 yards and two touchdowns. He was chosen for six **Pro Bowls**.

Allen was inducted into the **College Football Hall of Fame** in 2000 and the **Pro Football Hall of Fame** in 2003. He is the older brother of Damon Allen, who played quarterback for 23 seasons in the **Canadian Football League** and was inducted into the **Canadian Football Hall of Fame** in 2012.

ALL-PURPOSE YARDS. All-purpose yards is a **football** statistical measure that combines yards gained via **rushing**, receiving, **interception** returns, **punt** returns, **kickoff** returns, and **fumble** returns. The definition varies slightly between the **National Football League**, **Canadian Football League**, and **collegiate football**.

AMERICAN BOWL. The American Bowl was the name given to a series of **National Football League (NFL)** preseason games played outside the United States from 1986 to 2005. There were 79 games billed as the American Bowl during those 20 years, and 25 of the 32 NFL teams appeared in at least one of them. The first one was played on 3 August 1986, at Wembley Stadium in London, England, between the **Chicago Bears** and **Dallas Cowboys**. The 15 August 1994 game in Mexico City, Mexico, drew 112,376 **fans**, the largest attendance in NFL history. American Bowl games were also held in Tokyo, Japan; Montreal, Canada; Berlin, Germany; Barcelona, Spain; Toronto, Canada; Dublin, Ireland; Monterrey, Mexico; Vancouver, Canada; Sydney,

Australia; and Osaka, Japan. The series was abandoned in 2005, when the NFL decided to play regular-season games outside the United States. *See also* APPENDIX I (for a list of international NFL games).

AMERICAN FOOTBALL LEAGUE (AFL) (1960–1969). The American Football League (AFL) that began play in 1960 was the fourth major **professional football** league with that name and by far the most successful. It began in 1959, when **Lamar Hunt**, son of millionaire oilman H. L. Hunt, attempted to purchase a **National Football League (NFL)** franchise but was rebuffed. Several other wealthy businessmen were also attempting to get NFL franchises at that time and were also unsuccessful. They decided to form their own league in direct competition with the NFL. On 14 August 1959, the AFL was formally established, with franchises given to Dallas (Lamar Hunt), New York (sportscaster Harry Wismer), Houston (Kenneth S. "Bud" Adams, another wealthy Texas oilman), Denver (Bob Howsam), Los Angeles (Barron Hilton, hotel magnate), and Minneapolis–St. Paul (Max Winter). Later that year, Buffalo (**Ralph Wilson**) and Boston (Billy Sullivan) received franchises. World War II hero and former South Dakota governor **Joe Foss** was selected as league commissioner. After the Minneapolis group was able to join the NFL, they dropped out of the AFL and were replaced by Oakland (real estate developer Chet Soda) in January 1960.

A five-year television contract for roughly $10 million was signed in June. The eight teams that began the season were the Boston Patriots, **Buffalo Bills**, Houston Oilers, and Titans of New York in the East Division, and the Dallas Texans, **Denver Broncos**, Los Angeles Chargers, and **Oakland Raiders** in the West Division. The league began play on 9 September 1960, and teams played a 14-game schedule, with an AFL Championship Game on 1 January 1961, won by the Houston Oilers over the Los Angeles Chargers. Although most of the teams lost money, the fact that most were owned by wealthy businessmen enabled the league to stay afloat. In 1961, the Chargers, unable to compete successfully with the NFL's Los Angeles Rams, relocated to San Diego.

No other franchise changes occurred until 1963, when the Texans, faced with competition from the NFL's **Dallas Cowboys**, moved to Kansas City, Missouri, and played as the **Kansas City Chiefs**. The Titans of New York were taken over by the league midway through the 1962 season, as Wismer (one of the few league owners who was not extremely wealthy) went bankrupt. The franchise was sold to a group headed by David "Sonny" Werblin, a television executive, and renamed the **New York Jets**. Although the Jets continued to play at the Polo Grounds, they looked forward to the 1964 season, when they would be able to play at the newly built Shea Stadium in Queens.

The league's turning point occurred in 1964, when a new television contract for $36 million was signed. This enabled teams to entice college graduates to join the AFL, and **Joe Namath**, college star at the **University of Alabama**, was signed for an unprecedented $427,000. Other top players also received huge contracts, and a bidding war with the NFL ensued.

In April 1966, Commissioner Foss resigned and was replaced by Oakland Raiders' general manager **Al Davis**. Around the same time, representatives from both leagues met to discuss a prospective merger. Davis was not in favor of the merger, which was agreed upon and announced on 8 June 1966. In protest, Davis resigned on 25 July, and he was replaced by sportswriter Milt Woodard. The terms of the merger provided for a common **draft** of college players, an annual AFL–NFL Championship Game to be initially played in January 1967, and a merger into one league beginning with the 1970 season. The AFL added a franchise in Miami known as the **Miami Dolphins** for the 1966 season and another, the **Cincinnati Bengals**, for the 1968 season.

The first AFL–NFL Championship Game took place on 15 January 1967, at the **Los Angeles Memorial Coliseum**. The **stadium**, which seated nearly 100,000, was only about two-thirds full. The game between the NFL's **Green Bay Packers** and the AFL's Kansas City Chiefs was one sided, with the Packers prevailing, 35–10. The 1968 AFL–NFL World Championship Game was also an easy victory for Green Bay. The season-ending championship game would later be known as the Super Bowl, and it would become an annual sellout and a virtual national holiday. The AFL proved it could compete with the NFL when the New York Jets defeated the **Baltimore Colts** on 12 January 1969, in Miami, Florida, to become the first AFL team to win the Super Bowl. In its 10-year existence, the AFL produced 27 players, four **coaches**, and three executives who were later enshrined in the **Pro Football Hall of Fame**. *See also* APPENDIX E (for a list of league champions).

AMERICAN FOOTBALL LEAGUES (1926, 1936–1937, 1940–1941). Throughout **football** history there have been several professional leagues that were called the American Football League. The first one of significance was founded in 1926, by sports promoter Charles C. "C. C." Pyle. He signed the famed collegiate star **Harold "Red" Grange** to a contract in 1926, and then attempted to gain a franchise in the **National Football League (NFL)** for a team featuring Grange and known as the New York Yankees. When his application was refused, Pyle established his own league and called it the American Football League (AFL). In addition to the Yankees, the league had eight other teams, including the Boston Bulldogs, Brooklyn Horsemen (featuring several of the famed **Four Horsemen of Notre Dame**), Chicago Bulls, Cleveland Panthers, Los Angeles Wildcats, Newark Bears, Philadelphia

Quakers, and Rock Island Independents. The Wildcats were a traveling team based in Rock Island, Illinois, and the team was comprised mainly of players who attended college on the West Coast. The Independents had formerly been a member of the NFL.

The league did not do particularly well at the gate, and by the end of the season, only four teams remained. The Quakers finished in first place, with a record of 8–2. The Yankees were second, with a 10–5 record. The league folded following the season, but Pyle's Yankees were given an NFL franchise and competed in the league in 1927.

A second American Football League was created in 1936, by Dr. Harry A. March, a medical doctor and former part owner and president of the **New York Giants** of the NFL. After a dispute with **George Preston Marshall**, owner of the Boston Redskins NFL franchise, March sold his interest in the Giants and formed his own league in direct competition with the NFL. The league consisted of the Boston Shamrocks, Cleveland Rams, New York Yankees, Pittsburgh Americans, Syracuse (later Rochester) Braves, and Brooklyn (later Rochester) Tigers. The Shamrocks won the 1936 league championship with an 8–3 record. In 1937, the Shamrocks, Yankees, Americans, and Rochester Tigers returned. Cleveland joined the NFL and was replaced by the Los Angeles Bulldogs (a team that actually played in Los Angeles, unlike earlier Los Angeles teams that were road teams). The **Cincinnati Bengals** replaced the Braves team that had folded. The Bulldogs won in 1937 by winning all eight of their games. The Americans folded midway through the season, as did the entire league following the season.

In 1940, a third American Football League was formed, unrelated to the first two AFLs. It had six teams, which included the Boston Bears, Buffalo Indians, Cincinnati Bengals, Columbus Bullies, Milwaukee Chiefs, and New York Yankees. Several of these teams had previously been members of a minor league American Professional Football Association (a league unrelated to the NFL's predecessor of the same name). The Bullies won the 1940 league championship with an 8–1–1 record. In 1941, the Bears dropped out, resulting in a five-team league. New ownership of the Buffalo franchise changed their team nickname to the Tigers, and the Yankees nickname was changed to the Americans by their new owners. The Bullies repeated as league champions with a 5–1–2 record, edging out the Americans, who finished at 5–2–1. Although the league appeared to be in good financial position, the outbreak of World War II curtailed operations, and, when the war ended, the league was not resumed. *See also* AMERICAN FOOTBALL LEAGUE (1960–1969).

AMERICAN PROFESSIONAL FOOTBALL ASSOCIATION (APFA). *See* NATIONAL FOOTBALL LEAGUE.

ANDERSEN, MORTEN. B. 19 August 1960, Copenhagen, Denmark. Morten Andersen was raised in Struer, Denmark, and as a youth competed in gymnastics, **soccer**, handball, and long jumping. When he was a high school exchange student in 1977, he was first exposed to American **football** and played at Ben Davis High School in Indianapolis, Indiana. Andersen impressed college **coaches** with his kicking ability and received a scholarship to **Michigan State University**. In college, one of his kicks was a record-setting 63-yard **field goal**.

Andersen was chosen by the **New Orleans Saints** in the fourth round of the 1982 **National Football League (NFL) Draft** as the 86th overall selection. He played for the Saints from 1982 to 1994. From 1995 to 2000, he played for the **Atlanta Falcons**. At the age of 40, he was considered too old to play in the NFL, but he was signed by the **New York Giants** in 2001 and played the entire 16-game season with them. In 2002 and 2003, Andersen played for the **Kansas City Chiefs**. In 2004, he played for the **Minnesota Vikings**. He was briefly retired in 2005, but, in 2006, he was hired by the Atlanta Falcons to help instruct their placekicker. He did better than that and replaced him for 2006 and 2007.

Andersen played his final NFL game on 30 December 2007, at the age of 47, and made all three field goal attempts and all five extra point attempts to help lead Atlanta to a 44–41 victory over the **Seattle Seahawks**. He is the second-oldest player to play in the NFL (behind **George Blanda**), at 47 years and 133 days of age.

Andersen has played in more NFL games than any other player in the league. At six feet, two inches, and 215 pounds, the left-footed placekicker holds the NFL career record for games played, field goals made, and field goals attempted, and he is second to George Blanda in extra points made and attempted. In 1991, Andersen became the third NFL player to kick a field goal of 60 or more yards. In 1995, he was the first NFL player to kick three field goals of more than 50 yards in one game.

In his 25-year NFL career, Andersen played in 382 regular-season games, kicked 565 field goals in 709 attempts, including 40 of 50 yards or more, and booted 849 extra points in 859 attempts. In 11 postseason games, he kicked 23 of 23 extra points and 18 of 23 field goals. He played in seven **Pro Bowls**. Andersen's unfulfilled goal was to be the first NFL player to play past the age of 50, and he may yet reach this goal.

ARENA FOOTBALL. Arena football is a variety of **football** that is played indoors. It was invented in 1981 by James F. Foster and, in our legalistic society, was given a patent in 1987. (Can you imagine if James Naismith had been allowed to patent the game of basketball?) In arena football, the rules of the traditional outdoor game are modified so that there are only eight players on each team, and the field length is only 50 yards. **Punting** is not permitted, and teams may have backs in forward motion prior to the snap. Scoring is more prevalent than in regular football, and scores of 70–60 are not uncommon. The **Arena Football League** is currently the primary league for the sport. *See also* GARCIA, AARON.

ARENA FOOTBALL LEAGUE. The Arena Football League was founded in 1987 by James F. Foster, the inventor of **arena football**. The league competed from 1987 to 2008, suspended operations in 2009, and resumed in 2010. A modified version of American **football**, it is played in indoor arenas during the spring and summer months. A league championship is determined at the end of the season in the **ArenaBowl** championship game.

The league began operations in 1987 with just four teams, the Chicago Bruisers, Denver Dynamite, Pittsburgh Gladiators, and Washington Commandos. By 1992, it had grown to a 12-team league, and it was up to 15 teams in 1996. There have been as many as 19 teams in the league, and, in 2012, there were 17. In its more than 20-year existence, the league has had teams in nearly all parts of the country, from California to Connecticut, and the state of Washington to Florida.

The league has produced several players who later played outdoor football professionally in the **National Football League (NFL)**, among them **Super Bowl**–winning **quarterback** Kurt Warner and **kickers** Jay Feely and Rob Bironas (the NFL record holder with eight **field goals** in one game). It has also produced a division among football **fans** who either love the sport and follow it regularly or detest and ignore it. In recent years, the league's television coverage has expanded, and many games are televised nationally.

ARENABOWL. The ArenaBowl is the championship game of the **Arena Football League**. It was first played in 1987, and then annually through 2008. In 2009, the Arena Football League cancelled its season to restructure. After declaring bankruptcy, the league reorganized and returned to play in 2010, again using the ArenaBowl as its league championship. Although there is no need to (unlike the **Super Bowl** the ArenaBowl is played in the same calendar year as the league's regular season), the ArenaBowl uses roman numerals to distinguish one year's game from another. The 2011 ArenaBowl (known as ArenaBowl XXIV) was one of arena football's most exciting games, as the Jacksonville Sharks defeated the Arizona Rattlers in a game decided on the final play. The Sharks' 40-year-old **quarterback**, **Aaron Garcia**, who had played arena football for 18 years but had never played in an ArenaBowl, completed a **touchdown pass** with two seconds remaining in the game to give the Sharks the victory.

ARIZONA CARDINALS. The Arizona Cardinals are a **professional football** team in the National Football Conference West Division of the **National Football League (NFL)**. They are based in Glendale, Arizona, and, since 2006, play their home games at the 63,000-seat University of Phoenix Stadium. They are a charter member of the NFL and began play in 1920 as the Chicago Cardinals in the American Professional Football Association, the forerunner of the NFL. Their home field in 1920–1921 was Normal Park in Chicago, Illinois. In 1922, they moved to the 50,000-seat Comiskey Park in Chicago, where they played through 1925. From 1926 to 1928, they returned to Normal Park, and, in 1929, they went back to Comiskey Park, where they remained through 1958.

In 1944, the Cardinals and **Pittsburgh Steelers** merged and played one season as **Card-Pitt**, splitting home games between Wrigley Field in Chicago and Forbes Field in Pittsburgh. In 1959, they played four games at the 100,000-seat Soldier Field in Chicago, and two games at the 30,000-seat Metropolitan Stadium in Minneapolis, Minnesota. They moved to St. Louis, Missouri, in 1960, and played at the 30,000-seat Busch Stadium until 1965. In 1966, they began play at the new 60,000-seat Busch Memorial Stadium, which served as their home field through 1987. In 1988, they moved to Phoenix, Arizona. Known as the Phoenix Cardinals through 1993 and the Arizona Cardinals since then, they played home games at the 70,000-seat Sun Devil Stadium in Tempe, Arizona, until 2005.

The Cardinals have been one of the NFL's weakest franchises and have compiled a record of 501–710–39 in the 93 years from 1920 to 2012. In the 50 years prior to the merger with the **American Football League** in 1970, the Cardinals appeared in just two NFL Championship Games, in 1947 and 1948. They defeated the **Philadelphia Eagles** for the league title in 1947, but lost to them in a driving snowstorm in 1948. (In 1925, no postseason **playoff** was held, but the Cardinals were declared NFL champions, with a record of 11–2–1.) Since the merger in 1970, when the NFL has had a multitiered postseason playoff schedule, the Cardinals have qualified just six times. They lost in the divisional playoffs in 1974, 1975, 1998, and 2009; the first round in 1982; and the 2008 season's **Super Bowl** (1 February 2009 game). Their playoff record is just 6–7.

Cardinals' head **coaches** for three or more seasons include John "Paddy" Driscoll (1920–1922), Milan Creighton (1935–1938), Jimmy Conzelman (1940–1942, 1946–1948), Phil Handler (1943–1945, interim 1949, 1951), Ray Richards (1955–1957), Frank "Pop" Ivy (1958–1961), Wally Lemm (1962–1965), Charley Winner (1966–1970), Don Coryell (1973–1977), Jim Hanifan (1980–1985), Gene Stallings (1986–1989), Joe Bugel (1990–1993), Vince Tobin (1996–2000), Dave McGinnis (2000–2003), Dennis Green

(2004–2006), and Ken Whisenhunt (2007–2012). On 17 January 2013, Bruce Arians was hired as head coach for the 2013 season.

Among the Cardinals' best players have been 10 Hall of Famers, including **quarterbacks** John "Paddy" Driscoll and **Charley Trippi**; **halfback Ollie Matson**; **fullback Ernie Nevers**; **cornerbacks** Roger Wehrli and **Dick "Night Train" Lane**; offensive and defensive **lineman** Walt Kiesling; **safety** Larry Wilson; offensive **tackle Dan Dierdorf**; and **tight end** Jackie Smith. Other players of note include halfback Marshall Goldberg; cornerback/safety Aeneas Williams; quarterbacks Paul Christman, Jim Hart, Charley Johnson, Neil Lomax, and Kurt Warner; **wide receivers** Larry Fitzgerald, Mel Gray, Terry Metcalf, and Pat Tilley; **running backs** Ottis Anderson, Edgerrin James, and Jim Otis; Roy Green (who played both wide receiver on **offense** and defensive **back** on **defense** in the same game during the 1980s, one of the last players to do so); and fullback/**kicker** Marlin "Pat" Harder.

ARIZONA STATE UNIVERSITY (ASU). Arizona State University's (ASU) main campus is located in Tempe, Arizona. Their **football** program began in 1897, and, since then, through 2012, Sun Devils' teams have compiled a record of 554–354–23. In addition, they have competed in 26 postseason **bowl games**, with a record of 13–12–1. They have been selected as national collegiate champions twice, in 1970 and 1975. Home games since 1958 have been played at Sun Devil Stadium in Tempe. The facility's original seating capacity of 30,450 has been enlarged to its present 72,995. In 1978, ASU's football teams began competing in the Pacific-10 Conference (known as the **Pacific-12 Conference** since 2011) of the **National Collegiate Athletic Association**. Their main rival is the University of Arizona. Since 1899, the teams have met in a game for the Territorial Cup (so named because the two schools began playing prior to Arizona's statehood in 1912).

ASU's most successful **coach** was Frank Kush. Kush was their head coach from 1958 to 1979, and, while at ASU, he compiled a record of 176–54–1, with six victories in seven bowl appearances. He was inducted into the **College Football Hall of Fame** in 1995. Other notable coaches include Dan Devine (1955–1957, whose teams' record was 27–3–1), John Cooper (1985–1987), and Darryl Rogers (1980–1984).

ASU alumni in the College Football Hall of Fame include **cornerback** Mike Haynes, **wide receiver** John Jefferson, **guard** Randall McDaniel, **linebackers Pat Tillman** and Ron Pritchard, and **quarterback/punter** Danny White. Through 2012, there have been 227 **professional football** players who have attended ASU, with 219 in the **National Football League**, seven in the **American Football League**, and one in the **All-America Football Conference**. They include Hall of Famers Mike Haynes, John Henry Johnson,

Randall McDaniel, and Charley Taylor. Other ASU alumni who played professional football include Eric Allen, Raymond "Trace" Armstrong, Bob Breunig, Curley Culp, Mark Gastineau, Bruce Hardy, Jim Jeffcoat, Brian Jennings, Jason Kyle, Bob Lee, Mike Mercer, Mike Pagel, Jake Plummer, Dan Saleaumua, Derek Smith, Jerry Smith, Terrell Suggs, Danny Villa, Danny White, Darren Woodson, and Louis Wright. **Canadian Football League** Hall of Famer Junior Ah You also attended ASU.

ARMY. The United States Military Academy, located at West Point, New York, is more popularly known in collegiate sports circles as Army. Their **football** program began in 1890, and, since then, the Black Knights of the Hudson have compiled a record of 653–481–51. Traditionally, they did not compete in **bowl games**, but, in recent years, this has changed, and, since 1984, they have appeared in five of them, winning three. They have usually competed as an independent team, without **conference** affiliation, but, from 1998 to 2004, they were members of **Conference USA**. They have been selected as national collegiate champions five times, in 1914, 1916, 1944, 1945, and 1946. Home games have been played at the 38,000-seat Michie Stadium (pronounced Mike-ee) since 1924. In 1899, Army adopted a mule as their mascot.

Their main rival is the United States Naval Academy (known familiarly as **Navy**). The teams have met annually since 1890 (except for a few years) in a contest that during much of the 20th century was one of the most widely anticipated collegiate football games. The game is usually held in a neutral city, often Philadelphia, Pennsylvania. Navy leads the series, 57–49–7. Since 1972, the three major service academies (Army, Navy, and the Air Force Academy) have competed for the Commander-in-Chief's Trophy, awarded to the team with the best record against the other two schools.

Army's most successful **coach** was Earl "Red" Blaik. He led the Black Knights from 1941 to 1958, with a record of 121–33–10. From 1944 to 1946, they were undefeated, winning 27 games and being **tied** once.

There are 24 players in the **College Football Hall of Fame** who attended Army. Among them are **halfbacks** Bob Anderson, **Glenn Davis**, Pete Dawkins, and Harry Wilson; **fullback Felix "Doc" Blanchard**; **end** Bill Carpenter (known as "The Lonely End," since Army ran a formation in which he was positioned wide of the **line of scrimmage** and did not join the **huddle**); **quarterbacks** Arnold Galiffa and Doug Kenna; end/quarterback Don Holleder; **tackle** Alex Weyand; and **center** John "Cap" McEwan. Blanchard, Davis, and Dawkins were also **Heisman Trophy** winners.

Since West Point graduates are committed to service in the U.S. Army, there have not been many who have gone on to play **professional football**.

Through 2012, there have been just 28 who played in the **National Football League** and one in the **American Football League**. Among them are Bob Anderson, DeWitt "Tex" Coulter, Glenn Davis, Gene Filipski, John "J. D." Kimmel, Bob Mischak, Al Pollard, Hampton Pool, and Barney Poole. But there have been many military heroes who played football for Army. Among them are 1912 team members Dwight D. Eisenhower, who as general of the U.S. Army became president of the United States, and army general Omar Bradley. *See also* ARMY–NAVY GAME.

ARMY–NAVY GAME. Since 1890, the United States Military Academy (**Army**) has played the United States Naval Academy (**Navy**) in an annual **football** game. For various reasons, no games were played in 1894, 1895, 1896, 1897, 1898, 1909, 1917, 1918, 1928, or 1929. The game was usually played on the Saturday after Thanksgiving, although since the 1980s it has been moved to the first or second Saturday in December. In the 113 meetings through 2012, Navy has a slight edge over Army, with a record of 57–49–7 and 11 consecutive wins from 2002 to 2012. Although the first four games were played at the school's home fields (alternating between Army's location of West Point, New York, and Navy's Annapolis, Maryland, location), most of the other games have been played in Philadelphia, Pennsylvania. Games have also been played in New Jersey, New York, Maryland, Illinois, and California. For many of the earlier meetings, both Army and Navy were among the nation's best football teams, and the game was one of the most anticipated rivalries of the **college football** season. In recent years, however, both teams have rarely been among the top 25 nationally ranked teams, but, because of its tradition and military heritage, the game is televised nationally and is still one of the most widely followed sporting events.

ASSISTANT COACH. Since **football** has so many players (11 on **offense**, 11 on **defense**, and several specialists in the kicking aspect of the game), one **coach** cannot adequately instruct them all. Assistant coaches are used at all levels of the game. Assistant coaches are usually assigned duties for one type of position and, as such, there are offensive line coaches, defensive **back** coaches, receiving coaches, and so forth. In **professional football**, teams usually have one coach designated as offensive coordinator who helps the head coach prepare a game plan and calls most of the plays during the game. A defensive coordinator is also used to determine defensive alignments. Many assistant coaches progress to jobs as head coaches, but some remain specialists their entire career.

ASSOCIATION FOOTBALL. *See* SOCCER.

ATLANTA FALCONS. The Atlanta Falcons are a **professional football** team in the National Football Conference (NFC) South Division of the **National Football League (NFL)**. They joined the league in 1966 as an expansion team and played in the NFC East Division for one year, the NFC Coastal Division for three years, and the NFC West Division from 1970 to 2001, before moving to the NFC South Division in 2002. Their home games were played at the 60,000-seat Atlanta-Fulton County Stadium from 1966 to 1991, and at the 71,000-seat Georgia Dome since then. Their best season was 1998, when they won 14 of 16 games in the regular season but lost in the **Super Bowl** to the **Denver Broncos**. In 47 seasons of NFL play, the Falcons have compiled a regular-season record of 312–402–6 and a **playoff** record of 7–12. They lost the NFC Championship Game in 2004 and 2012, the division playoffs in 1978, 1980, 1991, 2002, and 2010. They lost in the first round, or **wild-card playoff** game, in 1982, 1995, 2008, and 2011.

Head **coaches** of the Falcons have included Norb Hecker (1966–1968), **Norm Van Brocklin** (1968–1974), Marion Campbell (1974–1976, 1987–1989), Pat Peppler (interim 1976), Leeman Bennett (1977–1982), Dan Henning (1983–1986), Jim Hanifin (interim 1989), Jerry Glanville (1990–1993), June Jones (1994–1996), **Dan (Edward) Reeves** (1997–2003), Wade Phillips (interim 2003), Jim Mora (2004–2006), Bobby Petrino (2007), **Emmitt Thomas** (interim 2007), and Mike Smith (2008–2012).

Although the Falcons have had four Hall of Famers play for them, including **Eric Dickerson**, Chris Doleman, Tommy McDonald, and **Deion Sanders**, of the four, only Sanders played more than two seasons with Atlanta. In addition to **cornerback** Sanders, Atlanta's best players have included **quarterbacks** Steve Bartkowski, Chris Chandler, Matt Ryan, and **Michael Vick**; **running backs** Jamal Anderson, William Andrews, Warrick Dunn, Dave Hampton, and Michael Turner; **wide receivers** Alge Crumpler, Tony Martin, Andre Rison, and Roddy White; defensive **end** Claude Humphrey; **center** Jeff Van Note; **tackle** Mike Kenn; **linebackers** Tommy Nobis and Jessie Tuggle; defensive **back** Rolland Lawrence; and **kicker Morten Andersen**.

ATLANTIC COAST CONFERENCE (ACC). The Atlantic Coast Conference is an organization of **major colleges** and universities that compete athletically in the **National Collegiate Athletic Association (NCAA)** Football Bowl Subdivision. It was established in 1953, and is based in Greensboro, North Carolina. In 2012, the 12 member schools included Boston College; Clemson University; Duke University; **Florida State University**; **Georgia Tech**; the University of Maryland, College Park; the **University of Miami**; the University of North Carolina at Chapel Hill; North Carolina State University at Raleigh; the University of Virginia; **Virginia Tech**; and Wake Forest

University. Changes to major conferences in the NCAA that have occurred since then will result in the University of Maryland leaving the ACC in 2014, the **University of Pittsburgh** and **Syracuse University** joining the ACC in 2013, and the University of Louisville joining the ACC at an unspecified future date. In addition, the **University of Notre Dame** will join the ACC for all sports except football and ice hockey.

AUBURN UNIVERSITY. Auburn University is located in Auburn, Alabama. Their **football** program began in 1892, and since then Auburn Tigers' teams have compiled a record of 699–401–45 through 2012. In addition, they have competed in 37 postseason **bowl games**, with a record of 22–13–2. They have been selected as national collegiate champions five times, in 1913, 1957, 1983, 1993, and 2010. Since 1932, Auburn football teams have competed in the **Southeastern Conference** of the **National Collegiate Athletic Association**. Their main rival is the **University of Alabama**. The teams have met annually since 1948 in a contest known as the Iron Bowl. Auburn's home field since 1939 is Jordan-Hare Stadium, expanded in 2003 to a seating capacity of 87,451.

Auburn's **coach** with the most longevity was Ralph "Shug" Jordan. He was their head coach from 1951 to 1975. He compiled a record of 176–73–6 in his 25 years. Other outstanding head coaches have included Pat Dye (1981–1992; 99–39–4), Terry Bowden (1993–1998; 47–17–1), and Tommy Tuberville (1999–2008; 85–40). There are four men who coached at Auburn who have been inducted into the **College Football Hall of Fame**. These include Jordan, Dye, John Heisman, and Mike Donahue. Heisman (for whom the **Heisman Trophy** is named) coached at Auburn from 1895 to 1899. Donahue coached from 1904 to 1906 and 1908 to 1922.

Auburn alumni in the College Football Hall of Fame include **quarterback/halfback/punter** Jimmy Hitchcock, **center** Walter Gilbert, quarterback Pat Sullivan, **running backs** Tucker Frederickson and Vincent "Bo" Jackson, **wide receiver** Terry Beasley, defensive **tackle** Tracy Rocker, and **fullback** Ed Dyas. Sullivan, Jackson, and quarterback **Cam Newton** each won the Heisman Trophy.

Through 2012, there have been 229 **professional football** players who have attended Auburn, 215 in the **National Football League**, 10 in the **American Football League**, and four in the **All-America Football Conference**. **Cleveland Browns'** center Frank Gatski is the only Auburn alumnus in the **Pro Football Hall of Fame**. Other Auburn players who have played professional football include Willie Anderson, William Andrews, James Brooks, Jason Campbell, Joe Childress, Al Del Greco, Dave Edwards, Tucker Frederickson, Wayne Gandy, Chris Gray, Kevin Greene, Dave Hill, Vincent

"Bo" Jackson, Chris Martin, Cam Newton, Neil O'Donoghue, Tony Richardson, Billy Ray Smith Sr., Takeo Spikes, Pat Sullivan, Gary Walker, Steve Wallace, Frank Warren, Ed West, and Gerald Williams.

AUDIBLE. An audible is a play called out loud (in code) at the **line of scrimmage** that is different from the play originally called in the **huddle**. This will occur when the **quarterback** sees that the way the **defense** is aligned will probably cause the originally called play to fail.

AUSTRALIAN RULES FOOTBALL. Australian rules football, or simply Australian football (also known as "footie"), is a variety of **football** played almost exclusively in Australia. It resembles **rugby** more than it does American or **Canadian football**. The game was played as early as 1859, and it features 18 players on each side propelling an elliptical-shaped, leather-covered ball down a large, grass field toward four **goalposts** (without crossbars) at the end of the field. The ball may be carried, kicked, or handballed (**passed** by hitting the ball with the fist). A player in possession of the ball may be **tackled** (only between the shoulders and knees) by an opponent, and, once tackled, they must relinquish possession of the ball. Six points are awarded for sending the ball between the inner two goalposts, and one point is scored if the ball goes between the two outer goalposts on either side. The professional Australian Football League is the sport's main league.

B

BACK. A back is a generic name for a position in **football**. The back begins a play positioned behind the **line of scrimmage**. Offensive backs are called **quarterbacks**, **halfbacks**, **fullbacks**, **running backs**, and occasionally **slotbacks** or tailbacks, depending on the team's formation. Defensive backs are usually in the third line of **defense** behind **linemen** and **linebackers** and can be designated as **cornerbacks**, defensive halfbacks, or **safeties**.

BACK JUDGE. *See* OFFICIALS.

BALTIMORE COLTS (1953–1983). *See* INDIANAPOLIS COLTS.

BALTIMORE COLTS (AAFC). The Baltimore Colts were a **professional football** team in the **All-America Football Conference (AAFC)** from 1947 to 1949. They replaced the **Miami Seahawks**, who were expelled from the league following the 1946 season. Home games were played at Municipal Stadium in Baltimore, Maryland. Although the Colts were not particularly successful in league play, with a record of 10–29–1 in three seasons, they were invited to join the **National Football League (NFL)** when the AAFC and NFL merged in 1950. That year proved to be the Colts' only season in the NFL, as they compiled a record of one win and 11 losses and finished seventh and last in the National Conference. The team was disbanded, although a new, unrelated franchise also called the Baltimore Colts began in the NFL in 1953.

In the brief four-year history of the first Colts' franchise, their best players included **quarterback Y. A. Tittle**, who later became a **Pro Football Hall of Fame** player for the **San Francisco 49ers** and **New York Giants**, **punter**/quarterback Adrian Burk, who went on to a substantial career with the **Philadelphia Eagles** and later became an NFL official, and **tackle** Art Donovan, who played most of his 12-year NFL career with the new Baltimore Colts franchise and is also a member of the Pro Football Hall of Fame. The Colts' head **coaches** included Cecil Isbell (1947–1949), Walter Driskill (interim 1949), and Clem Crowe (1950).

BALTIMORE RAVENS. The Baltimore Ravens are a **professional football** team in the American Football Conference (AFC) North Division of the **National Football League (NFL)**. They have been in the league since 1996. From 1996 to 2001, they played in the AFC Central Division. Home games in 1996 and 1997 were played at the 53,000-seat Memorial Stadium in Baltimore, Maryland. Since 1998, they have been played at the 70,000-seat M&T Bank Stadium in Baltimore (previously known as Ravens Stadium and PSI Stadium).

Owner Art Modell moved his **Cleveland Browns** team to Baltimore in 1996 to play as the Baltimore Ravens. In a move to placate the angry Cleveland **fans**, the NFL ruled that all Cleveland Browns history, records, team colors, and so forth would remain in Cleveland and that the Browns franchise would be suspended for three years. In 1999, an expansion team called the Cleveland Browns was added to the NFL.

From 1996 to 2012, the Ravens compiled a record of 150–121–1 in regular-season play and 10–7 in postseason **playoff** competition. Their best season was 2000, when they finished the regular season at 12–4 and then won four playoff games, including the **Super Bowl**. In 2012, they also won four playoff games including the Super Bowl but had a regular season record of 10–6. In 2006, they won their division, with a record of 13–3, but lost their first playoff game. In 2008 and 2011, they lost in the AFC Championship Game. They were defeated in the division playoff in 2006, 2009, and 2010, and in the **wild-card playoff** game in 2003.

Their **coaches** have included Ted Marchibroda (1996–1998), Brian Billick (1999–2007), and John Harbaugh (2008–2012). Although the Ravens are a relatively new team, they still have had four of their former players inducted into the **Pro Football Hall of Fame**, including **cornerback Deion Sanders**, offensive **tackle** Jonathan Ogden, **tight end Shannon Sharpe**, and **safety** Rod Woodson; however, all but Ogden played the bulk of their careers with other teams. The Ravens' best players have included **quarterbacks** Tony Banks, Kyle Boller, Joe Flacco, and Steve McNair; **running backs** Jamal Lewis and Ray Rice; **wide receivers** Mark Clayton and Derrick Mason; placekicker Matt Stover; defensive **back** Ed Reed; and **linebacker** Ray Lewis. The latter two stand a good chance for election to the Hall once they've retired.

BALTIMORE STALLIONS. The Baltimore Stallions were a **professional football** team in the **Canadian Football League (CFL)** in the 1994 and 1995 seasons. In those two years, the CFL experimented with placing teams in the United States. Among the several U.S.-based franchises, the Stallions were by far the most successful. In 1994, they won 12 of 18 regular-season games and two postseason games and lost in the **Grey Cup** to the **BC Lions**, 26–23. In 1995, they won 15 of 18 regular-season games and all three postseason games, including the Grey Cup, where they defeated the **Calgary Stampeders**, 37–20. The Stallions played their home games at the 53,000-seat Municipal Stadium in Baltimore, Maryland. Don Matthews **coached** the Stallions, and among their best players were **quarterback** Tracy Ham, **running back** Mike Pringle, **cornerback** Irvin Smith, **punter** Josh Miller, offensive **tackle** Shar Pourdanesh, offensive **guard** Mike Withycombe, and **kicker** Donald Igwebuike. After the 1995 season, the CFL decided not to continue with teams based in the United States. The Baltimore owners then moved their team to Canada, where they became the **Montreal Alouettes**.

BAUGH, SAMUEL ADRIAN "SAMMY," "SLINGIN' SAMMY." B. 17 March 1914, Temple, Texas. D. 17 December 2008, Rotan, Texas. Sammy Baugh attended Sweetwater High School in Sweetwater, Texas, where he played baseball, **football**, and basketball. He received a baseball scholarship to Washington State University, but, before enrolling there, hurt his knee and the scholarship offer was withdrawn. Instead, he attended Texas Christian University (TCU) and **quarterbacked** their football team in three **varsity** seasons, from 1934 to 1936. He led TCU to postseason bowl victories in the second annual **Sugar Bowl** on 1 January 1936, and the first **Cotton Bowl** on 1 January 1937.

Baugh, at six feet, two inches tall and 180 pounds, was selected by the **Washington Redskins** in the first round of the 1937 **National Football League (NFL) Draft** as the sixth overall selection. He signed with them and began a 16-year NFL career in 1937, leading them to the NFL championship that year. He also signed a contract with the St. Louis Cardinals Major League Baseball team and played shortstop for their highest-level minor-league teams, Rochester and Columbus, in 1938. In 53 games, he only batted .200. Since the Cardinals had another top shortstop prospect at that time, Marty Marion (who eventually played 13 years in the major leagues), Baugh decided to concentrate on football.

"Slingin' Sammy" led the Redskins to the NFL Championship Game in 1937, 1940, 1942, 1943, and 1945, winning the title in 1937 and 1942. He played tailback, **quarterback**, and defensive **back** and was the team's **punter**. By the time he retired, he had set NFL records in all three capacities, several of which he still held in 2012. In his 16-year NFL career, all with the Redskins, he appeared in 165 regular-season games, completed 1,693 **passes** in 2,995 attempts for 21,886 yards and 187 **touchdowns**, and carried the ball 324 times for nine touchdowns. Baugh was also one of the NFL's best punters, and he punted 338 times for a 45.1 yards per punt average. In 1940, he had an 85-yard punt, which stood as an NFL record until 1947. In each year from 1940 to 1944, he had the NFL's longest punt of the year.

After retiring from active play, Baugh was head football **coach** at Hardin-Simmons University from 1955 to 1959. In 1960, he was named head coach of the Titans of New York in the new **American Football League (AFL)**. He coached them in 1960 and 1961, followed by the Houston Oilers in 1964. Between AFL coaching jobs, he was an **assistant coach** at the University of Tulsa. He then left football to run his 7,600-acre ranch in West Texas. Baugh was inducted into the **College Football Hall of Fame** in 1951, and the **Pro Football Hall of Fame** as a charter member in 1963.

BC LIONS. The BC Lions are a team in the **Canadian Football League (CFL)**. They began play in the 1954 season in the Western Interprovincial Football Union, one of the forerunners of the CFL. From 1954 to 2012, their overall record is 484–490–24 in regular-season play and 20–27 in **playoff** competition. They have played in the **Grey Cup** 10 times and won six times (1964, 1985, 1994, 2000, 2006, and 2011). Their home field was the 32,000-seat Empire Stadium in Vancouver, British Columbia, from 1954 to 1982, and the 54,500-seat BC Place Stadium in Vancouver from 1983 to 2009. In 2010, they temporarily moved to the 27,000-seat Empire Field in Vancouver while a retractable roof was installed at BC Place.

The Italian-born Wally Buono **coached** the Lions from 2003 to 2011, longer than any other Lions' head coach. In 2012, defensive coordinator Mike Benevides was promoted to head coach and Buono remained as vice president and general manager. Dave Skrien (1961–1967) is the only other man to coach the Lions for more than five years. Among the Lions' best players have been **punter/kicker Lui Passaglia**, who played with them for 25 years, from 1976 to 2000; **quarterback Doug Flutie** and his brother, **wide receiver** Darren Flutie; **running back** Willie Fleming; **fullback** Sean Millington; **center** Al Wilson; **guards** Tom Hinton and Jamie Taras; **linebackers** Norm Fieldgate and Glen Jackson; defensive **linemen** Mike Cacic and Rick Klassen; and defensive **back** Larry Crawford.

BEDNARIK, CHARLES PHILIP "CHUCK." B. 1 May 1925, Bethlehem, Pennsylvania. Chuck Bednarik, son of Slovak immigrants, attended Bethlehem Catholic High School and Liberty High School in Bethlehem, Pennsylvania. After graduation, he served in the U.S. Air Force and was involved in 30 combat missions during World War II. Following his discharge from the service, Bednarik enrolled at the **University of Pennsylvania** in 1945. Since **college football** during that era had limited substitution rules, he played both **offense** and **defense**, as did most players during that time. At six feet, three inches tall and 230 pounds, he was a **center** on offense and **linebacker** on defense.

The recipient of the **Maxwell Award** in 1948 and third in voting for the **Heisman Trophy**, Bednarik was the overall first selection in the 1949 **National Football League (NFL) Draft**, and he was chosen by the **Philadelphia Eagles**. He played for the Eagles from 1949 to 1962, was selected for the **Pro Bowl** eight times in his career, and was the 1953 Pro Bowl Most Valuable Player. He helped lead the Eagles to the 1949 and 1960 NFL championships. Although the NFL's substitution rules were more liberal than those followed in college football, he still played both offense and defense, and, by the end of his career, he was the only player in the league doing so.

The NFL kept few statistics to measure the performance of centers and linebackers in that era. The only available statistics for Bednarik's 14-year career are the following: 169 regular-season games played (out of 172), 20 **interceptions** (one for a **touchdown**), and 21 **fumble** recoveries. In 1953, he also briefly served as a **punter** and recorded 12 punts for a 40.3 yards per punt average. Bednarik was inducted into the **Pro Football Hall of Fame** in 1967, and the **College Football Hall of Fame** in 1969. In 1995, the Maxwell Club began presenting an annual Chuck Bednarik Award to the best defensive collegiate football player in the United States.

BELICHICK, WILLIAM STEPHEN "BILL." B. 16 April 1952, Nashville, Tennessee. Bill Belichick is the son of Steve Belichick, a former **National Football League (NFL) fullback** with the **Detroit Lions** in 1941 and **football coach** at the United States Naval Academy (**Navy**). Bill attended Annapolis High School in Annapolis, Maryland, and was a football and lacrosse player there. After graduating, he spent one year at Phillips Academy before enrolling at Wesleyan University. At Wesleyan, he continued his athletic activity as a **center** and **tight end** on the football team and as a member of the lacrosse and squash teams.

After graduating from Wesleyan, Bill began a football coaching career in 1975 by working as a special assistant to **Baltimore Colts'** head coach Ted Marchibroda. From 1976 to 1990, he was employed as an **assistant coach** by the Detroit Lions (1976–1977), **Denver Broncos** (1978), and **New York Giants** (1979–1990), with the latter six years as defensive coordinator. In 1991, Bill was named head coach of the **Cleveland Browns** and coached them from 1991 to 1995. His record there was 36–44 in regular-season games and 1–1 in postseason games. In 1996, he worked as assistant coach under **Bill Parcells** of the **New England Patriots**.

Parcells moved to the **New York Jets** in 1997, and Belichick went with him. When Parcells resigned on 3 January 2000, Belichick was named as the

Jets' coach, but when Belichick was called to the podium at a press conference that day, he resigned the position. Later that month, he was hired by the Patriots as their head coach, a job he still holds in 2013.

In his 13 years as Patriots' head coach, his teams have compiled a regular-season record of 151–57 and a postseason record of 17–7, with **Super Bowl** wins in 2002, 2004, and 2005, and Super Bowl losses in 2008 and 2012.

BELL, DE BENNEVILLE "BERT." B. 25 February 1895, Philadelphia, Pennsylvania. D. 11 October 1959, Philadelphia, Pennsylvania. Bert Bell was born into a wealthy Philadelphia family. His father, John C. Bell, was an attorney who became the district attorney for Philadelphia and later Pennsylvania's attorney general. His mother, Fleurette deBenneville Myers, could trace her heritage back to pre–Revolutionary War days in Pennsylvania. Bert attended private schools for his elementary education and the Haverford School for his high school education. He played **football**, baseball, and basketball and was team captain in all three sports during his senior year. His father, a **University of Pennsylvania** alumnus and former football player, was named a trustee at Penn and insisted that Bert enroll there.

Bert majored in English and was the starting **quarterback**, defensive **back**, **punter**, and **punt returner** on the football team at Penn. He played in one of the first **Rose Bowl** games on 1 January 1917, in which Penn was defeated by Oregon. In December 1917, he was inducted into the U.S. Army, served in France in 1918, and was discharged as a sergeant in 1919. He returned to Penn but left in 1920 without graduating. He worked as an **assistant coach** of the football team at Penn during the 1920s and then became manager of the Ritz-Carlton Hotel. He became a stockbroker just prior to the Wall Street crash in 1929, with disastrous results. After his father helped cover his losses, he returned to football as a **coach** at Temple University.

In 1933, Bert decided to purchase a franchise in the **National Football League (NFL)**, and, although Bert's father disapproved of the idea, Bert and a few partners managed to raise the necessary franchise fee and acquired the franchise of the defunct Frankford Yellow Jackets. They named their new team the **Philadelphia Eagles** and entered the NFL in 1933. The team was not successful financially, and Bert suggested to the other NFL owners that a common **draft** of college players would be beneficial to the entire league. His suggestion was adopted, and, in 1936, the NFL conducted its first draft. Bell became the Eagles' head coach in 1936. He coached them through 1940 and had a won-lost record of 10–44–2, one of the worst coaching records in NFL history.

In a complicated series of transactions in 1940, Bell and **Art Rooney** wound up being partners in the **Pittsburgh Steelers** NFL team. Bell coached the Steelers for two games in 1941, before giving way to Aldo Donelli. In 1943, the Steelers merged with the Philadelphia Eagles and played as a combined team that year. The Steelers continued doing poorly financially.

In January 1946, the NFL owners fired NFL commissioner **Elmer Layden**, whom they felt was not acting strongly enough to combat a threat from a new professional league, the **All-America Football Conference (AAFC)**. They selected Bell as the new NFL commissioner. He then sold his interest in the Steelers to Rooney and, for the next 13 years, was league commissioner.

During his reign as commissioner, Bell oversaw the merger with the AAFC in 1950, handled a proposed game-fixing bribe situation, helped institute racial integration on teams, and helped set league policy, including local television blackouts during the rise of television. In 1950, he helped create the league's all-star game, the **Pro Bowl**. He was also praised for his ability to mediate owner disputes, and his recognition of the fledging NFL Players Association helped defuse a congressional antitrust hearing.

On 11 October 1959, while attending a Philadelphia Eagles game at Franklin Field in Philadelphia, Bell suffered a heart attack during the fourth quarter of the game and died later that day. He was inducted into the **Pro Football Hall of Fame** as a charter member in the category of contributor in 1963.

BERT BELL BENEFIT BOWL. *See* PLAYOFF BOWL.

BIG EAST CONFERENCE. The Big East Conference is an organization of **major colleges** and universities that compete athletically. It was established in 1979 and is based in Providence, Rhode Island. Only eight of the 16 member schools in 2012 compete in **conference football**. They are the University of Cincinnati, the University of Connecticut, the University of Louisville, the **University of Pittsburgh**, **Rutgers University**, the University of South Florida, **Syracuse University**, and Temple University. Seven of the other eight members, all private Catholic institutions, do not field football teams but compete in other conference sports. They are DePaul University, Georgetown University, Marquette University, Providence College, Seton Hall University, St. John's University, and Villanova University. In addition, the **University of Notre Dame**, while a member of the Big East Conference for other sports, plays football as an independent team. Loyola University Maryland is an associate conference member but does not play football.

The Big East Conference is one of the conferences that was greatly affected by the changes in conference affiliation in 2012. On 1 July 2013, Syracuse and Pittsburgh will leave to join the **Atlantic Coast Conference (ACC)**. On 1 July 2014, Louisville will leave for the ACC and Rutgers will leave for the **Big Ten Conference**. Additions to the Big East in 2013 are Temple

University (a football-only member in 2012), the University of Central Florida, University of Houston, University of Memphis, Southern Methodist University, and Tulane University. In 2014 East Carolina University will join as an associate member to play football in the Big East; in 2015, the United States Naval Academy will do likewise. The other major change in the Big East Conference is that the eight private Catholic schools also plan to leave the conference in the near future.

BIG EIGHT CONFERENCE. The Big Eight Conference was an organization of **major colleges** and universities that competed athletically. It was established in 1907 as the Missouri Valley Intercollegiate Athletic Association and officially renamed the Big Eight Conference in 1964, although it had previously been informally known by that name. The **conference** existed until 1996, when the members added four schools that had previously been members of the **Southwest Conference** and formed a new entity called the **Big 12 Conference**. For much of its existence, the winner of the Big Eight Conference received an automatic invitation to the **Orange Bowl** postseason game.

When the conference was dissolved in 1996, the members included the **University of Colorado**, Iowa State University, the University of Kansas, Kansas State University, the University of Missouri, the **University of Nebraska**, the **University of Oklahoma**, and Oklahoma State University. Former conference members were the **University of Iowa** (1907–1911), Washington University in St. Louis (1907–1928), Drake University (1908–1928), and Grinnell College (1918–1928).

BIG TEN CONFERENCE. The Big Ten Conference is an organization of **major colleges** and universities that compete athletically. Its headquarters are in Park Ridge, Illinois. It is the oldest major college athletic **conference** in the United States and was established in 1896 as the Intercollegiate Conference of Faculty Representatives with seven member schools, including the University of Chicago, the **University of Illinois**, the **University of Michigan**, the **University of Minnesota**, Northwestern University, **Purdue University**, and the **University of Wisconsin**. It was more commonly known as the Western Conference. In 1899, two schools, Indiana University and the **University of Iowa**, were added, and it was then informally called the Big Nine. In 1912, **Ohio State University** was added, and the conference was known as the Big Ten. In 1939, the University of Chicago withdrew, and the conference reverted to the Big Nine name until 1949, when the addition of **Michigan State University** restored the Big Ten name. In 1986, the conference was officially renamed the Big Ten Conference. In 1990, **Penn State University** joined, and, in 2011, the **University of Nebraska** was added. Although the addition of the last two schools increased the membership to greater than 10 schools, it was decided to retain the Big Ten name.

BIG 12 CONFERENCE. The Big 12 Conference is an organization of **major colleges** and universities that compete athletically. It was established in 1996 and is based in Irving, Texas. The **conference** was formed by adding four Texas schools (Baylor University, the **University of Texas, Texas A&M University**, and Texas Tech University) that had been part of the **Southwest Conference** to the eight schools that were members of the **Big Eight Conference** (the **University of Colorado**, Iowa State University, the University of Kansas, Kansas State University, the University of Missouri, the **University of Nebraska**, the **University of Oklahoma**, and Oklahoma State University). The Big 12 Conference considers itself a new entity and not an extension of the Big Eight Conference. In 2011, both Colorado and Nebraska withdrew, and, although the conference only has 10 members, it retained the name Big 12. In 2012, the University of Missouri and Texas A&M University also withdrew but they were replaced by West Virginia University and Texas Christian University.

BIRMINGHAM BARRACUDAS. The Birmingham Barracudas were a **professional football** team in the **Canadian Football League (CFL)** during the 1995 season. They played home games at the 71,000-seat Legion Field in Birmingham, Alabama. Their head **coach** was former **National Football League** player and coach Jack Pardee. He led them to a record of 10–8, good for third place in the CFL South Division. In their opening-round **playoff** game, they were defeated, 52–9, by the **San Antonio Texans**. The Barracudas' **quarterback**, Matt Dunigan, was later elected to the **Canadian Football Hall of Fame**. Other notable players include **wide receivers** Marcus Grant and Jason Phillips and Mexican-born **kicker** Luis Zendejas.

BLANCHARD, FELIX ANTHONY "DOC," "MR. INSIDE." B. 11 December 1924, McColl, South Carolina. D. 19 April 2009, Bulverde, Texas. Felix "Doc" Blanchard was the son of a physician who had played **college football** at Tulane University and Wake Forest University. Although Blanchard was born in South Carolina, his family moved several times, and he attended high school at St. Stanislaus College in Bay St. Louis, Mississippi, where he played **football**. Recruited by the United States Military Academy (**Army**) at West Point and several other schools, he chose the University of North Carolina, where his mother's cousin, Jim Tatum, was head **coach**. After playing on the North Carolina freshman team in 1942, he enlisted in the U.S. Army in 1943. In 1944, he enrolled at West Point and starred on their undefeated football teams from 1944 to 1946. At six feet tall and 205 pounds, he was used as a placekicker and **punter**, as well as **fullback** and **linebacker**. Along with **running back Glenn Davis**, Army had one of the best **running** attacks in collegiate football, and Blanchard was nicknamed "Mr. Inside" to Davis's nickname of "Mr. Outside."

As a junior in 1945, Blanchard won the James E. Sullivan Award presented by the Amateur Athletic Union to the "most outstanding amateur athlete in the United States." He was the first football player to receive the award, and, since then, only five other football players have won it. That same year, Blanchard also won two of the most prestigious football awards, the **Heisman Trophy** and **Maxwell Award**.

After graduating from West Point in 1947, Blanchard was commissioned as a second lieutenant in the U.S. Air Force and served until 1971, retiring as a colonel. Although he was **drafted** by the **Pittsburgh Steelers** of the **National Football League** as the third overall selection in 1946, he chose a military career and never played **professional football**. Blanchard was inducted into the **College Football Hall of Fame** in 1959.

BLANDA, GEORGE FREDERICK. B. 17 September 1927, Youngwood, Pennsylvania. D. 27 September 2010, Alameda, California. George Blanda had three careers in **professional football**. From 1949 to 1958, he was a **quarterback** and placekicker for the **Chicago Bears** of the **National Football League (NFL)**. When the **American Football League (AFL)** began in 1960, the Houston Oilers made him their starting quarterback, as well as their placekicker. From 1960 to 1966, he performed both roles for the Oilers. In 1967, at the age of 40, Blanda went to the **Oakland Raiders,** mainly as a placekicker, although he played a few games as their backup quarterback. He remained with the Raiders past his 48th birthday in 1975. His 26 years as an active player in pro football is the most in pro football in history, and his 26-year active career as a professional athlete is among the longest in any professional team sport.

A graduate of Youngwood High School in Youngwood, Pennsylvania, Blanda attended the University of Kentucky, where he played **linebacker** on **defense** and quarterback on **offense** for **Coach Paul "Bear" Bryant's football** teams. In his senior year at Kentucky, he led the team to a 9–3 record and an appearance in the **Orange Bowl**. He was chosen by the Chicago Bears in the 12th round of the 1949 NFL **Draft** as the 119th overall selection.

Blanda was six feet, two inches tall and weighed 215 pounds. He played with the Bears from 1949 to 1958, but was primarily used as a **kicker**. In 1953 and 1954, he was their starting quarterback but, from 1955 to 1958, was used as a backup quarterback. He retired in 1959 but returned in 1960 in the new AFL with the Houston Oilers as their starting quarterback. He played for them from 1960 to 1966 as quarterback and kicker and led them to the AFL championship in 1960 and 1961. In 1962, they reached the AFL Championship Game but were defeated in double **overtime** by the **Dallas Texans**. Blanda was released by the Oilers in 1967, at the age of 39, but he was signed by the Oakland Raiders. He played for Oakland, primarily as a kicker, from 1967 to 1975; was a member of the AFL championship team in 1967; and played on the losing side in the 1968 and 1969 AFL Championship Games. After the Raiders won the AFL championship in 1967, they played the **Green Bay Packers** in the second **Super Bowl** but were defeated by them.

In the 1970 season, Blanda, at the age of 43, had one of the most incredible series of games in a five-game period. On 25 October, he was used at quarterback as a substitute for the injured Daryle Lamonica, the Raiders starting quarterback. Blanda threw three **touchdown passes** to spark the Raiders to a 31–14 victory. The next week, he kicked a 48-yard **field goal** with three seconds left to gain a 17–17 **tie** against the **Kansas City Chiefs**. The following week, he threw a touchdown pass with 1:34 remaining and then kicked a 53-yard field goal (his third of the game) to win the game, 23–20, over the **Cleveland Browns** with three seconds left. The next week, his touchdown pass with 2:28 left in the game gave Oakland a 24–19 win over the **Denver Broncos**. On the fifth week, he kicked a field goal in the closing seconds to defeat the **San Diego Chargers**, 20–17.

Blanda played in 340 regular-season NFL and AFL games during his 26-years football career. He completed 1,911 passes in 4,007 attempts for 26,920 yards and 236 touchdowns. As a ball carrier, he ran 135 times for nine touchdowns. He kicked 335 field goals in 639 attempts and 943 extra points in 959 attempts. In his first two years in the NFL, Blanda was used as a **punter** and punted 22 times for an average of 36.8 yards per punt. In 1951, he was also used as a linebacker and recorded one pass **interception**. He also appeared in 19 **playoff** games and completed 89 of 189 passes for 1,190 yards and seven touchdowns. He made 49 of 49 extra points and 22 of 39 field goals in those games. Blanda was inducted into the **Pro Football Hall of Fame** in 1981.

BLITZ. A blitz is a defensive tactic in **football** in which defensive players not on the **line of scrimmage rush** the **quarterback**. Its use originated during the 1950s, and some of the early exponents of this tactic were Don Ettinger, Larry Wilson, and Dick LeBeau. The name is taken from "blitzkrieg," the German lightning war tactic during World War II. As a surprise move, it can be quite effective, but should the quarterback anticipate a blitz, he usually can throw and complete a short **pass** since the pass defender is rushing the quarterback and is out of position to defend the pass receiver.

BLOCK. A block is a move whereby an offensive player attempts to prevent the **defense** from reaching the **quarterback** or ball carrier by hitting the defensive player with his body. There are restrictions on how blocks can be made, and illegal blocks will result in a **penalty**. Blocking is the primary responsibility of **linemen**, although virtually all offensive players are required to block at one time or another.

BLOOD, JOHNNY. *See* MCNALLY, JOHN VICTOR "BLOOD."

BOISE STATE UNIVERSITY. Boise State University is located in Boise, Idaho. The school is a relatively young one and was founded as Boise Junior College in 1932. The following year, they began a **football** program. In 1968, they became Boise State College, a four-year school, and competed in the College Division (now known as Division II) of the **National Collegiate Athletic Association**. From 1968 to 2012, the Broncos have compiled a record of 389–147–2. Included in that total are 32 postseason **playoff** games and **bowl games**, where their record is 20–11–2. From 1970 to 1995, they were members of the Big Sky Conference. They moved to Division I and joined the Big West Conference in 1996. In 2001, they transferred to the **Western Athletic Conference**. In 2011, they became members of the **Mountain West Conference**. The Broncos were selected as national collegiate champions in 2006. Home games are played at the 33,000-seat Bronco Stadium located on the school campus. The stadium is unique in that since 1986, the field's artificial surface has been painted blue instead of the normal color of green. The Broncos' main rival is the University of Idaho. From 1971 to 2010, they played each other annually, and, since 2001, the winning team received the Governor's Trophy.

Chris Petersen has been Boise State's head **coach** from 2006 to 2012. From 2001 to 2005, Dan Hawkins was head coach. Boise State has one player, defensive **tackle** Randy Trautman, in the **College Football Hall of Fame**. Through 2012, the school has sent 50 players to the **National Football League (NFL)**. Among them are **linebacker** Dave Wilcox, who was inducted into the **Pro Football Hall of Fame** in 2000. Other Broncos in the NFL include Chris Carr, Daryn Colledge, Korey Hall, David Hughes, Jerry Inman, Bryan Johnson, Markus Koch, Quintin Mikell, Jeb Putzier, John Rade, Orlando Scandrick, Kimo von Oelhoffen, and Rick Woods.

BOOTLEG PLAY. In a bootleg play, the **quarterback** fakes a handoff to a **running back** but keeps the ball himself and **runs** in the opposite direction. **Frankie Albert** is credited for inventing the play. **Michael Vick** and **Fran Tarkenton** were two other quarterbacks who excelled at the play.

BOSTON BRAVES. *See* WASHINGTON REDSKINS.

BOSTON PATRIOTS. *See* NEW ENGLAND PATRIOTS.

BOSTON REDSKINS. *See* WASHINGTON REDSKINS.

BOSTON YANKS. The Boston Yanks were a **professional football** team in the **National Football League (NFL)** for five seasons. From 1944 to 1948, they played home games at the 35,000-seat Fenway Park in Boston, Massachusetts, also the home of the Boston Red Sox of Major League Baseball. Yanks' home games were also occasionally played at the 21,000-seat Manning Bowl in Lynn, Massachusetts (a Boston suburb), when the Red Sox had a game scheduled for Fenway Park. In their five seasons, the Yanks had a total won-lost record of 14–38–3 and finished between third and fifth place in the East Division each season. The 1945 team was merged with the Brooklyn Tigers due to the manpower shortage during World War II. Herb Kopf **coached** the team from 1944 to 1946, and Maurice "Clipper" Smith was the coach in 1947 and 1948. Among their best players were future **Pro Football Hall of Fame quarterback** Clarence "Ace" Parker, quarterback Frank "Boley" Danciewicz, and **end** Don Currivan. The team's owner was Ted Collins, manager of singer Kate Smith and former owner of the Original Celtics professional basketball team. After the 1948 NFL season, Collins folded the Yanks and organized a new NFL team called the New York Bulldogs, using quite a few of the Yanks to form his roster.

BOWL CHAMPIONSHIP SERIES (BCS). The Bowl Championship Series (BCS) is a somewhat complicated system that has been employed by the **National Collegiate Athletic Association (NCAA)** since 1998 in an attempt to determine a national collegiate football champion among its **major colleges**. The NCAA has designated certain schools as Football Bowl Subdivision schools (formerly known as Division I-A). In 2012, there were 124 such schools competing in 11 **conferences**, including four independent schools not playing in conferences. Only these 124 schools compete in the BCS, although only six of the conference winners receive automatic bowl entries. Schools from the five other conferences are considered at-large entries and may or may not be included depending on their overall ranking. Other lower-level NCAA schools with football programs compete in postseason **playoffs** to determine national championships for their divisions.

The BCS employs polls and various other selection methods, including measuring a school's strength of schedule, to determine the top 10 schools. The top two play in a BCS National Championship Game. Four major bowl venues are employed in the BCS series—the **Rose Bowl**, **Fiesta Bowl**, **Sugar Bowl**, and **Orange Bowl**—with the championship game rotating amongst the four.

From 1998 to 2012, there were 15 BCS National Championship Games, with the **University of Oklahoma** appearing in four. The **University of Alabama**, **Florida State University**, **Louisiana State University**, and **Ohio State University** have each played in three. The **University of Florida**, the **University of Southern California**, the **University of Texas**, and the **University of Miami** have been in two each, and **Auburn University**, the **University of Tennessee**, the **University of Nebraska**, the **University of Notre Dame**, **Virginia Tech**, and the University of Oregon one each. Alabama has won three times and Louisiana State, and Florida have each won twice. No other school has won more than once. *See also* APPENDIX K (for a list of national champions); APPENDIX O (for a list of Football Bowl Subdivision schools).

BOWL GAME. A bowl game is a postseason **football** game usually accompanied by additional festivities. College bowl games were traditionally played on **New Year's Day**, but in recent years they have been played from mid-December through early January. There have also been several collegiate rivalry games played during the regular season that have a bowl title, but the phrase is generally associated with postseason games. A few special professional games have also been called "bowl games," including the **Playoff Bowl**, **Pro Bowl**, and **Super Bowl**. *See also* APPENDIX C (for a list of Super Bowl champions); APPENDIX K (for a list of national champions); APPENDIX M (for a list of Rose Bowl champions).

BRADSHAW, TERRY PAXTON. B. 2 September 1948, Shreveport, Louisiana. Terry Bradshaw attended Woodlawn High School in Shreveport, Louisiana, where he led his team to the state class AAA high school **football** championship game. While in high school, he also was a member of the track team and twice set a national record in the javelin throw as a junior before surpassing it a third time in his senior year with a throw of 244 feet, 11 3/4 inches. Bradshaw attended Louisiana Tech University, where as **quarterback**, he led the nation with 2,890 yards **passing** in his junior year and 2,314 yards passing as a senior. Louisiana Tech had a record of 27–4 during those two seasons.

Bradshaw was the first overall selection in the 1970 **National Football League (NFL) Draft** and was chosen by the **Pittsburgh Steelers**. He played with them his entire professional career and led them to **Super Bowl** championships in 1975, 1976, 1979, and 1980. He was named the NFL Most Valuable Player in 1978 and the Super Bowl Most Valuable Player in 1979 and 1980.

In his 14-year NFL career, all with the Steelers, the six-foot, three-inch, 215-pound Bradshaw appeared in 168 regular-season games, completed 2,025 passes in 3,901 attempts for 27,989 yards and 212 **touchdowns**, ran 444 times for 2,257 yards and 32 touchdowns, and even **punted** eight times for an average of 28.1 yards. He also appeared in three **Pro Bowls**. Bradshaw's record as a starting quarterback in 158 games was 107–51. In **playoff** competition, he appeared in 19 games and completed 261 of 456 passes for 3,833 yards and 30 touchdowns. He carried the ball 52 times for 274 yards and three touchdowns.

After retiring from active play, Bradshaw has worked in television as a play-by-play analyst and also as a studio analyst. He has authored or coauthored five books and released six albums of country and western and gospel music. He was involved as a team sponsor in stock car racing, has done several television commercials, and has had several parts in Hollywood films and television shows. Bradshaw was inducted into the **Pro Football Hall of Fame** in 1989 and the **College Football Hall of Fame** in 1996.

BRADY, THOMAS EDWARD PATRICK, JR. "TOM." B. 3 August 1977, San Mateo, California. Tom Brady attended Junipero Serra High School in San Mateo, California, where he played both baseball as a catcher and **football** as a **quarterback**. In 1995, he was selected by the Montreal Expos in the 18th round of the 1995 Major League Baseball **Draft** but turned down their offer. He enrolled at the **University of Michigan** and was the backup quarterback to Brian Griese in 1996 and 1997. The following two years, Brady was the starting quarterback, and the school had a combined record of 20–5 those two seasons.

Brady was selected in the sixth round of the 2000 **National Football League (NFL) Draft** by the **New England Patriots** as the 199th choice. He began his professional career as a backup quarterback and played briefly in only one game in 2000. After quarterback Drew Bledsoe got injured early in the 2001 season, Brady became the Patriots' starting quarterback. Brady then started every game for New England until 2008. That year, an injury sidelined him in the first game, and he did not play again that season. He returned in 2009 and, through 2012, has again started every game for the Patriots. He has led New England to four **Super Bowls**, winning in 2002, 2004, and 2005, and losing in 2008 to the **New York Giants** after the Patriots won their first 18 games that year. In 2011, Brady became only the third NFL quarterback to **pass** for more than 5,000 yards in a season. His total of 5,235 yards would have been a new NFL record had not **Drew Brees** passed for 5,476 yards that same year.

Through the 2012 season, the six-foot, four-inch, 225-pound Brady has played in 177 regular-season NFL games in 13 seasons, started 175 games with a won-lost record of 136–39, and completed 3,798 passes in 5,958 attempts for 44,806 yards and 334 **touchdowns**. He has also carried the ball 402 times for 748 yards and 14 touchdowns, caught one pass for 23 yards, **punted** once for 36 yards, and appeared in eight **Pro Bowls**. In 24 **playoff** games, he completed 553 of 887 passes for 5,949 yards and 42 touchdowns. Brady also ran 56 times for 84 yards and three touchdowns and punted once for 48 yards. He was named the NFL Most Valuable Player in 2007 and 2010 and the Super Bowl Most Valuable Player in 2001 and 2003. He holds numerous NFL records, including most touchdown passes in one season, which he set in 2007, with 50. Brady stands a good chance of being elected to the **Pro Football Hall of Fame** once he retires.

BREES, DREW CHRISTOPHER. B. 15 January 1979, Austin, Texas. Drew Brees **quarterbacked** Westlake High School in West Lake Hills, Texas, an Austin suburb, to the 1996 Texas high school Class 5A state championship and had a 28–0–1 won-lost record in his final two high school seasons. He attended **Purdue University**. When he graduated in 2001, Brees had earned a degree in industrial management. While in college he managed to lead Purdue to its first **Rose Bowl** appearance in 34 years, win the **Maxwell Award** in 2000, and set **Big Ten Conference** records for most **passes** attempted, most passes completed, most passing yardage, and most **touchdown** passes.

Although he had an outstanding college career, Brees was thought by some to be too small, at six feet tall and 200 pounds, to be an effective professional quarterback, but he was selected by the **San Diego Chargers** as the first selection in the second round of the 2001 **National Football League (NFL) Draft**, the 32nd overall player chosen. He spent the 2001 season with the Chargers as the backup quarterback, appearing in only one game after veteran starting quarterback **Doug Flutie** suffered a concussion. Brees was the starting quarterback for the Chargers for the entire 2002 season, but he played poorly in 2003 and was replaced by Flutie. In 2004, Brees regained his starting role and was named the NFL Comeback Player of the Year after the Chargers recorded a 12–4 won-lost record and were American Football Conference West Division champions.

In 2006, Brees became a free agent and signed with the **New Orleans Saints**. He has played with the Saints through the 2012 season and led them to the **Super Bowl** championship in 2010, winning the Super Bowl Most Valuable Player Award in the process. In 2011, Brees set the NFL season record for passing yardage with 5,476, breaking **Dan Marino's** record set in 1984. He also regained the record for most pass completions in one season with 468, which he had originally set in 2008, at 413, and saw the record broken by **Peyton Manning** in 2010 at 450. During the 2012 season, Brees broke one of the longest-standing NFL records when he completed a touchdown pass in 54 straight games. **Johnny Unitas** had set the record in 1960 at 47 straight games.

Through the 2012 season, Brees has played in 170 regular-season NFL games in 12 seasons, started in 169 games and has a 99–70 record in those games, and completed 4,035 passes in 6,149 attempts for 45,919 yards and 324 **touchdowns**. He also carried the ball 298 times for 570 yards and nine touchdowns and caught six passes for 72 yards and one touchdown. In nine playoff games, he completed 262 of 392 passes for 2,980 yards and 22 touchdowns. He also ran 21 times for 29 yards and no touchdowns. Brees has appeared in seven **Pro Bowls**.

BROOKLYN DODGERS (AAFC). The Brooklyn Dodgers were a **professional football** team in the **All-America Football Conference (AAFC)** from 1946 to 1948. The team was unrelated to the former **National Football League** team. Home games were played at the 32,000-seat Ebbets Field in Brooklyn, New York (one of the five boroughs of New York City), also the home of Major League Baseball's Brooklyn Dodgers. In the Dodgers' three seasons, they had four head **coaches**, including Mal Stevens, Tom Scott, and Cliff Battles in 1946, Battles in 1947, and Carl Voyles in 1948. Among their best players were the versatile tailback/**punter**/kick **returner** Glenn Dobbs, **tackle** Martin Ruby, **back** Bob Hoernschemeyer, and **end** Saxon Judd. In three seasons they had a record of 8–32–2. They finished in a **tie** for second place in the East Division in 1946, third place in 1947, and fourth place in 1948. They merged with the **New York Yankees** of the AAFC to play as the **Brooklyn–New York Yankees** for the 1949 AAFC season.

BROOKLYN DODGERS (NFL). The Brooklyn Dodgers were a **professional football** team in the **National Football League (NFL)** from 1930 to 1944, although they changed their name to Brooklyn Tigers in 1944. In 1945, the Brooklyn team merged with the **Boston Yanks**. The NFL team started in 1930, after two Brooklyn businessmen, Bill Dwyer and Jack Depler, purchased the Dayton Triangles NFL franchise. Home games were played at the 32,000-seat Ebbets Field in Brooklyn, New York (one of the five boroughs of New York City), also the home of Major League Baseball's Brooklyn Dodgers. In their 15 years in the NFL, the Dodgers compiled a record of 60–100–9. Their best season was 1940, when, under **Coach** John "Jock" Sutherland, they finished in second place in the East Division with a record of 8–3. Since only the division leaders met in the NFL Championship Game during that era, the Dodgers never played a postseason game. George "Potsy" Clark, who coached the team from 1937 to 1939, was the only one of 10 Brooklyn head coaches to last more than two years. Future **Pro Football Hall of Fame** tailbacks Clarence "Ace" Parker and Benny Friedman, **tackle** Frank "Bruiser" Kinard, and **end** Morris "Red" Badgro were among the team's best players. Other notable players for the Dodgers include **fullback** Clarence "Pug" Manders, ends Jeff Barrett and Perry Schwartz, and **kicker** Ralph Kercheval.

BROOKLYN–NEW YORK YANKEES. The Brooklyn–New York Yankees were a **professional football** team in the **All-America Football Conference (AAFC)** in 1949. They were the result of a merger between the **Brooklyn Dodgers** and **New York Yankees** of the AAFC. In their one season in the league, playing at the 67,000-seat Yankee Stadium in the Bronx, New York (one of the five boroughs of New York City), they finished in third place in the seven-team league, with a record of 8–4, and lost to the **San Francisco 49ers** in the first round of the postseason **playoffs**. Among their better players were **halfback Claude "Buddy" Young**; **tackles** Martin Ruby and Arnie Weinmeister; **end** Barney Poole; and **punter** and **back Tom Landry**, who went on to become a **Pro Football Hall of Fame coach** with the **Dallas Cowboys**. Also on the team was Columbia University's star **linebacker**, Lou Kusserow, who, after a brief pro football career, became a producer for NBC, with five **Super Bowl** telecasts to his credit. The Yankees were disbanded when the AAFC merged with the **National Football League (NFL)** in 1950, and their players were distributed to the **New York Giants** and **New York Bulldogs** of the NFL.

BROOKLYN TIGERS. *See* BROOKLYN DODGERS (NFL).

BROWN, JAMES NATHANIEL "JIM." B. 17 February 1936, St. Simons, Georgia. Jim Brown is considered by some to be the greatest **running back** in **football** history. Although his career was relatively brief by modern standards (he only played nine seasons), in those nine years he led the **National Football League (NFL)** in **rushing** eight times. He is the only player to average more than 100 yards rushing per game throughout his NFL career.

Born on one of the Sea Islands off the coast of Georgia, Brown moved to Manhasset on Long Island, New York, when he was eight years old and was raised there. At Manhasset, he was a star in football, basketball, baseball, lacrosse, and track. He averaged 38 points per game playing basketball and set a Long Island high school record that was later broken by future Major League Baseball Hall of Famer Carl Yastrzemski. Brown continued to excel in football, basketball, and lacrosse at **Syracuse University**. He was inducted into the National Lacrosse Hall of Fame in 1983, and his plaque read in part, "Considered by many to be the greatest ever to play the game of lacrosse."

Brown was chosen by the **Cleveland Browns** in the first round of the 1957 NFL **Draft** as the sixth overall selection. As **fullback** for the Browns, the six-foot, two-inch, 230-pound Brown helped lead Cleveland to the NFL championship in his first season. In 1958, the Browns **tied** for their **conference** title but were defeated by the **New York Giants** in a tiebreaker **playoff** game. The Browns finished either second or third for the next five seasons and, in 1964, again won the NFL title. They played in the NFL Championship Game in 1965 but were defeated by the **Green Bay Packers**. Following that season, Brown retired from football at only 29 years of age.

Upon leaving the NFL, Brown decided to pursue an acting career after being in a film in 1964. Since then, he has appeared in more than 50 films, with many starring roles. *The Dirty Dozen* is one of his more memorable ones. In 2002, noted film director Spike Lee made a film about Brown's life entitled *Jim Brown: All American*.

In his nine-year NFL career, Brown played in 118 regular-season games, carried the ball 2,359 times for 12,312 yards and 106 **touchdowns**, and caught 262 **passes** for 2,499 yards and 20 touchdowns. He also completed four of 12 passes for 117 yards in **option plays**, but three of the four were for touchdowns. In the first five years of his professional career, he was also used for returning **kickoffs** and had an average of 22.3 yards per return for 29 kickoff returns. In four postseason games, he rushed 66 times for 241 yards and one touchdown, caught eight passes for 99 yards and no touchdowns, and returned six kicks for 167 yards. He played in the **Pro Bowl** in each one of his nine professional seasons. Brown still holds the record for most consecutive games started at fullback, with 118, even though the NFL only played 12 games per season in his first four years and 14 each season during the latter five years, in contrast to today's 16-game regular season. He was inducted into the **Pro Football Hall of Fame** in 1971 and the **College Football Hall of Fame** in 1995.

BROWN, PAUL EUGENE. B. 7 September 1908, Norwalk, Ohio. D. 5 August 1991, Cincinnati, Ohio. Paul Brown is one of the names mentioned in a discussion of the greatest **football coach** in history. He had winning teams at all levels of the sport, high school, college, and professional. Even when he served in the military, he coached one of the all-time great military teams. He is also the only person for which a **National Football League (NFL)** team is named (**Cleveland Browns**).

Brown was a graduate of the famed Washington High School (commonly known as **Massillon High School**) in Massillon, Ohio, where he was the **quarterback**, although he weighed barely 150 pounds. He began college at **Ohio State University**, but as a freshman quarterback there he found out that he was too small for that level of competition and transferred to Miami

University of Ohio. He lost a year of athletic eligibility in doing so and was only able to play two years at Miami.

After graduating from Miami in 1930, with a degree in education, he was hired by Severn School in Severna Park, Maryland (a preparatory school for the United States Naval Academy). He coached there for two years and compiled a won-lost record of 16–1–1 in that time. In 1932, he began coaching at his alma mater in Massillon and, from 1932 to 1940, put Massillon on the football map by achieving a record of 80–8–2, including a 35-game winning streak and six state high school championships. In 1940, Massillon outscored their opponents by 477–6. As a result of the school's success, a new 16,000-seat **stadium** was built as one of the largest high school stadiums in the country.

In 1941, Brown began coaching at Ohio State University. From 1941 to 1943, he compiled a record of 18–8–1 and led the Buckeyes to the national championship in 1942. He entered the U.S. Navy in 1944 as a lieutenant and was assigned to the Great Lakes Naval Station. His job there was to recruit a football team from all naval personnel. For two seasons, the Great Lakes team played other military teams, as well as colleges, and compiled a record of 15–5–2.

Following the war, Brown was signed to coach the Cleveland entry in the new **All-America Football Conference (AAFC)**. A newspaper contest was held to determine the team's name, and the team was called the Browns, named for the coach. During the four years that the AAFC was in existence, 1946 to 1949, the league was dominated by the Cleveland Browns as no other league has been either before or afterward. The Browns won the league championship all four years, amassing a won-lost record of 47–4–3 in the regular season and 5–0 in postseason games. Brown was one of the first coaches to employ black players, and **fullback** Marion Motley and **lineman** Bill Willis were two who starred for him in the AAFC.

When the AAFC and NFL merged for the 1950 season, the Browns continued their dominance of **professional football**, reaching the NFL Championship Game in each season from 1950 to 1955. They met a tougher opposition in the NFL and only won three of the six NFL Championship Games in which they played, in 1950, 1954, 1955. They also reached the NFL Championship Game in 1957.

Brown was known for his innovative ideas, which included using intelligence testing to evaluate players' learning potential, utilizing extensive classroom work to instruct players, and using film study to measure players' performance. He was one of the first professional coaches to insist on a dress code and expect certain behavior from his players to improve the image of professional players, and he was always one of the best-dressed coaches in his era. Brown experimented with calling offensive plays via electronic communication with the quarterback and, when that proved ineffective due to the limited technology of the day, alternated offensive **guards** who would relay his plays to the quarterback.

In 1961, Art Modell purchased a part ownership in the Browns. He and Brown did not see eye to eye, and Brown was fired in January 1963. In 1968, after staying away from the game for five seasons, Brown was offered the opportunity to be part owner, general manager, and coach of the new **American Football League** expansion franchise the **Cincinnati Bengals**. For eight seasons, Brown enjoyed these multiple roles and was able to lead the Bengals to the **playoffs** in only their third year of operation. After the 1975 season, Brown relinquished his coaching position but still remained as team president until his death in 1991. The Bengals reached the **Super Bowl** twice during the 1980s but were defeated in both the 1982 and 1989 games.

In 25 years as a professional football coach, Brown's teams had a record of 213–104–9 in regular-season play and 9–8 in the postseason. After Brown's death, his son, Mike, replaced him as president, general manager, and owner of the Bengals. Paul was inducted into the **Pro Football Hall of Fame** as a coach in 1967. In 2000, a new 65,000-seat football stadium was built in Cincinnati for use by the Bengals and was named Paul Brown Stadium. The 16,000-seat high school stadium in Massillon had been rededicated as Paul Brown Tiger Stadium years earlier.

BROWN, TIMOTHY DONELL "TIM." B. 22 July 1966, Dallas, Texas. Tim Brown attended Woodrow Wilson High School in Dallas, Texas. Although his **football** team won only five of 30 games during the three years he played on it, he still impressed enough people to be offered college scholarships to several major schools. He chose the **University of Notre Dame** and played for them from 1984 to 1987. Notre Dame's record was only 25–21 during that time, but Brown had an impressive career there as a **wide receiver** and kick **returner**. In 1987, he became the first player at his position to win the **Heisman Trophy**.

The six-foot-tall, 195-pound Brown was chosen by the Los Angeles Raiders in the first round of the 1988 **National Football League (NFL) Draft** as the sixth overall selection. He played for the Raiders in Los Angeles and Oakland for 16 years, from 1988 to 2003, and finished his NFL career with one year in Tampa Bay. Brown played in 255 regular-season games in the NFL. Through the 2012 season, only 29 players in the history of the league played in more games, and more than half of them were **kickers** or **punters**. **Jerry Rice** is the only other wide receiver to have played more NFL games then Brown.

Brown played on the losing side in the 26 January 2003 **Super Bowl**; was named to the **Pro Bowl** nine times; and in the regular season caught 1,094 **passes** for 14,934 yards and 100 **touchdowns, rushed** 50 times for 190 yards and one touchdown, and returned 251 punts and **kickoffs** for 4,555 yards and four touchdowns. In 12 postseason games he caught 45 passes for 581 yards and three touchdowns, ran three times for one yard, and returned four kickoffs for 68 yards and nine punts for 75 yards.

After retiring from active play, Brown has done some television work and attempted to start an auto racing team. In 2009, he was inducted into the **College Football Hall of Fame** and was a finalist for the **Pro Football Hall of Fame** the following year.

BRYANT, PAUL WILLIAM "BEAR." B. 11 September 1913, Fordyce, Arkansas. D. 26 January 1983, Tuscaloosa, Alabama. Paul Bryant attended Fordyce High School in Fordyce, Arkansas, and was a member of the 1930 Arkansas high school state champions as a **lineman** and defensive **end**. The six-foot, three-inch Bryant allegedly wrestled a circus bear while in high school and thus received the nickname "Bear," which remained with him throughout his adult life. He received an athletic scholarship to attend the **University of Alabama** but was required to attend high school in Tuscaloosa to complete his high school credits before he was allowed to matriculate at Alabama.

At Alabama, Bryant played from 1933 to 1935 and was a member of the **Southeastern Conference** champions in 1933 and 1934, as well as the national champions in 1934 that were victorious in the 1 January 1935 **Rose Bowl** over **Stanford University**. Also on those teams playing the **end** position was future **National Football League (NFL)** star **Don Hutson**, and, in later years, Bryant liked to describe himself as the "other end" on Alabama's championship team.

Bryant was selected by the **Brooklyn Dodgers** in the fourth round of the first NFL **Draft** ever held. It occurred in 1936, and Bryant was the 31st player selected. **Professional football** was not an especially lucrative career at that time, and Bryant elected to become a college **coach** instead. Bryant became an **assistant coach** at Union College, a small Baptist college in Jackson, Tennessee. He was there but a short while when he was offered an assistant's job at his alma mater, Alabama. He jumped at the opportunity and was an assistant there from 1936 to 1940. He moved to Vanderbilt University in 1940 and was employed as assistant coach. Following the 1941 football season, Bryant was offered the head coaching position at the University of Arkansas, but the attack on Pearl Harbor changed his plans and he enlisted in the U.S. Navy.

In 1942, Bryant was an assistant coach with a naval football team in Georgia and, in 1944, for a team in North Carolina. After being discharged with the rank of lieutenant commander, he was hired by the University of Maryland as their head coach in 1945. He only spent one year there, leading them to a 6–2–1 record before moving to the University of Kentucky. Bryant coached the Wildcats from 1946 to 1953, compiling a record of 60–23–5 in eight seasons, and he led them to the Southeastern Conference championship in 1950 and four postseason bowl appearances.

From 1954 to 1957, Bryant was the head coach at **Texas A&M University** and had a record of 25–14–2 with the Aggies in four years despite a 1–9 record in his first season there. That season would prove to be his only losing season in 38 years as a college head coach. In 1956, the Aggies were **Southwest Conference** champions.

Bryant returned to Alabama in 1958, and it was there that his Hall of Fame legacy was established. He was Alabama's head coach for 25 years, from 1958 to 1982, with a remarkable won-lost record of 232–46–9 as their coach. Alabama stood as conference champions or cochampions 13 times. His teams won national championship recognition in 1961, 1964, 1965, 1966, 1973, 1975, 1977, 1978, and 1979. Alabama did not play in a **bowl game** in Bryant's first year, 1958, but then played in one for each of the next 24 consecutive years, one of the most remarkable college coaching records of all time, made all the more so since there were far fewer bowl games in that era than there are now. More than 60 of his former players played professional football in the NFL or **American Football League**.

Bryant retired following the 1982 season at the age of 69 and died shortly afterward from a heart attack. In his 38 years of being a college head coach, his teams had only one losing season and compiled a record of 323–85–17, far more victories than any other college head coach at that time, although the record has since been surpassed. In 1986, he was selected to the **College Football Hall of Fame** for his coaching ability and success. In 1997, Bryant was honored on a U.S. commemorative postage stamp, along with **George Halas**, **Glenn "Pop" Warner**, and **Vince Lombardi**.

BUFFALO BILLS (AAFC). The Buffalo Bills were a **professional football** team in the **All-America Football Conference (AAFC)** from 1946 to 1949. In their first season in the league, they were called the Buffalo Bisons, but the team changed its name to the Bills for the 1947 season. Home games were played at the 35,000-seat Civic Stadium in Buffalo, New York (renamed War Memorial Stadium in 1960). In its four seasons in the league, the team had a record of 23–26–5. Playing in the league's four-team East Division, they finished third in 1946, second in 1947, and first in 1948 (after winning a tiebreaking **playoff** game against Baltimore). In the 1948 AAFC Championship Game, they were defeated by the West Division champion **Cleveland Browns**, 49–7. In the single division seven-team league in 1949, the Bills finished fourth. **Quarterback** George Ratterman was the star of the team from 1947 to 1949. Other top players included **halfback** and kick **returner** Chet Mutryn and **end** Al Baldwin. When the AAFC and **National Football League** merged in 1950, the Bills were dissolved, and Bills' owner Jim Breuil received a minority interest in the Cleveland Browns.

BUFFALO BILLS (NFL). The Buffalo Bills are a **professional football** team in the American Football Conference (AFC) East Division of the **National Football League (NFL)**. They began as a charter member of the **American Football League (AFL)** in 1960 and played in the AFL's East Division. Home games were played at the 46,000-seat War Memorial Stadium in Buffalo, New York, from 1960 to 1972. In 1973, the Bills moved to the newly built 80,000-seat Rich Stadium in Orchard Park, New York (a suburb of Buffalo). In 1998, the Rich company's naming rights expired, and the stadium was named **Ralph Wilson** Stadium in honor of the Bills' owner and founder. Wilson, still alive in 2013, has been the team's only owner in its 51-year existence.

In the Bills' 10 years in the AFL, they compiled an overall record of 65–69–6 in regular-season play and were 2–2 in postseason games. They won the AFL championship in 1964 and 1965 and were losers in the AFL Championship Game in 1966. In 1970, they joined the NFL in the AFC East Division when the AFL and NFL merged. Their regular-season record for 43 seasons in the NFL is 305–357–2, and their **playoff** record is 12–13. They were defeated in four consecutive **Super Bowls** from 1990 to 1993. In 1990 and 1991, they won 13 regular-season games each year, their best record. They lost the conference championship in 1988; lost in the divisional playoffs in 1974, 1980, 1981, 1989, and 1995; and lost in the **wild-card playoff** in 1996, 1998, and 1999.

Buffalo's most successful head **coach** was Marv Levy, who coached them from 1986 to 1997 and led them to four Super Bowls. Other head coaches for the Bills have been Garrard "Buster" Ramsey (1960–1961), Lou Saban (1962–1965, 1972–1976), Joe Collier (1966–1968), Harvey Johnson (1968, 1971), John Rauch (1969–1970), Jim Ringo (1976–1977), Chuck Knox (1978–1982), Kay Stephenson (1983–1985), Hank Bullough (1985–1986), Wade Phillips (1998–2000), Gregg Williams (2001–2003), Mike Mularkey (2004–2005), Dick Jauron (2006–2009), Perry Fewell (interim 2009), and Chan Gailey (2010–2012). On 6 January 2013, Doug Marrone was hired as head coach for the 2013 season.

The best players for the Bills include **Pro Football Hall of Fame running backs O. J. Simpson** and **Thurman Thomas, guards** Joe DeLamielleure and Billy Shaw, **quarterback Jim Kelly, wide receiver James Lofton**, and defensive **end** Bruce Smith. Other players of note include quarterback **Jack Kemp**, later a U.S. congressman and 1996 vice presidential candidate; quarterback Joe Ferguson; wide receivers Elbert Dubenion, Andre Reed, and Steve Tasker; nose **tackle** Fred Smerlas; guards Reggie McKenzie and Bob Kalsu (the only active NFL player killed in Vietnam); defensive tackle Tom Sestak; defensive **backs** George "Butch" Byrd, Booker Edgerson, and George Saimes; **linebacker** Darryl Talley; **fullback** Carlton "Cookie" Gilchrist; and **punter**/linebacker Paul Maguire.

BUFFALO BISONS. *See* BUFFALO BILLS (AAFC).

BUONICONTI, NICHOLAS ANTHONY "NICK." B. 15 December 1940, Springfield, Massachusetts. Nick Buoniconti attended Cathedral High School in Springfield, Massachusetts, and, as a sophomore, was a member of the 1955 Western Massachusetts Class AA **high school football** championship team. He played for the **University of Notre Dame** and, although only five feet, 11 inches tall and 220 pounds, played **guard** and **linebacker**. Notre Dame had some of the worst seasons in their history from 1959 to 1961, when Buoniconti was a team member, and, consequently, when he graduated he was not highly regarded by professional scouts.

Buoniconti was only chosen in the 13th round by the Boston Patriots in the 1962 **American Football League (AFL) Draft** as the 113th overall selection, and he was not selected in the **National Football League (NFL)** Draft. He surprised the experts by making the Patriots' team and playing with them for seven years, including playing on the AFL runner-up team in 1963. He was traded to the **Miami Dolphins** in 1969 and played seven more seasons with them. He played on the **Super Bowl** champions in 1973 and 1974 and the Super Bowl runners-up in 1972. In 1972, he was an integral part of the Miami team that went undefeated.

In Buoniconti's 14 years as a **professional football** player in the AFL and NFL, he played in 183 regular-season games and recorded 32 **interceptions**, but none were returned for **touchdowns**. In addition, he recovered six **fumbles** for two touchdowns. He was also credited with a **safety** in 1967. Buoniconti played in 13 **playoff** games and recorded two interceptions and one fumble recovery. He played in eight postseason all-star games, including six AFL All-Star Games and two NFL **Pro Bowls**.

While with the Patriots, Buoniconti earned a law degree, and, after retiring from professional football, he worked as an attorney. He was also president of the U.S. Tobacco Company and a cohost for a television series on football. In 1985, his son, Marc, was paralyzed while playing football at the Citadel. Since then, Nick has devoted much of his time to working with the Miami Project to Cure Paralysis, one of the world's leading spinal cord injury research centers. He was inducted into the **Pro Football Hall of Fame** in 2001.

BUSH, REGINALD ALFRED, II "REGGIE." B. 2 March 1985, San Diego, California. Reggie Bush attended Helix High School in La Mesa, California, and the **University of Southern California (USC)**. While at USC, he was used as a **running back** and kick **returner** and was awarded the **Heisman Trophy** following his junior year in 2005. From 2003 to 2005, USC compiled records of 12–1, 13–0, and 12–1, with victories in the **Rose Bowl** and **Orange Bowl** and a 41–38 loss to the **University of Texas** in the Rose Bowl. In 2003 and 2004, they were selected as national collegiate champions. The six-foot-tall, 200-pound Bush decided to leave school after his junior year and was chosen by the **New Orleans Saints** in the first round of the 2006 **National Football League (NFL) Draft** as the second overall selection. Bush's NFL career has not been nearly as spectacular as his college career, as injuries have limited his play. He was a member of the 2010 **Super Bowl** championship team, and he was traded to the **Miami Dolphins** prior to the 2011 season. That year, he had the best individual statistical season of his professional career, playing in 15 of 16 games and **rushing** for 1,086 yards, including one game with 203 yards rushing.

Through 2012, Bush has played seven NFL seasons and appeared in 91 regular-season games. He has carried the ball 967 times for 4,162 yards and 29 **touchdowns**, and caught 372 **passes** for 2,730 yards and 15 touchdowns. He has attempted only one pass, but it was **intercepted**. He has also been used for **punt** returns and has averaged 7.9 yards with four touchdowns for his 98 punt returns. In six **playoff** games, Bush has run 38 times for 200 yards and two touchdowns. He also caught 25 passes for 286 yards and two touchdowns and returned 11 punts for 144 yards and one touchdown.

In 2010, the **National Collegiate Athletic Association (NCAA)** completed an investigation into recruiting practices of the USC football team and disclosed that Bush had received improper gifts. As a result, USC was given four years of probation, was required to vacate their last two wins of 2004 and the entire 2005 season, was prohibited from playing in **bowl games** in 2010 and 2011, and forfeited 30 football scholarships. The Heisman Trophy Trust, donors of the Heisman Trophy, decided to nullify Bush's award and required him to return the trophy. Had Bush not run afoul of the NCAA, he likely would have eventually been selected for the **College Football Hall of Fame**, but since the NCAA decision it is quite unlikely.

BUTKUS, RICHARD MARVIN "DICK." B. 9 December 1942, Chicago, Illinois. At six feet, three inches tall and 245 pounds, Dick Butkus was one of the most imposing **linebackers** in **professional football** history, and he is considered by some to be the greatest of all time. He attended Chicago Vocational High School, where he played **fullback** on their football team and was named one of Chicago's best high school players. He played **center** and linebacker on the **University of Illinois varsity** teams from 1962 to 1964 and was a member of the **Big Ten Conference** championship team in 1963 that had a record of 8–1–1 that year and a victory in the **Rose Bowl**.

Butkus was selected by the **Chicago Bears** in the first round of the 1965 **National Football League (NFL) Draft** as the third overall pick, and also by the **Denver Broncos** in the second round of the 1965 **American Football League** Draft as the ninth overall selection. He signed with the Bears and played middle linebacker for them from 1965 to 1973.

In his nine-year NFL career, Butkus appeared in 119 regular-season games, **intercepted** 22 **passes**, and recovered 27 **fumbles**. His only **touchdown** came on a fumble recovery in the **end zone**. In 1972, he even carried the ball once on a fake **punt** and gained 28 yards when, as a punt **blocker**, the ball was snapped to him instead of the **punter**. During his career the Bears never reached the postseason **playoffs**. Butkus played in the **Pro Bowl** in each of his first eight NFL seasons.

Since retiring from active play, Butkus has done some television broadcasting, been featured in a few notable commercials, and appeared in more than 40 Hollywood films and television series. He was inducted into the **Pro Football Hall of Fame** in 1979 and **College Football Hall of Fame** in 1983.

C

CALGARY STAMPEDERS. The Calgary Stampeders are a team in the **Canadian Football League (CFL)**. They were founded in 1935 as the Calgary Bronks and changed their name to Stampeders (after the annual Calgary Stampede festival) in 1945. Calgary had fielded football teams as early as 1891, but those teams were unrelated to the present organization.

The Stampeders competed in the Western Interprovincial Football Union (WIFU) from 1936 until 1958, when the WIFU became part of the CFL. Since 1960, their home field has been McMahon Stadium, located in Calgary, Alberta, with seating expanded from its original 22,000-seat capacity to its present-day 38,000. Prior to the opening of McMahon Stadium, the Stamps played at the 10,000-seat Mewata Stadium, also in Calgary.

Calgary has played in the **Grey Cup** 13 times and has a 6–7 record in those games. Among their most notable head **coaches** have been Carl Cronin (1935–1938), Les Lear (1948–1952), Otis Douglas (1956–1960), Bobby Dobbs (1961–1964), Jerry Williams (1965–1968), Jim Duncan (1969–1973), Wally Buono (1990–2002), and John Hufnagel (2008–2012).

Former Stampeders in the **Canadian Football Hall of Fame** include Tony Anselmo, Willie Burden, **Doug Flutie**, Dean Griffing, Wayne Harris, Herman Harrison, John Helton, Alondra Johnson, Jerry Keeling, Earl Lunsford, Don Luzzi, Tony Pajaczkowski, Allen Pitts, Rocco Romano, Paul Rowe, and Harvey Wylie. Other Calgary players of note include Jamie Crysdale, Tom Forzani, Harry Hood, Stu Laird, and Mark McLoughlin.

CALIFORNIA, UNIVERSITY OF. The school popularly known as simply "California" is more properly called the University of California, Berkeley. Their football program began in 1882, and, since then, through 2012, Golden Bears' teams have compiled a record of 636–490–52. In addition, they have competed in 21 postseason **bowl games** with a record of 10–10–1 (2–5–1 in the **Rose Bowl** and 8–3 in other bowls). They have been selected as national collegiate champions five times from 1920 to 1923 and in 1927. Since 1915, California football teams have competed in the **Pacific-12 Conference** (formerly known by other names, including the Pacific Coast Conference) of the **National Collegiate Athletic Association**.

California's main rival is **Stanford University**. Since 1892, the teams have met nearly annually in a contest known simply as the "Big Game." Through 2012, the series stands at Stanford 53 victories, California 43 victories, and 10 ties. From 1906 to 1914, the schools met in annual **rugby** matches that are not reflected in that total. The 1982 game is noteworthy in that it ended with California, trailing 20–19, returning a **kickoff** for a **touchdown** with four seconds remaining in the game and using five **laterals** and **running** through the Stanford marching band that had started to come onto the field after mistakenly thinking that the game was over.

Among California's most noteworthy head **coaches** have been Andy Smith (1916–1925; 74–16–7), Leonard "Stub" Allison (1935–1944; 58–42–2), Lynn "Pappy" Waldorf (1946–1956; 67–32–4), and Jeff Tedford (2002–2012; 82–57). California coaches in the **College Football Hall of Fame** include Bill Ingram, Lawrence "Buck" Shaw, Andy Smith, and Lynn "Pappy" Waldorf.

California has 16 alumni in the Hall of Fame. They include **linemen** Stan Barnes, Rod Franz, Walter Gordon, Matt Hazeltine, Bob Herwig, Edwin "Babe" Horrell, Dan McMillan, Les Richter, and Ed White; **halfbacks** Vic Bottari and Sam Chapman; **fullback** Jackie Jensen (best known as the 1958 American League Most Valuable Player in Major League Baseball); **quarterbacks** Steve Bartkowski, **Joe Kapp**, and Craig Morton; and **end** Harold "Brick" Muller.

Through 2012, there have been 220 **professional football** players who have attended California, 212 in the **National Football League**, five in the **American Football League**, and three in the **All-America Football Conference**. They include **Pro Football Hall of Famer** Les Richter. Others are Chidi Ahanotu, Steve Bartkowski, David Binn, Jim Breech, Doug Brien, Isaac Curtis, Herman Edwards, Scott Fujita, Tarik Glenn, **Tony Gonzalez**, Matt Hazeltine, Joe Kapp, Ryan Longwell, Craig Morton, Chuck Muncie, Hardy Nickerson, Johnny Olszewski, Gary Plummer, **Aaron Rodgers**, Todd Steussie, Wesley Walker, Ray Wersching, Ed White, Sherman White, and Jim Wilks.

CALVILLO, ANTHONY. B. 23 August 1972, Los Angeles, California. Anthony Calvillo has claims to all three major North American countries. Born and raised in the United States, he is of Mexican American heritage and has become one of the greatest players in **Canadian Football League (CFL)** history. Calvillo attended La Puente High School in Los Angeles, where he played **football** and basketball. He began college at Mount San Antonio Junior College and was their **quarterback** for two years before transferring to Utah State University in 1992. As a senior, he helped lead Utah State to a 7–5 record, their first winning season in 13 years, and their first bowl victory.

Calvillo was not chosen in the 1994 **National Football League (NFL) Draft**, as he was considered too small, at six feet, one inch tall and 200 pounds, to be an effective NFL quarterback. He tried out for the **Las Vegas Posse**, a U.S.-based expansion team in the CFL, was successful, and made the team as their quarterback, but the team folded after one season. He then played for the **Hamilton Tiger-Cats** from 1995 to 1997 as their backup quarterback. In 1998, Calvillo signed as a free agent with the **Montreal Alouettes**, and he remained with them through the 2012 season. He has led them to the **Grey Cup** eight times in his 14 seasons with the team; won the Grey Cup championship in 2002, 2009, and 2010; and was named the Grey Cup Most Valuable Player in 2002. He was named the CFL's Most Outstanding Player in 2003, 2008, and 2009.

Through 2012, Calvillo has played in 322 regular-season games and completed 5,777 **passes** in 9,241 attempts for 78,494 yards and 449 **touchdowns**. He also **rushed** 676 times for 3,662 yards and 34 touchdowns. He is the CFL career leader in completed passes, passing yardage, and touchdowns passing. His total yards passing is the most in **professional football** and more than 6,000 yards greater than **Brett Favre's** NFL record.

CAMP, WALTER CHAUNCEY. B. 7 April 1859, New Britain, Connecticut. D. 14 March 1925, New York, New York. Walter Camp is known as the "Father of American **football**" due to his accomplishments as a player, **coach**, innovator, and rules maker during the early years of the sport. An excellent athlete, he competed in swimming, **running**, and tennis. After graduating from Hopkins Grammar School (a private college preparatory school in New Haven, Connecticut) he continued his education at **Yale University**, where he was a member of the football team. After graduation in 1880, he enrolled at Yale Medical College and continued playing football for Yale until 1882. Camp abandoned a medical career to work in his uncle's New Haven Clock Company in 1883 and eventually worked his way up to being the chairman of the board of directors of that firm.

Although Yale first began playing intercollegiate football in 1872, they did so without a head coach, as was customary in that era. In 1888, Camp became Yale's first head coach, and he retained that position until 1892. During those five years, Yale won 67 games and lost only two, and they took home the national championship in 1888, 1891, and 1892. Following Yale's last game in November 1892, Camp went west and coached **Stanford University** for four games in December 1892. He also coached Stanford University again in 1894 and 1895.

Camp was also a prolific author, and, in addition to editing an annual guide, he is credited with more than 20 books on football and other sports and more than 200 newspaper and magazine articles. He was a member of various football rules committees for 48 years. Among his contributions are the downs system; the points system; the **center** snap; the seven-man offensive line and four-man offensive backfield; and the concept of the **safety**, in which a defensive team is rewarded with two points for stopping the offensive team in its own **end zone**. He basically transformed the game from its **rugby** roots into the modern game known today. Along with Caspar Whitney, Camp is also credited with the selection of the earliest **All-American** teams. In 1951, he was selected as a charter member of the **College Football Hall of Fame** as a coach.

CAMPBELL, EARL CHRISTIAN. B. 29 March 1955, Tyler, Texas. During a relatively brief period from the mid-1970s until the mid-1980s, Earl Campbell was the premier **running back** in **football**. He won the **Heisman Trophy** in 1977, after leading the nation in **rushing** in college, and was the first overall selection of the Houston Oilers in the 1978 **National Football League (NFL) Draft**. In his rookie season in the NFL, Campbell was named Offensive Rookie of the Year, as well as Offensive Player of the Year.

Campbell attended John Tyler High School in Tyler, Texas, and led them to the Texas state high school championship in 1973. He went on to star at the **University of Texas**, gaining 4,443 yards in four years of collegiate play despite missing four games his junior year. When he completed his senior year, Campbell was the fifth leading collegiate rusher of all time. Despite being only five feet, 11 inches tall, he weighed between 220 and 240 pounds and had extremely powerful legs.

In his first three years in the NFL, Campbell led the league in rushing each year and, in 1980, amassed 1,934 yards, second only to **O. J. Simpson's** 2,003-yard record set seven years earlier. In his eight-year NFL career, Campbell played in 115 regular-season games, carried the ball 2,187 times for 9,407 yards and 74 **touchdowns**, and caught 121 **passes** for 806 yards but no touchdowns. In three option pass play attempts, his only completion went for a 57-yard touchdown. One of the other three pass attempts was **intercepted**. In eight postseason games, he rushed 135 times for 420 yards and four touchdowns, caught five passes for 45 yards and no touchdowns, and threw one **incomplete pass**.

Campbell's relatively early retirement from the NFL was precipitated by the abuse that his body took as a ball carrier. He became president of Earl Campbell Meat Products and briefly owned a restaurant in Austin, Texas. He was inducted into the **College Football Hall of Fame** in 1990 and the **Pro Football Hall of Fame** in 1991.

CANADIAN FOOTBALL. Canadian **football** is similar to American football in many respects. Both are modifications of **rugby** that originated in the

1860s. To the neophyte viewer, Canadian football looks just like the version played in the United States. Upon closer observation, however, there are several differences, some of them quite significant. Teams in Canada play with 12 men on each side versus the 11-man U.S. team. The 12th Canadian offensive player is an additional **back**, usually termed a **slotback**, and the 12th defensive player is a defensive back. Second, the field is 110 yards long from **goal line** to goal line and 65 yards wide, with 20-yard **end zones**. The American one is 100 yards long and 53 1/3 yards wide and has 10-yard end zones.

Possibly the greatest difference between the two games is that in Canada, a team has only three **downs** in which to gain 10 yards, whereas the American game allows four downs. This makes the Canadian game a more wide-open game in which **passing** is a greater factor. To facilitate the passing game, in Canada, all backfield players, exclusive of the **quarterback**, may be moving in any direction, including forward, when the ball is snapped. This is not permitted in American football. The American game only allows one back to be in motion, and it cannot include moving toward the **line of scrimmage**. The distance between the offensive and defensive teams at the line of scrimmage (known as the neutral zone) in American football is about 11 inches (the length of the football). In Canadian rules, a full yard is required.

One other significant rules difference that often makes the Canadian game a more exciting one to watch is that a **punt** receiver may not call for a **fair catch** in which the defenders may not **tackle** him, and he may not advance the ball. Canadian receivers must attempt to advance a punt, and their only protection is that the defenders must remain five yards from them while they are doing so.

One scoring rule difference provides for a single point (officially called a **"rouge"** but commonly called a single) if the ball is kicked out of the defending team's end zone or is elected not to be **run** out of the end zone. Quite a few other minor differences exist regarding timing, kicking, **overtimes**, position of the ball following a score, and certain penalties, but, in essence, the games are quite similar. Both games enjoy a huge fan base. *See also* ALBERT, FRANK CULLEN "FRANKIE"; CALVILLO, ANTHONY; CANADIAN FOOTBALL HALL OF FAME; CANADIAN FOOTBALL LEAGUE; CAPPELLETTI, GINO RAYMOND MICHAEL; CLEMONS, MICHAEL LUTRELL "MIKE," "PINBALL"; ETCHEVERRY, SAM; FLUTIE, DOUGLAS RICHARD "DOUG"; GRANT, HARRY PETER, JR. "BUD"; KAPP, JOSEPH ROBERT "JOE"; KEMP, JACK FRENCH; LEBARON, EDWARD WAYNE, JR. "EDDIE"; MARSHALL, JAMES LAWRENCE "JIM"; MOON, HAROLD WARREN "WARREN"; PASSAGLIA, LUI; THEISMANN, JOSEPH ROBERT "JOE."

CANADIAN FOOTBALL HALL OF FAME. The Canadian Football Hall of Fame is a museum in Hamilton, Ontario, devoted to **Canadian football**. The museum's collection of memorabilia began in 1962, but it was not until 1972 that a permanent home was established. In 1963, the first elections were held to induct individuals into the Hall as players and builders of the sport. As of 2012, there have been 258 people inducted, 185 players and 73 builders. The museum is open to the public year-round. *See also* APPENDIX B (for a list of inductees).

CANADIAN FOOTBALL LEAGUE (CFL). The sport of **football** in Canada is about as old as the American version. Both date to the 1860s, and both were originally variations of **rugby**. Organized **Canadian football** leagues began in the 1880s and were governed by the Canadian Rugby Football Union, an umbrella institution that determined rules for the sport. Two of the more important leagues were the Interprovincial Rugby Football Union (IRFU), founded in 1907, and the Western Interprovincial Football Union (WIFU), founded in 1936. Both gradually converted from amateur players to professional ones. In 1956, the two leagues formed an association called the Canadian Football Council, and, on 19 January 1958, it was renamed the Canadian Football League (CFL).

The IRFU consisted of three teams based in the province of Ontario, the **Hamilton Tiger-Cats**, **Ottawa Rough Riders**, and **Toronto Argonauts**, and one team in Quebec province, the **Montreal Alouettes**. The WIFU had teams in each of the four western Canadian provinces, including the **BC Lions** (based in Vancouver, British Columbia), **Calgary Stampeders** and **Edmonton Eskimos** (in Alberta), **Saskatchewan Roughriders** (in Regina, Saskatchewan), and **Winnipeg Blue Bombers** (in Manitoba). Initially, there was not an interlocking schedule, but the champions of the IRFU and WIFU divisions met in the **Grey Cup** final to determine the overall league champion.

In 1961, the two divisions of the CFL were renamed the Eastern Conference and Western Conference, and a limited schedule of interconference play was adopted. The league was exceptionally stable for a professional sports league, with the nine original franchises neither relocating nor changing names until 1982. The only significant change was renaming the two conferences as divisions for 1981. After the 1981 season, the Montreal Alouettes franchise folded but was replaced in 1982 by the Montreal Concordes. The Concordes played from 1982 to 1985 and were renamed the Alouettes for 1986 but then folded prior to the 1987 season. That year, the CFL only had eight teams, and to balance the divisions, the league moved Winnipeg from the Western Division to the Eastern Division.

In 1993, the CFL expanded to the United States and added the Sacramento Gold Miners team, based in Sacramento, California. The team was reasonably successful, and, in 1994, the league added three more U.S.-based teams, including the **Baltimore** (Maryland) **Stallions**, **Shreveport** (Louisiana) **Pirates**, and **Las Vegas** (Nevada) **Posse**. Baltimore was quite successful and reached the Grey Cup, but the Las Vegas team was not, on the field (only five wins in 18 games) or at the box office. The league continued its experiment in 1995, and, although the Las Vegas franchise folded, teams in Birmingham, Alabama (the **Birmingham Barracudas**), and Memphis, Tennessee (the **Memphis Mad Dogs**) were added, and the Sacramento team relocated to San Antonio, Texas, as the **San Antonio Texans**. The five U.S. teams were placed in the CFL South Division, while the eight Canadian teams played in the CFL North Division. Surprisingly, the Grey Cup was won by Baltimore, the only time in the cup's long history that it was not won by a Canadian team.

With mixed results in the United States, the CFL decided to return to a strictly Canadian-based league in 1996. The Baltimore Stallions moved to Montreal and were renamed the Montreal Alouettes. Ottawa dropped out of the league following the 1996 season, and the league continued as an eight-team operation until 2002. In 2002, a new team was placed in Ottawa called the **Ottawa Renegades**. They lasted through 2005. In 2008, the Ottawa franchise was awarded to a new owner with the possibility of a team playing there in 2014.

The CFL plays an 18-game schedule preceded by two weeks of preseason exhibition games. A three-week, six-team postseason **playoff** tournament is held, with the final game being the Grey Cup championship game. The season usually runs from July through November. *See also* CANADIAN FOOTBALL HALL OF FAME; APPENDIX G (for a list of Grey Cup champions).

CAPPELLETTI, GINO RAYMOND MICHAEL. B.26 March 1934, Keewatin, Minnesota. Gino Cappelletti attended Keewatin High School and the **University of Minnesota**. In college, he played **quarterback** and was also the Gophers' placekicker and **punter**. He was not **drafted** by the **National Football League (NFL)** and instead signed with the Sarnia Imperials of the Ontario Rugby Football Union (ORFU) in Canada as their quarterback. He played for them in 1955, and for Toronto Balmy Beach in 1956. Midway through the 1956 season, Cappelletti was drafted into the U.S. Army. After being discharged, he returned to Canada in 1958 and played in the ORFU with Sarnia.

In 1960, Cappelletti was signed by the Boston Patriots of the new **American Football League (AFL)** and, for the next 11 seasons, was one of their most important players. At six feet tall and 190 pounds, he was used as both a pass receiver and placekicker. In his first season, Cappelletti also played **cornerback**. He helped lead the Patriots to the AFL Championship Game in 1963 and was one of only 20 players to play all 10 of the years that the AFL was in existence and one of only three to play in all of their team's games (**Jim Otto** and **George Blanda** were the other two). During Boston's 10 years in the AFL, Cappelletti was their only player to score a **field goal**, and he scored all but one of their kicked extra points. In 1970, the Patriots became members of the NFL, and following that season Cappelletti retired.

In Cappelletti's 11-year professional AFL/NFL football career, he caught 292 passes for 4,589 yards and 42 **touchdowns** in 153 regular-season games. He was also Boston's placekicker and scored 176 field goals in 333 attempts and 342 of 353 extra points. His AFL career total of 1,100 points scored is that league's record, and in five of the league's 10 years he led the AFL in points scored. In 1960, Cappelletti also played cornerback on **defense** and **intercepted** four passes. In 1961, he completed his only pass attempt, and it went for a 27-yard touchdown. In two postseason games, he caught six passes for 181 yards and no touchdowns and kicked three of three extra points and five of six field goals. He played in five AFL All-Star Games, and, in 1964, he was named the AFL Player of the Year. After retiring from active play, Cappelletti became a sports announcer, and, from 1972 to 1978 and 1988 to 2012, he did the radio color commentary for the **New England Patriots**.

CARD-PITT. Card-Pitt was a team in the **National Football League (NFL)** in 1944. Although the previous season's NFL merger between the **Philadelphia Eagles** and **Pittsburgh Steelers** was due to the manpower shortage caused by World War II, in 1944 the league was faced with the problem of too many teams after the Cleveland Rams rejoined the league. An 11-team league was thought to be unwieldy, so league **officials** recommended that the Chicago Cardinals and Pittsburgh Steelers combine their squads and merge. The Chicago and Pittsburgh head coaches, Phil Handler and Walt Kiesling, managed the team together. Home games were split between Wrigley Field in Chicago, Illinois, and Forbes Field in Pittsburgh, Pennsylvania. The team had one of the worst seasons in NFL history, going winless in 10 games and being outscored 328–108. They also set a record for lowest team **punting** average, at 32.7 yards per punt. One of their players, Clint Wager (who later also played professional basketball), suffered one of the most freakish injuries that season when he fractured his skull by kicking himself in the head while practicing punting. Shortly after the 1944 season ended, the merger was dissolved, and the two teams fielded separate teams in the NFL for 1945.

CARLISLE INDIAN INDUSTRIAL SCHOOL. Carlisle Indian Industrial School was located in Carlisle, Pennsylvania, from 1879 to 1918. Their **football** program began in 1893 and lasted until 1917. In that time, the Indians compiled a record of 173–92–13. Although a small school with limited enrollment, they managed to play and defeat the best schools in the country, including **Army, Navy, Harvard University, Penn State University,** the University of Virginia, the **University of Pittsburgh,** the University of Cincinnati, the **University of Minnesota, Syracuse University,** the University of Chicago, the **University of Nebraska,** Georgetown University, and Brown University.

Carlisle's most successful **coach** was **Glenn "Pop" Warner**. He coached at Carlisle from 1899 to 1903, and again from 1907 to 1914. His teams won 113 games, lost 42, and **tied** 8 during his 13 years there. Carlisle's six alumni in the **College Football Hall of Fame** are **halfbacks Jim Thorpe** and **Joe Guyon, quarterbacks** Jimmy Johnson and Gus Welch, and **ends** Albert Exendine and Eddie Rogers. Coaches Pop Warner and George Woodruff are also enshrined there.

There were 19 **National Football League (NFL)** players who attended Carlisle, including Pete Calac, Joe Guyon, Nick "Long Time Sleep" Lassa, Jim Thorpe, Joe Little Twig, and Philip "Woodchuck" Welmas. Seventeen of the 19 played for the **Oorang Indians** in 1922 or 1923. Calac (1920–1926), Guyon (1920–1927), Little Twig (1922–1926), and Thorpe (1920–1928) also played for other NFL teams. William "Birdie" Gardner and Frank Lone Star were the only two professional players from Carlisle who did not play for Oorang. Thorpe was the last NFL player from Carlisle. Sally Jenkins's book *The Real All-Americans: The Team That Changed a Game, a People, a Nation* provides an in-depth study of the school; its impact on Native American society; and Warner, Thorpe, and the football program.

CAROLINA PANTHERS. The Carolina Panthers are a **professional football** team in the **National Football League (NFL)**. They joined the league in 1995 as an expansion team, along with the **Jacksonville Jaguars**. From 1995 to 2001, the Panthers played in the National Football Conference (NFC) West Division, and, since 2002, they have played in the NFC South Division. Home games are played at the 73,778-seat Bank of America Stadium in Charlotte, North Carolina, formerly known as Ericsson Stadium and Carolinas Stadium. From 1995 to 2012, the Panthers compiled a regular-season record of 132–156 and a postseason record of 6–4. Their best season was 2003, when they reached the **Super Bowl** but were defeated, 32–29, by the **New England Patriots** on a **field goal** with four seconds left in a game that many consider to be the most exciting Super Bowl to date. In 1996 and 2008, the

Panthers finished the regular season with records of 12–4, their best regular-season records. They were defeated in the NFC Championship Game in 1996 and 2005 and in the NFC division **playoffs** in 2008.

Panthers head **coaches** have included Dom Capers (1995–1998), George Seifert (1999–2001), John Fox (2002–2010), and Ron Rivera (2011–2012). Among their best players have been **quarterbacks** Kerry Collins and Jake Delhomme, **running backs** Michael Bates and DeAngelo Williams, **wide receivers** Muhsin Muhammad and Steve Smith, **tight end** Wesley Walls, defensive **end** Julius Peppers, **kicker** John Kasay, **linebackers** Jon Beason and Sam Mills, and defensive **tackle** Kris Jenkins. In 2011, they selected **Heisman Trophy** winner and **Auburn University** quarterback **Cam Newton** with the first overall selection in the NFL **Draft**.

CARR, JOSEPH FRANCIS "JOE." B. 22 October 1880, Columbus, Ohio. D. 20 May 1939, Columbus, Ohio. Joe Carr is one of the few members of the **Pro Football Hall of Fame** who did not attend high school. His formal education was limited to five years at St. Dominic's Elementary School in Columbus. At the age of 13, he left school to help his family by working at a machine shop. When he was 20 years old, he was employed by the Panhandle division of the Pennsylvania Railroad as a machinist, and it was there that his journey into the world of sports began. Carr also worked as assistant sports editor of the *Ohio State Journal*, a Columbus newspaper, in 1900. The following year, he formed a baseball team consisting primarily of railroad employees. He later formed a company football team known as the Columbus Panhandles. He was fortunate to have several husky members of the **Nesser family** on the team, and Carr's successful promotion of the Panhandles made them an extremely popular gate attraction.

In 1920, the Columbus Panhandles became members of the newly formed American Professional Football Association. The following year Carr replaced **Jim Thorpe** as league president. The league's name was changed to the **National Football League (NFL)** in 1922. During the next several years, Carr was primarily responsible for establishing order in the league by standardizing schedules and player contracts and taking a strong stand against gambling. He also worked on placing teams in major cities and minimizing franchise relocations. He was able to successfully counter the threat posed by other competitive leagues, including the **American Football League** in 1926 and another American Football League 10 years later. Carr remained NFL president until his death in 1939, by which time the NFL had established itself as a strong professional major league.

In 1925, Carr helped found the American Basketball League and became its first president. That league was the first professional basketball league to employ nearly all the game's top players and have franchises in most of the major cities east of the Mississippi River. He also was involved in baseball and, in 1927, became the owner of the Columbus minor league team. In 1933, he was named director of professional baseball's promotional department and was able to strengthen and organize its minor-league structure. Carr continued to run the NFL until his death from a heart attack in 1939.

The NFL's first annual Most Valuable Player Award was named the Joe F. Carr Trophy from 1938 to 1946. From 1955 to 1978, the Joe F. Carr Trophy was awarded to the NFL Player of the Year. Carr was inducted into the **Pro Football Hall of Fame** as a charter member in the category of contributor in 1963.

CENTER (CENTRE). The center (or centre in **Canadian football**) is an offensive **lineman** who snaps the ball between his legs back to a teammate (usually the **quarterback**) to begin each **down**. The center is then responsible for **blocking** players on the defensive team. On **punting** downs where the **punter** is 10 to 15 yards behind the line of scrimmage, a specialist at the center position, known as a long snapper, is often used instead of the team's regular center. Although it is an important position, there are few statistical measures of a center's ability, and consequently the center generally gets little publicity. Professional centers may play 10 or more years and still be virtually unknown to most **fans**. *See also* BEDNARIK, CHARLES PHILIP "CHUCK"; FORD, GERALD RUDOLPH, JR. "GERRY"; HEIN, MELVIN JACK "MEL"; OTTO, JAMES EDWIN "JIM."

CHALLENGE. Since the advent of instant **replay** on television, **football** rules have been modified so that a **coach** who feels that the **officials** erred in their call on a certain play may challenge that call and require the officials to examine the instant replay on a video screen to ensure that their original call was correct. The **National Football League** began this system in 1999. Coaches are allowed to challenge calls only twice in a game and must notify the officials by dropping a red handkerchief prior to the next play's inception. After review of the play, the official will announce either that the call is overturned and an adjustment is made, that the play is correct as called, or that the play stands as called since there is insufficient video evidence to overturn it. If the coach is incorrect with his challenge, his team is charged with a **timeout**. Calls made within the last two minutes of a half or in **overtime** cannot be challenged but are automatically reviewed by a replay official.

CHEERLEADER. Since the earliest days of **college football**, a small group of students has stood on the **sidelines** to encourage the **fans** in the stands to cheer on their team. Some of the original cheers used such nonsense words as the famed **Princeton University** "Locomotive cheer," which goes "Hip, hip! Rah, rah, rah! Tiger, tiger, tiger! Siss, siss, siss! Boom, boom, boom! Ah! Princeton! Princeton! Princeton!" As another example, **Virginia Tech's** nickname is the Hokies. It is a nonsense word that derives from a cheer written in 1896 that goes, "Hokie Hokie Hokie Hi; Tech Tech VPI; Solah-rex, Solah-rah; Poly Tech Vir-gin-ia; Ray Rah VPI; Team Team Team."

Cheerleading is predominantly done by female students, although a few males also participate, and it has evolved to include acrobatic stunts by cheerleaders. In recent years, **professional football** has also employed teams of scantily clad females to encourage their fans. They are primarily dance teams that perform set routines rather than lead the fans in cheers. In the early 1970s, the **Dallas Cowboys** were one of the first **National Football League** teams to have cheerleaders, and the Cowboy cheerleaders became nationally famous.

CHICAGO BEARS. The Chicago Bears are a **professional football** team in the National Football Conference (NFC) North Division of the **National Football League (NFL)**. They began playing as the Decatur Staleys and are the oldest team in the league, along with the Arizona (formerly Chicago) Cardinals. The Staleys originated in 1919, when a food starch manufacturer, the A. E. Staley Manufacturing Company of Decatur, Illinois, formed a company **football** team. Former **college football** player and Major League Baseball player **George Halas** was hired by Staley as a company representative and player-**coach** for the company's baseball and football teams. In 1920, the Staleys became one of the charter members of the American Professional Football Association, along with 13 other teams. After losing money in the 1920 season, owner Augustus E. Staley turned the team over to Halas in 1921. Halas moved the team to Chicago and played as the Chicago Staleys that year, winning the league championship. In 1922, the league was renamed the National Football League, and the Staleys were renamed the Chicago Bears.

In 1932, the Bears finished **tied** with the Portsmouth Spartans for the league championship and played a tiebreaker **playoff** game to determine the league champion. Due to extreme **weather** conditions, the game was played indoors at Chicago Stadium on a shortened field with other special rules and was won by the Bears. From 1933 to 1969, the Bears played in 10 NFL Championship Games and won in 1933, 1940 (by a record 73–0 score over the **Washington Redskins**), 1941, 1943, 1946, and 1963. Since 1970, when the **American Football League** and NFL merged and a postseason playoff system was established, the Bears have qualified for the playoffs 14 times and have a playoff record of 10–13. They won the **Super Bowl** in 1985 and lost it in 2006. They have also lost the NFC championship three times, the

1933 world champion Chicago Bears, coached by George Halas (#11) and featuring Bronko Nagurski (#3) and Red Grange (#77).
Mike Moran

divisional playoffs seven times, and the **wild-card playoff** twice. Their record for 93 seasons from 1920 to 2012 is 722–526–42 in the regular season and 17–18 in playoffs.

In Decatur, the team's home field was Staley Field. In Chicago, they played at the 40,000-seat Wrigley Field until 1970. From 1971 to 2001, they played at the 70,000-seat Soldier Field. While Soldier Field was being renovated in 2002, they played at the 69,000-seat Memorial Stadium in Champaign, Illinois. In 2003, they returned to the remodeled Soldier Field.

Owner George Halas was also their head coach for 40 seasons, longer than any other head coach in the NFL. He coached them from 1920 to 1929, 1933 to 1942, 1946 to 1955, and 1958 to 1967. During World War II, Luke Johnsos and Hartley "Hunk" Anderson simultaneously acted as head coaches from 1942 to 1945 while Halas served in the U.S. Navy. Other head coaches for the Bears have been Ralph Jones (1930–1932), John "Paddy" Driscoll (1956–1957), Jim Dooley (1968–1971), Abe Gibron (1972–1974), Jack Pardee (1975–1977), Neill Armstrong (1978–1981), **Mike Ditka** (1982–1992), Dave Wannstedt (1993–1998), Dick Jauron (1999–2003), and Lovie Smith (2004–2012). On 16 January 2013, Marc Trestman, a former **Canadian Football League** coach, was hired as head coach for the 2013 season.

The Bears have more individuals elected to the **Pro Football Hall of Fame** than any other team, with 30 through 2012. They include **backs George Blanda**, John "Paddy" Driscoll, **Harold "Red" Grange**, **Bobby Layne**, Sid

Luckman, George McAfee, **Bronko Nagurski**, **Gale Sayers**, and **Walter Payton**; **linemen** Doug Atkins, George Connor, Richard Dent, Mike Ditka, Dan Fortmann, Dan Hampton, Ed Healey, Bill Hewitt, Stan Jones, Walt Kiesling, William Lyman, George Musso, **Alan Page**, Joe Stydahar, George Trafton, and Clyde "Bulldog" Turner; **linebackers Dick Butkus**, Bill George, and Mike Singletary; coach and owner George Halas; and general manager Jim Finks. Layne, Kiesling, and Page were elected for their contributions with other teams, although they each played briefly in Chicago. Many of these players were from the single-platoon era and played both on **offense** and **defense**. Driscoll and Ditka also made major contributions as Bears' head coaches.

Other notable players for the Bears include **quarterbacks** Carl Brumbaugh, Rex Grossman, **Johnny Lujack**, Jim McMahon, and Billy Wade; **running backs** Neal Anderson, Rick Casares, Matt Forte, Willie Galimore, and **Brian Piccolo**; kick **returner/wide receiver Devin Hester**; wide receivers Willie Gault and Johnny Morris, **end** Harlon Hill, back Beattie Feathers, linebacker Brian Urlacher, defensive end Julius Peppers, and **kickers** Kevin Butler and Robbie Gould.

CHICAGO CARDINALS. *See* ARIZONA CARDINALS.

CHICAGO HORNETS. The Chicago Hornets were a **professional football** team in the **All-America Football Conference (AAFC)** from 1946 to 1949. They began in 1946, the first year of the league, as the Chicago Rockets and played three years under that name, until they were renamed for the 1949 season. Home games were played at the 100,000-seat Soldier Field in Chicago, Illinois. In 1950, the AAFC merged with the **National Football League (NFL)**, but the Hornets were not included in the merger and were disbanded. Their record for four years was 11–40–3. As the Rockets, they finished in fourth and last place in the Western Division each year, and, as the Hornets, they finished **tied** for fifth place in the seven-team divisionless league of 1949. Among their best players were **quarterback** Sammy Vacanti, all-purpose **backs** Bob Hoernschemeyer and Ray Ramsey, and **running back Elroy "Crazylegs" Hirsch**. Hirsch went on to a **Pro Football Hall of Fame** career with the Los Angeles Rams of the NFL.

CHICAGO ROCKETS. *See* CHICAGO HORNETS.

CHICAGO STALEYS. *See* CHICAGO BEARS.

CHUNG, JOHNNY "THE CELESTIAL COMET." Johnny Chung was a Hawaiian Chinese American sophomore **running back** at New Jersey's

Plainfield Teachers' College in 1941. The school's press secretary, Jerry Croyden, phoned the New York and Philadelphia newspapers weekly, and Chung's exploits on the **football** field appeared in several major newspapers, including the *New York Times*. The team was undefeated in part due to its "W" formation, in which the **ends** turned backward and faced the backfield. It was claimed that Chung owed much of his success to the wild rice he ate during the **halftime** intermission. Plainfield's team colors were puce and mauve, and their **coach** was "Hurry-Up Hoblitzel."

Chung was the product of the imagination of stockbroker Morris Newberger and radio announcer Alexander Dannenbaum. After six weeks of having Plainfield's results appear in the newspapers, reporter Walter "Red" Smith decided to visit Plainfield and interview Chung. After he discovered that the school and its star player were fictitious, the two hoaxers confessed. In their final press release, they wrote that Chung and several other players had become academically ineligible and, as a result, Plainfield terminated its schedule.

CINCINNATI BENGALS. The Cincinnati Bengals are a **professional football** team in the American Football Conference (AFC) North Division of the **National Football League (NFL)**. They began in 1968 as an expansion team in the **American Football League (AFL)**, and, in 1970, they became members of the NFL when the two leagues merged. From 1970 to 2001, they were placed in the AFC Central Division and, in 2002, moved to their present AFC North Division. While in the AFL, the Bengals played at the 35,000-seat Nippert Stadium. When they moved to the NFL, they played at the 59,000-seat Riverfront Stadium (renamed Cinergy Field in 1996) until 1999. They moved to the new 65,000-seat Paul Brown Stadium in 2000. All three venues are (or were) located in Cincinnati, Ohio.

Cincinnati's record for two seasons in the AFL was 7–20–1, where they finished in fifth and last place in the AFL's Western Division both years. For 43 seasons in the NFL, their regular-season record is 298–365–1, and their **playoff** record is 5–11. Their best seasons were in 1981 and 1988, when they had 12–4 records in the regular season and lost in the **Super Bowl** to the **San Francisco 49ers** each year. They lost the AFC division playoff four times (1970, 1973, 1975, 1990) and in the first round or **wild-card playoff** five times (1982, 2005, 2009, 2011, 2012).

The first head **coach** of the Bengals was the legendary **Paul Brown**. He coached them in the AFL and from 1970 to 1975 in the NFL. Other Bengals' head coaches have included Bill Johnson (1976–1978), Homer Rice (1978–1979), Forrest Gregg (1980–1983), Sam Wyche (1984–1991), David Shula (1992–1996), Bruce Coslet (1996–2000), Dick LeBeau (2000–2002), and Marvin Lewis (2003–2012).

Cincinnati's best players have included **quarterbacks** Ken Anderson, Norman "Boomer" Esiason, and Carson Palmer; **running backs** Cedric Benson, Corey Dillon, Pete Johnson, and Rudi Johnson; and **wide receivers Cris Collinsworth**, Isaac Curtis, Carl Pickens, and Chad Johnson (who since he wore number 85 had his name legally changed to **Chad Ochocinco**, which is Spanish for 85). Other top players are **Pro Football Hall of Fame** offensive **tackle** Anthony Muñoz, nose tackle Tim Krumrie, **cornerback** Ken Riley, **linebacker** Reggie Williams, **center** Bob Johnson, and **punter**/wide receiver Pat McInally.

CLEMONS, MICHAEL LUTRELL "MIKE," "PINBALL." B. 15 January 1965, Dunedin, Florida. Although Mike Clemons played in the **National Football League (NFL)**, he made his mark in **professional football** in the **Canadian Football League (CFL)**. He played **football** at Dunedin High School and the College of William and Mary, where he was used as a **running back** and return specialist. Although only five feet, five inches tall and 165 pounds, Clemons was selected by the **Kansas City Chiefs** of the NFL in the eighth round of the 1987 NFL **Draft** as the 218th overall selection. Surprisingly, he made the team and was used primarily as a **punt returner**. He appeared in eight games and returned 19 punts for an average of 8.5 yards per return. Clemons also carried the ball twice as a running back for a total of seven yards. The following year, he tried out for the **Tampa Bay Buccaneers** but was released from the team without appearing in a regular-season game.

Clemons's professional football fortunes improved in 1989, when he joined the **Toronto Argonauts** of the CFL. He acquired the nickname "Pinball" in Toronto due to his **running** style, since with his diminutive size and excellent balance he would bounce off of would-be **tacklers**. He played for the Argos from 1989 to 2000 and helped lead them to three **Grey Cup** Championships, in 1991, 1996, and 1997. In his 12-year CFL career, he played in 185 regular-season games, **rushed** 1,107 times for 5,341 yards and 31 **touchdowns**, caught 682 **passes** for 7,015 yards and 46 touchdowns, and completed five of nine passes for 85 yards and two touchdowns. He also returned 610 punts for 6,025 yards and eight touchdowns and 300 **kickoffs** for 6,349 yards. He holds the CFL records for most **all-purpose yards** in one season, with 3,840 in 1997, and career all-purpose yards, with 25,438.

Clemons retired from active play midway through the 2000 season and was named head coach of the Argonauts. In 2002, he was named president of the Argos and relinquished his head coaching duties. Midway through that season, he was named interim head coach and, at the end of the season, resigned the presidency to become the full-time head coach. In 2004, Clemons led the Argos to the Grey Cup, the first black CFL head coach to do so. He continued coaching through the 2007 season. He then resigned his coaching duties and was named the chief executive officer of the Argonauts. Clemons was inducted into the **Canadian Football Hall of Fame** in 2008.

CLEVELAND BROWNS (1946–1995). The Cleveland Browns began as a **professional football** team in the **All-America Football Conference (AAFC)** in 1946. Playing home games at the 80,000-seat Municipal Stadium in Cleveland, Ohio, they dominated the league, winning the league championship in each of the four years from 1946 to 1949 and compiling an overall record of 47–4–3, in addition to a record of 5–0 in **playoff** games. From 1947 to 1948, they won 18 consecutive games, including an undefeated season in 1948. From 19 October 1947 to 9 October 1949, the Browns were undefeated in 29 consecutive games, winning 27 and tying two. In 1950, they were one of the three teams that were added to the **National Football League (NFL)** with the merger of the two leagues.

The Browns continued their dominance of professional football as members of the NFL. From 1950 to 1969, they were NFL champions four times (1950, 1954, 1955, 1964). They also lost the NFL Championship Game seven times and the **conference** playoffs twice. Since 1970, they have not fared nearly as well. They and the **Detroit Lions** are the only two teams active that year that have not played in the **Super Bowl** (as of 2012). The original Browns reached the playoffs 10 times between 1970 and 1995, losing the conference championship three times, the divisional playoff four times, and the first round or **wild-card playoff** three times. From 1950 to 1995, the Browns' NFL record was 374–266–10 in regular-season play.

The Browns continued to play home games at Municipal Stadium until 1995. In 1996, Browns' owner Art Modell moved the team to Baltimore, Maryland, to play as the **Baltimore Ravens**. In a move to placate the loyal Browns **fans** who went berserk, removing seats, damaging restrooms, and setting fires following the Browns' final game in 1995, the NFL ruled that the Browns' franchise would be deactivated for three years, from 1996 to 1998. The league also stipulated that the Browns' name, colors, records, history, and archives would remain in Cleveland, and that the team formerly known as the Browns that moved to Baltimore would be considered a new franchise even though they were allowed to retain all player contracts of the former Browns.

Pro Football Hall of Famer Paul Brown was the Browns' head **coach** from 1946 to 1962, and it was after him that the "Browns" were named. He was replaced by Blanton Collier, who coached the team from 1963 to 1970. Other head coaches for the Browns included Nick Skorich (1971–1974), Forrest Gregg (1975–1977), Dick Modzelewski (interim 1977), Sam Rutigliano (1978–1984), Marty Schottenheimer (1984–1988), Leon "Bud" Carson (1989–1990), Jim Shofner (interim 1990), and **Bill Belichick** (1991–1995).

The Browns have had 21 former players honored by induction into the Pro Football Hall of Fame. They include **quarterback Otto Graham**; **fullbacks Jim Brown** and Marion Motley; **tackle/kicker Lou Groza**; **wide receivers** Dante Lavelli, Bobby Mitchell, and **Paul Warfield**; defensive **ends** Willie Davis and Len Ford; **guard** Bill Willis; offensive **linemen** Joe DeLamielleure, Frank Gatski, Gene Hickerson, and Mike McCormack; **running back Leroy Kelly**; and **tight end** Ozzie Newsome. In addition, Hall of Famers Doug Atkins, Willie Davis, **Len Dawson**, Henry Jordan, and Tommy McDonald all spent some time with the Browns, although their primary careers were with other NFL teams. Other notable Browns' players include quarterbacks Bernie Kosar, Frank Ryan, and Brian Sipe; wide receivers Ray Renfro and Mac Speedie; running backs Greg Pruitt and Mike Pruitt (no relation); and **linebacker** Walt Michaels. *See also* CLEVELAND BROWNS (1999–PRESENT).

CLEVELAND BROWNS (1999–PRESENT). The Cleveland Browns are a **professional football** team in the **National Football League (NFL)**. They were an expansion team in 1999 and are unrelated to a previous NFL franchise known as the Cleveland Browns that relocated to Baltimore in 1996 as the Ravens. From 1999 to 2001, the Browns were members of the American Football Conference (AFC) Central Division, and, since 2002, they have been in the AFC North Division. Since 1999, Browns' home games have been played at Cleveland Browns Stadium, a newly constructed facility on the former site of Municipal Stadium in Cleveland. In the 14 years that this new Browns' organization has existed, the team has only had two winning seasons, in 2002, when they had a record of 9–7, and 2007, when they were 10–6. They lost a **wild-card playoff** game in 2002, their only postseason **playoff** appearance. Their regular-season record for 14 years is 73–151.

Browns' head **coaches** have included Chris Palmer (1999–2000), Paul "Butch" Davis (2001–2004), Terry Robiskie (interim 2004), Romeo Crennel (2005–2008), Eric Mangini (2009–2010), and Pat Shurmur (2011–2012). On 10 January 2013, Robert Chudzinski was hired as head coach of the Browns for the upcoming season. Their best players have included **quarterbacks** Derek Anderson and Tim Couch; **running backs** Reuben Droughns, Peyton Hillis, and Jamal Lewis; **wide receivers** Braylon Edwards, Kevin Johnson, and Dennis Northcutt; **tackle** Joe Thomas; and defensive **lineman** Kenard Lang.

In a move to placate the loyal Browns **fans** who went berserk, removing seats, damaging restrooms, and setting fires following the former Browns' franchise final game in 1995, the NFL ruled that the Browns' franchise would be deactivated for three years, from 1996 to 1998. The league also stipulated that the Browns' name, colors, records, history, and archives would remain in Cleveland, and that the team formerly known as the Browns that moved to Baltimore as the Ravens would be considered a new franchise even though they were allowed to retain all player contracts of the former Browns. *See also* CLEVELAND BROWNS (1946–1995).

CLEVELAND RAMS. *See* ST. LOUIS RAMS.

COACH. The job of a **football** coach is a complex one. In addition to being the motivator of a large (40 to 100-plus players) group of individuals, he is responsible for knowing his opponents' strengths and weaknesses so that he can design a game plan for both the **offense** and **defense**, making the necessary changes to those plans during a game as conditions change, making the necessary personnel changes during the game to ensure that the best combination of players is on the field at all times, and meeting with the media before and/or after a game. On the high school level, a coach is also responsible for instructing his players in the rules and techniques required to play the game. In addition, he is held accountable for the success of the team, and if the team fails he is usually the first one to lose his job. As a result, the coach (usually termed the "head coach") will generally employ as many as a dozen **assistant coaches** to help carry out all these duties. *See also* ALLEN, GEORGE HERBERT; BROWN, PAUL EUGENE; BRYANT, PAUL WILLIAM "BEAR"; DOBIE, ROBERT GILMOUR "GLOOMY GIL"; GIBBS, JOE JACKSON; GRANT, HARRY PETER, JR. "BUD"; HALAS, GEORGE STANLEY, SR. "PAPA BEAR"; HAYES, WAYNE WOODROW "WOODY"; LAMBEAU, EARL LOUIS "CURLY"; LANDRY, THOMAS WADE "TOM"; LEAHY, FRANCIS WILLIAM "FRANK"; LOMBARDI, VINCENT THOMAS "VINCE"; MADDEN, JOHN EARL; NEALE, ALFRED EARLE "EARLE," "GREASY"; PARCELLS, DUANE CHARLES "BILL"; PATERNO, JOSEPH VINCENT "JOE," "JOEPA"; ROBINSON, EDWARD GAY "EDDIE"; ROCKNE, KNUTE KENNETH; SHULA, DONALD FRANCIS "DON"; STAGG, AMOS ALONZO; STRAM, HENRY LOUIS "HANK"; WARNER, GLENN SCOBEY "POP"; ZUPPKE, ROBERT CARL "BOB."

COFFIN CORNER. A **punter** often aims his kick so that the ball goes **out of bounds** between the **goal line** and the five-**yard line** to prevent a **punt** return. This area is known as the coffin corner. The *Coffin Corner* is also the title of the journal produced by the **Professional Football Researchers Association**.

COIN TOSS. A **football** game begins with the referee and representatives from each of the two teams meeting at midfield. The referee flips a coin, a visiting team player calls heads or tails, and the winner of the coin toss may elect to receive or **kick off** or select which goal to defend to begin the game. The opponent then has these choices to begin the second half. In recent years, an additional option has been added, which is that the winning team may defer the choice until the second half. A coin toss is also used at the start of **overtime**.

COLLEGE ALL-STAR GAME. The Chicago Charities College All-Star Game began in 1934 as a promotion by the *Chicago Tribune*. Arch Ward, sportswriter for the newspaper who was also responsible for the Golden Gloves amateur boxing tournament and who helped create Major League Baseball's All-Star Game, was the man who created this game as well. It was held during the summer at Chicago's Soldier Field and matched the previous season's **National Football League (NFL)** champions against a team of college senior players from the previous season. Proceeds from the game were donated to various Chicago-area charities. Of the first five games in the series, the All-Stars won two and **tied** two, but afterward, the pros dominated, winning most of the other games. A Most Valuable Player Award was given annually to a college player for his performance in the game.

As the season's first professional exhibition game, it drew well, and attendance exceeded 100,000 on several occasions. During the 1970s, however, as **professional football** became a big-money sport, **coaches** became reluctant to allow their top rookies to participate for fear of injury. and the game lost some of its luster. In 1974, the NFL players were on strike, and the game was cancelled.

The 1976 game proved to be the death knell. A heavy rain, accompanied by lightning, caused the game to be temporarily halted with 1:22 remaining in the third quarter. The **fans** became unruly and tore down the **goalposts**, and NFL commissioner **Alvin "Pete" Rozelle** decided not to resume the game. The following year, Chicago Tribune Charities, Inc. discontinued the event. Of the 42 games played from 1934 to 1976, the pros won 31, tied two, and lost nine.

COLLEGE FIGHT SONGS. Much of the spectacle of **college football** revolves around the student body. Many colleges have marching bands that play during the game and perform intricate march maneuvers at **halftime**. Quite a few also have their own fight songs, some nearly a century old, that have become recognizable even by nonfootball **fans**. Possibly the most famous is the **University of Notre Dame's** *Notre Dame Victory March*. Other well-known college fight songs include the **University of Michigan's** *The Victors* (praised by the famous bandleader and march composer John Philip Sousa as the greatest college fight song ever written) and the **University**

of Southern California's *Fight On*. **Georgia Tech's** fight song *Ramblin' Wreck from Georgia Tech* was even sung by U.S. vice president Richard Nixon and Soviet premier Nikita Khrushchev during a meeting in Moscow in 1959. Nixon did not know any Russian songs, but Khrushchev was familiar with the Georgia Tech song, as he had heard it sung on television on *The Ed Sullivan Show* by Georgia Tech's glee club.

COLLEGE FOOTBALL. The sport of American **football** has its origins in colleges in the United States during the latter half of the 19th century. As the sport became popular, professional teams and leagues developed in the early 20th century. More and more colleges began playing the sport, and its popularity far exceeded the professional game in the first half of the 20th century. It was not until the television age that **professional football** became more popular than college football. College football in the United States is administered by the **National Collegiate Athletic Association**, an organization that oversees all collegiate sports. Most colleges compete in leagues, called **conferences**, that contain between eight and 16 schools of roughly the same size and dedication to sports. Participants in college football are considered to be amateur athletes and are not permitted to be paid, although many receive full athletic scholarships for playing, valued at tens of thousands of dollars in the 21st century. The rules for college football in the 21st century differ slightly from those of professional football, but not in any significant manner except for **overtimes**. *See also* COLLEGE FOOTBALL HALL OF FAME; APPENDIX K (for Bowl Championship Series champions); APPENDIX L (for college champions); APPENDIX M (for Rose Bowl champions); APPENDIX N (for Heisman Trophy winners); APPENDIX O (for a list of Football Bowl Subdivision schools).

COLLEGE FOOTBALL HALL OF FAME. The College Football Hall of Fame is a museum devoted to **college football**. The Hall is administered by the National Football Foundation, which was founded in 1947 by General Douglas MacArthur, **Coach** Earl "Red" Blaik, and sportswriter **Grantland Rice**. Players and coaches were first inducted into the Hall in 1951, but it was not until 1978 that a permanent home was established with the memorabilia collection open to the public. The museum opened in Kings Mills, Ohio, adjacent to the Kings Island amusement park. In 1995, it was relocated to South Bend, Indiana, about two miles from the campus of the **University of Notre Dame**. Plans are to move the collection to Atlanta, Georgia, in 2013. As of 2012, there are 914 former college players inducted in the Hall out of the more than 4.7 million collegiate players of the sport since 1869. There also have been 197 coaches inducted.

COLLINSWORTH, ANTHONY CRIS "CRIS." B. 27 January 1959, Dayton, Ohio. Although born in Dayton, Ohio, Cris Collinsworth was raised in Florida. He attended Astronaut High School in Titusville, Florida, where he played **football** and ran track, excelling in both sports. The six-foot, five-inch, 190-pound Collinsworth played **quarterback** and **wide receiver** for the **University of Florida** from 1977 to 1980, and he graduated with a degree in accounting. He was chosen in the second round of the 1981 **National Football League (NFL) Draft** by the **Cincinnati Bengals** as the 37th overall selection. Collinsworth remained with the Bengals for eight seasons and was named to the **Pro Bowl** three times. In 1982, he played on the losing Bengals team in the **Super Bowl**.

From 1981 to 1988, Collinsworth played in 107 regular-season games and caught 417 **passes** for 6,698 yards and 36 **touchdowns**. In seven **playoff** games, he caught 21 passes for 354 yards and one touchdown. In 1985, he signed with Tampa of the **United States Football League** but failed their physical and returned to the Bengals.

Since retiring from active play, Collinsworth has received a law degree from the University of Cincinnati in 1991 and worked in television. He was a broadcaster for the 2005 Super Bowl and has covered the 2008 and 2010 **Olympic Games**, as well as football. In 2009, he was selected by NBC to replace **John Madden** for *Sunday Night Football*. Collinsworth's easygoing, knowledgeable style has earned him several Emmy Awards for his television work.

COLORADO, UNIVERSITY OF. The University of Colorado is located in Boulder, Colorado. Their **football** program began in 1890, and, since then, through 2012, Buffaloes' teams have compiled a record of 665–447–36. In addition, they have competed in 28 postseason **bowl games** with a record of 12–16. They were named national collegiate champions in 1990. Home games since 1924 have been played at Folsom Field, which, through a series of expansions, has been enlarged to seat 53,613 since 2010.

Colorado football teams have competed in several different **conferences** throughout the school's history. From 1948 to 1996, they were a member of the **Big Eight Conference**. When that conference was dissolved in 1996, the Buffaloes joined the newly formed **Big 12 Conference**. Their main rival is Colorado State University. The two teams played each other most years from 1893 to 1958. After a 24-year hiatus, the series was resumed in 1983. It is billed as the "Rocky Mountain Showdown," and the winner receives the Centennial Cup. Colorado leads the series 62–22–2.

Bill McCartney has **coached** the longest for Colorado. He coached from 1982 to 1994, with a record of 93–55–5, and led the team to its only national championship. Other successful Colorado coaches include Fred Folsom (1895–1999, 1901–1902, 1908–1915; 77–23–2), Myron Witham (1920–1931; 63–26–7), Dallas Ward (1948–1958; 63–41–6), Eddie Crowder (1963–1973; 67–49–2), Bill Mallory (1974–1978; 35–21–1), and Rick Neuheisel (1995–1998; 33–14).

The six Colorado alumni in the **College Football Hall of Fame** are **quarterback/running back** Bobby Anderson, **safety** Dick Anderson, **guards** Joe Romig and John Wooten, defensive **end** Alfred Williams, and **halfback** and future U.S. Supreme Court justice Byron "Whizzer" White. In 1994, running back Rashaan Salaam won the **Heisman Trophy**.

Through 2012, there have been 215 **professional football** players who have attended Colorado, 204 in the **National Football League**, eight in the **American Football League**, and three in the **All-America Football Conference**. They include Dick Anderson, Bill Bain, Mitch Berger, Greg Biekert, Cliff Branch, Pete Brock, Stan Brock, Tom Brookshier, Chad Brown, Frank Clarke, Boyd Dowler, Christian Fauria, Andre Gurode, Mark Haynes, Charlie Johnson, Matt Lepsis, Emery Moorehead, Chris Naeole, Whitney Paul, Tom Rouen, and Kordell Stewart.

CONERLY, CHARLES ALBERT, JR. "CHARLIE." B. 19 September 1921, Clarksdale, Mississippi. D. 13 February 1996, Memphis, Tennessee. No one in **New York Giants'** history played **quarterback** for more seasons than Charlie Conerly, yet his name is rarely mentioned today as one of the all-time great quarterbacks, and he has yet to be inducted into the **Pro Football Hall of Fame**, even though he played in four **National Football League (NFL)** Championship Games.

Conerly attended Clarksdale High School in Clarksdale, Mississippi, and the University of Mississippi, but his collegiate attendance was interrupted by a hitch in the U.S. Marine Corps during World War II. He began playing for the Mississippi **varsity** in 1942 and then returned to the team in 1946. In 1947, he helped lead the Rebels to a record of 9–2, the **conference** championship, and a postseason victory in the Delta Bowl. Conerly led all collegiate players with 133 completed **passes**, was named the collegiate player of the year by the Helms Foundation, and finished fourth in **Heisman Trophy** balloting.

Although he had played only one year of varsity **college football** and still had college eligibility remaining, the six-foot, one-inch, 185-pound Conerly was chosen by the **Washington Redskins** in the 1945 NFL **Draft** in the 13th round as the 127th overall selection. He returned to school though and did not sign a **professional football** contract until 1948. That same year, he signed with the New York Giants and played for them through the 1961 season.

In 1948, Conerly was the NFL's second leading passer, behind **Sammy Baugh**, completing 162 of 299 passes for 2,175 yards and 22 **touchdowns**. At the age of 27, he was named the 1948 NFL Rookie of the Year by the United Press football writers. In 1956, he led the Giants to the NFL championship and, in the next five years, helped lead the Giants to three more NFL Championship Games, although they came out on the short end of all three, including the memorable 1958 **overtime** loss to the **Baltimore Colts**. In 1959, Conerly was named the NFL Most Valuable Player by the Newspaper Enterprise Association. Following the 1961 season, Conerly, 40 years of age, retired.

In his 14-year NFL career, Conerly played in 161 regular-season games, all with the Giants, completed 1,418 passes in 2,833 attempts for 19,488 yards and 173 touchdowns, and carried the ball 270 times for 685 yards and 10 touchdowns. He was also used as the Giants' **punter** at the beginning and end of his career and punted 130 times for an average of 38.9 yards per punt. In six **playoff** games, he completed 48 passes in 92 attempts for 785 yards and four touchdowns, ran four times for 15 yards and one touchdown, and punted eight times for 342 yards. He played in the **Pro Bowl** in 1950 and 1956. In retirement, Conerly was the owner of several shoe stores in Mississippi. He was inducted into the **College Football Hall of Fame** in 1966.

Author's note: One of my prized possessions is a 1956 NFL Championship Game program autographed by Charlie Conerly to 13-year-old Johnny.

CONFERENCE. A conference is a collection of teams. It can be a subset of a league, as, for example, the **National Football League** is divided into the National Conference and American Conference, or it can be synonymous with league, as in the **Atlantic Coast Conference**, which is a group of colleges that compete against each other in sports. Most of the colleges in the United States compete athletically in leagues known as conferences. Conferences have traditionally been organized geographically, but in recent years this has not always been the case. The **Big Ten Conference** (originally known as the Intercollegiate Conference of Faculty Representatives) was organized in 1896 and is the oldest **major college** conference.

In 2012, there were 11 conferences among the **National Collegiate Athletic Association (NCAA)** Football Bowl Subdivision (FBS) schools and four schools that did not belong to any conference, known as independent teams. The FBS conferences include the Atlantic Coast Conference, **Big East Conference**, Big Ten Conference, **Big 12 Conference, Conference USA, Mid-American Conference, Mountain West Conference, Pacific-12 Conference, Southeastern Conference, Sun Belt Conference,** and **Western Athletic Conference**.

There were 13 conferences for the NCAA Football Championship Subdivision (FCS) schools, also with four unaligned independent teams. Those conferences are Big Sky Conference, Big South Conference, Colonial Athletic Association, **Ivy League**, Mid-Eastern Athletic Conference (MEAC), Missouri Valley Football Conference, Northeast Conference, Ohio Valley Conference, Patriot League, Pioneer Football League, Southern Conference, Southland Conference, and Southwestern Athletic Conference (SWAC). Both MEAC and SWAC are composed of historically black colleges and universities.

The NCAA has permitted conferences of 12 or more members to be split into divisions, with the division winners competing for the conference championship, thus most present-day conferences have at least 12 members, since this allows for an extra game and the extra television revenue derived from it.

CONFERENCE USA. Conference USA is an organization of **major colleges** and universities that compete athletically. It was established in 1995 and is based in Irving, Texas. Its 12 members in 2012 were the University of Alabama at Birmingham, the University of Central Florida, East Carolina University, the University of Houston, Marshall University, the University of Memphis, the University of Southern Mississippi, Rice University, Southern Methodist University, the University of Texas at El Paso, Tulane University, and the University of Tulsa.

Conference USA is one of the conferences that has experienced major changes in 2012. On 1 July 2013, it will lose Central Florida, Houston, and Southern Methodist to the **Big East Conference**. East Carolina and Tulane will move to the Big East Conference on 1 July 2014. Eight schools will move to Conference USA in 2013. They are the University of North Carolina at Charlotte, Florida Atlantic University, Florida International University, Louisiana Tech University, Middle Tennessee State University, the University of North Texas, Old Dominion University, and the University of Texas at San Antonio. *See also* CONFERENCE.

CONTINENTAL FOOTBALL LEAGUE (CFL). The Continental Football League (CFL) was a professional minor league that was in existence from 1965 to 1969. In those five seasons, the CFL grew from a 10-team league in 1965 primarily based in the eastern United States to a 22-team league with teams throughout the continental United States, from coast to coast and also in Hawaii, Canada, and Mexico. Among the teams in the league were the Hartford Charter Oaks, who were continually referred to by a Spooneresque public address announcer as the Hartford Artichokes. Some notable individuals associated with the league include A. B. "Happy" Chandler, former Major League Baseball commissioner who became the CFL's first commissioner; Jackie Robinson, Major League Baseball Hall of Famer who was the general manager of the CFL's Brooklyn Dodgers franchise; **Coach** Bill Walsh, who went on to become a three-time **Super Bowl**–winning coach in the **National**

Football League (NFL); and players Tom Kennedy, Otis Sistrunk, Ken Stabler, Sam Wyche, and **Garo Yepremian**, all of whom went on to substantial careers in the NFL. The league terminated operations in 1970 due to economic problems.

CONVERSION. After scoring a **touchdown**, a team is allowed to "convert" the score by playing an untimed **down** from scrimmage with the ball placed on the two- or three-**yard line** (high school, college, and professional rules differ, and **Canadian football** uses the five-yard line). They can kick the ball through the uprights for an additional point or **run** or **pass** the ball across the **goal line**. Since 1958, a run or pass has been worth two points in collegiate play. The **American Football League** adopted the two-point conversion rule in 1960, followed by the **National Football League** in 1994. The rule stems from **football's rugby** roots, in which scoring a touchdown was only important in that a **free kick** at the goal (or "try") was then awarded. In early football, the touchdown was only worth one point, while a successful try was worth four points.

CORNELL UNIVERSITY. Cornell University is located in Ithaca, New York. Their **football** program began in 1887, and, since then, through 2012, Big Red teams have compiled a record of 629–484–34. As a member of the **Ivy League** since 1955, they do not participate in postseason **bowl games**. As with many of the Ivy League schools, they have no one main rival, and all Ivy League games attract interest. Their series with neighboring Colgate (a non–Ivy League school) began in 1896. The schools have played most years since then, with Cornell leading the series 48–43–3.

Among Cornell's most successful **coaches** are the legendary **Glenn "Pop" Warner** (1897–1898, 1904–1906; 36–13–3), **Robert "Gloomy Gil" Dobie** (1920–1935; 82–36–7), Carl Snavely (1936–1944; 46–26–3), and George "Lefty" James (1947–60; 66–58–2). Cornell alumni in the **College Football Hall of Fame** include **quarterbacks** Chuck Barrett, George Pfann, and Clint Wyckoff; **halfbacks** Eddie Kaw, Ed Marinaro, and Win Osgood; **ends** Jerome "Brud" Holland, Jack O'Hearn, and Murray Shelton; and **linemen** Nick Drahos, Fred Sundstrom, and Bill Warner. Former Cornell coaches in the Hall are Bob Blackman, Robert "Gloomy Gil" Dobie, Percy Haughton, Carl Snavely, and Pop Warner.

Through 2012, there have been 38 **professional football** players who have attended Cornell, 34 in the **National Football League** and two each in the **American Football League** and **All-America Football Conference**. They include Kevin Boothe, DeWitt "Tex" Coulter, Fred Gillies, **Pete Gogolak**, Ed Marinaro, Tom McHale, Bob Nash, Seth Payne, Irvin "Bo" Roberson, Gary Wood, and Frank Wydo.

CORNERBACK. Cornerback is a defensive position on a **football** team. He is one of the players whose primary function is to prevent **pass** completions, and he is usually positioned behind the **linebackers** several yards behind the **line of scrimmage**. The name for the position is relatively new, beginning in the mid-1950s. Prior to that time, the position was simply referred to as a defensive **back**. *See also* SAFETY (POSITION).

COSELL, HOWARD WILLIAM, NÉE HOWARD WILLIAM COHEN. B. 25 March 1918, Winston-Salem, North Carolina. D. 23 April 1995, New York, New York. Howard Cosell "never played the game," as one of his books was entitled, yet he was one of the major factors in the rise of interest in **professional football** during the 1970s. Although born in North Carolina, Cosell was raised in Brooklyn, New York, and graduated from Alexander Hamilton High School in Brooklyn. He continued his education at New York University (NYU), earning a bachelor's degree in English, and followed that with a law degree, also from NYU.

Cosell served in the U.S. Army Transportation Corps during World War II and had achieved the rank of major when he was discharged. He began practicing law, specializing in union law. In 1953, he was offered a nonpaying job by ABC as a host of a radio show about Little League Baseball. After three years, Cosell decided he enjoyed radio more than law and convinced the head of ABC to give him a full-time radio position. Later, he was able to parlay his radio broadcasting into television work for ABC and was a sports anchorman from 1961 to 1974.

During that time, boxer Cassius Clay came into prominence, and Cosell befriended him. When Clay converted to Islam and changed his name to Muhammad Ali, Cosell was one of the few sportscasters to use the name Ali. Cosell also took a strong stand in favor of Ali when Ali was stripped of his heavyweight championship for his stand on the Vietnam War and refusal to serve in the military. After Ali won his Supreme Court battle and returned to boxing, Cosell was the primary announcer for many of Ali's fights.

In 1970, when ABC began an experiment televising **football** in prime time, Cosell was chosen, along with Keith Jackson and **Don Meredith**, to host *Monday Night Football*. The thrust of the show was to be entertaining, and Cosell was selected for his opinionated persona. The show turned out to be successful far beyond the expectations of ABC producer Roone Arledge and NFL commissioner **Alvin "Pete" Rozelle**. The chemistry between Cosell and the laid-back Meredith provided many memorable moments, and *Monday Night Football* became mandatory watching for much of America's male population. Although Cosell came across as pompous and arrogant at times and was voted as the favorite sports broadcaster by some and the least favorite by others, he definitely had people watching. During the height of his career in 1975, he hosted the entertainment television show *Saturday Night Live with Howard Cosell*. He also worked other sports, including baseball, and was one of the commentators during the massacre at the 1972 **Olympic Games** in Munich.

During the 1980s, Cosell became disenchanted with much of professional sports and withdrew from announcing boxing. He continued to do *Monday Night Football*, but, after criticizing ABC in one of his books, *I Never Played the Game*, he was dropped by the network. Cosell is best remembered for his voice; for his distinctive, deliberate delivery; and for "telling it like it is."

COTTON BOWL. The Cotton Bowl is both a venue and an event. The event, formally entitled the "Cotton Bowl Classic," is a postseason **college football bowl game** that has been played annually since 1 January 1937. The 92,000-seat venue where the game was played is called the Cotton Bowl, and it is located in Dallas, Texas. The game was traditionally played on **New Year's Day** and, for much of the series, featured a **Southwest Conference** team. With the increased impact of television on sports, traditions have changed, and, in 2010, the game was moved to the new **Cowboys Stadium** in Arlington, Texas, a Dallas suburb. In 2013, it was played on 4 January.

COWBOYS STADIUM. Cowboys Stadium is located in Arlington, Texas, a city midway between Dallas and Fort Worth. A domed **stadium** with a retractable roof, it seats 80,000 and can accommodate 110,000 **fans** using standing room. It features one of the world's largest high-definition television screens, which extends 180 feet in width and is situated above the **football field**. The facility opened in 2009 and is the home field of the **Dallas Cowboys** of the **National Football League (NFL)**. On 20 September 2009, for its regular-season opening game, an NFL record attendance of 105,121 saw the Dallas Cowboys lose to the **New York Giants**, 33–31. Cowboys Stadium was also the site of **Super Bowl** XLV on 6 February 2011.

COX, FREDERICK WILLIAM "FRED." B. 11 December 1938, Monongahela, Pennsylvania. Fred Cox attended Monongahela High School and the **University of Pittsburgh**. He was a **running back** and defensive **back**, as well as a **punter** and placekicker. Cox was not one of the top **draft** choices and was only chosen in the eighth round of the 1961 **National Football League (NFL)** Draft as the 110th overall selection by the **Cleveland Browns**. He was also drafted by the Titans of New York in the **American Football League** Draft in the 28th round as the 221st overall selection.

Cox signed with the Cleveland Browns of the NFL but was injured during his first **training camp** with them. **Coach Paul Brown** encouraged Cox to specialize in kicking, but as the Browns had future **Pro Football Hall of Famer Lou Groza** as their placekicker, Cox was cut. He was traded by the Browns to the **Minnesota Vikings** near the end of that preseason but, after playing just one exhibition game for the Vikings, was cut by them. He made the Vikings team in 1963 and remained with them for 15 seasons, playing in every one of their 210 regular-season games. In 1969, he set an NFL record for **kickers** by scoring 121 points and raised the record to 125 points in 1970. Cox also helped lead the Vikings to four **Super Bowls**, in 1970, 1974, 1975, and 1977.

In his NFL career, Cox kicked 282 of 455 **field goals** and 519 of 539 extra points in regular-season play. In his first 11 years in the league, he missed only three extra points (making 384 of 387), but, in his last four seasons, he missed 17 (making only 135 of 152). He also doubled as a punter in his first NFL season, averaging 38.7 yards per punt in 70 punts. In 18 postseason games, Cox kicked 38 of 40 extra points and 11 of 18 field goals. In 1970, he was named to the **Pro Bowl** after leading the league in field goals and field goal attempts.

Cox was a licensed chiropractor even while playing in the NFL. In 1972, while still an active player, he worked with another inventor and developed the Nerf football. His residuals from that invention enabled him to retire at the age of 50. In retirement, Cox is still active and is a licensed pilot who rebuilds airplanes.

CROSSBAR. *See* GOALPOSTS.

CROWLEY, "SLEEPY" JIM. *See* FOUR HORSEMEN OF NOTRE DAME.

CSONKA, LARRY RICHARD. B. 25 December 1946, Stow, Ohio. Larry Csonka attended Stow High School in Stow, Ohio, where he played defensive **end** and **running back**. He then went to **Syracuse University** and played **fullback** there from 1965 to 1967. He was selected by the **Miami Dolphins** in the first round as the eighth overall selection in the common **draft** held by both the **National Football League (NFL)** and **American Football League** in 1968. The six- foot, three-inch, 230-pound Csonka played for the Dolphins from 1968 to 1974 and helped to lead them to the **Super Bowl** in 1972, 1973, and 1974, winning it in 1973 and 1974.

In 1975, Csonka, along with Miami teammates Jim Kiick and **Paul Warfield**, signed with Memphis of the new **World Football League**. The league folded midway through the season, and the three players returned to the NFL in 1976. Csonka signed with the **New York Giants** and played for them from

1976 to 1978, before returning to Miami for his final **professional football** season.

In 146 regular-season NFL games, Csonka **rushed** 1,891 times for 8,081 yards and 64 **touchdowns**. He also caught 106 **passes** for 820 yards and four touchdowns. In 12 postseason games, he rushed 225 times for 891 yards and nine touchdowns and caught four passes for 26 yards and one touchdown. He was named Most Valuable Player in the 1973 Super Bowl, chosen as NFL Comeback Player of the Year in 1979, and selected for the **Pro Bowl** each year from 1970 to 1974.

After retiring from active play, Csonka has done television work, been a motivational speaker, and was a general manager of the Jacksonville team in the **United States Football League** during its brief existence in the mid-1980s. An outdoorsman, he has established a residence in Alaska and hosted several hunting and fishing television shows. He has also done some acting in feature films and a few episodes of various television series. Csonka was inducted into the **Pro Football Hall of Fame** in 1987 and the **College Football Hall of Fame** in 1989. In 2002, his uniform number 39 was retired by the Miami Dolphins, one of only three uniforms that they have retired.

DALLAS COWBOYS. The Dallas Cowboys are a team in the National Football Conference East Division of the **National Football League (NFL)**. They began in the NFL in 1960 as an expansion team and played home games at the 75,000-seat **Cotton Bowl** in Dallas, Texas, until 1970. In 1971, they moved to the 65,675-seat Texas Stadium in Irving, Texas, a suburb of Dallas. They played there through the 2008 season. In 2009, they moved to the 80,000-seat **Cowboys Stadium** in Arlington, Texas, located midway between Dallas and Fort Worth.

As an expansion team, the Cowboys began slowly, going winless in their inaugural season. After four more losing seasons, they won half their games in 1965 and, in 1966, reached the NFL Championship Game but lost to the **Green Bay Packers**. Since then, they have become the most successful NFL team. Their overall regular-season record from 1960 to 2012 is 456–340–6, but, from 1966 to 2012, it is 431–287–2. They have qualified for postseason play in 30 seasons, and their **playoff** record is 33–25. In their 52 years in the league, the Cowboys have won the **Super Bowl** five times (1971, 1977, 1992, 1993, 1995). They have also lost in the Super Bowl in 1970, 1975, and 1978. They lost in the conference championship six times, the division playoffs seven times, and the **wild-card playoff** five times. Prior to 1970, they also lost twice in the NFL Championship Game and twice in the conference playoffs. Their outstanding success has earned them the nickname "America's Team."

Tom Landry was the Dallas **coach** for 29 seasons, from their inception in 1960 through 1988. During his tenure, the Cowboys qualified for the playoffs in 17 of 18 years from 1966 through 1983 and reached the Super Bowl five times, winning twice. Other Dallas coaches have been Jimmy Johnson (1989–1993), Barry Switzer (1994–1997), Chan Gailey (1998–1999), Dave Campo (2000–2002), **Bill Parcells** (2003–2006), Wade Phillips (2007–2010), and Jason Garrett (2010–2012).

Notable players for the Cowboys include **Pro Football Hall of Fame quarterbacks Troy Aikman** and **Roger Staubach**; **wide receivers Bob Hayes** and **Michael Irvin**; **running backs Tony Dorsett** and **Emmitt**

Smith; offensive guard Larry Allen; offensive **tackle** Rayfield Wright; defensive tackles **Bob Lilly** and Randy White; and defensive **back** Mel Renfro. Other Cowboys' star players include quarterbacks **Don Meredith**, Craig Morton, Tony Romo, and Danny White; running backs Marion Barber, Don Perkins, and Duane Thomas; wide receivers Tony Hill, Drew Pearson, and Lance Rentzel; **linebacker** Chuck Howley; defensive back/wide receiver **Deion Sanders**; defensive **end** Harvey Martin; **cornerback** Larry Brown; linebacker/**center** Lee Roy Jordan; and **kicker** Rafael Septien.

DALLAS TEXANS (AFL). *See* KANSAS CITY CHIEFS.

DALLAS TEXANS (NFL). The Dallas Texans were a team in the **National Football League (NFL)** in the 1952 season. They replaced the defunct **New York Yanks** franchise and inherited many of the Yanks players. Texans' home games were initially played at the 75,000-seat **Cotton Bowl** in Dallas, Texas. Unable to meet the team's payroll after the team's seventh consecutive loss, team owner Giles Miller forfeited his ownership and returned the team to the league for the remainder of the season. The team's headquarters were moved to Hershey, Pennsylvania, and their two remaining home games were moved to other sites. After losing their first nine games, they defeated the **Chicago Bears**, 27–23, at Akron, Ohio, on **Thanksgiving Day**, 27 November 1952. Under head **coach** Jimmy Phelan, the Texans finished the season with a record of 1–11. They had several good players, including future **Pro Football Hall of Fame** defensive **end** Gino Marchetti and defensive **tackle** Art Donovan. Their **quarterback** was Frank Tripucka, and **halfbacks** were **Claude "Buddy" Young** and George Taliaferro. After the season, the franchise was awarded to a group headed by Carroll Rosenbloom, who established an NFL team in Baltimore, Maryland, named the **Baltimore Colts**.

DAVIS, ALLEN "AL." B. 4 July 1929, Brockton, Massachusetts. D. 8 October 2011, Oakland, California. Al Davis was best described as a renegade who was not afraid to oppose the cities of Los Angeles and Oakland or the **National Football League (NFL)** and its commissioner. Although born in Massachusetts, he was raised in Brooklyn, New York, and was a graduate of the famed Erasmus Hall High School in Brooklyn. He continued his education at Wittenberg University and graduated from **Syracuse University** with a degree in English.

In 1950, Davis was hired as an offensive line **coach** at Adelphi College and worked there for two years. He served in the U.S. Army in 1952 and 1953 and coached the **football** team at Fort Belvoir, Virginia, in those years. He was an **assistant coach** at the Citadel from 1953 to 1956, and the **University of Southern California** from 1957 to 1959.

Davis's big opportunity occurred in 1960, when he was hired as an assistant coach for the Los Angeles Chargers of the new **American Football League (AFL)**. He was their offensive ends coach through the 1962 season and was then signed by the **Oakland Raiders** as their head coach and general manager, although he was only 33 years of age. Under his helm, the Raiders, who had won just three games and lost 25 in the previous two seasons, won 10 of 14 games and finished in second place in their division. Davis was named AFL Coach of the Year for 1963.

In April 1966, Davis was named commissioner of the AFL. That position was short lived, however, as several of the league's owners wanted a merger with the NFL and Davis felt that it was not in the AFL's best interests. The merger agreement was signed anyway on 8 June 1966, and Davis resigned as AFL commissioner on 25 July 1966. Returning to the Raiders, he formed a partnership with two other men and became one of the team's owners, with a 10 percent share. He was no longer the team's coach but was the head of football operations and still controlled the decision making for the franchise. The Raiders won the AFL championship in 1967 and lost to the **Green Bay Packers** in the **Super Bowl**. They won the AFL Western Division championship the following two seasons but were defeated in the league's championship game and did not reach the Super Bowl.

In 1972, Davis became the new managing general partner despite objections from one of his partners and, after winning a subsequent suit, became the sole manager of the enterprise, retaining his general manager title even though he was not a majority owner. The team's fortunes continued to grow, and, from 1967 to 1985, the Raiders were one of the league's most successful teams, reaching the **playoffs** 15 times in 19 years and making it to the Super Bowl four times and winning three of the four. In 1980, Davis attempted to relocate the Raiders to Los Angeles, but a court injunction stopped him. Nonplussed, he sued the NFL in an antitrust action, was successful, and moved the Raiders to Los Angeles for the 1982 season, where they remained through 1994, when he returned them to Oakland.

In 1986, the competing **United States Football League (USFL)** also sued the NFL in an antitrust suit. Although he was an NFL owner, Davis sided with the USFL. While the USFL won that suit, they won only $3 in monetary damages, which effectively caused the league to fold. Davis again sued the league in 1995, claiming that they did not allow him to have a new **stadium** built in the Los Angeles area, and he moved his team back to Oakland.

During his career, Davis was responsible for hiring the first black head coach in modern **professional football** history (Art Shell) and the first female chief executive. After his death in 2011 due to heart failure, he received much praise for his accomplishments; however, the arrogant, brash manner in which he operated was not forgotten by some of the figures in his life. Davis was inducted into the **Pro Football Hall of Fame** as a contributor in 1992.

DAVIS, GLENN WOODWARD, "MR. OUTSIDE." B. 26 December 1924, Burbank, California. D. 9 March 2005, La Quinta, California. Glenn Davis began playing **football** at Bonita High School in Laverne, California. After graduating in 1943, he entered the United States Military Academy (**Army**). There, he starred in baseball, basketball, and track, but it was his football prowess that made him famous. He played for Army for four seasons from 1943 to 1946 and won the **Maxwell Award** in 1944 and the **Heisman Trophy** in 1946. Davis was also named the Male Athlete of the Year by the Associated Press in 1946. In his four years at Army, he helped the team compile a record of 34–2–1 and win the national championship in 1944, 1945, and 1946. The five-foot, nine-inch, 170-pound **halfback** was known as "Mr. Outside" to his teammate **Felix "Doc" Blanchard's** "Mr. Inside."

Davis was **drafted** by the **Detroit Lions** as the second overall selection in the 1947 **National Football League (NFL)** Draft, but he had to fulfill his military obligation first. In 1947, he and Blanchard appeared in a Hollywood film entitled *The Spirit of West Point*. During the filming, Davis hurt his knee. It never healed properly and caused his premature retirement from football in 1952.

In 1950, Davis signed with the Los Angeles Rams of the NFL, but his abilities were limited due to his knee injury. He played only two years of **professional football** and appeared in 23 regular-season games, in which he carried the ball 152 times for 616 yards and four **touchdowns**, caught 50 **passes** for 682 yards and five touchdowns, completed four passes in seven attempts for 102 yards and two touchdowns, returned 18 **punts** for an average of 6.1 yards per punt return, and returned 17 **kickoffs** for a 20.4 yards average kickoff return. In three postseason games, Davis carried the ball 20 times but gained only 15 yards. He also caught eight passes for 104 yards, including an 82-yard touchdown pass, and returned two punts for 22 yards. After his football career ended, he was employed by the *Los Angeles Times* as their special events director. Davis was inducted into the **College Football Hall of Fame** in 1961.

DAWSON, LEONARD RAY "LEN." B. 20 June 1935, Alliance, Ohio. Len Dawson is a **football** player who would never have become famous were it not for the creation of the **American Football League (AFL)**. A graduate of Alliance High School in Alliance, Ohio, he was a **quarterback**

and placekicker at **Purdue University** from 1954 to 1956. He was chosen in the first round of the 1957 **National Football League (NFL) Draft** by the **Pittsburgh Steelers** as the fifth overall selection. In his first NFL season in 1958, he served as the third-string quarterback behind Earl Morrall and **Jack Kemp** and played in only three games. The next season, he again was third string, behind **Bobby Layne** and Earl Morrall. Dawson was Layne's backup in 1960 and, in 1961, was traded to the **Cleveland Browns**, where he again played little as a backup quarterback. After his first five professional seasons, he had started only two games and completed 21 of 45 **passes** for 204 yards and two **touchdowns**.

After being released by the Browns, Dawson signed with the **Dallas Texans** of the AFL in 1962, and his career completely turned around. The **coach** of the Texans, **Hank Stram**, had been an **assistant coach** at Purdue while Dawson was there, and he was familiar with Dawson's abilities. Dawson became the Texans' starting quarterback in 1962 and led them to the AFL championship that year. For the next 14 years, he was the team's regular quarterback. In 1963, the Texans moved to Kansas City and became known as the **Kansas City Chiefs**. Dawson led the Chiefs to the 1966 AFL championship and a berth in the first **Super Bowl** game on 15 January 1967 against the **Green Bay Packers**. In 1969, Dawson again led the Chiefs to the Super Bowl, and this time they defeated the **Minnesota Vikings** on 11 January 1970 and became Super Bowl champions. Following that game, Dawson was selected as the Super Bowl Most Valuable Player.

In his 19-year combined NFL/AFL career, Dawson played in 211 regular-season games, completed 2,136 **passes** in 3,741 attempts for 28,711 yards and 239 touchdowns, and ran 294 times for 1,293 yards and nine touchdowns. In eight postseason games, he completed 107 of 188 passes for 1,497 yards and seven touchdowns. He also **rushed** 21 times for 103 yards and no touchdowns. He was selected for the AFL All-Star Game or **Pro Bowl** seven times. Following his retirement from active play, Dawson has worked in television as a sports director for a Kansas City television station and an analyst and host of a weekly football series. He was inducted into the **Pro Football Hall of Fame** in 1987.

DECATUR STALEYS. *See* CHICAGO BEARS.

DEFENSE (DEFENCE). The team not in possession of the ball is deemed to be on defense. The word is pronounced with the emphasis on the first syllable. In recent years, it has become customary for one or more **fans** to hold a pair of signs, one with the letter "D" and the other showing a picket fence to encourage the crowd to yell "Deee-Fense." *See also* OFFENSE (OFFENCE).

DEFENSIVE BACK. *See* BACK.

DEFENSIVE END. *See* END.

DEFENSIVE TACKLE. *See* TACKLE (POSITION).

DEFUNCT NATIONAL FOOTBALL LEAGUE FRANCHISES. In the early years of the American Professional Football Association (APFA) (later renamed the **National Football League [NFL]**), there were many franchises. Some lasted only one season, while a few were in the league for five or more seasons. The Akron (Ohio) Pros were the APFA's first champions in 1920. They remained in the league through the 1926 season but were renamed the Indians for that year. Their overall record was 27–26–11 for seven seasons. The Canton (Ohio) Bulldogs were NFL champions in 1922 and 1923. They played in the league from 1920 to 1923 and 1925 to 1926. Their overall record for six seasons was 38–19–11. From 1921 to 1923, they were undefeated in 25 straight games. They moved to Cleveland for 1924 and played as the Cleveland Bulldogs and again won the NFL championship. The Frankford (a Philadelphia suburb) Yellow Jackets played from 1924 to 1931 and were 1926 NFL champions. Their overall record was 69–45–15 for their eight seasons in the league.

In 1928, the Providence (Rhode Island) Steam Roller won the NFL championship. They played in the NFL from 1925 to 1931 and had an overall record of 41–32–11. Their home field was a converted outdoor velodrome. In 1929, in a six-day stretch from 5 November to 10 November, they played six league games but lost three and **tied** one. (Note: The Providence **football** team nickname was singular, unusual for its era, but a subsequent Providence professional basketball team's nickname was plural, the Steamrollers.)

Buffalo (New York) had a league franchise from 1920 to 1927 and 1929. They were known as the All-Americans from 1920 to 1923; the Bisons in 1924, 1925, 1927, and 1929; and the Rangers in 1926. Their overall record for nine seasons was 40–37–12. The All-Americans finished the 1921 season on 27 November with a record of 8–0–2 and claimed the league title. For some unknown reason, they agreed to play two additional games as exhibitions. They defeated Akron in Buffalo on 3 December and then traveled overnight to play the Chicago Staleys the next day. They were defeated by the Staleys, who then claimed the league title. The league's executive committee voted for the Staleys, who were named league champions.

Other early franchises that played five or more years were the Dayton (Ohio) Triangles (1920–1929; 18–51–8), Columbus (Ohio) Panhandles/Tigers (1920–1926; 13–45–3), Duluth (Minnesota) Kelleys/Eskimos (1923–

1927; 16–20–3), Hammond (Indiana) Pros (1920–1926; 7–28–4), Milwaukee Badgers (1922–1926; 16–27–6), Minneapolis (Minnesota) Marines/Red Jackets (1921–1924, 1929–1930; 6–33–3), Rochester (New York) Jeffersons (1920–1925; 8–27–4 [they were 0–21–2 in their last four seasons]), Rock Island (Illinois) Independents (1920–1925; 26–14–12), and the Pottsville (Pennsylvania) Maroons (1925–1928; 27–20–2)/Boston (Massachusetts) Bulldogs (1929; 4–4).

Early franchises that lasted two to four years were Cincinnati Reds (1933–1934; 3–14–1), Cleveland Indians/Bulldogs (1923–1925, 1927; 23–14–6), Cleveland Tigers/Indians (1920–1921; 5–9–2), Detroit Panthers (1925–1926; 12–8–4), Evansville (Indiana) Crimson Giants (1921–1922; 3–5–0), Kansas City (Missouri) Blues/Cowboys (1924–1926; 12–15–1), Louisville (Kentucky) Brecks/Colonels (1921–1923, 1926; 1–12–0), Muncie (Indiana) Flyers (1920–1921; 0–3), New York Yankees (1927–1928; 11–16–2), Orange/Newark (New Jersey) Tornadoes (1928–1929; 4–14–5), Oorang (Marion, Ohio) Indians (1922–1923; 4–16–0), Racine (Wisconsin) Legion/Tornadoes (1922–1924, 1926; 15–15–6), Staten Island (New York) Stapletons (1929–1932; 14–22–9), and Toledo (Ohio) Maroons (1922–1923; 8–5–4).

Teams that lasted only one season were the 1920 Chicago Tigers (2–5–1) and Detroit Heralds (2–3–3); the 1921 Cincinnati Celts (1–3–0), Detroit Tigers (1–5–1), New York Brickley Giants (0–2–0), Tonawanda (New York) Kardex (0–1), and Washington Senators (1–2); the 1923 St. Louis All-Stars (1–4–2); the 1924 Kenosha (Wisconsin) Maroons (1–4–1); the 1926 Brooklyn Lions (3–8–0), Hartford Blues (3–7–0), and Los Angeles Buccaneers (who played only road games and had a record of 6–3–1); the 1928 Detroit Wolverines (7–2–1); the 1931 Cleveland Indians (2–8–0); and the 1934 St. Louis Gunners (1–2–0).

DELAY OF GAME. Delay of game can be assessed against either the **offense** or **defense**. The most common cause for the offense is failure to snap the ball before the **play clock** reaches zero. The defense can be accused of delay of game for failure to allow a **tackled** player to get up to start the next play. The **penalty** is five yards.

DEMPSEY, THOMAS JOHN "TOM." B. 12 January 1947, Milwaukee, Wisconsin. Tom Dempsey was born without toes on his right foot and fingers on his right hand but did not let these limitations prevent him from participating in sports. He attended San Dieguito High School in Encinitas, California, and Palomar Junior College, where he played as a placekicker on their **football** team, wearing a special shoe and kicking with his truncated right foot. He also wrestled and was a weight thrower on the track and field team. Dempsey was not **drafted** by the **National Football League (NFL)** but received a tryout with the **New Orleans Saints** in 1969. In his second year with the team, in a game on 3 November 1970, he kicked four **field goals** in a game against the **Detroit Lions**, including the longest one in NFL history, at 63 yards, to win the game in the last few seconds. In that same game, he also kicked the shortest field goal in NFL history, at eight yards. (The **goalposts** in that era were on the **goal line**.) Dempsey played with the **Philadelphia Eagles** from 1971 to 1974, the Los Angeles Rams in 1975 and 1976, and the Houston Oilers in 1977, and he concluded his NFL career with two years with the **Buffalo Bills**. He led the league in field goal accuracy in 1971 and was named to the **Pro Bowl** in 1969.

In his 11-year NFL career, Dempsey played in 127 regular-season games and kicked 159 field goals in 258 attempts and 252 extra points in 282 attempts. He also appeared in four postseason games and kicked nine of 10 extra points but missed all four of his field goal attempts.

DENVER BRONCOS. The Denver Broncos are a **professional football** team in the American Football Conference (AFC) West Division of the **National Football League (NFL)**. They joined the **American Football League (AFL)** as a charter member in 1960. In their 10 years in the AFL, they were one of the weakest teams, with a losing record in each of nine years and finishing at 7–7 in 1962, their best season in that league. Their overall AFL record was 39–97–4. They entered the NFL in 1970 as a result of the AFL–NFL merger. In the NFL, they have fared much better. Although they did not reach the postseason **playoffs** until 1977, in the 29 years from that year through 2005, they have qualified for the playoffs in 17 seasons. They have played in six **Super Bowls**, winning in 1998 and 1999 and losing in 1977, 1986, 1987, and 1989. Their overall record in the NFL is 381–280–6 in regular-season competition and 18–17 in the playoffs. They lost the AFC championship in 1991 and 2005; in the divisional playoffs in 1978, 1984, 1996, 2011 and 2012; and in the **wild-card playoff** in 1979, 1983, 1993, 2000, 2003, and 2004.

Home games from 1960 to 2001 were played at Mile High Stadium in Denver, Colorado. The stadium's seating capacity was 51,706 in 1960 and was expanded to 76,273 in 1986. In 2001, a new **stadium** was built in the same general vicinity and also seats 76,000. It was called Invesco Field at Mile High, but the naming rights expired in 2011 and its present name is Sports Authority Field at Mile High.

The two most successful of the Broncos' head **coaches** have been **Dan (Edward) Reeves** (1981–1992), who led them to three Super Bowls, and Mike Shanahan (1995–2008), who coached them to their two Super Bowl championships. Other Broncos' head coaches have been Frank Filchock (1960–1961), Jack Faulkner (1962–1964), Mac Speedie (1964–1966), Ray Malavasi (interim 1966), Lou Saban (1967–1971), Jerry Smith (interim 1971), John Ralston (1972–1976), Robert "Red" Miller (1977–1980), Wade Phillips (1993–1994), Josh McDaniels (2009–2010), Eric Studesville (interim 2010), and John Fox (2011–2012).

The Broncos' best players have included **Pro Football Hall of Fame quarterback John Elway, running back** Floyd Little, **tight end Shannon Sharpe, cornerback** Willie Brown, and offensive **lineman** Gary Zimmerman. Other noteworthy players include quarterbacks Brian Griese, **Peyton Manning**, Craig Morton, Jason "Jake" Plummer, **Tim Tebow**, and Frank Tripucka; **wide receivers** Haven Moses, Rod Smith, and Lionel Taylor; running backs Terrell Davis and Sammy Winder; tight end Riley Odoms; **kicker** Jim Turner; **safeties** Steve Atwater, Austin Gonsoulin, Dennis Smith, and Billy Thompson; defensive **ends** Barney Chavous, Rulon Jones, and Paul Smith; **linebackers** Randy Gradishar, Tom Jackson, and Karl Mecklenburg; cornerback Louis Wright; and defensive end/linebacker Rich Johnson.

DETROIT LIONS. The Detroit Lions are a member of the National Football Conference North Division of the **National Football League (NFL)**. They began in 1930 as the Portsmouth Spartans and relocated to Detroit as the Lions in 1934. In 1932, as the Spartans, they took part in the NFL's first postseason Championship Game but were defeated by the **Chicago Bears**, 9–0. Although the game was played after the conclusion of the regular season, it is included in the teams' regular-season record by the NFL and was a **playoff** between two teams **tied** for the championship. It was played indoors due to the inclement **weather**. The Lions defeated the **New York Giants** to win the league championship in 1935. Detroit's best years were during the 1950s, when they played in the NFL Championship Game four times (1952, 1953, 1954, 1957, all against the **Cleveland Browns**) and won three of them (1952, 1953, 1957). The Lions have had one of the league's worst records and, since the 1970 merger, have qualified for the playoffs only 10 times. They have never reached the **Super Bowl** and lost once in the conference championship (41–10 to Washington in 1991), twice in the divisional playoffs, and seven times in the first round or **wild-card playoff**. The Lions' overall NFL regular-season record from 1930 to 2012 is 510–611–32. Their playoff record is 7–11.

In Portsmouth, Ohio (a town with a population of about 20,000), the Spartans played at the 8,200-seat Universal Stadium. In Detroit, Michigan, they played at the 25,000-seat University of Detroit Stadium from 1934 to 1937, and again in 1940. They used the 52,000-seat Briggs Stadium (renamed Tiger

Stadium in 1961) from 1938 to 1939 and 1941 to 1974. In 1975, they moved to the 82,000-seat Pontiac Silverdome, located in Pontiac, Michigan, about 35 miles northwest of Detroit. In 2002, they moved to the 65,000-seat Ford Field in Detroit.

Their head **coaches** have been Hal Griffen (1930), George "Potsy" Clark, (1931–1936, 1940), Earl "Dutch" Clark (1937–1938), Gus Henderson (1939), Bill Edwards (1941–1942), John "Bull" Karcis (interim 1942), Gus Dorais (1943–1947), Alvin "Bo" McMillin (1948–1950), Raymond "Buddy" Parker (1951–1956), George Wilson (1957–1964), Harry Gilmer (1965–1966), **Joe Schmidt** (1967–1972), Don McCafferty (1973), Rick Forzano (1974–1976), Tommy Hudspeth (1976–1977), Monte Clark (1978–1984), Darryl Rogers (1985–1988), Wayne Fontes (1988–1996), Bobby Ross (1997–2000), Gary Moeller (interim 2000), Marty Mornhinweg (2001–2002), Steve Mariucci (2003–2005), Dick Jauron (interim 2005), Rod Marinelli (2006–2008), and Jim Schwartz (2009–2012).

Lions' players who have been inducted into the **Pro Football Hall of Fame** include **quarterbacks** Earl "Dutch" Clark and **Bobby Layne**; **fullback** John Henry Johnson; **halfbacks** Bill Dudley and **Doak Walker**; **running back Barry Sanders**; defensive **backs** Lem Barney, Jack Christiansen, **Dick "Night Train" Lane**, and Dick LeBeau; **punter**/defensive back Yale Lary; **center/linebacker** Alex Wojciechowicz; linebacker Joe Schmidt; defensive **tackle** Curley Culp; offensive **lineman** Lou Creekmur; and **tight end** Charlie Sanders. Other players of note include quarterbacks Greg Landry, Milt Plum, Tobin Rote, and Matthew Stafford; halfback Bob Hoernschemeyer; running back Billy Sims; fullback Nick Pietrosante; **wide receivers** Gail Cogdill, Calvin Johnson, and Herman Moore; **ends** Cloyce Box and Dorne Dibble; **guard** Grover "Ox" Emerson; defensive tackles **Alex Karras** and Ndamukong Suh; **kicker**/linebacker Wayne Walker; and defensive lineman Les Bingaman.

DICKERSON, ERIC DEMETRIC. B. 2 September 1960, Sealy, Texas. Eric Dickerson played **football** and ran track at Sealy High School. As a high school senior, he won the Texas state high school 100-yard dash and led his team to the state class AA **high school football** championships. He attended Southern Methodist University from 1979 to 1982, where he helped lead them to **Southwest Conference** championships in 1981 and 1982 and a 21–1–1 won-lost record in those two years.

Dickerson was selected by the Los Angeles Rams in the first round of the 1983 **National Football League (NFL) Draft** as the second overall selection. He played with the Rams from 1983 to 1987. In 1984, he **rushed** for an NFL record 2,105 yards for the season. He was traded to the **Indianapolis**

Colts after three games with the Rams in 1987, played with the Colts through 1991, and played his last two NFL seasons with the Los Angeles Raiders in 1992 and **Atlanta Falcons** in 1993. Dickerson retired after being traded to the **Green Bay Packers** in 1993 and failing a physical examination before playing for them.

In his 11-year NFL career, Dickerson played in 146 regular-season games, ran 2,996 times for 13,259 yards and 90 **touchdowns**, and caught 281 **passes** for 2,137 yards and six touchdowns. He attempted two passes on **option plays**, was **intercepted** once, and completed the other pass for a 15-yard touchdown. In seven postseason games, he ran 148 times for 724 yards and three touchdowns and caught 19 passes for 91 yards and one touchdown. He played in six **Pro Bowls**.

After retiring from active play, Dickerson has done work on television and was the **sideline** reporter for *Monday Night Football* in 2000 and 2001. He also owns a sports memorabilia company. He was inducted into the **Pro Football Hall of Fame** in 1999.

DIERDORF, DANIEL LEE "DAN." B. 29 June 1949, Canton, Ohio. Dan Dierdorf attended Glenwood High School in Canton, Ohio, where he played **football**. He went to the **University of Michigan** and played offensive **tackle** on their **varsity** football team from 1968 to 1970. In those three years, Michigan had won-lost records of 8–2, 8–3, and 9–1, and the team played in the **Rose Bowl** following the 1969 season.

The six-foot, four-inch, 250-pound **lineman** was chosen by the St. Louis Cardinals in the 1971 **National Football League (NFL) Draft** in the second round as the 43rd overall selection. Dierdorf played his entire NFL career, from 1971 to 1983, with them. Although a versatile offensive lineman (he played **guard**, **tackle**, and **center**), there are no official statistical measures of his performance except that he played in 160 regular-season games and three **playoff** games and recovered seven **fumbles**. He played in six **Pro Bowl** games.

Following retirement from active play, Dierdorf became a television broadcaster. He was a member of the *Monday Night Football* broadcast team from 1987 to 1998, along with Al Michaels and **Frank Gifford**. The trio formed one of the most popular broadcast teams for that event. He also covered the 1988 **Olympic Games** and later, professional boxing. He continues to be one of the better football analysts and now covers the NFL on a weekly basis for CBS. He also is a coowner of a St. Louis steakhouse with former Cardinals **quarterback** Jim Hart and part owner of a St. Louis radio station. Dierdorf was inducted into the **Pro Football Hall of Fame** in 1996 and the **College Football Hall of Fame** in 2000.

DITKA, MICHAEL KELLER, JR. "MIKE," NÉE MICHAEL KELLER DYCZKO JR. B. 18 October 1939, Carnegie, Pennsylvania. Mike Ditka is one of the few people in **football** who had an outstanding professional playing career and also an outstanding **coaching** career. Born Michael Dyczko, the family name was changed to Ditka while Mike was still a youth. He attended Aliquippa High School in Aliquippa, Pennsylvania, a suburb of Pittsburgh. As was common during the 1950s, he played baseball, basketball, and football in high school, as each sport during that time had definite seasons. He continued his education at the **University of Pittsburgh**, where he played **tight end** on **offense**, defensive **end**, and was the **punter** on the football team. During his three years on Pitt's **varsity** team, 1958 to 1960, the team had a record of 15–11–4.

Ditka was selected by the **Chicago Bears** in the first round (fifth overall selection) of the 1961 **National Football League (NFL) Draft**, and by the Houston Oilers in the first round (eighth overall) of the **American Football League** Draft. A six-foot, three-inch, 230-pound tight end, he signed with the Bears and played for them for the next six years. In 1967, he was traded to the **Philadelphia Eagles**, played two years for them, and finished his NFL career with four years with the **Dallas Cowboys**. In 1963, with the Bears, he was a member of the NFL champions. With the Cowboys, he was a member of the 1971 **Super Bowl** runners-up and 1972 Super Bowl champions.

In his 12-year NFL playing career, Ditka played in 158 regular-season games, caught 427 **passes** for 5,812 yards and 43 **touchdowns**, and also recovered two **fumbles** for touchdowns. In seven postseason games, he caught 11 passes for 107 yards and one touchdown. He played in five **Pro Bowl** games.

Ditka retired after the 1972 season and was hired by the Cowboys as an **assistant coach**. During that time, he coached in three more Super Bowl games. In 1982, the Chicago Bears offered him the head coaching job, which he accepted. He coached the Bears from 1982 to 1992 and led them to the Super Bowl championship in 1986. He had an outstanding record of 106–62 in regular-season games with the Bears and was 6–6 in **playoff** games. After a 5–11 record in 1992, he was let go by the Bears. In 1997, he was hired by the **New Orleans Saints** as their head coach but did not fare as well and only had a 15–33 record there.

Ditka has since spent his time working as a television analyst for NFL games. He is also the owner of three restaurants; a part owner of the **Arena Football League** team the Chicago Rush; and one of the investors in the new **Elite Football League of India**. He was inducted into the **College Football Hall of Fame** in 1986 and the **Pro Football Hall of Fame** in 1988.

DOBIE, ROBERT GILMOUR "GLOOMY GIL." B. 31 January 1878, Hastings, Minnesota. D. 23 December 1948, Hartford, Connecticut. Although he gained his nickname later in life as a pessimistic college **coach**, Robert "Gloomy Gil" Dobie had every right to be gloomy. He lost his mother at the age of four and his father at the age of eight and was raised at the Minnesota State Public School for Dependent and Neglected Children as a ward of the state. At various times in his childhood, he was a foster child and was raised by different families for short periods of time. At the age of 17, Dobie was released from the protection of the state and declared self-supporting. He enrolled at Hastings High School at the age of 17, at a time when many high school students were graduating, and was on their first **football** team in 1898, playing both **end** and **halfback** at 150 pounds. He graduated in 1899, at age 20, and enrolled at the **University of Minnesota**. He played end on the Minnesota **varsity** football team in 1899 and **quarterback** the following two years. In 1900 and 1901, Minnesota had a record of 19–1–3 and outscored their opponents, 482–41. In 1902, Dobie was unable to play football for financial reasons. He graduated in 1904 with a bachelor of laws degree.

From 1903 to 1905, Dobie was an **assistant coach** of the football team at the University of Minnesota and simultaneously the head coach of the Minneapolis South High School team. The 1903 South High team went undefeated and won the state championship after losing nine of their players to internal disputes.

In 1906, Dobie became head coach at the North Dakota Agricultural College (now known as North Dakota State University). He led them to eight consecutive victories in two years. He then went to the **University of Washington** in 1908 and began the most incredible nine years of **college football** coaching in history. From 1908 to 1916, Washington did not lose a single game and had a record of 58–0–3.

In 1917, Dobie was named head coach of the United States Naval Academy (**Navy**), and it was there that his remarkable victory string came to an end. After winning their first game of the season, Navy lost to West Virginia, 7–0, on 6 October 1917. Dobie's undefeated streak of 70 consecutive college football games may never be approached. That loss proved to be Navy's only one that season. Dobie coached Navy for two more seasons, losing only one game in each of those seasons. He then spent the next 16 years as the coach of the **Cornell University** football team, where he compiled a record of 82–36–7 from 1920 to 1935. In 1921, 1922 and 1923, Cornell was voted by some organizations as the best collegiate football team in the nation, after winning all eight games on their schedule in each of those three years. Dobie's final three years as a college football coach were spent at Boston College, where from 1936 to 1938 he had a record of 16–6–5. In 33 years of coaching college football, his combined record was 186–45–15. He was inducted into the **College Football Hall of Fame** as a charter member in 1951.

DORSETT, ANTHONY DREW "TONY." B. 7 April 1954, Rochester, Pennsylvania. Tony Dorsett is one of only three men who have played in a **Super Bowl** and whose son has also played in a Super Bowl. Of those three, only Tony (Super Bowls 1978 and 1979) and his son Anthony (2000 and 2003) have played in more than one Super Bowl game. Tony was a star athlete at Hopewell High School in Aliquippa, Pennsylvania (a suburb of Pittsburgh), as a member of both their basketball and **football** teams. He continued his stellar amateur football career at the **University of Pittsburgh**, where in four years, from 1973 to 1976, he was second in the nation in **rushing** as a freshman, set a Pittsburgh career rushing yardage record in his sophomore year, and set a Pittsburgh single-game rushing record with 303 yards as a junior. In addition, as a senior, he led the nation in rushing, led Pittsburgh to the national championship, and was awarded the **Heisman Trophy**, among other honors. He was the first collegiate football player to rush for more than 6,000 yards and set the all-time record at 6,082 (since broken) for his four years at Pitt. During his scholastic years, his name was pronounced with the accent on the first syllable, but after he became a professional he changed the pronunciation to accent the second syllable.

The five-foot, 11-inch, 190-pound **running back** was selected by the **Dallas Cowboys** in the first round of the 1977 **National Football League (NFL) Draft** as the second overall selection, and he remained with the Cowboys for the next 11 seasons. In his first year with the team, in addition to being named the NFL Offensive Rookie of the Year, Dorsett helped lead the Cowboys to the Super Bowl championship, becoming the first player to be a member of the national collegiate champions one year and Super Bowl champions the following year. In 1978, he again helped Dallas reach the Super Bowl, but this time they were defeated. Dorsett was traded to the **Denver Broncos** in 1988 and concluded his NFL career after one season with them.

In his 12-year NFL career, Dorsett played in 173 regular-season games, ran 2,936 times for 12,739 yards and 77 **touchdowns**, and caught 398 **passes** for 3,554 yards and 13 touchdowns. He also attempted eight passes on **option plays** and completed only two, but one of those was for a touchdown. He **fumbled** 90 times and recovered 17 fumbles, including one for a touchdown. In 17 postseason games, he ran 302 times for 1,383 yards and nine touchdowns and caught 46 passes for 403 yards and one touchdown. He was selected for the **Pro Bowl** four times.

Dorsett was inducted into both the **College Football Hall of Fame** and **Pro Football Hall of Fame** in 1994. In 2001, his high school, Hopewell High School, renamed their **football field** Tony Dorsett Stadium. His son Anthony also attended the University of Pittsburgh and played defensive **back** in the NFL from 1996 to 2003, making Super Bowl appearances in 2000 with the **Tennessee Titans** and 2003 with the **Oakland Raiders**.

DOWN. A down is the basic unit of play in **football**. A team is allowed four downs (three downs in **Canadian football**) to either advance the ball 10 yards or score a **touchdown** or **field goal**. If they successfully advance 10 or more yards, it is called a **first down**, and they are entitled to four more downs. A down takes place when the official places the ball on the field and an offensive player (nearly always the **center**) snaps the ball backward to a teammate (usually the **quarterback**), who then either **runs** with the ball, hands the ball to a teammate, or **passes** the ball. After the ball carrier has been **tackled** or run **out of bounds**, play stops and the ball is placed at the line of his forward progress to begin the next down.

DRAFT. The draft is a process whereby all teams in a league take turns selecting prospective players from a pool. The selection is usually done in inverse order to the team's previous year's performance. The drafted player may then only sign a contract with the team that selects him. Teams will sometimes trade established players to another team for the right to that team's future draft selection. The **National Football League** annual college draft was begun on 8 February 1936, after a suggestion by **Philadelphia Eagles** owner **Bert Bell** was implemented. Drafts have also been conducted to fairly distribute players from disbanded teams (dispersement drafts) and stock expansion teams (expansion drafts).

DRAW PLAY. The draw play is a **running** play that at first appears to be a **passing** play. The **quarterback** drops back as if to pass but hands the ball to a **running back**, who runs straight ahead. A variant is a quarterback draw play, in which after the quarterback drops back as if to pass, he keeps the ball and runs straight ahead.

DROPKICK. A dropkick is a type of kick that can be used in an attempt for a **conversion** or **field goal**. It also may be used in a **free kick** situation. The **kicker** drops the ball and then kicks it after it makes contact with the ground. It is rarely used in modern-day **football**, as the shape of the ball makes it hard to control after it bounces. In the early days of football, it was a common method, since the ball used was much rounder. To encourage this unusual play, **arena football** awards a bonus point for a dropkicked extra point or field goal.

EDMONTON ESKIMOS. The Edmonton Eskimos are a team in the **Canadian Football League (CFL)**. They were founded in 1949. Although there were **football** teams bearing the same name as early as 1895, they were unrelated to the present-day Eskimos team. Contrary to the belief of some, they are not composed of indigenous peoples (as was the case of the **Oorang Indians** of the **National Football League**). The Eskimos began play in the Western Interprovincial Football Union in 1949, which, in 1958, became a part of the CFL. They are a community-owned team of 80 local shareholders, although shares are no longer offered publicly. Home games since 1978 have been played at the 60,000-seat Commonwealth Stadium located in Edmonton, Alberta. Prior to 1978, they played at the 20,000-seat Clarke Stadium, also in Edmonton. Edmonton has been one of the most successful CFL franchises, and, for 34 years, from 1972 through 2005, the team reached the **playoffs** each year, the most consecutive seasons of playoff activity for any North American team in any sport. They have played in 21 **Grey Cups**, winning 13, including five consecutive championships from 1978 to 1982.

Unlike many of the other CFL teams, Edmonton's **coaching** situation has been relatively stable, with most of their head coaches serving for four or more years. Among the more notable Edmonton coaches have been Annis Stukus (1949–1952), Frank "Pop" Ivy (1954–1957), Eagle Keys (1959–1963), Neill Armstrong (1964–1969), Ray Jauch (1970–1977), Hugh Campbell (1978–1982), Jackie Parker (1983–1987), Joe Faragalli (1987–1990), Ron Lancaster (1991–1997), and Danny Maciocia (2005–2008).

Edmonton players honored on their Wall of Honour include Frank Anderson, Danny Bass, Johnny Bright, Tommy Joe Coffey, Rod Connop, Dave Cutler, Ron Estay, Dave Fennell, Sean Fleming, Don Getty, Larry Highbaugh, Danny Kapley, Brian Kelly, Oscar Kruger, Normie Kwong, John LaGrone, George McGowan, Rollie Miles, **Warren Moon**, Chris Morris, Frank Morris, Roger Nelson, Jackie Parker, Willie Pless, Tom Scott, Tom Wilkinson, Henry "Gizmo" Williams, and Larry Wruck.

ELITE FOOTBALL LEAGUE OF INDIA. The Elite Football League of India is a professional American **football** league that began play on 22

September 2012. The league was originally slated to have 12 teams, each based in a city throughout the Indian subcontinent, including one team each in the nations of Pakistan and Sri Lanka but only had eight teams when the 2012 season began. The league is being backed by several prominent American investors, including former **National Football League (NFL)** players **Mike Ditka**, **Michael Irvin**, and **Ron Jaworski**. Brandon Chillar, one of only four NFL players of Indian descent, is also an investor. The league employs primarily Indian **rugby** players to staff the teams. The eight teams are the Bangalore Warhawks, Mumbai Gladiators, Pune Marathas, Kolkata Vipers, Delhi Defenders, Pakistan Wolfpack, Colombo Lions, and Kandy Skykings. The league played 26 games in the 2012 season with all games played at the 25,000-seat Sugathadasa Stadium in Colombo, Sri Lanka. The season ended on 10 November 2012 with the Pune Marathas having the best record at 6–2. Whether such a novel undertaking will be successful remains to be seen.

ELLER, CARL. B. 25 January 1942, Winston-Salem, North Carolina. Carl Eller attended Atkins High School in Winston-Salem. At six feet, six inches tall and 245 pounds, Eller was an imposing **lineman** who played both offensive and defensive **tackle** at the **University of Minnesota**. In his sophomore year, he helped lead them to a 21–3 victory in the **Rose Bowl**. In 1964, he was selected in the first round of both the **National Football League (NFL)** and **American Football League (AFL) Drafts**, by Buffalo in the AFL as the fifth overall selection and by Minnesota in the NFL as the sixth overall selection.

Eller signed with the **Minnesota Vikings** of the NFL and became an important member of their line, playing defensive **end** from 1964 to 1978. The Vikings reached the **Super Bowl** four times (1970, 1974, 1975, 1977) while Eller was with them, although they were defeated each time. Their front line of Eller, **Jim Marshall**, **Alan Page**, and Gary Larsen (and later Doug Sutherland) were nicknamed the "Purple People Eaters" by the media.

After 15 years with the Vikings, Eller concluded his NFL career in 1979 with the **Seattle Seahawks**. As a defensive lineman, there are few statistical records of his NFL accomplishments. He started 209 of 225 regular-season games in 16 years, recovered 23 **fumbles**, made one **interception**, and scored two **safeties** by sacking opposing **quarterbacks** in the **end zone**. Although sacks were not an official NFL statistic during Eller's career, he is credited unofficially with 130 1/2 while a Viking and is their all-time leader in that category. In 18 postseason games, he recorded 10 1/2 sacks and one safety. He was selected for the **Pro Bowl** six times and, in 1971, was named the NFL Defensive Player of the Year.

In retirement, Eller has worked as a drug and alcohol substance abuse counselor and founded several clinics in the Minneapolis area. He also appeared in several Hollywood films. He was inducted into the **Pro Football Hall of Fame** in 2004 and the **College Football Hall of Fame** in 2006.

ELWAY, JOHN ALBERT, JR. B. 28 June 1960, Port Angeles, Washington. John Elway is one of the rare modern athletes who played more than one professional sport. In baseball, he was a good outfielder who batted .318 and fielded 1.000 in 1982 with the Oneonta Yankees of the Class A New York–Pennsylvania League. After completing his senior year at **Stanford University** and being selected first overall by the **Baltimore Colts** in the 1983 **National Football League (NFL) Draft**, Elway decided to concentrate on **football** and gave up a possibly promising baseball career.

The son of a high school and **college football** coach, Elway played his final three years of high school at Granada Hills High School in Granada Hills, California, a suburb of Los Angeles. In high school, he starred in both baseball and football and was selected by the Kansas City Royals in the 1979 Major League Baseball Draft but turned down their offers and selected Stanford among the many college football scholarship offers he also received. He played both football and baseball at Stanford from 1979 to 1983. In four years of football, he had 774 **pass** completions for 9,349 yards and 77 **touchdowns** in 42 games; however, Stanford's football team only had a record of 20–23–1 during Elway's tenure. In his last college football game against the **University of California**, Stanford was the victim of "The Play," in which the game ended when California, trailing 20–19, returned a **kickoff** for a touchdown with four seconds remaining in the game, using five **laterals** and **running** through the Stanford marching band, which had started to come onto the field after mistakenly thinking that the game was over.

After being drafted by the Baltimore Colts in 1983, Elway was reluctant to play for them, since they were one of the worst teams in the league at the time. He threatened to not play football but play baseball instead unless he was traded to a contending team. The Colts traded him to the **Denver Broncos** a few months later, and Elway played his entire 16-year NFL career with the Broncos. In 1987, he was voted the NFL Most Valuable Player. Elway led Denver to **Super Bowl** appearances in 1987, 1988, 1990, 1998, and 1999, and he is the only **quarterback** to start in five Super Bowls. The Broncos were defeated in their first three Super Bowl games but won the last two. Elway was selected as the Super Bowl Most Valuable Player for the 1999 game.

During his lengthy career, Elway played in 234 regular-season games, starting in 231 of them, and had a won-lost record of 148–82–1. He completed 4,123 passes in 7,250 attempts for 51,475 yards and 300 touchdowns; ran 774 times for 3,407 yards and 33 touchdowns; and caught three passes, including one for a touchdown. He was occasionally used as a backup **punter** and **punted** seven times for an average of 36.1 yards per punt. In 22 postseason games, Elway completed 355 passes in 651 attempts for 4,964 yards and 27 touchdowns and ran 94 times for 461 yards and six touchdowns. He was selected for nine **Pro Bowls**.

Elway retired in 1999 after leading the Broncos to the Super Bowl championship. Since then, he has been involved in several business enterprises. He owned five automobile dealerships in the Denver area and three in Southern California, as well as two Denver-area steakhouses. He is also part owner of an **Arena Football League** team; does radio work; and, in 2011, became executive vice president of football operations for the Denver Broncos. Elway was inducted into the **College Football Hall of Fame** in 2000 and the **Pro Football Hall of Fame** in 2004.

ENCROACHMENT. Encroachment is an infraction that occurs when a defensive player crosses the **line of scrimmage** and makes contact with an offensive player prior to the ball being snapped. The **official** will blow the whistle, indicating a stoppage of play, and advance the ball five yards to enforce the **penalty** without allowing the play to begin. *See also* OFFSIDES.

END. End is a **football position** that is the leftmost and rightmost player on the offensive or defensive line. In modern-day football on offense, one end usually lines up next to the **tackle** and is known as the **tight end**, while the other end lines up several yards away from the tackle on the other side of the field and is known as the **split end**. The ends are the only **linemen** that can catch **passes** or **run** with the ball. The ends' primary functions are to be a pass receiver on some plays and a **blocker** on other plays. The defensive end's primary function is to tackle the **quarterback** or knock down passes.

END AROUND. The end around is a type of offensive play in which the **end runs** behind the **quarterback** and is handed the ball to begin a running play.

END ZONE. The end zone is a 10-yard area (20 yards in **Canadian football**) immediately following the **goal line** that marks the extreme boundary of the **football field**.

ETCHEVERRY, SAM. B. 20 May 1930, Carlsbad, New Mexico. D. 29 August 2009, Montreal, Quebec, Canada. Sam Etcheverry attended high school in Albuquerque, New Mexico, and college at the University of Denver. He played on the Denver **varsity** from 1949 to 1951. Undrafted by the **National Football League (NFL)**, he signed with the **Montreal Alouettes** of the Interprovincial Rugby Football Union (IRFU) (forerunners of the **Canadian**

Football League [CFL]) in 1952 and played nine seasons with them. After being traded to the **Hamilton Tiger-Cats** in 1960, Etcheverry left the CFL and signed with the St. Louis Cardinals of the NFL, playing his last two seasons of **professional football** with them. He won the CFL's Most Outstanding Player Award in 1954. He also led the Alouettes to three straight **Grey Cup** games from 1954 to 1956, but they were defeated by the **Edmonton Eskimos** each year.

Etcheverry played in 122 CFL games as the Montreal **quarterback**, completing 1,944 **passes** for 30,435 yards and 183 **touchdowns**. He also ran for 20 touchdowns. Nicknamed "The Rifle," the five-foot, 11-inch, 185-pound Etcheverry led the IRFU in passing yardage each year from 1954 to 1959 and had one game in 1954 in which he passed for 586 yards and another one in 1956 in which he passed for 561 yards. He also served as the team's **punter** and had 514 **punts** for an average of 39.4 yards per punt during his CFL career. In his two years in the NFL, he played in all 28 regular-season games, completed 154 of 302 passes for 1,982 yards and 16 touchdowns, carried the ball 41 times for 78 yards and no touchdowns, and punted 59 times for an average of 38.6 yards per punt in 1962. The Cardinals did not reach the postseason in the two years Etcheverry was with them. He returned to the CFL in 1970 as the Montreal **coach** and led them to the Grey Cup championship that year. He remained as Montreal coach for two more seasons. Etcheverry was inducted into the **Canadian Football Hall of Fame** in 1969.

EXTRA POINT. *See* CONVERSION.

F

FACE MASK. The face mask is a series of iron bars affixed to a player's **helmet** to prevent facial injuries. Its use became popular in the 1950s. **Bobby Layne** was one of the last players in the **National Football League** to play without one. Grabbing the opponent's face mask to aid in tackling him is subject to a 15-yard **penalty**.

FAIR CATCH. On **punts** that are exceptionally high or short, the punt **returner** may wave one hand in the air to signal for a fair catch. In that case, he may not advance the ball and the **defense** may not **tackle** him. **Canadian football** does not have this rule and, consequently, all punt returners are subject to be tackled; however, the defense must stay at least five yards from him to allow him to catch the ball before they can attempt to tackle him. *See also* NO YARDS.

FANS. Because **football** has a relatively short season, fans are able to purchase season tickets more readily than in other team sports. As a result, some fans have strong attachments to their teams. Through their excessive **cheerleading** attempts, quite a few fans have become minor celebrities in their own right. One such diehard fan is "Fireman Ed" of the **New York Jets**. A retired fireman (Edwin M. Anzalone) who wears his fireman's hat and a Jets jersey to all the games, he has become a self-appointed cheerleader. More than half a dozen times during a game, he will stand and face the crowd to lead them in a cheer of J-E-T-S. Other super fans include "Barrel Man" (Tim McKernan), fan of the **Denver Broncos** who wore a barrel similar to the barrel a rodeo clown would wear at nearly all Broncos home games from 1967 to 2007, when he had to retire for health issues. "Chief Zee" (Zema Williams) is a **Washington Redskins'** fan who wears an Indian headdress and carries a tomahawk and has been present at Redskins' home games since 1978. "Crazy Ray" (Wilford Jones) was a former vendor at **Dallas Cowboys'** games, and, from 1962 until his death in 2007, he wore a traditional Western outfit with 10-gallon hat and missed only three Cowboys home games. The "Hogettes," a group of a dozen Washington Redskins' male fans who wear dresses and pig-snout masks, have been attending Redskins' home games since 1983. On 11 January 2013, the Hogettes announced that they would be retiring although they would still attend Redskins' games. During the 1980s, Washington's offensive line was known as the "Hogs," and many Redskins' fans would attend their games wearing pig-snout masks.

In 2000, the **Pro Football Hall of Fame** created a special exhibit on super fans and selected representatives from each of the NFL teams to be honored at the Hall in Canton. Super fans of **college football** include Giles Pellerin, who attended 797 consecutive **University of Southern California** games, home and away, from 1925 through 1998. His streak ended when he died of a heart attack during a game at the age of 91. **University of Alabama** fan Dick Coffee has seen more than 700 consecutive games, and, if all goes well, will surpass Pellerin's record in 2014. In recent years, more and more fans attend football games in costume with the hopes of being shown on television.

FAVRE, BRETT LORENZO. B. 10 October 1969, Gulfport, Mississippi. When Brett Favre retired for the third (and most likely final) time following the 2010 **football** season, he had established many of the **National Football League's (NFL)** career records as a **quarterback**. His most remarkable one, in the opinion of many, is starting 297 consecutive NFL regular-season games. He attended Hancock North Central High School in Kiln, Mississippi, and played baseball and football there with his father, Irvin Favre, as **coach** of the football team. Brett received a scholarship to the University of Southern Mississippi and was their quarterback from 1987 to 1990. During that time, the team had a record of 29–17.

Favre was chosen in the second round of the 1991 NFL **Draft** by the **Atlanta Falcons** as the 33rd overall selection. He played briefly with the Falcons in 1991 and was their third-string quarterback that year, appearing in only two games and attempting only four **passes** with none complete. He was traded to the **Green Bay Packers** in 1992. Favre started the season as the backup quarterback to Don Majkowski. After Majkowski was injured in the third game of the season, Favre became the starter. He started every game for the Packers from 27 September 1992 through 2007. During that time, he compiled a regular-season won-lost record of 160–93 and led the Packers to the **Super Bowl** in 1997 and 1998, winning it in 1997.

Favre announced his retirement on 4 March 2008, but he later changed his mind. Meanwhile, the Packers had committed to making **Aaron Rodgers** their quarterback for 2008 and did not want Favre back to lead the team. After substantial negotiations between Favre and the Packers, they agreed to trade him to the **New York Jets** for the 2008 season.

With the Jets, Favre started every game, continuing his consecutive streak, but he was inconsistent and the team finished the season with a 9–7 record and did not qualify for the postseason **playoffs**. Favre retired again on 11 February 2009. After being officially released by the Jets, he decided to try playing again and signed with the **Minnesota Vikings**. He played the 2009 and 2010 seasons with them. In 2009, he again started every game, had an outstanding year, and nearly led the Vikings to the Super Bowl. They had a 12–4 regular-season record but lost in **overtime** in the NFL **conference** championship to the **New Orleans Saints**.

In 2010, Favre started the first 12 games of the season, but the Vikings did not do as well as they had done the previous year. On 5 December 2010, he started the game but suffered an injury to his shoulder shortly after the start of the game and was unable to play the remainder of the contest. His consecutive game streak ended the following week, when he was unable to play. He came back two weeks later, on 20 December 2010, to play what was his final NFL game, as he suffered a concussion and was unable to play the remainder of the season. He retired for what is most likely the final time at the end of the season.

In his 20-year NFL career, Favre played in 302 regular-season games, started 298 of them, and had a won-lost record of 186–112. He completed 6,300 passes in 10,169 attempts for 71,838 yards and 508 **touchdowns** and ran 602 times for 1,844 yards and 14 touchdowns. In 24 postseason games, he completed 481 passes in 791 attempts for 5,855 yards and 44 touchdowns and ran 52 times for 72 yards and one touchdown. He was selected for the **Pro Bowl** 11 times.

Favre's list of NFL career records and achievements appears endless and includes most passes completed, with 6,300 (more than 1,300 more than **Dan Marino**, who is in second place); most passes attempted, with 10,169 (Marino is second with 8,358); most passing yardage, with 71,838 (Marino is second with 61,361); and most passing touchdowns, with 508 (Marino is second with 420). On the negative side, Favre also holds the career record for most passes **intercepted**, with 336, and most times sacked, with 525. He will undoubtedly be inducted into the **Pro Football Hall of Fame** once he is eligible.

FIELD GOAL. A field goal is a scoring play worth three points that is accomplished by kicking the ball through the uprights. It is generally done via a placekick, but, in **football's** earlier days, a **dropkick** was used. In the past half century, kicking specialists have been used for this purpose, but previously a position player usually doubled as the team's **kicker**. **Quarterback George Blanda** was one of **professional football's** most accomplished kickers, as was **tackle Lou Groza** and **end Pat Summerall**.

FIELD JUDGE. *See* OFFICIALS.

FIESTA BOWL. The Fiesta Bowl is an annual postseason college **bowl game** that is the newest of the major bowl games. It was first played on 27 December 1971. From 1971 to 2006, it was played in Tempe, Arizona, at Sun Devil Stadium. The stadium's capacity was increased from 50,000 in 1971 to its present 71,000. In 2006, the game was moved to the 63,400-seat University of Phoenix Stadium in Glendale, Arizona. Although the game originally was played a week or so before **New Year's Day**, as it grew in importance it was moved, and, since 1982, it has been played on New Year's Day in most years. Originally, a **Western Athletic Conference (WAC)** team was one of the participants, but, in 1978, both the University of Arizona and **Arizona State University** moved to the Pacific-10 Conference, and the WAC agreement was terminated. Since then, the bowl has usually attracted top-level teams and is one of the more prestigious bowl games.

FIFTH DOWN. In **football** history there have been a few instances where the **officials** lost track of the **downs** and erroneously allowed a team a fifth down. Four notable ones in **college football** are the **Cornell University**–Dartmouth College game of 16 November 1940, the **Ohio State University**–**University of Wisconsin** game of 8 November 1941, the **University of Miami**–Tulane University game of 14 October 1972, and the **University of Colorado**–University of Missouri game of 6 October 1990.

At Memorial Field in Hanover, New Hampshire, on 16 November 1940, Cornell, which had won 18 straight games in two years, faced Dartmouth. The home team, Dartmouth, had a 3–0 lead with less than one minute remaining in the game. Cornell had the ball on Dartmouth's six-**yard line** and gained three yards on **first down**, one yard on second down, and no yards on third down. On fourth down, after Cornell was penalized five yards for **delay of game**, they attempted a **pass** that went **incomplete**. Although possession should have gone to Dartmouth, the referee inexplicably gave the ball to Cornell. On their fifth down, they completed a pass for the winning **touchdown**. Following the game, after reviewing films, Cornell sent a telegram to Dartmouth offering to forfeit the game. Dartmouth accepted, and the final result was recorded as a 3–0 Dartmouth victory.

In the Ohio State–Wisconsin game, Wisconsin's second touchdown came as a result of an erroneous fifth down, but it did not impact the game's result, as Ohio State won, 46–34. In the fourth quarter of the Miami–Tulane game, with Tulane ahead, 21–17, Miami had the ball on Tulane's 32-yard line. The officials had lost track of the downs due to a **penalty**, and Miami was given a fifth-down opportunity. They capitalized on it with a 32-yard pass play for a touchdown and won, 24–21.

Fifty years after the infamous Cornell–Dartmouth game, another college football game was decided by an official's mistake. With 40 seconds remaining in the game at Faurot Field in Columbia, Missouri, and Colorado trailing, 31–27, Colorado completed a pass near the Missouri **goal line**. On first down, the Colorado **quarterback spiked** the ball to stop the game clock. They called a **running** play on second down and were stopped just short of the goal and then called for a **time-out**. The officials failed to move the down indicator on the **sideline**, so that when time resumed it still read second down, although it should have read third down. Colorado again tried to run and again was stopped short of the goal. As the down indicator now read third down instead of fourth down, the Colorado quarterback spiked the ball in an attempt to stop the clock. That should have given possession to Missouri, as Colorado had failed to score after four downs. But since the indicator now erroneously read fourth down, the Colorado quarterback carried the ball over the goal line with a **quarterback sneak**, and Colorado was awarded the winning touchdown. The final score, which was not overturned, was Colorado 33, Missouri 27.

50-YARD LINE. An American **football field** is 100 yards long from one **goal line** to the other. The 50-**yard line** marks the halfway point of the line and is also known as midfield. (**Canadian football** uses a 110-yard field, thus their midfield is the 55-yard line.)

1ST AND 10. The offensive team is allowed four **downs** to advance the ball 10 yards. Once they do so, they are allowed another four downs until they either score, lose possession via **fumble** or **interception**, **punt** the ball to their opponent, or are unsuccessful on fourth down and the ball reverts to their opponent. When they start their series of downs, it is usually referred to as 1st (down) and 10 (yards to go). *1st and Ten* was also the name of a situation comedy series from 1984 to 1991 that featured **O. J. Simpson**.

FIRST DOWN. A first **down** is achieved when a team has advanced the ball 10 or more yards from their initial starting position within four or fewer attempts. In the **National Football League**, a team is credited with a first down if they score a **touchdown** regardless of the number of yards gained on the play. College and high school rules differ slightly in that if the **line of scrimmage** for the first down is inside the 10-**yard line**, no first down is credited for a touchdown.

FLAG FOOTBALL. *See* TOUCH FOOTBALL.

FLANKER. *See* WIDE RECEIVER.

FLEA FLICKER. A flea flicker is a play in **football** meant to catch the opponent by surprise. The **quarterback** hands off to a **running back**, who, after taking a few steps forward, turns and flips the ball back to the quarterback, who then **passes** the ball downfield. **University of Illinois coach Bob Zuppke** is credited with inventing the play in 1910.

FLORIDA, UNIVERSITY OF. The University of Florida is located in Gainesville, Florida. Their **football** program began in 1906, and, since then, through 2012, the Gators have compiled a record of 660–367–40. In addition, they have competed in 40 postseason **bowl games**, with a record of 20–20. They have been selected as national collegiate champions five times, in 1984, 1985, 1996, 2006, and 2008. Home games have been played at Ben Hill Griffin Stadium since 1930. The stadium, originally known as Florida Field, was renamed for alumnus and benefactor Ben Hill Griffin in 1989, and the facility has been gradually expanded so that it presently seats 88,548.

Since 1932, Florida football teams have competed in the **Southeastern Conference (SEC)** of the **National Collegiate Athletic Association**. They have rivalries with many of the SEC schools. They have played **Florida State University** annually since 1964 and hold a 34–21–2 advantage in the series. The series with the **University of Georgia** dates back to 1915, with Georgia leading 48–40–2. A recent addition to that series is the Okefenokee Oar, which is the trophy that has been awarded to the victor since 2009.

Florida's most successful **coach** was former Florida player Steve Spurrier. After playing 10 years of **professional football** in the **National Football League (NFL)**, he turned to coaching. From 1990 to 2001, he coached the Gators to a record of 122–27–1. Other successful Florida coaches have been Ray Graves (1960–1969; 70–31–4), Doug Dickey (1970–1978; 58–43–2), Galen Hall (1984–1989; 40–18–1), and Urban Meyer (2005–2010; 65–15).

There are six Florida alumni in the **College Football Hall of Fame**. They include **linebacker** Wilber Marshall, **running back Emmitt Smith**, **quarterback** Steve Spurrier, **wide receiver** Carlos Alvarez, **end** Dale Van Sickel, and defensive end Jack Youngblood. Florida coaches in the Hall are Charlie Bachman, Doug Dickey, and Ray Graves. Steve Spurrier and quarterbacks Danny Wuerffel and **Tim Tebow** were both **Heisman Trophy** winners.

Through 2012, there have been 258 professional football players who have attended Florida, 246 in the NFL, 10 in the **American Football League**, and two in the **All-America Football Conference**. They include Raymond "Trace" Armstrong, Lomas Brown, Cooper Carlisle, Kevin Carter, Rick Casares, Don Chandler, Wes Chandler, **Cris Collinsworth**, Bobby Joe Green, Rex

Grossman, John James, Jevon Kearse, Wilber Marshall, Nat Moore, Bernie Parrish, Mike Peterson, Maurkice Pouncey, Emmitt Smith, Steve Spurrier, Fred Taylor, Tim Tebow, John L. Williams, and Jack Youngblood.

FLORIDA STATE UNIVERSITY. Florida State University is located in Tallahassee, Florida. Although the school was founded in 1851, it did not begin a **football** program until 1947, since beginning in 1905 it was the Florida State College for Women and did not become coeducational until 1947. Since then, through 2012, their teams have compiled a record of 460–223–15. In addition, they have competed in 42 postseason **bowl games**, with a record of 25–14–2 and one game won but vacated. They have been selected as national collegiate champions seven times, in 1980, 1987, 1992, 1993, 1994, 1996, and 1999. Since 1992, Florida State football teams have competed in the **Atlantic Coast Conference** of the **National Collegiate Athletic Association (NCAA)**.

The school's nickname is the Seminoles, and although in recent years the NCAA has frowned upon the use of Native American names for school nicknames (and even required some schools to change them), the Seminole Tribe of Florida has officially allowed the school to retain it. The Seminoles' home field since 1950 has been Doak Campbell Stadium, which throughout the years has been expanded from its original seating capacity of 15,000 to its present one of 82,300. Florida State's two main rivals are the **University of Florida** and the **University of Miami**. Florida leads their series with the Seminoles, 34–21–2, and Miami leads their series, 31–26. Since 2002, the Florida Cup has been awarded to the team defeating the other two teams in the same year.

Since beginning their football program in 1947, Florida State has employed nine head **coaches**. Bobby Bowden was coach for 34 years, from 1976 to 2009, and he compiled a record of 316–97–4, nearly 75 percent of the school's victories. Bill Peterson coached from 1960 to 1970, with a record of 62–42–11.

The five Florida State alumni in the **College Football Hall of Fame** are **wide receiver**s Fred Biletnikoff and Ron Sellers; middle **guard** Ron Simmons; **cornerback Deion Sanders**; and **quarterback** and **Heisman Trophy** winner Charlie Ward, who at six feet, two inches tall was deemed to be too short to play **professional football**, so he became a professional basketball player and played 11 years in the National Basketball Association. Coaches Bobby Bowden and Darrell Mudra are also enshrined in the Hall. Quarterback Chris Weinke played Minor League Baseball for six years and then enrolled at Florida State. In 2000, at the age of 28, he became the oldest Heisman Trophy winner.

Through 2012, there have been 229 professional football players who have attended Florida State, 216 in the **National Football League** and 13 in the **American Football League**. They include Fred Biletnikoff, Anquan Boldin, Derrick Brooks, Terrell Buckley, Leroy Butler, Laveraneus Coles, Zack Crockett, Warrick Dunn, Jessie Hester, Sebastian Janikowski, Brad Johnson, Ken Lanier, Anthonia "Amp" Lee, Orpheus Roye, Deion Sanders, Rohn Stark, William "Tra" Thomas, and Javon Walker.

FLUTIE, DOUGLAS RICHARD "DOUG." B. 23 October 1962, Manchester, Maryland. Doug Flutie was a **football** player who recorded memorable moments in **college football**, **Canadian football**, and the **National Football League (NFL)**. He was born in Maryland, spent much of his youth in Florida, and lived most of his teenage years in Massachusetts. He attended Natick High School in Natick, Massachusetts, a suburb west of Boston. In high school, Flutie played baseball, basketball, and football. He did not receive many scholarship offers and accepted one from Boston College. He played **quarterback** on the football team there from 1981 to 1984. In those four years, the Eagles improved each season, with records of 5–6, 8–3–1, 9–3, and 10–2. They played in postseason **bowl games** the last three years. In his senior year, Flutie was the recipient of the **Heisman Trophy**.

One of the most memorable moments of Flutie's college career occurred on 23 November 1984, when Boston College, led by Flutie, played the **University of Miami**, led by future NFL quarterback Bernie Kosar. The teams traded scores for much of the game, and Miami led, 45–41, with 28 seconds remaining in the game. Boston College had the ball on their own **22-yard line**. With the ball near midfield and only six seconds left, Flutie threw a **Hail Mary pass** into the **end zone** that was caught for the game-winning **touchdown**.

Despite his excellent career at Boston College and his last-minute heroics in the Miami game, Flutie was thought to be too small, at five feet, 10 inches and 180 pounds, to be able to play successfully in the NFL, thus he signed with the new **United States Football League (USFL)** prior to the NFL **Draft**. When the 1985 draft occurred, he was only selected in the 11th round by the Los Angeles Rams as the 285th overall selection. He played the 1985 season with the New Jersey Generals of the USFL and had a good year, completing 134 of 281 passes for 2,109 yards and 13 touchdowns in 15 games and leading the Generals to a second-place finish in their **conference**. The USFL folded in 1985, and Flutie signed with the NFL.

In 1986, Flutie was traded by the Rams to the **Chicago Bears**, and he played four games for the Bears as a backup quarterback. He was traded to the **New England Patriots** during the 1987 season and played for them in 1988 and 1989, mainly as a backup, although he did start nine games in 1988.

In 1990, Flutie went to Canada and played in the **Canadian Football League (CFL)** from 1990 to 1997, where he had the best years of his professional career. In 1991, he passed for a CFL (and **professional football**) record 6,619 yards. This record has not been surpassed as of the 2012 season. He completed 466 of 730 pass attempts, both also CFL records at the time, although both have since been surpassed. That same year, he also had one game in which he passed for 582 yards (just four yards short of the CFL record at that time). Flutie had several other excellent years in the CFL, passing for 6,092 yards in 1992 (third best all-time in the CFL) and setting the CFL record with 48 touchdown passes in 1994.

Flutie played for the **BC Lions** in 1991 and 1992, the **Calgary Stampeders** from 1992 to 1995, and the **Toronto Argonauts** in 1996 and 1997. He led Calgary to the **Grey Cup** game in 1995 and the Argos to the Grey Cup championship in 1996 and 1997. While with the Lions, Flutie's younger brother, Darren, was one of the **wide receivers** on that team. Darren later played for Edmonton and Hamilton in a 12-year CFL career and was a member of Grey Cup champions in 1994 and 1999. He is fourth all-time with 14,359 receiving yards and holds the record (as of 2012) for most **playoff receptions**. In eight years of CFL football, Flutie played in 135 regular-season games, completed 2,975 passes in 4,844 attempts for 41,355 yards and 270 touchdowns, and carried the ball 704 times for 4,660 yards and 66 touchdowns.

He returned to the NFL in 1998 with the **Buffalo Bills**. After a few games, he became the Bills' starting quarterback and played in 10 games that year and 15 games in 1999. In 2000, Flutie reverted to the role of backup. After being released by the Bills, he signed with the **San Diego Chargers** in 2001. He started all 16 games for them that season, but, by 2002, he was again a second-string quarterback. He remained with the Chargers in that role through 2004. After being released by the Chargers in early 2005, Flutie signed with the New England Patriots as **Tom Brady's** backup. Flutie appeared in only five games for the Patriots, but, in their final regular-season game on 1 January 2006, he ended his professional football career by successfully **dropkicking** an extra point, the first such kick in the NFL since 1941.

Flutie retired in 2006 at the age of 43. In his 12-year NFL career, he played in 92 regular-season games, completed 1,177 passes in 2,151 attempts for 14,715 yards and 86 touchdowns, and ran 338 times for 1,634 yards and 10 touchdowns. In two postseason games, he completed 32 of 67 passes for 494 yards and two touchdowns and ran six times for 41 yards and no touchdowns. He was inducted into the **College Football Hall of Fame** in 2007 and the **Canadian Football Hall of Fame** in 2008, joining his brother there, who had been inducted the previous year.

FLYING WEDGE. The flying wedge was a type of **football** play in which the ball carrier was surrounded by teammates in a "V" formation. It was originally a military tactic and is still occasionally used by police riot squads. It was originated by **Harvard University** in 1892 but banned two years later due to the numerous injuries that occurred during its use.

FOOTBALL (EQUIPMENT). The ball used in the sport of football is also called a football. Originally, a nearly round ball was used, as in **rugby**, but throughout the years the ball has become more elongated for ease in **passing** it. A modern-day football is an inflated rubber lining filled to a pressure of about 13 pounds per square inch that is covered by leather and laced. The leather is stamped with a pebble-grain texture to aid in gripping the ball. The ball's total weight is between 14 and 15 ounces.

FOOTBALL (SPORT). The word *football* means different things. It describes a game, as well as the ball used to play the game. In most parts of the world, it refers to a game that is known in the United States as **soccer** or association football. In Australia and Ireland, they play two other quite different games known as football, which, outside those countries, are referred to as **Australian rules football** and **Gaelic football**. The popular game known simply as football in the United States is called American football, or **gridiron** in most other countries. A Canadian version (with slightly different rules) is known as **Canadian football**. Although this game is primarily a North American sport, it has grown internationally, with a European league and one that began play on the Indian subcontinent in 2012. An organization known as the **International Federation of American Football** administers competition internationally and has attempted to have the International Olympic Committee include the sport in future **Olympic Games**.

American football is a game usually played outdoors, with 11 players on a team on the field at a time. Substitutes are permitted, and most teams employ 40 or more players. The game originated in the latter part of the 19th century in American colleges and is a derivative of **rugby**. Through the 19th century, the game continually evolved with significant rules changes almost annually. By 1912, the game was defined nearly identically to the game now played in 2012. During the past 100 years, only minor changes to the rules have occurred, although the equipment, techniques, and size of the participants have changed significantly.

The modern-day field is 100 yards long by 53 1/3 yards wide, with end zones of 10 yards at each end of the field. A set of "H"-shaped wooden **goalposts** are placed at each **goal line**. A leather-covered ball with an inflated rubber lining known as a **football** is used. The object of the game is for a team to carry the ball over their opponent's goal line either by **running** with it or catching it when thrown. A team has four attempts (called **downs**) to advance the ball 10 yards or score. If it fails to do so, the opposing team then gains possession of the ball. The defensive team attempts to halt the progress of the offensive team by **tackling** the player with the ball or forcing him **out of bounds**. Additional scoring occurs by kicking the ball over the crossbar and between the uprights. Although the sport is known as "football," kicking of the ball is relatively minimal, and the game is predominantly one of running, **passing**, and tackling. As the game is quite physical, extensive protective equipment is worn and has significantly evolved as players have become bigger and more powerful.

The game is played by amateurs in high schools and colleges, as well as professionals, and, since the mid-20th century, it has become the most popular sport in the United States. Younger children not yet in high school often play organized football in various **Pop Warner Leagues** similar to Little League Baseball leagues. Variants of the sport include **six-man football** (popular at smaller high schools), flag or **touch football** (a noncontact variety popular as a social activity), and **arena football** (a patented indoor variety played professionally using a smaller football field). In recent years, **women** have begun playing the sport; however, the women's game is far less popular than the men's version.

In the United States, the major **professional football** league, the **National Football League (NFL)**, has grown significantly since its beginning in 1920. It has gone from a 12-team league in 1959 to its present 32 teams. It has also become a multibillion dollar business. In 2011, *Forbes* magazine estimated the worth of an average NFL team at $1.04 billion. Extensive television coverage has made the sport the most popular American spectator sport, and the professional championship game, the **Super Bowl**, has virtually become a national holiday on the first Sunday in February.

FOOTBALL FIELD. American **football** was originally played outdoors on a grass field. While most games are still held on this same surface, with the advent of domed **stadiums**, many games are no longer subject to the **weather** conditions. With the rise of domed stadiums, artificial turf surfaces have been developed and are often used, even in some outdoor stadiums, for ease of maintenance. The dimensions of the American football field are 100 yards long between the **goalposts**, with 10-yard **end zones** at each end. The width is 160 feet (53 1/3 yards). **Canadian football** uses a slightly larger field that is 110 yards long and 65 yards wide with 20-yard end zones. The indoor variety of football, known as **arena football**, uses a playing area that is 50 yards long and 85 feet wide (28 1/3 yards) with eight-yard end zones.

FOOTBALL FILMS. Since Hollywood first began producing films, the sport of **football** has had more than its share. Football-themed pictures appeared as early as 1911, when *Brown of Harvard* was first made. In 1925, the well-known silent comedian Harold Lloyd made *The Freshman*, a film about a **college football** player that was included in the National Film Registry in 1990, along with such classic films as *Fantasia*, *It's a Wonderful Life*, and *Rebel without a Cause*. One of the Marx Brothers' films, *Horsefeathers*, released in 1932, features Groucho Marx as a university president who hires Chico and Harpo Marx to help his school win a big football game against a rival school.

The 1940 film *Knute Rockne: All-American* was one of the first biographical films of a football personality. It features future president of the United States Ronald Reagan in a memorable role as the dying **University of Notre Dame** football player **George Gipp**. *Jim Thorpe: All-American*, released in 1951, stars Burt Lancaster as **Jim Thorpe** in another biography of a football star.

Paper Lion, the 1968 film based on writer George Plimpton's attempts at playing professional football, features several **Detroit Lions'** players. One of them, **Alex Karras**, did so well acting in it that he began a film career following his retirement from football. Burt Reynolds's 1974 film *The Longest Yard*, about a prison football team, was a box-office success that was remade in 2005.

Other notable football films include *Any Given Sunday* (1999), *Black Sunday* (1977), *Brian's Song* (1971), *Friday Night Lights* (2004), *Leatherheads* (2008), *North Dallas Forty* (1979), *Remember the Titans* (2000), *Rudy* (1993), *Two-Minute Warning* (1976), *The Waterboy* (1998), and *We Are Marshall* (2006).

Although many of these films have received good ratings and have done well at the box office, the only ones to have earned major Academy Awards are *The Blind Side* (best actress Sandra Bullock, 2010) and *Jerry Maguire* (best supporting actor Cuba Gooding Jr., 1997). *The Blind Side* was also nominated for best picture. *Heaven Can Wait* received nine nominations in 1979, including best picture, but it only won one for art direction and set direction. *Jerry Maguire* received five nominations, including best picture, but won only one Oscar.

As football gained in popularity throughout the latter half of the 20th century, the number of films with a football theme increased exponentially, and, in the 21st century, there have been one or more football films released each year. *See also* FOOTBALL PLAYERS WHO WERE ACTORS; APPENDIX P (for a list of football films).

FOOTBALL PLAYERS WHO WERE ACTORS. There have been quite a few **professional football** players who turned to acting after their **football**

careers ended. Among them are **Jim Brown**, Johnny Mack Brown, Bernie Casey, Terry Crews, Ben Davidson, **Alex Karras**, Howie Long, Ed Marinaro, **Joe Namath**, **Merlin Olsen**, Mark Schlereth, **O. J. Simpson**, **Bubba Smith**, Woody Strode, Carl Weathers, Herm Wedemeyer, and Fred Williamson.

Jim Brown was probably the best former football player who later became a successful actor. He has appeared in more than 50 Hollywood films and television series from 1964 to 2012, with *The Dirty Dozen* being one of his more memorable ones. Carl Weathers had only a brief career as a **linebacker** for the **Oakland Raiders** and **BC Lions** from 1970 to 1973, but he became famous as Apollo Creed in the Sylvester Stallone *Rocky* series. Johnny Mack Brown was a **college football** star at the **University of Alabama** who was the Most Valuable Player in the 1926 **Rose Bowl** game. Professional football was not a viable career option for him after college graduation, and he went directly into a film career, since his good looks made him a sought-after actor. From 1927 to 1965, he appeared in more than 160 films, the vast majority of them Westerns. In 1960, Brown was honored with a star on the Walk of Fame in Hollywood. O. J. Simpson also had an outstanding **National Football League** career. He has appeared in more than 25 films and television series, including featured roles in the *Naked Gun* series with Leslie Nielsen. His film career undoubtedly would have been more extensive had he not encountered his difficulties with the law in the 1990s.

Woody Strode was one of the few black players during the 1940s. He played only one season with the Los Angeles Rams in 1946 but went on to establish himself as one of Hollywood's leading black actors, appearing in more than 90 films in 50 years, including *Spartacus*, for which he was nominated for a Golden Globe as best supporting actor in 1961. Hawaiian-born Herm Wedemeyer played two seasons in the **All-America Football Conference** and then became a regular as "Duke" in the *Hawaii Five-O* television series.

Alex Karras, who had an exceptional sense of humor, showed the range of his acting abilities by playing the memorable character Mongo in Mel Brooks's 1974 comedy *Blazing Saddles*, and by his sensitive portrayal of Babe Didrickson Zaharias's husband, George Zaharias, during her bout with terminal cancer in the 1975 film *Babe*. He also starred in the television series *Webster* from 1983 to 1989 and appeared in more than 30 other films and television episodes.

Numerous other professional football players have appeared in only a handful of films, often playing themselves or fictional football players or **coaches**. Among them are **Y. A. Tittle** (*Any Given Sunday*), **Michael Irvin** (*The Longest Yard*, 2005 version), Bill Romanowski (*The Longest Yard*, 2005 version), **Brett Favre** (*Reggie's Prayer*), **Dan Marino** (*Ace Ventura, Pet Detective*), Bill Goldberg (*The Longest Yard*, 2005 version), Bob Sapp (*Conan the Barbarian*, 2011 version), **Terry Bradshaw** (*The Cannonball Run*), Lyle

Alzado (*Ernest Goes to Camp*), **Dick Butkus** (*Any Given Sunday*), John Matuszak (*North Dallas Forty*), **Lawrence Taylor** (*Any Given Sunday*), Brian Bosworth (*The Longest Yard*, 2005 version), **Elroy "Crazylegs" Hirsch** (*Unchained*), **Ray Nitschke** (*The Longest Yard*, 1974 version), Frank McRae, Roosevelt Grier, **Mike Ditka**, Roman Gabriel, and Ed O'Neil. Such football-themed films as *Any Given Sunday*, *The Longest Yard*, and *North Dallas Forty* have frequently used many professional football players in minor roles.

Several other notable actors, including Ronald Reagan (later president of the United States and a football player at Eureka College), John Wayne (**University of Southern California**), Burt Reynolds (**Florida State University**), Mark Harmon (**University of California, Los Angeles**), Dean Cain (**Princeton University**), Donald Gibb (University of New Mexico), and Forest Whitaker (California State Polytechnic University, Pomona), were accomplished scholastic football players. *See also* FOOTBALL FILMS; PROFESSIONAL FOOTBALL PLAYERS WHO WERE PROFESSIONAL WRESTLERS.

FOOTBALL POSITIONS. In the early days of **football**, the 11 players had specific position names. On **offense**, the seven players who played up front on the **line of scrimmage** were left **end**, left **tackle**, left **guard**, **center**, right guard, right tackle, and right end. These players were also known as **linemen**, with the tackles, guards, and center referred to as interior linemen. The backfield was composed of a **quarterback**, left and right **halfbacks**, and **fullback**. The defensive linemen had similar names to the offensive linemen, while the four defensive backfield players were simply labeled as defensive **backs**. Players also usually played on both offense and **defense**.

In modern football, players specialize and normally play only offense or defense. Offensive positions are usually called **wide receiver**, left tackle, left guard, center, right guard, right tackle, and **tight end** on the line of scrimmage, and quarterback, halfback, fullback, and wide receiver in the backfield. The tight end may also line up on the left side of the line of scrimmage, with the wide receiver on the right. The halfback and fullback are sometimes referred to as **running backs**. Although offensive alignments may vary, football rules require exactly seven offensive players to be positioned on the line of scrimmage for the snap of the ball to start a **down**.

Defensive positions are left end, left tackle, right tackle, right end on the line of scrimmage, left outside **linebacker**, middle linebacker, right outside linebacker immediately behind the defensive linemen, left **cornerback**, strong **safety**, free safety, and right cornerback positioned further back. Modern defenses are quite flexible, and teams may use more or less than four players on the line of scrimmage.

Depending on the offensive or defensive alignment, other position names occasionally used include **slotback**, tailback, wingback, middle guard, nose tackle, **split end**, **strong side** linebacker, and **weak side** linebacker. On **punting** plays, the center is usually referred to as a long snapper, one of the four backfield players will be the **punter**, and the defensive team will have one or two players positioned deep behind the line of scrimmage to be punt **returners**. On place kicking plays, a **kicker** (or placekicker) and **holder** will replace two of the backs. On **kickoffs**, players outside of the kicking team's kicker and receiving team's kick returner usually do not have special position names.

FORD, GERALD RUDOLPH, JR. "GERRY," NÉE LESLIE LYNCH KING JR. B. 14 July 1913, Omaha, Nebraska. D. 26 December 2006, Rancho Mirage, California. Before he became president of the United States in 1974, Gerald Ford had been one of the best **college football** players of the 1930s when he played **center** for the **University of Michigan**.

Ford had a difficult start in life. His parents separated 16 days after he was born and were divorced six months later. In 1916, his mother remarried to Gerald Rudolff Ford, and, although her son was never formally adopted, they called him Gerald Rudolff Ford Jr. Raised in Grand Rapids, Michigan, Gerald became an Eagle Scout in the Boy Scouts of America. He attended Grand Rapids South High School, became captain of their **football** team, and was named to the Grand Rapids All-City **high school football** team.

Ford was about six feet tall and 195 pounds when he went to the University of Michigan and played center and **linebacker** there. As a sophomore and junior in 1932 and 1933, he helped lead the Wolverines to a record of 15–0–1 and the cochampionship of the **Big Ten Conference** each year. In his senior year, however, the team slumped and only won one of eight games. He was chosen to play in the East-West Shrine Game on 1 January 1935 and, later that year, in the **College All-Star Game** against the **National Football League (NFL) Chicago Bears** on 29 August 1935.

In 1935, Ford legally changed his name from Leslie King to Gerald Ford and modified the spelling of his middle name to the more common Rudolph. After graduating in 1935 with a bachelor of arts degree in economics, he was offered a contract to play in the NFL but turned it down to enter **Yale University** Law School. He was also the boxing **coach** at Yale, as well as the **assistant coach** of the football team. Because of his full-time coaching duties, Ford was not accepted to Yale Law School until 1937, and he graduated from there in 1941.

Ford enlisted in the U.S. Navy in 1942 and participated in World War II in the Pacific Theater. After his discharge from the service, he entered local politics and, in 1949, won the congressional seat from Grand Rapids. He retained that position until 1973. From 1965 to 1973, he was the minority leader of the House of Representatives. After Vice President Spiro Agnew resigned in October 1973, Ford was nominated to replace him. After approval by the Senate and separate approval by the House of Representatives, Ford was sworn in on 6 December 1973 as the 40th vice president of the United States. After the resignation of President Richard M. Nixon on 9 August 1974, he became the 38th president of the United States. Although he ran for reelection in 1976, Ford was defeated by Jimmy Carter. At his death in 2006, he was 93 years of age and is the oldest-lived president. He is also the only U.S. president who once played football against the Chicago Bears.

FOSS, JOSEPH JACOB "JOE." B. 17 April 1915, Sioux Falls, South Dakota. D. 1 January 2003, Scottsdale, Arizona. Although Joe Foss played some **football** at the University of South Dakota as a second-string **guard**, he is not remembered as a football player. He served as the **American Football League's (AFL)** first commissioner from 1960 to 1966. While in that position, he helped the league grow to be a viable competitor with the **National Football League (NFL)** and laid the groundwork for the subsequent merger with the NFL, which took place two months after he resigned as AFL commissioner on 7 April 1966.

Foss accomplished many more important things in his life. During World War II, he served in the U.S. Marine Corps as a fighter pilot. He was the country's leading "ace" and was credited with shooting down 26 Japanese aircraft. He was awarded the Congressional Medal of Honor in 1943. After being released from active duty in 1945, he started the Joe Foss Flying Service, a charter flight service and flight instruction school. He remained in the Air National Guard and was recalled to active duty during the Korean War. Foss eventually earned the rank of brigadier general.

Foss served two terms in the South Dakota House of Representatives and, in 1955, was elected governor of South Dakota, a post in which he served through 1959. After a brief time in industry, he was hired as the commissioner of the newly formed AFL. From 1964 to 1967, he also hosted *The American Sportsman* television show and later hosted and produced his own syndicated show, *The Outdoors*. In 1972, Foss was hired by KLM Royal Dutch Airlines as director of public affairs. In 1988, he became the president of the National Rifle Association. He died on **New Year's Day** 2003, two months after suffering a severe stroke.

FOUR HORSEMEN OF NOTRE DAME. In describing the results of the **University of Notre Dame** upset of **Army** at the Polo Grounds on 18 October 1924, sportswriter **Grantland Rice** of the *New York Herald Tribune* wrote, "Outlined against a blue-gray October sky, the Four Horsemen rode again. In dramatic lore their names are Death, Destruction, Pestilence, and Famine. But those are aliases. Their real names are Stuhldreyer, Crowley, Miller, and Layden." Notre Dame capitalized on this article and billed their backfield as "The Four Horsemen" in publicizing their team, taking advantage of a popular Rudolph Valentino movie of that era, *The Four Horsemen of the Apocalypse*.

Notre Dame finished the 1924 season undefeated, at 9–0, and then defeated **Stanford University** in the **Rose Bowl** and were named national collegiate **football** champions. The **quarterback** was Harry Stuhldreyer (Harry Augustus Stuhldreyer, B. 14 October 1901, Massillon, Ohio. D. 26 January 1965, Pittsburgh, Pennsylvania). After graduation from Notre Dame, he briefly played **professional football** and then became head football **coach** at Villanova University and later the **University of Wisconsin**. He was inducted into the **College Football Hall of Fame** in 1958.

One **halfback** was "Sleepy" Jim Crowley (James Harold Crowley, B. 10 September 1902, Chicago, Illinois. D. 15 January 1986, Scranton, Pennsylvania). Crowley also briefly played pro football before beginning a **college football** coaching career. After coaching at the **University of Georgia**, **Michigan State University**, and Fordham University, he served in the U.S. Navy during World War II. Following the war, he was named commissioner of the new **All-America Football Conference (AAFC)** in 1946. After just one season as commissioner, Crowley resigned to become part owner and coach of the Chicago Rockets of the AAFC. After the team finished at 1–13, he quit football and moved to Pennsylvania, where he worked as an insurance salesman and station manager of a television station. From 1925 to 1950, he also worked as a boxing referee and in 1930 awarded Max Schmeling the world's heavyweight championship on a foul over Jack Sharkey—the only time that a world's heavyweight title changed hands in that manner. Crowley later became the chairman of the Pennsylvania State Athletic Commission and was inducted into the College Football Hall of Fame in 1966.

The other halfback was Don Miller (Donald Charles Miller, B. 29 March 1902, Defiance, Ohio. D. 28 July 1979, Cleveland, Ohio). Miller coached football at **Georgia Tech** and **Ohio State University** from 1925 to 1932, and he then pursued a career in law. He was inducted into the College Football Hall of Fame in 1970.

The fourth Horseman, **fullback Elmer Layden**, also played professional football briefly and then went into coaching. From 1925 to 1933, he coached at Columbia College in Iowa and Duquesne University. In 1934, he was named coach of his alma mater, Notre Dame, and he remained there through

1940. In 1941, Layden was chosen as the commissioner of the **National Football League**, and he held that position until 1946. He then became a successful businessman in Chicago and was inducted into the College Football Hall of Fame in 1951 as a charter member.

FOUTS, DANIEL FRANCIS "DAN." B. 10 June 1951, San Francisco, California. Dan Fouts was one of the **National Football League's (NFL)** best players who never had the chance to compete in an NFL Championship Game or **Super Bowl**. He began high school at Marin Catholic High School in Kentfield, California, a suburb of San Francisco, but after his sophomore year he transferred to St. Ignatius College Preparatory for his final two years. Fouts played **quarterback** on the **football** team at both schools and received a scholarship to the University of Oregon. He was the quarterback of the Oregon **varsity** from 1970 to 1972. In 33 games, he completed 482 **passes** in 956 attempts for 5,995 yards and 37 **touchdowns**.

Fouts was picked by the **San Diego Chargers** in the third round of the 1973 NFL **Draft** as the 64th overall selection. He played for the Chargers from 1973 to 1987 and was the Chargers' starting quarterback for most of that time. During those 15 seasons, the Chargers only reached the postseason **playoffs** four times, from 1979 to 1982, and the team did not advance past the **conference** championship game. Despite the team's losing record, Fouts had some excellent individual statistical performances and was the NFL leader in passing yardage each season from 1979 to 1982. He set the NFL record for passing yardage in one season in 1979, with 4,082 yards; broke the record in 1980, with 4,715 yards; and broke it again the following year, with 4,802 yards. He retired following the 1987 season.

In his 15-year NFL career, Fouts played in 181 regular-season games, started 171 of them, and had a won-lost record of 86–84–1. He completed 3,297 passes in 5,604 attempts for 43,040 yards and 254 touchdowns and ran 224 times for 476 yards and 13 touchdowns. In seven postseason games, he completed 159 passes in 286 attempts for 2,125 yards and 12 touchdowns and ran eight times for 15 yards and no touchdowns. He was selected for the **Pro Bowl** six times.

After retiring, Fouts became a broadcaster, and he has become one of the better ones. In that capacity, he also worked for two years on *Monday Night Football*. He was inducted into the **Pro Football Hall of Fame** in 1993.

FRANKFORD YELLOW JACKETS. *See* PHILADELPHIA EAGLES.

FREE KICK. A free kick occurs in two situations, by the team scored upon following a **safety**, and by the receiving team following a **fair catch** of a

punt or **kickoff**. There are minor rules variations for the two scenarios. The kicking team may put the ball into play by either a punt or placekick without using a tee. A free kick following a fair catch may also be used as a **field goal** attempt.

FREE SAFETY. *See* SAFETY (POSITION).

FULLBACK. Fullback is an offensive position. He is generally stationed next to or behind the **quarterback**. In modern-day **football**, he is usually employed as a **blocker** but may occasionally **run** with the football in short yardage situations. He is generally one of the more powerful players on the team.

FUMBLE. A fumble occurs when an offensive player who has possession of the ball drops it. The ball may then be claimed by either the **offense** or **defense** by falling on it and **holding** it. *See also* MUFF.

G

GAELIC FOOTBALL. Gaelic **football** is a sport played almost exclusively in Ireland, and one of its most popular spectator sports. The game is a cross between **soccer** and **rugby** and is more like either of those two games than it is like American or **Canadian football**. It is played by teams of 15 players on each side on a grass field with "H"-shaped **goalposts** at each end of the field that have a net behind them. The ball is rounder than an American football or rugby ball and is similar to a soccer ball or volleyball. The object is to kick or punch the ball over the crossbar between the goalposts to score one point or kick the ball into the net to score three points. As in soccer, a goalkeeper protects the net.

GARCIA, AARON. B. 20 October 1970, Sacramento, California. Aaron Garcia attended Grant Union High School in Sacramento. While there, he played **football** and basketball. In two years as **quarterback**, he **passed** for 5,800 yards, with 57 **touchdown** passes, and set the California state high school record in those categories. He enrolled at Washington State University in 1988 but was **redshirted** his first year. He quarterbacked the team in 1989, but midway through the 1990 season he was replaced by future **National Football League (NFL)** star Drew Bledsoe. In 1991, Garcia transferred to Sacramento State College, where he finished his **college football** career.

The six-foot, one-inch, 195-pound Garcia went undrafted by the NFL, and he joined the **Arena Football League** in 1995. He began with the Arizona Rattlers in 1995 and went on to play for the Connecticut Coyotes in 1996, the New Jersey Red Dogs in 1997 and 1998, the Iowa Barnstormers from 1998 to 2000, the New York Dragons from 2001 to 2008, and the Jacksonville Sharks in 2010 and 2011.

The highlight of his **arena football** career was the 2011 season, when he became one of the few quarterbacks to pass for more than 50,000 yards in a professional career and led Jacksonville to the Arena Football League championship by passing for the winning touchdown on the final play of the **ArenaBowl** to give Jacksonville the victory over the Arizona Rattlers, 73–70. Through the 2012 season, Garcia has played in the Arena Football League for 18 seasons (missing 2009, when the league suspended operations) and completed 4,151 passes in 6,503 attempts for 52,056 yards and 1,125 touchdowns. He also carried the ball 226 times for 450 yards and 46 touchdowns. He is still active in the league with the San Jose Sabercats in 2013.

GEORGIA, UNIVERSITY OF. The University of Georgia is located in Athens, Georgia. Their **football** program began in 1891, and, since then, through 2012, Bulldogs' teams have compiled a record of 733–384–51. In addition, they have competed in 48 postseason **bowl games**, with a record of 27–18–3. They have been selected as national collegiate champions five times, in 1927, 1942, 1946, 1968, and 1980. Sanford Stadium has been the site of Georgia's home games since 1929. The **stadium's** seating capacity is presently 92,746, a substantial increase from its original capacity of 30,000. A unique aspect of the stadium is the privet hedges that surround the facility, leading to the saying that Georgia games are played "Between the Hedges."

Since 1932, Georgia football teams have competed in the **Southeastern Conference (SEC)** of the **National Collegiate Athletic Association (NCAA)**. Georgia's rivalries are with other SEC schools, and they have played more than 50 games with each of eight other schools. The series with **Auburn University** is billed as the "Deep South's Oldest Rivalry" and dates back to 1892. The two schools have met 116 times and are exactly even at 54–54–8. Georgia leads 63–39–5 over **Georgia Tech** in a series that began in 1893, and Georgia has a record of 48–40–2 against the **University of Florida**.

Georgia's two most notable head **coaches** have been Wally Butts and Vince Dooley. Butts coached from 1939 to 1960, with a record of 140–86–9, and Dooley's record from 1964 to 1988 is 201–77–10. Mark Richt took over in 2001 and, through 2012, has compiled a record of 118–40–0.

Georgia alumni in the **College Football Hall of Fame** include placekicker Kevin Butler; **fullback** Bill Hartman; **safeties** Terry Hoage and Jake Scott; **halfbacks** Bob McWhorter, Frank Sinkwich, and **Charley Trippi**; **running back Herschel Walker**; **quarterbacks** John Rauch and **Fran Tarkenton**; **end** Vernon Smith; and **tackle** Bill Stanfill. Coaches Wally Butts, Jim Donnan, Vince Dooley, and **Glenn "Pop" Warner** have also been enshrined in the Hall. Sinkwich and Walker each won the **Heisman Trophy**.

Through 2012, 266 **professional football** players have attended Georgia, 252 in the **National Football League**, four in the **American Football League**, and 10 in the **All-America Football Conference**. They include Champ Bailey, Zeke Bratkowski, Kevin Butler, Philip Daniels, Terrell Davis, Ray Donaldson, Rodney Hampton, Len Hauss, Garrison Hearst, John Kasay, Morris "Mo" Lewis, Guy McIntyre, Randy McMichael, Jimmy Orr, Jake Scott, Richard Seymour, Bill Standfill, Mack Strong, Fran Tarkenton, Charley Trippi, Bobby Walden, Herschel Walker, and **Hines Ward**.

GEORGIA INSTITUTE OF TECHNOLOGY. *See* GEORGIA TECH.

GEORGIA TECH. Georgia Institute of Technology, more popularly known as Georgia Tech, is located in Atlanta, Georgia. Their **football** program began in 1892, and, since then, through 2012, Yellow Jackets' teams have compiled a record of 673–450–43. In addition, they have competed in 41 postseason **bowl games**, with a record of 23–18. They have been selected as national collegiate champions six times, in 1917, 1928, 1951, 1952, 1956, and 1990. Their home field since 1913 is Grant Field, which was officially renamed Bobby Dodd Stadium at Historic Grant Field in 1988 and has a present-day seating capacity of 55,000.

Since 1979, Georgia Tech football teams have competed in the **Atlantic Coast Conference** of the **National Collegiate Athletic Association**. Their main rival is the **University of Georgia**. Georgia leads, 63–39–5, over Georgia Tech in a series that began in 1893. Tech's fight song, published in 1908 and still in use today, is *Ramblin' Wreck from Georgia Tech*. One of Georgia Tech's most famous games is their 1916 game with Cumberland College, which the Yellow Jackets won by a score of 222–0.

From 1904 to 1966, Georgia Tech only had three head **coaches** of their football teams. John Heisman (for whom the **Heisman Trophy** is named) coached from 1904 to 1919, had a record of 104–29–7, and was the coach for the Cumberland College game. Bill Alexander coached from 1920 to 1944. His record was 134–95–15. Bobby Dodd coached from 1945 to 1966, with a record of 165–64–8. In more recent years, both George O'Leary (1994–2001; 52–33) and Paul Johnson (2008–2012; 40–26) have had successful careers coaching the Yellow Jackets.

Georgia Tech alumni in the **College Football Hall of Fame** include **centers** Maxie Baughan, George Morris, Larry Morris, and Peter Pund; **guard** Ray Beck; **tackle** Bobby Davis; **end**/tackle Bill Fincher; **halfbacks** Allen "Buck" Flowers and Everett Strupper; halfback/tackle **Joe Guyon**; **safety** Randy Rhino; and defensive end Pat Swilling. Coaches Bill Alexander, Bobby Dodd, and John Heisman have also been enshrined in the Hall.

Through 2012, 162 **professional football** players have attended Georgia Tech, 152 in the **National Football League**, six in the **American Football League**, and four in the **All-America Football Conference**. Pro players who have attended Georgia Tech include Maxie Baughan, Keith Brooking, Marco Coleman, Bill Curry, Nick Ferguson, Joe Guyon, Drew Hill, Kent Hill, Dorsey Levens, Bill Lothridge, Dave Lutz, Larry Morris, Mark Pike, Lucius Sanford, Billy Shaw, Billy Shields, Daryl Smith, Larry Stallings, Pat Swilling, and Reggie Wilkes. *See also* GEORGIA TECH 222, CUMBERLAND COLLEGE 0.

GEORGIA TECH 222, CUMBERLAND COLLEGE 0. On 7 October 1916, **Georgia Tech** defeated Cumberland College by the unbelievable score of 222–0 at Georgia Tech's home field, Grant Field in Atlanta, Georgia. Tech scored 63 points in each of the first two quarters, 54 in the third quarter and 42 in the final quarter. At **halftime**, it was agreed to shorten the length of the second half by 15 minutes, thus the lower second-half totals. Georgia Tech scored 32 **touchdowns** and 30 of 32 extra points. Neither team scored a **first down**, as Georgia Tech scored a touchdown on every set of downs, although not on every play, as has sometimes been written. Other game statistics are sketchy, and various totals have been published. One set of statistics states that Cumberland **fumbled** nine times and was **intercepted** six times. They had a total of minus 96 yards **rushing** and completed two of 18 **passes** for 14 yards. Georgia Tech, on the other hand, rushed 40 times for 1,620 yards.

There were several factors for the one-sided score. Cumberland, a small school in Lebanon, Tennessee, had cancelled its **football** program but booked the game with Georgia Tech prior to cancelling the program. Georgia Tech insisted that the game be played or else Cumberland would have had to pay $3,000 (a considerable sum in those days) to Georgia Tech if the game was forfeited. Cumberland's student manager of their baseball team, George E. Allen (not the famous football **coach**, but a man who was later involved in politics as the secretary of the Democratic National Committee), recruited 14 students to travel to Atlanta to play the game. The second reason is that college teams in that era were ranked based on the number of points they scored, and John Heisman, Georgia Tech's coach, did not feel that was a valid measure, so he deliberately ran up the score to illustrate his point. A third reason is that the previous year, Cumberland's baseball team had defeated Georgia Tech, 22–0, and was alleged to have used professional players in doing so, thus there was an element of revenge involved.

There are a few quotes from the game's participants, although they may be apocryphal. It is worth mentioning Coach John Heisman's halftime speech, part of which went as follows: "We're ahead but you just can't tell what those Cumberland players have up their sleeves. They may spring a surprise. Be alert, men." The following appeared in the *Atlanta Journal*: "As a general rule, the only thing necessary for a touchdown was to give a Tech **back** the ball and holler, 'Here he comes' and 'There he goes.'" After a Cumberland player fumbled the ball, another player shouted to him to pick it up: "Pick it up yourself, you dropped it." The Cumberland College website has a play-by-play account of the game.

GIBBS, JOE JACKSON. B. 25 November 1940, Mocksville, North Carolina. To some sports **fans**, Joe Gibbs is known as a successful stock car racing car owner. To others, he is known as a successful **National Football League (NFL)** head **coach**. He is, in fact, both. He was born in stock car country, North Carolina, but was raised in Southern California and attended Santa Fe High School in Santa Fe Springs, California. He also went to Cerritos Junior College and San Diego State University (SDSU). He played **quarterback** on his school's **football** teams. After his college graduation in 1964, Gibbs was hired as an **assistant coach** of the football team at his alma mater, San Diego State. He remained in that position through 1966, while earning his master's degree there.

Gibbs was offensive line coach at **Florida State University** from 1967 to 1968, and at the **University of Southern California** from 1969 to 1970. In 1971, he moved to the University of Arkansas, where he coached their **running backs** until 1972. When Don Coryell, Gibbs's former college coach at SDSU, became the head coach of the St. Louis Cardinals of the NFL in 1973, he hired Gibbs as his offensive backfield coach. Gibbs held that job until 1977. He became offensive coordinator for the **Tampa Bay Buccaneers** in 1978 and in 1979, and then went back to work for Coryell as offensive coordinator of the **San Diego Chargers**.

In 1981, Gibbs became the head coach of the **Washington Redskins**, a position he held through 1992. During that time, his Redskins went to the **Super Bowl** four times, winning in 1983, 1988, and 1992, and losing in 1984. He retired from coaching in 1993 citing health problems and, from 1994 to 1997, did television work.

In 1992, he formed Joe Gibbs Racing, a National Association for Stock Car Auto Racing team, with Dale Jarrett as his driver from 1992 to 1994. Subsequent drivers for that team were Bobby Labonte from 1995 to 2005, J. J. Yeley from 2006 to 2007, and Kyle Busch from 2008 to 2012. Gibbs added other cars, and Tony Stewart, Joey Logano, and Denny Hamlin have also driven for him. Joe Gibbs Racing drivers have won the major series (now known as the Sprint Cup) three times, including Bobby Labonte in 2000 and Tony Stewart in 2002 and 2005. Gibbs branched out into drag racing in 1995 and sponsored vehicles in each of three National Hot Rod Association categories.

In 2004, Gibbs was coaxed out of (football) retirement and returned to coach the Redskins with the added title of team president. He coached Washington through 2007, but the Redskins did not fare as well as in his initial turn coaching them. The team reached the postseason **playoffs** only twice in those four years.

Upon retiring from coaching in 2008, Gibbs retained the position of advisor to the Redskins and returned to spend more time with his racing endeavors. In 16 years as an NFL head coach, he compiled a regular-season record of 167–84 and a postseason playoff record of 17–7. He was inducted into the **Pro Football Hall of Fame** as a coach in 1996.

GIFFORD, FRANCIS NEWTON "FRANK." B. 16 August 1930, Santa Monica, California. According to Frank Gifford's 1993 autobiography, *The Whole Ten Yards*, by the time he entered high school he had lived in 47 different towns. He was raised during the Depression, and his father worked as a "roughneck" in the oil fields. When a new field was opened, the family (Frank, his parents, and his two siblings) would move to the new location. Fortunately, by the time he entered high school, the family's situation was more stable, and Gifford was able to complete four years at Bakersfield High School in Bakersfield, California. Although he was a good athlete, Gifford was a poor student, and, after his high school graduation, he was unable to receive an athletic scholarship to the **University of Southern California (USC)** because of his grades. He enrolled at Bakersfield Junior College, improved his grades, and then received a scholarship to USC. He was a **halfback** for the Trojans from 1949 to 1951.

Gifford was selected by the **New York Giants** in the first round of the 1952 **National Football League (NFL) Draft** as the 11th overall pick. He played for the Giants through 1964 as both an offensive and defensive halfback and, in his later years, a **wide receiver**. He was a member of the 1956 NFL championship team and played on the losing side in the NFL Championship Games of 1958, 1959, 1962, and 1963. Gifford missed the entire 1961 season due to a concussion he had sustained in the ninth game of 1960. He retired from active play following the 1964 season. In 1956, he was named the NFL Most Valuable Player.

In his 12-year NFL career, Gifford played in 136 regular-season games, ran 840 times for 3,609 yards and 34 **touchdowns**, and caught 367 **passes** for 5,434 yards and 43 touchdowns. He also completed 29 passes in 63 attempts for 823 yards and 14 touchdowns. At the beginning of his NFL career, he was also used as a **punt** and kick **returner**, and he returned 25 punts for an average return of 4.8 yards and 23 **kickoffs** for an average return of 25.8 yards. He did not score any touchdowns as a returner. In 1953 and again in 1956, Gifford was used as a backup placekicker, and he kicked two **field goals** in seven attempts and 10 extra points in 11 attempts. In six postseason games, he ran 48 times for 241 yards and no touchdowns and caught 17 passes for 236 yards and three touchdowns. He played in eight **Pro Bowls**.

After retiring, Gifford began a second career as a sportscaster. In 1971, he became a member of the *Monday Night Football* team and remained one of their announcers through 1997. Besides working football games, he handled a variety of other sporting broadcast assignments, including the **Olympic Games**, and he has cohosted *Good Morning America* with his wife, Kathie Lee Gifford, on occasion. He was inducted into the **College Football Hall of Fame** in 1975 and the **Pro Football Hall of Fame** in 1977.

GIPP, GEORGE. B. 18 February 1895, Laurium, Michigan. D. 14 December 1920, South Bend, Indiana. George Gipp attended Calumet High School in Calumet, Michigan, on the Upper Peninsula, but did not play **football** there. He enrolled at the **University of Notre Dame** in 1917, with the intention of playing center field on their baseball team but was recruited for the football team by Notre Dame **coach Knute Rockne** prior to the start of the baseball season. Six feet tall and 175 pounds, he became one of Notre Dame's first star players. He played **halfback, quarterback**, and defensive **back** and was the team's **punter, kicker**, and kick **returner**. From 1917 until his death in 1920, Gipp compiled 2,341 yards **rushing**, tallied 1,789 yards **passing**, scored 21 **touchdown**s, kicked 27 extra points, and **intercepted** five passes. During that time, he also averaged 38 yards per punt, 14 yards per punt return, and 22 yards per **kickoff** return. Gipp's career rushing yardage was not surpassed at Notre Dame until 1978. He led Notre Dame to undefeated 9–0 records in both 1919 and 1920, and Notre Dame was considered the national collegiate champions on some postseason polls each of those years.

In 1920, Gipp was selected by **Walter Camp** to the **All-American** football team and became the first Notre Dame player to receive that honor. Had he not succumbed to pneumonia and a related streptococcal throat infection in December of his senior year, he would probably be just another excellent collegiate player who has been forgotten by history; however, on his deathbed, in talking with Coach Knute Rockne, Gipp supposedly told Rockne, "I've got to go, Rock. It's all right. I'm not afraid. Some time, Rock, when the team is up against it, when things are wrong and the breaks are beating the boys, ask them to go in there with all they've got and win just one for the Gipper. I don't know where I'll be then, Rock. But I'll know about it, and I'll be happy."

Rockne later used this story in a **halftime** speech to motivate his Notre Dame team in a 1928 game against **Army**. Rockne, himself, died young in a plane crash in 1931, and a 1940 film, *Knute Rockne: All-American*, was made about his life. In the film, actor Ronald Reagan, the future 40th president of the United States, played the part of George Gipp and delivered the famous deathbed speech. Later in life, Reagan was often referred to as "The Gipper." George Gipp was inducted into the **College Football Hall of Fame** as a charter member in 1951.

GOAL LINE. The goal line is the line at each end of the field 100 yards apart (110 yards in **Canadian football**). The object of the game of **football** is to be in possession of the ball and cross the goal line with it to score a **touchdown**, worth six points. This can be accomplished by **running** with the ball over the goal line or being positioned past the goal line in the **end zone** and catching a **pass** there.

GOALPOSTS. The goalposts are an H-shaped structure in the center of the field at the back of the **end zone** 10 yards behind the **goal line**. The horizontal part of the H is known as the crossbar. The two vertical parts are known as the uprights. There is a set of goalposts at each end of the field. After scoring a **touchdown**, a team may elect to kick the ball above the crossbar between the uprights to score one point. At any time during the game, the offensive team may elect to attempt to kick the ball above the crossbar and through the uprights to score a **field goal**, worth three points. In collegiate football, a tradition developed where, after a particularly noteworthy victory, the winning school's students would physically attempt to climb the goalposts and tear them down. Modern football has discouraged this practice.

GOGOLAK, PETER KORNEL "PETE." B. 18 April 1942, Budapest, Hungary. Pete Gogolak was born in Hungary and moved with his family to Ogdensburg, New York, in 1957, following the Hungarian Revolution. A **soccer** player in his native land, he was exposed to American **football** at Ogdensburg Free Academy, since the school did not have a soccer team but did have a football team. After graduating, he enrolled at **Cornell University** and proceeded to revolutionize the game of American football. He was used as a placekicker and kicked the ball with the side of his foot, as a soccer player would kick a soccer ball, rather than the traditional straight-on kick, with the toe making contact with the ball, that American football players used.

Gogolak was successful at Cornell, but, upon graduation in 1964, he was surprised that there were no **National Football League (NFL)** teams interested in him. The **Buffalo Bills** of the **American Football League (AFL)** decided to take a chance and selected him in the 12th round of the 1964 AFL **Draft** as the 92nd player chosen. He played for the Bills in 1964 and 1965, made 76 of 77 extra points and 47 of 75 **field goals**, and helped lead the Bills to the AFL championship both years.

At that time, the AFL was competing with the NFL for fan support, although neither league attempted to sign the other league's star players under a "gentlemen's agreement." The **New York Giants** of the NFL were having a difficult time competing with the **New York Jets** of the AFL after the Jets signed **quarterback Joe Namath** to a huge contract and the Giants' stars of the 1950s and early 1960s were aging and the team's performance was declining. In 1966, the Giants offered the six-foot, one-inch, 190-pound Gogolak a contract and became the first NFL team to "steal" an AFL star player. This action helped to escalate the war between the two leagues, which eventually resulted in a merger agreement in 1967.

With the Giants from 1966 to 1974, Gogolak continued his effective kicking, but he was unable to bring the team a championship. He did, however, help the team improve to second place in their division each season from 1967 to 1970. In 1970, Gogolak scored 107 points in 14 games, a team record that was not broken until 1983, and it was then topped in a 16-game season. When he retired following the 1974 season, Gogolak was the Giants' all-time leading scorer, a distinction he still holds. He also holds the Giants' career records for most field goals and extra points.

In his 11-year combined AFL/NFL career, Gogolak played in 149 regular-season games and kicked 173 field goals in 294 attempts and 344 extra points in 354 attempts. He was also used as a **punter** in 1969 and had 12 **punts** for an average of 40.9 yards per punt. In two postseason games, he made all four extra point attempts and five of seven field goal attempts. His brother, Charlie, also was a **kicker** in the NFL from 1966 to 1972 for the **Washington Redskins** and **New England Patriots**. He still holds the record for most extra points kicked in one game, ironically against the Giants and his brother Pete.

GONZALEZ, ANTHONY DAVID "TONY." B. 27 February 1976, Torrance, California. Tony Gonzalez was raised in Southern California and attended Huntington Beach High School, where he played baseball, **football**, and basketball. After graduating, he attended the **University of California** and continued playing baseball and football. Although California's football teams did not have winning seasons during Gonzalez's years there, the basketball team fared better. In 1997, as a six-foot, five-inch, 240-pound junior, Gonzalez helped lead the Golden Bears to the third round of the **National Collegiate Athletic Association** Basketball Tournament. He decided to skip his senior year in college and was chosen by the **Kansas City Chiefs** in the first round of the 1997 **National Football League (NFL) Draft** as the 13th overall selection.

Gonzalez played for the Chiefs from 1997 to 2008, and for the **Atlanta Falcons** from 2009 to 2012. He is considered by many to be one of the best **tight ends** in NFL history. He holds the league record for tight ends for most **pass receptions** in one season, with 102 in 2004. He also holds NFL career records for tight ends for most **touchdowns**, receptions, and yardage. His career total receptions in second only to **Jerry Rice** among all players, regardless of position.

In his 16-year NFL career through 2012, Gonzalez has played in 254 regular-season games (all but two of his team's scheduled games) and caught 1,242 passes for 14,268 yards and 103 touchdowns. He also carried the ball twice on **end around** plays for 14 yards total. In 2001, he completed his only pass attempt for 40 yards. He has played in 13 **Pro Bowls**. Unfortunately for Gonzalez, neither his Kansas City nor his Atlanta teams have reached the **Super Bowl** during his career with them. In fact, he has only played in seven postseason games, with 30 receptions for 286 yards and four touchdowns.

GOODELL, ROGER S. B. 19 February 1959, Jamestown, New York. Roger Goodell is the son of New York senator Charles Goodell. His family moved to Bronxville, New York, when Roger was 12 years old, and he attended Bronxville High School. He played baseball, basketball, and **football** in high school and was the captain of all three teams. He attended Washington & Jefferson College and graduated with a degree in economics, but injuries prevented him from participating in sports.

In 1982, Goodell began as an intern in the **National Football League (NFL)** office and, the following year, was hired by the **New York Jets** as an intern. From 1984 to 1987, he worked in the public relations department of the NFL. In 1987, he became an assistant to **Lamar Hunt**, the president of the American Football Conference. Goodell went on to hold a variety of positions in the NFL office and, in 2001, was named executive vice president and chief operating officer. After Commissioner **Paul Tagliabue** announced his retirement, Goodell was selected by the league owners to be NFL commissioner effective 1 September 2006. His most challenging task during his tenure was handling the labor dispute in 2011, which was resolved with a new 10-year collective bargaining agreement that does not expire until 2021. As of 2013, Goodell is still league commissioner.

GRAHAM, OTTO EVERETT, JR. B. 6 December 1921, Waukegan, Illinois. D. 17 December 2003, Sarasota, Florida. Otto Graham was one of the greatest all-time winners in professional sports. He played one year of professional basketball and was a member of the 1945–1946 National Basketball League (NBL) champion Rochester Royals. In 10 years of **professional football** with the **Cleveland Browns**, he led them to a league title in five consecutive seasons. They were the losers in the league Championship Game the next three seasons and then won two more league championships.

Graham attended Waukegan Township High School in Waukegan, Illinois, where his father was the school's band director and Otto played cornet in the school band. Graham also found the time to play baseball, **football**, and basketball. He then went to Northwestern University and continued his multifaceted activities. He was a **halfback** and tailback, as well as **punter** and placekicker in football, playing on the **varsity** from 1941 to 1943.

Graham was selected in the first round of the 1944 **National Football League (NFL) Draft** by the **Detroit Lions** as the fourth overall selection, but his first obligation was to serve in the U.S. Coast Guard. While in the service, he played football for the North Carolina Pre-Flight Cloudbusters service team. He was signed by **Coach Paul Brown** to a contract for the Cleveland Browns in the new **All-America Football Conference (AAFC)** and began play with them in 1946.

Prior to joining the Browns, Graham played one season of professional basketball with the Rochester Royals of the NBL. Among his teammates on the Royals that season were future Basketball Hall of Famers Bob Davies, Al Cervi, and William "Red" Holzman, as well as future Major League Baseball players Del Rice and Chuck Connors. The Royals won the NBL championship that season, with Graham playing 32 games and averaging 5.2 points per game.

The AAFC began play in 1946, and Graham abandoned his basketball career for football. Under the leadership of head coach Paul Brown and featuring Graham at **quarterback**, Marion Motley at **running back**, and **Lou Groza** playing offensive **tackle** and placekicking, the Browns compiled a record of 47–4–3 in the regular season and 5–0 in postseason and won the AAFC championship each year from 1946 to 1949. In 1950, the AAFC and NFL merged, and the Browns continued their winning ways. From 1950 to 1955, their record was 58–13–1 in the regular season. They played in the NFL Championship Game in each of those six years and won in 1950, 1954, and 1955. Graham retired following the 1955 season, and, as of 2012, the Browns have won only one league championship since.

In his 10-year combined AAFC/NFL career, Graham played in 126 regular-season games, completed 1,464 **passes** in 2,626 attempts for 23,584 yards and 174 **touchdowns**, and ran 405 times for 882 yards and 44 touchdowns. He was also used as a **punt returner** in his first three years with the Browns and returned 23 punts for an average of 11.4 yards per return. In 1946, he scored a touchdown on an **interception** return, and, in 1951, he recovered a **fumble** in the **end zone** for another touchdown. In postseason play, Graham appeared in 13 **playoff** games, completed 159 of 300 passes for 2,101 yards and 14 touchdowns, ran 73 times for 359 yards and six touchdowns, intercepted a pass for four yards, returned five punts for 20 yards, and returned one **kickoff** for 46 yards.

After Graham retired, he served as head coach of the U.S. Coast Guard Academy's football team from 1959 to 1965. He was hired as head coach of the **Washington Redskins** in 1966 and coached them through 1968. They did not perform exceptionally well, and his three-year record with the team was just 17–22–3.

In 1974, Graham returned to the U.S. Coast Guard Academy, where he coached until 1975. His record for nine years there was a respectable 44–32–1. He remained at the academy as athletic director until 1984. Graham was inducted into the **College Football Hall of Fame** in 1956 and the **Pro Football Hall of Fame** in 1965.

GRAMBLING STATE UNIVERSITY. Grambling State University is a historically black university located in Grambling, Louisiana. Their **football** program began in 1928, and, since then, through 2012, Tigers' teams have compiled a record of 516–231–18. In addition, they have competed in 26 postseason **bowl games** with a record of 18–8–0. Through 2012, there has never been a historically black college and university (HBCU) selected as the nation's champion college team, but Grambling has been named Black College National Champion nine times, in 1955, 1972, 1975, 1980, 1983, 1992, 2001, 2002, and 2008. They were also Black College National Cochampions five times, in 1967, 1974, 1977, 2000, and 2005. Since 1958, Grambling football teams have competed in the Southwestern Athletic Conference of the **National Collegiate Athletic Association (NCAA)**. Their main rival is Southern University, in a contest referred to as the "Bayou Classic." The series is currently even at 30 wins apiece.

Although nearly all of Grambling's opponents have been other HBCU schools, since the 1970s, non-HBCU schools have scheduled games with the Tigers. Grambling holds victories over California State University, Fullerton (twice); California State University, Long Beach; California State University, Sacramento; the University of Hawaii (three times); the University of Nevada; Nicholls State University (twice); Northwestern State University (LA) (twice); Oregon State University (twice); Portland State University; and Temple University. They were defeated by Boston University, the University of Houston, Louisiana Tech, the University of Louisiana at Monroe, the University of Louisville, North Dakota State University, Oklahoma State University, the **University of Pittsburgh**, San Jose State University, Southern Methodist University, Stephen F. Austin State University, Texas Christian University, and Washington State University. Grambling has also met non-HBCU schools in NCAA Division 1-AA **playoff** games, defeating the University of Delaware in 1973, losing to Western Kentucky University in 1973, and losing to **Boise State University** in 1980.

One of the highlights of any Grambling State football game is the Grambling Tiger Marching Band. The band started in 1926, and, after Conrad Hutchinson Jr. became band director in 1952, the school's band became one of the best and most popular marching bands in the country. After performing at **halftime** of the 1964 **American Football League (AFL)** Championship Game in San Diego, they became nationally famous. The high-stepping, fast-paced 104-member band also performed at halftime for the first **Super Bowl** in Los Angeles in 1968 and has since performed throughout the country, as well as overseas.

The man most responsible for Grambling's football success was head **coach Eddie Robinson**, who coached for 55 years, more than any other **college football** coach. From 1941 to 1997, his teams won 408 games, lost 167, and **tied** 16. One of his former students, Doug Williams, a **National Football League (NFL)** Super Bowl–winning **quarterback**, succeeded Robinson and coached Grambling from 1998 to 2003, compiling a record of 53–17. Williams returned as coach in 2011 and had a record of 8–4 that year but was only 1–10 in 2012. Along with Coach Robinson, the four Grambling alumni in the **College Football Hall of Fame** are **tackles** Junious "Buck" Buchanan and Gary Johnson, quarterback Doug Williams, and **fullback** Paul "Tank" Younger.

Through 2012, there have been 110 **professional football** players who attended Grambling State, 99 in the NFL and 11 in the AFL. They include Garland Boyette, Willie Brown, Junious "Buck" Buchanan, Willie Davis, Andrew Glover, James Harris, Gary Johnson, Charlie Joiner, Ernie Ladd, Albert Lewis, Frank Lewis, Clifton McNeil, John Mendenhall, Woody Peoples, Jake Reed, Rosey Taylor, Bennie Thompson, Everson Walls, Sammy White, Doug Williams, Nemiah Wilson, Willie Young, and Paul "Tank" Younger.

GRANGE, HAROLD EDWARD "RED," "THE GALLOPING GHOST." B. 13 June 1903, Forksville, Pennsylvania. D. 28 January 1991, Lake Wales, Florida. Harold "Red" Grange was the most popular **football** player in the 1920s, and he is considered to be the football symbol of the Golden Age of Sport, along with Babe Ruth in baseball, Jack Dempsey in boxing, Bill Tilden in tennis, and Bobby Jones in golf. Born in Pennsylvania, Grange moved with his family to Wheaton, Illinois, when he was five years old and was raised there. He attended Wheaton High School and participated in baseball, football, basketball, and track in each of his four years there.

Grange attended the **University of Illinois** and starred on their **varsity** football team from 1923 to 1925. A fast, powerful runner, six feet tall and 180 pounds, he played **halfback**. In his first varsity football game, on 6 October 1923, he scored three **touchdowns**. That season, he lead the Illini to an undefeated season and the national championship. In 1924, Grange had one of the greatest days in **college football** history. On 18 October, in the first game played at the University of Illinois' new Memorial Stadium in Champaign,

Harold "Red" Grange, football's entry in the Golden Age of Sport.
Mike Moran

Illinois, he returned the opening **kickoff** against the **University of Michigan** 95 yards for a touchdown. He then ran for touchdowns of 67, 56, and 44 yards in the first quarter. With the limited substitution rules in effect in that era, he did not play in the second quarter. In the third quarter, Grange ran for another touchdown, this time only 12 yards. He threw a **pass** in the fourth quarter for yet another score. By the end of the game he had run for five touchdowns; passed for one touchdown; and compiled 212 yards **rushing**, 64 yards passing, and 126 yards on kickoff returns. Illinois defeated Michigan, 39–14, ending Michigan's 20-game undefeated streak. During his senior year, 1925, Grange had another 200-yard day, when he was credited with 237 yards rushing on a muddy field in a defeat of the **University of Pennsylvania**. Grange's college totals for 20 games were 3,362 yards rushing and 253 yards in 14 pass **receptions**. He scored 31 touchdowns and completed 40 passes in 82 attempts for 575 yards. His totals would have been even greater had he played in all 23 games that season.

Grange played his final college game on Saturday, 21 November 1925, and, by Monday, he had signed with the **Chicago Bears** to play the final five games of their **National Football League (NFL)** season for $2,000 a game plus a share of the gate receipts. His first NFL game was on **Thanksgiving Day**, 26 November, and drew around 50,000 **fans** to see him play for the Chicago Bears against the Chicago Cardinals. This was reported by the Associated Press as nearly 40,000 more fans than had ever seen a **professional football** game previously. Grange hired promoter Charles C. "C. C." Pyle to be his manager. On 6 December, the Bears played the **New York Giants** at the Polo Grounds in New York and drew 70,000 fans. This saved the season for the Giants, who had been drawing poorly all year, and provided owner **Tim Mara** with the necessary cash to continue operating the franchise.

Pyle's promotional abilities earned Grange an additional $3,000 that night, as he was also the referee of an American Basketball League contest between the Original Celtics and the Washington Palace team in New York. By 7 December, Grange had signed a motion picture contract, and newspapers were estimating that he had earned $500,000 in the two weeks following his last college game by his share of the gate receipts and various other endorsements that Pyle had obtained for him.

In 1926, after a contract dispute with the Bears, Grange and Pyle formed their own football league, the **American Football League**. Pyle's team, the New York Yankees, featured Grange. The league failed, but the Yankees became members of the NFL in 1927. Grange injured his knee during that season and did not play in 1928. He returned to the Bears in 1929 and played for them through 1934. He was a member of Chicago's NFL championship team in 1932 and played for the Bears in the first NFL Championship Game in 1933.

Official statistics from Grange's professional career in the NFL are incomplete. In his eight years in the NFL, he scored at least 21 rushing touchdowns, 10 receiving touchdowns, and one touchdown on an **interception** return, and he passed for 10 touchdowns. He is also credited with at least two extra points. After retiring from the Bears, Grange worked as a motivational speaker and television football announcer. He was inducted into the **College Football Hall of Fame** in 1951 as a charter member, and also as a charter member to the **Pro Football Hall of Fame** in 1963.

GRANT, HARRY PETER, JR. "BUD." B. 20 May 1927, Superior, Wisconsin. Although Bud Grant was a star basketball player and a member of the National Basketball Association (NBA) champion Minneapolis Lakers in 1950, his major impact on the sports world was in the game of **football**. As a youth, he overcame polio and became active in sports. At Superior High School in Superior, Wisconsin, he played football, baseball, and basketball. After graduating in 1945, Grant enlisted in the U.S. Navy and was stationed at the Great Lakes Naval Training Center, where he played on their football team under **Coach Paul Brown**. After being discharged from the service, he enrolled at the **University of Minnesota**, where he played all three sports. In his three years as an offensive and defensive **end** on the Minnesota football **varsity** team, from 1947 to 1949, the team had a record of 20–7.

In December 1949, following the football season, Grant was declared academically ineligible for basketball, so he quit school and signed a professional contract with the Minneapolis Lakers of the NBA. At six feet, three inches tall and 195 pounds, he was the Lakers backup forward behind their starters and future Hall of Famers Vern Mikkelsen and Jim Pollard. He played the remainder of the 1949–1950 season with the Lakers, and they went on to win the league title. Two days after they defeated the Syracuse Nationals to win the NBA championship, Grant was selected by the Lakers in the fourth round of the NBA **Draft** in one of the peculiarities of that era's NBA. He continued with the Lakers in the 1950–1951 season and then quit professional basketball to play football. Grant played in 96 regular-season games during his two NBA seasons and averaged 2.6 points per game. He also played in 17 **playoff** games and averaged 3.2 points per game in playoff competition.

Grant had been chosen in the first round of the 1950 **National Football League (NFL)** Draft by the **Philadelphia Eagles** as the 14th overall selection, and, after deciding to concentrate on professional basketball at first and playing two seasons in the NBA, he elected to try **professional football** in 1951 and played with the Eagles as a defensive end. In 1952, he switched to offensive end and was second in the league in **pass receptions** and reception yardage. Grant played in all 12 games in each of his two years in the NFL,

1951 and 1952. In 1952, as an offensive end, he caught 56 passes for 997 yards and seven **touchdowns**.

In 1953, when he did not receive a contract that he thought was sufficient, Grant left the NFL to play for the **Winnipeg Blue Bombers** of the Western Interprovincial Football Union (WIFU) in Canada, a forerunner of the **Canadian Football League**. He played for the Blue Bombers from 1953 to 1956 as an offensive end and was selected to the WIFU all-star team in 1953, 1954, and 1956. He led the league in pass receptions each of those three years. In 1953, Grant was on the losing side in the **Grey Cup** final. In four seasons, he played in 64 regular-season games and caught 216 passes for 3,200 yards and 13 touchdowns.

In 1957, Grant became Winnipeg's coach and coached them from 1957 to 1966. In those 10 seasons, his teams compiled a record of 102–56–2 in regular-season games and 13–4 in playoff games. The Blue Bombers reached the Grey Cup final in six of the 10 years and were Grey Cup champions in 1958, 1959, 1961, and 1962.

Grant returned to the NFL in 1967 as the coach of the **Minnesota Vikings**. In his first year as their coach, the team only had a record of 3–8–3. They improved in 1968 and made the postseason playoffs for the first time in their history. From 1968 to 1978, the Vikings reached the playoffs in 10 of the 11 years and played in the **Super Bowl** in 1970, 1974, 1975, and 1977, albeit on the losing side in each of those four years. Grant retired as head coach after the 1983 season but was coaxed out of retirement to coach in 1985. Since that time, he has served the Vikings as a consultant and devotes much of his time to the outdoors and environmental conservation issues. He was inducted into the **Canadian Football Hall of Fame** as a builder in 1983 and the **Pro Football Hall of Fame** as a coach in 1994.

GREEN BAY PACKERS. The Green Bay Packers are one of the most famous teams in **professional football**. They began play in 1921 in the American Professional Football Association, the forerunner of the **National Football League (NFL)**. They have been the most successful team in the league, winning 13 championships—nine prior to the 1970 merger—and four **Super Bowls**. Their overall record from 1921 to 2012 is 690–530–36. They were named NFL champions in 1929, 1930, and 1931 based on their won-lost record. They won NFL championship **playoff** games in 1936, 1939, 1944, 1961, 1962, and 1965. They won the first two Super Bowls in 1966 and 1967, and won again in 1996 and 2010. Their overall postseason playoff record since 1921 is 29–17. They lost the NFL Championship Game in 1938 and 1960; an NFL Western Division tiebreaker playoff game in 1941; the Super Bowl in 1997; the National Football Conference (NFC) championship in 1995 and 2007; the NFC divisional playoff games in 1972, 1993, 1994, 2001, 2003, 2011, and 2012; an NFL second-round playoff in 1982; and the **wild-card playoff** in 1998, 2002, 2004, and 2009.

The Packers have played their home games at four different facilities, all in the city of Green Bay, Wisconsin, including Hagemeister Park in 1921 and 1922, Bellevue Park in 1923 and 1924, City Stadium from 1925 to 1956, and the New City Stadium (renamed **Lambeau Field**) since then. The seating capacity at Lambeau Field has gradually been increased from its initial 32,000 to its present-day 73,128. From 1933 to 1994, games were also played in the Milwaukee, Wisconsin, metropolitan area at Borchert Park in Milwaukee in 1933, Wisconsin State Fair Park in West Allis from 1934 to 1951, Marquette Stadium in 1952, and Milwaukee County Stadium from 1953 to 1994.

The Green Bay Packers are unique in that they represent a city with a population of only about 100,000 and are a publicly owned corporation that does not pay dividends, with about 110,000 shareholders holding about 4.5 million shares of stock. Packers' games have been sold out since 1960, and the waiting list for season tickets has more names than there are seats at Lambeau Field. Less than 100 tickets become available annually.

Their owner and head **coach** for 29 seasons (1921–1949) was **Earl "Curly" Lambeau**. Other Packers' head coaches include Gene Ronzani (1950–1953), Ray McLean (interim 1953, full season 1958), Hugh Devore (interim 1953), Lisle Blackbourn (1954–1957), **Vince Lombardi** (1959–1967), Phil Bengtson (1968–1970), Dan Devine (1971–1974), **Bart Starr** (1975–1983), Forrest Gregg (1984–1987), Lindy Infante (1988–1991), Mike Holmgren (1992–1998), Ray Rhodes (1999), Mike Sherman (2000–2005), and Mike McCarthy (2006–2012).

The Packers have 22 former players and coaches in the **Pro Football Hall of Fame**, second only to the **Chicago Bears**, who have 27. They include coaches Vince Lombardi and Earl "Curly" Lambeau (also a **halfback**); **quarterbacks** Arnie Herber and Bart Starr; offensive **backs** Tony Canadeo, Clarke Hinkle, **Paul Hornung**, **John "Blood" McNally**, and **Jim Taylor**; **end Don Hutson**; **wide receiver James Lofton**; offensive **linemen** Forrest Gregg, **Cal Hubbard**, Mike Michalske, and Jim Ringo; defensive linemen Willie Davis, Henry Jordan, and **Reggie White**; **linebackers Ray Nitschke** and Dave Robinson; and defensive backfield players **Herb Adderley** and Willie Wood.

Other noteworthy Packers players include quarterbacks **Brett Favre** and **Aaron Rodgers**; halfback Cecil Isbell; **running backs** Donny Anderson, Edgar Bennett, John Brockington, Jim Graboski, and Ahman Green; tailbacks Joseph "Red" Dunn and Verne Lewellen; ends and wide receivers Lavvie Dilweg, Boyd Dowler, Donald Driver, Billy Howton, Greg Jennings, Max

McGee, and Sterling Sharpe; offensive linemen Bill Curry, **Jerry Kramer**, and Fuzzy Thurston; defensive back Bob Jeter; linebacker Lee Roy Caffey; **kicker/punter** Don Chandler; nose **tackle** B. J. Raji; and **cornerback** Charles Woodson.

GREY CUP. The Grey Cup can be considered the **Super Bowl** of **Canadian football**. Its heritage, however, predates the Super Bowl by more than half a century. The phrase "Grey Cup" refers to both a trophy and the Canadian **football** game played for that trophy. The cup was donated and first presented by the governor general of Canada, Albert Henry George Grey, the 4th Earl Grey, to the winner of a contest on 4 December 1909 between the University of Toronto Varsity Blues and the Toronto Parkdale Canoe Club. The contest determined the best amateur **rugby** football team in Canada. Throughout the years, the Grey Cup has been contested annually (with the exception of 1916 to 1919), and the game is now played to determine the champion of the **Canadian Football League**. Until 1940, the site was the home field of one of the two contesting teams, but since then a neutral field has often been used and the game played in various cities throughout Canada, usually near the end of November. The game played on 25 November 2012, in Toronto, was the 100th in the series.

Unlike most other sports trophies, the actual Grey Cup is displayed throughout Canada at various events. It usually resides at the **Canadian Football Hall of Fame** but can be borrowed for display at events as diverse as a golf tournament or marketing exhibition. It has even traveled to Afghanistan to visit Canadian troops at Kandahar Air Base. *See also* APPENDIX G (for a list of Grey Cup champions).

GRIDIRON. A gridiron is a surface with parallel lines. A **football field** is often referred to as a gridiron due to the markings on early fields. The game of American **football** is sometimes also referred to as "gridiron football," especially in countries outside the United States.

GRIESE, ROBERT ALLEN "BOB." B. 3 February 1945, Evansville, Indiana. Bob and Brian Griese are a father and son who both played **quarterback** in the **National Football League (NFL)** and were members of **Super Bowl** teams, although Brian, as a backup quarterback, did not get to play in the Super Bowl game. Bob Griese played football for Rex Mundi High School in Evansville, Indiana, a Catholic high school that was only in existence from 1958 to 1972. After graduation, as an outstanding student athlete in baseball, basketball, and **football**, he was offered a football scholarship to **Purdue University** but also played on Purdue's baseball and basketball teams. Griese was Purdue's starting quarterback in his three **varsity** seasons there, from 1964 to 1966. During that time, Purdue compiled a record of 22–7–1, and the team emerged victorious in the **Rose Bowl** following the 1966 season.

The six-foot, one-inch, 190-pound Griese was selected in the first round of the 1967 National Football League–**American Football League (AFL)** common **draft** as the fourth overall selection by the **Miami Dolphins**. He played his entire **professional football** career with the Dolphins, initially in the AFL, and then the NFL, after the two leagues merged in 1970. He was a member of three Super Bowl teams, in 1972, 1973, and 1974, and was a Super Bowl champion the latter two years. In 1972, the Dolphins won all 14 games in the regular season and three **playoff** games, including the Super Bowl, to finish the season undefeated. They were the first NFL team to accomplish this feat and, through the 2012 season, the only NFL team to complete a season undefeated and untied.

In his 14-year NFL career, Griese played in 161 regular-season games, starting 151 of them. His won-lost record was 92–56–3. He completed 1,926 **passes** in 3,429 attempts for 25,092 yards and 192 **touchdowns** and ran 261 times for 994 yards and seven touchdowns. In 12 postseason games, he completed 112 of 208 passes for 1,467 yards and 10 touchdowns and ran 13 times for 84 yards and no touchdowns.

After retiring from active play, Griese turned to the broadcast booth and worked as a color commentator for several networks for both college and professional football games. His son, Brian, played **college football** for the **University of Michigan** and for Denver, Miami, Tampa Bay, and Chicago in the NFL from 1998 to 2008. Brian was a member of the 1998 Super Bowl-winning **Denver Broncos**, although as third-string quarterback he played in only one game that season and did not appear in the Super Bowl. He was also a member of the 2006 **Chicago Bears** who lost in the Super Bowl that season. Once again he was a backup quarterback and did not play in the Super Bowl game. Bob Griese was inducted into the **College Football Hall of Fame** in 1984 and the **Pro Football Hall of Fame** in 1990.

GRIFFIN, ARCHIE MASON. B. 21 August 1954, Columbus, Ohio. Archie Griffin is the only person to ever win the **Heisman Trophy** twice. As a **fullback** at Columbus' Eastmoor High School, he led his team to the city championship with a 267-yard effort in the championship game. He played four seasons at **Ohio State University** from 1972 to 1975, winning the Heisman Trophy in both 1974 and 1975. In those four years, Ohio State had a record of 40–5–1 and played in the **Rose Bowl** all four seasons. Griffin set a **National Collegiate Athletic Association** record (since broken) with 5,589 yards on 924 carries while at Ohio State.

Griffin was selected in the first round of the 1976 **National Football League (NFL) Draft** by the **Cincinnati Bengals** as the 24th overall selection. His **professional football** career was not nearly as successful as his college career, and his lack of size (five feet, nine inches and 190 pounds) as a **running back** was a factor. In his seven-year NFL career, all with the Bengals from 1976 to 1982, he played in 98 regular-season games, ran 691 times for 2,808 yards and seven **touchdowns**, and caught 192 **passes** for 1,607 yards and six touchdowns. On **option plays**, Griffin completed three of four passes for 39 yards and two touchdowns. He also returned 22 **kickoffs** for an average of 21.0 yards per return. In three postseason games, he ran five times for 25 yards and caught three passes for 14 yards. He played in the 1982 **Super Bowl**, where his Bengals lost to the **San Francisco 49ers**, 26–21. In his final season, injuries limited him to just 12 **rushing** attempts and 39 yards gained. Griffin was with the Bengals in 1983 but was on the injured reserve list and did not play. In 1984, he made a brief comeback with Jacksonville in the **United States Football League**.

After retiring from active play, Griffin returned to Ohio State, where he obtained his master's degree in business administration. He was assistant athletic director at Ohio State and president of the Ohio State Alumni Association. He also was on the board of directors for an insurance company in Columbus and is a part owner of a Minor League Baseball team. His younger brother, Keith, also played in the NFL. Archie was inducted into the **College Football Hall of Fame** in 1986.

GROZA, LOUIS ROY "LOU," "THE TOE." B. 25 January 1924, Martins Ferry, Ohio. D. 29 November 2000, Columbia Station, Ohio. Lou Groza was not only one of the premier **kickers** in **professional football** for more than 20 years, he was also one of the best offensive **tackles** of his era. He attended Martins Ferry High School in Martins Ferry, Ohio, where he played **football**, baseball, and basketball and was team captain in all three sports. The basketball team was state champion in 1941, and the football team was cochampion later that year. After graduating from high school, Groza entered **Ohio State University** and played football for **Coach Paul Brown**. He was only there one year before he was drafted into the U.S. Army.

Groza served three years during World War II. After his discharge from the military, he was signed by the **Cleveland Browns** of the new **All-America Football Conference (AAFC)**, where Brown was the head coach. Groza, at six feet, three inches and 240 pounds, remained with the Browns as their offensive tackle and placekicker as they joined the **National Football League (NFL)** in 1950 and played with them through 1959. He retired in 1960 following a back injury but was coaxed back into the NFL in 1961 solely as a placekicker and played the next seven years, retiring at the age of 42.

With the Browns, Groza was a member of the AAFC championship team each year from 1946 to 1949. In 1950, the Browns entered the NFL and again won their league championship. During his years with Cleveland, the Browns won the NFL title in 1950, 1954, 1955, and 1964, and lost in the NFL Championship Game in 1951, 1952, 1953, 1957, and 1965. In Groza's 21-year professional career, he played in the league Championship Game 13 times.

During his lengthy AAFC/NFL career, Groza played in 268 regular-season games and kicked 264 **field goals** in 481 attempts and 810 extra points in 833 attempts. He also caught a **pass** for a 23-yard **touchdown** in 1950. In 16 postseason games, he was a perfect 44 of 44 in extra point attempts and 13 of 27 in field goal attempts. There are no official statistics that adequately measure his play as a **lineman**. He played in nine **Pro Bowls**. When he retired, Groza held most of the NFL career kicking records, but they have since been surpassed. He is still fourth all-time in extra points made and third in extra points attempted.

Lou's younger brother, Alex, was the center for the 1948 and 1949 national collegiate basketball champions at the University of Kentucky. He also won a gold medal with the U.S. Men's **Olympic** Basketball Team in 1948 and played three seasons in the National Basketball Association. In a statistical anomaly, in 1950, both Alex and Lou lead their respective professional leagues in field goal percentage, although the statistic measured two different events. Lou was inducted into the **Pro Football Hall of Fame** in 1974.

GUARD. Guard is both an offensive and defensive **football position**. The two offensive guards line up on either side of the **center**. Their primary role is to **block** the opposition from reaching the ball carrier or **quarterback**. The **defense** may employ a player known as a nose guard to play opposite the offensive team's center. The nose guard's primary function is to attempt to stop the ball carrier on a **running** play or **tackle** the quarterback on an attempted **passing** play. On some teams, the nose guard was formerly known as the middle guard.

GUY, WILLIAM RAY "RAY." B. 22 December 1949, Swainsboro, Georgia. Ray Guy is acclaimed by many as the best **punter** in **football** history. He attended Thomson High School in Thomson, Georgia. At the University of Southern Mississippi, the six-foot, three-inch, 195-pound Guy played **safety** and occasionally **quarterback**, in addition to **punting** and placekicking. On 18 November 1972, he kicked a then-record 61-yard **field goal** in a heavy snowstorm. He also was credited with a 93-yard punt in college. He was the first punter to be selected in the first round of the **National Football League**

(**NFL**) **Draft**, when the **Oakland Raiders** chose him in 1973 as the 23rd overall selection.

One factor that made Guy an exceptional punter was his lengthy **hang time**. From 1973 to 1986, he played in 207 consecutive regular-season games with the Raiders, had a 42.4 yards per punt average for his NFL career, and was voted to the **Pro Bowl** seven times. In the postseason, he played in 22 games and had 111 punts for a 42.4 yards per punt average. He won three **Super Bowl** rings with the Raiders, in 1977, 1981, and 1984.

In 2000, the Greater Augusta Sports Council began presenting an annual Ray Guy Award to the nation's best collegiate punter. Since his retirement, Guy has also conducted periodic kicking camps throughout the country to instruct high school players in the kicking game. He was inducted into the **College Football Hall of Fame** in 2004 and has been a seven-time finalist and five-time semifinalist for the **Pro Football Hall of Fame** but, as of 2013, has not yet been enshrined there.

GUYON, JOSEPH NAPOLEON "JOE." B. 26 November 1892, White Earth, Minnesota. D. 27 November 1971, Louisville, Kentucky. Joe Guyon was a Native American of the Ojibwa Nation (also known as Chippewa). He was known as O-Gee-Chidah in Anishinaabe, the native tongue of the Ojibwe. He played **halfback** for **Coach Glenn "Pop" Warner** at the **Carlisle Indian Industrial School** in 1912 and 1913. During those two seasons, Carlisle's **football** teams had a record of 23–3–2. He later attended Keewatin Academy from 1914 to 1916 and **Georgia Tech** in 1917 and 1918, where he was coached by John Heisman and played **tackle**. On 3 November 1917, against Vanderbilt University, Guyon was used as a **back** and recorded an incredible 344 yards **rushing** in just 12 carries. Georgia Tech was national champion that year.

In 1919, Guyon began playing **professional football** for the Canton Bulldogs, coached by **Jim Thorpe**, a former star at Carlisle. The following year, the Bulldogs joined the newly formed American Professional Football Association, the predecessor of the **National Football League (NFL)**. The five-foot, 10-inch, 195-pound Guyon played various back positions for several teams from 1920 to 1927, including two years, 1922 and 1923, with the **Oorang Indians**, an NFL team comprised solely of Native Americans. Ironically, one of the NFL teams he played with was the Kansas City Cowboys in 1925. He concluded his NFL career by playing for the **New York Giants** in 1927 and helping them win the NFL championship that year. Unfortunately for modern-day football **fans**, Guyon's NFL statistics are incomplete. He scored at least 10 **touchdowns**, seven rushing, one receiving, and two on **interception** returns. He also kicked at least 13 extra points.

From 1920 to 1936, Guyon played the outfield in Minor League Baseball, where he had a lifetime batting average of .329. He was also a manager in the minors for three different teams in 1931, 1932, and 1936. Guyon worked as a baseball coach at Union University in 1924 and 1926, and at Clemson University from 1928 to 1931. From 1931 to 1933, he was the **high school football** coach at St. Xavier High School in Louisville, Kentucky. Guyon was inducted into the **Pro Football Hall of Fame** in 1966 and the **College Football Hall of Fame** in 1971.

HAIL MARY. A Hail Mary is a desperation **pass** thrown into the **end zone** with a few seconds remaining in the half or the game. The name derives from the **quarterback** throwing the ball and saying a prayer that it will be caught. **Roger Staubach**, in 1975, is said to be the originator of the expression. *See also* FLUTIE, DOUGLAS RICHARD "DOUG."

HALAS, GEORGE STANLEY, SR. "PAPA BEAR." B. 2 February 1895, Chicago, Illinois. D. 3 October 1983, Chicago, Illinois. George Halas was one of the founding fathers of the **National Football League (NFL)**. He was a member of the league when it organized in 1920 as the American Professional Football Association (APFA) and was still **coaching** in the league in 1967. He was a graduate of Crane Technical High School in Chicago, Illinois, and the **University of Illinois** with a degree in civil engineering. He played **football**, baseball, and basketball at Illinois and was a member of their 1918 **Big Ten Conference** cochampionship team. After graduation, Halas served in the U.S. Navy and played football for the Great Lakes Naval Station team. During World War I, the **Rose Bowl** invited service teams to participate, and he played **end** on the victorious Great Lakes team in the 1 January 1919 Rose Bowl game. Halas caught a 32-yard **touchdown pass** and **intercepted** a pass, returning it for 77 yards before being **tackled** on the three-**yard line**. For his efforts, he was named the 1919 Rose Bowl Most Valuable Player.

Halas signed with the New York Yankees Major League Baseball team and played right field for them in 12 games in 1919, batting only .091 with just two hits in 22 times at bat. He also played for their minor-league farm team, the St. Paul Saints, and appeared in 39 games with a .274 batting average.

Halas was given a job by the A. E. Staley Company, a starch manufacturer in Decatur, Illinois, as a sales representative and player on their company baseball team, as well as player-coach of their company football team. In 1920, he represented the company at a meeting held in Canton, Ohio, with representatives from other independent football teams. This gathering resulted in the formation of the APFA. The Decatur Staleys were one of the 14 teams that played in the inaugural year of that league. The six-foot, one-inch, 180 pound Halas played end and also coached the team. The Staleys won more games than any of the other APFA teams and finished with a record of 10–1–2, but they were placed second in the league standings, behind the Akron Pros, who finished at 8–0–3.

In 1921, Augustus E. Staley had had enough of **professional football** and transferred control of the team to Halas, who relocated them to Chicago. That year, the Staleys finished with a record of 9–1–1 and were declared champions of the league, even though the Buffalo All-Americans disputed their claim and league historians feel that Buffalo was swindled out of the title. The following year, the APFA was renamed the National Football League, and Halas renamed his Staleys the **Chicago Bears**.

He continued as player-coach through 1928 and coached the team in 1929 but did not play. In 1930, Halas retained team ownership but did not coach. Ralph Jones was the team's coach from 1930 to 1932, and he led the Bears to the NFL championship in 1932. Halas returned as coach in 1933, and, once again, the Bears were league champions; this time, however, the league was divided into two divisions and an NFL Championship Game was held after the regular season matching the two division winners.

Halas continued as the Bears' coach through the 1942 season and led them to the NFL Championship Game in 1934, 1937, 1940, 1941, and 1942. They demolished the **Washington Redskins** in the 1940 NFL championship by the record-setting score of 73–0 and won the championship over the **New York Giants** in 1941, 37–9. The team lost the NFL Championship Game in 1934, 1937, and 1942.

Following the 1942 season, at the age of 47, Halas enlisted in the U.S. Navy and served until 1946, when he was discharged with the rank of captain. He returned to the Bears for the 1946 season and was their coach through 1955. His former Great Lakes teammate John "Paddy" Driscoll coached the Bears in 1956 and 1957, but Halas returned as coach in 1958 and remained in that capacity through the 1967 season. In that time, the Bears won the league championship again in 1946 and 1963.

Halas was the Bears' owner until his death in 1983 from pancreatic cancer, although from 1963 to 1979, his son, George Jr., was the team's president. In Halas's 40 years as the Bears' coach, his teams had a record of 318–148–31 and won six NFL championships. In 1997, he was honored on a U.S. commemorative postage stamp, along with **Paul "Bear" Bryant**, **Glenn "Pop" Warner**, and **Vince Lombardi**. Halas was inducted into the **Pro Football Hall of Fame** as a charter member in the category of coach in 1963.

HALFBACK. Halfback is an offensive **football position**. Teams generally use two halfbacks who are stationed near the **quarterback** behind the **line of scrimmage** and whose functions are to **run** with the ball, **block**, or receive a **pass**. Modern football offensive alignments often use one halfback as a **wide**

receiver whose primary function is to catch passes. Modern terminology often refers to the other halfback as a **running back**, and his primary role is to carry the ball.

HALFTIME. Halftime is the intermission between the first and second halves of a **football** game. The length of the intermission varies but is generally between 10 and 20 minutes. In **National Football League** rules, the length is officially 12 minutes. There is also a two-minute intermission between the first and second quarters and between the third and fourth quarters. The **National Collegiate Athletic Association** uses a 20-minute halftime intermission with a one-minute intermission between quarters. Television requirements often lengthen the intermission intervals.

College football traditionally featured performances by the home school's marching band and occasionally the visiting team's band as well. **Professional football** also used to feature performances by marching bands. In recent years, however, this is rarely the case in professional football, although most colleges still maintain the tradition. Modern halftime entertainment in professional football often features routines by dance teams, contests for selected **fans**, or ceremonies honoring former players or alumni.

HAMILTON TIGER-CATS. The Hamilton Tiger-Cats are a **professional football** team in the **Canadian Football League (CFL)**. They were founded in 1950 by a merger of the Hamilton Tigers and Hamilton Wildcats. In 1869, the Hamilton Football Club began, and, in 1873, the club was renamed the Hamilton Tigers. In 1907, they joined the new Interprovincial Rugby Football Union (IRFU). The Hamilton Wildcats began play in the Ontario Rugby Football Union (ORFU) in 1941. In 1948, the Wildcats moved to the IRFU, and the Tigers moved to the ORFU. After the merger in 1950, the Tiger-Cats played in the IRFU, which became part of the CFL in 1958. The Tiger-Cats have played home games at the 29,600-seat Ivor Wynne Stadium in Hamilton, Ontario, since 1950. A proposed new **stadium**, tentatively called Pan-American Stadium, is scheduled to open in Hamilton in 2014.

The team has played in 18 **Grey Cup** games since 1950, winning eight of them. Their most notable head **coaches** include Carl Voyles (1950–1955), Jim Trimble (1956–1962), Ralph Sazio (1963–1967), Jerry Williams (1972–1975), Al Bruno (1983–1990), Ron Lancaster (1998–2003), and Marcel Bellefeuille (2008–2011).

Canadian Football Hall of Fame players who played for Hamilton include John Barrow, Tommy Joe Coffey, Grover Covington, Rocky DiPietro, Matt Dunigan, Bernie Faloney, Darren Flutie, Tony Gabriel, Garney Henley, Ellison Kelly, Joe Montford, Angelo Mosca, Peter Neumann, Hal Peterson,

Ralph Sazio, Vince Scott, Dave S. Sprague, Don Sutherin, Brian Timmis, Earl Winfield, and Ben Zambiasi. Other notable Hamilton players include Damon Allen, Chuck Ealey, Danny McManus, and Don McPherson.

HANG TIME. Hang time is a measure of the time a **punted football** is in the air. The advantage of a high hang time is that the punting team's players have more time to get downfield to stop a punt return. **Ray Guy** and Reggie Roby were **punters** known for their ability to achieve a high hang time.

HARRIS, FRANCO. B. 7 March 1950, Fort Dix, New Jersey. Franco Harris played in the **National Football League (NFL)** for 13 years, yet he is remembered most for one catch that he made during his rookie year. On 23 December 1972, with his **Pittsburgh Steelers** losing, 7–6, in the American Football Conference divisional **playoff** game with no **time-outs** left, 22 seconds remaining in the game, and the ball on the **Oakland Raiders' 40-yard line**, Pittsburgh **quarterback Terry Bradshaw's pass** was deflected and caught at the shoe tops by Harris, who continued **running** with it and scored the winning **touchdown**. The play was dubbed the **"Immaculate Reception"** by Pittsburgh sportswriter Myron Cope.

Harris attended Rancocas Valley Regional High School in Mount Holly Township, New Jersey, and continued his education at **Penn State University**. He played on the **varsity** from 1969 to 1971 and shared the team's running **offense** with Lydell Mitchell. During those three years, the Nittany Lions were undefeated in 1969 and had a record of 29–4, with victories in the **Orange Bowl** in 1969 and **Cotton Bowl** in 1971.

Harris was selected by the Pittsburgh Steelers in the first round of the 1972 NFL **Draft** as the 13th overall selection. The six-foot, two-inch, 230-pound Harris was the Steelers' **running back** and **fullback** for the next 12 seasons. He played on four **Super Bowl** championship teams during that time and was voted the 1974 Super Bowl Most Valuable Player. After being refused a pay raise following the 1983 season, he was released by the Steelers and signed with the **Seattle Seahawks** as a free agent. After one season with the Seahawks, he retired. At the time of his retirement, Harris was third in career **rushing** yardage behind **Jim Brown** and **Walter Payton** but has since slipped to 13th place on that list.

In his 13-year NFL career, Harris played in 173 regular-season games, ran 2,949 times for 12,120 yards and 91 touchdowns, and caught 307 passes for 2,287 yards and nine touchdowns. In 19 postseason games, he ran 400 times for 1,556 yards and 16 touchdowns and caught 51 passes for 504 yards and one touchdown. He played in nine **Pro Bowls**.

Since retiring from active play, he and Mitchell have become partners in a bakery and a sausage company. In 2008, Harris was one of Pennsylvania's

21 presidential electors and cast his ballot for Barack Obama in the electoral college vote. He was inducted into the **Pro Football Hall of Fame** in 1990.

HARRISON, MARVIN DANIEL. B. 25 August 1972, Philadelphia, Pennsylvania. Marvin Harrison attended Roman Catholic High School in Philadelphia and **Syracuse University**. He graduated from Syracuse in 1995 with a degree in retailing. As a **wide receiver** there, the six-foot, 175-pound Harrison set a school record for career receiving yardage.

Harrison was chosen by the **Indianapolis Colts** in the first round of the 1996 **National Football League (NFL) Draft** as the 19th overall selection. He played with the Colts from 1996 to 2008 and was a member of the Colts' winning **Super Bowl** team in 2007. In 2002, he caught 143 **passes** and set the NFL season record in that category. Harrison also holds numerous less significant NFL records. These include most consecutive seasons, with at least 10 **touchdown receptions**, with eight; and most receiving yards in a four-season period, with 6,322 from 1999 to 2002.

In his 13-year professional career, Harrison played in 190 of 208 regular-season games. He is third on the all-time list of NFL pass catchers with 1,102 passes caught, sixth all-time with 14,580 yards on receptions, and ninth all-time with 128 touchdowns. He was also used as a **punt returner** his first year in the league and returned 18 punts for 177 yards. In 16 postseason games, Harrison caught 65 passes for 883 yards and two touchdowns. He was named to the **Pro Bowl** team eight times. A knee injury in 2007 caused him to miss most of that season, and, after playing in 2008, he decided to retire. Harrison owns several businesses in Philadelphia, including a car wash and a sports bar.

HARVARD STADIUM. Harvard Stadium is one of the oldest **football** venues in the United States. It was built in 1903 and remains in continuous use by the **Harvard University** football team. It was also the home of the Boston Patriots of the **National Football League** in 1970. The facility's seating capacity has been as much as 57,166, but structural modifications throughout the years have reduced the present-day capacity to 30,323. Changes made in 2006 included the addition of lights; the change from natural grass to an artificial turf; and the removal of ivy from the walls of the stadium, which helped give rise to the phrase "**Ivy League**." On 27 February 1987, Harvard Stadium was named a National Historic Landmark.

HARVARD UNIVERSITY. Harvard University is located in Cambridge, Massachusetts, a suburb of Boston. Their **football** program began in 1873, and, since then, through 2012, Crimson teams have compiled a record of 830–383–50. Their only postseason **bowl game** was the 1920 **Rose Bowl**, in which they defeated the University of Oregon, 7–6. Since then, as a member of the **Ivy League**, they do not compete in bowl games. Harvard has been selected as national collegiate champions 12 times, but none since 1921. They were selected in 1874, 1875, 1890, 1898, 1899, 1901, 1908, 1910, 1912, 1913, 1919, and 1920. Their main rival is **Yale University**. The teams have met nearly annually since 1875 in a contest simply known as "The Game." Through 2012, Yale leads in the series, 65–56–8. Since 1903, Harvard has played home games at the historic **Harvard Stadium** in Boston, which currently seats 30,323 and is the oldest **stadium** in the United States still in use.

Harvard's most notable **coach** was Percy Haughton. He coached the Crimson from 1908 to 1916 and had a record of 72–7–5. His remarkable winning percentage of .887 was actually bettered by several 19th-century and early 20th-century Harvard coaches who coached for fewer years, including co-coaches George Stewart and George Adams (1890–1892; 34–2; .944), co-coaches George Stewart and Everett Lake (1893; 12–1; .923); William Cameron Forbes (1897–1898; 21–1–1; .935), Benjamin Dibblee (1899–1900; 20–1–1; .932), John Farley (1902; 11–1; .917), and Bill Reid (1901, 1905–1906; 30–3–1; .897). More recent Harvard coaches that have been successful include Bob Fisher (1919–1925; 43–14–5), John Yovicsin (1957–1970; 78–42–5), Joe Restic (1971–1993; 117–97–6), and Tim Murphy (1994–2012; 128–61).

There are 17 Harvard alumni in the **College Football Hall of Fame** and three former Harvard coaches. They are **fullbacks** Charley Brewer, Ned Mahan, and Bill Reid; **end** Dave Campbell; **halfbacks** Eddie Casey, George Owen, and Percy Wendell; **quarterbacks** Charles Daly and Barry Wood; **guards** Bob Fisher, Endicott "Chub" Peabody, and Stan Pennock; end/halfback Huntington Hardwick; **centers** Ben Ticknor and William H. Lewis (the first African American **college football** player and future U.S. assistant attorney general); **tackle** Marshall Newell; and coaches Dick Harlow, Percy Haughton, and Lloyd Jordan. One of the more illustrious Harvard graduates in the College Football Hall of Fame is tackle Hamilton Fish III, who lived to the age of 102 and followed in the footsteps of his grandfather and father and became a U.S. congressman. His son also became a congressman. Through 2012, there have been 28 **National Football League** players who have attended Harvard and one **American Football League** player, including Matt Birk, John Dockery, Ryan Fitzpatrick, Dan Jiggetts, Isaiah Kacyvenski, and Pat McNally.

HAYES, ROBERT LEE "BOB," "BULLET BOB." B. 20 December 1942, Jacksonville, Florida. D. 18 September 2002, Jacksonville, Florida. At one time in his life, Bob Hayes was the world's fastest human. He won the 100-meter dash in the 1964 **Olympic Games** in 10.0 seconds, equaling the world record. He also ran the anchor leg for the U.S. team in that Olympics and won a second gold medal when that team also set a world record. In 1963, he set the world record for the 100 yards and the indoor record for 60 yards. Hayes attended Matthew Gilbert High School in Jacksonville, Florida, and played **football**, as well as ran track. In 1958, he was a member of the state's high school championship football team. He then enrolled at Florida A&M University, a historically black school.

Based on his track exploits, Hayes was selected by the **Dallas Cowboys** in the seventh round (88th overall) in the 1964 **National Football League (NFL) Draft** and by the **Denver Broncos** in the 14th round (105th overall) in the 1964 **American Football League (AFL)** Draft. He signed with neither team to preserve his amateur status and eligibility for the Olympic Games, held that year in Tokyo in October.

After his triumph in the Olympic Games, Hayes signed with the Dallas Cowboys and began his **professional football** career with them in 1965. A powerful runner, at six feet tall and 185 pounds, he played as a **pass** receiver and **punt** and **kickoff returner**. His incredible speed (giving him the nickname "Bullet Bob") caused a change in defensive strategy, as no single defensive **back** was able to keep up with him and zone pass **defenses** began to be used. Hayes played for the Cowboys from 1965 to 1974 and was a member of their losing **Super Bowl** team in 1971 and Super Bowl championship team in 1972. He concluded his professional football career in 1975, playing a few games for the **San Francisco 49ers**.

In his 11-year NFL career, Hayes played in 132 regular-season games, caught 371 passes for 7,414 yards and 71 **touchdowns**, and ran 24 times for 68 yards and two touchdowns. As a kick and punt returner, he returned 23 kickoffs for a 25.3-yard average return and returned 104 punts for an 11.1-yard average return and three touchdowns. In 14 postseason games, he caught 31 passes for 492 yards and two touchdowns, ran once for 16 yards, and returned one kickoff for 16 yards and 12 punts for 151 yards. Hayes played in three **Pro Bowls**. He was inducted into the **Pro Football Hall of Fame** in 2009.

HAYES, WAYNE WOODROW "WOODY." B. 14 February 1913, Clifton, Ohio. D. 12 March 1987, Upper Arlington, Ohio. Woody Hayes was one of **football's** most dedicated, hardworking, and single-minded **coaches**. He hated to lose, and that desire eventually proved to be his downfall. He attended Newcomerstown High School in Newcomerstown, Ohio, a small town in northeastern Ohio between Akron and Columbus. He played **center** on his high school's football team and continued his education at Denison University, where he played **tackle**. After his graduation in 1935, Hayes was an **assistant coach** at Mingo Junction High School from 1935 to 1936, and New Philadelphia High School in 1937. In 1938, he became head coach at New Philadelphia and held that position until 1940.

Hayes enlisted in the U.S. Navy in 1941 and served during World War II until he was honorably discharged with the rank of lieutenant commander. Following his discharge, he was hired as head coach at his alma mater, Denison University. He coached there from 1946 to 1948, and Denison was undefeated in both 1947 and 1948, with a 19-game winning streak that began in 1946.

Hayes was offered the head coaching position at Miami University of Ohio and was there in 1949 and 1950, finishing the 1950 season with a 9–1 record and postseason victory. **Ohio State University** hired him next, and it was there that he spent the rest of his coaching career, from 1951 to 1978. During his 28 seasons at Ohio State, his teams compiled a record of 205–61–10, won nine national championships, and had a 4–4 record in **Rose Bowl** games and a 1–2 record in other major **bowl games**.

Hayes's final game as head coach was the Gator Bowl game on 29 December 1978. As the game neared its end, Ohio State was trailing Clemson by two points, 17–15. Ohio State had the ball and was driving toward a possible game-winning score when a Clemson defensive player **intercepted** the ball. As he was pushed **out of bounds**, Hayes ran toward him and punched him and then ran after the referee. Hayes was ejected from the game and no further incident ensued. The day after the game, Hayes was fired, ending a 28-year career at Ohio State. He was known for his volatile temper and had been involved in previous incidents, although none quite as severe as that one, which incidentally was broadcast on national television.

Hayes remained at Ohio State and worked in the U.S. Navy recruiting office. As a naval historian, he hosted a television series during the 1980s about World War II. He was inducted into the **College Football Hall of Fame** as a coach in 1983 and died in his sleep of an apparent heart attack in 1987.

HEAD COACH. *See* COACH.

HEAD LINESMAN. *See* OFFICIALS.

HEFFELFINGER, WILLIAM WALTER "PUDGE." B. 20 December 1867, Minneapolis, Minnesota. D. 2 April 1954, Blessing, Texas (some sources erroneously list the date as 5 April, but an Associated Press obituary appears in 3 April 1954 newspapers). William "Pudge" Heffelfinger is hardly a household name today, but, in the 19th century, he was one of **football's** best-known names. After graduating from Central High School in Minneapolis, Minnesota, he was a member of **Yale University's** football teams from 1888 to 1891. He also won the Yale heavyweight boxing championship, was a weight thrower on the track team, and was a rower on the **varsity** crew. A big man for his era, at six feet, three inches and 195 pounds, he played **guard** on the football team and was considered to be the greatest **lineman** in the sport at that time. During the four years that Heffelfinger was part of the team, Yale's football squad compiled a record of 54–2, outscored opponents 2,329–49, and was national champions in 1888 and 1891. Yale's won-lost record and points scored for and against in that time were as follows: 1888, 13–0/694–0; 1889, 15–1/661–31; 1890, 13–1/486–18; 1891, 13–0/488–0.

After his graduation from Yale, Heffelfinger worked in a railroad office in Omaha, Nebraska. As was the custom of the times, local athletic associations often scheduled football games against one another, with some of the better players receiving expense money. Heffelfinger joined the Chicago Athletic Association in 1892. Later that year, he was paid a bonus of $500, in addition to his $25 expenses to play for the Allegheny Athletic Association in a game against the Pittsburgh Athletic Club. He thus became the first "official" **professional football** player. In 1896, he was again paid by Allegheny and received $100 for each of two games.

Heffelfinger was employed by the **University of California** in 1893 as their football **coach** and led them to a record of 5–1–1. The following year, Lehigh University hired him as football coach. They finished the 1894 season with a record of 5–9. In 1895, he returned home to Minnesota and coached the **University of Minnesota's** team to a 7–3 record. From 1896 to 1910, Heffelfinger was a volunteer coach at Minnesota and often helped the Yale football team as well. Even though he was nearly 50 years of age, he would still scrimmage with the college players.

Heffelfinger founded Heffelfinger Publications and published an annual entitled *Heffelfinger's Football Facts*. In Minneapolis, he was involved in a shoe business and real estate, was an elected county commissioner, and ran for U.S. Congress in 1930 unsuccessfully. He retired to Blessing, Texas, where he died. Heffelfinger was inducted into the **College Football Hall of Fame** as a charter member in 1951.

HEIN, MELVIN JACK "MEL." B. 22 August 1909, Redding, California. D. 31 January 1992, San Clemente, California. Mel Hein was raised in the state of Washington and attended Burlington Union High School in Burlington, Washington, playing basketball as well as **football**. As an offensive **center** and defensive **lineman** on the football team, he was named the county's Most Valuable Player his senior year. He attended Washington State University, where he helped lead the Huskies to the **Rose Bowl** in 1931.

Following graduation in 1931, Hein signed with the **New York Giants** of the **National Football League (NFL)**. He played both center and **linebacker** with the Giants from 1931 to 1945, logging nearly 60 minutes of every game for 15 seasons, 170 regular-season games and eight **playoff** games in total. The Giants played in the NFL Championship Game seven times during Hein's career, winning the title in 1934 and 1938 and losing in 1933, 1935, 1939, 1941, and 1944. They also finished **tied** with the **Washington Redskins** in 1943 but lost a playoff to determine the division champion. Hein was named the NFL Most Valuable Player in 1938 and selected to play in the first four **Pro Bowls** from 1938 to 1941.

In 1943, Hein was assistant professor of physical education and head **coach** at Union College while still playing in the NFL. After he retired from the NFL, he became a coach and shared the coaching responsibilities of the **Los Angeles Dons** for three games in 1947. He was also an **assistant coach** with the **New York Yankees** and Los Angeles Rams of the NFL and the **University of Southern California**. From 1966 to 1969, Hein was the supervisor of **officials** of the **American Football League (AFL)**. After the AFL–NFL merger in 1970, he was the supervisor of officials of the American Football Conference of the NFL. Hein was inducted into the **College Football Hall of Fame** in 1954 and the **Pro Football Hall of Fame** as a charter member in 1963.

HEISMAN TROPHY. The Heisman Trophy is the most prestigious individual collegiate **football** award. It was originally presented by the Downtown Athletic Club (DAC) in 1935 to the player deemed to be the most outstanding player in collegiate football and was known simply as the Downtown Athletic Club Trophy. Following the death of the DAC's athletic director, John Heisman, a former **college football** player and **coach**, the award was renamed the Heisman Memorial Trophy.

Following the events of 11 September 2001, the DAC was closed. The club was located south of the World Trade Center, and, while not damaged, the area in which it was located was closed to the public during the cleanup. As a result, the club declared bankruptcy in 2002. The Yale Club took over responsibility for the Heisman Trophy and, from 2002 to 2004, made the presentation. Since 2005, the Heisman Trust has presented the award.

The recipients have invariably been offensive **backs** and receivers. Charles Woodson, a **cornerback** and **punt returner** who won the award in 1997, is the lone exception. Through 2012, 37 different schools have been represented by Heisman Trophy winners, with the **University of Notre Dame**, **Ohio State University**, and the **University of Southern California** each having seven recipients. The award is usually presented to a player who is in his senior year at school, although from 2007 to 2009 it went to a sophomore. **Archie Griffin, running back** from Ohio State, is the only person to win the award twice. He won it in 1974 and 1975. In 2012, Johnny Manziel of **Texas A&M** became the first freshman to win the award. *See also* APPENDIX N (for a list of winners).

HELMET. The **football** helmet is a protective device covering most of the player's head. Modern helmets also contain a **face mask**. The use of protective head gear began in the 1890s. The helmet was made of leather and offered some protection. As players became bigger, stronger, and faster, better helmets were designed out of various synthetic plastic materials.

HESTER, DEVIN. B. 4 November 1982, Riviera Beach, Florida. Devin Hester is one of the **National Football League's (NFL)** most exciting players of the 21st century. A return specialist, through the 2012 season, he has scored five **touchdowns** on **kickoff** returns, including two in one game on 11 December 2006, and an NFL record 12 touchdowns on **punt** returns (four in 2007, another NFL record). Hester also has a 108-yard touchdown **run** on a missed **field goal** attempt. In the 4 February 2007 **Super Bowl**, he scored a touchdown on the opening kickoff with a 92-yard return, the first time this has been accomplished in Super Bowl history.

Hester attended Suncoast Community High School in Riviera Beach, Florida, and the **University of Miami** in Florida. While at Miami, he played both **offense** and **defense** and was a kick **returner** on **special teams**. In his four years in college, Miami compiled a record of 41–9 and played in a **bowl game** each of the four years.

Hester was chosen by the **Chicago Bears** in the second round of the 2006 NFL **Draft** as the 57th overall selection and has played for the Bears from 2006 to 2012 as a defensive **back, wide receiver**, and return specialist. In his seven-year NFL career through 2012, Hester has played in 107 regular-season games, caught 217 **passes** for 2,807 yards and 14 touchdowns, and run 30 times for 80 yards and no touchdowns. As one of the NFL's greatest return specialists, he has returned 246 punts for an average return of 12.1 yards and 12 touchdowns and returned 170 kickoffs for an average return of 23.9 yards and five touchdowns, including touchdown runs of 96, 97, and 98 yards. He has played in five postseason games, caught two passes for four yards and no touchdowns, returned nine kickoffs for 214 yards and one touchdown, and 11 punts for 78 yards and no touchdowns.

HIGH SCHOOL FOOTBALL. In many high schools in the United States, **football** is one of the school sports. High school football rules vary slightly from **college football** and **professional football**, with the major one being the length of the game. The National Federation of State High School Associations is the national body that sets the rules for high school play. In some parts of the country, most notably Texas and Ohio, high school football is nearly as popular as the college and professional game. In many parts of the country, high school football is played on Friday night so as not to conflict with the college games on Saturday or the professional games on Sunday. Top high school players are actively recruited by colleges, and scholarships are offered to them. Throughout much of the 20th century, high school athletes often played football in the fall, played basketball in the winter, and played baseball or ran track in the spring, although in recent years players have begun to specialize in just one sport.

HIRSCH, ELROY "CRAZYLEGS." B. 17 June 1923, Wausau, Wisconsin. D. 28 January 2004, Madison, Wisconsin. Elroy Hirsch played **football** at Wausau High School in Wausau, Wisconsin. He attended the **University of Wisconsin** in 1942 and, while playing **halfback** there, was nicknamed "Crazylegs" by a Chicago sportswriter for his unusual **running** style. He enrolled in the U.S. Navy V-12 college training program as a Marine Corps officer candidate and was required to transfer to the **University of Michigan** in 1943 to participate in the program. At Michigan, Hirsch played football, basketball, and baseball and was a broad jumper on the track team. In 1945, he played football for the El Toro marine team.

Hirsch was picked by the Cleveland Rams in the first round of the 1945 **National Football League (NFL) Draft** as the fifth overall selection, but he signed with the Chicago Rockets of the new **All-America Football Conference (AAFC)**. He played with the Rockets from 1946 to 1948 but was injured for much of that time and only played in 24 of their scheduled 42 games. One of those injuries was a skull fracture, and for added protection following the injury, he became one of the first players to wear a plastic **helmet**, similar to ones used today, rather than the leather one used by his contemporaries. In 1949, Hirsch was signed by the Rams, who had since moved to Los Angeles, and he played for them for the next nine seasons at **end** and halfback. In 1951, he set the NFL season record for most yards gained as a **pass** receiver, with 1,495 in 12 games. The record lasted until 1984, when it was broken by Roy Green in a 16-game season.

In his 12-year combined AAFC/NFL career, Hirsch played in 127 regular-season games, ran 207 times for 687 yards and three **touchdowns**, made an additional touchdown after receiving a **lateral**, and caught 387 passes for 7,029 yards and 60 touchdowns. He also threw 22 passes and completed 12 for 156 yards and one touchdown. He was used as a **punt** and kick **returner** and had 21 punt returns for an average of 13.6 yards per punt and 21 **kickoff** returns for an average return of 27.0 yards per kickoff. Hirsch scored one touchdown on a punt return and one on a kickoff return. As was common for players of his era, he also played **defense** and recorded 15 **interceptions** and two **fumble** recoveries. He was also occasionally used as a placekicker and made nine extra points in 12 attempts. With the Rams, Hirsch played in the NFL Championship Game in 1949, 1950, 1951, and 1955 and was a member of the NFL champions in 1951. He played in the **Pro Bowl** in 1951, 1952, and 1953.

Hirsch played himself in a 1953 Hollywood film about his life entitled *Crazylegs*. He followed that role with the lead in the 1955 prison film *Unchained* (which featured the poignant song "Unchained Melody"). He also had a leading role in the 1957 film *Zero Hour* and appeared in numerous television dramas.

After retiring from the NFL, Hirsch was an assistant to the president of the Rams and director of athletics at the University of Wisconsin. He was inducted into the **Pro Football Hall of Fame** in 1968 and the **College Football Hall of Fame** in 1974. He died of natural causes at the age of 80 while living at an assisted living facility. *See also* FOOTBALL FILMS.

HOLDER. The holder is a **football position** on placekicking plays (**field goals** and **conversions**). The holder receives the snap from the **center** and places the ball down on its end so that the placekicker can kick it. The holder is usually either a **punter** or backup **quarterback** who has good hands and is used to handling the **football**.

HOLDING. Holding, or illegal use of hands, is an infraction that results in a **penalty**. Offensive **linemen** are not allowed to use their hands on the outside of a defender's body while **blocking**. The penalty is 10 yards. The ball is moved back 10 yards and the **down** is replayed. Defensive holding can be assessed when a defender uses his hands to push or hold an offensive **pass** receiver beyond five yards past the **line of scrimmage**. The penalty is five yards. The ball is advanced and an automatic **first down** is credited.

HOMECOMING. Homecoming is an annual event at most colleges and universities and many high schools in the United States. A weekend is set aside, usually during the **football** season if the school has a team, and alumni are invited back to attend special events, dinners, and a sports event. This tradition began at some schools in the early 20th century.

HOPKINS, EDWARD J. "TED." *See* NESSER FAMILY.

HORNUNG, PAUL VERNON "GOLDEN BOY." B. 23 December 1935, Louisville, Kentucky. Paul Hornung was one of the **National Football**

League's (**NFL**) best-looking players during the 1950s and 1960s and was nicknamed "Golden Boy" for his blond hair and good looks. He also was one of the league's best players, and, since he scored both **touchdowns** and kicked extra points and **field goals**, he set an NFL scoring record that was not broken for 46 years, and then only because the schedule had increased from 12 to 16 games per team.

Hornung attended Bishop Benedict Joseph Flaget High School in Louisville, Kentucky, where he played baseball, basketball, and **football** for each of his four years there. He received a scholarship to the **University of Notre Dame** and played on the **varsity** football team in 1954, 1955, and 1956. Extremely versatile, he played **quarterback**, **halfback**, and defensive **back** and was also their **punter**, placekicker, and kick **returner**. During those four years, the Fighting Irish had records of 9–1, 8–2, and 2–8. Yet, even though they had a poor record of 2–8 in 1956, Hornung was still awarded the **Heisman Trophy** as the nation's best collegiate player. He is the only player from a losing team ever to receive the award.

Hornung was selected by the **Green Bay Packers** as the first overall choice in the 1957 NFL **Draft** and played his entire **professional football** career with them, from 1957 to 1966. In 1957 and 1958, the Packers did not do well and finished last in the NFL West Division. In 1959, **Vince Lombardi** became their **coach**, and they improved to third place. By 1960, they were one of the league's best teams and reached the NFL Championship Game but were defeated by the **Philadelphia Eagles**. The Packers were NFL champions in 1961 and 1962.

Following the 1962 season, NFL commissioner **Alvin "Pete" Rozelle** conducted an investigation and found that there were some players associating with known gamblers. In an effort to ensure the integrity of the game, he suspended indefinitely Hornung and **Alex Karras** of the **Detroit Lions**, two of the league's best players, for gambling. Both were banned from play in 1963 but were reinstated in 1964. Consequently, the Packers did not repeat as league champions in 1963, although they finished second in their division and won the consolation **bowl game** between second-place teams, the Bert Bell Benefit Bowl (also known as the **Playoff Bowl** or Runner-Up Bowl). The Packers also played in that game in 1964 but were losers that year. They repeated as NFL champions in 1965 and 1966 and played and won the first National Football League–**American Football League** Championship Game (later known as the **Super Bowl**) on 15 January 1967. Hornung, however, was unable to play in that game, as he suffered a pinched nerve in his neck during the season. He was selected by the **New Orleans Saints** in the expansion draft in 1967 but did not sign with them and retired.

In his nine-year NFL career, Hornung played in 104 regular-season games, ran 893 times for 3,711 yards and 50 touchdowns, and caught 130 **passes** for

1,480 yards and 12 touchdowns. He attempted 55 passes and completed 24 of them for 383 yards and five touchdowns. Hornung was also Green Bay's placekicker for most of his career and kicked 66 field goals in 140 attempts and 190 extra points in 194 attempts. In 1958, he returned **kickoffs** as well and, in 10 returns, averaged 24.8 yards per return. In five postseason games, he ran 67 times for 323 yards and three touchdowns, caught 12 passes for 111 yards and no touchdowns, completed one pass in six attempts for 21 yards, and was successful on five extra points in five attempts and five field goals in six attempts. Hornung played in the **Pro Bowl** in 1959 and 1960 and was named the NFL Most Valuable Player in 1961. He led the NFL in points scored in 1959, 1960, and 1961 and set the NFL record, with 176 points, in 1960.

After retiring, Hornung became a real estate investor and also produced and hosted a weekly sports television program. He was inducted into the **College Football Hall of Fame** in 1985 and the **Pro Football Hall of Fame** in 1986.

HOUSTON OILERS. *See* TENNESSEE TITANS.

HOUSTON TEXANS. The Houston Texans are a **professional football** team in the American Football Conference (AFC) of the **National Football League (NFL)** that began play in 2002. Home games are played at the 71,500-seat Reliant Stadium in Houston, Texas. In their first 11 seasons in the NFL through 2012, they have compiled a won-lost record of 77–99. Their best seasons were 2011 and 2012, when they finished in first place in the AFC South Division. Through the 2012 season, they qualified only twice for the postseason **playoffs**. The Texans won their first wild-card game and lost in the division playoff in both 2011 and 2012. Among their better players have been **quarterbacks** Matt Schaub and Taylor "T. J." Yates; **linebackers** Brian Cushing and DeMeco Ryans, both NFL Defensive Rookies of the Year; **running back** Domanick Williams; and **wide receiver** Andre Johnson. Texans' **coaches** have included Dom Capers (2002–2005) and Gary Kubiak (2006–2012).

HUBBARD, ROBERT CALVIN "CAL." B. 31 October 1900, Keytesville, Missouri. D. 17 October 1977, St. Petersburg, Florida. Cal Hubbard is the only man enshrined in both the Baseball Hall of Fame (inducted in 1976) and **Pro Football Hall of Fame** (charter member inducted in 1963). He was also inducted into the **College Football Hall of Fame** in 1962. He attended Keytesville High School in Keytesville, Missouri, and Centenary College. At Centenary, he played from 1922 to 1924 for Alvin "Bo" McMillin, one of **college football's** legendary **coaches**. When McMillin left Centenary to coach at Geneva College, Hubbard followed him there to conclude his college education, playing for McMillin in 1926. At six feet, four inches tall and 250 pounds, Hubbard was a huge man for his era and was a dominating **lineman** both on **offense** and **defense**.

Hubbard signed with the **New York Giants** of the **National Football League (NFL)**, played for them in 1927 and 1928, and then moved to the **Green Bay Packers** from 1929 to 1933. In 1934, he was hired by **Texas A&M University** as an **assistant coach**. He was coaxed into returning to the Packers in 1935. The following year, he concluded his NFL career by playing for the New York Giants and Pittsburgh Pirates.

In nine NFL seasons, Hubbard appeared in 105 regular-season games as both an offensive and defensive lineman, playing both **tackle** and **end**. He scored two **touchdowns** while in the league, one in 1930 as a receiver and one in 1935 on an **interception**. He played on four NFL championship teams, the 1927 Giants and 1929, 1930, and 1931 Packers.

Hubbard began umpiring baseball in the minor leagues while still an active **football** player and, in 1936, was promoted to the major leagues. He umpired in the American League from 1936 to 1951, when an off-season hunting accident damaged his vision and he had to retire. He worked in four World Series and three All-Star Games. From 1954 to 1969, Hubbard was supervisor of umpires for the American League.

HUDDLE. In **football**, a huddle usually occurs prior to the beginning of each play. The offensive team gathers in a circle around the **quarterback**, who then calls the next play and the count when the ball should be snapped. The defensive team also huddles to discuss their alignment. The huddle was first used during the 1920s. In recent years, some teams play without using a huddle (a no-huddle offense) and communicate information at the **line of scrimmage** via verbal codes. This strategy makes it more difficult for the defensive team to get set.

HUFF, ROBERT LEE "SAM." B. 4 October 1934, Edna Gas, West Virginia. Sam Huff was raised in a coal mining camp in West Virginia. He attended Farmington High School in Farmington, West Virginia, where his team was undefeated in 1951. He played **guard** and **tackle** for the University of West Virginia for four years, from 1952 to 1955, and while there helped the Mountaineers to a record of 31–7.

Huff was selected by the **New York Giants** in the 1956 **National Football League (NFL) Draft** in the third round as the 30th overall choice. With the Giants, he was converted to **linebacker** and became one of the greatest linebackers of his era. He helped lead the Giants to the 1956 NFL championship and the NFL Championship Game in 1958, 1959, 1961, 1962, and 1963. With the Giants in 1960, an episode of the television series *The Twentieth Century* was produced entitled "The Violent World of Sam Huff," one of the first shows glamorizing a defensive football player. Huff was wired for sound during an exhibition game, and the show helped promote the violence inherent in **professional football**. He was traded to the **Washington Redskins** in 1964 and played five seasons for them, retiring after the 1969 season.

In his 13 years in the NFL, in 168 regular-season games, Huff **intercepted** 30 **passes** and recovered 17 **fumbles**. He scored five defensive **touchdowns**, two as a result of interceptions and three via fumble recoveries. In seven postseason games, he had one interception. He played in five **Pro Bowls**.

After retiring from active play, Huff worked as an **assistant coach** for the Redskins in 1970, did radio commentary for Giants and Redskins football broadcasts, was a salesman for Marriott Corporation and eventually became their vice president of sports marketing, raised thoroughbred racehorses, and made an unsuccessful attempt running for a seat in Congress. He was inducted into the **College Football Hall of Fame** in 1980 and the **Pro Football Hall of Fame** in 1982.

HUNT, LAMAR. B. 2 August 1932, El Dorado, Arkansas. D. 13 December 2006, Dallas, Texas. Lamar Hunt was a major contributor to the growth of many different sports in North America. As such, he has been honored by induction into the National Soccer Hall of Fame (1982), International Tennis Hall of Fame (1993), and **Pro Football Hall of Fame** (1972). He was the son of Texas oil magnate H. L. Hunt, possibly the richest man in the world at the time of his death in 1974 and the inspiration for the television series *Dallas*. Lamar attended prestigious private schools, including Culver Military Academy, and was a graduate of the Hill School, located in a suburb of Philadelphia. At Southern Methodist University, he was on the **football** team as a substitute and did not receive much playing time. He graduated in 1956 with a bachelor's degree in geology.

Hunt attempted to purchase a **National Football League (NFL)** franchise in 1959 but was unsuccessful. Undaunted, he met with other businessmen who were also seeking to join the NFL, including Kenneth Stanley "Bud" Adams Jr., another wealthy Texas oilman, and the result was that in August 1959, the **American Football League (AFL)** was formed to directly compete with the established NFL. Hunt would be the owner of the AFL team the **Dallas Texans**, and Adams would own the Houston Oilers.

The league began play in 1960, but Hunt's Dallas team, while successful on the field (1962 AFL champions), did not do well at the box office as a result of their direct competition with the NFL's **Dallas Cowboys**. In 1963, he moved the Texans to Kansas City, Missouri, where they played as the **Kansas City Chiefs**. The Chiefs continued to succeed and won two more AFL championships in the decade. Hunt retained ownership of the Chiefs until his death, at which time his son, Clark, became their chairman.

As the AFL and NFL competed for talent, player salaries began to escalate, and the two leagues decided that a merger would be in both of their best interests. Hunt was one of the owners who led that initiative, and, on 8 June 1966, a merger plan was agreed upon. As part of the terms of the merger, a season-ending contest between the NFL champion and AFL champion was agreed upon to take place following the 1966 season. The game was initially called the AFL–NFL Championship Game, although in a letter from Hunt to NFL commissioner **Alvin "Pete" Rozelle**, he kiddingly called it a "**Super Bowl**." That name would later be used by the media, and the NFL adopted it as the official name for the event.

Hunt developed an interest in soccer and, in 1967, founded a soccer team, the Dallas Tornado, which played in the United Soccer Association. That league merged with the National Professional Soccer League in 1968 to form the North American Soccer League, which lasted through 1984. In 1996, Hunt helped found Major League Soccer and owned two teams in that enterprise and later purchased a third.

In 1968, he founded World Championship Tennis, which organized a tour for male professional tennis players and helped the growth of the open era in that sport. Hunt also opened two amusement parks in Kansas City during his lifetime. Since 1984, the winner of the American Football Conference championship has received the Lamar Hunt Trophy. The United States Soccer Federation has held a Lamar Hunt U.S. Open Cup tournament since 1999. He died in 2006 as a result of prostate cancer.

HUTSON, DONALD MONTGOMERY "DON." B. 31 January 1913, Pine Bluff, Arkansas. D. 26 June 1997, Rancho Mirage, California. Don Hutson was in a class by himself during his 11 years in the **National Football League (NFL)**, from 1935 to 1945. When he retired following the 1945 season, he held nearly every NFL **pass** receiving record. He began playing **football** for Pine Bluff High School in Pine Bluff, Arkansas, and continued at the **University of Alabama**. Hutson was also a member of the Alabama baseball and track teams. He played on the Alabama **varsity** from 1932 to 1934. During those three years, Alabama had a record of 25–4–1, outscoring their opponents 646–113. They were **conference** champions or cochampions twice, had an undefeated 10–0 record in 1934, and were **Rose Bowl** victors in 1934.

The six-foot, one-inch, 180-pound Hutson signed **professional football** contracts with both the **Brooklyn Dodgers** and **Green Bay Packers**. The problem was resolved when NFL president **Joe Carr** intervened and awarded Hutson to the Packers. On his first play in the NFL, Hutson caught a pass and scored an 85-yard **touchdown**. He was named the NFL Most Valuable Player in both 1941 and 1942; was a member of the NFL champions in 1936, 1939, and 1944; and played on the losing side in the 1938 NFL Championship Game. He led the league in pass receiving yardage seven times, pass **receptions** eight times, and pass receiving touchdowns nine times. In addition to his prowess as a receiver he was also an outstanding placekicker and defensive **safety**, leading the league in **interceptions** one season, interception yardage another season, points after touchdown made and attempted three times, and **field goals** made once.

In his 11-year NFL career, Hutson played in 116 regular-season games, caught 488 passes for 7,991 yards and 99 touchdowns, and ran 62 times for 284 yards and three touchdowns. He completed only one of 11 passes, but it was good for a 38-yard touchdown in 1943. He also kicked extra points and field goals and scored seven field goals in 17 attempts and 172 extra points in 183 attempts. On **defense**, Hutson recorded 30 interceptions and returned one for an 84-yard touchdown in 1943, and he was credited with two other defensive touchdowns in his career. He was inducted into the **College Football Hall of Fame** as a charter member in 1951 and the **Pro Football Hall of Fame** as a charter member in 1963.

I

ICE BOWL. The "Ice Bowl" was the name given to the **National Football League (NFL)** championship game between the **Green Bay Packers** and **Dallas Cowboys** in Green Bay, Wisconsin, on 31 December 1967. The temperature at the start of the game was 15 degrees below zero Fahrenheit, and, during the game, the 15-mile-per-hour wind resulted in a windchill factor of approximately 40 degrees below zero. The game was won by Green Bay, 21–17, on a **quarterback sneak** by **Bart Starr** with 13 seconds remaining in the game. On a frozen **football field**, the Packers had failed to score twice from the one-**yard line** before Starr, led by a **block** thrown by **guard Jerry Kramer**, was able to cross the **goal line**.

The extreme **weather** caused the field's underground heating system to malfunction, and the field was slick as ice. The marching band was unable to perform, as several band members' instruments froze to their lips. Several players were unable to start their cars and had to make alternate arrangements to get to the **stadium**. The referees were unable to blow their whistles during the game and used hand signals to control play. Several players developed frostbite.

One of the offshoots of the game is that television announcer **Frank Gifford**, a former **football** player, interviewed the losing **quarterback**, **Don Meredith**, after the game, a practice that had not been done before. It resulted in an honest, emotional dialogue with Meredith and subsequently led to his being selected as one of the announcers on *Monday Night Football*.

ILLINOIS, UNIVERSITY OF. The University of Illinois is located in Champaign, Illinois. Their **football** program began in 1890, and, since then, through 2012, Fighting Illini teams have compiled a record of 574–535–50. In addition, they have competed in 17 postseason **bowl games**, with a record of 8–9. They have been selected as national collegiate champions five times, in 1914, 1919, 1923, 1927, and 1951. Illinois was a charter member of the **Big Ten Conference** when it was created in 1896. Home games have been played at Memorial Stadium since 1923. The **stadium** currently has a seating capacity of 62,000.

One of their main rivals is **Ohio State University**. The two teams have played since 1925 for a trophy known as Illibuck. The trophy was originally a live turtle, but, since its passing in 1927, a wooden replica has been used. Ohio State leads the series, 58–26–2. The two schools also played 13 times between 1902 and 1924, with Illinois ahead, 7–4–2. Another traditional rival is **Purdue University**. Illinois and Purdue have played since 1905, with Illinois leading the series, 42–40–6. Since 1943, the teams have played for the Purdue Cannon trophy, with Purdue having the advantage, 33–27–2. From 1945 to 2008, Illinois and Northwestern competed for the Sweet Sioux Tomahawk trophy. Illinois had the lead in that series, 33–29. Since 2009, the trophy has been known as the Land of Lincoln Trophy, and the series is tied at two games each.

Illinois' most famous **coach** was **Bob Zuppke**. He coached the Illini for 29 years, from 1913 to 1941. His record in that time was 131–81–12. His successor, Ray Eliot, coached from 1942 to 1959, with a record of 83–73–11. Zuppke's predecessor, Arthur Hall, was also quite successful as an Illinois coach. He coached from 1907 to 1912 and had a record of 27–10–3.

There are 11 Illinois alumni in the **College Football Hall of Fame** and four former Illinois coaches. They are **guards** Alex Agase and Bernie Shively; **safety** Al Brosky; **center/linebacker** Dick Butkus; **end** Chuck Carney; **halfbacks** J. C. Caroline, **Harold "Red" Grange**, Bart Macomber, and **Claude "Buddy" Young**; **fullback** Jim Grabowski; **wide receiver** David Williams; and coaches Bob Blackman, Ed Hall, George Woodruff, and Bob Zuppke.

Through 2012, there have been 253 **professional football** players who have attended Illinois, 238 in the **National Football League**, six in the **American Football League**, and nine in the **All-America Football Conference**. They include Les Bingaman, Ed Brady, Bill Brown, Dick Butkus, J. C. Caroline, Dave Diehl, Doug Dieken, Jeff George, Harold "Red" Grange, **George Halas**, Don Hansen, Brad Hopkins, Ernie McMillen, Bobby Mitchell, **Ray Nitschke**, Ed O'Bradovich, Preston Pearson, Neil Rackers, Simeon Rice, Scott Studwell, Bob Trumpy, Laurie Walquist, Abe Woodson, and Claude "Buddy" Young.

"IMMACULATE RECEPTION." The "Immaculate Reception" is the name given by Pittsburgh sportscaster Myron Cope to a catch made by **Franco Harris** of the **Pittsburgh Steelers** in a **National Football League** American Football Conference **playoff** game against the **Oakland Raiders** at Pittsburgh on 23 December 1972. Pittsburgh trailed, 7–6, with 22 seconds remaining and no **time-outs** left. They had the ball at Oakland's 40-**yard line** on fourth **down**. The **pass**, thrown by Pittsburgh **quarterback Terry Bradshaw**, was deflected, and Harris caught the ball at his shoe tops and ran for the game-winning **touchdown**. A controversy developed regarding the deflection, since both a Pittsburgh and Oakland player appeared to have touched the ball. Had only a Pittsburgh player deflected the ball, it would have been an illegal play, but after the **officials** conferred, they agreed that the ball had indeed touched the Oakland player. Some players later speculated that the officials favored Pittsburgh for fear of riots had the play not been called a touchdown. Subsequent viewing of the film and interviews with the players has failed to provide definitive answers, and the catch remains controversial.

INCOMPLETE PASS. An incomplete **pass** is a pass that is not caught by an offensive player or **intercepted** by a defensive player.

INDIANAPOLIS COLTS. The Indianapolis Colts are a **professional football** team in the American Football Conference (AFC) South Division of the **National Football League (NFL)**. They began as the Baltimore Colts in the NFL in 1953, but, in 1984, the team moved to Indianapolis in a controversial departure that included moving vans leaving the Colts' facilities in Maryland in the middle of the night. Although the Colts began as a new team with new owners in 1953, their franchise history, through a series of relocations, ownership changes, and team name changes, can actually be traced back to the Dayton Triangles, one of the original teams that founded the American Professional Football Association, the NFL's predecessor, in 1920.

From 1953 to 1983, the Colts played home games at the 47,000-seat Memorial Stadium in Baltimore, Maryland. In 1984, they moved to the 60,000-seat Hoosier Dome (later renamed RCA Dome) in Indianapolis, Indiana, where they played until 2007. In 2008, they moved to the 63,000-seat Lucas Oil Stadium, a new domed facility also in Indianapolis.

From 1953 to 1969, the Colts played in the NFL Western Conference. When the NFL expanded to 16 teams in 1967, they split their conferences into divisions and the Colts played in the Coastal Division of the Western Conference. In 1970, the NFL and **American Football League (AFL)** merged and became a 26-team league. The Colts, along with the **Cleveland Browns** and **Pittsburgh Steelers**, were placed in the AFC, with the Colts in the East Division. They remained there until 2002, when another realignment occurred, and they were placed in the AFC South Division.

Through 2012, the Colts' overall regular-season record is 464–415–7, and their **playoff** record is 19–21. Prior to the advent of the **Super Bowl**, the Colts won the NFL championship in 1958 (defeating the **New York Giants** in the first NFL **overtime** game) and 1959 (again defeating the Giants). They lost the NFL Championship Game in 1964. They also lost a conference tiebreaker playoff in 1965. In 20 years of NFL postseason play since the AFL–NFL merger in 1970, they have lost in the **wild-card playoff** six times (including two in overtime), the divisional playoffs eight times, and the conference championships three times. They have played in four Super Bowls, winning in 1970 and 2006 and losing in 1968 and 2009.

Head **coaches** have included Keith Molesworth (1953), Wilbur "Weeb" Ewbank (1954–1962), **Don Shula** (1963–1969), Don McCafferty (1970–1972), John Sandusky (interim 1972), Howard Schnellenberger (1973–1974), Joe Thomas (interim 1974), Ted Marchibroda (1975–1979, 1992–1995), Mike McCormack (1980–1981), Frank Kush (1982–1984), Hal Hunter (interim 1984), Rod Dowhower (1985–1986), Ron Meyer (1986–1991), Rick Venturi (interim 1991), Lindy Infante (1996–1997), Jim Mora (1998–2001), Tony Dungy (2002–2008), Jim Caldwell (2009–2011) and Chuck Pagano (2012). Pagano was diagnosed with leukemia in September 2012 and Colts' offensive coordinator Bruce Arians acted as interim head coach for 12 games during the season.

The Colts' best players include **Pro Football Hall of Fame quarterback Johnny Unitas**, **wide receiver** Raymond Berry, defensive **tackle** Art Donovan, **linebacker** Ted Hendricks, **tight end** John Mackey, defensive **end** Gino Marchetti, **halfback Lenny Moore**, offensive **lineman** Jim Parker, and **running backs** Marshall Faulk and **Eric Dickerson**. Other top players include quarterbacks Bert Jones, **Peyton Manning**, and Earl Morrall; running backs Joseph Addai, Edgerrin James, and Lydell Mitchell; **fullback** Alan Ameche; wide receivers **Marvin Harrison**, Jimmy Orr, and Reggie Wayne; and defensive end Dwight Freeney.

INTENTIONAL GROUNDING. Intentional grounding occurs when the **quarterback** is in the **pocket** and deliberately throws the ball to an area where there are no eligible receivers in an attempt to avoid being **tackled**. He is permitted to do so if he is outside the pocket. The **penalty** is loss of **down**, and the ball is placed at the spot where the ball was thrown. If it occurs in the **end zone**, the penalty is a **safety**.

INTERCEPTION. An interception occurs when a **pass** is caught by the defensive team. The player intercepting the ball is allowed to **run** with it and will occasionally return it for a **touchdown**. In modern terminology, this is sometimes called a "pick six."

INTERNATIONAL FEDERATION OF AMERICAN FOOTBALL (IFAF). The International Federation of American Football (IFAF) was established in 1998, with one of its goals being the eventual inclusion of American **football** in the **Olympic Games**. Based in La Courneuve, France, it has 62 member nations on six continents. An IFAF World Cup tournament has been held every four years since 1999. Japan was champion in 1999 and 2003, and the United States (which did not enter previously) was the 2007 and 2011 champion. IFAF also sponsors a Women's World Cup and a boys' Junior World Cup. Since the United States has many more players than other countries, they have participated in the World Championship under extremely restrictive rules that have made most American football players ineligible. Other similar regional American football federations include the European Federation of American Football, the Pan American Federation of American Football, the Asian Federation of American Football, and the Oceania Federation of American Football.

IOWA, UNIVERSITY OF. The University of Iowa is located in Iowa City, Iowa. Their **football** program began in 1889, and, since then, through 2012, Hawkeyes' teams have compiled a record of 585–520–38. In addition, they have competed in 26 postseason **bowl games**, with a record of 14–11–1. They have been selected as national collegiate champions four times, in 1921, 1956, 1958, and 1960. Since 1899, Iowa football teams have competed in the **Big Ten Conference** of the **National Collegiate Athletic Association**. Home games since 1929 have been played at the 70,000-seat Kinnick Stadium (known simply as Iowa Stadium until 1972). The **stadium** is named for Iowa's **Heisman Trophy** winner, Nile Kinnick, who was killed during a training flight in World War II.

Since 1935, Iowa's rivalry with the **University of Minnesota** is played for the Floyd of Rosedale Trophy. The bronze trophy is that of a pig whose origins stem from a bet between the governors of Minnesota and Iowa, with a live pig as the bet's stake. Minnesota leads the series, 41–35–2. The Iowa–Iowa State rivalry has been played for the Cy-Hawk Trophy since 1977. Iowa leads that series, 39–22.

Iowa's most notable **coaches** have been Howard Jones (1916–1923; 42–17–1), Eddie Anderson (1939–1949; 35–33–2), Forest Evashevski (1952–1960; 52–27–4), Hayden Fry (1979–1998; 143–89–6), and Kirk Ferentz (1999–2012; 100-74). There are nine Iowa alumni in the **College Football Hall of Fame** and five former Iowa coaches. They are **quarterbacks** Aubrey Devine, Randy Duncan, and Chuck Long; **guard** Calvin Jones; **tackles** Alex Karras and Fred "Duke" Slater; **halfback** Nile Kinnick; **fullback** Gordon Locke; **linebacker** Larry Station; and coaches Eddie Anderson, Forest Evashevski, Hayden Fry, Howard Jones, and Ed "Slip" Madigan.

Through 2012, there have been 241 **professional football** players who have attended Iowa, 233 in the **National Football League**, six in the **American Football League**, and two in the **All-America Football Conference**. They include John Alt, Jason Baker, Mark Bortz, Rudy Bukich, Dallas Clark, Joe Devlin, Quinn Early, Mike Goff, Ron Hallstrom, Ronnie Harmon, Jonathan Hayes, Merton Henks, Jay Hilgenberg, Wally Hilgenberg, Bob Jeter,

Nate Kaeding, Alex Karras, Paul Krause, Joe Laws, John Niland, Reggie Roby, Andre Tippett, **Emlen Tunnell**, and Casey Wiegmann.

IRVIN, MICHAEL JEROME. B. 5 March 1966, Fort Lauderdale, Florida. Michael Irvin was raised in Fort Lauderdale. He first attended Piper High School in Sunrise, Florida, and then transferred to St. Thomas Aquinas in Fort Lauderdale. The six-foot-tall, 205-pound **wide receiver** attended the **University of Miami** in Miami, Florida. He helped lead the Hurricanes to an undefeated season and a national college championship in 1987. In his four years at Miami, Irvin's teams had a record of 41–8 and **bowl game** appearances in each of those four years.

Irvin was selected by the **Dallas Cowboys** in the first round of the 1988 **National Football League (NFL) Draft** as the 11th overall choice. He played for the Cowboys from 1988 to 1999 and was a member of three **Super Bowl** championship teams, in 1993, 1994, and 1996. He played in 159 regular-season games and caught 750 **passes** for 11,904 yards and 65 **touchdowns**. In 16 postseason games, he caught 87 passes for 1,315 yards and eight touchdowns. Irvin was selected for the **Pro Bowl** each year from 1991 to 1995. In 1995, he set an NFL record by having 11 games with 100 or more yards receiving in each. In 1999, he sustained an injury to his spinal cord, which, although fortunately nonparalytic, ended his playing career.

In retirement, Irvin has worked in television and radio as a **football** commentator. He has also appeared in two Hollywood feature films, including a costarring role in the 2005 film *The Longest Yard*, as well as several episodes of television shows. He was inducted into the **Pro Football Hall of Fame** in 2007. *See also* FOOTBALL FILMS.

IVY LEAGUE. The Ivy League is an organization of eight **major colleges** and universities that compete in sports. In **football**, they are grouped in the **National Collegiate Athletic Association** Football Championship Series. The Ivy League was officially established in 1954, although its eight schools have a long tradition of competing against one another, with most of their football programs originating in the 19th century. All eight schools are located in the northeastern United States and are among the most prestigious scholastically. Seven of the eight were founded prior to the American Revolution, with **Cornell University** being founded in 1865, the newest institution and only exception. The league's headquarters are based in Princeton, New Jersey. Since the league's inception, the eight member schools are Brown University, Columbia University, Cornell University, Dartmouth College, **Harvard University**, the **University of Pennsylvania**, **Princeton University**, and **Yale University**.

JACKSON, HAROLD LEON. B. 6 January 1946, Hattiesburg, Mississippi. Harold Jackson attended Rowan High School in Hattiesburg, Mississippi, and Jackson State University. As Jackson State is a historically black university, and during Jackson's years there their **football** teams had good but not outstanding results, he was overlooked by professional scouts and was not selected until the 12th round of the 1968 **National Football League (NFL) Draft**. He was chosen by the Los Angeles Rams and was the 323rd player picked. He only played two games for the Rams in the 1968 season and was traded to the **Philadelphia Eagles** in 1969. A five-foot, 10-inch, 175-pound **wide receiver**, he played for the Eagles from 1969 to 1972 and twice led the NFL in receiving yardage. Jackson was traded back to the Rams and played for them from 1973 to 1977. He was with the **New England Patriots** from 1978 to 1981 and concluded his NFL career with one season with the **Minnesota Vikings** and one season with the **Seattle Seahawks**.

In his 16-year NFL career, Jackson played in 208 regular-season games, caught 579 **passes** for 10,372 yards and 76 **touchdowns**, and ran 33 times for 181 yards and no touchdowns. In 10 postseason games, he caught 24 passes for 548 yards and five touchdowns. He played in five **Pro Bowls**. After retiring from active play, Jackson worked as an **assistant coach** for the New England Patriots, **Tampa Bay Buccaneers**, and **New Orleans Saints** of the NFL, as well as for Baylor University.

JACKSONVILLE JAGUARS. The Jacksonville Jaguars are a **professional football** team in the **National Football League (NFL)**. They joined the league as an expansion team in 1995. They have competed in the American Football Conference (AFC) South Division since 2002 and, prior to that, in the AFC Central Division. Home games are played at the 70,000-seat EverBank Field in Jacksonville, Florida, formerly known as Alltel Stadium and Jacksonville Municipal Stadium. From 1995 to 2012, the Jaguars have compiled a regular-season record of 140–148 and a postseason record of 5–6. Their best season was 1999, when their regular-season record was 14–2 and they lost in the AFC championship. They also reached the 1996 AFC

Maurice Jones-Drew, star running back of the Jacksonville Jaguars.
Jacksonville Jaguars

championship. They lost in the divisional **playoffs** in 1998 and 2007 and the **wild-card playoff** in 1997 and 2005.

Through 2012, the Jaguars have only had four head **coaches**. These have been Tom Coughlin from 1995 to 2002, Jack Del Rio from 2003 to 2011, Mel Tucker, who took over for the last five games in 2011, and Mike Mularkey in 2012. On 17 January 2013, Gus Bradley was hired as the Jacksonville head coach for the 2013 season. Jacksonville's best players have included **tackle** Tony Boselli; **wide receivers** Jimmy Smith and Mike Thomas; **quarterbacks** Mark Brunell, David Garrard, and Byron Leftwich; and **running backs** Maurice Jones-Drew, James Stewart, and Fred Taylor.

JAWORSKI, RONALD VINCENT "RON," "JAWS," "THE POLISH RIFLE." B. 23 March 1951, Lackawanna, New York. Ron Jaworski attended Lackawanna High School in western New York, where he **quarterbacked** their **football** team, as well as played baseball and basketball. He was **drafted** by the St. Louis Cardinals of Major League Baseball but turned down their offer to attend Youngstown State University in Ohio. At Youngstown State, he quarterbacked their **offense** in a unique formation called the "Sidesaddle T," a variation of the single wing formation, in which the quarterback stands two or three feet behind the **center** at a 45-degree angle to the **line of scrimmage**. The formation apparently was successful, since in his senior year, 1972, he was the fifth-ranked small-college **passing** quarterback in the nation.

Jaworski was drafted by the Los Angeles Rams in the second round of the 1973 **National Football League (NFL) Draft** as the 37th overall selection. Although he joined the Rams in 1973, he spent the entire season on their **taxi squad** as their third-string quarterback and did not play in an NFL game. The six-foot, two-inch, 195-pound Jaworski only appeared in five games in 1974, but, in 1975, he played in 14 games as a result of injuries to the Rams' other two quarterbacks. In 1976, he again was a backup and only played in five games. He was traded to the **Philadelphia Eagles** in 1977, and his NFL career took off. He became the Eagles' starting quarterback for the next 10 seasons and, in 1980, led them to the **Super Bowl**, where they were defeated by the **Oakland Raiders**. That season, he was also named to the **Pro Bowl** and was the recipient of the Bert Bell Award as the NFL Player of the Year. After the Eagles released him following the 1986 season, Jaworski signed with the **Miami Dolphins** as the backup quarterback to **Dan Marino**. He did not get into a game that year and played briefly for the Dolphins in 1988. His final year as a professional player was with the **Kansas City Chiefs**, where he again filled a backup role and played in only six games.

In his 15-year NFL career, spanning 17 seasons, Jaworski played in 188 regular-season games and started 143 of them. His 116 consecutive starts as a

NFL quarterback set a record that was later eclipsed by **Brett Favre**. Jaworski had a won-lost record of 73–69–1 as a starter. He completed 2,187 passes in 4,117 attempts for 28,190 yards and 179 **touchdowns** and ran 257 times for 859 yards and 16 touchdowns. In nine postseason games, he completed 126 passes in 271 attempts for 1,669 yards and 10 touchdowns and ran 21 times for 50 yards and one touchdown.

After retiring from active play, Jaworski has worked as a television announcer and, from 2007 to 2011, was one of the three announcers on *Monday Night Football*. He also owns two golf and country clubs in New Jersey, and his company, Ron Jaworski Golf Management, manages two other golf facilities. He is part owner of the Philadelphia Soul of the **Arena Football League** and is one of the investors in the **Elite Football League of India**.

JOHNSON, CHAD JAVON. *See* OCHOCINCO, CHAD JAVON.

JONES, DAVID D. "DEACON." B. 9 December 1938, Eatonville, Florida. Deacon Jones attended Hungerford High School in Eatonville, Florida, where he played baseball, **football**, and basketball. In 1957, he played football for one year at the historically black college South Carolina State. After being involved in a civil rights demonstration, his scholarship was revoked. He then transferred to Mississippi Valley State University (then known as Mississippi Vocational College), where he played in 1960.

Since he played at a relatively unknown school and consequently had little national publicity, Jones was not chosen until the 14th round of the 1961 **National Football League (NFL) Draft** by the Los Angeles Rams as the 186th overall selection. At six feet, five inches tall and 270 pounds, he is a huge man with huge hands. (I met him a few years ago, and my hand was buried in his during a handshake.) With the Rams, Jones played defensive **end** alongside Roosevelt Grier, **Merlin Olsen**, and Lamar Lundy in a front line known as the "Fearsome Foursome." Jones became known for his head slap, which he would give the opposing **lineman** before attempting to **run** past him to get at the **quarterback**. He remained with the Rams from 1961 to 1971. He was traded by the Rams to the **San Diego Chargers** in 1972 and played two years with them before moving to Washington for his final NFL season in 1974.

In his 13-year NFL career, Jones played in 191 regular-season and three postseason games of a possible 199 games. He recorded 15 **fumble** recoveries and two **interceptions** and two safeties when he sacked opposing quarterbacks in the **end zone**. Although the NFL did not officially record sacks during the years that Jones was in the league, his unofficial sack totals include record-setting numbers. His unofficial total in 1967 was 26, and the following year it was 24, both surpassing the official league record of 22 1/2. In Jones's last regular-season NFL game, on 15 December 1974, with his **Washington Redskins** leading, 41–0, the team allowed him to kick the final extra point, which he did successfully.

Since retiring from active play, Jones has been involved in a number of activities. He has appeared in several feature films and television series, worked as a television football analyst, done corporate promotional work, and runs the Deacon Jones Foundation. He was inducted into the **Pro Football Hall of Fame** in 1980.

JONES, ED LEE "TOO-TALL." B. 23 February 1951, Jackson, Tennessee. The six-foot, nine-inch, 270-pound Ed "Too-Tall" Jones attended Merry High School in Jackson, Tennessee, and Tennessee State University. He was the first overall choice in the 1974 **National Football League (NFL) Draft** and was taken by the **Dallas Cowboys**. He was a defensive **end** from 1974 to 1989 for the Cowboys and as part of their "Doomsday **Defense**" played in the 1976, 1978, and 1979 **Super Bowls**. Dallas won only in 1978.

In 1979, Jones retired from the NFL to pursue professional boxing and trimmed his weight from 275 to 250 pounds. From November 1979 to January 1980, he competed in six professional bouts. He won his first bout, a six-rounder, by decision, and then won his next five by knockout. His opponents were all mediocre, and, after his brief experiment in the ring, he realized that he was "too tall" to effectively compete in the ring and returned to the Cowboys for the 1980 football season.

As a defensive end, his performance cannot be adequately measured by statistics. During his 15 years in the NFL, Jones played in 224 regular-season games (more than any other Dallas Cowboys player), recovered 19 **fumbles**, and made three **interceptions**. **Quarterback** sacks were not officially recorded during much of Jones's NFL career, but, from 1982 to 1989, he recorded 57 1/2 sacks, with an unofficial total of 106 sacks for his career. In 19 postseason games, he recorded an additional 5.5 sacks, made one interception, and recovered one fumble. He played in three **Pro Bowls**. In retirement, Jones has worked as a public speaker and made a few television commercials.

JURGENSEN, CHRISTIAN ADOLPH "SONNY." B. 23 August 1934, Wilmington, North Carolina. Sonny Jurgensen was a **quarterback** with a strong arm. The legendary **coach Vince Lombardi** once stated that Jurgensen was "the best I have seen." As a youth, Jurgensen participated in several sports, including baseball, basketball, tennis, and **football**. He won the city tennis championship and was a pitcher on a sandlot baseball team that won the city title. At New Hanover High School in Wilmington, North Carolina, he played football and baseball for four years and basketball for his last three. He was a member of the state **high school football** championship team as a junior, when he was the team's backup quarterback. At Duke University, he played defensive **back** and also quarterback on the **varsity** from 1954 to 1956. During those three years, Duke compiled a record of 20–8–3, and the Blue Devils were **conference** champions and **Orange Bowl** victors in 1954 and conference cochampions in 1955.

Jurgensen was chosen by the **Philadelphia Eagles** in the fourth round of the 1957 **National Football League (NFL) Draft** as the 43rd overall selection. In his first four years with the Eagles, he was a backup quarterback and saw little action; however, he was a member of the NFL championship team in 1960. After Eagles' quarterback **Norm Van Brocklin** retired in 1961, Jurgensen became the starter for the next two and a half seasons. In 1961, his first year as the starting quarterback, Jurgensen **tied Johnny Unitas's** NFL record with 32 **touchdown passes** in a season. (That record lasted for only one year, as **Y. A. Tittle** broke it the following season, and since then it has been surpassed many times.) In 1961, Jurgensen also set the NFL season record with 3,723 yards passing. That record lasted until 1967, when he again surpassed it with 3,747 passing yards in 14 games. This time the record stood until 1979, when **Dan Fouts** passed for 4,082 yards in a 16-game season.

In 1964, Jurgensen was traded to the **Washington Redskins**, and it was as a Redskin that his NFL career prospered. He remained with the Redskins for 11 years before retiring at the age of 40 following the 1974 season. With Washington, he led the NFL three times in passes completed and passes attempted and twice in pass completion percentage. Jurgensen's Redskins played in the 14 January 1973 **Super Bowl**, but by then he had been reduced to being the backup quarterback.

In his 18-year NFL career, Jurgensen played in 218 regular-season games, completed 2,433 passes in 4,262 attempts for 32,224 yards and 255 touchdowns, and ran 181 times for 493 yards and 15 touchdowns. He played in only one postseason game, although he was on the roster for several others. In that game, in 1974, he completed six passes in 12 attempts for 78 yards and no touchdowns. After retiring from active play, Jurgensen became a television commentator for football. He was inducted into the **Pro Football Hall of Fame** in 1983.

KANSAS CITY CHIEFS. The Kansas City Chiefs are a **professional football** team in the **National Football League (NFL)**. They began as a charter member of the **American Football League (AFL)** in 1960 as the Dallas Texans and played home games at the 75,000-seat **Cotton Bowl** in Dallas, Texas. After the 1962 season, the Texans relocated to Kansas City, Missouri, where they have played as the Kansas City Chiefs since then. They played home games at the 35,000-seat Municipal Stadium in Kansas City until 1971. Since 1972, they have played at the 76,000-seat Arrowhead Stadium, also in Kansas City.

The Texans'/Chiefs' regular-season record for 10 years in the AFL was 87–48–5, one of the best records in that league. They were 5–1 in AFL **playoff** competition. They won the AFL championship three times, including a double-**overtime** victory over the Houston Oilers, 20–17, in 1962, and played in two of the first four **Super Bowls**, losing the first one in 1966, 35–10, to the **Green Bay Packers** and winning the fourth one over the **Minnesota Vikings**, 2–7. In 1970, they joined the NFL in the American Football Conference (AFC) West Conference. In 43 years of NFL play, their overall regular-season record is 317–340–7, and their playoff record is 3–12. Since joining the NFL, the Chiefs have not done nearly as well as they did in the AFL. Their NFL playoff record shows six losses in the **wild-card playoff**; five losses in the divisional playoff, including a double-overtime loss in 1971; and one loss in the AFC championship to the **Buffalo Bills** in 1993.

The team's best head **coach** was the innovative **Hank Stram**, who led them from 1960 to 1974. Other head coaches have been Paul Wiggin (1975–1977), Tom Bettis (interim 1977), Marv Levy (1978–1982), John Mackovic (1983–1986), Frank Gansz (1987–1988), Marty Schottenheimer (1989–1998), Gunther Cunningham (1999–2000), Dick Vermeil (2001–2005), Herman Edwards (2006–2008), Todd Haley (2009–2011), and Romeo Crennel (2011–2012). On 4 January 2013, Andy Reid signed a five-year contract to be head coach and general manager of the Chiefs. Reid had been head coach of the Philadelphia Eagles from 1999 to 30 December 2012.

The best players for the Texans/Chiefs have included **Pro Football Hall of Famers quarterback Len Dawson**; **linebackers** Bobby Bell, Willie Lanier, and Derrick Thomas; defensive **tackles** Junious "Buck" Buchanan and Curley Culp; offensive tackle Willie Roaf; and **cornerback Emmitt Thomas**. Other top players have been **kicker Jan Stenerud**, **running backs** Abner Haynes and Priest Holmes, **tight ends** Fred Arbanas and **Tony Gonzalez**, offensive **linemen** Will Shields and Jim Tyrer, and **wide receiver** Otis Taylor.

KAPP, JOSEPH ROBERT "JOE." B. 19 March 1938, Santa Fe, New Mexico. Joe Kapp is one of the few players to play in the **Rose Bowl**, **Grey Cup**, and **Super Bowl**. He is also one of the few professional players with Hispanic heritage, as his mother was Mexican American. He is a graduate of William S. Hart High School in Newhall, California, a suburb of Los Angeles. After **quarterbacking** his **high school football** team, he received an athletic scholarship to the **University of California**. He played on the California **varsity** from 1956 to 1958. Although the team did poorly his first two years, with a record of 4–16, they did much better during his senior year and had a record of 7–4, were Pacific Coast Conference champions, and played in the 1 January 1959 Rose Bowl.

Kapp was selected in the 18th round of the 1959 **National Football League (NFL) Draft** by the **Washington Redskins** as the 209th overall choice. He was not contacted by the Redskins, however, and accepted an offer to play in the **Canadian Football League (CFL)**. He played for the **Calgary Stampeders** in 1959 and 1960 and, after one game in 1961, was traded to the **BC Lions**, a team new to the CFL that year. Only two years later, in 1963, Kapp led the Lions to the Grey Cup, where they were defeated by the **Hamilton Tiger-Cats**. The following year, the Lions became Grey Cup champions after defeating the Tiger-Cats in a rematch. Kapp remained with the Lions through the 1966 season and then decided to try the NFL.

His rights were obtained by the **Minnesota Vikings** in one of the few player trades between the NFL and CFL. One of the reasons that the Vikings sought Kapp was that their general manager was Jim Finks, who had been Kapp's general manager at Calgary. Minnesota's **coach, Harry "Bud" Grant**, had been a CFL coach while Kapp played in that league and was familiar with Kapp's abilities. Kapp played for the Vikings as their starting quarterback from 1967 to 1969 and led them to the Super Bowl on 11 January 1970, where they were defeated by the **Kansas City Chiefs**.

One of Kapp's best days as a quarterback occurred on 28 September 1969, when he **tied** the NFL record by completing seven **passes** for **touchdowns** in a 52–14 victory over the **Baltimore Colts**. He was the fifth NFL quarterback to achieve that feat, and none have done it since. Ironically, the second NFL quarterback to throw seven touchdown passes in one game, Adrian Burk, was one of the **officials** (back judge) when Kapp tied his record.

Kapp had not signed his player contract for the 1969 season and thus became a free agent in 1970. He signed with the Boston Patriots but had a poor season. Following the season, NFL commissioner **Alvin "Pete" Rozelle** demanded that Kapp sign a standard player contract, but Kapp refused. Consequently, the Patriots did not allow Kapp to play for them, and he retired. He sued the NFL for restraint of trade in an antitrust lawsuit, and, while he won a summary judgment, he did not receive any monetary damages. A subsequent agreement was made and a cash settlement received by the NFL Players Association as a result of Kapp's suit.

In his four-year NFL career, Kapp played in 51 regular-season games and started in 48 of them. He compiled a won-lost record of 24–21–3. He completed 449 passes in 918 attempts for 5,911 yards and 40 touchdowns and ran 119 times for 611 yards and five touchdowns. In four postseason games, he completed 61 of 101 passes for 835 yards and three touchdowns and ran 27 times for 160 yards and two touchdowns.

In retirement, Kapp has done some acting in bit parts and, in 1982, was hired by his alma mater, California, as their head coach. He coached five years, from 1982 to 1986, and had a record of 20–34–1. One of the more memorable highlights of his college coaching career was California's last-second win over **Stanford University** in their last game of the season. With four seconds left to play and Stanford leading California, 20–19, California received the **kickoff** and kept **lateraling** the ball while advancing toward the **goal line**. Midway through the play, the Stanford marching band started to come onto the field, thinking the game was over. After five laterals, Kevin Moen, of California, ran through the band and scored the winning touchdown as time expired. In 1990, Kapp returned to the CFL as general manager of the BC Lions but was fired before the season ended. He was inducted into the **Canadian Football Hall of Fame** in 1984 and the **College Football Hall of Fame** in 2004.

KARRAS, ALEXANDER GEORGE "ALEX." B. 15 July 1935, Gary, Indiana. D. 10 October 2012, Los Angeles, California. Alex Karras played 12 seasons in the **National Football League (NFL)** and was one of the better defensive **tackles** during that time, yet he was probably better known for his portrayal of "Mongo" in the Mel Brooks film *Blazing Saddles*, his three years on *Monday Night Football*, and his television series *Webster*. Karras was raised in Gary, Indiana, and was a graduate of Emerson High School in Gary, where he played on both the offensive and defensive lines. He received a scholarship to the **University of Iowa** and played both ways on the Hawkeyes' **varsity** from 1955 to 1957. As a junior, he helped lead Iowa to a record of 9–1 and a victory in the **Rose Bowl** on 1 January 1957. The following year,

Iowa had a record of 7–1–1, and Karras won the **Outland Trophy** as the nation's best collegiate **lineman**. He also finished second in the voting for the **Heisman Trophy** as the best collegiate player regardless of position. That award has traditionally been given to an offensive **back**, and Karras is one of few linemen in the history of the Heisman Trophy to finish that strongly in the voting.

Karras was picked by the **Detroit Lions** in the first round of the 1958 NFL **Draft** as the 10th overall selection. The six-foot, two-inch, 245-pound tackle played with the Lions his entire **professional football** career. During his time with the team, they finished as runners-up in their division from 1960 to 1962 and played in and won the first three editions of the Bert Bell Benefit Bowl (also known as the **Playoff Bowl** or Runner-Up Bowl).

Karras was part owner of Lindell AC, a famed sports bar in Detroit. In 1963, NFL commissioner **Alvin "Pete" Rozelle** urged him to divest his interest in the establishment, citing reports of gambling there. It was then disclosed that Karras had placed bets on NFL games, which was strictly against NFL policy. He and **Green Bay Packers** star **halfback Paul Hornung** were suspended for the 1963 season but were both reinstated for the 1964 season. During his time off, Karras became a professional wrestler, an activity that he had engaged in briefly prior to his NFL career.

A knee injury sustained in 1970 brought an end to Karras's playing career during the 1971 preseason. In his 12 years in the NFL, he had 16 **fumble** recoveries and four **interceptions** in 161 regular-season games and one postseason game. In 1962, he was credited with a **safety** when he sacked **quarterback** Billy Wade of the **Chicago Bears** in the **end zone**. Karras played in four **Pro Bowls**.

In 1968, Karras played himself in the Hollywood film *Paper Lion*, a film based on writer George Plimpton's book about Plimpton's adventures with the Detroit Lions as a prospective quarterback in 1963. Karras had one of the larger parts among the players who played themselves and received critical acclaim. He decided to pursue a full-time acting career after his retirement from **football** and appeared in more than 30 films and television shows in a variety of roles, ranging from the memorably comic "Mongo" in *Blazing Saddles*, to a poignant portrayal of Babe Didrickson Zaharias's husband, George Zaharias, in the film *Babe*. In *Babe*, he plays opposite actress Susan Clark, whom he later married and starred with in the television series *Webster*.

From 1974 to 1976, Karras was **Don Meredith's** replacement as an announcer for *Monday Night Football*, and his good sense of humor made him one of the series' best announcers. When Meredith decided to return to the program, Karras resumed his acting career.

Alex had several relatives who also played in the NFL. His older brother Lou was a defensive lineman from 1950 to 1952 with the **Washington Redskins**. His other older brother, Ted, was a lineman from 1958 to 1966 for four different NFL teams, including the Lions in 1965, when he was a teammate of Alex. Ted's son, Ted Karras Jr., appeared in one game for Washington in 1987. Alex was inducted into the **College Football Hall of Fame** in 1991. *See also* FOOTBALL FILMS.

KELLY, JAMES EDWARD "JIM." B. 14 February 1960, Pittsburgh, Pennsylvania. Jim Kelly attended East Brady High School in East Brady, Pennsylvania, a suburb of Pittsburgh. While there, he starred in both **football** and basketball. He received a scholarship to the **University of Miami** and helped establish their football program. He was their **quarterback** from 1979 to 1982 and led them to a record of 30–15 during that time. In 1982, his senior year, he suffered a severe shoulder injury, and his play was limited.

Kelly was chosen by the **Buffalo Bills** in the first round of the **National Football League (NFL) Draft** as the 14th overall selection. He instead chose to play for the Houston Gamblers of the new **United States Football League (USFL)**. In 1984, he was the league's Most Valuable Player and Rookie of the Year, as he completed 370 **passes** in 587 attempts for 5,219 yards and 44 **touchdowns**. Kelly had similar statistics the following season, with 360 completions in 567 attempts for 4,623 yards and 39 touchdowns. In one game, on 24 February 1985, he passed for a USFL league record 574 yards, 20 yards more than the NFL record. After the league folded in 1986, Kelly signed with the Bills of the NFL. He played for the Bills from 1986 to 1996 and led them to the **Super Bowl** four consecutive times from 1990 to 1993. Unfortunately, the Bills were unable to win any of those four games.

In his 11-year NFL career, Kelly played and started in 160 regular-season games, had a won-lost record of 101–59, completed 2,874 passes in 4,779 attempts for 35,467 yards and 237 touchdowns, and ran 304 times for 1,049 yards and seven touchdowns. In 17 postseason games, he completed 322 passes in 545 attempts for 3,863 yards and 21 touchdowns and ran 44 times for 161 yards and no touchdowns. He played in five **Pro Bowls**.

After he retired, Kelly devoted much of his life to his son, Hunter, born 14 February 1997, who had a rare degenerative nerve disease and finally succumbed to its effects in 2005. He has since established the Hunter's Hope Foundation, with the mission of finding a cure for the condition. Kelly also runs a kids' football camp during the summer. He was inducted into the **Pro Football Hall of Fame** in 2002.

KELLY, LEROY. B. 20 May 1942, Philadelphia, Pennsylvania. Leroy Kelly attended Simon Gratz High School in Philadelphia and Morgan State

University. He was chosen by the **Cleveland Browns** in the eighth round of the 1964 **National Football League (NFL) Draft** as the 110th overall selection. Kelly played for the Browns from 1964 to 1973. Six feet tall and 200 pounds, he was a **running back** for the Browns as both a **halfback** and **fullback**, and he was also used as a **punt** and kick **returner**. Kelly was a member of the NFL champions his rookie year, 1964, and he played on the losing side in the NFL Championship Game in 1965, 1968, and 1969. After retiring from the Browns, he played one season for the Chicago Fire of the **World Football League (WFL)** in 1974. In 1975, he served as an **assistant coach** in the WFL for the Philadelphia Bell.

In his 10-year NFL career, Kelly played in 136 regular-season games, ran 1,727 times for 7,274 yards and 74 **touchdowns**, caught 190 **passes** for 2,281 yards and 13 touchdowns, and completed three of 16 passes for 93 yards and two touchdowns. As a punt and **kickoff** returner, he returned 94 punts for an average of 10.5 yards per return and three touchdowns and 76 kickoffs for a 23.5-yard average and no touchdowns. In 1967, he was used briefly as the team's backup punter and punted 10 times for a 40.7-yard average. In eight postseason games, Kelly **rushed** for 417 yards and two touchdowns in 100 carries, caught 18 passes for 190 yards and one touchdown, and returned two kickoffs for 64 yards and eight punts for 110 yards but had no touchdowns as a returner. He played in six **Pro Bowls**. Kelly was inducted into the **Pro Football Hall of Fame** in 1994. His brother, Pat, played Major League Baseball from 1967 to 1981.

KEMP, JACK FRENCH. B. 13 July 1935, Los Angeles, California. D. 2 May 2009, Bethesda, Maryland. Jack Kemp was a man whose contribution to American history was much more than just being a successful **football** player. He was a graduate of Fairfax High School in Los Angeles, where he played **quarterback** on the football team. Since he was only five feet, 10 inches tall and 175 pounds, he did not think he would make the team as a quarterback at the major California universities, so he enrolled at Occidental College, a smaller school in Los Angeles that competed in the **National Collegiate Athletic Association** College Division. In addition to playing quarterback at Occidental, Kemp also played defensive **back** and was a **punter** and placekicker. He was also a javelin thrower on their track and field team.

Kemp was chosen by the **Detroit Lions** in the 17th round of the **National Football League (NFL) Draft** in 1957 and was the 203rd player selected. He was far from being the last player chosen, as the draft that year spanned 30 rounds and 360 players. He was cut by the Lions but managed to secure a position with the **Pittsburgh Steelers** as their backup quarterback, along with **Len Dawson**, behind starter Earl Morrall. Kemp spent the next season on the **taxi squad** of the **San Francisco 49ers** and then the **New York Giants**.

In 1959, he was on the roster of the **Calgary Stampeders** of the **Canadian Football League (CFL)** as backup quarterback to **Joe Kapp** but never got into a game.

Kemp's big opportunity in **professional football** occurred in 1960, when he was offered a job with the Los Angeles Chargers of the new **American Football League (AFL)**. He started most of their games that season and helped lead them to the AFL Championship Game, where they were defeated by the Boston Patriots. In 1961, the Chargers moved to San Diego, and Kemp again brought them to the AFL Championship Game, but they again fell short by a **touchdown**.

In 1962, Kemp suffered a broken finger after two games of the regular season. Chargers' **coach** Sid Gillman attempted to "hide" Kemp and placed him on the waiver list. **Buffalo Bills** coach Lou Saban spotted Kemp on that list, and the Bills claimed Kemp for the waiver price of $100. Kemp recovered and was able to play the last four games of the season for the Bills. Kemp remained with the Bills through the 1969 season, although he missed the entire 1968 campaign with a knee injury. He led the Bills to the AFL Championship Game in 1964, 1965, and 1966. They defeated the Chargers in 1964 and 1965 and lost to the **Kansas City Chiefs** in 1966. Had they won the latter game, they would have played in the first **Super Bowl**.

Kemp's two sons, Jeff and Jimmy, also played professional football. Jeff was a backup quarterback for four teams in the NFL from 1981 to 1991 and appeared in 96 games during that time. His best year was 1984, when he started 13 games for the Los Angeles Rams, had a 9–4 record, and helped them reach the **playoffs**. Jimmy also played quarterback, mostly as a backup, for six teams in the CFL from 1994 to 2002.

In his 10-year combined NFL–AFL career, Jack Kemp played in 122 regular-season games, starting 105 of them, and had a won-lost record of 65–37–3. He completed 1,436 **passes** in 3,073 attempts for 21,218 yards and 114 touchdowns and ran 356 times for 1,150 yards and 40 touchdowns. In his first year in the NFL with Pittsburgh, he was also briefly used as a punter, and he punted twice for a 27.5-yard average. In six postseason games, Kemp completed 78 of 160 passes for 1,126 yards and two touchdowns and ran 15 times for 39 yards and one touchdown.

Kemp's second and more notable career began in 1971. He had previously been interested in politics and had worked for Barry Goldwater and Ronald Reagan while still an active player during the 1960s. Kemp ran for Congress in 1970 as a Republican in the Buffalo-area congressional district and was elected, with his term of office beginning on 3 January 1971. He was reelected every two years and served in Congress until 3 January 1989. In 1988, he ran for U.S. president in the Republican primary elections but withdrew midway through the campaign. He was chosen by President George H. W.

Bush as the secretary of housing and urban development and, on 13 February 1989, took office in that position and served four years. In 1996, Kemp ran for vice president of the United States on the Republican ticket with Bob Dole as president, but they were defeated by the incumbent team of President Bill Clinton and Vice President Al Gore. In 2009, after Kemp died from cancer, he was awarded the Presidential Medal of Freedom posthumously by President Barack Obama.

KICK RETURNER. *See* RETURNER.

KICKER. The kicker (or placekicker) on a **football** team is responsible for kicking off and attempting extra points and **field goals** via placekicks. Throughout much of the first 100 years of football, the kicker also played another position on **offense** and/or **defense**. In recent years, however, most teams employ specialists whose sole function is to kick. *See also* ANDERSEN, MORTON; BLANDA, GEORGE FREDERICK; DEMPSEY, THOMAS JOHN "TOM"; GROZA, LOUIS ROY "LOU," "THE TOE"; STENERUD, JAN; STRONG, ELMER KENNETH "KEN"; SUMMERALL, GEORGE ALLEN "PAT"; YEPREMIAN, GARABED SARKIS "GARO."

KICKING TEE. A kicking tee is a small plastic platform usually with prongs and a depression in the center designed to hold a **football** about one inch above the ground. It is used for **kickoffs** but is not allowed to be used for **field goal** attempts in the **National Football League**. The **Canadian Football League** and some high schools do permit its use for field goal attempts. Use of a tee for field goal attempts was formerly permitted in **college football** but was banned in 1988.

KICKOFF. A kickoff is used to begin a **football** game and also to begin play following a **touchdown** or successful **field goal**. It can also be used following a **safety**, although a **punt** is also allowed at that time. The team kicking off lines up at a specific **yard line**, and the ball is placed on a **kicking tee**. The receiving team lines up throughout the field 10 or more yards away from the kicking team. Once the ball has traveled 10 yards, either team may recover the ball. For many years, the kickoff line was the 40-yard line of the kicking team, but in recent years the **National Football League** and **National Collegiate Athletic Association** have moved the line back to the 30- or 35-yard line. *See also* ONSIDE KICK; TOUCHBACK.

KRAMER, GERALD LOUIS "JERRY." B. 23 January 1936, Jordan, Montana. Although Jerry Kramer probably made more than 5,000 **blocks** in his **National Football League (NFL)** career, he is remembered most for one block that he made in one game. During the famous "**Ice Bowl**" NFL Championship Game on 31 December 1967, Kramer's block enabled **quarterback Bart Starr** to score the winning **touchdown** with 16 seconds remaining in the game, and Kramer became world famous.

Kramer is a product of the Rocky Mountain area of the United States. Born in Montana, his family moved to northern Utah and then to Idaho. He attended Sandpoint High School in Sandpoint, Idaho, where he played **football**. He was offered a scholarship to the University of Idaho and continued his excellent play as a **lineman** there.

Kramer was selected by the **Green Bay Packers** in the fourth round of the 1958 NFL **Draft** as the 39th overall choice. At that time, the Packers were not the powerful team they would become in the next decade, and, in Kramer's first NFL season, they won only one of 12 games. In 1959, **Vince Lombardi** was hired as the Packers' coach and, in a short period of time, completely turned the team around. In 1960, they reached the NFL Championship Game but were defeated by the **Philadelphia Eagles**. From 1961 to 1967, Green Bay won the NFL championship five times in seven years. Kramer, a six-foot, three-inch, 245-pound **guard**, was an integral part of that team, and he played with the winning Packers in the first two American Football League–National Football League Championship Games (now known as the **Super Bowl**). He retired following the 1968 season.

There are no official statistics that measure Kramer's abilities as an offensive lineman for 11 years and 130 regular-season and nine postseason games in the NFL. He was used as Green Bay's placekicker in 1962, 1963, and 1968 and made 29 **field goals** in 54 attempts and 90 of 95 extra points. In a postseason game in 1962, he was successful in three of five field goals and one of one extra points. He played in three **Pro Bowls**.

Kramer coauthored three books with Dick Schaap about his years with the Packers. He retired to a ranch in Idaho and also worked as president of Single Source Telecommunication, a payphone outsourcing company. One of his sons, Jordan (named for teammate Henry Jordan), played briefly in the NFL in 2003 and 2004 as a **linebacker** with the **Tennessee Titans**. Surprisingly, as of 2012, Jerry Kramer has not yet been inducted into the **Pro Football Hall of Fame** (although he has been nominated several times). Yet, he was named to the NFL 50th Anniversary All-Time Team in 1969, and nine of his Packer teammates have become Hall of Famers.

LAMBEAU, EARL LOUIS "CURLY." B. 9 April 1898, Green Bay, Wisconsin. D. 1 June 1965, Sturgeon Bay, Wisconsin. Before there was **Vince Lombardi**, there was Earl "Curly" Lambeau. Lambeau was one of the founders of the **Green Bay Packers** and their **coach** from 1921 to 1949. He attended Green Bay East High School in Green Bay, Wisconsin, and played several sports, captaining the **football** team his senior year. He continued his education at the **University of Notre Dame** and, as a freshman in 1918, played under Coach **Knute Rockne**. A severe illness caused him to drop out of school following that year.

Lambeau worked as a shipping clerk at the Indian Packing Company in Green Bay and formed a football team in 1919, calling them the **Green Bay Packers**. They played other independent teams in the Midwest and, in 1921, joined the one-year-old American Professional Football Association (renamed the **National Football League [NFL]** in 1922). Lambeau both coached and played for the Packers. At five feet, 10 inches tall and 185 pounds, Lambeau played tailback and was the team's placekicker from 1921 to 1929. He then retired as a player but continued to coach the team through the 1949 season. As coach, he led Green Bay to NFL championships in 1929, 1930, 1931, 1936, 1939, and 1944. They were also losers to the **New York Giants** in the NFL Championship Game in 1938.

Lambeau left the Packers in 1950 and served two years as coach of the Chicago Cardinals and two more as coach of the **Washington Redskins**. During his 33 years as an NFL head coach, his teams compiled a cumulative record of 226–132–22. As a player and coach, Lambeau was one of the first to take advantage of the forward **pass** and was a strong advocate of its use as an offensive weapon.

When Lambeau played in the NFL from 1921 to 1929, there were no official statistics kept that can accurately measure his performance. The limited amount of statistical information available shows that he kicked at least six **field goals** and 20 extra points and scored 12 **touchdowns**, eight by **rushing** and three as a pass receiver. As a charter member, Lambeau was inducted into the **Pro Football Hall of Fame** as a coach in 1963. After his death from a heart attack in 1965, the Packers renamed their home **stadium Lambeau**

Field. The "Lambeau Leap," which is executed when a Green Bay player jumps into the **end zone** stands in celebration of a touchdown, is also named after Lambeau.

LAMBEAU FIELD. Lambeau Field in Green Bay, Wisconsin, the home field of the **Green Bay Packers**, is one of the storied sports venues in North America. Owned by the City of Green Bay and opened in 1957 as City Stadium with a seating capacity of 32,500, it was the first **stadium** to be built expressly for a **National Football League (NFL)** team. Throughout the years, the seating capacity has been gradually increased so that in 2012 the facility could hold 73,128 spectators. In 1965, it was renamed in honor of the founder of the Green Bay Packers, **Earl "Curly" Lambeau**, who had died earlier that year. The Packers have played in the same stadium longer than any other NFL team, with the 2012 season being their 56th at Lambeau Field.

LANDRY, THOMAS WADE "TOM." B. 11 September 1924, Mission, Texas. D. 12 February 2000, Dallas, Texas. Tom Landry was a good **professional football** player, but, more importantly, was one of the sport's all-time best **coaches**. Landry played **high school football** at Mission High School in Mission, Texas, and, as **quarterback**, led the team to an undefeated season his senior year. He enrolled at the **University of Texas** but, after only one semester, enlisted in the U.S. Army Air Corps. During World War II, he took part in 30 missions over Europe as a bomber copilot. After his discharge from the service, he returned to the University of Texas and played **fullback** and defensive **back** for them. From 1946 to 1948, Texas had a record of 25–6–1, and they emerged victorious in the **Sugar Bowl** on 1 January 1948, as well as the **Orange Bowl** on 1 January 1949.

Landry was selected by the **New York Giants** as a "future" player in the 20th round of the 1947 **National Football League (NFL) Draft** as the 184th overall choice, even though he still had two years of college eligibility remaining. In 1948, he was also drafted by the **New York Yankees** of the **All-America Football Conference (AAFC)**. He signed with them after they offered him a modest signing bonus. Landry played for the Yankees in 1949 and was primarily used as a **punter**, although he also played some at **halfback** and occasionally returned **punts** and **kickoffs**. The AAFC merged with the NFL in 1950, and the Yankees folded, with their players being mostly absorbed by the New York Giants and New York Bulldogs (renamed the **New York Yanks**) of the NFL. From 1950 to 1955, Landry played for the Giants and was used as their punter and defensive back, and occasionally quarterback and offensive halfback. He was also a punt and kick **returner** at times.

In his seven-year combined AAFC–NFL playing career, Landry played in 82 regular-season games and punted 389 times for an average of 40.9 yards per punt. He also **intercepted** 32 **passes** and recovered 10 **fumbles** and scored three **touchdowns** on interception returns and two on fumble recoveries. In two postseason games, he punted 11 times for an average of 51.6 yards and **rushed** three times for minus two yards. Although Landry was primarily a defensive back and punter, in 1952, as a quarterback, he completed 11 passes in 47 attempts for 172 yards and one touchdown. He also rushed 36 times for 131 yards and one touchdown and caught six passes for 109 yards. In addition, he returned 15 punts for an average of 9.7 yards per punt return and six kickoffs for an average of 16.2 yards per kickoff return.

In 1954, Landry began serving as **assistant coach** and defensive coordinator of the Giants, but, by 1956, he retired from playing and was strictly the defensive coordinator. The Giants' offensive coordinator at that time was **Vince Lombardi**, later to become one of the league's greatest head coaches. In 1960, Landry was named head coach of the expansion **Dallas Cowboys**. Although the Cowboys were winless in their first season (with a 31–31 **tie** game against the Giants in their next-to-last game being their season highlight), Landry was retained as coach. He gradually improved the team, and, by 1966, they were Western Conference champions, with a 10–3–1 record. The Cowboys did not have a losing record from 1966 to 1985 and played in the **Super Bowl** five times during that span, winning in 1972 and 1978. They became one of the NFL's most popular teams and were referred to as "America's team." Landry continued as coach until 1988, when new team owner Jerry Jones fired him after a 3–13 season. This decision was an extremely unpopular one among players and **fans** alike.

Landry's record for 29 seasons as head coach was 250–162–6 in regular-season games and 20–16 in **playoff** competition. From 1966 to 1985, his teams reached the playoffs in all but two years. He was inducted into the **Pro Football Hall of Fame** as a coach in 1990 and died from leukemia in 2000.

LANE, RICHARD "DICK," "NIGHT TRAIN." B. 16 April 1927, Austin, Texas. D. 29 January 2002, Austin, Texas. Dick "Night Train" Lane was one of the most feared defensive **backs** during the 1950s and early 1960s. At six feet, one inch tall and 190 pounds, he was an exceptionally strong **tackler** whose necktie tackles have since been banned by the **National Football League (NFL)**. He holds the NFL record for most **interceptions** in a season, with 14, attained in a 12-game season. Even though the NFL has played a 16-game season since 1978, as of 2012 the record has yet to be broken. In 1969, Lane was selected as the best **cornerback** in **professional football's** first 50 years.

Lane is one of the few NFL players who never played senior **college football**. Abandoned as an infant, he was found by a woman named Ella Lane, who raised him and adopted him. He played **football**, baseball, and basketball at the segregated L. C. Anderson High School in Austin. He helped lead the football team to the 1944 state Negro high school championship. Lane attended Scottsbluff Junior College for one year and then joined the U.S. Army. After being discharged from the service, he worked in an aircraft plant.

In 1952, Lane asked for a tryout with the NFL champion Los Angeles Rams. He made the team as a defensive back and, in his first year, set an NFL record for interceptions in a season that has yet to be broken. The 1952 Rams finished in a **tie** for first place in their division of the NFL but lost a tiebreaker game to the **Detroit Lions**. This was the closest that Lane came to playing in a Championship Game during his years as a professional player. He played for the Rams in 1952 and 1953, and the Chicago Cardinals from 1954 to 1959, and he concluded his NFL career with the Detroit Lions from 1960 to 1965.

In his 14-year NFL career, Lane played in 157 regular-season games, intercepted 68 **passes**, and recovered 11 **fumbles**. He scored five **touchdowns** on interception returns, one touchdown on a fumble recovery, and another on a **blocked field goal**. He was also credited with a **safety** in 1952, when he tackled an opposing ball carrier in the **end zone**. Although primarily a defensive player, Lane was occasionally used on **offense**, and he caught eight passes for 253 yards. In 1955, one of those pass **receptions** was for a 98-yard touchdown. He played in seven **Pro Bowls**.

After retiring, Lane worked as an assistant to the owner of the Lions, **coached** at Central State University and Southern University, and was the director of the Police Athletic League in Detroit. His second marriage was to jazz singer Dinah Washington, but she died of a sleeping pill overdose during their first year of marriage. Lane was inducted into the **Pro Football Hall of Fame** in 1974.

LARGENT, STEPHEN MICHAEL "STEVE." B. 28 September 1954, Tulsa, Oklahoma. Steve Largent attended Putnam City High School in Oklahoma City, graduating in 1972. From 1972 to 1976, he was at the University of Tulsa, from which he graduated with a bachelor of science degree in biology. He played on the Tulsa **football** teams from 1973 to 1975. In each of those four years, Tulsa was the Missouri Valley Conference champion or cochampion. As a **wide receiver**, Largent played in 33 games and caught 136 **passes** for 2,385 yards and 32 **touchdowns**.

Largent was picked in the fourth round of the 1976 **National Football League (NFL) Draft** by the Houston Oilers as the 117th overall selection. He was then traded to the expansion **Seattle Seahawks** and played his entire

NFL career with them, from 1976 to 1989. At five feet, 11 inches tall and 185 pounds, he was not tall for a pass receiver and was not particularly fast, but he was one of the best receivers in his era. When he retired after the 1989 season, Largent held the NFL career record for most pass **receptions**, reception yardage, and receiving touchdowns, but, as the game has changed in recent years, with the emphasis on passing greatly increased, his career records have been surpassed by many players.

In his 14-year NFL career, Largent played in 200 regular-season games, caught 819 passes for 13,089 yards and 100 touchdowns, and ran 17 times for 83 yards and one touchdown. He also completed two passes in seven attempts for 29 yards. In his first two years in the league, he was used as a **punt** and kick **returner** and returned eight punts and eight **kickoffs** for an average of 8.5 yards per punt return and 19.5 yards per kickoff return. In 1985 and again in 1989, Largent was credited with an extra point, when, as the kick **holder**, a bad snap from the **center** caused him to **run** for the extra point. (With the rules change in 1994, that would now be scored a two-point **conversion**, but at that time it was only worth one point.) In seven postseason games, Largent caught 23 passes for 434 yards and four touchdowns. He played in seven **Pro Bowls**. In 1989, the Seattle Seahawks established the Steve Largent Award, presented annually to the team contributor who best exemplifies the spirit, dedication, and integrity of Steve Largent. Largent, himself, was the first recipient of the award.

After retiring from football, Largent pursued a career in politics and was elected to Congress in 1994 as a representative from Oklahoma. He won three successive elections and served until 2002. He ran for governor of Oklahoma in 2002 and was defeated in a close election. In 2003, he became the president and chief executive officer of CTIA,The Wireless Association. Largent was inducted into the **Pro Football Hall of Fame** in 1995.

LAS VEGAS POSSE. The Las Vegas Posse was a team in the **Canadian Football League (CFL)** in 1994. Home games were played at the 36,000-seat Sam Boyd Stadium in Whitney, Nevada, a suburb of Las Vegas. Their record was 5–13, last in their division. Poor attendance (one game had only 2,350 as the announced attendance) resulted in their last home game being played in Edmonton, Alberta, Canada, and caused the franchise to fold after just one season. The Posse's head **coach** was Ron Meyer, a former coach at the University of Nevada, Las Vegas, as well as in the **National Football League**. One of their players was rookie **quarterback Anthony Calvillo**, who went on to an outstanding career in the CFL (three-time winner of the league's Most Outstanding Player Award) with Hamilton and Montreal and was still active in 2012.

LATERAL. A lateral is a sideward or backward **pass**. It can be thrown by any ball carrier. In present-day **football**, it is seldom employed. The famous **University of California–Stanford University** game in 1982 employed five laterals on a last-second **kickoff** return to enable California to score a **touchdown** and win the game.

LAYDEN, ELMER FRANCIS. B. 4 May 1903, Davenport, Iowa. D. 30 June 1973, Chicago, Illinois. Elmer Layden was a graduate of Davenport High School in Davenport, Iowa, where he played both basketball and **football** and ran on the track team. He continued his education at the **University of Notre Dame** and was a six-foot-tall, 160-pound **fullback** in the famed Notre Dame backfield that was nicknamed the **"Four Horsemen of Notre Dame"** by sportswriter **Grantland Rice**. Layden's final football game at Notre Dame was on 1 January 1925, in the **Rose Bowl**, where he scored three **touchdowns** to lead the undefeated Fighting Irish to a 27–10 victory over previously undefeated **Stanford University** and win the national collegiate championship. Following the football season, Layden played on the Notre Dame basketball team.

After graduating from Notre Dame, Layden was named **coach** of Columbia College in Iowa (now known as Loras College) and coached there in 1925 and 1926. He also briefly played **professional football** in the **American Football League** in 1926. In 1927, he moved to Duquesne University as head coach, coached there until 1933, and was named the Notre Dame head coach in 1934. His coaching record at Loras was 8–5–2; at Duquesne, 48–16–6; and at Notre Dame, 47–13–3.

In 1941, Layden was selected as the first commissioner of the **National Football League (NFL)**, and he resigned from his coaching position at Notre Dame. (Prior NFL chief executives **Jim Thorpe**, **Joe Carr**, and Carl Storck had held the title of league president.) Layden served as NFL commissioner until January 1946, when it was felt by several of the NFL owners that he was not strong enough to combat the threat posed by the newly created rival **All-America Football Conference**.

After leaving the NFL, Layden became an executive with General American Transportation in Chicago, a lessor of railroad cars (later known as GATX), and he remained with them until 1968, when he retired at the age of 65. He was inducted into the **College Football Hall of Fame** as a charter member in 1951.

LAYNE, ROBERT LAWRENCE "BOBBY." B. 19 December 1926, Santa Anna, Texas. D. 1 December 1986, Lubbock, Texas. Bobby Layne was one of the toughest **quarterbacks** in **National Football League (NFL)** history and one of the few players active during the 1960s that played without a **face mask**. At Highland Park High School in Dallas, Texas, he was a teammate of **Doak Walker**, who would later be his teammate with the **Detroit Lions** in the NFL. Layne attended the **University of Texas** and played **football** there from 1944 to 1947. During those four years, Texas had a record of 33–8, with victories in the **Cotton Bowl** and **Sugar Bowl**. In the 1 January 1946 Cotton Bowl, Layne, a sophomore, accounted for all 40 of his team's points in their 40–27 victory over Missouri. He ran for four **touchdowns, passed** for two others, and kicked four of six extra points. He also starred as a pitcher on the Texas baseball team.

Layne was selected by the **Chicago Bears** as the third overall choice in the 1948 NFL **Draft**, and also by the **Baltimore Colts** in the 1948 **All-America Football Conference** Draft as the second overall pick. He signed with the Bears but was relegated to third-string quarterback behind **Sid Luckman** and **Johnny Lujack**, both future **Pro Football Hall of Famers**. After one season in Chicago, Layne was traded to the New York Bulldogs. He played with them for only one year before being traded to the Detroit Lions. He starred with the Lions and led them to the NFL Championship Game in 1952, 1953, 1954, and 1957, although in 1957 he shared the quarterback role with Tobin Rote and did not play in the Championship Game. They met the **Cleveland Browns** in all four title games and won all except 1954.

Layne was traded to the **Pittsburgh Steelers** after two games in 1958, and an apocryphal story is that he put a curse on the Lions franchise, saying that they would not win for 50 years. As of the 2012 season, the "curse of Bobby Layne" has come true, and the Lions have not reached the final round of the NFL **playoffs** and are one of only two teams active in 1958 to have never played in the **Super Bowl**. Layne remained with the Steelers through the 1962 season.

In his 15-year NFL career, Layne played in 175 regular-season games, completed 1,814 passes in 3,700 attempts for 26,768 yards and 196 touchdowns, and ran 611 times for 2,451 yards and 25 touchdowns. He was occasionally used as a placekicker and kicked 34 **field goals** in 50 attempts and 120 of 124 extra points. After retiring, he worked as an **assistant coach** for the Steelers. He was inducted into the Pro Football Hall of Fame in 1967.

LEAHY, FRANCIS WILLIAM "FRANK." B. 27 August 1908, O'Neill, Nebraska. D. 21 June 1973, Portland, Oregon. Frank Leahy attended Winner High School in Winner, South Dakota, where he was a member of their **football** team. He then went to the **University of Notre Dame** and played **tackle** for three years for the legendary football **coach Knute Rockne** from 1928 to 1930. The Fighting Irish had a record of only 5–4 in 1928, but they were undefeated national champions in 1929 and 1930, winning 19 games during those two years.

After graduating in 1931, Leahy was employed by Georgetown University as an **assistant coach**. He moved to **Michigan State University** the following year and Fordham University the year after that. At each of these three schools, he specialized in coaching line play. He remained at Fordham through 1938 and, while there, coached their famous line the "Seven Blocks of Granite," which featured **Vince Lombardi** as one of the **linemen**. From 1935 to 1938, Fordham had a record of 24–3–7 and outscored their opponents 630–120. Their 1937 team was undefeated in eight games and allowed only 16 points. In 1939, Leahy became head coach of Boston College. In 1939, he led them to a record of 9–2 and a postseason appearance in the **Cotton Bowl**. He improved on that performance in 1940, leading the Terriers to the national championship with an undefeated 11–0 season and **Sugar Bowl** postseason victory.

Leahy was offered an opportunity to coach his alma mater, Notre Dame, in 1941 and accepted it. He coached them from 1941 to 1943; served in the U.S. Navy in 1944 and 1945; and returned to coach Notre Dame from 1946 until 1953, when ill health caused him to resign. Leahy spent a total of 11 years as head coach at Notre Dame. During that time, the Fighting Irish compiled a record of 87–11–9; were national champions in 1943, 1946, 1947, and 1949; and were undefeated in 1941, 1946, 1947, 1948, 1949, and 1953, including a consecutive 39-game winning streak from 28 September 1946 to 30 September 1950.

Leahy's only experience with **professional football** occurred in 1960, when he served as general manager for one season for the Los Angeles Chargers of the newly formed **American Football League**. He later worked as an executive for a vending machine company in Oregon. He was inducted into the **College Football Hall of Fame** as a coach in 1970.

LEBARON, EDWARD WAYNE, JR. "EDDIE." B. 7 January 1930, San Rafael, California. At only five feet, seven inches tall and 165 pounds, Eddie LeBaron was one of the smallest men to play **professional football** and the shortest to play **quarterback**. He played **high school football** at Oakdale High School in Oakdale, California, and collegiate **football** at the College of the Pacific. In college, in addition to quarterbacking on **offense**, he played **safety** on **defense** and was also the team's **punter**. In LeBaron's four years at Pacific, 1946 to 1949, the school had a record of 33–9–2 and played in four **bowl games**. In 1949, the team won all 11 games, and LeBaron **passed** for a school record 1,282 yards. He also set school season records for most **touchdowns** passing (16) in 1947 and highest punting average (40.5 yards per **punt**) in 1948.

After graduation, LeBaron served in the U.S. Marine Corps as a lieutenant during the Korean War and was awarded the Purple Heart and Bronze Star for heroism. He was **drafted** by the **Washington Redskins** of the **National Football League (NFL)** in the 10th round (123rd overall) in 1950 and, after being discharged from the service, began playing with them in 1952. In 1952, the 22-year-old LeBaron shared quarterback duties with the legendary **Sammy Baugh**, then 38 years old. The following year, LeBaron again shared the quarterback position, this time with rookie Jack Scarbath. LeBaron, however, was the team's primary punter in each of those years.

In 1954, he played in Canada for the **Calgary Stampeders** after his college **coach**, Larry Siemering, had just been named as their coach. After just one season in Calgary, Siemering was replaced, and LeBaron returned to the Redskins for 1955. He was their main punter but again shared the quarterback role. By 1957, LeBaron became Washington's main quarterback and started all 12 games, although he was no longer used as a punter.

In 1960, LeBaron was selected by the **Dallas Cowboys** in the expansion draft, and he became their starting quarterback through the 1961 season. In 1962 and 1963, LeBaron's final year as a professional football player, he helped tutor Cowboys' quarterback **Don Meredith** and, as such, only appeared in a few games.

In his 11-year NFL career, LeBaron played in 134 regular-season games, started in 81 of those games, had a 26–52–3 record as a starter, completed 898 passes in 1,796 attempts for 13,399 yards and 104 touchdowns, and ran 202 times for 650 yards and nine touchdowns. During the seasons in which he was used as a punter, he punted 171 times for an average of 40.9 yards per punt. In his first season, 1952, LeBaron also kicked six extra points in seven attempts. His NFL teams did not play in any postseason games. He played in four **Pro Bowls**.

After retiring, LeBaron practiced law and did some sports announcing. From 1977 to 1985, he was an executive with the **Atlanta Falcons**, first as general manager and later as executive vice president. He was inducted into the **College Football Hall of Fame** in 1980.

LILLY, ROBERT LEWIS "BOB." B. 26 July 1939, Throckmorton, Texas. Bob Lilly played **high school football** at Throckmorton High School in Throckmorton, Texas, through his junior year. During his senior year, he and his family moved to Pendleton, Oregon, where he completed his high school education at Pendleton High School. He returned to Texas for college and attended Texas Christian University (TCU). At TCU from 1958 to 1960, he helped lead the **defense** to limit their opposition to just 247 points in 32 games, an average of less than eight points per game. TCU's record during those three years was 20–9–3. They were Southwest Conference cochampions in 1958 and champions in 1959.

The six-foot, five-inch, 260-pound defensive **lineman** was selected in the first round of the 1961 **National Football League (NFL) Draft** by the **Dallas Cowboys** as the 13th overall choice, and by the **Dallas Texans** in the second round of the **American Football League** Draft as the 14th overall selection. Lilly chose the Cowboys and played with them from 1961 to 1974. He began as a defensive **end** but was moved to defensive **tackle** after his first two seasons with the team. He was a member of the 1972 **Super Bowl** champions and played on the losing side in the 1966 and 1967 NFL Championship Games and 1971 Super Bowl.

As a defensive lineman, there are no official statistics that adequately measure Lilly's performance. In his 14-year NFL career, Lilly played in all 14 regular-season games each year for a total of 196 games. He also appeared in an additional 14 postseason games. He **intercepted** one **pass** and returned it 17 yards for a **touchdown**. Lilly also recovered 18 **fumbles** and returned three of them for touchdowns, including one of 42 yards. Sacks were not officially recorded during his pro career. He appeared in 11 **Pro Bowls**.

After retiring from active play, Lilly pursued his interest in photography and has become a professional photographer. His photography hobby began, ironically, as a result of his football prowess when he received a 35mm camera plus a year's supply of film for being named to the Kodak Coaches' All-American team in 1961 following his senior year at TCU. Lilly was inducted into the **Pro Football Hall of Fame** in 1980 and the **College Football Hall of Fame** in 1981.

LINE JUDGE. *See* OFFICIALS.

LINE OF SCRIMMAGE. The line of scrimmage is an imaginary line crossing the spot where the ball is placed at the start of a **down**. Neither team can cross this line until the ball has been snapped. In **Canadian football**, the **defense** must play one yard behind the line of scrimmage. *See also* LINEMAN.

LINEBACKER. A linebacker is a defensive player in the row of players immediately behind the defensive **linemen**. Linebackers are generally quick and strong **tacklers**. Most teams generally employ three linebackers on a defensive set. *See also* FOOTBALL POSITIONS.

LINEMAN. The football term *lineman* refers to a player who lines up on the **line of scrimmage** on either **offense** or **defense**. Interior offensive linemen are the two **tackles**, the two **guards**, and the **center**. Defensive linemen are generally two tackles and two **ends**. Both offensive and defensive linemen tend to be the largest players on their teams and, in modern-day **football**, are often 300 pounds or heavier. *See also* FOOTBALL POSITIONS; LINEBACKER.

LIPSCOMB, EUGENE ALLEN "GENE," "BIG DADDY." B. 9 August 1931, Uniontown, Alabama. D. 10 May 1963, Baltimore, Maryland. Gene "Big Daddy" Lipscomb was one of the **National Football League's (NFL)** legendary players. One of the largest players of his era, at six feet, six inches tall and weighing around 300 pounds, he was one of the most feared defensive **linemen** and was known for his head smack (legal at that time) to opposing offensive linemen.

Orphaned at the age of 11 after his mother was murdered, Lipscomb was raised by his grandparents in Detroit. He played **football** for Miller High School in Detroit. He enlisted in the U.S. Marine Corps and was assigned to Camp Pendleton. There he was spotted by a scout for the Los Angeles Rams and was signed by them in 1953, after being discharged from the service. Lipscomb played with them from 1953 to 1955 and was then traded to the **Baltimore Colts**. With the Colts from 1956 to 1960, as a defensive **tackle**, he played in the memorable **overtime** NFL Championship Game won by the Colts over the **New York Giants** in 1958 and was a member of the NFL champion Colts again in 1959. In 1961, Lipscomb was traded to the **Pittsburgh Steelers** and was a member of that team when he was found dead of a heroin overdose in 1963.

In his 10-year NFL career, Lipscomb played in 112 regular-season and two **playoff** games, made one **interception**, and recovered seven **fumbles**. He was also credited with a **safety** in 1960, when he tackled ball carrier C. R. Roberts in the **end zone**. He played in three **Pro Bowls**. Lipscomb worked in the off-season as a professional wrestler from 1959 to 1961.

LOFTON, JAMES DAVID. B. 5 July 1956, Fort Ord, California. James Lofton attended George Washington High School in Los Angeles, California. He played **football** in high school as a **quarterback** on **offense** and **safety** on **defense**. He attended **Stanford University** from 1974 to 1978. At Stanford, he competed in track, in addition to football, and was the **National Collegiate Athletic Association** long jump champion in 1978.

A six-foot, three-inch, 190-pound **wide receiver**, Lofton was chosen in the first round of the 1978 **National Football League (NFL) Draft** by the **Green Bay Packers** as the sixth overall selection and played for them from 1978 to 1986. He played for the Los Angeles Raiders from 1987 to 1988 and **Buffalo Bills** from 1989 to 1992 and spent his final year in **professional football** in

1993 with the Raiders and **Philadelphia Eagles**. With the Bills, he played in three **Super Bowls** from 1991 to 1993 but was on the losing side each time.

In his 16-year NFL career, Lofton played in 233 regular-season games, caught 764 **passes** for 14,004 yards and 75 **touchdowns**, and ran 32 times for 246 yards and one touchdown. In 12 postseason games, he caught 41 passes for 759 yards and eight touchdowns. He also **rushed** three times for 55 yards and one touchdown. He played in eight **Pro Bowls**.

Since retiring from active play, Lofton has worked as a television analyst for pro football games and been an **assistant coach** for the **San Diego Chargers** and **Oakland Raiders**. One of his three sons, David, has played professional football in the **Canadian Football League**. Lofton was inducted into the **Pro Football Hall of Fame** in 2003.

LOMBARDI, VINCENT THOMAS "VINCE." B. 11 June 1913, Brooklyn, New York. D. 3 September 1970, Washington, D.C. Vince Lombardi is considered one of **professional football's** greatest **coaches**, if not *the* greatest. A deeply religious man who attended daily Mass throughout his adult life, he began high school at Cathedral Preparatory Seminary (then known as the Catholic College of the Immaculate Conception), a six-year school designed to prepare students for the Roman Catholic priesthood. After completing the four high school years, Lombardi decided that the priesthood was not his vocation. He then spent one year at St. Francis Preparatory High School, where he starred on their **football** team.

Lombardi received a football scholarship to Fordham University and began there in 1933. Although relatively short in stature, at five feet, eight inches tall, he was stocky at 180 pounds and played the offensive and defensive line. During that era, under coach "Sleepy" Jim Crowley, one of Notre Dame's famed **Four Horsemen**, Fordham was a **major college** contender and had records of 6–2, 5–3, 6–1–2, and 5–1–2 from 1933 to 1936. Team publicist Tim Cohane, later a nationally renowned sportswriter, nicknamed the Fordham offensive line the "Seven Blocks of Granite," and Lombardi was one of those seven blocks.

After graduation in 1937, Lombardi attempted several things, including Fordham Law School, but, in 1939, he accepted a position at St. Cecilia's High School in Englewood, New Jersey, where his former teammate, and one of the other seven blocks, Andy Palau, had just been named head football coach. Lombardi served as Latin, physics, and chemistry teacher, in addition to being an **assistant coach**. In 1942, he was promoted to head coach. In 1947, he was hired as the freshman football and basketball coach at his alma mater, Fordham. In 1948, he was an assistant coach of the Fordham **varsity** football team. In 1949, Lombardi was hired by Colonel Earl "Red" Blaik to be his assistant at the United States Military Academy. There he observed Blaik's insistence on military discipline, which, when coupled with Lombardi's spiritual discipline, helped produce the man who later succeeded as a professional football coach.

In 1954, Lombardi was hired by the **New York Giants** of the **National Football League (NFL)** as their offensive coordinator. He, along with the Giants' defensive coordinator **Tom Landry**, another future **Pro Football Hall of Fame** head coach, produced an NFL championship team in 1956. After another season in which the Giants reached the NFL Championship Game in 1958, Lombardi was offered the job of head coach of the **Green Bay Packers** in 1959.

Lombardi was Packers head coach from 1959 to 1967, and, in those nine years, he produced five NFL championship teams (1961, 1962, 1965, 1966, 1967), with the last two of those teams also winning the first two **Super Bowls**. The Packers also reached the NFL Championship Game in 1960 but were defeated by the **Philadelphia Eagles**. In 1963, the Packers had an excellent record of 11–2–1, with their only two losses being to the **Chicago Bears**, who finished at 11–1–2. Lombardi retired as coach following his second Super Bowl victory in 1967, although he remained the Packers' general manager. In his nine years at Green Bay, his record was 89–29–4.

In 1969, Lombardi was named head coach of the **Washington Redskins**. The Redskins had not had a winning season since 1955, but, under Lombardi, they had a record of 7–5–2 and finished second in their division. In 1970, he was diagnosed with cancer and died prior to the start of the football season. Following his death, the trophy given to the winning Super Bowl team was named the Vince Lombardi Trophy, and it was first presented on 17 January 1971 to the **Baltimore Colts**.

Lombardi was inducted into the Pro Football Hall of Fame as a coach in 1971. In 1986, he was selected to the **College Football Hall of Fame** for his coaching abilities and success as a player. In 1997, he was honored on a U.S. commemorative postage stamp, along with **George Halas**, **Glenn "Pop" Warner**, and **Paul "Bear" Bryant**. A theater production about his life entitled *Lombardi* opened in New York in 2010 and closed 22 May 2011 after 244 performances.

LONG SNAPPER. *See* CENTER.

LOS ANGELES CHARGERS. *See* SAN DIEGO CHARGERS.

LOS ANGELES DONS. The Los Angeles Dons were a **professional football** team in the **All-America Football Conference (AAFC)** from 1946 to

1949. They were owned by a group headed by Chicago real-estate executive and racetrack owner Benjamin Lindheimer and included among its owners actors Bob Hope, Bing Crosby, and Don Ameche and movie producer Louis B. Mayer. Home games were played at the 90,000-seat Los Angeles Coliseum in Los Angeles, California. Among their best players were tailback/**quarterback** Glenn Dobbs, **fullback** John Kimbrough, future **Pro Football Hall of Fame end** Len Ford, **punter**/fullback Bob Reinhard, **guard** Bill Radovich, and **kicker** Ben Agajanian. The Dons finished in third place in the four-team Western Division in each of their first three seasons and were **tied** for fifth place in the seven-team league in 1949. Their won-lost record for the four years was 25–27–2. The team was disbanded in 1950, when the AAFC merged with the **National Football League**.

LOS ANGELES MEMORIAL COLISEUM. The Los Angeles Memorial Coliseum was built in 1923 and is one of the largest sports facilities in the United States. Located in Los Angeles, California, it has a present-day seating capacity of 93,607, although at times in its history its capacity exceeded 100,000. It has been used as the home field for more different **professional football** teams than any other arena, including the **Los Angeles Dons** of the **All-America Football Conference** from 1946 to 1949, the Los Angeles Rams of the **National Football League (NFL)** from 1946 to 1979, the Los Angeles Chargers of the **American Football League (AFL)** in 1960, the Los Angeles Raiders of the NFL from 1982 to 1994, the Los Angeles Express of the **United States Football League** from 1983 to 1985, the Los Angeles Dragons of the Spring Football League in 2000, and the Los Angeles Xtreme of the **XFL** in 2001. In addition, the first AFL–NFL Championship Game, later known as the **Super Bowl**, was played there in 1967. The coliseum was also the site of the NFL **Pro Bowl** from 1951 to 1972, and again in 1979.

The coliseum is also used by both the **University of Southern California** and the **University of California, Los Angeles**, as their home field for **football**, and it was the site of athletics events in both the 1932 and 1984 **Olympic Games**. It was even used briefly by the Los Angeles Dodgers of Major League Baseball from 1958 to 1961, although its oval configuration did not make for a properly shaped baseball park, and its extremely short left-field fence (251 feet) required a 42-foot screen to prevent an inordinate number of home runs. Some players, notably Wally Moon, were able to adapt their swing and hit high pop flies that cleared the screen for home runs. In 1984, the coliseum was designated a National Historic Landmark. *See also* STADIUM.

LOS ANGELES RAIDERS. *See* OAKLAND RAIDERS.

LOS ANGELES RAMS. *See* ST. LOUIS RAMS.

LOUISIANA STATE UNIVERSITY (LSU). Louisiana State University (LSU) is located in Baton Rouge, Louisiana. Their **football** program began in 1893, and, since then, through 2012, Tigers' teams have compiled a record of 722–372–46. In addition, they have competed in 44 postseason **bowl games**, with a record of 22–21–1. They have been selected as national collegiate champions seven times, in 1908, 1935, 1936, 1958, 1962, 2003, and 2007. Since 1932, LSU football teams have competed in the **Southeastern Conference (SEC)** of the **National Collegiate Athletic Association**. Home games since 1924 have been played at Tiger Stadium in Baton Rouge, which currently has a seating capacity of 92,542.

The Tigers have rivalries with several schools. Tulane was a more formidable rival during the earlier part of the 20th century, but in recent years has deemphasized their athletic program, and while they still meet LSU on the **football field**, the series has become one sided. LSU leads 69–22–7 and, since 1948, has only lost four of the last 42 meetings. LSU's series with the University of Mississippi dates back to 1894, with the Tigers holding a 57–39–4 advantage. The series between LSU and Mississippi is even more one sided, as LSU leads that one 70–33–3, going back to 1896. The **University of Alabama** holds the advantage over LSU, at 47–25–5, in contests beginning in 1895. Although LSU played **Auburn University** in 1901, they only met 24 times through 1981. Since then, the two Tigers' teams have played nearly annually and have built a rivalry in the SEC. LSU leads the series (unofficially named the Tiger Bowl), 26–20–1.

LSU's most notable **coaches** have been Bernie Moore (1935–1947; 83–39–6), Paul Dietzel (1955–1961; 46–24–3), Charles McClendon (1962–1979; 137–59–7), Bill Arnsparger (1984–1986; 26–8–2), Nick Saban (2000–2004; 48–16), and Les Miles (2005–2012; 85–21). LSU alumni in the **College Football Hall of Fame** are **halfbacks** Billy Cannon (a **Heisman Trophy** winner), Abe Mickal, Charles Alexander, and Jerry Stovall; **cornerback** Tommy Casanova; **quarterback/end** George "Doc" Fenton; and ends Ken Kavanaugh and Gus Tinsley. Former LSU coaches Dana X. Bible, Mike Donahue, Lawrence "Biff" Jones, Charlie McClendon, and Bernie Moore have also been enshrined.

Through 2012, there have been 286 **professional football** players who have attended LSU, 273 in the **National Football League**, 10 in the **American Football League**, and three in the **All-America Football Conference**. They include Joseph Addai, Mel Branch, Billy Cannon, Eugene Daniel, Tommy Davis, Alan Faneca, Kevin Faulk, Dennis Gaubatz, Charlie Hennigan, Stan Humphries, Bert Jones, William "Dub" Jones, Brian Kinchen,

Kevin Mawae, Fred Miller, Johnny Robinson, Jerry Stovall, **Jim Taylor**, Henry Thomas, **Y. A. Tittle, Steve Van Buren**, and Roy Winston.

LUCKMAN, SIDNEY "SID." B. 21 November 1916, Brooklyn, New York. D. 5 July 1998, Aventura, Florida. Sid Luckman is probably the greatest **football** player to call Columbia University his alma mater. He was a graduate of Erasmus Hall High School in Brooklyn, New York. The school, founded in 1786 by Dutch settlers, was the oldest high school in New York City. The school boasts of many famous alumni in various fields, including boxing promoter Bob Arum, basketball player Billy Cunningham, football owner **Al Davis**, singer Neil Diamond, chess champion Bobby Fischer, actress Lainie Kazan, writer Bernard Malamud, detective writer Mickey Spillane, actress/singer Barbra Streisand, and actress Mae West.

After a standout career as a baseball and football player at Erasmus Hall, Luckman enrolled at Columbia University, even though he did not receive an athletic scholarship. He played on the Columbia **varsity** from 1936 to 1938 as a **halfback** or tailback in the single-wing formation and was also the team's **punter** and placekicker. During his senior year, he finished third in the voting for the **Heisman Trophy**.

Luckman was selected by the **Chicago Bears** in the 1939 **National Football League (NFL) Draft** as the second overall selection. **George Halas**, owner and **coach** of the Bears, selected Luckman because of his strong throwing arm and converted him into a **T formation quarterback**. Luckman initially did not want to play **professional football** and was preparing to work for his father-in-law's trucking company, but Halas offered him a substantial contract to sign with the Bears and Luckman accepted.

With Luckman, the Bears became the first professional team to use the T formation as their primary offensive formation, and, with Luckman as quarterback, the team reached the NFL Championship Game in five of the next eight seasons, winning the league title in 1940, 1941, 1943, and 1946, and being defeated by the **Washington Redskins** in 1942. Chicago's triumph over the Redskins in the 1940 NFL Championship Game by a score of 73–0 remains the highest-scoring and most one-sided game in NFL history, regular-season or **playoff** games.

In 1943, Luckman enlisted in the U.S. Merchant Marine and, while stationed in the United States, was able to play most games for the Bears, although he was not available for team practices. That year, he also won the league's Most Valuable Player Award, as he compiled a then NFL season record of 2,194 yards **passing**. On 14 November 1943, in a game against the **New York Giants**, he passed for 433 yards and a record seven **touchdowns**. That single-game record still stands as of 2012, although it has been matched on four other occasions.

In his 12-year NFL career, Luckman played in 128 regular-season games, completed 904 passes in 1,744 attempts for 14,686 yards and 137 touchdowns, and ran 204 times for minus 239 yards and four touchdowns. On **defense**, he **intercepted** 17 passes and returned one for a touchdown. Luckman was also a punter and had 230 **punts** for an average of 38.6 yards per punt. In 1947, he even scored an extra point. During the war years, he was also occasionally used as a punt **returner** and returned 11 punts for a 9.7-yard average. In six postseason games, Luckman completed 45 of 85 passes for 661 yards and seven touchdowns, ran 17 times for 36 yards and two touchdowns, punted 22 times for 863 yards, returned four punts for 42 yards, and intercepted three passes for 42 yards.

Luckman retired after the 1950 season and was employed by the Chicago firm Cel-U-Craft, of which he eventually became president. He was inducted into the **College Football Hall of Fame** in 1960 and the **Pro Football Hall of Fame** in 1965.

LUJACK, JOHN CHRISTOPHER, JR. "JOHNNY." B. 4 January 1925, Connellsville, Pennsylvania. Johnny Lujack attended Connellsville High School in Connellsville, Pennsylvania, where he played **football** but was not even named to the Pennsylvania all-state team. A six-foot-tall, 185-pound **quarterback**, he was surprised when he received a scholarship to the **University of Notre Dame** in 1942, as he did not think he was that good a football player. After two years in college, he served in the U.S. Navy for two years, returning to school in 1946.

After leading Notre Dame to the national championship and an undefeated season, he was **drafted** by the **Chicago Bears** of the **National Football League (NFL)** in the first round as the fourth overall selection in the 1946 draft. Lujack returned to school, and, after again leading the Irish to an undefeated season and the national championship in 1947, he was awarded the 1947 **Heisman Trophy**. In addition to playing quarterback, he also played defensive **back** and found time to be on Notre Dame's basketball, baseball, and track teams.

Lujack signed with the Bears in 1948 and played with them for four years in the NFL. His early retirement was due to the fact that he had built a successful insurance business, and he could not afford the time to play **professional football**. In addition to quarterbacking and playing defensive back, he was also the Bears' placekicker and even did a little **punting**. He played in 45 regular-season games in four years and completed 404 **passes** in 808 attempts for 6,295 yards and 41 **touchdowns**. He also ran for 742 yards and 21 touchdowns and, on **defense**, **intercepted** 12 passes. He kicked 130 of 136 extra points and four of nine **field goals**. In one postseason game (a 1950 division tiebreaker against the Los Angeles Rams), Lujack completed 15 of 29 passes for 193 yards and no touchdowns, ran three times for two yards, and kicked two extra points in two attempts.

After retiring from football, Lujack continued his insurance business, was an **assistant coach** at Notre Dame for two years, and then had an automobile dealership in Dubuque, Iowa. He was inducted into the **College Football Hall of Fame** in 1960.

MADDEN, JOHN EARL. B. 10 April 1936, Austin, Minnesota. John Madden was one of the **National Football League's (NFL)** best **coaches** but became better-known as a **football** color commentator. He was born in Minnesota and moved with his family to the West Coast as a youth. He is a graduate of Jefferson High School in Daly City, California, a San Francisco suburb. A big man, he played both offensive and defensive line in high school and college. He continued his education and football playing at the University of Oregon, transferred to the College of San Mateo (a junior college), and transferred once more to California Polytechnic State University in San Luis Obispo.

Madden was chosen by the **Philadelphia Eagles** in the 1958 NFL **Draft** in the 21st round as the 244th overall selection. He suffered a career-ending knee injury in **training camp** and never got to play in a regular-season NFL game. He turned to coaching and was hired as an assistant at Allan Hancock College in 1960. In 1962, after receiving a master's degree in education, Madden became the head football coach at Allan Hancock. In 1963, he was hired by Coach Don Coryell at San Diego State University and was there through 1966. In 1967, Madden became an **assistant coach** for the **Oakland Raiders** of the **American Football League (AFL)**. In 1969, although just 32 years of age, he was promoted to head coach of the Raiders.

In his first year as a **professional football** head coach, Madden led the Raiders to the best record in the AFL, 12–1–1, but they were defeated by the **Kansas City Chiefs** in the AFL Championship Game. In 1970, the AFL merged with the NFL, and the Raiders became members of the NFL. The now 26-team league was divided into two **conferences** and each conference into three divisions. The Raiders finished atop their division but again were defeated one game shy of the **Super Bowl**.

Although they continued to have winning records and reaching the **playoffs**, Oakland did not qualify for the Super Bowl until the 1976 season, and the team defeated the **Minnesota Vikings** on 9 January 1977 to become Super Bowl champions. After two more seasons, Madden retired at only 42 years of age. In his 10 seasons as head coach, the Raiders never had a losing record and reached the postseason playoffs in eight of the 10 seasons. His teams had a record of 103–32–7 in the regular season and 9–7 in the postseason. He was the youngest NFL coach to record 100 victories.

In 1979, Madden embarked on his second career, that of color commentator for professional football games. His down-to-earth, straightforward, knowledgeable style made him a **fan** favorite. From 1979 to 2008, he worked in that capacity for each one of the four major networks that telecast NFL games at one time or another. For much of that time, he was teamed with **Pat Summerall**. Madden later worked for four years on *Monday Night Football*, teaming with Al Michaels from 2002 to 2005.

Madden was known for his dislike of flying, stemming, he claimed, from claustrophobia due to his large size (six feet, four inches tall and probably near 300 pounds). As a result, during the first few years of his broadcast career, he traveled almost exclusively by train. During the 1980s, he reached an agreement with a bus manufacturer and, since then, has traveled in a personalized bus dubbed the Madden Cruiser. He officially retired from broadcasting in 2009 with the simple statement, "It's time." He was inducted into the **Pro Football Hall of Fame** as a coach in 2006.

MAJOR. In **Canadian football**, a **touchdown** is also referred to as a major score.

MAJOR COLLEGE. The term *major college* is popularly used in referring to Division I Football Bowl Subdivision and Division I-AA Football Championship Subdivision colleges of the **National Collegiate Athletic Association**.

MANNING, ELISHA ARCHIBALD "ARCHIE." B. 19 May 1949, Drew, Mississippi. Archie Manning may go down in **football** history as the father of two of the league's best **quarterbacks** of all time, but he himself was a talented quarterback. He attended Drew High School in Drew, Mississippi, and the University of Mississippi. At Ole Miss, he was the **varsity** quarterback from 1968 to 1970. During that time, the Rebels compiled a record of 22–10–1 and played in a postseason **bowl game** each year. Manning finished fourth in the voting for the **Heisman Trophy** in 1969 and third in 1970.

Manning was taken by the **New Orleans Saints** in the first round of the 1971 **National Football League (NFL) Draft** as the second overall selection. He played for the Saints from 1971 to 1981 and was their starting quarterback for most of that time, missing the entire 1976 season due to a shoulder injury. The Saints, however, did not have a strong team during that era and, in those 11 years, managed only one season in which they did not lose more than they won. In that year, 1979, they finished second in the National Football

Conference West Division with a record of 8–8. In 1982, after appearing in just one game for the Saints, Manning was traded to the Houston Oilers. He was traded to the **Minnesota Vikings** midway through the 1983 season and finished his NFL career with them in 1984.

In his 13-year NFL career, Manning played in 151 regular-season games, started 139 of them, and had a won-lost record of 35–101–3 in those games. He did not play in any **playoff** games in his career and was not a member of a team that reached the playoffs. He completed 2,011 **passes** in 3,642 attempts for 23,911 yards and 125 **touchdowns** and ran 384 times for 2,197 yards and 18 touchdowns. He was selected for the **Pro Bowl** in 1978 and 1979.

Manning was inducted into the **College Football Hall of Fame** in 1989. He is the father of three sons, Cooper, Peyton, and Eli. Cooper was an outstanding high school **wide receiver** but was diagnosed with a spinal condition that precluded him from continuing to play football. Both **Peyton Manning** and **Elisha "Eli" Manning** reached the NFL and have starred as quarterbacks there, each leading his team to a victory in the **Super Bowl**. In retirement, Archie Manning has done some radio and television work and runs a football camp in the summer.

MANNING, ELISHA NELSON "ELI." B. 3 January 1981, New Orleans, Louisiana. Eli Manning is the youngest of **Archie Manning's** sons but may eventually be considered as the best **football** player of the three. He is a graduate of the Isidore Newman School, a private college preparatory school in New Orleans, and, unlike his brother, Peyton, followed in his father's footsteps by attending the University of Mississippi. He played **quarterback** for Ole Miss from 2000 to 2003 and was the starter for the last three seasons. During those four years, the school had a record of 31–18 and played in postseason **bowl games** in three of the four years. Eli completed 841 **passes** in 1,383 attempts for 10,286 yards and 84 **touchdowns** in 43 games.

Manning was chosen by the **San Diego Chargers** as the first overall selection in the 2004 **National Football League (NFL) Draft**. He had stated that he did not want to play for the Chargers, and, as a result, he was immediately traded to the **New York Giants** for quarterback Philip Rivers. Manning has played for the Giants from 2004 to 2012 and, during those nine years, has had less impressive statistics than his older brother, **Peyton Manning**, although Eli has still been one of the NFL's best quarterbacks during that time.

In 2012, he surpassed Peyton in **Super Bowl** victories and also Super Bowl Most Valuable Player (MVP) Awards as he led the Giants to a second Super Bowl win in the 5 February 2012 game and won his second Super Bowl MVP Award. Eli had previously led the Giants to the Super Bowl championship in 2008 and was named MVP in that game. Peyton's **Indianapolis Colts** have reached the Super Bowl twice during his years as their quarterback but have only won one of the two games. Peyton was named MVP in that game. Eli's 2011 season was highlighted by his ability to bring the Giants victories after trailing in the fourth quarter six times during the regular season and twice more in the **playoffs**, including the Super Bowl.

Through the 2012 season, Eli has played in 137 NFL games in nine seasons, started in 135 of them, and compiled a won-lost record of 78-57. He has completed 2,612 passes in 4,457 attempts for 31,527 yards and 211 touchdowns. He has also carried the ball 213 times for 395 yards and four touchdowns. In 11 postseason games, he has completed 219 passes in 356 attempts for 2,516 yards and 17 touchdowns and **rushed** for 34 yards and no touchdowns in 19 attempts. Eli has appeared in three **Pro Bowls**.

MANNING, PEYTON WILLIAMS. B. 24 March 1976, New Orleans, Louisiana. Peyton Manning is the son of **Archie Manning**, a former **National Football League (NFL) quarterback**. Peyton's brother, **Elisha "Eli" Manning**, is also an NFL quarterback. Peyton is a graduate of the Isidore Newman School, a private college preparatory school in New Orleans. He led them to a 34–5 record in three years as a starting quarterback. He continued his education at the **University of Tennessee**, where he played from 1994 to 1997. Although he completed his degree requirements in three years, he returned as a graduate student in 1997. In his four years there, the Volunteers had a record of 40–9, were **Southeastern Conference** champions in 1997, and played in postseason **bowl games** all four years. Manning set more than a dozen significant individual records while at Tennessee. These included most **passing** attempts in a career, season, and game; most pass completions in a career and game; most passing yards in a career, season, and game; highest pass completion percentage in a career and season; and most **touchdowns** passing in a career and game.

Manning was selected by the **Indianapolis Colts** as the first overall choice in the 1998 NFL **Draft**. He played for the Colts from 1998 to 2010. In 2011, after signing a five-year contract extension, he developed a neck problem and was sidelined the entire season. From 1998 to 2010, he started in every game for the Colts and led them to a **Super Bowl** victory in 2007 and was named the game's Most Valuable Player. The Colts also reached the Super Bowl in 2010 but were defeated by the **New Orleans Saints**. Manning was named the league's Most Valuable Player in 2003, 2004, 2008, and 2009. He also holds several NFL records, including most seasons with more than 4,000 yards passing and most consecutive regular-season wins as a starting quarterback. On 7 March 2012, the Colts released the 35-year-old Manning, making him a free agent and enabling him to pursue offers from any other professional team. On 20 March 2012, he was signed by the **Denver Broncos**.

Through the 2012 season, Manning has played in and started 224 NFL games in 15 seasons, with a won-lost record of 154–70. He completed 5,082 passes in 7,793 attempts for 59,487 yards and 436 touchdowns. He also carried the ball 369 times for 728 yards and 17 touchdowns. In 20 postseason games, he has completed 481 passes in 761 attempts for 5,679 yards and 32 touchdowns and **rushed** for 26 yards and three touchdowns in 24 attempts. Manning has appeared in 12 **Pro Bowls**. Should his health hold out, he will undoubtedly be enshrined in the **Pro Football Hall of Fame** when he becomes eligible.

MARA, TIMOTHY JAMES "TIM." B. 29 July 1887, New York, New York. D. 16 February 1959, New York, New York. Tim Mara began his business life as a legal bookmaker in early 20th-century New York. A school dropout at the age of 13, he began work as a theater usher, then moved to selling newspapers, and later became a runner for bookmakers (a legal occupation at that time). By the age of 18, he began his own bookmaking business.

National Football League (NFL), league president **Joe Carr** wanted to establish a franchise in New York. He was referred to Mara after his first choice, boxing promoter Billy Gibson, refused the offer. Although he knew nothing about the sport, Mara had a friend, Dr. Harry L. March, who did, and March encouraged Mara to buy the franchise for $500. March was hired as the team's secretary and was able to take over much of the day-to-day operations.

The **New York Giants** began play in 1925, and, although the franchise lost money, Mara fortunately had enough and was able to survive. He overcame his first season's substantial losses by booking the **Chicago Bears**, with their star **Harold "Red" Grange**, as opponents for the Giants' final game of the season. The game drew exceptionally well, and Mara was able to recoup his losses. The Giants became one of the NFL's more successful teams and won the league championship in 1927. During the next 20 years, they played in the NFL Championship Game eight times from 1933 to 1946 and were league champions in 1934 and 1938. They were able to withstand competition from other New York–, Staten Island–, and Brooklyn-based professional teams in both the NFL and other leagues. Following World War II, the Giants went into somewhat of a decline, although they continued to be popular in New York. The 1956 team again won the NFL championship, and the 1958 team lost to the **Baltimore Colts** in a memorable **overtime** game for the league title.

Mara died in 1959, after having witnessed the game that has been called by some the "greatest game in **football** history." After his death, ownership remained in the Mara family, and Tim's oldest son, Jack, took over. Upon Jack's premature death at the age of 57 in 1965, Tim's son, **Wellington Mara**, became the owner. As of 2012, the Mara family still owns the New

Tim Mara, first owner of the New York Giants.
Mike Moran

York Giants. As a charter member, Tim Mara was inducted into the **Pro Football Hall of Fame** as a contributor in 1963.

MARA, WELLINGTON TIMOTHY. B. 14 August 1916, Rochester, New York. D. 25 October 2005, Rye, New York. Wellington Mara was born into a **football** family and remained a part of the **National Football League** his entire life. His father, **Tim Mara**, was the owner of the **New York Giants**, and, as a youth, Wellington was a ball boy for them. He attended the Loyola School (high school) and Fordham University. After graduating from Fordham, he began work with the Giants organization. He was assistant to the president and team treasurer in 1937 and team secretary from 1938 to 1940. Mara served in the U.S. Navy during World War II and returned and was the Giants' vice president and secretary from 1945 to 1958, vice president from 1959 to 1965, president from 1966 to 1990, and president and chief executive officer from 1990 until his death in 2005. One of his major contributions to the league was his recommendation that teams share television revenue. This enabled teams in smaller markets to prosper along with those in the major cities. He was a well-liked team executive who cared for the well-being of his players. Mara was inducted into the **Pro Football Hall of Fame** as a contributor in 1997.

MARINO, DANIEL CONSTANTINE, JR. "DAN." B. 15 September 1961, Pittsburgh, Pennsylvania. Dan Marino played **professional football** for the same team for more than 240 games, one of only 11 players and the only **quarterback** to do so. He was a graduate of Central Catholic High School in Pittsburgh, Pennsylvania, where he starred in both baseball and **football**. Selected by the Kansas City Royals in the fourth round of the 1979 Major League Baseball **Draft**, he decided to continue his education and enrolled at the **University of Pittsburgh**. He was Pittsburgh's quarterback from 1979 to 1982. During those four years, Pitt had records of 11–1, 11–1, 11–1, and 9–3.

Marino was selected by the **Miami Dolphins** in the first round of the 1983 **National Football League (NFL)** Draft as the 27th overall selection. He played with the Dolphins from 1983 through 1999 and was their starting quarterback for all but two of his 242 regular-season games. Although he compiled an excellent 147–93 won-lost record as Miami's starter and led them to the postseason **playoffs** in 10 of his 17 years, he was only able to lead them to the **Super Bowl** once, in 1985, where they were defeated by the **San Francisco 49ers**.

Marino retired from active play following the 1999 season. At that time, he was the NFL career leader in **passes** attempted, passes completed, passing yardage, and passing **touchdowns**, but all four of these records have since been surpassed by **Brett Favre**. Through the 2012 season, Marino is still in second or third place in all four categories. In his 17-year NFL career Marino, played in 242 regular-season games, started in 240 of them, and had a won-lost record of 147–93. He completed 4,967 passes in 8,358 attempts for 61,361 yards and 420 touchdowns and ran 301 times and scored nine touchdowns but only gained 87 yards. In 18 postseason games, he completed 385 passes in 687 attempts for 4,510 yards and 32 touchdowns and ran 15 times for one yard and one touchdown. He played in nine **Pro Bowls**.

Toward the end of his career, Marino dabbled briefly in auto racing, becoming a coowner of a stock car team in 1998. The team was unsuccessful and lasted only one season. Marino also owned several restaurants in Florida and has appeared in several Hollywood films. He was inducted into the **College Football Hall of Fame** in 2002 and the **Pro Football Hall of Fame** in 2005.

MARSHALL, GEORGE PRESTON. B. 11 October 1896, Grafton, West Virginia. D. 9 August 1969, Georgetown, District of Columbia. George Preston Marshall attended Friends Select School in Washington, D.C., and

Randolph-Macon College. He served in the military in World War I. He inherited a chain of laundries in the Washington, D.C., area and built a small, family owned business into a 57-store enterprise.

In 1925, Marshall owned the Washington Palace Five, a team in the new American Basketball League, the first professional basketball league that had teams in most of the major cities in the eastern United States. The team folded midway through the 1927–1928 season. Marshall then turned his interest to **football** and, along with three partners, purchased a **National Football League (NFL)** franchise in 1932. They placed a team in Boston, calling it the Boston Braves.

In 1933, the partners left, and Marshall had sole ownership of the team. He renamed the team the Redskins. Although the team was successful, winning the NFL East Division in 1936, it did not draw well, and Marshall moved the Redskins–**Green Bay Packers** NFL Championship Game to the Polo Grounds in New York with the hope of drawing more **fans**. In 1937, he relocated the Redskins to Washington, D.C., where they remain as of 2012. From 1932 to 1969, his Redskins reached the NFL Championship Game six times, winning NFL championships in 1937 and 1942.

Marshall remained owner of the **Washington Redskins** until his death in 1969 and was one of the more innovative owners. To mimic the more popular college game in the 1930s, he added a Redskins' marching band, created a Redskins' fight song ("Hail to the Redskins"), and held **halftime** shows. He helped bring about a standard schedule, with each NFL team playing the same number of games, splitting the league into two divisions, with the winners playing an NFL Championship Game, and splitting gate receipts between both teams.

Marshall also helped convince the NFL's Rules Committee to liberalize the forward **pass** rules and move the **goalposts** from the back of the **end zone** to the **goal line** to encourage more **field goals**. This latter rule change backfired against him in 1945, when, in the NFL Championship Game, Redskins' **quarterback Sammy Baugh** attempted to pass from his own end zone and the pass hit the goalpost, resulting in a **safety** against the Redskins. The two-point safety was the margin of difference, as the Cleveland Rams defeated the Redskins, 15–14. Marshall was so upset at this outcome that he had the rule changed the following season so that a pass striking the goalpost was simply an **incomplete pass**.

One area that Marshall was far from innovative in was race relations. Because Washington was the southernmost NFL city during the 1930s and 1940s, he attempted to attract fans throughout the southern United States. In that regard, he had strong views on segregation. When he first became an owner, there were several black players in the NFL, but, after 1933, there were none until after World War II. Marshall's publicly stated views on integration included the statement that, "We'll start signing Negroes when the Harlem Globetrotters start signing whites." (Marshall was probably unaware that during the World War II years, the Globetrotters did feature a white player, Bob Karstens, who actually invented several of the "reems" that were later made popular by Goose Tatum and Meadowlark Lemon.)

Marshall's Redskins were the last NFL team to integrate, and the team did so only after being ordered to do so by secretary of the interior Stewart Udall, who threatened to revoke Washington's lease on D.C. Stadium, a federally owned facility. **Running back** Bobby Mitchell became the first black player for the Redskins in 1962, after having been acquired in a trade with the **Cleveland Browns**.

Marshall was also known for his frugality in dealing with his players and his penchant for micromanaging his team to the extent of calling in plays to his **coaches** during games and ordering player substitutions. Despite his shortcomings, he was inducted into the **Pro Football Hall of Fame** as a charter member in the category of contributor in 1963.

MARSHALL, JAMES LAWRENCE "JIM." B. 30 December 1937, Danville, Kentucky. Jim Marshall played **professional football** for 21 years, appeared in four **Super Bowls**, and held the **National Football League (NFL)** record for most consecutive games played, yet he is remembered by many **fans** for one play in one game. On 25 October 1964, in a game against the **San Francisco 49ers**, he picked up a **fumble** and ran 66 yards with it to the **end zone** and threw the ball out of the end zone in celebration of what he thought was a **touchdown**. Unfortunately, he got twisted around after recovering the ball and ran the wrong way. Fortunately for him, the resulting **safety** did not cause his team to lose the game.

Marshall played football on two undefeated teams at East High School in Columbus, Ohio. He attended **Ohio State University** and played on their **varsity** in 1957 and 1958. The 1957 team was national champion and won the **Rose Bowl**. During those two years, Ohio State had a record of 15–2–2. Although Marshall was a defensive **lineman**, in one game against **Purdue University** in 1958, which ended in a 14–14 **tie**, he scored 12 of Ohio State's 14 points by returning a fumble for one touchdown and **intercepting** a **pass** for another. He left school after his junior year and played the 1959 season for the **Saskatchewan Roughriders** of the **Canadian Football League (CFL)**. In the CFL, Marshall played primarily as a defensive lineman but did play some **offense**, catching three passes for 43 yards and one touchdown.

Marshall was **drafted** by the **Cleveland Browns** of the NFL in 1960 in the fourth round as the 44th overall selection. He played for the Browns in

1960 and was traded to the expansion **Minnesota Vikings** in 1961. He spent the rest of his NFL career with the Vikings and played in the Super Bowl in 1970, 1974, 1975, and 1977, unfortunately on the losing side in each of those four games. A six-foot, four-inch, 250-pound defensive **end**, he, along with **Alan Page**, **Carl Eller**, and Gary Larsen (and later Doug Sutherland) made up the Vikings' front four linemen dubbed the "Purple People Eaters" by the media. When Marshall retired following the 1979 season, he held the NFL records for most consecutive regular-season games played, with 282, and most consecutive regular-season games as a starter, with 270, although both records have since been surpassed. He still holds the NFL career record for most opponents' fumbles recovered, with 30, including his infamous one.

In his 20-year NFL career, Marshall played in every one of his team's games, including 282 regular-season games and 19 postseason games. He had one interception and 30 fumble recoveries, with one being for a touchdown. He was also credited with a safety in 1968, when he sacked Green Bay **quarterback Bart Starr** in the end zone.

Marshall's love for adventure has had him pursuing skydiving, scuba diving, and snowmobiling. During one snowmobile expedition in Wyoming in 1971, he nearly died when his group of 16 snowmobilers got caught in a blizzard. One member of the party did die from exposure. After retiring from football, he worked as a stockbroker, insurance broker, real estate broker, owner of a limousine service, and television commentator. Although not yet inducted into the **Pro Football Hall of Fame**, Marshall is a worthy candidate and may someday be enshrined there.

MASSILLON HIGH SCHOOL. Washington High School (commonly known as Massillon High School) in Massillon, Ohio, has had one of the most famous **high school football** programs. Their football program began in 1894, and, since then, through 2012, the Tigers have compiled a record of 821–249–35. Their home field since 1939 is one of the largest high school football **stadiums** in the country, with a seating capacity of 16,600. Originally known as Tiger Stadium, it was renamed Paul Brown Tiger Stadium in 1976. The Tigers' chief rival throughout the years has been McKinley High School of Canton.

Massillon's most famous **coach** was **Paul Brown**. A Massillon alumnus, he was their head coach from 1932 to 1940 and had a record of 80–8–2, including a 35-game winning streak. Brown went on to coach at **Ohio State University** and, in **professional football**, in the **All-America Football Conference** and **National Football League (NFL)**, with the **Cleveland Browns** and, later, the **Cincinnati Bengals** of the NFL. From 1935 to 1940, Massillon was named the Ohio state high school champions. In the 1940 season, the team scored 477 points to their opponents' six.

Through 2010, 23 NFL players have attended Massillon, including Andy Alleman, Shawn Crable, Horace Gillom, brothers Jim and Lindell Houston, Tommy Jones, Willie Spencer, Chris Spielman, and Harry Stuhldreyer (one of the famed **Four Horsemen of Notre Dame** and a member of the **College Football Hall of Fame**).

MATSON, OLLIE GENOA, II. B. 1 May 1930, Trinity, Texas. D. 19 February 2011, Los Angeles, California. Ollie Matson was one of the premier **running backs** during the 1950s and was once traded for nine players in a nine-for-one-player deal. He attended George Washington High School in San Francisco, City College of San Francisco, as well as the University of San Francisco. During his senior year at the University of San Francisco, he was the nation's leading collegiate **rusher** in both yardage and **touchdowns** and helped lead his school to a record of 9–0. Although the Dons were undefeated and untied, they were also uninvited to a **bowl game**, possibly because most of the bowl games in that era were held in the southern United States and both Matson and star **lineman Burl Toler** were black.

National Football League (NFL) Draft by the Chicago Cardinals as the third overall selection. He deferred signing with the Cardinals until after the **Olympic Games**, where he competed for the U.S. track and field team in Helsinki, Finland, and won a bronze medal for his third-place finish in the 400 meter **run** and a silver medal as a member of the U.S. 4 x 400 meter relay team that was runner-up to Jamaica.

At six feet, two inches tall and 220 pounds, Matson played **halfback** and was a powerful runner and good **pass** receiver. He also returned **punts** and **kickoffs** throughout much of his professional career. He played with the Cardinals from 1952 to 1958 but missed the 1953 season while he was doing military duty that year. On 23 March 1959, he was traded by the Cardinals to the Los Angeles Rams for seven players and two future draft choices. The trade did not help either team significantly, however, as the Cardinals, who had finished in fifth place in the NFL East Division in 1958, finished in sixth place in 1959, and the Rams, who had finished second in the NFL West Division in 1958, also finished in sixth place in 1959. Matson played for the Rams from 1959 to 1962 and the **Detroit Lions** in 1963. He concluded his professional career with the **Philadelphia Eagles** from 1964 to 1966.

In his 14-year NFL career, Matson played in 171 regular-season games, ran 1,170 times for 5,173 yards and 40 touchdowns, and caught 222 passes for 3,285 yards and 23 touchdowns. He also had 143 kickoff returns and 65 punt returns for averages of 26.2 yards per kickoff return and 9.2 yards per punt return and returned three punts and six kickoffs for touchdowns. Playing on **defense**, he also **intercepted** three passes and scored a touchdown on a **fumble** recovery. Matson never played in a postseason game, but he did play in six **Pro Bowls**. He was inducted into the **Pro Football Hall of Fame** in 1972 and the **College Football Hall of Fame** in 1976.

MAXWELL AWARD. In 1935, the Maxwell Football Club of Philadelphia, a social club, was formed by **Bert Bell**, then owner of the **Philadelphia Eagles** and later commissioner of the **National Football League**. Its initial purpose was to promote safety in American **football**. In 1937, the club began awarding an annual trophy to the best collegiate football player. The award is one of the most prestigious, although it lacks the level of media publicity garnered by the **Heisman Trophy**.

MCELHENNY, HUGH EDWARD "THE KING." B. 31 December 1928, Los Angeles, California. Hugh McElhenny graduated from George Washington Preparatory High School in Los Angeles and continued his education at Compton Junior College. He was a teammate of future **National Football League (NFL)** player **Joe Perry** on the **football** team at Compton and helped lead them to the 1948 National Junior College Championship. McElhenny then attended the **University of Washington** for his final three years of college.

A six-foot, one-inch, 195-pound **halfback** nicknamed "The King," McElhenny was selected by the **San Francisco 49ers** in the first round of the 1952 NFL **Draft** as the ninth overall pick. He played with the 49ers from 1952 to 1960 and then was taken by the **Minnesota Vikings** in the expansion draft in 1961. He spent two years with the Vikings and one year each with the **New York Giants** and **Detroit Lions**. Although the 49ers had above-average teams, the closest they came to the NFL title game was in 1957, when they **tied** the Detroit Lions for first place in the NFL West Conference but were defeated by them in a **playoff** for first place. McElhenny did get to play in an NFL Championship Game in 1963 with the Giants but was on the losing side in that game.

In his 13-year NFL career, McElhenny played in 143 regular-season games, ran 1,124 times for 5,281 yards and 38 **touchdowns**, and caught 264 **passes** for 3,247 yards and 20 touchdowns. As a **kickoff** and **punt returner**, he returned 126 punts and 83 kickoffs for averages of 23.1 yards per kickoff return and 7.3 yards per punt return. He returned two punts for touchdowns. McElhenny also completed two of seven passes on **option plays** for 13 yards and one touchdown. In two postseason games, he **rushed** 21 times for 101 yards and no touchdowns, caught eight passes for 116 yards and one touchdown, and returned one kickoff for 47 yards and two punts for 19 yards. He competed in six **Pro Bowls**.

After retiring from the NFL, McElhenny became vice president of the Washington Transit Authority in Seattle, Washington. He was inducted into the **Pro Football Hall of Fame** in 1970 and the **College Football Hall of Fame** in 1981.

MCNABB, DONOVAN JAMAL. B. 25 November 1976, Chicago, Illinois. Donovan McNabb was a multisport star at Mount Carmel High School in Chicago, Illinois. In addition to leading the **football** team to a state championship in his sophomore year, he played on the basketball team alongside future National Basketball Association player Antoine Walker, was on the track and field team, and even played volleyball for one semester. McNabb received a scholarship to play football for **Syracuse University**. He was **redshirted** his freshman season and then started every game for the Orangemen the next four seasons. In 49 games from 1995 to 1998, Syracuse had a record of 35–14, and McNabb completed 548 **passes** in 938 attempts for 8,389 yards and 77 **touchdowns**. In addition, he **rushed** 465 times for 1,561 yards and 19 touchdowns. Syracuse played in a postseason **bowl game** in each of the four years McNabb was on the roster, winning two and losing two. During one of the two seasons he played on Syracuse's basketball team, 1996, the Orangemen reached the **National Collegiate Athletic Association** final game, contested against his high school teammate, Walker, who was then with Kentucky.

McNabb was taken by the **Philadelphia Eagles** in the 1999 **National Football League (NFL) Draft** in the first round as the second overall selection. He played for the Eagles from 1999 to 2009 and took them to the **Super Bowl** in 2005, but they were defeated by the **New England Patriots**, 24–21. He was traded to the **Washington Redskins** in 2010 and played one season with them as their starting **quarterback**. After losing eight of the Redskins' first 13 games, he was benched for the final three games of the season. McNabb was traded to the **Minnesota Vikings** just prior to the start of the 2011 season, but, after winning just one of the team's first six games, he was benched in favor of rookie quarterback Christian Ponder. On 1 December 2011, McNabb was released by the Vikings at his request. He had hoped to sign with another NFL team but was unable to do so.

Through the 2011 season, McNabb played in 167 NFL games in 13 seasons and started 161 of them, with a won-lost record of 98–62–1. He completed 3,170 passes in 5,374 attempts for 37,276 yards and 234 touchdowns. He also carried the ball 616 times for 3,459 yards and 29 touchdowns and caught five passes but lost seven yards while doing so. In 16 postseason games, McNabb completed 341 passes in 577 attempts for 3,752 yards and 24 touchdowns and ran 72 times for 422 yards and four touchdowns. He has appeared in six **Pro Bowls**. In 2012, McNabb was not signed by any NFL team, and his professional playing career may have reached an end.

MCNALLY, JOHN VICTOR "BLOOD." B. 27 November 1903, New Richmond, Wisconsin. D. 28 November 1985, Palm Springs, California. John "Blood" McNally was one of **football's** all-time characters. He graduated from high school at the age of 14, but there is no record of him playing organized high school sports. He then enrolled at St. John's College in Minnesota and, during his junior year, was a member of the football, baseball, basketball, and track and field teams. Prior to his college graduation, McNally decided to try his fortune playing **professional football**. To ensure his remaining college eligibility, he used an alias and, after seeing the Rudolph Valentino film *Blood and Sand*, decided to use the name "Johnny Blood." A friend of his used the name "Sand."

McNally became a **National Football League (NFL)** player in 1925 with the Milwaukee Badgers. He moved to the Duluth Eskimos in 1926 and 1927 and the Pottsville Maroons in 1928 before settling with the **Green Bay Packers** in 1929. He remained with them through 1933, played for the Pittsburgh Pirates in 1934, went back to the Packers in 1935 and 1936, and was hired as player-**coach** of the Pirates in 1937. McNally served in that capacity again in 1938, and, in 1939, he retired from playing but remained the Pirates' coach. With the Packers from 1929 to 1931 and again in 1936, he was a member of the NFL championship team. In his professional career, the six-foot, one-inch, 190-pound McNally was primarily used as a **back** and occasionally as a **punter** and placekicker.

In his 14-year NFL career, McNally played in 137 regular-season games. Official league records are incomplete for that era, but he scored at least five **rushing touchdowns** and 37 receiving touchdowns. He scored five touchdowns on **interceptions** and one each on a **punt** return and **kickoff** return. He also **passed** for four touchdowns and kicked three extra points.

During World War II, McNally served as a cryptographer and, following the war, returned to St. John's to complete his degree in economics. He coached at St. John's from 1950 to 1952 and had a record of 13–9. He was replaced at St. John's by John Gagliardi, who began coaching there in 1953 and has coached them continuously through 2012. Gagliardi is the winningest coach in collegiate football, with a record of 489–138–11 in 60 seasons through 2012. He announced his retirement on 19 November 2012. McNally was inducted into the **Pro Football Hall of Fame** as a charter member in 1963.

MEMPHIS MAD DOGS. The Memphis Mad Dogs were a **professional football** team in the **Canadian Football League (CFL)** in 1995. **Coached** by former college coach Franklin "Pepper" Rodgers, they won nine of 18 CFL games and finished fourth in the South Division. They played home games at the 62,000-seat Liberty Bowl Memorial Stadium in Memphis, Tennessee. Their **quarterback** was Damon Allen, one of the CFL's greatest players and holder of the all-time **professional football** record for most **passing** yards, with 72,381. Other players of note on the Mad Dogs were **wide receiver** Joe Horn and Nigerian-born **kicker** Donald Igwebuike. Due to their poor attendance, the Mad Dogs franchise folded after the 1995 season.

MEREDITH, JOSEPH DON "DON," "DANDY DON." B. 10 April 1938, Mount Vernon, Texas. D. 5 December 2010, Santa Fe, New Mexico. Don Meredith is best remembered by many as **Howard Cosell's** sidekick on *Monday Night Football*, but he was also one of the better **quarterbacks** in the **National Football League (NFL)** during his nine years as a player. A graduate of Mount Vernon High School in Mount Vernon, Texas, about 100 miles northeast of Dallas, he played both **football** and basketball while a student there and graduated second in his class (contrary to the hillbilly country bumpkin role he later played on *Monday Night Football*). He enrolled at Southern Methodist University and was their quarterback from 1957 to 1959.

Meredith was selected by the **Chicago Bears** in the third round of the 1960 NFL **Draft** as the 32nd overall choice and was traded by to the **Dallas Cowboys**, an expansion team in 1960. The **Dallas Texans** of the **American Football League** also selected Meredith as a "territorial choice," but Meredith signed with the NFL.

Meredith played with the Cowboys from 1960 through 1968. He began as the backup quarterback to **Eddie LeBaron**, and it was not until 1962 that he started most of the games for Dallas. In 1966 and 1967, he led the Cowboys to the NFL Championship Game, but they were defeated by the **Green Bay Packers** each year. The 1967 loss was particularly difficult, as the temperature at the start of the game was 15 degrees below zero, leading to that contest being referred to as the "**Ice Bowl**." That game, however, indirectly led to Meredith's postplaying career, as following the game, television announcer **Frank Gifford** interviewed Meredith and he came across exceptionally well. (It was rare in that era for a losing player to be interviewed.) Several years later, when the broadcast team for *Monday Night Football* was being selected, Gifford nominated Meredith to be one of the original announcers. Meredith retired as an active player after the 1968 season.

In his nine-year NFL career, Meredith played in 104 regular-season games, started 85 of them, and had a won-lost record of 48–33–4. He completed 1,170 **passes** in 2,308 attempts for 17,199 yards and 135 **touchdowns** and ran 242 times for 1,216 yards and 15 touchdowns. In four postseason games, he completed 39 of 78 passes for 551 yards and three touchdowns and ran eight times for 42 yards and no touchdowns. He played in three **Pro Bowls**.

Meredith holds the unusual NFL record of most consecutive games with two or more touchdown passes, with 13, compiled from 17 October 1965 to 9 October 1966, and is **tied** with three other players for that distinction.

In 1970, Meredith was chosen to be one of the three announcers for the ABC television experiment *Monday Night Football*. Howard Cosell and Keith Jackson were the other two. Frank Gifford, an original choice, had a contractual commitment and recommended Meredith. The show turned out to be successful far beyond anyone's expectations. A big part of the success was the interplay between the straightlaced, conservative, arrogant Cosell and the laid-back, country boy persona that Meredith adopted. After three years of *Monday Night Football*, Meredith began to lose interest and quit the show in pursuit of acting roles. He did do football announcing work for NBC on Sunday afternoon games with Curt Gowdy. After three years of varied success as an actor, Meredith returned to *Monday Night Football* from 1977 to 1984.

A private person, Meredith kept out of the limelight for most of the time following his retirement from *Monday Night Football*. The former quarterback died of a brain hemorrhage in 2010. He was inducted into the **College Football Hall of Fame** in 1982.

MIAMI, UNIVERSITY OF. The University of Miami is located in Miami, Florida. Their **football** program began in 1927, and, since then, through 2012, Hurricanes' teams have compiled a record of 554–313–19. In addition, they have competed in 37 postseason **bowl games**, with a record of 19–18. They have been selected as national collegiate champions nine times, in 1983, 1986, 1987, 1988, 1989, 1990, 1991, 2000, and 2001. For much of their history, Miami competed as an independent team. But, from 1991 to 2003, they were members of the **Big East Conference**, and, since 2004, Miami football teams have competed in the **Atlantic Coast Conference** of the **National Collegiate Athletic Association**.

Their main rivals are the **University of Florida** and **Florida State University**. Miami leads Florida State, 31–26. They also lead Florida, 28–26, in a series played for the Seminole War Canoe Trophy. Since 2002, Miami, Florida, and Florida State have battled for the Florida Cup, which is awarded to the team that defeats the other two in the same season. Miami has won three of the six cups that have been awarded.

Miami's most noted **coaches** include Andy Gustafson (1948–1963; 93–65–3), Howard Schnellenberger (1979–1983; 41–16), Jimmy Johnson (1984–1988; 52–9), Dennis Erickson (1989–1994; 63–9), Paul "Butch" Davis (1995–2000; 51–20), and Larry Coker (2001–2006; 60–15). Miami alumni in the **College Football Hall of Fame** are **safety** Bennie Blades, **fullback** Don Bosseler, defensive **tackle** Russell Maryland, defensive **end** Ted Hendricks, and **quarterbacks** Gino Torretta and Arnold Tucker. Former Miami coaches in the Hall are Andy Gustafson, Jack Harding, and Jimmy Johnson. Miami's two **Heisman Trophy** winners are Vinny Testaverde and Gino Torretta.

Through 2012, there have been 288 **professional football** players who have attended Miami, 276 in the **National Football League** and 12 in the **American Football League**. They include Ottis Anderson, Jessie Armstead, Pete Banaszak, Micheal Barrow, Bennie Blades, Rubin Carter, Dan Conners, Jeff Feagles, Chuck Foreman, Dennis Harrah, Ted Hendricks, **Devin Hester**, **Michael Irvin**, Edgerrin James, **Jim Kelly**, Cortez Kennedy, Bernie Kosar, Ray Lewis, Santana Moss, **Jim Otto**, Clinton Portis, Ed Reed, Warren Sapp, Jeremy Shockey, Vinny Testaverde, and Reggie Wayne.

MIAMI DOLPHINS. The Miami Dolphins are one of the most successful **professional football** teams in the **National Football League (NFL)**. They joined the **American Football League (AFL)** in 1966 as an expansion team and played in the Eastern Division. When the two leagues merged in 1970, they became members of the NFL's American Football Conference East Division. Home games were played at the 80,000-seat Miami **Orange Bowl** in Miami, Florida, until 1986. Since 1987, they have been played at the 75,000-seat Sun Life Stadium in Miami Gardens, Florida, originally known as Joe Robbie Stadium and subsequently known by a variety of names, as naming rights have been sold several times.

In their four years in the AFL, the Dolphins never won more than five games in one season and had an overall record of 15–39–2. Beginning in 1970, when they played in the NFL, their fortunes changed, and, from 1970 to 1985, they won 10 or more games in 13 of those 16 seasons. Their record for the 43 seasons from 1970 to 2012 is 392–270–2 in regular-season play and 20–20 in postseason **playoff** competition. Their best season, undoubtedly, was 1972, when they won all 17 games they played, 14 in the regular season and three in the playoffs. The following year, 1973, they won 12 of 14 games in the regular season, three more in the playoffs, and again won the **Super Bowl**. They have competed in the playoffs in 22 seasons and were defeated in the **wild-card playoff** game five times, lost in the divisional playoff game 10 times, lost in the AFC Championship Game in 1985 and 1992, lost in the Super Bowl three times (1971, 1982, 1984), and were Super Bowl winners twice (1972, 1973).

One of the reasons for their early success was their head **coach**, **Don Shula**. He was their coach from 1970 to 1995, and his teams had 24 winning seasons in those 26 years. Other Miami head coaches have been George Wilson (1966–1969), Jimmy Johnson (1996–1999), Dave Wannstedt (2000–2004), Jim Bates (interim 2004), Nick Saban (2005–2006), Malcolm "Cam" Cameron

(2007), Tony Sparano (2008–2011), Todd Bowles (2011), and Joe Philbin (2012).

The best players for the Dolphins include **wide receiver Paul Warfield**, **fullback Larry Csonka**, **centers** Jim Langer and Dwight Stephenson, **quarterbacks Bob Griese** and **Dan Marino, guard** Larry Little, and **linebacker Nick Buoniconti**. All are now enshrined in the **Pro Football Hall of Fame**. Hall of Famer Cris Carter, a wide receiver, also played for Miami briefly in his final NFL season. Other top players for Miami include **safeties** Dick Anderson and Jake Scott, Most Valuable Player of the 1972 Super Bowl; quarterbacks Earl Morrall and David Woodley; **kicker Garo Yepremian**; guard Bob Kuechenberg; wide receivers Mark Clayton, Mark Duper, and Nat Moore; linebacker Zach Thomas; **tackle** Richmond Webb; defensive **linemen** Bob Baumhower, Doug Betters, Bill Standfill, and Jason Taylor; and **tight end** Jim Mandich.

MIAMI SEAHAWKS. The Miami Seahawks were a **professional football** team in the **All-America Football Conference (AAFC)** in 1946. They played in the league's first game on 6 September 1946, at Cleveland's Municipal Stadium, where they were defeated by the **Cleveland Browns**, 44–0. Although the Seahawks' home games were played at the 70,000-seat Burdine Stadium (renamed the **Orange Bowl** in 1959), they never drew more than 10,000 **fans** to one of their games. The team only won three of 14 games, finishing fourth and last in the Eastern Division. After losing more than $80,000, they were expelled from the league and replaced by the **Baltimore Colts** in 1947. Of the 47 men (17 veterans, 30 rookies) who played for the Seahawks in 1946, only 13 (three veterans, 10 rookies) played pro football in subsequent years. **Halfback** William "Dub" Jones was the only Seahawk who went on to a substantial career in the AAFC and **National Football League**.

MICHIGAN, UNIVERSITY OF. The University of Michigan is located in Ann Arbor, Michigan. Their **football** program, one of the oldest in the nation, began in 1878, and, since then, through 2012, Wolverines' teams have compiled a record of 883–295–38. This is the most victories and highest winning percentage (.750) in **major college football** history. In addition, they have competed in 42 postseason **bowl games**, with a record of 20–22. They have been selected as national collegiate champions 16 times, in 1901, 1902, 1903, 1904, 1918, 1923, 1925, 1926, 1932, 1933, 1947, 1948, 1964, 1973, 1985, and 1997. From 1901 to 1904, the Wolverines were undefeated and had a record of 43–0–1. In 1905, they won 12 games and lost only one, the one loss (to Chicago, 2–0) coming in the season's last game and ending a 56-game undefeated streak in which they won 55 and **tied** one. Following the

1901 season, they defeated **Stanford University**, 49–0, in the Tournament of Roses game, the forerunner of the **Rose Bowl**. The 1901 to 1905 teams were known as the "point-a-minute" teams and scored 2,821 points to their opponents' 42.

Michigan was one of the charter members of the **Big Ten Conference** in 1896. Since 1927, Michigan has played home games at Michigan Stadium, the largest **stadium** in the United States, with a seating capacity of 109,901. Built in 1927, with a seating capacity of 72,000, it was enlarged by 1951 to 101,001, and to its present number in subsequent years. Since 26 October 1975, Michigan's home attendance for every game has surpassed 100,000.

Their main rivals are **Michigan State University**, the **University of Minnesota**, the **University of Notre Dame**, and **Ohio State University**. Michigan and Minnesota compete for the Little Brown Jug, one of the country's oldest sports' trophies. Michigan leads, 68–22–3, in that series. Michigan has the advantage over Michigan State, 68–32–5, in a series dating back to 1898. Since 1953, the two schools have competed for the Paul Bunyan Trophy, and Michigan also leads, 35–24–2. Michigan and Notre Dame have had two of the most prestigious football programs in the country. Their first meeting was in 1887. They have played only 40 times, but many of their games have featured two of the nation's top teams. Michigan leads that series, 23–16–1. Michigan and Ohio State first met in 1897. Since then, they have played nearly annually, as both schools have been in the Big Ten Conference since its inception. Michigan leads, 58–44–6.

The two most memorable head **coaches** at Michigan are Fielding "Hurry-Up" Yost and Glenn "Bo" Schembechler. Yost coached 25 years, from 1901 to 1926, missing 1924. His record was 165–29–11. Schembechler was coach from 1969 to 1989. His teams won 85 percent of their Big Ten Conference games, and his overall record was 194–48–5. Herbert "Fritz" Crisler (1938–1947; 71–16–3) and Bennie Oosterbaan (1948–1958; 63–33–4) were two other outstanding Michigan head coaches.

Michigan alumni in the **College Football Hall of Fame** are **quarterbacks** Pete Elliott, Benny Friedman, and Harry Newman; **linemen** Benny Benbrook, **Dan Dierdorf**, Reggie McKenzie, Merv Pregulman, Germany Schulz, Ernie Vick, Albert Wistert, Alvin Wistert, and Francis "Whitey" Wistert (three brothers); **safeties** Dave Brown and Tom Curtis; **ends** and **wide receivers** Anthony Carter, Desmond Howard, Ron Kramer, Jim Mandich, and Bennie Oosterbaan; **halfbacks** Bob Chappuis, Chalmers "Bump" Elliott, Tom Harmon, Willie Heston, **Elroy "Crazylegs" Hirsch**, Ron Johnson, Harry Kipke, and Bill Morley; **fullbacks** Johnny Maulbetsch and Bob Westfall; and end/fullback Neil Snow. Coaches Herbert "Fritz" Crisler, George Little, Glenn "Bo" Schembechler, Elton "Tad" Wieman, and Fielding "Hurry-Up" Yost are also enshrined in the Hall. Another of Michigan's top players was **center Gerald Ford**, who, in 1974, became the 38th president of the United States. Michigan's three **Heisman Trophy** winners are Tom Harmon; Desmond Howard; and **cornerback/kick returner** Charles Woodson, the only nonoffensive player to win the award.

Through 2012, there have been 335 **professional football** players who have attended Michigan, 321 in the **National Football League**, six in the **American Football League**, and eight in the **All-America Football Conference**. They include John Anderson, Tim Biakabutuka, David Bowens, **Tom Brady**, Dave Brown, Anthony Carter, Todd Collins, Dan Dierdorf, John "Jumbo" Elliott, Jay Feely, Len Ford, Elvis Grbac, Brian Griese, Ali Haji-Sheikh, James Hall, Jim Harbaugh, Tom Harmon, Elroy "Crazylegs" Hirsch, Steve Hutchinson, Mike Kenn, Ron Kramer, Ty Law, Randy Logan, Tom Mack, Reggie McKenzie, Trevor Pryce, Jon Runyan, Amani Toomer, Rick Volk, and Charles Woodson.

MICHIGAN STATE UNIVERSITY (MSU). Michigan State University (MSU) is located in East Lansing, Michigan. Their **football** program began in 1885, and, since then, through 2012, Spartans' teams have compiled a record of 638–426–44. In addition, they have competed in 23 postseason **bowl games**, with a record of 9–14–0. Home games since 1923 have been played at Spartan Stadium, which has a present-day seating capacity of 75,000. MSU has been selected as national collegiate champions six times, in 1951, 1952, 1955, 1957, 1965, and 1966. Since 1953, MSU football teams have competed in the **Big Ten Conference** of the **National Collegiate Athletic Association**.

The Spartans play several rivals in trophy games. The series with the **University of Notre Dame** has been played for the Megaphone Trophy since 1949. The two first met in 1897. Notre Dame leads the series 33–26–1 for the trophy and 47–28–1 overall. The series with the **University of Michigan** began in 1898. Michigan leads, 68–32–5. Since 1953, the two teams have played for the Paul Bunyan Trophy, and Michigan has that advantage as well, 35–24–2. Since 1950, MSU and the University of Indiana have played for the Old Brass Spittoon trophy, with MSU leading the series, 42–12–1. The two schools only played four times prior to 1950, and Indiana won three and **tied** one.

The **coach** most associated with MSU football is Hugh "Duffy" Daugherty. He coached the Spartans for 19 years, from 1954 to 1972, and led them to four of their six national championships. His overall record was 109–69–5. John Macklin (1911–1915; 29–5–0), **"Sleepy" Jim Crowley** (1929–1932; 22–8–3), Charlie Bachman (1933–1942, 1944–1946; 70–34–10), Clarence "Biggie" Munn (1947–1953; 54–9–2), Nick Saban (1995–1999; 35–24–1), and Mark Dantonio (2007–2012; 51–28) are other MSU head coaches with excellent records. Coaches Charlie Bachman, Duffy Daugherty, Clarence "Biggie" Munn, and Frank "Muddy" Waters have been inducted into the **College Football Hall of Fame**, along with former Spartan players **tackle** Don Coleman, **halfback** Johnny Pingel, **wide receiver** Gene Washington, defensive **end** Charles "Bubba" Smith, **safety** Brad Van Pelt, and **linebacker** George Webster.

Through 2012, there have been 268 **professional football** players who have attended MSU, 251 in the **National Football League**, 16 in the **American Football League**, and one in the **All-America Football Conference**. They include Flozell Adams, **Herb Adderley**, **Morten Andersen**, Fred Arbanas, Carl Banks, Ed Budde, Plaxico Burress, Lynn Chandnois, Joe DeLamiellieure, Al Dorow, Billy Joe DuPree, Derrick Mason, Earl Morrall, Muhsin Muhammad, Julian Peterson, Andre Rison, Rich Saul, Charles "Bubba" Smith, Willie Thrower (the first black **quarterback** in the NFL), Brad Van Pelt, Gene Washington, George Webster, Lorenzo White, and Ray Wietecha.

MID-AMERICAN CONFERENCE. The Mid-American Conference is an organization of **major colleges** and universities that compete athletically. It was established in 1946 and is based in Cleveland, Ohio. Its 12 members in 2011 were the University of Akron, Ball State University, Bowling Green State University, the State University of New York at Buffalo, Central Michigan University, Eastern Michigan University, Kent State University, Miami (Ohio) University, Northern Illinois University, Ohio University, the University of Toledo, and Western Michigan University. In 2012, the University of Massachusetts joined the conference as a football-only member.

MIDDLE GUARD. *See* GUARD.

MILLER, DON. *See* FOUR HORSEMEN OF NOTRE DAME.

MINNESOTA, UNIVERSITY OF. The University of Minnesota is located in the twin cities of St. Paul and Minneapolis, Minnesota. Their **football** program began in 1882, and, since then, through 2012, Golden Gophers' teams have compiled a record of 649–479–44. In addition, they have competed in 15 postseason **bowl games**, with a record of 5–10. They have been selected as national collegiate champions seven times, in 1904, 1934, 1935, 1936, 1940, 1941, and 1960. In 1896, Minnesota became a charter member of the **Big Ten Conference**. Home games since 2009 have been played at the 50,000-seat TCF Bank Stadium. Minnesota previously used the 64,000-seat Hubert H. Humphrey Metrodome (1982–2008), the 56,000-seat Memorial

Stadium (1924–1981), and the 20,000-seat Northrop Field (prior to 1924) as their home fields.

Since 1903, the Golden Gophers have played the **University of Michigan** nearly annually in a contest for the Little Brown Jug, one of the country's oldest sports' trophies. Michigan leads the series, 68–22–3. Minnesota's rivalry with the **University of Wisconsin** has seen 121 games since 1890. Since 1948, the winner of their annual game has been awarded the Paul Bunyan's Axe trophy. Minnesota leads the series, 59–55–8.

Minnesota's most successful **coach** was Henry L. "Doc" Williams. He led them from 1900 to 1921 and had a record of 136–33–11. Bernie Bierman, coach for 16 seasons, from 1932 to 1941 and 1945 to 1950, also had an outstanding record of 93–35–6 and five national championships. Murray Warmath (1954–1971; 87–78–7) and Glen Mason (1997–2006; 64–57–0) also had successful careers with the Golden Gophers.

Minnesota has 18 alumni and four former coaches in the **College Football Hall of Fame**. They are **quarterbacks** John McGovern and Sanford "Sandy" Stephens; **halfbacks** George "Sonny" Franck, Paul Giel, Francis "Pug" Lund, and Bruce Smith (a **Heisman Trophy** winner); **fullback** Herb Joesting; **ends** Bert Baston, Bobby "Rube" Marshall, and Eddie Rogers; **linemen** Bobby Bell, Tom Brown, **Carl Eller**, **Bronko Nagurski** (the legendary **tackle** on **defense** and fullback on **offense**), **Leo Nomellini**, Clayton Tonnemaker, Ed Widseth, and Dick Wildung; and coaches Bernie Bierman, Herbert "Fritz" Crisler, Lou Holtz, and Henry L. "Doc" Williams. **Robert "Gloomy Gil" Dobie**, who played end and quarterback for Minnesota from 1900 to 1902 and was later an **assistant coach** there, is also a member of the College Football Hall of Fame and was inducted for his success as head coach at four other schools.

Through 2012, 234 **professional football** players have attended Minnesota, 218 in the **National Football League**, five in the **American Football League**, and 11 in the **All-America Football Conference**. They include Marion Barber, Bobby Bell, **Gino Cappelletti**, Tyrone Carter, Carl Eller, Keith Fahnhorst, Gale Gillingham, Matt Herkenhoff, Greg Larson, Karl Mecklenburg, Mike Mercer, Leo Nomellini, Charlie Sanders, Gordie Soltau, Milt Sunde, Clayton Tonnemaker, and John Williams, as well as **Harry "Bud" Grant** and Tony Dungy (better known as **Super Bowl**-winning head coaches).

MINNESOTA VIKINGS. The Minnesota Vikings are a **professional football** team in the **National Football League (NFL)**. They began play in the NFL Western Conference in 1961 as an expansion team. In 1967, when the league split into four divisions, they were placed in the Central Division.

Adrian Peterson, star running back of the Minnesota Vikings.
Minnesota Vikings

After the merger with the **American Football League (AFL)** in 1970, the Vikings were members of the National Football Conference (NFC) Central Division until 2001. In 2002, they became members of the NFC North Division. Their home field through 1981 was the 48,000-seat Metropolitan Stadium in Bloomington, Minnesota, a suburb of Minneapolis. Since 1982, the Vikings have played home games at the 64,000-seat Hubert H. Humphrey Metrodome in Minneapolis, Minnesota. The **stadium** features an inflatable domed roof that collapsed in December 2010 as a result of heavy snow accumulation, forcing the Vikings to play a home game in Detroit and a second contest outdoors at the **University of Minnesota's** TCF Bank Stadium.

In the nine years that the Vikings played in the NFL prior to the merger with the AFL in 1970, they compiled a regular-season record of 52–67–7. In 1967, three of their 14 games ended in **ties**. Their **playoff** record for those nine years was 2–2. The Vikings lost the Western Division playoffs in 1968, and, in 1969, they reached the **Super Bowl**, where they were defeated by the **Kansas City Chiefs**, 23–7. The Vikings' overall regular-season record in 52 years of NFL competition is 426–355–9, and in playoff competition it is 19–27. Their best seasons were 1969 and 1973, when they won 12 of 14 games in the regular season and reached the Super Bowl but lost. In 1998, they finished the regular season at 15–1 but lost in the NFC championship to the **Atlanta Falcons**, 30–27, in **overtime**. In 26 years of postseason playoff competition, they have lost in the **wild-card** round six times, were defeated in the division playoffs or second round 12 times, lost in the NFC championship five times (twice in overtime), and were defeated in the Super Bowl four times (1969, 1973, 1974, 1976).

Their best head **coach** was **Harry "Bud" Grant**, a former **professional football** (both NFL and **Canadian Football League**) and basketball player (Minneapolis Lakers in the National Basketball Association). He was coach from 1967 to 1983 and again in 1985. All four of the Vikings' Super Bowl appearances came during his tenure. Other Minnesota coaches include **Norm Van Brocklin** (1961–1966), Les Steckel (1984), Jerry Burns (1986–1991), Dennis Green (1992–2001), Mike Tice (2001–2005), Brad Childress (2006–2010), and Leslie Frazier (2010–2012).

The Vikings' best players have included **Pro Football Hall of Fame quarterbacks Warren Moon** and **Fran Tarkenton; running back Hugh McElhenny; tight end** Dave Casper; **wide receiver** Cris Carter; **safety** Paul Krause; defensive **linemen** Chris Doleman, **Carl Eller, Alan Page**, and John Randle; offensive linemen Jim Langer, Randall McDaniel, Ron Yary, and Gary Zimmerman; and **kicker Jan Stenerud**. Other outstanding players for Minnesota include quarterbacks Daunte Culpepper, Randall Cunningham, **Brett Favre**, and **Joe Kapp**; running backs Bill Brown, Chuck Foreman,

Dave Osborne, Adrian Peterson, and Robert Smith; **center** Mick Tinglehoff; wide receivers John Gilliam, **Randy Moss**, **Ahmad Rashad**, and Gene Washington; **linebacker** Scott Studwell; and defensive linemen Gary Larsen and **Jim Marshall**. During the Vikings' best years, the 1970s, their defensive line of Page, Eller, Marshall, and Larsen (and Larsen's replacement, Doug Sutherland) were dubbed the "Purple People Eaters" by the media (named after the Sheb Wooley popular song of the 1950s since their uniforms were purple and they "ate up" the opposition).

MONDAY NIGHT FOOTBALL. *Monday Night Football* began in 1970 as an experiment by ABC and quickly became an American institution. **Alvin "Pete" Rozelle**, commissioner of the **National Football League (NFL)**, was looking to expand television coverage during the 1960s and decided to experiment with night football. Although the NFL had played a few Saturday night games during the early 1950s, the league had not yet achieved the extensive **fan** interest that it would later in the decade, and the games did not achieve high ratings.

As the NFL fan base greatly increased during the 1960s, Rozelle wanted to try again. Although the networks were initially unreceptive to the idea of preempting their regular family television programming in the evening, Rozelle convinced ABC (then the least-watched and lowest-rated network) to televise a weekly game on Monday nights. Once the agreement was made, ABC producer Roone Arledge decided to try a different slant on the broadcast and emphasize its entertainment value.

With that in mind, he hired **Howard Cosell**, a former lawyer turned sportscaster whose style of broadcasting was argumentative and controversial. Along with Cosell, Arledge attempted to hire an established football play-by-play announcer, and, since his first two choices of Vince Scully and Curt Gowdy were unavailable, he settled for Keith Jackson, an experienced, capable announcer. Arledge then sought a color analyst and tried to hire **Frank Gifford**, the former **New York Giants** NFL player who had been working as a football color analyst in New York, but he was also unavailable. Gifford suggested **Don Meredith**, a recently retired former **Dallas Cowboys quarterback** who had come across quite well when interviewed by Gifford following the Cowboys' loss in the infamous "**Ice Bowl**" game that Meredith had quarterbacked.

The first *Monday Night Football* telecast took place on 21 September 1970, during a game between the **New York Jets** (defending NFL champions) and **Cleveland Browns** in Cleveland. The interplay between the pompous, opinionated Cosell and the laid-back, humorous Meredith turned out to be much more entertaining than expected, and the event soon became must-see television for a large portion of American males.

The following year, Gifford became available, and he replaced Jackson as the play-by-play reporter, even though he had previously only been a color analyst. The team of Gifford, Meredith, and Cosell had exceptional chemistry, and the show became an outstanding success. The three worked together through the 1973 season. By 1974, Meredith had lost interest and left the broadcast team to pursue an acting career. Former NFL star Fred Williamson replaced him but lasted only a few games before being replaced by **Alex Karras**, another former NFL player with an excellent sense of humor who later worked as an actor. Meredith returned in 1977 and worked on the show until 1984. Cosell continued until 1983. Gifford did play-by-play through 1985 and was replaced by Al Michaels but continued as a color analyst through 1997. Other color analysts used during the 1980s at one time or another included former players **Fran Tarkenton, O. J. Simpson, Joe Namath,** and **Dan Dierdorf**. One of the best announcing combinations occurred from 2002 to 2005, when **John Madden** joined Al Michaels.

The series remained on ABC until 2006, when the Entertainment and Sports Programming Network cable channel better known as ESPN, owned by ABC, took over the broadcasts. Although the show is still highly rated, the announcing chemistry that Gifford, Meredith, and Cosell had during the broadcast's early years has been lost.

MONK, JAMES ARTHUR "ART." B. 5 December 1957, White Plains, New York. Art Monk, a distant relative of jazz great Thelonious Monk, attended White Plains High School and **Syracuse University**. He was a **wide receiver** at Syracuse for four years, from 1976 to 1979. Although Syracuse's **football** teams did not fare particularly well during those four years, with a record of just 19–26, the six-foot, three-inch, 210-pound Monk led the team in receiving in each of his last three years and caught the eye of professional scouts.

Monk was chosen in the first round of the 1980 **National Football League (NFL) Draft** by the **Washington Redskins** as the 18th overall selection. He played for the Redskins for 14 years, from 1980 to 1993, and finished his NFL career with one year with the **New York Jets** and one year with the **Philadelphia Eagles**. He was a member of the **Super Bowl** champions in 1983, 1988, and 1992 and was on the losing side in the 1984 Super Bowl. In 1984, Monk became the first NFL player to record more than 100 **receptions** in a season. His record of 106 catches remained the NFL record until 1992. Monk also held the NFL record for most career receptions, but it was broken by **Jerry Rice** in 1995.

In his 16-year NFL career, Monk played in 224 regular-season games, caught 940 **passes** for 12,721 yards and 68 **touchdowns**, and ran 63 times for

332 yards and no touchdowns. He only attempted two passes and completed one for a 46-yard gain. In 15 postseason games, he caught 69 passes for 1,062 yards and seven touchdowns. He also ran six times for 17 yards and no touchdowns. He played in three **Pro Bowls**.

After retiring from active play, Monk cofounded Alliant Merchant Services, an electronic payment services company. He is also involved with the Art Monk Football Camp. He was inducted into the **Pro Football Hall of Fame** in 2008.

MONTANA, JOSEPH CLIFFORD, JR. "JOE." B. 11 June 1956, New Eagle, Pennsylvania. Joe Montana is one of only two **quarterbacks** to start and win four **Super Bowls**. (**Terry Bradshaw** is the other.) Montana is also one of several **National Football League (NFL)** star quarterbacks to be raised in western Pennsylvania. He attended Ringgold High School in Monongahela, Pennsylvania, about 25 miles south of Pittsburgh. He played baseball, **football**, and basketball in high school; was a member of the league basketball championship team; and was a good enough player to be offered a basketball scholarship to North Carolina State University. Montana became Ringgold's starting quarterback on their football team during his junior year. He later accepted a football scholarship to the **University of Notre Dame**.

Montana was at Notre Dame for five football seasons, from 1974 to 1978, but he did not play on the **varsity** as a freshman due to Notre Dame policy and was **redshirted** in 1976 due to a shoulder separation that he had suffered prior to the start of that season. He did not become the starting quarterback until the fourth game of the 1977 season. That year, he led the Fighting Irish to nine consecutive victories, a victory over the **University of Texas** in the **Cotton Bowl**, and the national championship. In 1978, Montana led Notre Dame to a 9–3 season and another Cotton Bowl victory.

Montana was selected by the **San Francisco 49ers** in the third round of the 1979 NFL **Draft** as the 82nd overall choice. He began his **professional football** career in 1979 with the 49ers as their backup quarterback and only started one game. He started seven games in 1980 but became the fulltime starting quarterback in 1981. That year, he led the 49ers to a 13–3 regular-season record and the Super Bowl championship. This was the first time that the 49ers had reached the NFL Championship Game since joining the league in 1950. Montana led them to a second Super Bowl title in 1985.

In 1986, a severe back injury limited Montana to just eight games, but he made a fine comeback and won two more Super Bowls in 1989 and 1990. During the 1990 season, Montana led the 49ers to the best record in the NFL that year, at 14–2, but they were defeated by the **New York Giants** in the National Football Conference championship game. Montana suffered an elbow injury in that game and, as a result, missed the entire 1991 season and was only able to play in one game in 1992. In 1993, he was traded to the **Kansas City Chiefs** and played his last two NFL seasons with them, retiring after the 1994 season.

In his 15-year NFL career, Montana played in 192 regular-season games, started in 164 of those games, and had a won-lost record of 117–47. He completed 3,409 **passes** in 5,391 attempts for 40,551 yards and 273 **touchdowns** and ran 457 times for 1,676 yards and 20 touchdowns. In 23 postseason games, he completed 460 of 734 passes for 5,772 yards and 45 touchdowns and ran 63 times for 314 yards and two touchdowns.

After retiring from the NFL, Montana became the owner of a vineyard in the Napa Valley in California and produces wines under the name Montagia Wines. He was inducted into the **Pro Football Hall of Fame** in 2000.

MONTREAL ALOUETTES. The Montreal Alouettes are a team in the **Canadian Football League (CFL)**. The original Montreal **football** team was founded in 1872 as the Montreal Football Club. After several name changes (Montreal AAA Winged Wheelers, 1919–1935; Montreal Indians, 1936–1937; Montreal Cubs, 1938; Montreal Royales, 1939–1941), they were renamed the Alouettes (Larks) in 1946 and became members of the Interprovincial Rugby Football Union (IRFU). In 1958, the IRFU became part of the new CFL. The Alouettes played in the CFL through the 1981 season. The franchise was folded, but new ownership was found and a new Montreal franchise, known as the Concordes, began play in 1982 using Alouette players. In 1986, the Concordes were renamed the Alouettes but only lasted until 24 June 1987, when the team was disbanded.

In 1994, the CFL decided to expand into the United States, and one of the new teams was the **Baltimore Stallions**. Although the Stallions were successful, most of the other U.S.-based teams were not, and the Baltimore ownership decided to move their team to Montreal in 1996 and play as the Montreal Alouettes, which they have done through 2012.

Teams named the Montreal Alouettes have appeared in the **Grey Cup** 18 times since 1946 and have won seven. The Alouettes franchise in existence from 1946 to 1981 had a record of 4–6, and the Alouettes franchise in existence from 1996 to 2012 has a record of 3–5. The Concorde/Alouettes teams of 1982 to 1987 did not reach the Grey Cup. The Stallions were 1–1 in the Grey Cup in their two years in the league.

Since 1997, the Alouettes have played most home games at the 25,000-seat Percival L. Molson Stadium in Montreal, Quebec. They have also used Olympic Stadium in Montreal, a much larger **stadium** that seats 66,000 for football. Throughout their history, the team has also played at Delorimier

Stadium (1946–1953) and the Autostade (1968–1971, 1973–1976), both located in Montreal.

Among Montreal's **coaches** have been Lew Hayman (1946–1951), Douglas "Peahead" Walker (1952–1959), **Sam Etcheverry** (1970–1972), Marv Levy (1973–1977), Joe Scannella (1978–1981), Don Matthews (2002–2006), and Marc Trestman (2008–2012).

Canadian Football Hall of Fame players who played for the Alouettes include Junior Ah You, Peter Dalla Riva, George Dixon, Sam Etcheverry, Terry Evanshen, Gene Gaines, Dickie Harris, John O'Quinn, Tony Pajaczkowski, Hal Patterson, Mike Pringle, Herb Trawick, Pierre Vercheval, and Virgil Wagner. Other players of note include future Hall of Famer **Anthony Calvillo**, the all-time **professional football passing** yardage leader; Pierre Desjardins; Vince Ferragamo; Frank Filchock; and Billy "White Shoes" Johnson.

MONTREAL CONCORDES. *See* MONTREAL ALOUETTES.

MOON, HAROLD WARREN "WARREN." B. 18 November 1956, Los Angeles, California. Warren Moon is one of only two men inducted into both the **Canadian Football Hall of Fame** and **Pro Football Hall of Fame**. He was known for having one of the strongest throwing arms in **football** history. He attended Alexander Hamilton High School in Los Angeles, California, where he was the **quarterback** during his senior year. He continued his education at West Los Angeles College, a two-year junior college. Although Moon was recruited by four-year colleges, they wanted to convert him to other positions, since it was uncommon at the time for **major colleges** to have black quarterbacks. He insisted on playing quarterback, thus his decision to enroll at a two-year school. After playing successfully at West Los Angeles in 1974, he was offered a scholarship to the **University of Washington**, where he was allowed to play his best position, quarterback. He played three seasons at Washington, appeared in 31 games, and completed 129 **passes** in 496 attempts for 3,277 yards and 19 **touchdowns**. Washington had a record of 21–13 during those three years, and Moon led the Huskies to a 10–2 record and a **Rose Bowl** victory his senior year.

Despite the fact that he was a Rose Bowl–winning quarterback, Moon was not **drafted** by the **National Football League (NFL)**, possibly because there were few black quarterbacks in the NFL during that period. He decided to play in the **Canadian Football League (CFL)** and, from 1978 to 1983, starred with the **Edmonton Eskimos**. In his six years in the CFL, he played in 94 regular-season games and completed 1,369 passes in 2,382 attempts for 21,228 yards and 144 touchdowns. He also carried the ball 330 times for

1,700 yards and 16 touchdowns. From 1978 to 1982, the Eskimos won the **Grey Cup** each year, an unprecedented feat in the long history of that event and one that has yet to be equaled. Moon and Tom Wilkinson split the quarterback position for the first four years of that streak.

After establishing himself as one of the great CFL players of all time, Moon was offered the opportunity to play in the NFL in 1984. He signed with the Houston Oilers and was their starting quarterback for the next 10 seasons. Although he helped the Oilers reach the **playoffs** in seven consecutive seasons, from 1987 to 1993, they could never win more than one playoff game in any of those years. Moon was traded to the **Minnesota Vikings** in 1994 and played for them through 1996. In 1997, after being released by the Vikings at the age of 40, he signed with the **Seattle Seahawks** and played two seasons for them as their starting quarterback. A free agent again in 1999, he was signed by the **Kansas City Chiefs** as a backup quarterback and appeared in just three games in two seasons with them before finally retiring at the age of 44.

Moon's best NFL seasons were 1990 and 1991, when he led the NFL in pass attempts, pass completions, and passing yardage and was named the NFL Offensive Player of the Year in 1990. On 16 December 1990, he passed for 527 yards in one game, the second most in NFL history. He is among the top five NFL career leaders in pass attempts, pass completions, and passing yardage despite the fact that he played the first six years of his professional career in the CFL.

In his 17-year NFL career, Moon played in 208 regular-season games, starting in 203 of them for a won-lost record of 102–101. He completed 3,988 passes in 6,823 attempts for 49,325 yards and 291 touchdowns and ran 543 times for 1,736 yards and 22 touchdowns. In 10 postseason games, he completed 259 of 403 passes for 2,870 yards and 17 touchdowns and ran 35 times for 114 yards and no touchdowns. He played in nine **Pro Bowls**. Moon was inducted into the Canadian Football Hall of Fame in 2001 and the Pro Football Hall of Fame in 2006.

MOORE, LEONARD EDWARD "LENNY." B. 25 November 1933, Reading, Pennsylvania. Lenny Moore, known as the "Reading Rocket" when he played **football** for Reading High School, continued his scholastic football playing at **Penn State University**. He was on the Penn State **varsity** from 1953 to 1955, and the six-foot, one-inch, 195-pound **halfback** was one of the best collegiate runners in the nation during that time. Penn State compiled a record of 14–9 in those three years, while Moore **rushed** for 2,380 yards and 23 **touchdowns** in 382 attempts. He also averaged 15.8 yards per **punt** return, with one touchdown in 24 returns and 24.3 yards per **kickoff** return in 23 returns.

Moore was selected by the **Baltimore Colts** in the first round of the 1956 **National Football League (NFL) Draft** as the ninth overall choice and played for the Colts for the next 12 years. He was a member of the Colts' NFL championship teams in 1958 and 1959 and played on the losing side in the 1964 NFL Championship Game. During his NFL career, Moore led the league in rushing yards per attempt four times, touchdowns twice, and rushing yardage and points scored once each. From 1963 to 1965, he scored at least one touchdown in 18 straight games, a record equaled only in 2005 by **LaDainian Tomlinson**.

In his 12-year NFL career, Moore played in 143 regular-season games, ran 1,069 times for 5,174 yards and 63 touchdowns, caught 363 **passes** for 6,039 yards and 48 touchdowns, and completed three of 12 passes for 33 yards and two touchdowns. He was also used as a kickoff and punt **returner** and returned 14 punts and 49 kickoffs for averages of 4.0 yards per punt return and 24.1 yards per kickoff return. One of his kickoff returns went for a 92-yard touchdown. Moore also recovered one **fumble** for a touchdown. In four postseason games, he ran 33 times for 104 yards and no touchdowns and caught 13 passes for 246 yards and one touchdown. He was selected for the **Pro Bowl** in seven seasons. Moore was inducted into the **Pro Football Hall of Fame** in 1975.

MOORE, ROBERT "BOBBY" EARL. *See* RASHAD, AHMAD.

MOSS, RANDY GENE. B. 13 February 1977, Rand, West Virginia. Randy Moss attended DuPont High School in Belle, West Virginia, where he participated in four sports, **football**, basketball, baseball, and track. In football, he helped lead DuPont to the state high school championship in 1992 and 1993 as a **wide receiver**, defensive **back**, kick **returner**, placekicker, and **punter**. He was named West Virginia High School Football Player of the Year in 1994. In basketball, one of his teammates was future National Basketball Association star Jason Williams. In 1993 and 1994, Moss was named West Virginia High School Basketball Player of the Year. In 1992, as a sophomore, he competed in track and won the West Virginia state championship in both the 100 meters and 200 meters sprints.

Moss initially signed a letter of intent to attend the **University of Notre Dame**, but after being involved in a fight in his senior year, Notre Dame withdrew his application. Moss then enrolled at **Florida State University**, but after completing his freshman year there again got into trouble and was dropped by Florida State. He then applied to Marshall University in West Virginia and played two seasons there, 1996 and 1997. At Marshall, in 1996, he helped lead them to an undefeated 15–0 season and the NCAA Division 1-AA national championship. In 1997, Marshall moved to the NCAA Division 1, had a commendable record of 10–3, and was the **Mid-American Conference** champion.

Moss was selected by the **Minnesota Vikings** in the first round of the 1998 **National Football League (NFL) Draft** as the 21st overall selection. Because of his widely publicized scrapes with the law, several NFL teams did not choose him. He played for the Vikings from 1998 to 2004 as a wide receiver. Following the 1998 season, Moss was named the NFL Offensive Rookie of the Year. He was traded to the **Oakland Raiders** in 2005 and played for them in 2005 and 2006. In 2007, he was again traded, this time to the **New England Patriots**. That year, the Patriots were undefeated in the regular season, the only team to ever win all their games in a 16-game season, but they were defeated by the **New York Giants** in the **Super Bowl**. Moss set an NFL record with 23 **touchdown receptions** for the season. Moss's NFL career appeared to end in 2010. After playing four games that season for the Patriots, he was traded to the Minnesota Vikings. He only played four games there and was released. The **Tennessee Titans** signed him, and he played the final eight games of the season for them. He retired prior to the 2011 season. His retirement lasted only one season as he signed a contract with the San Francisco 49ers in March 2012 and appeared in all 16 regular-season games and all three playoff games (including the Super Bowl for them in 2012).

Through 2012, Moss has played in 14 NFL seasons and has appeared in 218 regular-season games, caught 982 **passes** for 15,292 yards and 156 touchdowns, and run 25 times for 159 yards and no touchdowns. He also completed four of eight passes for 106 yards, with two passes going for touchdowns. In the early part of his NFL career, he was also used as a **punt** returner and averaged 9.0 yards on 18 returns, with one touchdown. In 15 postseason games, Moss caught 54 passes for 977 yards and 10 touchdowns. He also ran once for 14 yards and returned three punts for 34 yards. He played in six **Pro Bowls**. In 2008, Moss became part owner of Randy Moss Motorsports, an organization that sponsors vehicles in the National Association for Stock Car Auto Racing truck series.

MOUNTAIN WEST CONFERENCE. The Mountain West Conference is an organization of **major colleges** and universities that compete athletically in the **National Collegiate Athletic Association** Football Bowl Subdivision. It was established in 1999 and is based in Colorado Springs, Colorado. Its membership in 2012 consisted of the United States Air Force Academy; **Boise State University**; California State University, Fresno; Colorado State University; the University of Nevada, Las Vegas; the University of Nevada,

Reno; the University of New Mexico; San Diego State University; and the University of Wyoming. In addition, the University of Hawai'i is a member for football only. In 2013, the conference will add San Jose State University and Utah State University.

MUFF. A muff, as distinguished from a **fumble**, is an attempt at catching a **punted** ball in which the **punt returner** never has possession. A play is ruled a fumble if the ball carrier has possession of the **football** and then loses it. A muffed ball may not be advanced by the recovering team, while a fumbled ball can be advanced.

N

NAGURSKI, BRONISLAU "BRONKO." B. 3 November 1908, Rainy River, Ontario, Canada. D. 7 January 1990, International Falls, Minnesota. Of the nearly 100 **National Football League (NFL)** players born in Canada, Bronko Nagurski is by far the most outstanding. At six feet, two inches tall and 225 pounds, he was exceptional both as a **fullback** on **offense** and a **tackle** on **defense**. His strength was legendary, and stories are told of him **running** into a brick wall following a **touchdown** run and breaking the bricks.

Raised near the Canadian border in International Falls, Minnesota, he played **football** at International Falls High School, which did not have a very good football team. The **coach** of nearby Bemidji High School heard of Nagurski and had him transfer to Bemidji High for his senior year. Unfortunately for both the coach and Nagurski, International Falls High School protested the move and the Minnesota High School Athletic Association prohibited Nagurski from playing for Bemidji, although he was allowed to practice with the team.

After graduating from high school, the muscular Nagurski was allegedly discovered by **University of Minnesota** football coach Clarence "Fats" Spears while Nagurski was plowing a field on his family's farm. Spears got Nagurski to enroll at Minnesota, and Nagurski played both fullback and defensive tackle there from 1927 to 1929. In those three years, Minnesota football teams compiled a record of 18–4–2.

Following the 1929 season, **Chicago Bears** owner/coach **George Halas** signed Nagurski to a **professional football** contract, and, for the next eight years, he played for the Bears. He helped lead Chicago to the NFL championship in 1932 and 1933, as well as to the NFL Championship Game in 1934 and 1937, in which the team was defeated by the **New York Giants** in 1934, followed by the **Washington Redskins**. Nagurski retired following the 1937 season. Since the NFL was experiencing a manpower shortage during World War II, he was coaxed back to play for the Bears in 1943 but was used primarily as both an offensive and defensive **lineman** that year, with limited appearances as a **running back**. He again helped the Bears win the NFL championship.

When he retired following the 1937 season, Nagurski became a professional wrestler. In an era during which professional wrestling bore much more credibility than today's version, Nagurski became the world heavyweight champion. He continued as a professional wrestler until 1960. He then opened an automobile service station in International Falls, which he ran for the next 18 years.

During Nagurski's nine years in the NFL, official statistics were not well kept. He played in 97 regular-season games and scored at least 25 **rushing** touchdowns. He also completed 32 of 77 **passes** for seven touchdowns and caught 11 passes for 134 yards. He also scored four extra points. Nagurski was inducted into the **College Football Hall of Fame** as a charter member in 1951 and also the **Pro Football Hall of Fame** as a charter member in 1963. He was also inducted into the Professional Wrestling Hall of Fame in 2011. Nagurski's son, Bronko Nagurski Jr., had a successful career at the **University of Notre Dame** and, from 1959 to 1966, as an offensive lineman for the **Hamilton Tiger-Cats** in the **Canadian Football League**.

NAMATH, JOSEPH WILLIAM "JOE," "JOE WILLIE." B. 31 May 1943, Beaver Falls, Pennsylvania. Joe Namath is best known for the record-breaking **professional football** contract he signed with the **New York Jets** in January 1965, after completing his college eligibility. He attended Beaver Falls High School in Beaver Falls, Pennsylvania, about 30 miles northwest of Pittsburgh. He was a multisport athlete in high school, playing baseball, basketball, and **football**. Although he was offered opportunities to play professional baseball, Namath bowed to his mother's concern that he receive a college education and stayed with football. He accepted a scholarship to the **University of Alabama** and played on their **varsity** football team from 1962 to 1964 under famed head **coach Paul "Bear" Bryant**. During his three years as Alabama **quarterback**, he completed 203 **passes** in 374 attempts for 2,713 yards and 25 **touchdowns**. Namath also carried the ball 190 times for 655 yards. Alabama compiled a record of 29–4, played in major **bowl games** each year, and was national champion in 1964.

Namath was selected by the New York Jets as the first overall choice in the 1965 **American Football League (AFL) Draft** (actually held on 28 November 1964, before the **college football** season had concluded). The competing **National Football League (NFL)** also held their draft that day, and Namath was selected in the first round by the St. Louis Cardinals as the 12th overall choice. On 2 January 1965, immediately following his last college game (a 21–17 loss to the **University of Texas** in the **Orange Bowl**), Namath signed a contract with the New York Jets for an amount reported to be in excess of $400,000, an astronomical amount for that era.

The six-foot, two-inch, 205-pound Namath played quarterback for the Jets from 1965 to 1976 and concluded his professional football career with one season with the Los Angeles Rams in 1977. He began slowly with the Jets in 1965 and only started in nine of the team's 14 games but finished strong and was named the AFL Rookie of the Year. In 1966, he began the season as the Jets' full-time starter and led the league in pass attempts, pass completions, and passing yardage. Namath had another excellent year in 1967, again leading in those three categories and becoming the first NFL or AFL quarterback to pass for more than 4,000 yards in one season. His season total of 4,007 yards passing was not surpassed until 1979, and it was done in a 16-game season rather than the 14-game season that Namath played.

The highlight of Namath's career occurred on 12 January 1969, when, after "guaranteeing" a Jets victory, he fulfilled his promise by leading the 17-point underdog Jets to a 16–7 win over the **Baltimore Colts** in the **Super Bowl** and was named the game's Most Valuable Player. The Jets became the first AFL team to defeat an NFL team in that event.

In 1970, Namath's knees began to give him trouble, and, for the rest of his career, although he had some outstanding games, and did, in fact, lead the NFL in passing yardage in 1972, he never regained his initial abilities. From 1970 to 1973, he was only able to play in half of New York's scheduled games.

In 1972, Namath had one memorable game against the Colts, defeating them 44–34 and passing for 496 yards (third highest in NFL history to that point), with six touchdowns, to Colts' quarterback **Johnny Unitas's** 376 yards and three touchdowns. Namath played his final professional season for the Los Angeles Rams but only appeared in four games as a backup quarterback.

In his 13-year combined AFL–NFL career, Namath played in 140 regular-season games, started in 130 of those games, had a won-lost record of 62–63–4, completed 1,886 passes in 3,762 attempts for 27,663 yards and 173 touchdowns, ran 71 times for 140 yards and seven touchdowns, and recovered one **fumble** for another touchdown. In three postseason games, he completed 50 passes in 117 attempts for 636 yards and three touchdowns. Namath also **rushed** twice for 15 yards and no touchdowns. He appeared in five AFL All-Star Games and NFL **Pro Bowls**.

During his career, Namath's flamboyant personality resulted in his nickname, "Broadway Joe." In 1969, he and several other athletes opened an upscale bar called Bachelors III in New York City. In an effort to protect the NFL's image, Commissioner **Alvin "Pete" Rozelle** made Namath relinquish his share of the ownership, although, in a compromise, allowed him to retain ownership in a couple of the bar's branches outside of New York. Namath also enhanced his playboy image by wearing a full-length fur coat on the **sidelines** during NFL games.

After retiring from active play, Namath appeared in several Hollywood films and television shows and worked one season as an analyst on *Monday Night Football*. He also later opened several bars named Broadway Joe's in New York and Tuscaloosa, Alabama. In 2006, he reenrolled at the University of Alabama to complete his degree requirements and graduated in 2007. He was inducted into the **Pro Football Hall of Fame** in 1985.

NATIONAL ASSOCIATION OF INTERCOLLEGIATE ATHLETICS (NAIA). The National Association of Intercollegiate Athletics (NAIA) was founded in 1937 as the National Association of Intercollegiate Basketball (NAIB). Dr. James Naismith (inventor of basketball) and others organized a tournament for small colleges to be held in Kansas City, Missouri, to determine a national champion. Eight schools were invited to that first tournament, which was won by Central Missouri State University. In 1952, the NAIB was renamed as the National Association of Intercollegiate Athletics and sponsorship of tournaments in additional sports was begun. In 1956, the NAIA began holding postseason **football** tournaments to determine their national champion. As of 2012, Texas A&I University (now known as Texas A&M University, Kingsville) has won seven NAIA national championships, one more than Carroll College and Westminster College, each of whom have six. The NAIA currently sponsors events in more than 20 sports and has more than 300 member institutions.

NATIONAL COLLEGIATE ATHLETIC ASSOCIATION (NCAA). The National Collegiate Athletic Association (NCAA) is an organization of more than 1,200 U.S. colleges and universities and coordinates athletic activities in these schools. It administers programs in about 25 different sports and organizes national championships. The NCAA was founded on 3 February 1906 as the Intercollegiate Athletic Association of the United States (IAAUS) as a result of President Theodore Roosevelt requesting the presidents of three major **Ivy League** schools to take steps to improve the safety of collegiate athletics. In 1910, the IAAUS was renamed the National Collegiate Athletic Association.

In 1973, the NCAA organized competition into three divisions, Division I, Division II, and Division III, with Division III schools not permitted to offer athletic scholarships. In 1978, Division I was split into two divisions, I and I-AA, for **football**. Divisions I-AA, Division II, and Division III each have a postseason **playoff** system to determine a division champion, but Division I does not. Since 1998, it has had a **Bowl Championship Series** in which two teams, based on their season records, are matched and play a championship game at one of several bowl sites. In 2006, Division I and Division I-AA were renamed Football Bowl Subdivision (FBS) (formerly Division I) and Football Championship Subdivision (FCS) (formerly Division I-AA).

The NCAA was headquartered in the Kansas City metropolitan area from 1951 to 1999 but is now located in Indianapolis, Indiana. Its president since 2010 has been Mark Emmert. *See also* APPENDIX L (for a list of college champions); APPENDIX O (for a list of Football Bowl Subdivision schools).

NATIONAL FOOTBALL LEAGUE (NFL). The National Football League (NFL) is the major **professional football** league in the United States and has been so for more than 90 years. It was founded in Canton, Ohio, on 20 August 1920, at a meeting held at the Hupmobile automobile dealership owned by Ralph Hay, owner of the Canton Bulldogs professional football team. Other participants at the meeting were representatives of the Akron Pros, Dayton Triangles, and Cleveland Tigers professional football teams. The proposed league was named the American Professional Football Conference. At a subsequent meeting, which included representatives of two teams from Indiana (the Hammond Pros and Muncie Flyers), three teams from Illinois (the Rock Island Independents, Decatur Staleys, and Racine Cardinals [based in Chicago]), and the Rochester Jeffersons (based in New York), the 10-team league was renamed the American Professional Football Association (APFA), and **Jim Thorpe** was named league president. Four additional teams, the Buffalo (New York) All-Americans, Detroit (Michigan) Heralds, Chicago (Illinois) Tigers, and Columbus (Ohio) Panhandles, also joined the league for its first season.

During the 1920s, the league was a relatively loose organization of professional football clubs. They did not play similar schedules, and membership varied from 10 to 22 teams. The team with the best won-lost record (disregarding **tie** games) was declared the league champion. Following the league's first season, **Joe Carr**, owner of the Columbus Panhandles, was named league president. He worked on standardizing schedules and player contracts and making the league a viable professional organization. The league was renamed the National Football League for the 1922 season and has retained that name since.

In 1926, a competitive league, the **American Football League**, began operation but did not last for more than one season. The NFL continued but, by 1932, had decreased to just eight teams. The 1932 season ended in a first-place tie between the Portsmouth Spartans and **Chicago Bears**, and a one-game tiebreaker game was played between the two teams to determine the league champion. The success of this game gave the league owners the idea to split the league into two divisions, an East Division and a West Division, and play an NFL Championship Game following the regular season between the two division champions. This was begun in 1933 and continues to this day, although in recent years a postseason **playoff** tournament exists with more than just two teams.

The NFL continued as the major professional league and successfully withstood challenges from two other leagues, also both named American Football League (one in 1936–1937 and one in 1940–1941). During World War II, the NFL continued operation, although the number of teams and number of games played were reduced. In 1946, the **All-America Football Conference (AAFC)** provided additional competition, but, by 1950, the AAFC had merged with the NFL. During the 1950s, the NFL continued to gain **fans** as games began to be televised. The 1958 NFL Championship Game between the **New York Giants** and **Baltimore Colts** was tied at the end of 60 minutes, and the league played its first nonexhibition **overtime** game. The drama produced by this game helped the NFL increase its popularity even more.

In 1960, another competing league, also called the American Football League, presented the NFL with its greatest challenge, but, in 1966, an agreement was reached to merge the two leagues effective with the 1970 season. As part of the merger agreement, an annual Championship Game between the two leagues was begun in 1967. This game, later named the **Super Bowl**, has virtually become an American national holiday.

The final event that cemented the NFL the most popular league in American sports occurred in 1970, when ABC began televising NFL games on Monday nights on a broadcast known as *Monday Night Football*. Since then, the league has continued to expand and add teams. As of 2012, the NFL has 32 teams throughout the United States. *See also* APPENDIX C (for a list of Super Bowl champions); APPENDIX D (for a list of league champions).

NATIONAL FOOTBALL LEAGUE GAMES PLAYED INTERNATIONALLY. Since 1976, the **National Football League (NFL)** has experimented with playing preseason games outside the United States and Canada. The first such game was played on 16 August 1976 in Tokyo, Japan, between the St. Louis Cardinals and **San Diego Chargers**. From 1986 through 2005, the NFL played an international preseason game billed as the **American Bowl** nearly every year and, in some years, played more than one such game. Games were played in Australia, England, Germany, Ireland, Japan, Mexico, and Spain. Since 2005, the NFL has played regular-season games in Mexico, England, and Canada. International popularity of the sport led to the creation of the **World League of American Football**. *See also* APPENDIX I (for a list of international NFL games).

NATIONAL FOOTBALL LEAGUE PLAYERS BORN OUTSIDE THE UNITED STATES. Through 2012, the **National Football League (NFL)** has employed more than 20,000 players. Although most have been born in the United States, there have been more than 500 born in other countries. With the rise of **soccer**-style kicking specialists in the 1960s and 1970s, most NFL teams have employed a **kicker** born in Europe or Latin America. In addition, there have been several players born abroad but raised in the United States, for example, **Steve Van Buren**, **Leo Nomellini**, and Ted Hendricks. In recent years, many native **Samoans** and Tongans have also developed an interest and ability for American **football**, and the NFL has had more than 50 native Pacific Islanders. *See also* APPENDIX J (for a list of foreign-born NFL players).

NAVY. The United States Naval Academy, known in the sports world simply as Navy, is located in Annapolis, Maryland. Their **football** program began in 1879, and, since then, through 2012, Midshipmen teams have compiled a record of 658–526–56. In addition, they have competed in 18 postseason **bowl games**, with a record of 7–10–1. They were selected as national collegiate champions once in 1926. Navy has competed as an independent team since the start of its football program. Home games since 1959 have been played at the 34,000-seat Navy–Marine Corps Memorial Stadium in Annapolis.

Their main rival is the United States Military Academy (**Army**). The teams have met annually since 1890 (except for a few years) in a contest that, during much of the 20th century, was one of the most widely anticipated collegiate football games. The game is usually held in a neutral city, often Philadelphia, Pennsylvania. Navy leads the series, 57–49–7. Since 1972, the three major service academies (Army, Navy, and the Air Force Academy) have competed for the Commander-in-Chief's Trophy, awarded to the team with the best record against the other two schools.

Navy's most notable **coach** was Eddie Erdelatz. He coached from 1950 to 1958, with a record of 50–26–8. From 1959 to 1964, Wayne Hardin, who succeeded Erdelatz, also had a fine record of 38–22–2. **Robert "Gloomy Gil" Dobie**, coach from 1917 to 1919, had an 18–3–0 record in his brief stint as coach. In 2007, Ken Niumatalolo became Navy's coach and has compiled a record of 40–26 through 2012.

Navy has 20 alumni in the **College Football Hall of Fame**. They are **quarterback** Roger Staubach; **ends** Ron Beagle and Dick Duden; **halfbacks** Joe Bellino, Buzz Borries, Jack Dalton, Tom Hamilton, Anthony "Skip" Minisi, and Clyde Scott; **linemen** George Brown, John "Babe" Brown, Slade Cutter, Steve Eisenhauer, Bob Reifsnyder, Richie Scott, Don Whitmeyer, and Frank Wickhorst; **fullback** Jonas Ingram; **running back** Napoleon McCallum; and safety Chet Moeller. In addition, coaches Robert "Gloomy Gil" Dobie, Bill Ingram, and George Welsh are also honored there. Bellino and Staubach are Navy's two **Heisman Trophy** winners.

Since players enrolled at the Naval Academy have a military obligation following graduation, there have only been a few who have pursued a **professional football** career. Through 2010, there have been just 25 **National Football League** players (also one **All-America Football Conference** player and two **American Football League** players) who have attended Navy, including Joe Bellino, Bob Hoernschemeyer, Max Lane, Napoleon McCallum, Phil McConkey, Todd Peterson, Ed Sprinkle, Roger Staubach, and Mike Wahle. *See also* ARMY–NAVY GAME.

NEALE, ALFRED EARLE "EARLE," "GREASY." B. 5 November 1891, Parkersburg, West Virginia. D. 2 November 1973, Lake Worth, Florida. Earle "Greasy" Neale had a substantial sports career as a player and **coach** in both baseball and **football**. He was also an accomplished golfer, basketball player, and contract bridge player. He received the nickname "Greasy" as a youth when he called one of his friends "Dirty Face" and the boy replied by calling Neale "Greasy." The name stuck, and he was known as "Greasy" throughout his adult life.

Neale was a graduate of Parkersburg High School in Parkersburg, West Virginia, and West Virginia Wesleyan College. He began playing Minor League Baseball in 1912 with the London Tecumsehs in the Class C Canadian League. He played for several minor-league teams from 1912 to 1915, before being promoted to the major leagues. He played Major League Baseball with the Cincinnati Reds from 1916 to 1922, and again in 1924. In 1921, he also played briefly with the Philadelphia Phillies. Neale played in 768 major-league games and had a career batting average of .259. He played all three outfield positions and was the right fielder for the winning Reds team in the 1919 World Series and the team's leading hitter, with a .357 batting average. In 1930, he played one more season of Minor League Baseball with the Clarksburg Generals in the Class C Middle Atlantic League.

Neale also played **professional football** in the years prior to the advent of the American Professional Football Association. He played **end** for **Jim Thorpe's** Canton Bulldogs in 1917, the Dayton Triangles in 1918, and the Massillon Tigers in 1919. While still an active player, he began working as a **college football** head coach and was employed by Muskingum College in 1915, West Virginia Wesleyan in 1916 and 1917, Marietta College in 1919 and 1920, Washington & Jefferson College in 1921 and 1922, the University of Virginia from 1923 to 1928, and West Virginia University from 1931 to 1933. He was an **assistant coach** at **Yale University** from 1934 to 1940. In

16 years as a college head coach, Neale compiled a record of 82–54–11. His 1921 Washington & Jefferson team was undefeated, at 10–0, and was invited to the **Rose Bowl**, where the school met an undefeated **University of California** team and held them to a scoreless **tie** even though California was a two- or three-**touchdown** favorite entering the game.

Neale was a player-coach with the independent Dayton Triangles professional team in 1918 and the head coach of the independent Ironton Tanks in 1930. In 1941, he became coach of the **Philadelphia Eagles** of the **National Football League (NFL)** and coached them for a decade, leading them to NFL championships in 1948 and 1949. As of 2012, the Eagles are the only NFL team to win back-to-back championships by shutout scores in the Championship Games. Neale was inducted into the **College Football Hall of Fame** as a coach in 1967 and the **Pro Football Hall of Fame** as a coach in 1969.

NEBRASKA, UNIVERSITY OF. The University of Nebraska is located in Lincoln, Nebraska. Their **football** program began in 1890, and, since then, through 2012, Cornhuskers' teams have compiled a record of 842–328–41. In addition, they have competed in 49 postseason **bowl games**, with a record of 24–25. They have been selected as national collegiate champions 11 times, in 1970, 1971, 1980, 1981, 1982, 1983, 1984, 1993, 1994, 1995, and 1997. Nebraska's home field since 1923 is Memorial Stadium in Lincoln. Its seating capacity has been gradually expanded throughout the years to its present 81,067.

In 1907, Nebraska became a charter member of the Missouri Valley Intercollegiate Athletic Association, later renamed the **Big Eight Conference**. That conference dissolved in 1996, and Nebraska became a member of the newly created **Big 12 Conference**. In 2011, Nebraska left the Big 12 to join the **Big Ten Conference**, which is comprised mainly of northern midwestern schools. Nebraska's main rival had been the **University of Oklahoma**, but since Nebraska has changed conferences, the rivalry most likely will not be continued. From 1912 to 2010, Nebraska and Oklahoma met 86 times, with Oklahoma ahead, 45–38–3.

Coaches Bob Devaney (1962–1972; 101–20–2) and Tom Osborne (1973–1997; 255–49–3) have been responsible for more than 40 percent of Nebraska's victories and 45 of Nebraska's 48 bowl appearances. Nebraska's 15 alumni in the **College Football Hall of Fame** are **linemen** Forrest Behm, Bob Brown, Rich Glover, Wayne Meylan, Dave Rimington, Will Shields, Ed Weir, and Grant Wistrom; **halfback/end** Guy Chamberlin; **fullbacks** Sam Francis and George Sauer; halfbacks Bobby Reynolds and Johnny Rodgers; **running back** Mike Rozier; and end Clarence Swanson. Coaches Dana X. Bible, Bob Devaney, Lawrence "Biff" Jones, Tom Osborne, Fielding Yost, and Eddie Robinson (not the same man who coached **Grambling State University**) have also been enshrined. Tim Crouch, Johnny Rodgers, and Mike Rozier have each won the **Heisman Trophy**.

Through 2012, there have been 328 **professional football** players who have attended Nebraska, 318 in the **National Football League**, eight in the **American Football League**, and two in the **All-America Football Conference**. They include Charley Brock, Bob Brown, Josh Brown, Kris Brown, Mike Brown, Roger Craig, John Dutton, Vince Ferragamo, Pat Fischer, Irving Fryar, Ahman Green, Ed Husmann, Sam Koch, Bernie Masterson, Ron McDole, Carl Nicks, Johnny Rodgers, Mike Rozier, Mike Rucker, Will Shields, Neil Smith, Ndamukong Suh, Mick Tinglehoff, LaVerne Torczon, Kyle Vanden Bosch, Freeman White, and Grant Wistrom.

NESSER FAMILY.
  HOPKINS, EDWARD J. "TED." B. 5 December 1890, Canton, Ohio. D. 8 March 1973, Canton, Ohio.
  NESSER, ALFRED LOUIS "AL." B. 6 June 1893, Columbus, Ohio. D. 11 March 1967, Akron, Ohio.
  NESSER, CHARLES T. "CHARLIE." B. 1902, Columbus, Ohio. D. 26 February 1970, Franklin County, Ohio.
  NESSER, FRANK B. B. 3 June 1899, Columbus, Ohio. D. 1 November 1953, Amanda, Ohio.
  NESSER, FREDERICK W. "FRED." B. 10 September 1897, Columbus, Ohio. D. 2 July 1967, Columbus, Ohio.
  NESSER, JOHN. B. 25 April 1876, Triere, Germany. D. 29 July 1931, Columbus, Ohio.
  NESSER, PHILIP GREGORY "PHIL." B. 10 December 1880, Triere, Germany. D. 9 May 1959, Columbus, Ohio.
  NESSER, RAYMOND "RAY." B. 22 March 1898, Columbus, Ohio. D. 2 September 1969, Columbus, Ohio.
  NESSER, THEODORE, JR. "TED." B. 5 April 1883, Denison, Ohio. D. 7 June 1941, Columbus, Ohio.
  SCHNEIDER, JOHN GEORGE. B. 15 February 1894, Columbus, Ohio. D. 13 May 1957, Columbus, Ohio.
  The Nesser family of Columbus, Ohio, was one of the most famous families in early **football** history. Theodore Nesser, a German immigrant, settled in Ohio in the 1880s to work for the Pennsylvania Railroad. He designed a steam engine for the railroad, but they disregarded his patent, while using the engine. He quit and started a plumbing business in Columbus, Ohio. He and his wife had a large family of 12 children. Seven of the boys worked as boilermakers for the Panhandle Division of the Pennsylvania Railroad, and all enjoyed playing football in their spare time.

Columbus Panhandles, pre-NFL champions: the six Nesser brothers and eight of their friends.
Mike Moran

The Columbus Panhandles' **professional football** team was organized in 1901, and the Nesser brothers were invited to participate. Six of them did so at various times. Ironically, the largest Nesser brother, 325-pound Pete Nesser, did not play football. The Panhandles became one of football's most popular and successful teams. When the American Professional Football Association (APFA) was organized in 1920, the Columbus Panhandles were one of the league's charter teams.

Nesser brothers Al, Frank, Fred, John, Phil, and Ted all played in the APFA. Ted's son Charlie (Charles T. Nesser) also played in the league. Brother Ray did not, although he did appear in team photos with his other brothers. The 1921 Columbus Panhandles had six Nesser brothers, son Charlie Nesser, nephew Ted Hopkins, and brother-in-law John Schneider. John Nesser was 46 years old and the oldest player in **National Football League** history until 1973, when **George Blanda** surpassed him.

NEVERS, ERNEST ALONZO "ERNIE." B. 11 June 1902, Willow River, Minnesota. D. 3 May 1976, San Rafael, California. Ernie Nevers is one of very few men to have played **professional football**, baseball, and basketball, and he played all three professional sports in the same year, 1927. (Famed baseball player Jackie Robinson also played semiprofessional football and basketball in his lifetime.) Nevers began high school at Superior Central High School in Superior, Wisconsin. After his family moved to the West Coast, he concluded his high school years at Santa Rosa High School in Santa Rosa,

California. There, he helped lead the football team to the state championship in 1920. He continued his education at **Stanford University** and played for their **varsity** football team from 1923 to 1925. During those three years, Stanford had a record of 21–5–1. They played in the 1 January 1925 **Rose Bowl** but were defeated by the **University of Notre Dame**. That eagerly anticipated game matched two famous **coaches**, **Glenn "Pop" Warner** of Stanford and **Knute Rockne** of Notre Dame, as well as two undefeated teams. It also featured the Notre Dame backfield known as the **Four Horsemen of Notre Dame**. In that game, Nevers, who had just recuperated from a broken ankle and had been in a cast less than a week before, played all 60 minutes and carried the ball 34 times for 114 yards, only 13 yards less than all Four Horsemen combined. Nevers also played excellent **defense**; had a **pass interception**; and was Stanford's **punter**, with an average of 42 yards per **punt**.

In January 1926, Nevers organized a professional football team, the Jacksonville All-Stars, but the effort was unsuccessful and abandoned after two exhibition games against established NFL teams. He was signed by the St. Louis Browns of Major League Baseball as a pitcher and appeared in 11 games, with a 2–4 won-lost record. Nevers played two more years for the Browns and had a lifetime career record of 6–12 in three seasons.

After the 1926 baseball season concluded, Nevers was signed by the Duluth Eskimos of the **National Football League (NFL)**. At six feet, one inch tall and 205 pounds, he was considered a big man and played in 13 NFL games for the Eskimos as a **fullback** and placekicker, and an additional 16 exhibition games for the Eskimos when they traveled as a barnstorming team. In 1927, during the basketball season, he played for a barnstorming team in St. Louis, Missouri, as well as with Eskimos (who he also coached) in the NFL. He also pitched for the Browns once again.

Nevers did not play football in 1928 but returned to the NFL in 1929 with the Chicago Cardinals. On 28 November 1928, in a **Thanksgiving Day** game against the **Chicago Bears**, he set an NFL record that, as of the 2012 season, has never been equaled. He scored all 40 of his team's points (on six **touchdowns** and four extra points), as the Cardinals defeated the Bears, 40–6. Nevers played two more seasons with the Cardinals in 1930 and 1931 and doubled as their coach during those two years. In 1939, he again coached the Cardinals but did not play for them.

Nevers played five years in the NFL, appearing in 54 regular-season games. Complete official statistics are not available for his NFL career, but he scored at least 38 touchdowns **rushing** and kicked seven **field goals** and 52 extra points. At the start of World War II, he enlisted in the U.S. Marine Corps. He served in the Pacific, and, at one point, he and his battalion were reported missing. When they were found on a deserted island, several had died and Nevers was severely ill. After the war, Nevers was involved with organizing the Chicago Rockets of the new **All-America Football Conference**. He subsequently worked in the San Francisco Bay Area for several beer, wine, and liquor distributors. He was inducted into the **College Football Hall of Fame** in 1951 as a charter member and also the **Pro Football Hall of Fame** as a charter member in 1963.

NEW ENGLAND PATRIOTS. The New England Patriots are a **professional football** team in the American Football Conference East Division of the **National Football League (NFL)**. As the Boston Patriots, they were a charter member of the **American Football League (AFL)** in 1960. They played home games at the 10,000-seat Nickerson Field in Boston, Massachusetts, from 1960 to 1962; the 37,000-seat Fenway Park in Boston from 1963 to 1968; and the 26,000-seat Alumni Stadium in Chestnut Hill, Massachusetts, a Boston suburb, in 1969.

The Patriots became members of the NFL in 1970. In that year, they used the 50,000-seat **Harvard Stadium** in Boston as their home field. In 1971, a new facility seating 60,000 was built in Foxborough, Massachusetts, about 30 miles southwest of Boston. The Patriots were then renamed the New England Patriots. The **stadium**, originally named Schaefer Stadium, was renamed Sullivan Stadium from 1983 to 1989, and finally Foxboro Stadium was the team's home through the 2001 season. In 2002, they moved to the new 68,756-seat Gillette Stadium in Foxborough.

The Patriots' AFL regular-season record was 63–68–9, and their **playoff** record was 1–1 from 1960 to 1969. In 1963, they lost the AFL Championship Game to the **San Diego Chargers**, 51–10. Since joining the NFL, they have been one of the most successful teams in the league, amassing a regular-season record of 363–301 and a playoff record of 23–16 in 19 playoff seasons. In the 16 years from 1996 to 2012, they have qualified for the playoffs in 13 years. They have played in seven **Super Bowls**, winning in 2001, 2003, and 2004 and losing in 1985, 1996, 2007, and 2011. The Patriots lost in the AFC championship in 2006 and 2012, the divisional playoff six times, and the first round or **wild-card playoff** four times. From 5 October 2003 through 24 October 2004, they won 21 consecutive games. In 2009, they became the first NFL team to have an undefeated regular season since the league expanded to a 16-game season. The Patriots also won their first two playoff games for 18 consecutive victories that season but were defeated by the **New York Giants** in the Super Bowl.

The Patriots' most successful head **coach** has been **Bill Belichick**, who, from 2000 to 2012, has led them to the Super Bowl five times. Other Patriots head coaches include Lou Saban (1960–1961), Mike Holovak (1961–1968),

Clive Rush (1969–1970), John Mazur (1970–1972), Phil Bengtson (interim 1972), Chuck Fairbanks (1973–1978), Hank Bullough (interim 1978), Ron Erhardt (1978–1981), Ron Meyer (1982–1984), Raymond Berry (1984–1989), Rod Rust (1990), Dick MacPherson (1991–1992), **Bill Parcells** (1993–1996), and Pete Carroll (1997–1999).

New England's best players have included **Pro Football Hall of Famers guard** John Hannah, **linebacker Nick Buoniconti**, **running back** Curtis Martin, and **cornerback** Mike Haynes. Other stars include **quarterbacks** Drew Bledsoe, **Tom Brady**, Steve Grogan, and **Vito "Babe" Parilli**; **wide receivers** Deion Branch, Troy Brown, Stanley Morgan, and Wes Welker; **kickers Gino Cappelletti** and Adam Vinatieri; **fullback** Jim Nance; running backs Sam Cunningham and Corey Dillon; defensive **linemen** Julius Adams, Bob Dee, and Jim Lee Hunt; offensive **tackle** Bruce Armstrong; linebackers Tedy Bruschi, Steve Nelson, Andre Tippett, and Mike Vrabel; **center** Jon Morris; and **tight end** Ben Coates.

NEW ORLEANS SAINTS. The New Orleans Saints are a **professional football** team in the National Football Conference (NFC) South Division of the **National Football League (NFL)**. They entered the league in 1967 and were initially placed in the Capitol Division of the then 16-team NFL. They were transferred to the Century Division for the 1968 season and returned to the Capitol Division in 1969. In 1970, the NFL merged with the **American Football League**, and a new divisional structure was created. The Saints were then placed in the West Division of the NFC and remained there through 2001. In 2002, the NFL changed from a six-division organization to an eight-division one, and the Saints became members of the NFC South Division.

The Saints' home field was originally the 80,000-seat Tulane Stadium in New Orleans, Louisiana (site of the **Sugar Bowl**, and often referred to as the Sugar Bowl), until 1974. In 1975, they moved into the 76,000-seat domed **stadium** the Louisiana Superdome, also in New Orleans, and have remained there since then, with the exception of 2005, when the effects of Hurricane Katrina caused them to move their home games to three other venues. That year they played four games at the 91,000-seat Tiger Stadium in Baton Rouge, Louisiana; three games at the 65,000-seat Alamodome in San Antonio, Texas; and one game at the 80,000-seat Giants Stadium in East Rutherford, New Jersey.

In their 46-year existence, the Saints have amassed a won-lost record of 306–395–5 in regular-season play and 6–8 in **playoff** competition. Although they were one of the league's weakest teams during their first 20 years, failing to qualify for postseason competition until 1987 or win a postseason game until 2000, they have since become much more competitive, reaching the conference championship in 2006 and winning the **Super Bowl** in 2009. They have been five-time losers in the **wild-card playoff** (1987, 1990, 1991, 1992, 2010) and were defeated in the divisional playoff in 2000 and 2011.

The team's head **coaches** have been Tom Fears (1967–1970), J. D. Roberts (1970–1972), John North (1973–1975), Ernie Hefferle (interim 1975), **Hank Stram** (1976–1977), Dick Nolan (1978–1980), Dick Stanfel (interim 1980), O. A. "Bum" Phillips (1981–1985), Wade Phillips (interim 1985), Jim Mora (1986–1996), Rick Venturi (interim 1996), **Mike Ditka** (1997–1999), Jim Haslett (2000–2005), and Sean Payton (2006–2011). On 20 March 2012, league commissioner **Roger Goodell** suspended Payton for one year for his awareness of a team "bounty" system that rewarded defensive players for injuring their opponents. In 2012, Aaron Kromer and Joe Vitt acted as co-coaches during Payton's suspension, which was ended on 22 January 2013.

The Saints' best players include **Pro Football Hall of Famers** defensive end Doug Atkins, **running back Earl Campbell**, **linebacker** Rickey Jackson, offensive **tackle** Willie Roaf, and **fullback Jim Taylor**. Other stars with the Saints include **quarterbacks Drew Brees**, Billy Kilmer, and **Archie Manning**; running backs **Reggie Bush**, Deuce McAllister, Pierre Thomas, and Ricky Williams; **wide receivers** Danny Abramowitz, Joe Horn, and Eric Martin; offensive tackle Jahri Evans; defensive **lineman** La'Roi Glover; linebackers Sam Mills and Pat Swilling; and **kickers Morten Andersen** and **Tom Dempsey**, who, in 1970, set the record for the longest **field goal** with a 63-yard kick with two seconds remaining in the game to win it for the Saints, 19–17.

NEW YEAR'S DAY. Since the first **bowl game** on 1 January 1902, New Year's Day has always been a special day for **football** games. Many of the major bowl games, including the **Rose Bowl**, **Sugar Bowl**, **Cotton Bowl**, and **Orange Bowl**, have traditionally been played on New Year's Day. In recent years, however, with the proliferation of other bowl games, many of them are played throughout December and January.

NEW YORK BULLDOGS. *See* NEW YORK YANKS.

NEW YORK GIANTS. The New York Giants are a **professional football** team in the National Football Conference (NFC) East Division of the **National Football League (NFL)**. They entered the league in 1925 and are one of the oldest franchises in the league. From 1925 to 2012, their overall record is 654–538–33. Prior to 1970, the Giants played in 14 NFL Championship Games (including several historic ones) but won only three of them (1934, 1938, 1956). In 1927, the Giants were named NFL champions by virtue of their regular-season won-lost record. Since the NFL merged with the **American Football League** in 1970, the Giants have qualified for the **playoffs** in 15 seasons, with a playoff record of 20–11. They won the **Super Bowl** in 1986, 1990, 2007, and 2011 and lost in 2000. They lost in the divisional playoffs six times and the **wild-card playoff** four times.

The Giants' home field was the 55,000-seat Polo Grounds from 1925 to 1955, a field they shared with the Major League Baseball team of the same name. They played at the 67,000-seat Yankee Stadium in the Bronx borough of New York from 1956 to 1973. While Yankee Stadium was being refurbished in 1973 and 1974, the Giants played home games at the 64,000-seat **Yale Bowl** in New Haven, Connecticut, and, in 1975, at the 60,000-seat Shea Stadium in Flushing, New York, in the borough of Queens. In 1976, they moved to a new 80,000-seat facility, Giants Stadium, in East Rutherford, New Jersey, in an area popularly known as the Meadowlands, but the team continued to be known as the "New York" Giants, even though they no longer played in either New York City or the state of New York. They played there until 2010, when the 82,000-seat New Meadowlands Stadium was built adjacent to Giants Stadium. This facility was renamed MetLife Stadium in 2011.

Their head **coaches** have been Bob Folwell (1925), Joseph "Doc" Alexander (1926), Earl Potteiger (1927–1928), Roy Andrews (1929–1930), Benny Friedman (interim 1930), Steve Owen (1931–1953), Jim Lee Howell (1954–1960), Allie Sherman (1961–1968), Alex Webster (1969–1973), Bill Arnsparger (1974–1976), John McVay (1976–1978), Ray Perkins (1979–1982), **Bill Parcells** (1983–1990), Ray Handley (1991–1992), **Dan (Edward) Reeves** (1993–1996), Jim Fassel (1997–2003), and Tom Coughlin (2004–2012).

The Giants have 28 former players or executives in the **Pro Football Hall of Fame**, the second most of any NFL franchise. They are **quarterbacks** Benny Friedman, Arnie Herber, **Fran Tarkenton**, and **Y. A. Tittle**; **halfbacks, fullbacks,** and **running backs Larry Csonka, Frank Gifford, Joe Guyon,** Alphonse "Tuffy" Leemans, **Hugh McElhenny, Ken Strong,** and **Jim Thorpe**; offensive **linemen** Roosevelt Brown, **Mel Hein**, Pete Henry, **Cal Hubbard,** and Steve Owen; **ends** and **wide receivers** Morris "Red" Badgro, Ray Flaherty, and Don Maynard; defensive **backs** and **linebackers** Harry Carson, **Sam Huff, Lawrence Taylor,** and **Emlen Tunnell**; and defensive linemen Andy Robustelli and Arnie Weinmeister. In addition, Coach Bill Parcells and owners **Tim Mara** and **Wellington Mara** have also been inducted. Several of the aforementioned players, however, did not play the majority of their careers with the Giants.

Other of the Giants' top players include quarterbacks **Charlie Conerly, Eli Manning,** and Phil Simms; running backs Tiki Barber, Tucker Frederickson,

Rodney Hampton, Brandon Jacobs, Joe Morris, and Alex Webster; ends **Kyle Rote** and Del Shofner; tailback Francis "Hap" Moran; wide receivers Plaxico Burress and Amani Toomer; defensive back Erich Barnes; defensive ends Michael Strahan and Osi Umenyiora; defensive **tackle** Roosevelt Grier; **punter**/back **Tom Landry**; **kicker**/end **Pat Summerall**; punter Don Chandler; and kickers Brad Daluiso and **Pete Gogolak**.

NEW YORK JETS. The New York Jets are a **professional football** team in the American Football Conference (AFC) East Division of the **National Football League (NFL)**. They began as a charter member in the **American Football League (AFL)** in 1960, when they were known as the Titans of New York (more popularly, the New York Titans). In 1963, their name was changed to the New York Jets. From 1960 to 1963, they played home games at the 55,000-seat Polo Grounds on Manhattan Island in New York City. In 1964, they moved their home games to the new 60,000-seat Shea Stadium in Flushing, New York, in the borough of Queens. In 1984, they moved to the 80,000-seat Giants Stadium in East Rutherford, New Jersey, although they retained the name "New York" Jets and shared the **stadium** with the New York Giants of the NFL. In 2010, the Giants and Jets moved to a new 80,000-seat facility located adjacent to Giants Stadium called the New Meadowlands Stadium. Naming rights were subsequently sold, and, in 2011, the arena was known as MetLife Stadium.

In the Titans'/Jets' 10 years in the AFL, they played in its Eastern Division. Their overall record was 69–65–6 in regular-season play and 2–1 in postseason action. They won the 1968 **Super Bowl**, the first AFL team to do so. In 1969, they lost the division **playoffs** to the **Kansas City Chiefs**. They joined the NFL in 1970 after the merger of the AFL and NFL and were placed in the AFC East Division, where they have remained through the 2012 season. In 43 years of NFL competition, their overall record is 296–366–2 in the regular season and 10–12 in the postseason. Their best season in the NFL was 1998, when they won 12 of 16 regular-season games and lost in the AFC Championship Game. They have only appeared in the playoffs in 12 of their 41 NFL seasons and lost in the AFC championship four times (1982, 1998, 2009, 2010), the divisional playoffs three times (1986 in double **overtime**, 2002, 2004 in overtime), and the **wild-card playoff** five times (1981, 1985, 1991, 2001, 2006).

Titans'/Jets' **coaches** have included **Sammy Baugh** (1960–1961), Clyde "Bulldog" Turner (1962), Wilbur "Weeb" Ewbank (1963–1973), Charley Winner (1974–1975), Ken Shipp (interim 1975), Lou Holtz (1976), Mike Holovak (interim 1976), Walt Michaels (1977–1982), Joe Walton (1983–1989), Bruce Coslet (1990–1993), Pete Carroll (1994), Rich Kotite (1995–1996),

Mark Sanchez, quarterback of the New York Jets.
New York Jets

Bill Parcells (1997–1999), Al Groh (2000), Herman Edwards (2001–2005), Eric Mangini (2006–2008), and Rex Ryan (2009–2012).

The franchise's best players include **Pro Football Hall of Famers quarterback Joe Namath**, **running backs** Curtis Martin and John Riggins, **end** Don Maynard, and defensive **back** Ronnie Lott. Other of their best players include running backs Emerson Boozer, Freeman McNeil, and Matt Snell; quarterbacks Ken O'Brien, Chad Pennington, Mark Sanchez, and Vinny Testaverde; **linebacker** Larry Grantham; defensive back Darrelle Revis; defensive **lineman** Joe Klecko; defensive ends Mark Gastineau and Gerry Philbin; **wide receivers** Jerricho Cotchery, Santana Moss, Al Toon, and Wesley Walker; offensive **tackles** Winston Hill and Marvin Powell; and **kicker** Pat Leahy.

NEW YORK TITANS. *See* NEW YORK JETS.

NEW YORK YANKEES. The New York Yankees were a **professional football** team in the **All-America Football Conference (AAFC)** from 1946 to 1948. They were one of the more successful teams in the league and finished first in the Eastern Division in both 1946 and 1947, although they lost the AAFC Championship Game both years to the **Cleveland Browns**. Home games were played at the 70,000-seat Yankee Stadium, also the home of the Major League Baseball team of the same name. Among the Yankees' top players were **quarterback** Clarence "Ace" Parker, **fullback Claude "Buddy" Young**, and quarterback/**punter**/**returner** Orban "Spec" Sanders. In 1949, the Yankees merged with the **Brooklyn Dodgers** and played as the **Brooklyn–New York Yankees**.

NEW YORK YANKS. The New York Yanks were a team in the **National Football League (NFL)** from 1949 to 1951 and should not be confused with the **New York Yankees**, a team in the **All-America Football Conference (AAFC)** from 1946 to 1948. In 1949, Ted Collins, former owner of the **Boston Yanks**, was awarded a new NFL franchise and called it the New York Bulldogs, although he used quite a few former Yanks to fill out his roster. The Bulldogs played at the 55,000-seat Polo Grounds in New York, also the home of the **New York Giants** baseball and football teams. The Bulldogs were unsuccessful, finishing fifth and last in the NFL East Division with a record of 1–10–1. Their **quarterback**, **Bobby Layne**, went on to a **Pro Football Hall of Fame** career with the **Detroit Lions**.

For the 1951 season, the Bulldogs were renamed the New York Yanks and played at the 70,000-seat Yankee Stadium, which they shared with the New York Yankees Major League Baseball team. The 1951 team featured George Ratterman at **quarterback** and numerous former AAFC New York Yankees' players, including Lou Kusserow, Barney Poole, Orban "Spec" Sanders, and **Claude "Buddy" Young**. The Yanks finished third, with a record of 7–5. In 1951, after the team compiled a record of 1–9–2, the team was dissolved. The rights to the NFL franchise were sold to a group of Dallas investors, and a team called the **Dallas Texans** replaced the Yanks in the NFL for the 1952 season.

NEWTON, CAMERON JERRELL "CAM." B. 11 May 1989, College Park, Georgia. Cam Newton was raised in College Park, Georgia, and attended Westlake High School in Atlanta, where he played both **football** and basketball. In football, he played **quarterback**, along with his older brother, Cecil Newton Jr., who played **center** and later played in the **National Football League (NFL)**. Cam began his college career at the **University of Florida** in 2007 and, as a freshman, was a backup quarterback to future **Heisman Trophy** winner **Tim Tebow**. The following year, Newton suffered an ankle injury in Florida's first game and became a medical **redshirt** for the remainder of the season. In 2009, he transferred to Blinn Junior College and led them to the National Junior College Athletic Association championship. In 2010, he again transferred schools, this time to **Auburn University**. He led the Tigers to an undefeated season, at 14–0, and the national championship, after they defeated the University of Oregon, 22–19, in the Bowl Championship Series Championship Game. Newton won the Heisman Trophy as well. He decided to forgo his final season of college eligibility and was selected as the first overall choice in the 2011 NFL **Draft** by the **Carolina Panthers**.

In his first NFL season, Newton set more than a dozen league rookie records, including most **passing** yardage in his first NFL game, with 422 yards; most passing yardage in a game by a rookie, with 432 yards; most passing yardage in a season by a rookie, with 4,051 yards; and most **touchdowns rushing** by a quarterback in one season, with 13. He became the first NFL player with more than 4,000 yards passing and 500 yards rushing in one season.

In his first two professional seasons, Newton started all 32 games for Carolina but only had a won-lost record of 13–19. He completed 590 passes in 1,002 attempts for 7,920 yards and 40 touchdowns. He also carried the ball 253 times for 1,447 yards and 22 touchdowns. He was selected as an alternate to the **Pro Bowl** in 2011. As long as he remains healthy, Newton appears to have a bright future in the NFL.

NFL EUROPA. *See* WORLD LEAGUE OF AMERICAN FOOTBALL.

NFL EUROPE. *See* WORLD LEAGUE OF AMERICAN FOOTBALL.

NITSCHKE, RAYMOND ERNEST "RAY." B. 29 December 1936, Elmwood Park, Illinois. D. 8 March 1998, Venice, Florida. Ray Nitschke had a difficult youth. He was orphaned at the age of 13 and raised by his two older brothers. He attended Proviso High School in Maywood, Illinois, and played **fullback** on the freshman **football** team. During his sophomore year, he did poorly academically and was not allowed to play sports. Nitschke improved his grades and was able to return to sports in his junior year, **quarterbacking** the football team on **offense** and playing **safety** on **defense**. He was a catcher and outfielder on the baseball team and also played basketball.

Although his baseball prowess brought him an offer to play in the major leagues, Nitschke declined and accepted a football scholarship to the **University of Illinois** instead. He began there at quarterback but was moved to fullback on offense and **linebacker** on defense. Although Illinois did not have exceptional teams during Nitschke's years there, his play at linebacker was noticed and he was selected by the **Green Bay Packers** in the third round of the 1958 **National Football League (NFL) Draft** as the 36th overall selection. Nitschke played with the Packers his entire 15-year NFL career, from 1958 to 1972, and was a member of their NFL championship teams in 1961, 1962, and 1965, and **Super Bowl** championship teams in 1966 and 1967.

The Packers also reached the NFL Championship Game in 1960 but were defeated by the **Philadelphia Eagles**.

Nitschke played in 190 regular-season games in his 15 years in the NFL and recorded 25 **interceptions** and returned two for **touchdowns**. He also recovered 23 **fumbles**. In his final regular-season game, on 17 December 1972, he was on the receiving end of a **pass**, when, on a **blocked field goal** attempt, **holder** Ron Widby passed the ball to Nitschke, who gained 34 yards on the play. In 10 postseason games, Nitschke had one interception for nine yards, two fumble recoveries, and one **kickoff** return of 18 yards. Surprisingly, he only played in one **Pro Bowl** game. In 1969, while still an active player, he was selected to the NFL 50th Anniversary All-Time Team. Nitschke was inducted into the **Pro Football Hall of Fame** in 1978.

NO YARDS. In **Canadian football**, all **punts** must be run back by the receiving team. A **fair catch**, as in American **football**, is not allowed. The defending team must remain five yards or more from the ball **returner** until he touches the ball, otherwise it is a no yards **penalty** of five or 15 yards, depending on the circumstances of the infraction.

NO-HUDDLE OFFENSE. A no-huddle **offense** occurs when the offensive team starts a **down** without **huddling** to call the play. The **quarterback** will use verbal signals to notify the team of the play to be run. It is often used by a team trying to complete a down quickly because the time remaining is short. It is also sometimes run during the game to confuse the **defense** and prevent them from being able to make substitutions.

NOMELLINI, LEO JOSEPH "THE LION." B. 19 June 1924, Lucca, Italy. D. 17 October 2000, Stanford, California. Leo Nomellini was one of the strongest men to ever play **professional football**. Born in Italy, he came to the United States with his family at the age of four. He was raised in Chicago, Illinois, and attended Crane Technical High School but did not play **high school football** because he was required to work to help support his family. Nomellini served in the U.S. Marine Corps and, while there, was introduced to **football**. After being discharged from the service, he enrolled at the **University of Minnesota** in 1946. At six feet, three inches tall and 260 pounds, he played offensive and defensive **tackle** for the Gophers' football team for four years and also was on the wrestling and track teams. He was the **Big Ten Conference** wrestling champion and a shot-putter on the track team. During his four years at Minnesota, the football team had a record of 25–11.

Nomellini was picked by the **San Francisco 49ers** in the first round of the 1950 **National Football League (NFL) Draft** as the 11th overall selection.

He played either offensive or defensive tackle in every single game for the 49ers from 1950 through 1963, 174 regular-season games and one postseason game. In his professional career, he recovered one **fumble**, scored two **safeties**, returned one **punt** for a **touchdown**, returned four **kickoffs** for an average of 12.5 yards per return and even carried the ball once for a five-yard gain. He played in 10 **Pro Bowls**.

During the off-season, Nomellini worked as a professional wrestler, mainly in the Midwest and on the West Coast, and was one of the more popular ones and held a tag-team championship on multiple occasions. He later worked for a title insurance company in the San Francisco area. He was inducted into the **Pro Football Hall of Fame** in 1969 and the **College Football Hall of Fame** in 1977.

NOSE GUARD. *See* GUARD.

NOTRE DAME, UNIVERSITY OF. For many people, the name Notre Dame is synonymous with **football**. The University of Notre Dame is located in Notre Dame, Indiana, a suburb of South Bend. Their football program began in 1887, and, since then, through 2012, Fighting Irish teams have compiled a record of 850–285–41. In addition, they have competed in 32 postseason **bowl games**, with a record of 15–17. They have been selected as national collegiate champions 21 times, in 1919, 1920, 1924, 1927, 1929, 1930, 1938, 1943, 1946, 1947, 1949, 1953, 1964, 1966, 1967, 1970, 1973, 1977, 1988, 1989, and 1993. Since 1932, Notre Dame football teams have competed as independent teams. Home games are played at Notre Dame Stadium, an 80,000-seat facility that has been used since 1930.

The Fighting Irish have no single main rival but, throughout the years, have played several teams on a more or less regular basis. The **University of Southern California** and Notre Dame have played 84 times, with Notre Dame leading, 44–35–5, in a game played for the "Jeweled Shillelagh." Notre Dame and **Michigan State University** play for the "Megaphone Trophy," with Notre Dame leading, 33–26–1. Notre Dame and **Purdue University**, both located in Indiana, have had a long series of games dating back to 1896. They play for the Shillelagh Trophy, and Notre Dame leads 56–26–2 in that series. The United States Naval Academy (**Navy**) has met Notre Dame annually since 1927, but the Fighting Irish generally have a more powerful team, and, consequently, they lead that series, 73–12–1, with 43 consecutive victories from 1964 to 2006, before they were defeated in triple **overtime** in 2007. During the 1940s, both Notre Dame and United States Military Academy (**Army**) had strong teams, and their annual game was highly anticipated by **fans** and alumni. Notre Dame leads that series, 38–8–4.

As Notre Dame has won more than 70 percent of its games throughout its history, there have been quite a few Notre Dame head **coaches** who have compiled outstanding records. Their most famous coach, who has been immortalized in film (*Knute Rockne: All-American*, with Pat O'Brien playing the coach and Ronald Reagan as **George Gipp**), is **Knute Rockne**. He coached the Irish from 1918 until his death in a plane crash on 31 March 1931. His record was 105–12–5, and he led them to six national championships. **Frank Leahy**, coach from 1941 to 1943 and 1946 to 1953, had a record nearly as good, at 87–11–9. Ara Parseghian coached the team from 1964 to 1974, with a record of 95–17–4. Other Notre Dame coaches who each won more than 80 percent of their games are James Faragher (1902–1903; 14–2–2), Thomas Barry (1906–1907; 12–1–1), Victor Place (1908; 8–1–0), Frank "Shorty" Longman (1909–1910; 11–1–2), Jack Marks (1911–1912; 13–0–2), Jesse Harper (1913–1917; 34–5–1), and Ed McKeever (1944; 8–2–0). Of the 29 men who have coached the Irish for more than one game, only one, Joe Kuharich (1959–1962; 17–23), had a losing record.

Notre Dame's 43 alumni in the **College Football Hall of Fame** include **quarterbacks** Angelo Bertelli, Frank Carideo, Ralph Guglielmi, **Paul Hornung**, John Huarte, **Johnny Lujack**, Harry Stuhldreyer, **Joe Theismann**, and Bobby Williams; **halfbacks** "Sleepy" Jim Crowley, George Gipp, Johnny Lattner, Creighton Miller, Don Miller, Marchy Schwartz, and William Shakespeare; **fullbacks** Ray Eichenlaub, **Elmer Layden**, and Louis Salmon; halfback/fullback Emil "Red" Sitko; **ends** and **wide receivers Tim Brown**, Dave Casper, Bob Dove, Leon Hart, Ken McAfee, and Wayne Millner; **linemen** Heartley "Hunk" Anderson, Ross Browner, Jack Cannon, George Connor, Ziggy Czarobski, Bill Fischer, Jerry Groom, Frank Hoffman, Jim Martin, Bert Metzger, Edgar Miller, Fred Miller, **Alan Page**, John Smith, Adam Walsh, Tommy Yarr, and Chris Zorich; and **linebacker** Jim Lynch. Coaches Dan Devine, Jesse Harper, Lou Holtz, Frank Leahy, Ara Parseghian, and Knute Rockne have also been enshrined. Seven Notre Dame players have won the **Heisman Trophy**. They are Angelo Bertelli, Tim Brown, Leon Hart, Paul Hornung, John Huarte, Johnny Lattner, and Johnny Lujack.

Through 2012, there have been 517 **professional football** players who have attended Notre Dame, the most of any school. There have been 477 in the **National Football League**, 13 in the **American Football League**, and 27 in the **All-America Football Conference**. They include Mark Bavaro, Angelo Bertelli, Jerome Bettis, Steve Beuerlein, Robert "Rocky" Bleier, Tim Brown, Ross Browner, **Nick Buoniconti**, John Carney, Dave Casper, George Connor, Art Donovan, Dave Duersen, Bob Golic, Ralph Guglielmi, Terry Hanratty, Leon Hart, Craig Hentrich, Paul Hornung, George Izo, Frank "Bucko" Kilroy, Bob Kuechenberg, Joe Kuharich, George Kunz,

Earl "Curly" Lambeau, Daryle Lamonica, Johnny Lattner, Dorsey Levens, Johnny Lujack, Dick Lynch, Jim Martin, **John "Blood" McNally**, **Joe Montana**, Alan Page, Nick Pietrosante, Myron Pottios, George Ratterman, Joe Scibelli, Hunter Smith, Jack Snow, Monty Stickles, Dick Szymanski, Joe Theismann, Frank Tripucka, Justin Tuck, Frank Varrichione, Ricky Watters, and Bryant Young.

OAKLAND RAIDERS. The Oakland Raiders are a **professional football** team in the American Football Conference West Division of the **National Football League (NFL)**. They began as a charter member of the **American Football League (AFL)** in 1960 and, in their 10 years in that league, compiled one of the AFL's best records, at 77–58–5 in the regular season. In AFL **playoffs**, they were 3–3. They won the AFL championship in 1967 but were defeated by the **Green Bay Packers** in the **Super Bowl**.

The Raiders became members of the NFL in 1970 as a result of the merger between the AFL and NFL. In their 43 years in the NFL, through 2012, their overall record is 353–305–6 in the regular season and 22–15 in postseason play. As one of the NFL's most powerful teams during the 1970s and 1980s, they won the Super Bowl in 1976, 1980, and 1983, but lost the AFC championship in 1970, 1973, 1974, 1975, and 1977. The Raiders also lost the 2002 Super Bowl, their last playoff appearance through the 2012 season. Their overall NFL postseason record shows 25 years reaching the playoffs, with three Super Bowl wins, one Super Bowl loss, seven AFC championship losses, five divisional playoff losses, and two **wild-card playoff** losses.

The Raiders played home games at the 59,000-seat Kezar Stadium in San Francisco, California, in 1960; the 69,000-seat Candlestick Park, also in San Francisco, in 1961; the 22,000-seat Frank Youell Field in Oakland from 1962 to 1965; and the 63,000-seat Oakland–Alameda County Coliseum from 1966 to 1981. In 1982, they moved to the 93,000-seat **Los Angeles Memorial Coliseum** and were renamed the Los Angeles Raiders. They played there through the 1994 season and then returned to Oakland and again played at Oakland–Alameda County Coliseum, which, from 1998 through 2012, went through a series of name changes depending upon the corporation that purchased the naming rights.

The Raiders' most effective head **coach** was **John Madden**, who, from 1969 through 1978, led them to a regular-season record of 103–32–7, seven AFC Championship Games, and a victory in the 1976 Super Bowl. Other Raiders' head coaches have been Eddie Erdelatz (1960–1961), Marty Feldman (1961–1962), Bill Conkwright (interim 1962), **Al Davis** (1963–1965),

John Rauch (1966–1968), Tom Flores (1979–1987), Mike Shanahan (1988–1989), Art Shell (1989–1994, 2006), Mike White (1995–1996), Joe Bugel (1997), Jon Gruden (1998–2001), Bill Callahan (2002–2003), Norv Turner (2004–2005), Lane Kiffin (2007–2008), Tom Cable (2008–2010), Hue Jackson (2011), and Dennis Allen (2012).

The Raiders' best players include **Pro Football Hall of Famers running back Marcus Allen, wide receiver** Fred Biletnikoff, **tight end** Dave Casper, **quarterback/kicker George Blanda, center Jim Otto, guard Gene Upshaw, tackle** Art Shell, defensive **end** Howie Long, defensive tackle Warren Sapp, **linebacker** Ted Hendricks, defensive **back** Jack Tatum, and **cornerbacks** Mike Haynes and Willie Brown. Other top Raider players include quarterbacks Daryle Lamonica and Ken Stabler, wide receiver **Tim Brown**, **punter Ray Guy**, defensive back Fred Williamson, running backs Clem Daniels and Marv Hubbard, and linebacker Phil Villapiano.

OCHOCINCO, CHAD JAVON, NÉE CHAD JAVON JOHNSON. B. 9 January 1978, Miami, Florida. Chad Johnson attended Miami Beach Senior High School. He graduated in 1997 and enrolled at Langston University, a historically black university, but did not play **football** there. Later that year, he transferred to Santa Monica Community College, where he played for two seasons. In 2000, he transferred to Oregon State University, where he helped lead his team to an 11–1 record and a victory over the **University of Notre Dame** in the **Fiesta Bowl**.

A six-foot, one-inch, 190-pound **wide receiver**, Ochocinco (then known as Chad Johnson) was selected by the **Cincinnati Bengals** in the second round of the 2001 **National Football League (NFL) Draft** as the 36th player chosen that year. He quickly became a **fan** favorite with his flamboyant personality. He gained more than 1,000 yards receiving each year from 2002 to 2007 and led the NFL in that category in 2006. Wearing uniform number 85, he gave himself the nickname "Ochocinco," Spanish for 85. On 29 August 2008, he had his name legally changed to Chad Javon Ochocinco and has been known by that name since then. In 2011, he was traded to the **New England Patriots** but was primarily used as a backup and had his worst professional season. He was briefly a member of the **Miami Dolphins** in 2012 but was cut from the team following his arrest for domestic violence.

In his 11-year NFL career, Ochocinco played in 166 regular-season games, caught 766 **passes** for 11,059 yards and 67 **touchdowns**, and ran 24 times for 175 yards and no touchdowns. In three postseason games, he caught seven passes for 108 yards and no touchdowns. He has played in six **Pro Bowls**.

With his penchant for trying new things, Ochocinco has appeared as the guest host for a professional wrestling show, ridden a bull in a Professional

Bull Riders event, tried out for a Major League Soccer team during the NFL lockout in 2011, hosted his own television show, appeared in a Hollywood film, competed in *Dancing with the Stars* and finished fourth, and raced and defeated a thoroughbred racehorse. He is definitely one of football's most unique characters.

OFFENSE (OFFENCE). In **football**, the offense (pronounced with the accent on the first syllable) is the team in possession of the ball. *See also* DEFENSE.

OFFENSIVE TACKLE. *See* TACKLE.

OFFICIALS. Modern-day college and **professional football** is officiated by a crew of seven on-field officials. To properly administer a game played by 22 active players on a field more than 100 yards long and 50 yards wide, each of the seven officials has specific duties. The referee (who wears a white cap to distinguish him from the other officials, who wear black caps) is in charge of the crew and responsible for starting play, communicating details of penalties and other information to both teams and spectators, reviewing plays via instant **replay**, and watching for rule infractions by certain players depending on the type of play. At the start of each play from scrimmage, he is usually positioned behind the offensive team.

The umpire usually stands behind the defensive team and is primarily responsible for determining the legality of **blocking** and line play. Because the players are generally coming toward him, his is the most dangerous position, and collisions between players and the umpire are not uncommon.

The head linesman is positioned to the side of the field at the **line of scrimmage** and is responsible for determining **offsides** or **encroachment** and judging plays near the **sideline**. He is also the official who marks forward progress of the **offense** and sets the ball ready for play.

The line judge is positioned opposite the head linesman at the other side of the field and has similar responsibilities for determining infractions. The field judge is positioned downfield on the same side as the line judge. His primary job is determining interference during **passing** plays. He also watches the sideline for **out of bounds** situations. The side judge has similar duties to the field judge and is positioned on the opposite side of the field from the field judge. The back judge is also positioned downfield but is in the center of the field. He is also primarily concerned with the legality of passing plays.

In addition, each of the officials has specific responsibilities regarding game timing, legality of substitutions, and legality of kicks. The officials work together and confer at times to ensure that their decisions are correct. *See also* TOLER, BURL ABRON, SR.

OFFSETTING PENALTIES. When players on both the **offense** and **defense** commit an infraction on the same play, the ruling is "offsetting penalties" and the **down** is replayed. This is true regardless of the nature of the penalties, thus a 15-yard **penalty** by the defense can be nullified by a 5-yard penalty by the offense and vice versa.

OFFSIDES. Offsides is a type of infraction that occurs when an offensive **lineman**, after coming to a set position, moves before the **center** snaps the ball. To enforce the **penalty**, the official moves the ball back five yards and the **down** is replayed. An offsides penalty can also be called against the **defense** if they cross the **line of scrimmage** prior to the ball being snapped. *See also* ENCROACHMENT.

OHIO STATE UNIVERSITY, THE (OSU). The Ohio State University (OSU) is located in Columbus, Ohio. Their **football** program began in 1889, and, since then, through 2012, Buckeyes' teams have compiled a record of 818–293–53. In addition, they have competed in 43 postseason **bowl games**, with a record of 19–23 and one win vacated due to recruiting infractions. They have been selected as national collegiate champions 13 times, in 1933, 1942, 1944, 1954, 1957, 1961, 1968, 1969, 1970, 1973, 1974, 1975, and 2002. Home games since 1922 have been played at Ohio Stadium, the nation's fourth-largest **stadium**, upgraded in 2007 to have a seating capacity of 102,329. Since 1913, OSU football teams have competed in the **Big Ten Conference** of the **National Collegiate Athletic Association**. Their main rival is the **University of Michigan**. The two teams have met nearly every year since 1895, with Michigan holding a 58–44–6 lead in the series, with the 2010 OSU victory vacated.

Paul Brown, who went on to have much success as a **professional football coach**, got his start at OSU and had a record of 18–8–1 from 1941 to 1943. OSU's most famous coach, however, has been **Wayne "Woody" Hayes**. He coached the Buckeyes from 1951 to 1978 and had a record of 205–61–10, but his coaching career came to a shameful end in 1978. During the postseason Gator Bowl against Clemson University, Clemson player Charlie Bauman **intercepted** an OSU **pass** and was **run out of bounds**. The frustrated Hayes then punched Bauman. After the game, Hayes was fired by the OSU administration. Hayes's next three successors at Ohio State, Earl Bruce, John Cooper, and Jim Tressel, all had outstanding careers with the Buckeyes. Bruce was 81–26–1 from 1979 to 1987, Cooper was 111–43–4 from 1988 to 2000, and Tressel was 94–22 (with 12 wins in 2010 considered as vacated) from 2001 to 2010.

Ohio State alumni in the **College Football Hall of Fame** are **quarterback** Rex Kern; **halfbacks** Howard "Hopalong" Cassady, Eddie George, **Archie**

Griffin, Charles "Chic" Harley, Vic Janowicz, and Gaylord Stinchcomb; **fullback** Bob Ferguson; halfback/quarterback Les Horvath; **ends** Wes Fesler and Jim Houston; **linemen** Warren Amling, Jim Daniell, John Hicks, Gomer Jones, Jim Parker, Jim Stillwagon, Aurealius Thomas, Bill Willis, and Gust Zarnas; **linebackers** Randy Gradishar and Chris Spielman; and **safety** Jack Tatum. Former OSU coaches in the Hall are Earle Bruce, John Cooper, Wayne "Woody" Hayes, Howard Jones, Francis Schmidt, and John Wilce. The Buckeyes are **tied** with the **University of Notre Dame** and the **University of Southern California** for the most **Heisman Trophies**, with seven. Howard "Hopalong" Cassady, Eddie George, Archie Griffin (twice), Les Horvath, Vic Janowicz, and Troy Smith have all won the prestigious award.

Through 2012, there have been 382 **professional football** players who have attended OSU, the third most of any school. There have been 371 in the **National Football League**, six in the **American Football League**, and five in the **All-America Football Conference**. They include Cris Carter, Joey Galloway, Eddie George, Randy Gradishar, **Lou Groza**, Santonio Holmes, Jim Houston, Vic Janowicz, Thomas "Pepper" Johnson, Dante Lavelli, Dick LeBeau, Nick Mangold, **Jim Marshall**, Tom Matte, Mike Nugent, Jim Otis, Orlando Pace, Jim Parker, Dick Schafrath, Matt Snell, Chris Spielman, Jack Tatum, Mike Tomczak, Tom Tupa, Jim Tyrer, Bob Vogel, Mike Vrabel, **Paul Warfield**, Bill Willis, and Antoine Winfield.

OKLAHOMA, UNIVERSITY OF. The University of Oklahoma is located in Norman, Oklahoma. Their **football** program began in 1895, and, since then, through 2012, their team, known as the Oklahoma Sooners, has compiled a record of 802–295–52. In addition, they have competed in 46 postseason **bowl games**, with a record of 27–18–1. They have been selected as national collegiate champions 17 times, in 1915, 1949, 1950, 1953, 1955, 1956, 1957, 1967, 1973, 1974, 1975, 1978, 1980, 1985, 1986, 2000, and 2003. Home games since 1923 have been played at Oklahoma Memorial Stadium, renamed Gaylord Family Oklahoma Memorial Stadium in 2002. When the **stadium** was built in 1923, it had a seating capacity of 500. Throughout the years, the facility has been gradually expanded to its present capacity of 82,112.

Oklahoma football teams competed in the **Big Eight Conference** from 1920 to 1995. In 1996, the Big Eight added four schools from the defunct **Southwest Conference** and became a new entity known as the **Big 12 Conference**. Oklahoma's main rivals were the **University of Texas** and the **University of Nebraska**. In the series with Texas, the teams have met in most years since 1900 in a contest known as the Red River Rivalry. Texas leads the series, 59–43–5. From 1912 to 2010, Nebraska and Oklahoma met 86 times, with Oklahoma being ahead, 45–38–3. In 2011, Nebraska joined the **Big Ten Conference**, and the rivalry has been effectively ended.

Oklahoma has had four head **coaches** who each coached more than 10 years and 100 games. Bennie Owen was coach from 1905 to 1926 and compiled a record of 122–54–16. Charles "Bud" Wilkinson was in charge from 1947 to 1963. His record was 145–29–4 and includes a record 47-game winning streak and six national championships. Barry Switzer, coach from 1973 to 1988, won 157 games, lost 29, and **tied** four. Bob Stoops, coach from 1999 to 2012, has a record of 149–37.

The 20 Oklahoma alumni in the **College Football Hall of Fame** include **quarterback Troy Aikman**; **halfbacks** Tommy McDonald, Steve Owens, Greg Pruitt, Billy Sims, Clendon Thomas, and Billy Vessels; **fullbacks** Forest Geyer and Claude Reeds; **running back** Joe Washington; **ends** Keith Jackson, Jim Owens, and Walter "Waddy" Young; and **linemen** Tom Brahaney, Kurt Burris, Tony Casillas, J. D. Roberts, Lee Roy Selmon, Jerry Tubbs, and Jim Weatherall. In addition, Oklahoma coaches Lawrence "Biff" Jones, Bennie Owen, Barry Switzer, Jim Tatum, and Clarence "Bud" Wilkinson have been inducted in the Hall. Oklahoma's five **Heisman Trophy** winners are Sam Bradford, Steve Owens, Billy Sims, Billy Vessels, and Jason White.

Through 2012, there have been 310 **professional football** players who have attended Oklahoma, 298 in the **National Football League**, eight in the **American Football League**, and four in the **All-America Football Conference**. They include Troy Aikman, Jason Belser, Bobby Boyd, Sam Bradford, Dexter Bussey, Scott Case, Tony Casillas, Mark Clayton, Prentice Gautt, Kelly Gregg, Tommie Harris, Lee "Pop" Ivy, Keith Jackson, Edward "Wahoo" McDaniel, Tommy McDonald, Derland Moore, Ralph Neely, Adrian Peterson, Greg Pruitt, Lance Rentzel, Lee Roy Selmon, Clendon Thomas, Keith Traylor, Jerry Tubbs, and Joe Washington.

OLSEN, MERLIN JAY. B. 15 September 1940, Logan, Utah. D. 11 March 2010, Duarte, California. Although Merlin Olsen was a star **professional football** player for 15 years, he is probably better known for his postfootball acting career in the television shows *Little House on the Prairie*, *Aaron's Way*, and *Father Murphy*. A 1958 graduate of Logan High School, he attended Utah State University from 1958 to 1962 and starred as a defensive **tackle** from 1959 to 1961. During his three years as a member of the **varsity**, the Aggies compiled a record of 23–9–1, were **conference** cochampions twice, and played in two **bowl games**. Olsen won the **Outland Trophy** following his senior year and was also named Most Valuable Player in the Hula Bowl all-star game that year. During his junior and senior years, Utah State's **defense**, led by Olsen, set team records for fewest points allowed per game.

The six-foot, five-inch, 270-pound Olsen was chosen by the Los Angeles Rams in the first round of the 1962 **National Football League (NFL) Draft** as the third overall selection, an unusual distinction for a defensive **lineman**. He remained with the Rams for 15 seasons and was named to the **Pro Bowl** in every season except his last. During Olsen's career, the Rams had winning records in 10 of the 15 seasons and reached the postseason **playoffs** six times but could never advance past the conference championship round, and, consequently, Olsen never appeared in a **Super Bowl**.

Olsen played in all of his team's 208 regular-season games and nine postseason games. His only **touchdown** occurred in the final game of his first NFL season, when he returned an **interception** 20 yards for a score. He also recovered 10 **fumbles**, including one in 1965 that he returned 59 yards before being tackled and one in the postseason.

Before retiring from active play, Olsen turned to acting and appeared in several films and television shows. He also worked as an analyst on NFL **football** coverage, which included a Super Bowl telecast, and did several **Rose Bowl** telecasts and multiple commercials. He was inducted into the **College Football Hall of Fame** in 1980 and the **Pro Football Hall of Fame** in 1982. Diagnosed with peritoneal mesothelioma in 2009, Olsen succumbed to the disease in March 2010.

OLYMPIC GAMES. The 1904 Olympic Games, in St. Louis, Missouri, was a very loosely structured event, with contests in various sports held from July through November, in conjunction with the Louisiana Purchase Exposition. A **soccer (football)** tournament was held from 16 November to 23 November, with the Galt Football Club of Canada being named champion. An American football game between two Native American schools, the Haskell Institute and **Carlisle Indian Industrial School**, won by Carlisle, 38–4, was also held in St. Louis on 27 November. This can be looked at as a demonstration event, although during that era the International Olympic Committee (IOC) did not give formal recognition to demonstration sports. At the Olympic Games in Los Angeles, California, in 1932, an American football game was played as a formal demonstration sport.

An all-star game between seniors from three West Coast colleges (the **University of California, Stanford University**, and the **University of Southern California**) and three East Coast colleges (**Harvard University, Yale University,** and **Princeton University**) was played on 8 August 1932, at the **Los Angeles Memorial Coliseum**, before 60,000 spectators, with the West Coast team winning, 7–6. Players on both teams lived at the Olympic Village with the other Olympic athletes.

One of the functions of an Olympic demonstration sport is to expose the game to people from countries that do not play the sport. A second function is to invite the IOC to possibly include the sport as an official Olympic sport. As of 2012, the IOC has yet to officially include football in the Olympic Games, although with the founding of the **International Federation of American Football** in 1998, steps have been taken in this direction.

ONSIDE KICK. An onside kick is a strategic maneuver by the kicking team during a **kickoff**. Rather than kick the ball as far as possible, as is generally the case in a kickoff, the ball will be kicked only a few yards (but at least 10 yards) in an attempt to recover possession by the kicking team. This play usually occurs late in a game when a team is behind in the score and they feel there is insufficient time to regain possession via normal defensive play.

OORANG INDIANS. The Oorang Indians were one of the most unusual teams in professional sports history. They were a **professional football** team in the fledgling **National Football League (NFL)** in 1922 and 1923. The team was owned by Walter Lingo, a breeder of Airedale dogs and owner of the Oorang Kennels. Lingo was a friend of **Jim Thorpe**, a Sac and Fox Indian and a man considered to be among the greatest athletes of all time. Lingo purchased an NFL franchise for $100 and used it as a basis for advertising his Airedales. The team, based in LaRue, Ohio, a town of less than 1,000 people, was to be a traveling team, with all games played on the road. Thorpe was player-**coach** and recruited only Native Americans for the squad, which featured players from nine different Indian tribes. **Halftime** shows featured the Airedales performing tricks and the Indians performing dances and tomahawk-throwing exhibitions. **Football** was secondary to Airedale promotion. As a result, the team won only three of nine games in 1922, and one of 11 games in 1923. The novelty wore off after two seasons, and Lingo dissolved the team. Players on the team, in addition to Thorpe, included future **Pro Football Hall of Famer Joe Guyon** and quite a few others who used their tribal names, including Arrowhead, Eagle Feather, Gray Horse, Joe Little Twig, Xavier Downwind, and Nicholas "Long Time Sleep" Lassa.

OPTION PLAY. The option play, much more popular in high school or collegiate play than in professional play, occurs when the **quarterback** keeps the ball and **runs** toward the side with a **back** nearby. If the quarterback is about to be **tackled**, he **laterals** the ball to the back. In modern-day **football**, there are many variants of this play. Since professional defensive players are much faster and quarterbacks who run this play get tackled more often, with consequent liability for injury, professional teams seldom use this play. **Tim Tebow** and **Michael Vick** are two modern-day exceptions in the **National Football League** and have been successful running it from time to time.

ORANGE BOWL. The Orange Bowl is a postseason college **bowl game**. It was first played on 1 January 1935, and, along with the **Sun Bowl** and **Sugar Bowl**, it is the second-oldest bowl game. Until recent years, it was always played on **New Year's Day** (or 2 January if New Year's fell on a Sunday). From 1935 to 1937, it was played at Miami Field in Miami, Florida, and, from 1938 to 1996 and again in 1999, it was played at Burdine Stadium (renamed the Miami Orange Bowl in 1959). That venue's seating capacity was only 23,000 in 1938 but was gradually expanded to more than 80,000 throughout the years. Since 1997, with the exception of 1999, the game has been played at a 75,000-seat **stadium** in Miami Gardens, Florida, that has gone through several name changes. It was originally called Joe Robbie Stadium and, in 2012, was known as Sun Life Stadium.

For much of the event's history (1968–1998), one of the teams selected was the champion of the **Big Eight Conference**, and, as a result, the **University of Oklahoma**, with 18 appearances and 12 victories, leads all schools in Orange Bowl history. The **University of Nebraska**, with 17 appearances and eight victories, is second. With the creation of the **Bowl Championship Series (BCS)** in 1998, the Orange Bowl has been affiliated with either the **Big East Conference** or **Atlantic Coast Conference**. In 2001, 2005 and 2013, the Orange Bowl hosted the BCS National Championship Game.

OTTAWA RENEGADES. The Ottawa Renegades were a team in the **Canadian Football League (CFL)** for four seasons, from 2002 to 2005. They suspended operations in 2006. Their record for those years was 23–49. They did not make the postseason **playoffs** and finished in third or fourth place in the East Division in each of those years, with a best record of 7–11 in 2003 and 2005. Home games were played at the 26,500-seat Frank Clair Stadium in Lansdowne Park, Ottawa, Ontario. The team was **coached** by Joe Paopao. Among their best players were defensive **back** Korey Banks, **quarterback** Kerry Joseph, and **wide receiver** Markus Howell.

OTTAWA ROUGH RIDERS. The Ottawa Rough Riders were a team in the **Canadian Football League (CFL)** from 1958 to 1996. They were founded in 1876 as the Ottawa Football Club. In 1898, they were named the Rough Riders after Theodore Roosevelt's Spanish American war regiment. From 1925 to 1930, they were known as the Ottawa Senators but reverted to the Rough Riders in 1931. The team played in various leagues until 1907, when they became one of the charter members of the Interprovincial Rugby Football Union and, in 1958, joined the new CFL. Although there were only eight teams in the CFL, two of them had similar names, the **Saskatchewan Roughriders** and the Ottawa Rough Riders. Ottawa played in 15 **Grey Cups**, winning nine of them, with a record of 5–2 in the CFL (1960, 1968, 1969, 1973, and 1976). Ottawa's home field from 1908 until 1996 was Lansdowne Park, in Lansdowne Park, Ottawa, Ontario. The facility was renamed Frank Clair Stadium in 1993.

Frank Clair (1956–1969) had the longest stint as head **coach**. Other notable Ottawa head coaches included Tom Little (1904–1911), Clem Crowe (1951–1954), Jack Gotta (1970–1973), and George Brancato (1974–1984). **Canadian Football Hall of Famers** who played for Ottawa include Damon Allen, Less Browne, Jerry Campbell, Tom Clements, Abe Eliowitz, Eddie Emerson, Tony Gabriel, Tony Golab, Conredge Holloway, Russ Jackson, Ron Lancaster, Ken Lehmann, Dave McCann, Rudy Phillips, Bob Simpson, David Sprague, Ron Stewart, Dave Thelen, Andrew Tommy, Joe Tubman, Whit Tucker, and Kaye Vaughan.

In 1996, the Rough Riders folded their operation and withdrew from the CFL. In 2002, a new team, the **Ottawa Renegades**, played in the CFL, but they only lasted through the 2005 season. Plans have been made for another Ottawa team to join the CFL for the 2014 season.

OTTO, JAMES EDWIN "JIM." B. 5 January 1938, Wausau, Wisconsin. Jim Otto played **professional football** for 15 years and has the scars to prove it. He had 28 knee operations and multiple joint replacements and, in 2007, had to have a leg amputated as a result of an infection stemming from his injuries. Otto began playing **football** at Wausau High School and received a scholarship to play for the **University of Miami** in Florida, where he played **center** on **offense** and **linebacker** on **defense**. He was not **drafted** by the **National Football League (NFL)** and signed with the **Oakland Raiders** of the **American Football League (AFL)** in their inaugural season, 1960. The six-foot, two-inch, 255-pound Otto played center for the Raiders from 1960 to 1974 and wore the unusual uniform number of 00. He was a member of the 1966 AFL champions and played on the losing side in the second **Super Bowl** in 1967. The following two seasons, Otto played in the AFL Championship Game, but the Raiders were defeated both times. During his career, he was considered the premier center in the AFL.

In his 15-year combined AFL–NFL career, Otto played in all of his team's 210 regular-season and 13 postseason games. Unfortunately, as a center, no official statistics were kept that can measure his effectiveness, although in the 1972 **playoff** game against the **Pittsburgh Steelers**, won by Pittsburgh with **Franco Harris's "Immaculate Reception"** in the last few seconds of the game, early in the game, a **pass** from Ken Stabler was tipped at the **line of scrimmage**, and Otto caught it and ran five yards with it for his only offensive statistical accomplishment. He played in the AFL All-Star Game or

Pro Bowl every year from 1961 to 1972. In 1970, he was named to the AFL All-Time Team.

After retiring from active play, Otto became the owner of several Burger King restaurants, owned a walnut orchard, invested in real estate, and worked for Raiders' owner **Al Davis** on various special projects. He was inducted into the **Pro Football Hall of Fame** in 1980, in his first year of eligibility.

OUT OF BOUNDS. If the ball (or player carrying the ball) touches or goes over the **sidelines**, it is considered to be out of bounds, and the following play will begin on the **yard line** in which the out of bounds occurred. In **professional football**, the time clock is stopped when an out of bounds situation occurs. This leads to a strategic decision late in games when a player will deliberately **run** out of bounds to stop the clock.

OUTLAND TROPHY. The Outland Trophy is an award presented by the Football Writers Association of America to a collegiate interior offensive or defensive **lineman**. The award has been presented since 1946 and is considered to be among the most prestigious individual awards. It is named for John H. Outland, a 19th-century **football** player at William Penn College, the University of Kansas, and the **University of Pennsylvania**. Outland later became a physician and served as a surgeon during World War I. Linemen from the **University of Nebraska** have won the award nine times. Dave Rimington, **center** for Nebraska, is the only player to win the award twice, in 1981 and 1982.

OVERTIME. Overtime is a relatively recent addition to **football**. For most of football's history, if the score was **tied** at the end of the game, the result was a tie. To determine a champion, **professional football** provided that in the championship game, if the score was tied, additional 15-minute periods would be played, but the game would end upon the first score. This is known as "**sudden-death**" overtime. The 1958 **National Football League (NFL)** Championship Game between the **Baltimore Colts** and **New York Giants** was the first important game played that was decided by an overtime period (although the experiment had been tried several years earlier in a preseason game). In 1974, the NFL decided to employ overtime for regular-season games, although in those games, if the score is still tied at the end of a 15-minute overtime period, the result is a tie.

In 1996, the **National Collegiate Athletic Association (NCAA)** adopted overtime for all games. Unlike the NFL's sudden-death overtime, the NCAA overtime places the ball on the 25-**yard line**, and each team has four **downs** to attempt to score, alternating possessions until one team outscores their opponent. **Canadian football** also has dual possession overtime rules similar to American colleges.

OWENS, TERRELL ELDORADO "T. O." B. 7 December 1973, Alexander City, Alabama. Terrell Owens was one of the most flamboyant characters in **professional football** during the 21st century. He was known for his exuberant and innovative (if often excessive) celebrations following **touchdown receptions**. He attended Benjamin Russell High School in Alexander City, Alabama, where he played **football**, baseball, and basketball. After graduating, he received an athletic scholarship to the University of Tennessee at Chattanooga. In addition to playing football, he also played basketball and ran track in college. His 1995 Chattanooga basketball team reached the **National Collegiate Athletic Association** championships, although they lost their first-round game. In his four seasons at Chattanooga, from 1992 to 1995, the football team did not have a single winning season and had a combined record of 13–31. As a result, Owens was not exceptionally visible to professional football scouts, and he was not chosen until the third round of the 1996 **National Football League (NFL) Draft** as the 89th overall selection. He was picked by the **San Francisco 49ers**.

A six-foot, three-inch, 225-pound **wide receiver**, Owens played for San Francisco from 1996 to 2003, the **Philadelphia Eagles** in 2004 and 2005, the **Dallas Cowboys** from 2006 to 2008, the **Buffalo Bills** in 2009, and the **Cincinnati Bengals** in 2010. With the Eagles, he played in the 2005 **Super Bowl**. He caught nine **passes** for 122 yards in that game, but it was not enough, as the Eagles lost, 24–21, to the **New England Patriots**. During his career, he led the league in receiving touchdowns and recorded more than 1,000 yards receiving in nine seasons.

In his 15-year NFL career, Owens played in 219 regular-season games, caught 1,078 passes for 15,934 yards and 153 touchdowns, and ran 39 times for 251 yards and three touchdowns. In his first two seasons, he was occasionally used as a kick **returner** and returned five **kickoffs** for an average of 15.6 yards per return. In 11 postseason games, Owens caught 54 passes for 751 yards and five touchdowns and completed one pass in one attempt for 25 yards and no touchdowns. He played in six **Pro Bowls**.

Owens was not signed by any team for the 2011 NFL season, but, in 2012, he signed with the Allen Wranglers to play indoor football in the Indoor Football League, a relatively minor league in that sport. He only lasted four months with the Wranglers and was dropped from the team for failure to play in two games and not showing up for a scheduled appearance at a children's hospital. As he is among the top 10 all-time in the NFL in touchdowns, pass receptions, and receiving yardage, there is a good chance that he will eventually be enshrined in the **Pro Football Hall of Fame**.

P

PACIFIC-12 CONFERENCE (PAC-12). The Pacific-12 Conference (Pac-12) is an organization of **major colleges** and universities that compete athletically in the **National Collegiate Athletic Association**. It was established in 1915 as the Pacific Coast Conference. Since then, it has been known as the Athletic Association of Western Universities (1959–1968), the Pacific-8 (1968–1978), and the Pacific-10 (1978–2012). The **conference** is based in Walnut Creek, California. Its 12 members in 2012 were the University of Arizona; **Arizona State University**; the University of California, Berkeley; the **University of California, Los Angeles**; the **University of Colorado** at Boulder; the University of Oregon; Oregon State University; the **University of Southern California**; **Stanford University**; the University of Utah; the **University of Washington**; and Washington State University.

PAGE, ALAN CEDRIC. B. 7 August 1945, Canton, Ohio. Alan Page is a graduate of Central Catholic High School in Canton. A star **football** player in high school, he received a scholarship to the **University of Notre Dame**. He played defensive **end** at Notre Dame from 1964 to 1966 and was a member of the national champions in 1964 and 1966. In his three years on the Notre Dame **varsity**, the school had a record of 25–3–2.

Page was chosen by the **Minnesota Vikings** in the first round of the 1967 **National Football League (NFL) Draft** as the 15th overall selection. The six-foot, four-inch, 245-pound Page played with the Vikings from 1967 to 1978. He was traded to the **Chicago Bears** midway through the 1978 season and finished his career with them in 1981.

In his 15-year NFL career, Page played in all of his teams' 218 regular-season games and 19 postseason games. He had two **interceptions** and 23 **fumble** recoveries in the regular season and one interception and one fumble recovery in the postseason. Two of his fumble recoveries went for **touchdowns**, including one 77-yard return in 1970. In 1969, he also recorded a touchdown after receiving a **lateral**. Page was credited with three **safeties**, including two in 1971, and was selected for the **Pro Bowl** nine times. He took up **running** as a conditioning aid and, in 1979, became the first active NFL player to complete a marathon. He later ran and completed a 100-kilometer race.

As a resident of Canton, one of Page's summer jobs was working on the construction of the **Pro Football Hall of Fame**. He was inducted into the Hall in 1988 and is the only person to have worked on the construction of the building who is enshrined there. He was also inducted into the **College Football Hall of Fame** in 1993.

Page was an NFL Players Association representative from 1970 to 1974 and 1976 to 1977 and was a member of the organization's Executive Committee from 1972 to 1975. In 1978, he received his law degree from the **University of Minnesota** and worked for a law firm in the off-season while continuing to play football. He was appointed special assistant attorney general of Minnesota in 1985 and was later promoted to assistant attorney general. In 1992, Page was elected an associate justice of the Minnesota Supreme Court and was subsequently reelected in 1998, 2004, and 2010. He has been awarded honorary doctorates from nine universities.

PARCELLS, DUANE CHARLES "BILL." B. 22 August 1941, Englewood, New Jersey. Although Bill Parcells's father is an attorney, Bill did not want to follow in his father's footsteps and wanted to be a professional athlete. He attended River Dell Regional High School in Oradell, New Jersey, and was a pitcher on the baseball team, **quarterback** on the **football** team, and **center** on the basketball team. He continued his education at Colgate University but transferred to the Municipal University of Wichita (later known as Wichita State University), where he was a **linebacker** and offensive **lineman** on the football team. Parcells graduated from Wichita with a degree in physical education and was selected by the **Detroit Lions** of the **National Football League (NFL)** in the seventh round of the 1964 NFL **Draft** as the 89th overall selection. He did not make the team and decided to pursue a career in **coaching**.

Parcells began as an **assistant coach** coaching the linebackers at Hastings College in 1964. In 1965, he moved to Wichita State in the same role. From 1966 to 1969, he was an assistant at the United States Military Academy (**Army**) and was the defensive coordinator for the latter two years. While at Army, he also helped Bob Knight with the basketball team. During the next decade, Parcells continued to move from college to college as an assistant football coach and was at **Florida State University** (1970–1972), Vanderbilt University (1973–1974), Texas Tech (1975–1977), and the Air Force Academy (1978). At Air Force, he was head coach and compiled a record of 3–8.

In 1979, Parcells received an offer to coach **professional football** and spent the remainder of his coaching career in that capacity. Although he accepted the offer from **New York Giants'** coach Ray Perkins to be their defensive coordinator, he quit before the regular season and started to work for a land development company in Colorado. By 1980, he decided to return to football and was hired by the **New England Patriots** as linebackers coach. In 1981, the Giants rehired him as defensive coordinator, and, in 1983, he became their head coach. Although their record for his first season was just 3–12–1, by 1986 he had turned the Giants around and they were **Super Bowl** champions that year. After leading the Giants to a second Super Bowl in 1990, Parcells retired.

He spent the next two years as a television analyst but, by 1993, decided to return to the NFL as a coach. He was hired as head coach of the New England Patriots. In four years as their coach, he brought them from a losing record to the Super Bowl in 1996. After the Patriots lost the Super Bowl, Parcells went searching for new challenges and was hired by the **New York Jets** for the 1997 season. He coached the Jets from 1997 to 1999 and then retired from coaching again, although he remained as the Jets' general manager for one more season.

In 2003, Parcells again came out of retirement and was hired by the **Dallas Cowboys**. He coached them through 2006 and, frustrated with their lack of success, retired yet again. In 2008, he was hired by the **Miami Dolphins** as their executive vice president of football operations but remained in the front office and did not coach the team. In 2013, Parcells was elected to the **Pro Football Hall of Fame**.

PARILLI, VITO "BABE." B. 7 May 1929, Rochester, Pennsylvania. In Babe Parilli's long **professional football** career, he played for six teams in three leagues, and, after he retired, he **coached** in two other leagues. He was born and raised in western Pennsylvania, in the same area as such successful **National Football League (NFL) quarterbacks** as **George Blanda, Jim Kelly, Johnny Lujack, Dan Marino, Joe Montana, Joe Namath,** and **Johnny Unitas**, among others. Parilli attended Rochester High School in Rochester, Pennsylvania. He began as a **fullback** but was moved to quarterback. He enrolled at the University of Kentucky and helped lead the Wildcats to a record of 28–8, a **Southeastern Conference** championship, and three bowl appearances during his three years as the **varsity** quarterback for coach **Paul "Bear" Bryant** from 1949 to 1951.

At six feet, one inch tall and 195 pounds, Parilli was chosen by the **Green Bay Packers** in the first round of the 1952 NFL **Draft** as the fourth overall selection. He was the Packers' backup quarterback to Tobin Rote in 1952 and 1953. Parilli played in Canada for the **Ottawa Rough Riders** in 1954 and 1955. He returned to the NFL in 1956 with the **Cleveland Browns** but again was used as a backup quarterback. He spent 1957 and 1958 with the Packers as backup to **Bart Starr**. Parilli returned to Canada in 1959 for another year as the Rough Riders' quarterback.

The turning point in Parilli's professional football career occurred in 1960. In that year, the **American Football League (AFL)** began operations, and, for the league's entire 10-year existence, he played in the AFL, one of only 20 players to do so. He began in 1960 with the **Oakland Raiders** as the backup to Tom Flores. In 1961, Parilli moved to Boston and had the best years of his AFL career there, becoming their starting quarterback in 1962 and remaining as such through 1967. In 1963, he led the Patriots to the AFL Championship Game, but they were defeated by the **San Diego Chargers**. Parilli finished his professional football playing career with the **New York Jets** in 1968 and 1969 as backup to Joe Namath, another western Pennsylvania player who also had played for Bear Bryant in college, although in Namath's case he played for Bryant at the **University of Alabama**. With the Jets in 1968, Parilli was a member of the AFL's first **Super Bowl** championship team. Although Parilli was just a backup quarterback on that team, he was most valuable to the Jets as a placekick **holder** and was considered to be one of the most reliable holders in league history.

In his 15-year combined NFL–AFL career, spanning 18 years, Parilli played in 189 regular-season games, started 101 of those contests, and had a won-lost record of 49–46–7. He completed 1,552 **passes** in 3,330 attempts for 22,681 yards and 178 **touchdowns** and ran 383 times for 1,522 yards and 23 touchdowns. He also scored one touchdown on a **fumble** recovery. Parilli was used as a **punter** in three seasons and **punted** 89 times for an average of 39.4 yards per punt. He appeared in five postseason games, two as the starting quarterback with the Patriots in 1963 and three with the Jets as backup quarterback and placekick holder in 1968 and 1969. He completed 28 of 65 passes for 489 yards and two touchdowns and ran twice for 10 yards. After retiring from active play, Parilli worked as head coach in the new **World Football League** and later coached in **arena football**. He was inducted into the **College Football Hall of Fame** in 1982.

PASS. One of the most effective offensive plays is a pass play. After the offensive player (ordinarily the **quarterback**) receives the ball from the **center** to start a **down**, he may elect to pass the ball forward to a teammate. The passer must be behind the **line of scrimmage** when attempting a forward pass. Only certain players (**backs**, **ends**, and **wide receivers**) are eligible to receive a pass. On occasion, a player other than the quarterback may attempt a pass, but he must be behind the line of scrimmage, and the receiver must be an eligible pass receiver. In the early days of **football**, passing was severely restricted and seldom attempted, but, as the rules changed (and the shape of the ball changed), passing became an integral part of a team's offense. Since the 1940s, the forward pass has become the major offensive weapon of most teams, and players at the quarterback position are selected both for arm strength and throwing accuracy. To be a successfully completed forward pass, the receiver must have complete possession of the ball before hitting the ground and must have at least one foot (two in **professional football**) in bounds. *See also* PASS INTERFERENCE; RECEPTION.

PASS INTERFERENCE. Pass interference is a **penalty** when the defensive player interferes with the offensive player's attempt to catch the ball. It is the most severe penalty in **football** since the ball is placed at the spot of the foul (the one-**yard line** if it occurs in the **end zone**) and can result in a gain of 50 yards or more. It can also be called on the offensive team if the **official** rules that the offensive player interfered with the defender.

PASSAGLIA, LUI. B. 7 June 1954, Vancouver, British Columbia, Canada. Lui Passaglia was one of the greatest players in **Canadian Football League (CFL)** history, although he remains unknown to most American **football fans** south of Canada. At Notre Dame Regional Secondary School in East Vancouver, Canada, he played **quarterback** on their football team. After graduating from high school, he attended Simon Fraser University in Burnaby, British Columbia, a suburb of Vancouver. In college, he was a **kicker**, **punter**, and **wide receiver**.

Passaglia was chosen by the **BC Lions** in the 1976 CFL **Draft** in the first round as the fifth overall selection. He remained with the Lions for the next quarter century, playing in 408 regular-season games from 1976 to 2000 (more than 25 more than the **National Football League's** leader in games played, **Morten Andersen**). During that time, Passaglia played on three **Grey Cup** championship teams (1985, 1994, 2000) and two Grey Cup runners-up (1983, 1988). His **field goal** with no time remaining won the 1994 cup for the Lions.

Passaglia is the CFL career record holder for most points (3,991), extra points (1,045 of 1,048, including 550 consecutive), field goals (875 of 1,203), and **rouges** (309). He also scored two **touchdowns**, one in his very first CFL game and the other in his last regular-season CFL game. He is also second all-time with 3.142 **punts** and holds the CFL record for longest punt, at 89 yards. After retiring from active play at the age of 46, Passaglia continued to work for the Lions as their director of community relations. He was inducted into the **Canadian Football Hall of Fame** in 2004.

PATERNO, JOSEPH VINCENT "JOE," "JOEPA." B. 21 December 1926, Brooklyn, New York. D. 22 January 2012, State College, Pennsylvania. Joe Paterno had an outstanding career as a **college football coach**, but it ended tragically in a few short weeks in the fall of 2011. Paterno attended Brooklyn Prep and graduated in 1944. He was drafted into the U.S. Army and served in Korea. Upon his discharge, he enrolled at Brown University and played **quarterback** on **offense** and **cornerback** on **defense** under Coach Charles "Rip" Engle. After graduating from Brown in 1950, he followed Engle to **Penn State University**, where he became an assistant football coach. He remained as Engle's assistant until 1965, when Engle retired.

Paterno was named head coach in 1966 and retained that position until November 2011. During that time, his teams compiled a record of 409–136–3, with five undefeated seasons and five national championships. They played in postseason **bowl games** 37 times in 45 seasons. His bowl won-lost record was 24–12–1, and he won more bowl games than any other college coach. More than 240 players that Paterno coached at Penn State while a head coach there have played **professional football** in the **National Football League**. He was inducted into the **College Football Hall of Fame** as a coach in 2007.

On 29 October 2011, Paterno recorded his 409th victory as a head coach in a game played in an unusual October blizzard and won by Penn State, 10–7, over the **University of Illinois**. One week later, 5 November, one of Paterno's **assistant coaches**, Jerry Sandusky, was accused of child sexual abuse in a series of incidents allegedly occurring between 1994 and 2009. Although Paterno was not accused of any misconduct, he was accused of being aware of some of Sandusky's activities and of not doing enough to stop him. On 8 November, the Board of Trustees of Penn State, in a severe overreaction, terminated the 84-year-old Paterno, who had been a member of their staff for 61 years. Within the next month, it was revealed that Paterno had cancer and, on 22 January 2012, he was dead. In a ridiculous overreaction to the situation, the **National Collegiate Athletic Association** on 23 July 2012 ruled that Penn State's 112 victories from 1998 to 2011 were vacated and thus Paterno's career record number of victories was reduced to 298.

PAYTON, WALTER JERRY "SWEETNESS." B. 25 July 1954, Columbia, Mississippi. D. 1 November 1999, South Barrington, Illinois. Walter Payton was one of the **National Football League's (NFL)** greatest **running backs**. He began high school at the all-black John J. Jefferson High School in Columbia, Mississippi. While he was there, Columbia began to integrate their schools, and Jefferson was merged with the all-white Columbia High School. Payton played **football** and basketball and was a long jumper on the track team.

Payton continued his education at Jackson State University, a historically black school. He played football there from 1971 to 1974. In addition to playing **halfback**, he was the team's **punter** and placekicker. During his four years there, the Tigers had a record of 33–9–1 and were **conference** cochampions twice. In 1972, as a sophomore, Payton scored 46 points in one game on seven **touchdowns** and two two-point **conversions**. In four years, he scored a record 464 points and **rushed** for 3,563 yards. He graduated in 1975 with a degree in communications and was taken in the first round of the NFL **Draft** by the **Chicago Bears** as the fourth overall selection.

A five-foot, 10-inch, 200-pound powerful runner, he played with the Bears through 1987 and was a member of their 1986 **Super Bowl**–winning team. His best year was 1977, when he gained a league-leading 1,852 yards (the third highest in the NFL at that time) in 14 games for an average of 132.3 yards per game, still the third highest in NFL history. On 20 November 1977, he rushed for an NFL record 275 yards in 40 carries in a game against the **Minnesota Vikings**. That record remained for 23 years before being surpassed.

Payton's older brother, Eddie, also a Jackson State alumnus, played in the NFL for five years between 1977 and 1982. He appeared in 65 games (including six games against his brother's Bears team), primarily as a **punt** and kick **returner** and occasionally as running back. Payton's son, Jarrett, also played **professional football** briefly in the NFL in 2005 with the **Tennessee Titans** as a running **back**, and in the **Canadian Football League** and **World League of American Football**. Sean Payton, an NFL player and **coach**, is unrelated to the Walter Payton family.

When Payton retired in 1987, he was the NFL's all-time leading rusher in attempts, yardage, and touchdowns, but all three records have since been surpassed by **Emmitt Smith**. Payton still ranks second in attempts and yardage and fourth in touchdowns. In his 13-year NFL career, he played in 190 regular-season games, ran 3,838 times for 16,726 yards and 110 touchdowns, and caught 492 **passes** for 4,538 yards and 15 touchdowns. He also completed 11 of 34 passes for eight touchdowns. In his first three years in the league, when he was also occasionally used as a kick returner, he returned 17 **kickoffs** for an average of 31.7 yards per return. In 1975, he also punted once for 39 yards. In nine postseason games, Payton ran 180 times for 632 yards and two touchdowns, caught 22 passes for 178 yards and no touchdowns, completed one of two passes for 19 yards and one touchdown, and returned three kickoffs for 57 yards.

After retiring from active play, Payton founded Walter Payton, Inc. and was involved in a variety of businesses, including real estate, nursing homes, travel agencies, and restaurants. He became interested in motor sports and established Payton-Coyne Racing with partner Dale Coyne and sponsored

Indy-style racing cars. In 1988, he was invited to become a member of the Board of Directors of the Chicago Bears, an honor that few former players are ever offered. Payton was inducted into the **Pro Football Hall of Fame** in 1993 and the **College Football Hall of Fame** in 1996. He died in 1999 of a rare liver ailment.

PENALTY. Football teams may incur penalties for various rules infractions. One or more of the **officials** will drop a handkerchief (called a flag) when they spot a rules infraction. When the play is concluded, the referee will signal the cause of the penalty and ask the offending team if they wish to accept the result of the play or the additional yardage and replay of the **down**. The most common causes for penalties are **offsides**; **encroachment** or false start; **pass interference**, either defensive or offensive; **intentional grounding**; **face mask** infractions; illegal use of hands or **holding**; illegal **blocks**; **unsportsmanlike conduct**; unnecessary roughness; roughing the passer (or **kicker**); and, in **Canadian football**, **no yards**.

PENN STATE UNIVERSITY. The Pennsylvania State University is located in State College, Pennsylvania. Familiarly known as Penn State, their **football** program began in 1881, and, since then, through 2012, the Nittany Lions' teams have compiled a record of 836–365–43. In addition, they have competed in 44 postseason **bowl games**, with a record of 27–15–2. They have been selected as national collegiate champions seven times, in 1911, 1912, 1969, 1981, 1982, 1986, and 1994. Home games since 1960 have been played at the 106,572-seat Beaver Stadium, the second largest **stadium** in the United States. Penn State has the unusual team nickname of the Nittany Lions, supposedly due to the mountain lions that once roamed nearby Mount Nittany.

In 1993, Penn State became the 11th member of the **Big Ten Conference**. Prior to that, they competed as an independent team. Since joining the Big Ten, Penn State's schedule of opponents has changed significantly, and former rivalries with the **University of Pittsburgh**, West Virginia University, the University of Maryland, and **Syracuse University** are no longer played. They are attempting to develop new rivalries with other Big Ten schools, including **Michigan State University**, the **University of Minnesota**, and **Ohio State University**. Their series with Michigan State is played for the Land Grant Trophy, and the one with Minnesota is for the Governor's Victory Bell.

Penn State's most successful **coach** was **Joe Paterno**. He coached the Nittany Lions from 1966 to 2011 and was responsible for nearly half of the school's victories. His record for 45 years was 409–136–3 and 24–12–1 in bowl games. He was the football coach at a **major college** longer than anyone else in history, passing **Amos Alonzo Stagg's** record of 41 years in 2007.

Paterno was inducted into the **College Football Hall of Fame** in 2007 but continued to coach the team although in his 80s. Other effective Penn State head coaches have included Bob Higgins, who coached Penn State from 1930 to 1948 and had a record of 91–57–11, and Charles "Rip" Engle, Paterno's predecessor from 1950 to 1965. Engle also had an outstanding record of 104–48–4.

There are 17 Penn State alumni in the College Football Hall of Fame. They are **quarterbacks** Glenn Killinger, Richie Lucas, and Gene "Shorty" Miller; **halfbacks** John Cappelletti (a **Heisman Trophy** winner), Pete Mauthe, and Harry Wilson; **running backs** Lydell Mitchell and Curt Warner; **ends** Ted Kwalick, Dave Robinson, and Dexter Very; **linemen** Keith Dorney, Mike Reid, Glenn Ressler, and Steve Suhey; and **linebackers** Jack Ham and Dennis Onkota. Penn State coaches in the Hall are Hugo Bezdek, Charles "Rip" Engle, Dick Harlow, Bob Higgins, and Joe Paterno.

Through 2012, there have been 328 **professional football** players who have attended Penn State, 319 in the **National Football League**, seven in the **American Football League**, and two in the **All-America Football Conference**. They include LaVar Arrington, brothers Chris and Matt Bahr, Stew Barber, Todd Blackledge, Kyle Brady, Kerry Collins, Chuck Drazenovich, Bobby Engram, Robbie Gould, Roosevelt Grier, Jack Ham, **Franco Harris**, Mike Hartenstine, Dick Hoak, Jeff Hostetler, Bill Lenkaitis, Kareem McKenzie, Matt Millen, **Lenny Moore**, Mike Munchak, Milt Plum, Tom Rafferty, Dave Robinson, Mickey Shuler, Dave Szott, Curt Warner, and Steve Wisniewski. On 5 November 2011, one of Paterno's **assistant coaches**, Jerry Sandusky, was accused of child sexual abuse in a series of incidents allegedly occurring between 1994 and 2009. While Paterno was not accused of any misconduct, it was disclosed that he was apparently aware of some of Sandusky's activities. On 8 November, the Board of Trustees of Penn State, in a severe overreaction, terminated the 84-year-old Paterno, who had been a member of their staff for 61 years. Within the next month, it was revealed that Paterno had cancer and, on 22 January 2012, he was dead. In a ridiculous overreaction to the situation, the **National Collegiate Athletic Association** on 23 July 2012 ruled that Penn State's 112 victories from 1998 to 2011 were vacated.

PENNSYLVANIA, UNIVERSITY OF. The University of Pennsylvania is located in Philadelphia, Pennsylvania. Their **football** program is one of the oldest in the country, as it began in 1876. Through 2012, Quakers' teams have compiled a record of 820–474–42. As members of the **Ivy League**, which bans football **bowl games** for its members, they do not play in any bowl contests. Prior to the league's formation, however, Penn was invited to play in the third **Rose Bowl** on 1 January 1917, where they were defeated by the University of Oregon. They have been selected as national collegiate champions six times, in 1894, 1895, 1897, 1904, 1908, and 1924. Penn's home games since 1895 have been played at Franklin Field, one of the oldest **stadiums** in the country. Its current seating capacity is 52,593. Penn was one of the charter members of the Ivy League when it was formed in 1956. As with many of the Ivy League schools, they have no one rival, but all games with other Ivy League teams attract interest.

Pennsylvania's most outstanding **coach** was George Woodruff. He coached the Quakers from 1892 to 1901 and had a record of 124–15–2. Carl Williams followed from 1902 to 1907. His record was nearly as good, at 60–10–4. Other noteworthy Penn coaches include Lou Young (1923–1929; 49–15–2), George Munger (1938–1953; 82–42–10), and Al Bagnoli (1992–2012; 142–66).

Pennsylvania alumni in the **College Football Hall of Fame** include **quarterback** Vince Stevenson; **halfbacks** Francis "Reds" Bagnell, Bill Hollenback, Anthony "Skip" Minisi, Bob Odell, and Win Osgood; **fullbacks** George Brooke, Leroy Mercer, and Jack Minds; **end** Hunter Scarlett; **center** Chuck Bednarik; **guard**/end Charlie Gelbert; guards Truxton Hare and Charles "Buck" Wharton; **tackles** Ed McGinley and George Savitsky; center/tackle Bob Torrey; and tackle/halfback John Outland (for whom the **Outland Trophy** is named). Penn coaches in the Hall are Harvey Harman, John Heisman, George Munger, Andy Smith, and George Woodruff.

Through 2012, there have been 59 **professional football** players who have attended Penn, 52 in the **National Football League (NFL)**, one in the **American Football League**, and six in the **All-America Football Conference**. They include Chuck Bednarik, Eddie Bell, Jim Finn, Tex Hamer, Lou Little (later college head coach for 33 years at Georgetown University and Columbia University), Tim Mazzetti, Brent Novoselsky, Bob Oristaglio, Frank Reagan, John Schweder, and Walt Stickel. **Bert Bell**, NFL commissioner from 1946 to 1959, was also a good player for Penn (although he did not play professional football) but was inducted in the **Pro Football Hall of Fame** for his administrative abilities.

PENNSYLVANIA STATE UNIVERSITY. *See* PENN STATE UNIVERSITY.

PERRY, FLETCHER JOSEPH "JOE," "THE JET." B. 27 January 1927, Stephens, Arkansas. D. 25 April 2011, Tempe, Arizona. Joe Perry is the only **Pro Bowler** who became a pro bowler. As a star **fullback** for the **San Francisco 49ers**, he played in the **National Football League's (NFL)** Pro Bowl in 1952, 1953, and 1954. An avid ten-pin bowler, he joined the Professional Bowlers Association tour after his retirement from **professional football**.

Perry was raised in Los Angeles and enrolled at David Starr Jordan High School. After graduation, he served in the U.S. Navy and played for the Alameda Naval Air Station team. Along with future **Pro Football Hall of Fame** player **Hugh McElhenny**, Perry played on national junior college championship teams at Compton Junior College in 1946 and 1947. Extremely fast, at six feet tall and 200 pounds, and known as "The Jet," Perry was signed by the San Francisco 49ers of the **All-America Football Conference (AAFC)** in 1948, although he was undrafted. In 1949, he played in the AAFC Championship Game, where the 49ers were defeated by the **Cleveland Browns**. Perry played with the 49ers as they joined the NFL in 1950 and remained with them through 1960. In 1961 and 1962, he was with the **Baltimore Colts** and concluded his NFL career with the 49ers in 1963.

In 1954, Perry became the first African American to be named the NFL Most Valuable Player. In his 16-year combined AAFC–NFL career, he played in 181 regular-season games, ran 1,929 times for 9,723 yards and 71 **touchdowns**, and caught 260 **passes** for 2,021 yards and 12 touchdowns. He also completed three of 11 passes for 79 yards and one touchdown. At the start of his professional career, Perry was also used as a **kickoff returner**, and he returned 33 kickoffs for an average of 23.0 yards per return, including one for an 87-yard touchdown. In 1953 and 1954, he was also occasionally used as a placekicker and made one **field goal** in six attempts and six of seven extra points. In 1948, as a defensive **back**, he recorded one **interception**. In three postseason games, he ran 23 times for 85 yards and no touchdowns.

After retiring from active play, Perry worked as a sales executive for a wine distributor, owned a bowling supply store, and worked for the 49ers organization. He was inducted into the Pro Football Hall of Fame in 1969. After his death from dementia in 2011, his brain was donated to Boston University, where researchers examined it and that of NFL **running back** John Henry Johnson, who also died that year, in an attempt to determine the relationship between brain trauma and football.

PERRY, WILLIAM ANTHONY "REFRIGERATOR," "THE FRIDGE." B. 16 December 1962, Aiken, South Carolina. William Perry attended Aiken High School and Clemson University. As a freshman at Clemson in 1981, he helped lead the Tigers to a 12–0 record and the national college championship. In four years at Clemson, his school compiled a record of 37–6–2. A mammoth defensive **tackle** who weighed between 325 and 375 pounds at six feet, two inches tall, earning him the nickname "Refrigerator" for his size, he was selected in the first round of the 1985 **National Football League (NFL) Draft** by the **Chicago Bears** as the 22nd overall pick.

Perry was a **fan** favorite, as he was occasionally used as a **fullback** in short yardage situations, either as a **blocker** or ball carrier. During his rookie year, 1985, he carried the ball seven times and scored two **touchdowns** during the regular season. He also caught a four-yard **pass** for a third touchdown, as the Bears compiled a record of 17–1 and reached the **Super Bowl**. With the Bears leading the **New England Patriots**, 37–7, in the third quarter of the Super Bowl, Perry scored a touchdown on a one-yard **run** and helped to lead the Bears to the championship.

Perry played for the Bears from 1985 to 1993 but only carried the ball three more times, losing two yards and not scoring any more touchdowns. In 1993, he was traded to the **Philadelphia Eagles** midseason and concluded his NFL career with the Eagles in 1994. In his nine years in the NFL, he played in 138 games and recorded 29 1/2 sacks and two **fumble** recoveries. In 1996, he made a comeback and played in the **World League of American Football** for the London Monarchs.

Perry's younger and smaller brother (six feet, one inch tall and 285 pounds), Michael Dean, also played defensive tackle in the NFL from 1988 to 1997 for the **Cleveland Browns**, **Denver Broncos**, and **Kansas City Chiefs**. While not the celebrity that the Refrigerator was, he was a more accomplished player and was selected for the **Pro Bowl** six times.

After retiring from active play, William attempted to capitalize on his fame in a variety of ways. He appeared in a hot-dog-eating contest; a celebrity boxing event against the seven-foot, seven-inch, 225-pound former basketball player Manute Bol; a Toughman boxing contest; a World Wrestling Federation battle royal; and several commercials and television shows. He also had his own brand of barbecue sauce and was director of football operations for a team in the Continental Indoor Football League.

In 2008, Perry began dealing with a series of serious health issues that nearly ended his life. He was an alcoholic since his days with the Bears, and that, combined with a mouth infection following some dental work, resulted in Guillain-Barre Syndrome, a disease of the nervous system. The disease, coupled with his excess weight, rendered him a virtual paraplegic. In 2009, an attack of pneumonia nearly resulted in his death. Perry's weight plummeted to 190 pounds and led to a diagnosis of chronic inflammatory demyelinating polyneuropathy. By September 2010, he had recovered and returned to his 350-plus-pound weight, but the various illnesses have left him wheelchair bound.

PHILADELPHIA EAGLES. The Philadelphia Eagles are one of the oldest teams in the **National Football League (NFL)**. They began in 1933 and were a replacement for the Frankford Yellow Jackets franchise, although they did not retain the Yellow Jackets' ownership or players. Since 1970, the Eagles played in the East Division of the National Football Conference.

In their 80 NFL seasons through 2012, they have had six different home fields, all in Philadelphia, Pennsylvania. From 1933 to 1935, they used the 18,000-seat Baker Bowl. The mammoth 102,000-seat Philadelphia Municipal Stadium was their home from 1936 to 1939 and again in 1941. They played at the 23,000-seat Shibe Park (renamed Connie Mack Stadium in 1954) in 1940 and from 1942 to 1957. The **University of Pennsylvania's** 60,000-seat Franklin Field was their home from 1958 to 1970. The 65,000-seat Veterans' Memorial Stadium was used from 1971 to 2002. Lincoln Financial Field, which seats 68,000, has been their home since 2003. In 1943, due to the manpower shortage caused by World War II, the Eagles merged with the **Pittsburgh Steelers**. They were nicknamed the "Steagles" by **fans**, although their official name was the Philadelphia Eagles. Two of their six home games were played at Forbes Field in Pittsburgh.

From 1933 to 2012, Philadelphia's overall record is 521–561–26 in regular-season play and 19–19 in postseason play. Prior to the merger in 1970, they played in the NFL Championship game four times, losing in 1947 and winning in 1948, 1949, and 1960. Since the merger and the more extensive postseason, they have qualified for the **playoffs** 19 times. They lost in the **Super Bowl** in 1980 and 2004; the NFL conference championship in 2001, 2002, 2003, and 2008; the divisional playoffs six times; and the **wild-card playoff** seven times.

Their head **coaches** have been Lud Wray (1933–1935); **Bert Bell**, future NFL commissioner (1936–1940); **Earle "Greasy" Neale** (1941–1950); Walt Kiesling (co-coach with Neale in 1943); Wayne Millner (1951); Alvin "Bo" McMillin (interim 1951); Jim Trimble (1952–1955); Hugh Devore (1956–1957); Lawrence "Buck" Shaw (1958–1960); Nick Skorich (1961–1963); Joe Kuharich (1964–1968); Jerry Williams (1969–1971); Ed Khayat (1971–1972); Mike McCormack (1973–1975); Dick Vermeil (1976–1982); Marion Campbell (1983–1985); Fred Bruney (interim 1985); James "Buddy" Ryan (1986–1990); Rich Kotite (1991–1994); Ray Rhodes (1995–1998); and Andy Reid (1999–2012). On 16 January 2013, Charles "Chip" Kelly was hired as head coach for the 2013 season.

Former Eagles players in the **Pro Football Hall of Fame** include **linebacker/centers** Chuck Bednarik and Alex Wojciechowicz; offensive **tackle** Bob Brown; defensive **ends** Richard Dent and **Reggie White**; offensive ends **Mike Ditka**, Bill Hewitt (the last NFL player to play without a **helmet**), and **Pete Pihos**; **quarterbacks Sonny Jurgensen** and **Norm Van Brocklin**; **halfbacks Ollie Matson** and **Steve Van Buren**; **wide receivers James Lofton**, Cris Carter, Tommy McDonald, and **Art Monk**; and center Jim Ringo.

Coaches Bert Bell and Earle "Greasy" Neale are also enshrined there. Carter, Dent, Ditka, Lofton, Matson, Monk, Ringo, and Van Brocklin were primarily inducted for their work with other teams and Bell for his work as NFL commissioner.

Other Eagles of note include quarterbacks Randall Cunningham, Roman Gabriel, **Ron Jaworski**, **Donovan McNabb**, Norm Snead, and **Michael Vick**; **running backs** Timmy Brown, Wilbert Montgomery, Clarence Peaks, Brian Westbrook, and Tom Woodeschick; receivers Harold Carmichael, Jack Ferrante, DeSean Jackson, Mike Quick, and Pete Retzlaff; linebackers Bill Bergey and Dave Lloyd; defensive **backs** Tom Brookshier and Brian Dawkins; defensive tackle Jerome Brown; offensive tackles Jerry Sisemore, Stan Walters, and Al Wistert; **punter/safety** Bill Bradley; and **kicker** David Akers. See also PHIL-PITT STEAGLES.

PHIL-PITT STEAGLES. The "Steagles" was the nickname given to the merged **Philadelphia Eagles–Pittsburgh Steelers professional football** team that played in the **National Football League (NFL)** in 1943. As a result of players being drafted to serve in World War II, the Philadelphia Eagles had only 16 men under contract, while the Pittsburgh Steelers had but six. Steelers' owner **Art Rooney** suggested the merger, which occurred, with four home games to be played in Philadelphia and two in Pittsburgh. Although the team was officially known as the Philadelphia Eagles, it became popularly known as Phil-Pitt or the "Steagles." **Earle "Greasy" Neale**, Philadelphia's **coach**, and Walt Kiesling, Pittsburgh's coach, were named as co-coaches, although the two men did not get along. They resolved their differences by putting Neale in charge of the **offense** and Kiesling in charge of the **defense**. Surprisingly, the Steagles finished the season with a record of 5–4–1, good for third place in the Eastern Division, one game behind the **New York Giants** and **Washington Redskins**, who **tied** for first place. Among the Steagles' best players were **halfback** Jack Hinkle, **end** Tony Bova, **lineman** Frank "Bucko" Kilroy, and **quarterback** Allie Sherman. Following the season, the merger was dissolved, although the Steelers played the 1944 NFL season as a merged team with the Chicago Cardinals. An excellent account of the Steagles can be found in *Last Team Standing* (2006), by Matthew Algeo. See also CARD-PITT.

PHOENIX CARDINALS. See ARIZONA CARDINALS.

PICCOLO, LOUIS BRIAN "BRIAN." B. 31 October 1943, Pittsfield, Massachusetts. D. 16 June 1970, New York, New York. Although Brian Piccolo was born in New England, he was raised in Fort Lauderdale, Florida.

He attended Central Catholic High School in Fort Lauderdale and played baseball and **football** there. He received a football scholarship to Wake Forest University and was a **running back** from 1962 to 1964. During his three **varsity** years, Wake Forest had won-lost records of 0–10, 1–9, and 5–5. The school's lack of success hurt Piccolo's chances at **professional football**. Despite the fact that he was named **Atlantic Coast Conference** player of the year in 1964 and led the nation in **rushing**, he was not **drafted** by any teams in the **National Football League (NFL)** or **American Football League**.

Piccolo was signed as a free agent in 1965 by the **Chicago Bears** but remained on their **taxi squad** for the season as a reserve under contract who could practice with the team but could not play in league games. He made the team in 1966, playing primarily on **special teams**. In 1967, he was a backup running back to **Gale Sayers**, and, by 1969, he was the starting **fullback**.

While the sport had been integrated for two decades, roommate assignments were still segregated. As the nation began to change, this segregation was gradually eliminated, and Piccolo and Sayers were roommates. Since they played similar positions, they soon became good friends. A film about the relationship between the two men, *Brian's Song*, was released in 1971 and warmly received.

On 16 November 1969, Piccolo had difficulty breathing during a game against Atlanta. He went for a medical examination, where it was disclosed that he had cancer. He had several surgeries to combat the disease, but, on 16 June 1970, he succumbed to the ailment. In his brief four-year NFL career, Piccolo played in 51 regular-season games and no postseason games, ran 258 times for 927 yards and four **touchdowns**, and caught 58 **passes** for 537 yards and one touchdown. In 1969, he was also used as a **punt returner** and returned nine punts for an average of 4.8 yards per punt. *See also* FOOTBALL FILMS.

PICK SIX. *See* INTERCEPTION.

PIGSKIN. Pigskin is a slang term for a **football**. In the early days of the game, leather made from pig's hide was used to cover an inflated rubber ball, but this is no longer the case, and modern-day footballs are an inflated rubber bladder encased in a pebble-grained cowhide leather cover.

PIHOS, PETER LOUIS "PETE." B. 22 October 1923, Orlando, Florida. D. 16 August 2011, Winston-Salem, North Carolina. Pete Pihos (pronounced Pea-hoce) was a graduate of Austin High School in Chicago, Illinois. While in high school, his father, Louis, a Greek immigrant, was murdered. Pete played offensive and defensive **end** at Indiana University in 1942 and 1943, served in the U.S. Army in Europe in 1944, and returned to school as a **fullback** in 1945 and 1946. At six feet, one inch tall and 210 pounds, he was taken by the **Philadelphia Eagles** in the fifth round of the 1945 **National Football League (NFL) Draft** as the 41st overall selection, even though he still had college eligibility remaining.

Pihos joined the Eagles in 1947 and played with them through the 1955 season. The Eagles lost the 1947 NFL Championship Game but won the league championship in 1948 and 1949. In his nine-year NFL career, Pihos played in 107 of 108 regular-season games, caught 373 **passes** for 5,619 yards and 61 **touchdowns**, and ran only nine times for minus 4 yards. In 1952, he recovered a **fumble** for a touchdown. He was occasionally used as a **returner** during the first few years of his career and returned one **punt** for a 26-yard touchdown and six **kickoffs** for an average of 11.0 yards per return. In four postseason games, Pihos caught seven passes for 83 yards and one touchdown, **intercepted** one pass for 11 yards, and returned one kickoff for 14 yards.

Pihos retired following the 1955 season at the age of 32 and claimed that baseball great Joe DiMaggio had once given him advice to retire from professional sports while still on top. After retiring, he worked as an **assistant coach** at Tulane University, and as a sales manager for a construction company. He was inducted into the **College Football Hall of Fame** in 1966 and the **Pro Football Hall of Fame** in 1970. Pihos spent the last 10 years of his life as a victim of Alzheimer's disease, to which he finally succumbed at the age of 87.

PITTSBURGH, UNIVERSITY OF. The University of Pittsburgh is located in Pittsburgh, Pennsylvania. Their **football** program began in 1890, and, since then, through 2012, Panthers' teams have compiled a record of 672–483–41. In addition, they have competed in 29 postseason **bowl games**, with a record of 12–17. They have been selected as national collegiate champions 11 times, in 1910, 1915, 1916, 1918, 1929, 1931, 1936, 1937, 1976, 1980, and 1981. Since 1991, Pittsburgh football teams have competed in the **Big East Conference** of the **National Collegiate Athletic Association**. For their first 101 years, they played as an independent team. Their home field was the 60,000-seat Pitt Stadium from 1925 to 1999. Since 2001, their home field has been the 65,000-seat Heinz Field. Pitt's main rival is West Virginia University. The teams have met in most years since 1895 in a contest known as the Backyard Brawl. Pitt leads the series, 61–40–3.

Pittsburgh's most successful **coach** was Dr. John B. "Jock" Sutherland. He was their head coach from 1924 to 1938 and compiled a record of 111–20–12. Other noteworthy Pitt coaches include **Glenn "Pop" Warner**

(1915–1923; 60–12–4), John Michelosen (1955–1965; 56–49–7), Jackie Sherrill (1977–1981; 50–9–1), Walt Harris (1997–2004; 52–44), and Dave Wannstedt (2005–2010; 42–31).

Pittsburgh alumni in the **College Football Hall of Fame** include **quarterback Dan Marino**; **halfbacks** Tom Davies, **Tony Dorsett** (a **Heisman Trophy** winner), and Joe Thompson; **fullback**/halfback Marshall Goldberg; fullback George McLaren; **ends Mike Ditka**, Joe Donchess, and Joe Skladany; end/halfback Hube Wagner; **linemen** Jim Covert, Ave Daniell, Bill Fralic, Hugh Green, Mark May, Bob Peck, and Herb Stein; and **linebacker Joe Schmidt**. Coaches Glenn "Pop" Warner, Jock Sutherland, Clark Shaughnessy, and Len Casanova are also enshrined.

Through 2012, there have been 287 **professional football** players who have attended Pitt, 284 in the **National Football League**, two in the **American Football League**, and one in the **All-America Football Conference**. They include Ruben Brown, Matt Cavanaugh, Sam Clancy, **Fred Cox**, Mike Ditka, Chris Doleman, Anthony Dorsett (son of Tony Dorsett), Tony Dorsett, Larry Fitzgerald, Marshall Goldberg, Hugh Green, Russ Grimm, Keith Hamilton, Craig "Iron-Head" Heyward, Rickey Jackson, Andy Lee, Mike Lucci, Dan Marino, Paul Martha, Curtis Martin, Mark May, Dave Moore, John Reger, Darrelle Revis, Joe Schmidt, Marty Schottenheimer, Ed Sharockman, **Tony Siragusa**, Mark Stepnoski, Joe Stydahar, Jim Sweeney, and Joe Walton.

PITTSBURGH PIRATES. *See* PITTSBURGH STEELERS.

PITTSBURGH STEELERS. The Pittsburgh Steelers are a **professional football** team in the American Football Conference (AFC) North Division of the **National Football League (NFL)**. They began play in 1933 as the Pittsburgh Pirates and changed their name to Steelers beginning in 1940. During World War II, due to the manpower shortage, the Steelers played two seasons, 1943 and 1944, merged with another NFL team. The 1943 entry was merged with the **Philadelphia Eagles** and was known as **Phil-Pitt** and popularly referred to by the nickname conferred on them by sportswriters and their **fans**, the "Steagles." The 1944 team merged with the Chicago Cardinals and was simply known as **Card-Pitt**. The Steelers played in the Eastern Division of the NFL from 1933 to 1969, with the exception of the 1944 season, when the Card-Pitt team played in the Western Division. In 1970, when the **American Football League (AFL)** and NFL merged leagues, the newly formed NFL reassigned three former NFL teams to the new AFC to provide for a more balanced league. The Steelers were assigned to the AFC Central Division, where they remained until 2002, when another league reorganization placed them in the AFC North Division. The Steelers were founded by

Art Rooney and have remained in the Rooney family since their inception, with Art's son, **Dan Rooney**, taking over upon Art's death in 1988 and Dan's son, Art II, assisting him in recent years.

The Pirates/Steelers used the 41,000-seat Forbes Field in Pittsburgh, Pennsylvania, as their home field from 1933 to 1963. (As Phil-Pitt and Card-Pitt, they also played home games at their merged partners' fields, Shibe Park in Philadelphia, and Comiskey Park in Chicago.) Beginning in 1958, the Steelers also played some home games at the 60,000-seat Pitt Stadium in Pittsburgh. They continued splitting home games between the two parks until 1963. In 1964, Pitt Stadium became their exclusive home field, and they remained there until 1970, when they moved into the new 59,000-seat Three Rivers Stadium in Pittsburgh, where they played until 2000. In 2001, the 65,000-seat Heinz Field was built in Pittsburgh, and they have played there since.

From 1933 to 2012, the Steelers' overall record is 561–511–20. Prior to the 1970 merger, the Steelers did not play in an NFL Championship Game. Their best effort was in 1947, when they **tied** for the Eastern Division title but lost to the Philadelphia Eagles in a tiebreaker **playoff**. Since the 1970 merger, the Steelers have been one of the NFL's best teams and have qualified for the postseason playoffs 25 times in 42 years. Their playoff record is 33–20. They have won the **Super Bowl** six times, more than any other team. They were champions in 1974, 1975, 1978, 1979, 2005, and 2008. They also lost twice in the Super Bowl, 1995 and 2010. They were defeated in the **conference** championships seven times, the divisional playoffs seven times, and the first round or **wild-card playoff** four times.

From 1969 to 2012, the Steelers have only had three head **coaches**, Chuck Noll (1969–1991), Bill Cowher (1992–2006), and Mike Tomlin (2007–2012). Prior to that, their coaches were Forrest "Jap" Douds (1933), Albert "Luby" DiMeolo (1934), Joe Bach (1935–1936, 1952–1953), **John "Blood" McNally** (1937–1939), Walt Kiesling (1939–1940, 1941–1944, 1954–1956), Aldo Donelli (interim 1941), **Bert Bell** (1941), Jim Leonard (1945), John "Jock" Sutherland (1946–1947), John Michelosen (1948–1951), Raymond "Buddy" Parker (1957–1964), Mike Nixon (1965), and Bill Austin (1966–1968).

There are 21 former Pittsburgh players in the **Pro Football Hall of Fame**. They are **quarterbacks Terry Bradshaw**, **Len Dawson**, and **Bobby Layne**; offensive **backs** Bill Dudley, **Franco Harris**, John Henry Johnson, John "Blood" McNally, and Marion Motley; **wide receivers** John Stallworth and **Lynn Swann**; offensive **linemen** Dermontti Dawson, **Cal Hubbard**, Walt Kiesling, and Mike Webster; defensive linemen Joe Greene and Ernie Stautner; **linebackers** Jack Ham and Jack Lambert; and defensive backs/**cornerbacks** Mel Blount, Jack Butler, and Rod Woodson. Owners Art Rooney and Dan Rooney; head coach Chuck Noll; and league commissioner and part-owner of the Steelers, Bert Bell, are also Hall of Famers. Former Pittsburgh quarterback Jim Finks is also in the Hall of Fame as an executive for his contributions with other NFL teams.

Among other noteworthy Steelers' players are quarterbacks Neil O'Donnell, **Ben Roethlisberger**, and Kordell Stewart; **running backs** Jerome Bettis, Robert "Rocky" Bleier, John Fuqua, Rashard Mendenhall, and Willie Parker; wide receivers Gilbert "Buddy" Dial, Santonio Holmes, and **Hines Ward**; **tight ends** Larry Brown, Bennie Cunningham, and Elbie Nickel; offensive linemen Alan Faneca, Turkish-born Tunch Ilkin, and Jon Kolb; defensive linemen L. C. Greenwood, Casey Hampton, and Dwight White; linebackers James Harrison, Greg Lloyd, Joey Porter, and Andy Russell; cornerback Carnell Lake; **safeties** Troy Polamalu and Donnie Shell; **kicker** Gary Anderson; and **punter** Bobby Walden.

PLACEKICKER. *See* KICKER.

PLAY CLOCK. In both **professional football** and **collegiate football**, teams are required to snap the ball to begin a play within a certain number of seconds or they are penalized five yards for **delay of game**. In **Canadian football**, teams are allowed 20 seconds from the time the referee whistles the play to begin. The **National Football League (NFL)** allows 40 seconds from the end of the previous **down** or, in certain situations, 25 seconds after the referee whistles the play to begin. Collegiate football currently uses restrictions similar to those in the NFL, with minor modifications.

PLAYBOOK. A playbook is a bound collection of a **football** team's offensive and defensive plays with which team members must become familiar.

PLAYOFF BOWL. From 1960 to 1969, the **National Football League (NFL)** played a consolation game between the runner-up teams in the Eastern Division and Western Division. The game's official name was the Bert Bell Benefit Bowl, although it was usually referred to as the Playoff Bowl or Runner-Up Bowl. It was held at the **Orange Bowl** in Miami, Florida, and was created to give the NFL added national television exposure at a time when the league was being threatened by the newly created **American Football League (AFL)**. The game was played the week following the NFL Championship Game, which, from 1967 to 1969, was the week prior to the AFL–NFL Championship Game (**Super Bowl**). The game was unpopular with players and **fans**, and, after the AFL–NFL merger in 1970, it was dropped since the new **playoff** structure created more nationally televised postseason play.

PLAYOFFS. In **professional football**, following the last game of the regular season, a series of playoff games are played to determine the league champion. None were contested in the **National Football League (NFL)** from 1920 to 1932. From 1933 to 1966, the two division winners met in a single championship game. In several of those years, teams that **tied** for the division lead played a special tiebreaker game to determine the division winner. Following the 1966 season, the NFL champion played the **American Football League (AFL)** champion in what was originally called the AFL–NFL Championship Game but was later known as the **Super Bowl**. From 1967 to 1969, after the NFL became a 16-team league divided into four divisions, a preliminary round of division playoffs was played, with those winners playing in the NFL Championship Game and that winner going on to the Super Bowl.

After the AFL–NFL merger in 1970, the NFL became a 26-team entity structured into two **conferences** (American and National), with each conference divided into three divisions. A four-team divisional playoff was held for each conference, with the three division winners and the team with the next best regular-season record taking part. The division winners then met in the conference championships, and the two conference champions played in the Super Bowl.

This playoff pattern continued until 1978, when the league, now featuring 28 teams, invited one more team from each conference to join the playoff series and added a **wild-card playoff** game in each conference, matching the two teams with the worst record of the five playoff teams in that conference and extending the playoff series to four weeks. In 1990, an additional wild-card team from each conference was added to the postseason playoff tournament, and, this structure, with 12 teams qualifying for the playoffs, is still in existence in 2013.

National Collegiate Athletic Association college football teams also have playoff series at all levels, except the highest level. In 2012, it was announced that beginning with the 2014 season a four-team playoff series will be held. The **National Association of Intercollegiate Athletics** has a playoff tournament, as does the **Canadian Football League**.

POCKET. The pocket is formed by **blockers** in front of and to the sides of the **quarterback** to enable him to gain time to oversee his downfield receivers to attempt to **pass** to them.

POINT AFTER TOUCHDOWN (PAT). *See* CONVERSION.

POLLARD, FREDERICK DOUGLASS "FRITZ." B. 27 January 1894, Chicago, Illinois. D. 11 May 1986, Silver Spring, Maryland. Fritz Pollard was one of the first black players in the **National Football League (NFL)** and the league's first black **coach**, even though today he is mostly forgotten by modern-day **football fans**. He attended Lane Tech High School in Chicago, where he was a member of the track team. He went to Brown University and played in the 1916 **Rose Bowl** as a member of their football team. Pollard played for Brown in 1915 and 1916. Brown had a record of 13–5–1 in those years and was invited to the Tournament of Roses game on 1 January 1916, where they were defeated by Washington State University in the second game in what is now known as the Rose Bowl. Pollard became the first African American to play in that event.

The fleet five-foot, nine-inch, 165-pound Pollard signed with the Akron Pros in 1920 and played tailback for them during the inaugural season of the American Professional Football Association (APFA), the forerunner of the NFL. He helped lead Akron to an undefeated season, at 8–0–3, and the league championship. The following season, Pollard was named Akron's co-coach, along with Elgie Tobin. Akron again had a fine season, at 8–3–1, but was surpassed for the league title by the Buffalo Americans, at 9–1–2, and Chicago, at 9–1–1. Pollard played for Milwaukee in 1922; was member of Hammond in 1923; played 13 games for Hammond, Providence, and Akron in 1925; and concluded his NFL career in 1926. Following the 1926 season, the NFL removed all six of the black players in the league, although one or two played briefly in subsequent years. In 1923 and 1924, Pollard played for an independent team, the Gilberton Cadamounts, in Pennsylvania. In 1928, he organized his own independent team, the Chicago Black Hawks, an all-black touring team that lasted for several seasons, until the Depression.

In his six years in the APFA/NFL, he appeared in 49 games and scored at least 12 **touchdowns** and three extra points. Afterward, Pollard, an entrepreneur, owned coal companies in New York and Chicago, ran a theatrical booking agency, had a movie studio, organized an investment company, and published a weekly newspaper, in addition to coaching football at Lincoln University in Philadelphia. He was inducted into the **College Football Hall of Fame** in 1954 and the **Pro Football Hall of Fame** in 2005.

POP WARNER LEAGUES. In 1934, famed **college football coach Glenn "Pop" Warner**, along with Joe Tomlin, a New York stockbroker, began a youth football program in Philadelphia emphasizing scholarship as well as **football**. There were no age restrictions, and some players were in their 20s. The program, named the Pop Warner Conference, grew, and, by 1947, there were more than 100 teams involved. Since most of the players were 15 years old or younger, special rules were established. Although Warner died in 1954 of throat cancer, the program continued to grow in the 1950s, and, in 1959,

Pop Warner Little Scholars was officially established as a nonprofit organization. The program continued to grow and became the football equivalent of Little League Baseball, with more than 3,000 teams by 1970. In the 21st century, the organization claims more than 400,000 boys and girls, ages five to 16, on more than 5,000 teams worldwide. The organization also conducts programs on cheerleading, flag football, and dance and presents annual award recognition for academic excellence.

PORTSMOUTH SPARTANS. *See* DETROIT LIONS.

PRAIRIE VIEW A&M UNIVERSITY. Prairie View A&M University is located in Prairie View, Texas, about 45 miles northwest of Houston. A historically black school, their **football** program began in 1907, and, since then, through 2012, Panthers' teams have compiled a record of 401–459–34. From 1907 to 1965, they had an excellent record of 271–107–30 and were black college national champions five times, in 1953, 1954, 1958, 1963, and 1964. Since 1966, their fortunes have declined, and, from 1966 to 2012, their record is just 127–350–4. From 28 October 1989 to 26 September 1998, they had a record 80-game losing streak. In 11 games in 1991, the Panthers were outscored, 617–48, with 20 of their 48 points coming in their final game. From 1928 to 1962, they hosted a postseason **bowl game** called the Prairie View Bowl. Their record in those 34 contests was 21–12–1. The one **tie**, on 1 January 1958, against Texas Southern, was notable in that the score was 6–6, and all six points scored by Prairie View were the result of safeties. Prairie View also competed in six other bowl games, with a record of 3–3. Since 1923, the Panthers have competed in the Southwestern Athletic Conference (SWAC). Home games have been played at the 6,000-seat Edward L. Blackshear Field since 1960.

Prairie View's most successful **coach** was Bill Nicks. He was their head coach from 1945 to 1965 and compiled a record of 126–40–8. He was inducted into the **College Football Hall of Fame** in 1999. Another outstanding Panthers' coach was Sam Taylor, coach from 1931 to 1943, with a record of 70–32–15. Coach Henry Frazier III turned the program around and, from 2004 to 2010, compiled a record of 43–31 and led the Panthers to the SWAC championship in 2009.

There are no Prairie View alumni in the **College Football Hall of Fame**, but, through 2012, there have been 27 **professional football** players in the **National Football League (NFL)** and three in the **American Football League** who have attended Prairie View, including Sam Adams, Charlie Brackins (one of the earliest black **quarterbacks** in the NFL), Clem Daniels, John "Bo" Farrington, Ken Houston, Jim Hunt, Jim Kearney, Jim Mitchell, Alvin Reed, Otis Taylor, and Clarence "Sweeny" Williams.

PREVENT DEFENSE. A prevent **defense** (pronounced PREE-vent DEE-fense, with the accent on the initial syllables) occurs late in the game when the defensive team has the lead and the offensive team needs to score with little time remaining in the game. The defensive backs, and also **linebackers**, station themselves much further downfield than they usually play and allow the offensive **quarterback** to complete short **passes** but try to prevent a long pass. This maneuver occasionally backfires, as an efficient quarterback will complete several short passes and is able to move the ball effectively despite any additional defensive measures.

PRINCETON UNIVERSITY. Princeton University is located in Princeton, New Jersey. The school is credited with playing the first intercollegiate **football** game on 6 November 1869, and, since then, through 2012, Tigers' teams have compiled a record of 795–391–50. As a member of the **Ivy League** since 1955, they do not compete in postseason **bowl games** and have never done so. They have been selected as national collegiate champions 28 times, more than any other school. They were named champions in 1869, 1870, 1872, 1873, 1874, 1875, 1877, 1878, 1879, 1880, 1881, 1884, 1885, 1886, 1889, 1893, 1894, 1896, 1898, 1899, 1903, 1906, 1911, 1920, 1922, 1933, 1935, and 1950. From 1914 to 1996, they played home games at the 42,000-seat Palmer Stadium, one of the oldest football **stadiums** in the country. Since 1998, they have played home games at Princeton University Stadium, which seats 27,773. They do not have one main rival, but most of their Ivy League opponents have played Princeton for many years, and each game is significant.

Princeton's most notable head **coaches** have been Bill Roper (1906–1908, 1910–1911, 1919–1930; 89–28–16), Herbert "Fritz" Crisler (1932–1937; 35–9–5), Charlie Caldwell (1945–1956; 70–30–3), Dick Colman (1957–1968; 75–33), and Steve Tosches (1987–1999; 78–50–2). There are 21 Princeton alumni in the **College Football Hall of Fame**. They are **quarterbacks** Hobart "Hobey" Baker (the only player inducted into both the College Football Hall of Fame and Hockey Hall of Fame), Philip King, and Don Lourie; **fullbacks** Knowlton Ames, Cosmo Iacavazzi, and Jim McCormick; **halfbacks** Alex Moffett and Dick Kazmaier (a **Heisman Trophy** winner); **ends** Gary Cochran and Art Poe; and **linemen** Harold Ballin, Hector Cowan, John Dewitt, Hollie Donan, Bill Edwards, Ed Hart, Art Hillebrand, Stan Keck, Langdon Lea, John Weller, and Art Wheeler. Princeton coaches in the Hall are Charlie Caldwell, Dick Colman, Herbert "Fritz" Crisler, Bill Roper, and Elton "Tad" Wieman.

Through 2011, 30 **professional football** players, 27 in the **National Football League**, one in the **American Football League**, and two in the **All-America Football Conference**, have attended Princeton. They include

Carl Barisich, Bob Beattie, Karl Chandler, Jason Garrett (later head coach of the **Dallas Cowboys**), Charlie Gogolak, Oscar "Dutch" Hendrian, Dennis Norman, and Ross Tucker.

PRO BOWL. The Pro Bowl (officially the AFC–NFC Pro Bowl since 1971) is the **National Football League's (NFL)** all-star game. Since 1980 (except for 2010), the contest has been played at the 50,000-seat Aloha Stadium in Honolulu, Hawaii, and is looked on as a reward for players doing well during the NFL season. The main goal for the players in the game is to avoid injury, so several special rules are in effect to help accomplish this. As a result, the game is often a high-scoring offensive display, like the 55–52 game in 2003, the 59–41 game of 2012, or the 62–35 game of 2013. The game takes place the week after the **Super Bowl** and, in recent years, has occurred in February, although from 2011 to 2013 it was played the week before the Super Bowl.

The NFL began playing all-star games in 1939 and played five annual games, held at various sites, from January 1939 to December 1942, matching an all-star team against the league champions. The game was abandoned for the next several years and resumed in 1951, matching all-star teams from the league's two **conferences**. The 93,000-seat **Los Angeles Memorial Coliseum** was the site from 1951 to 1972, although the **stadium** was often less than half-full. Various venues were used from 1973 to 1979 before Honolulu was chosen.

While players consider it a honor to be selected for the game, the physical demands of **football** often cause many of them to skip the game, citing injuries. In the 1976 Pro Bowl, since so many of the NFL's top **quarterbacks** were injured, **Philadelphia Eagles'** backup quarterback, Mike Boryla, who had started only five games that season, was selected to play on the National Football Conference team. Boryla, the son of professional basketball star Vince Boryla, had an outstanding game and threw two **touchdown passes** in the final minutes to help his team win the Pro Bowl. *See also* COLLEGE ALL-STAR GAME.

PRO FOOTBALL HALL OF FAME. The Pro Football Hall of Fame is located in Canton, Ohio. It was opened in 1963 and is open to the public year-round. As of 2013, there have been 280 men enshrined in the Hall, 241 former players, 22 **coaches**, and 17 contributors. The Hall also maintains an extensive Archives and Information Center that is open to researchers by appointment. *See also* APPENDIX A (for a list of inductees).

PROFESSIONAL FOOTBALL. Professional sports differ from amateur sports in that some or all participants are paid for playing, and professional teams attempt to recoup their expenses by charging admission to their games. In amateur sports, often played by schools, while admission may be charged, players do not receive any reimbursement, except possibly to cover their expenses.

Professional **football** began in the 1890s, as sporting associations began to hire players for important games. The first recorded professional player was **William "Pudge" Heffelfinger**, when the Allegheny Athletic Association of Pittsburgh, Pennsylvania, paid him $500 plus $25 in expenses to play for them in a game against the Pittsburgh Athletic Club on 12 November 1892. Other clubs soon followed suit, and, by the early 1900s, there were teams and leagues of professional players.

It was not until 1920 that a stable organization of professional teams was created. The league, originally known as the American Professional Football Association, was renamed the **National Football League (NFL)** and is in existence today as one of the most important organizations in professional sports worldwide. Other professional football leagues have attempted to challenge the NFL but have failed. **Canadian football's** most important professional league, the **Canadian Football League**, has been in existence since 1958. *See also* ALL-AMERICA FOOTBALL CONFERENCE; AMERICAN FOOTBALL LEAGUE (1960–1969); AMERICAN FOOTBALL LEAGUES (1926, 1936–1937, 1940–1941); ARENA FOOTBALL LEAGUE; CONTINENTAL FOOTBALL LEAGUE; ELITE FOOTBALL LEAGUE OF INDIA; UNITED FOOTBALL LEAGUE; UNITED STATES FOOTBALL LEAGUE; WORLD FOOTBALL LEAGUE; WORLD LEAGUE OF AMERICAN FOOTBALL; XFL.

PROFESSIONAL FOOTBALL PLAYERS WHO PLAYED OTHER PROFESSIONAL SPORTS. For the first half of the 20th century, students who pursued sports activity in high school or college often played **football** in the fall, basketball in the winter, and baseball or track in the spring. Consequently, after graduation, those who turned to professional sports sometimes played more than one sport professionally. In more recent times, the effort required to play a sport at a high level has encouraged specialization, and it has become uncommon for students to excel at more than one sport.

Individuals who played **professional football** and also Major League Baseball include Cliff Aberson, Morris "Red" Badgro, Norm Bass, Charlie Berry, Joe "Howard" Berry, Larry Bettencourt, Lyle Bigbee, Tom Brown, Garland Buckeye, Bruce Caldwell, Ralph Capron, Jim Castiglia, Chuck Corgan, Paul "Shorty" Desjardien, D. J. Dozier, Chuck Dressen, Paddy Driscoll, Oscar "Ox" Eckhardt, Steve Filipowicz, Paul Florence, Walter French, Wally Gilbert, Norm Glockson, Frank Grube, Bruno Haas, **George Halas**, Henry

"Hinkey" Haynes, Carroll Hardy, Drew Henson, Chad Hutchinson, Vincent "Bo" Jackson, Charles "Lefty" Jamerson, Vic Janowicz, Rex Johnston, Brian Jordan, Matt Kinzer, Bert Kuczynski, Pete Layden, Jim Levey, Dean Look, Walter "Waddy" MacPhee, Howard Maple, Walt Masters, John Mohardt, **Ernie Nevers**, Ossie Orwoll, Clarence "Ace" Parker, Al Pierotti, Everett "Pid" Purdy, Dick Reichle, **Deion Sanders**, Johnny Scalzi, Richard "Red" Smith, Evar Swanson, **Jim Thorpe**, Andy Tomasic, Joe Vance, Ernie Vick, Tom Whelan, Mike Wilson, Harry "Hoge" Workman, Ab Wright, Tom Yewcic, Russ Young, and Joe Zapustas. Fred Crolius, Christy Mathewson, **Earle "Greasy" Neale**, and Rube Waddell all played Major League Baseball and pro football prior to the formation of the NFL. In addition, three notable Major League Baseball umpires, **Cal Hubbard**, Hank Soar, and Frank Umont, all played in the NFL, although none of the three played Major League Baseball.

Players of both professional football and professional basketball include Neal Adams, Lou Barle, Connie Mack Berry, Ted Cook, Hal Crisler, Harold "Cookie" Cunningham, Armand Cure, Jack Dugger, Don Eliason, Dick Evans, Len Ford, Ted Fritsch, Gorham Getchell, **Otto Graham**, **Harry "Bud" Grant**, Vern Huffman, Bob MacLeod, Joel Mason, Max Morris, Ray Ramsey, Frank Sachse, Ted Scalissi, Otto Schnellbacher, Bill Schroeder, Bob Shaw, Jim Spruill, George Svendsen, Clint Wager, Ron Widby, John Wiethe, George Wilson, and Lonnie Wright. Nearly all of these men played pro basketball in the National Basketball League (1937–1949) or Basketball Association of America (1946–1949). The only ones who did not were Harry "Bud" Grant (National Basketball Association, 1949–1951) and Ron Widby and Lonnie Wright (who both played in the American Basketball Association, 1967–1972).

Athletes who competed in the **Olympic Games** (OG) and also played professional football in the American Professional Football Association (APFA), **National Football League (NFL)**, or **American Football League (AFL)** include the following:

Jim Thorpe (OG 1912, athletics: high jump, long jump, pentathlon [gold medal], decathlon [gold medal]; NFL 1920–1928)
Gene Vidal, father of author Gore Vidal (OG 1920, athletics: decathlon; APFA 1921)
John Spellman (OG 1924, light heavyweight freestyle wrestling [gold medal]; NFL 1925–1932)
Jim Bausch (OG 1932, athletics: decathlon [gold medal]; NFL 1933)
Jack Riley (OG 1932, heavyweight freestyle wrestling [silver medal]; NFL 1933)
Sam Francis (OG 1936, athletics: shot put; NFL 1937–1940)

Glenn Morris (OG 1936, athletics: decathlon [gold medal]; NFL 1940)
Jack Torrance (OG 1936, athletics: shot put; NFL 1939–1940)
Clyde Scott (OG 1948, athletics: 110m hurdles [silver medal]; NFL 1949–1952)
Milt Campbell (OG 1952, athletics: decathlon [silver medal]; OG 1956, athletics: decathlon [gold medal]; NFL 1957)
Ollie Matson (OG 1952, athletics: 400m **run** [bronze medal], 4x400m relay [silver medal]; NFL 1952–1966)
Glenn Davis (OG 1956, athletics: 400m hurdles [gold medal]; OG 1960, athletics: 400m hurdles [gold medal], 4x400m relay [gold medal]; NFL 1960–1961)
Frank Budd (OG 1960, athletics: 100m, 4x100m relay; NFL 1962–1963)
Ray Norton (OG 1960, athletics: 100m, 200m, 4x100m relay; NFL 1960–1961)
Irvin "Bo" Roberson (OG 1960, athletics: long jump [silver medal]; AFL 1961–1966)
Henry Carr (OG 1964, athletics: 200m [gold medal], 4x400m relay [gold medal]; NFL 1965–1967)
Bob Hayes (OG 1964, athletics: 100m [gold medal], 4x100m relay [gold medal]; NFL 1965–1975)
Curley Culp (OG 1968, wrestling [on team, did not compete]; AFL/NFL 1968–1981)
Jim Hines (OG 1968, athletics: 100m [gold medal], 4x100m relay [gold medal]; AFL/NFL 1969–1970)
Tommie Smith (OG 1968, athletics: 200m [gold medal]; AFL 1969)
Larry Burton (OG 1972, athletics: 200m; NFL 1975–1979)
Gerald Tinker (OG 1972, athletics: 4x100m relay [gold medal]; NFL 1974–1975)
Johnny "Lam" Jones (OG 1976, athletics: 100m, 4x100m [gold medal]; NFL 1980–1984)
James Owens (OG 1976, athletics: 110m hurdles; NFL 1979–1984)
Willie Gault (OG 1980, United States did not compete; NFL 1983–1993)
Renaldo Nehemiah (OG 1980, United States did not compete; NFL 1982–1984)
Ron Brown (OG 1984, athletics: 100m, 4x100m [gold medal]; NFL 1984–1991
Sam Graddy (OG 1984, athletics: 100m [silver medal], 4x100m relay [gold medal]; NFL 1987–1992)
Michael Bates (OG 1992, athletics: 200m [bronze medal]; NFL 1993–2003)
James Jett (OG 1992, athletics: 4x100m relay [gold medal]; NFL 1993–2002)
Herschel Walker (OG 1992, two-man bobsleigh; NFL 1986–1997)

In addition, several pro football players have pursued other professional sports. Norm Bass, who played both pro football and Major League Baseball, was stricken with rheumatoid arthritis after his career ended. He then competed at the Paralympic Games in 2000 and won a silver medal in table tennis. Herschel Walker competed in mixed martial arts. Tom Zbikowski boxed professionally while in college and then returned to the ring after playing in the NFL.

Other football players who tried boxing include Ray Edwards, Mark Gastineau, Ernest "Tex" Hamer, Alonzo Highsmith, **Ed "Too-Tall" Jones**, Jevon Langford, Leif Larsen, George Linberger, Roy Lumpkin, **Al Nesser**, Earl Nolan, Charlie Powell, Ray Richards, Fred "Duke" Slater, George Trafton, Adrian White, Craig Wolfley, and Roy Young. Powell was probably the most accomplished boxer and fought former heavyweight champions Floyd Patterson and Muhammad Ali and defeated heavyweight contenders Harold Carter, Charley Norkus, and Nino Valdes.

There have also been a few Canadian professional football players who also played professional ice hockey. They include Bob Berry, Lionel Conacher, Gerry James, and Edward "Butch" Songin. Roy "Red" Storey scored three **touchdowns** to lead the **Toronto Argonauts** to the 1938 **Grey Cup** championship and was later a well-known National Hockey League referee. Hobart "Hobey" Baker was an outstanding football player for **Princeton University** and also a top amateur ice hockey player. He is the only man who is a member of both the **College Football Hall of Fame** and Hockey Hall of Fame. *See also* PROFESSIONAL FOOTBALL PLAYERS WHO WERE PROFESSIONAL WRESTLERS.

PROFESSIONAL FOOTBALL PLAYERS WHO WERE PROFESSIONAL WRESTLERS. Although modern professional wrestling can be categorized more as entertainment than sport, there have been quite a few **football** players who have pursued ring careers, some with exceptional success. One of the most popular professional wrestlers was Dick "The Bruiser" Afflis. As a **lineman**, he played in every game for the **Green Bay Packers** from 1951 to 1954. In 1954, he turned to professional wrestling and, for the next 30 years, was one of its main attractions. **Leo Nomellini** played offensive or defensive **tackle** in every game for the **San Francisco 49ers** from 1950 to 1963 and was named to the **Pro Football Hall of Fame** in 1969 and **College Football Hall of Fame** in 1977. In the off-season, he worked as a professional wrestler.

Other **professional football** players who wrestled professionally include Monty Brown, Darren Drozdov (who became a quadriplegic after an accident in the wrestling ring), Bill Goldberg, John Heidenreich, **Alex Karras**, Ernie

Ladd, **Gene "Big Daddy" Lipscomb,** Ed "Wahoo" McDaniel, Steve McMichael, **Bronko Nagurski**, Brian Pillman, and Don Stansauk (who wrestled as Hard-Boiled Haggerty). Frank Leavitt played briefly with the New York Brickley Giants of the American Professional Football Association in 1921, before becoming a professional wrestler known as "Man Mountain Dean." Gus Sonnenberg, although only five feet, six inches tall, was one of the better linemen in the **National Football League (NFL)** from 1923 to 1930 and was a member of the 1928 NFL champion Providence Steam Roller. He wrestled from 1928 to 1942 and was a professional wrestling world champion. Several wrestling promotions during the 1990s featured professional football players. Players who appeared in only one or two of these wrestling promotions include Bill Fralic, Russ Francis, Kevin Greene, Harvey Martin, Bart Scott, **Lawrence Taylor**, and **Reggie White**. Afflis, McDaniel, Nagurski, and Sonnenberg are all members of the Pro Wrestling Hall of Fame.

PROFESSIONAL FOOTBALL RESEARCHERS ASSOCIATION (PFRA). The Professional Football Researchers Association (PFRA) was formed in 1979 by Bob Carroll, a noted **football** expert. The association produces a bimonthly newsletter, the *Coffin Corner*; maintains a website; and has an online forum in which researchers can ask questions and update members with information. The PFRA also maintains several committees, including the "Hall of Very Good" committee, which selects several players each year who have been overlooked by the **Pro Football Hall of Fame** and have had noteworthy careers. The PFRA has nonprofit status as a section 501c3 organization. Their website is www.profootballresearchers.org.

PUNT. If a team decides that they do not have a good chance of gaining the necessary yards for a **first down** via **running** or **passing**, they may choose to kick the ball to the opposition. This is done by snapping the ball back to a player, known as a **punter**, who stands about 10 yards behind the **line of scrimmage**. After receiving the snap, the punter drops the ball and kicks it before it touches the ground. In modern-day **football**, a punt almost invariably occurs only on a fourth-down situation, although in earlier times teams often punted on earlier downs to gain field position.

PUNT, PASS, AND KICK (PPK). Punt, **Pass**, and Kick (PPK) is a national contest sponsored by the **National Football League (NFL)** for youngsters ages six to 15. Participants are judged for distance and accuracy in three football disciplines: punting the football, passing the football, and placekicking the football. Local winners compete for national championships in age groups. In recent years, the final PPK competition has taken place during a

NFL **playoff** game. In 1992, Kendra Wecker, a 10-year-old girl, made the finals in her age group, competing on an equal basis with boys. She later became a professional basketball player in the Women's National Basketball Association.

PUNT RETURNER. *See* RETURNER.

PUNTER. A punter is a specialist who is used mainly in fourth-**down** situations to **punt** the ball to the opposition. *See also* GUY, WILLIAM RAY "RAY"; WATERFIELD, ROBERT STANTON "BOB."

PURDUE UNIVERSITY. Purdue University is located in West Lafayette, Indiana. Their **football** program began in 1887, and, since then, through 2012, Boilermakers' teams have compiled a record of 583–507–48. In addition, they have competed in 17 postseason **bowl games**, with a record of 9–8. Purdue was a charter member of the **Big Ten Conference** in 1896. Home games since 1924 have been played at the 62,000-seat Ross-Ade Stadium. The Boilermakers were selected as national collegiate champion in 1931. Their main rival is Indiana University. The teams have met annually since 1925 for a trophy known as the "Old Oaken Bucket." Purdue leads the series, 58–27–3, and had a record of 14–10–3 in games with Indiana prior to 1925.

Purdue's most notable **coaches** have been Jimmy Phelan (1922–1929; 35–22–5), Noble Kizer (1930–1936; 42–13–3), Kenneth "Jack" Mollenkopf (1956–1969; 84–39–9), Jim Young (1977–1981; 38–19–1), and Joe Tiller (1997–2008; 87–62). There are nine Purdue alumni in the **College Football Hall of Fame**. They include **quarterbacks Bob Griese**, Mark Herrmann, and Mike Phipps; **halfbacks** Otis Armstrong, Chalmers "Bump" Elliot, Cecil Isbell, Leroy Keyes, and Elmer Oliphant; and **guard** Alex Agase. Coaches Kenneth "Jack" Mollenkopf, Jim Phelan, Andy Smith, and Jim Young are also enshrined there.

Through 2012, there have been 262 **professional football** players who have attended Purdue, 243 in the **National Football League**, 12 in the **American Football League**, and seven in the **All-America Football Conference**. They include Alex Agase, Mike Alstott, Otis Armstrong, Erich Barnes, Dick Barwegan, Gregg Bingham, **Drew Brees**, Dave Butz, Gary Danielson, **Len Dawson**, Cris Dishman, Jim Everett, Ross Fichtner, Ed Flanagan, Jeff George, Abe Gibron, Mel Gray, Bob Griese, Cecil Isbell, Leroy Keyes, Matt Light, Lamar Lundy, Elmer Oliphant, Kyle Orton, Curtis Painter, Mike Phipps, Mike Pruitt, Darryl Stingley, Keena Turner, Rod Woodson, and Jeff Zgonina. Although not a star player at Purdue, **Hank Stram** played football there but became best known as the coach of the **Kansas City Chiefs** of the NFL and is enshrined in the **Pro Football Hall of Fame**.

PYLON. A pylon is a cone-shaped marker placed on each corner of the **goal line** to aid **officials** in determining whether a player is in bounds when he crosses the goal line.

Q

QUARTERBACK. The quarterback is the player who directs a **football team's offense**. He lines up behind the **center**; receives the snap to begin play; and either hands the ball off to a **running back**, **passes** the ball to a teammate, or **runs** with the ball. It is the position requiring the most skill and, in **professional football**, is usually the highest paid.

QUARTERBACK SNEAK. A quarterback sneak is a play in which the **quarterback** keeps the ball and plunges forward behind the **blocking** of his offensive line. It is usually run when less than one yard is needed for a **first down**.

R

RANKINGS. Because **college football** teams play relatively few games, especially when compared with other sports, one way of establishing comparative strengths has been the use of rankings. Several newspapers began ranking college teams in the 1930s. The Associated Press has done so each season since 1936. Another poll, the Coaches Poll, reflects the voting of college coaches. Originally sponsored by the United Press, in recent years the poll is carried out by various other media organizations.

For much of college football history, the collegiate champion was determined by various polls. Several ranking systems attempted to use "scientific" methods and employed strength of schedule, amount of points scored, and regional section of the country. In 1924, Dr. Frank Dickinson created one of these polls, and, through 1940, the Dickinson System was one of the major ranking systems used in college football. Since 1998 and the formation of the **Bowl Championship Series (BCS)**, the national collegiate champion at the highest level has been awarded to the winner of the BCS National Championship Game, although rankings and polls are used to determine the teams that play in that game.

RASHAD, AHMAD, NÉE ROBERT "BOBBY" EARL MOORE. B. 19 November 1949, Portland, Oregon. Bobby Moore attended Mount Tahoma High School in Tacoma, Washington. He received a **football** scholarship to the University of Oregon and played for them beginning in 1969, initially as a **wide receiver** and then as a **running back**. After graduating from Oregon, at six feet, two inches tall and 205 pounds, he was selected by the St. Louis Cardinals of the **National Football League (NFL)** in the 1972 NFL **Draft** in the first round as the fourth overall choice. He played for the Cardinals in 1972 as Bobby Moore, but, before the 1973 season, he changed his name to Ahmad Rashad as he converted to a branch of the Muslim faith. After playing the 1973 season with the Cardinals and the 1974 season with the **Buffalo Bills**, he was traded to the **Minnesota Vikings**, where he spent the remainder of his NFL career. He played in three **Super Bowls** with the Vikings, in 1974, 1975, and 1977, but was on the losing side each time.

In his 10-year NFL career, Rashad played in 139 regular-season games, caught 495 **passes** for 6,831 yards and 44 **touchdowns**, and ran 10 times for 52 yards and no touchdowns. In his first year, he was used as a **kickoff returner** and averaged 20.8 yards in 20 returns. In 1974, he scored two touchdowns on **fumble** returns. In eight postseason games, Rashad caught 21 passes for 303 yards and one touchdown. He played in four **Pro Bowls**. Since retiring from active play following the 1982 NFL season, Rashad has moved into television, where, in addition to doing football commentary, he has hosted several nonfootball shows and appeared in several television series. He was inducted into the **College Football Hall of Fame** in 2007.

RECEPTION. In **football**, a reception is another word for a completed **pass**.

REDSHIRT. In collegiate sports in the United States, a player may be included on a team and practice with the team but not play for one season. That season does not count against the four-year eligibility limit. The player is termed a *redshirt*. This was originally done so that players who had incurred injuries would not be penalized and lose a year's eligibility, but it has been changed so that any player whose career a **coach** wants to defer may be redshirted. The term originated with the requirement that these players wear red shirts for team practices.

REEVES, DANIEL EDWARD "DAN." B. 19 January 1944, Rome, Georgia. Although Dan Reeves played **professional football** for eight years and played for the 1972 **Super Bowl** champions, he is best known for the 27 years he spent as a **National Football League (NFL) assistant coach** and head **coach** and the seven other Super Bowls in which he participated in that capacity. His participation in nine Super Bowls is more than any other player or coach. Reeves attended Americus High School in Americus, Georgia, and the University of South Carolina. He played **football**, baseball, and basketball in high school. He **quarterbacked** South Carolina from 1962 to 1964. The school's record during those three years was only 8–18–4, and, consequently, Reeves received little attention from professional football scouts and was not **drafted** by the NFL.

He was offered a Major League Baseball contract by the Pittsburgh Pirates but chose instead to sign with the **Dallas Cowboys** of the NFL. Reeves was initially slotted to be used as a **safety** on **defense** but was instead moved to offensive **halfback**. For each of the eight years of his NFL playing career, the Cowboys reached the **playoffs**. A knee injury suffered in 1968 limited his play during the last few years of his career, but Reeves did get to play in two Super Bowls, on the losing side in 1971 and with the Super Bowl champions in 1972.

In his eight-year NFL career, Reeves played in 100 regular-season games, ran 535 times for 1,990 yards and 25 **touchdowns**, and caught 129 **passes** for 1,693 yards and 17 touchdowns. He also completed 14 passes in 32 attempts for two touchdowns and returned five **kickoffs** for an average of 20.2 yards per return. In addition, in 1971, he ran for an extra point. In the postseason, Reeves played in eight games and ran 36 times for 91 yards and one touchdown, caught 15 passes for 163 yards and no touchdowns, and completed his only pass for a 50-yard touchdown. In 1970, he was named a player–assistant coach of the Cowboys and had those dual roles during his last three seasons as an active player.

After retiring following the 1972 season, Reeves entered the business world in 1973 but, in 1974, was rehired by the Cowboys as their backfield coach. In 1977, he was promoted to offensive coordinator and, in 1981, was hired by the **Denver Broncos** as their head coach. He coached the Broncos from 1981 to 1992 and led them to the Super Bowl as American Football Conference champions following the 1986, 1987, and 1989 seasons. In 1993, Reeves became head coach of the **New York Giants** and was with them for four seasons. After compiling a record of 31–33 with the Giants, he left to join the **Atlanta Falcons** as their coach for the 1997 season. In 1998 he led the Falcons to the best record in their history, 14–2; the National Football Conference title; and a berth in the Super Bowl. In that contest, they were defeated by Reeves's former team, the Denver Broncos. Reeves remained as Falcons coach through the 2003 season but resigned with three games remaining that year. He has since done radio color commentary for NFL games and is also employed as a motivational speaker.

REEVES, DANIEL FARRELL "DAN." B. 30 June 1912, New York, New York. D. 15 April 1971. Daniel Farrell Reeves is the other Dan Reeves in **professional football** history, the wealthy one who grew up on Fifth Avenue in New York City. His father owned a grocery chain that was sold to Safeway Stores, and Reeves was raised in an environment of comfort. He attended the Newman School in Lakewood, New Jersey, and Georgetown University. At Newman, Reeves was captain of the **football** team. He left Georgetown prior to obtaining a degree and worked in the family grocery business. In 1941, he purchased a two-thirds interest in the **National Football League (NFL)** team the Cleveland Rams. Reeves also became part owner of the Jersey City Giants, a minor-league football team. In 1943, he joined a Wall Street firm, Adler, Coleman and Company. He served with the Army Air Corps during World War II as a second lieutenant and was promoted to captain prior to his discharge in 1945. Even though the Rams won the NFL championship in 1945, Reeves decided to move the team to the West Coast and transferred them to Los Angeles.

An innovator, Reeves became the first NFL owner to hire black players since the league put an unofficial ban on them in 1933 after **George Preston Marshall** became an NFL team owner. Reeves hired Kenny Washington and Woody Strode. Although Strode only played that one season, he went on to excel in Hollywood as an actor, with featured roles in more than 90 films in a career lasting more than 50 years. Washington played three seasons as one of the NFL's better **running backs**, averaging 6.1 yards per carry and 15.1 yards per **pass reception**. That same year, Reeves founded his own Wall Street firm, Daniel Reeves and Company, but the following year he transferred his seat on the New York Stock Exchange to an associate.

The postwar Los Angeles Rams faced a challenge at the box office from the **Los Angeles Dons** of the new **All-America Football Conference (AAFC)**, but Reeves and the Rams survived, as he took on several new partners. Once the AAFC folded following the 1949 season, the Rams had the Los Angeles market to themselves. Reeves was the first NFL owner to employ a full-time scouting staff and hired **Alvin "Pete" Rozelle** as publicity director. Rozelle went on to become commissioner of the NFL.

The Rams were one of the NFL's more successful teams during the 1950s and played in the NFL Championship Game in 1949, 1950, 1951, and 1957 but only won the NFL title in 1951. They did well financially, playing at the 100,000-seat **Los Angeles Memorial Coliseum** and drawing crowds in excess of 100,000. In 1962, Reeves bought out his partners and became sole owner of the franchise. In 1966, **George Allen** became head coach, and although there were personality conflicts between him and Reeves, the Rams prospered on the playing field and became title contenders, although they did not win an NFL title during the 1960s. Reeves was inducted into the **Pro Football Hall of Fame** as a contributor in 1967 and died at the relatively young age of 58 from Hodgkin's disease in 1971.

REFEREE. *See* OFFICIALS.

REPLAY. With the advent of videotape in the 1960s and its subsequent use for instant replay of a live event, sports have changed significantly. The first use of instant replay for a **football** game occurred in 1963, when the **Army–Navy game** used it to show Army's final **touchdown** a second time. In recent years, as the technology has been perfected and multiple television cameras are routinely employed, both the **National Football League** and **National Collegiate Athletic Association** have allowed their **officials** to consult video replay to ensure that questionable calls are made correctly. *See also* CHALLENGE.

RETURNER. When a team kicks off or **punts** the ball, the opposing team sends one or more players downfield to act as kick or punt returners. Their function is to catch the ball and **run** upfield with it. A returner is usually one of the fastest players on the team, and several **Olympic** sprint champions have played **professional football** in that role.

RICE, HENRY GRANTLAND "GRANTLAND." B. 2 November 1880, Murfreesboro, Tennessee. D. 13 July 1954, New York, New York. Grantland Rice was one of the few sportswriters who could write poetry. He was a graduate of Montgomery Bell Academy and Vanderbilt University, both located in Nashville, Tennessee. After his college graduation in 1901, he began working for newspapers in the southern United States, among them the *Atlanta (GA) Journal*, *Cleveland (TN) News*, and *Nashville Tennessean*.

A sports enthusiast who had played **college football**, Rice became a sportswriter. During the 1920s, he helped popularize the "Golden Age of Sports" and wrote about many of the top sports personalities of that era. He also wrote quite a bit of sports poetry, and his columns often featured a poem. His picturesque, imaginative style coined the phrase "the **Four Horsemen**" in writing of the **University of Notre Dame's** backfield in 1924, and his *New York Herald Tribune* article on the Notre Dame–**Army** game at the Polo Grounds began in the following manner: "Outlined against a blue-gray October sky, the Four Horsemen rode again. In dramatic lore their names are Death, Destruction, Pestilence, and Famine. But those are aliases. Their real names are Stuhldreyer, Crowley, Miller, and Layden."

Following **Walter Camp's** death in 1925, Rice continued Camp's selection of an annual **All-American** football team published in *Collier's* magazine until 1947. During the 1930s, Rice's columns began to be syndicated in newspapers across the country, and his fame spread. Although his poetic style may seem out of place in today's faster-paced, "tell it like it is" sporting world, the elegance of his phrases are still enjoyable to read. One of his more famous phrases from a poem entitled "Alumnus Football" reads, "When the One Great Scorer comes to write against your name/He marks—not that you won or lost—but how you played the game."

Rice died following a stroke in 1954 and has since been honored by the Football Writers of America with the annual Grantland Rice Memorial Award, presented to an outstanding college player. The Grantland Rice Bowl, an annual college postseason **bowl game** played from 1964 to 1977, paid tribute to him, and the J. G. Taylor Spink Award was presented posthumously to Rice in 1966 by the Baseball Writers' of Association of America.

RICE, JERRY LEE. B. 13 October 1962, Crawford, Mississippi. Jerry Rice is thought by many to be the greatest **wide receiver** in **National Football League (NFL)** history and certainly has the statistical record to support that claim. He was also selected by NFL Films as the greatest player in NFL history, a more debatable position. Rice began playing football at B. L. Moor High School in Crawford, Mississippi. Although he played well and was named All-State **end**, he did not receive a scholarship offer from a **National Collegiate Athletic Association (NCAA)** Division I school and went to Mississippi Valley State University, a historically black school, where he played from 1981 to 1984. In those four years, he caught 301 **passes** for 4,693 yards and 50 **touchdowns**. During his senior year, Mississippi Valley won nine of their first 10 games, outscoring their opponents 609–236 in those 10 games, and was selected to play in the NCAA Division I-AA postseason **playoffs**. They lost their first-round playoff to Louisiana Tech, but Mississippi Valley and Rice received enough publicity that he was selected in the first round of the 1985 NFL **Draft** by the **San Francisco 49ers** as the 16th overall choice.

Rice played for the 49ers from 1985 to 2000 and led the NFL in pass **reception** yardage and also pass reception touchdowns six times each. With the 49ers, he played in the **Super Bowl** three times, in 1989, 1990, and 1995, and was a member of the winning team each time. He was named the Super Bowl Most Valuable Player following the 1989 game. A knee injury in the opening game of the 1997 season caused him to miss virtually the entire season. He attempted a comeback in the 49ers' 15th game that year but reinjured the knee and missed the remainder of the season. He was able to come back the following year and was nearly his usual self, as he played in all 16 regular-season games and caught 82 passes for 1,157 yards. Following the 2000 season, Rice signed with the **Oakland Raiders** and played the next three and a half years with them, ending his career with the **Seattle Seahawks** after being traded to them six games into the 2004 season. During that season, he actually played in 17 regular-season games, since the Seahawks had their bye week while Rice was playing for Oakland, a feat accomplished by only a handful of players in the modern-day NFL.

When Rice retired, he held several major NFL career records, including most passes caught (400 more than the second-place player), most pass receiving yardage (nearly one and a half times greater than the second-place player), and most receiving touchdowns. In his 20-year NFL career, he played in 303 regular-season games, caught 1,549 passes for 22,895 yards and 197 touchdowns, and ran 87 times for 645 yards and 10 touchdowns. He also completed three passes in 10 attempts for one touchdown and scored another touchdown on a **fumble** recovery. In 29 postseason games, Rice caught 151 passes for 2,245 yards and 22 touchdowns and ran seven times for 44 yards. His only pass attempt was incomplete. He played in 13 **Pro Bowls**, 11 of them in his first 11 seasons. After retiring, Rice has experimented with playing professional golf. He was inducted into the **College Football Hall of Fame** in 2006 and the **Pro Football Hall of Fame** in 2010.

ROBESON, PAUL LEROY. B. 9 April 1898, Princeton, New Jersey. D. 23 January 1976, Philadelphia, Pennsylvania. Paul Robeson is best remembered as a concert singer, actor, and political activist who ran afoul of the U.S. government's Cold War anti-Communist policies. But in his youth he was one of the nation's best collegiate **football** players. Robeson's father, the Reverend William Drew Robeson, was a former slave who served in the Union Army during the Civil War, earned a degree from Lincoln University, and became a Presbyterian minister. Paul followed in his father's accomplishments and surpassed him by far.

Paul attended Somerville High School in Somerville, New Jersey, where he participated in the school's theatrical productions, in addition to playing several sports, including football. He won an academic scholarship to **Rutgers University** as only the third African American student ever enrolled there and played football, baseball, and basketball and was also on the track and field team. Robeson even found time to be a member of the debate team and glee club. For four years, from 1915 to 1918, he played on the Rutgers football team and helped lead them to a record of 22–6–3 in that time. He was selected to **Walter Camp's All-American** football team and declared the "greatest ever defensive **end**." Academically, Robeson was a member of Phi Beta Kappa and was class valedictorian.

In 1919, Robeson enrolled in New York University Law School and also worked as an **assistant coach** of the Lincoln University football team. He transferred to Columbia Law School the following year and, while there, was recruited to play **professional football** in the newly created American Professional Football Association (APFA), the forerunner of the **National Football League (NFL)**. At six feet, three inches tall and 220 pounds, Robeson was one of the larger football players of his era and played both **tackle** and end. He appeared in 13 APFA games in 1921 and 1922 and scored at least one **touchdown** on a **fumble** recovery. He played for the Akron Pros in 1921 and the Milwaukee Badgers in 1922.

Robeson graduated from Columbia in 1923 and began an extensive theatrical and concert career, appearing in more than a dozen Hollywood films and Broadway theater performances, including *Othello* and *Show Boat*, as well as becoming a top recording artist, with such songs as "Old Man River." He established residency in London, England; performed in Europe; and visited the Soviet Union. He also became an outspoken political activist and, following World War II, was blacklisted by the U.S. government in its anti-Communist fervor, although he was never a member of the Communist Party.

Robeson was one of the most accomplished African Americans in U.S. history yet, in his lifetime, was never accorded the proper acclaim due him. Posthumously, he has been recognized significantly, and his football accomplishments were acknowledged when he was inducted into the **College Football Hall of Fame** in 1995.

ROBINSON, EDWARD GAY "EDDIE." B. 13 February 1919, Jackson, Louisiana. D. 3 April 2007, Ruston, Louisiana. Eddie Robinson is one of the greatest **college football coaches** in college **football** history. At the time of his retirement from coaching in 1997, he had compiled more football coaching victories than any other college head coach. Yet, he played down his accomplishments, saying, "The real record I have set for over 50 years is the fact that I have had one job and one wife." Robinson was a graduate of McKinley Senior High School in Baton Rouge, Louisiana, and Leland College. In 1941, Robinson was hired by the Colored Industrial and Agricultural Institute of Lincoln Parish (now known as **Grambling State University**) as their football coach. In his first year there, his team had a record of only 1–5–1. He completely turned around the team's fortunes in 1942, and the team won all nine games and lost none. The following two seasons, Grambling State did not field a football team due to World War II.

At Grambling, Robinson initially operated with a miniscule budget, and, in addition to coaching the football team, at various times he also worked at Grambling High School coaching boys' and girls' basketball, coaching baseball, and directing the band. Robinson earned a master's degree from the **University of Iowa** in 1954 and continually emphasized the need for an education to his players. He was proud of the fact that nearly all of the members of his teams went on to receive their degrees.

In 1949, one of Robinson's pupils, Paul "Tank" Younger, was signed by the Los Angeles Rams of the **National Football League (NFL)** and starred in the league at **fullback** for 10 seasons. Younger was the first player from a historically black college to play in the NFL, and, as a result of his success, Grambling State was added to the lists of schools watched by **professional football** scouts.

Although Grambling initially played only other black schools either at their home field or in Grambling, Louisiana, during the 1960s, Robinson began taking his team to large cities and played before large crowds in big **stadiums**. They traveled to such metropolitan areas as New York, Chicago, and Los Angeles. During the 1970s, as the civil rights movement had made significant inroads, Grambling occasionally scheduled and defeated nonblack schools. Even today, there are usually one or two nonconference games against nonblack schools on Grambling's schedule.

In Robinson's 55 years of coaching at Grambling, there were 99 of his former players who played in the NFL or **American Football League**. Four of his former players are enshrined in the **College Football Hall of Fame**, including Junius "Buck" Buchanan, Gary "Big Hands" Johnson, Doug Williams, and Paul "Tank" Younger. Robinson's record from 1941 to 1997 was 408–165–15. His teams won 17 Southwest Athletic Conference championships and nine Black College National Championships. From 1960 to 1986, his teams had 27 consecutive winning seasons.

Shortly after he retired following the 1997 season, Robinson was diagnosed with Alzheimer's disease. He succumbed to its effects in 2007. He was inducted into the College Football Hall of Fame as a coach in 1997.

ROCKNE, KNUTE KENNETH, NÉE KNUT LARSEN ROKNE. B. 4 March 1888, Voss, Norway. D. 31 March 1931, Bazaar, Kansas. Knute Rockne was one of **football's** most famous **coaches**. He was immortalized following his death in an airplane crash at the height of his career. Born in a small town in Norway, he immigrated with his family to Chicago, Illinois, when he was about five years old. He attended North West Division High School in Chicago and played football and ran track there. After graduation, he worked for the U.S. Postal Service while saving money to attend college. In 1910, Rockne enrolled at the **University of Notre Dame** to study pharmacy. He played **end** on the football team and was selected to the 1913 **All-American** team. Notre Dame was undefeated in both 1912 and 1913.

Rockne began work at Notre Dame as a laboratory assistant to Father Julius A. Nieuwland, a renowned chemist who later contributed to the development of a form of synthetic rubber that became a product of the DuPont chemical company. Rockne was a lecturer in the Notre Dame chemistry department and helped out with various sports programs, including their football team.

In 1918, Rockne was made head coach of the Notre Dame football team, and, for the next 13 years, Notre Dame was one of the American collegiate football powers. They won nearly 90 percent of their games, and Rockne's record was 105–12–5. In an era with no official national football champion, Notre Dame was given that distinction by one or more polls in 1919, 1920, 1924, 1927, 1929, and 1930. They were undefeated in 1919, 1920, 1924, 1929, and 1930 and lost only one game in each of 1921, 1922, 1923, 1926, and 1927. In 1924, they were victors in the **Rose Bowl**, their only appearance in the long history of that event.

As a player and as a coach, Rockne was one of the first to emphasize the use of the forward **pass**, which, in that era, still had several restrictions in its execution. He was an excellent motivator and promoter and helped make Notre Dame synonymous with **college football**. Among his students were several who made a major impact on the sport, namely **Earl "Curly" Lambeau**, **Frank Leahy**, and **Elmer Layden**, to name just a few.

Knute Rockne, the innovative coach who made Notre Dame synonymous with college football.
Mike Moran

In 1930, while traveling from Kansas City, Missouri, to Los Angeles, California, to participate in the filming of *The Spirit of Notre Dame*, the small plane on which Rockne was flying crashed in a wheat field in Kansas, killing all eight people onboard. Rockne's death was lamented as a national tragedy. The 1940 Hollywood film *Knute Rockne: All-American*, starring Pat O'Brien as Rockne and Ronald Reagan as **George Gipp**, helped preserve his legacy in American history. He was a charter member of the **College Football Hall of Fame**, where he was inducted as a coach in 1951. See also FOOTBALL FILMS.

RODGERS, AARON CHARLES. B. 2 December 1983, Chico, California. Aaron Rodgers was born in Chico, California, and raised in Oregon but returned to Chico to attend high school at Pleasant Valley High School. He starred on their **football** team as **quarterback** and set several school records in the process; however, his relatively small stature (five feet, 10 inches tall and 165 pounds) discouraged colleges from offering him scholarships and he enrolled at local Butte Community College. While there, he led them to their **conference** championship and a ranking of second in the nation, which attracted the attention of **major colleges**. Rodgers was offered a scholarship to the **University of California** and played for them in 2003 and 2004. During those two seasons, the football team compiled a record of 18–8 and appeared in a **bowl game** each year. Rodgers decided to pass up his senior year to enter the **National Football League (NFL) Draft** and was selected in the first round of the 2005 NFL Draft by the **Green Bay Packers** as the 24th overall pick.

Rodgers spent most of his first three NFL seasons as the backup to **Brett Favre** and played in only seven games during that time. He got his chance to be a starting quarterback in 2008, when Favre retired. After Rodgers was named as the Packers starter for 2008, Favre came out of retirement but was traded to the **New York Jets**. From 2008 to 2012, Rodgers has been the Packers' starting quarterback in every game that he has played. He led them to the **Super Bowl** championship in the 2010 season and was named the Super Bowl Most Valuable Player following that game. In 2011, he led the Packers to a nearly undefeated season, losing only one regular-season game, but they were upset by the **New York Giants** in the division **playoff** game. He managed to establish an all-time NFL quarterback rating of 122.5 and won the 2011 NFL Most Valuable Player Award for his efforts.

Rodgers's performance during his first few NFL seasons has established him as one of the league's elite quarterbacks. Through the 2012 season, he has played in 85 NFL games in eight seasons. He has started in 78 games and has a won-lost record of 52–26. He has completed 1,752 **passes** in 2,665 attempts for 21,661 yards and 171 **touchdowns**. He has also carried the ball 303 times for 1,442 yards and 18 touchdowns and appeared in three **Pro Bowls**. In nine postseason games, Rodgers has completed 193 passes in 292 attempts for 2,312 yards and 18 touchdowns and run 29 times for 173 yards and three touchdowns.

ROETHLISBERGER, BENJAMIN TODD "BEN." B. 2 March 1982, Lima, Ohio. Ben Roethlisberger played **football**, baseball, and basketball and was team captain in all three sports at Findlay High School in Findlay, Ohio. He was a **wide receiver** until his senior year, as the **coach's** son, Ryan Hite, was the **quarterback**. In college, Roethlisberger went to the other Miami University, in Oxford, Ohio, in the Miami Valley part of the state. He was **redshirted** his freshman year, but, the following year, as a redshirt freshman, he became the starting quarterback. In three years at Miami, he played in 38 games and completed 854 **passes** in 1,304 attempts for 10,829 yards and 80 **touchdowns**. The team had a record of 27–11 from 2001 to 2003 and was the **Mid-American Conference** champion in 2003, with a 13–1 season record.

Roethlisberger bypassed his senior year in college and was selected by the **Pittsburgh Steelers** in the first round as the 11th overall choice in the 2004 **National Football League (NFL) Draft**. In 2004, he was selected as the NFL Offensive Rookie of the Year. He has played for the Steelers from 2004 through 2012. During that time, he has led Pittsburgh to the **Super Bowl** three times, winning in 2006 and 2009 and losing in 2011. Roethlisberger is one of the largest quarterbacks in the NFL, at six feet, five inches tall and 245 pounds, but he is agile and does not hesitate to scramble out of the **pocket** in an attempt to find an open receiver. His size also makes him difficult to **tackle**.

Through the 2012 season, Roethlisberger has played in 127 NFL games in nine seasons, starting in 126 of them, with a won-lost record of 87–39. He has completed 2,374 passes in 3,762 attempts for 29,844 yards and 191 touchdowns. He has also carried the ball 318 times for 1,036 yards and 14 touchdowns. In addition, he has **punted** four times for an average of 33.3 yards and appeared in two **Pro Bowls**. In 14 postseason games, Roethlisberger has completed 248 passes in 409 attempts for 3,150 yards and 20 touchdowns and run 61 times for 203 yards and three touchdowns. He also punted once for 25 yards.

ROONEY, ARTHUR JOSEPH, SR. "ART." B. 27 January 1901, Coultersville, Pennsylvania. D. 25 August 1988, Pittsburgh, Pennsylvania. Art Rooney Sr. was the oldest of nine children of Pittsburgh-area saloon keeper Dan Rooney. He attended Duquesne Prep High School in Pittsburgh, was a good athlete, and played baseball and **football**. He also enjoyed boxing and was one of the better amateur boxers in the United States and competed in the national Amateur Athletic Union championships in the lightweight class. During the 1920s, Rooney played semiprofessional football and also Minor League Baseball. He played baseball for the Wheeling Stogies in the Class C Middle Atlantic League. He also managed them briefly in 1925, during which time he was the league leader in games, runs, hits, and stolen bases and had the league's second-highest batting average, at .369. Rooney's brother, Dan Rooney, who later became a Catholic priest and missionary in China, was his teammate and finished third in the league in batting.

During the late 1920s, Art became a heavy gambler and, in his words, was "one of the country's biggest and most successful horse players." Later in his life, he became the owner of a horse breeding farm in Maryland and the owner of several racetracks, both horse and dog. In 1933, he purchased a franchise in the **National Football League (NFL)** and named the team the Pittsburgh Pirates after the Major League Baseball team of the same name. In 1940, he sold the Pirates to Alexis Thompson. Rooney then bought a share of the **Philadelphia Eagles** and traded it to Thompson, who wanted a team closer to his home in New York, and Rooney regained ownership of the Pittsburgh franchise. He renamed the team the Steelers for the 1940 season, and the team has retained that name since.

During World War II, the manpower shortage caused the Steelers to merge their team with the Philadelphia Eagles and play the 1943 NFL season as Philadelphia-Pittsburgh, or **Phil-Pitt**, or as **fans** and sportswriters called them, the "Steagles." In 1944, the Pittsburgh team merged with the Chicago Cardinals and played that season as **Card-Pitt**.

Although Rooney was one of the league's more popular owners, his teams never reached the NFL Championship Game until the 1970s. During that decade, they became one of the league's best teams and won the **Super Bowl** four times between 1975 and 1980. By then, Rooney's sons, Dan and Art Jr., had been given control of team operations, although Art Sr. remained as the team's chairman of the board until his death in 1988. Art Sr. was one of the best-liked team owners in football and was inducted into the **Pro Football Hall of Fame** as a contributor in 1964.

ROONEY, DANIEL MILTON "DAN." B. 20 July 1932, Pittsburgh, Pennsylvania. Dan Rooney is the son of **Art Rooney**, owner of the **Pittsburgh Steelers**. Dan has also been a significant contributor to the **National Football League (NFL)**. He attended North Catholic High School in Pittsburgh and played **quarterback** on their **football** team. He continued his education at Duquesne University, graduating with an accounting degree. Since the 1960s, he has been active in the day-to-day management of team activities and, in 1975, was named the team's president. In 1988, following the death of his father, Dan became the controlling owner of the Steelers. After turning 70 years of age, he has begun to turn control of the team over to his son, Art Rooney II.

Dan was one of the key owners involved in the 1982 collective bargaining agreement with the NFL players and was instrumental in ending the players' strike that year. He also worked toward adding a salary cap, which was accomplished in 1993. One of his more important accomplishments is the so-called "Rooney Rule." This NFL regulation, implemented in 2003, requires that any team hiring a head coach or general manager must interview at least one minority candidate. In 2009, this rule was expanded to include all senior football operations positions in the NFL.

Dan was inducted into the **Pro Football Hall of Fame** as a contributor in 2000. In 2009, he was selected by President Barack Obama to be the U.S. ambassador to Ireland.

ROSE BOWL (EVENT). The Rose Bowl is an annual postseason **college football** game. It was first played in 1902 and is nicknamed "The Grandaddy of Them All." It is played on **New Year's Day** in Pasadena, California, following the Tournament of Roses Parade, which predates the game by 12 years, first being held in 1890. Since 1923, the game has been played at **Rose Bowl Stadium**, a massive facility that seated more than 100,000 **fans** for much of its history but now has a seating capacity of 94,392. The first game, in 1902, was called the "Tournament East-West Football Game," and it matched the undefeated, untied, and unscored upon **University of Michigan** Wolverines against **Stanford University**, a local team with a more modest record of 3–1–2. Michigan had won all 10 of their games and scored 506 points while doing so. They prevailed, 49–0, against Stanford in a game that was terminated by Stanford with eight minutes remaining.

It was not until 1 January 1916 that a second Tournament East-West Football Game was played, but since then the event (renamed the Rose Bowl in 1923) has been played annually at Pasadena on 1 January (2 January if the first falls on a Sunday), with only a few exceptions. In 1942, due to security concerns, the game was moved to Durham, North Carolina. In 2002 and 2006, the game was played for the **Bowl Championship Series (BCS)** National Championship and was moved to a later date during the first week of the new year.

For much of the game's history, the contest featured a representative of the **Big Ten Conference** and one from the Pacific Coast Conference. As a result, the **University of Southern California** has appeared in the event 33 times, with 24 victories, and the University of Michigan has played in 20 Rose

Bowls, with only eight victories. In 1918 and 1919, the Rose Bowl featured two military service teams each year. Since 1998, with the formation of the BCS, the Rose Bowl has been one of the venues that hosts a BCS **bowl game**. *See also* APPENDIX M (for a list of champions).

ROSE BOWL (STADIUM). Rose Bowl Stadium is located in Pasadena, California, a suburb of Los Angeles. It was opened in 1922 and has been the site of the **Rose Bowl** game each year since 1 January 1923, with the exception of 1942, when wartime travel restrictions caused the game to be played in Durham, North Carolina. The present-day seating capacity is 94,392, although in earlier years, with bleacher-type seating, more than 100,000 **fans** attended games there. The 1973 Rose Bowl drew 106,869 spectators.

The Rose Bowl Stadium has also been used as the home field for the **University of California, Los Angeles**, since 1982. In 1983, it hosted the **Army–Navy game**, the only time that event has been held west of the Mississippi River. The California Institute of Technology, located in Pasadena and popularly known as Caltech, also used the **stadium** as its home field for football until 1993, when they no longer fielded a team. The facility was used for both the 1932 and 1984 **Olympic Games**, and the Olympic **soccer** final in 1984 drew 101,799 onlookers, the largest attendance for a soccer match in the United States. In 1987, Rose Bowl Stadium was designated as a National Historic Landmark.

ROTE, WILLIAM KYLE, SR. "KYLE." B. 27 October 1927, San Antonio, Texas. D. 15 August 2002, Baltimore, Maryland. Kyle Rote Sr. is a graduate of Thomas Jefferson High School in San Antonio, Texas, where he played both basketball and **football**. From 1948 to 1950, he played at Southern Methodist University, where in his first two seasons he played alongside **Doak Walker**. During Rote's three years on the Southern Methodist **varsity**, the team had a record of 20–9–2 and played in the 1 January 1949 **Cotton Bowl**. Following the 1950 season, Rote was runner-up to Vic Janowicz of **Ohio State University** in the voting for the **Heisman Trophy**.

The six-foot-tall, 200-pound Rote was selected by the **New York Giants** as the first overall selection in the 1951 **National Football League (NFL) Draft** and played **halfback** and **end** for them from 1951 to 1961. Although a **punter** in college, he was never used by the Giants in that capacity.

In his 11-year NFL career, Rote played in 121 regular-season games, caught 300 **passes** for 4,797 yards and 48 **touchdowns**, and ran 231 times for 871 yards and four touchdowns. He also completed six of 20 passes for two touchdowns. In his first two seasons in the NFL, he was also used as a **kickoff returner** and returned 12 kickoffs for an average of 24.6 yards per return. In five postseason games, Rote caught nine passes for 191 yards and one touchdown. He played in four **Pro Bowls** and helped the Giants win the 1956 NFL championship and reach the NFL finals in 1958, 1959, and 1961.

Rote was one of the Giants' team captains and also one of the founders of the NFL Players Association in the early 1950s and its first president. After retiring from active play, he became a sportscaster in the New York area, working for both local stations and networks. His son, Kyle Jr., became a top **soccer** player and was a three-time winner of the *Superstars* made-for-television sports competition. Rote's cousin, Tobin Rote, was a **quarterback** in the NFL and **American Football League** from 1950 to 1966. Kyle Rote Sr. was inducted into the **College Football Hall of Fame** in 1964. He died of pneumonia following hernia surgery in 2002, at the age of 74.

ROUGE. In **Canadian football**, a rouge is scored when the **offense** kicks the ball into their opponent's **end zone** on either a **punt** or missed **field goal** and the ball is not brought out by the receiving team. A rouge (also called a single) is worth one point. The team scored upon then receives the ball at their own 35-**yard line** to begin the next play.

ROZELLE, ALVIN RAY "PETE." B. 1 March 1926, South Gate, California. D. 6 December 1996, Rancho Santa Fe, California. Pete Rozelle was the **National Football League (NFL)** commissioner who had the greatest impact on the game and made it into America's most popular sport. He was raised in Southern California and was a graduate of Compton High School in Compton, California, where he played both baseball and basketball. After his high school graduation in 1944, he served in the U.S. Navy. After his discharge from the service, he enrolled at the University of San Francisco and graduated in 1950. After college, Rozelle worked at various public relations jobs, one of which was for the Los Angeles Rams of the NFL, and, in 1957, he became their general manager. In 1960, following the sudden death of league commissioner **Bert Bell**, Rozelle was selected as commissioner of the NFL. He retained that position until 1989 and, in that time, increased the league's fortunes many times over.

In 1960, Rozelle's first challenge was the threat posed by the newly created **American Football League**, and, by 1970, he had worked to merge the two leagues into one powerful organization. He also helped improve the NFL's television contracts and implemented revenue sharing so that the NFL teams in smaller markets could successfully compete. Rozelle was a strong advocate of having NFL games aired on prime-time television, and his push for *Monday Night Football* proved to be a major factor in making the NFL the most-watched sport in the United States. His challenges during the 1970s and 1980s, which he met successfully, included two more attempts at rival leagues, the **World Football League** and **United States Football League**, and labor problems during the 1980s, which resulted in two player strikes.

One of the few negative aspects about Rozelle's career as NFL commissioner concerned his handling of the league's schedule following the assassination of President John F. Kennedy on 22 November 1963. He was advised by Pierre Salinger, the White House press secretary and a former University of San Francisco classmate of Rozelle's, that the president was a big sports fan and would have wanted the NFL to play the Sunday following his death. Rozelle went along with that decision, and the NFL played a full schedule on Sunday, 24 November. Rozelle was severely criticized for this decision by players, **fans**, and the media and, in later years, said that it had been his worst mistake, but that mistake was nearly forgotten after the next two decades, during which time he worked tirelessly in establishing the NFL as the most powerful sports league in the United States. Rozelle was inducted into the **Pro Football Hall of Fame** as a contributor in 1985, while still active as commissioner.

RUGBY. Rugby is a sport that can be considered the ancestor of American **football**. It originated at the Rugby School in Rugby, Warwickshire, England, and is played (predominantly in former British Empire countries) in two variants, rugby union and rugby league. The concept of a team moving a ball toward a goal and being prevented from doing so by physically tackling the player with the ball was carried over to American football.

RUN. A **football** team can advance the ball by either running with the ball or **passing** it to a player who will then run. Plays that do not involve passing are referred to as runs. *See also* RUSHING.

RUNNING BACK. A running back is a **football position** whose primary function is to receive the ball from the **quarterback** and **run** downfield with it. He may also be called upon to run downfield without the ball to catch a **pass** or assist with **blocking** if he is not the ball carrier.

RUSHING. The **football** term *rushing* is used to designate yardage gained by **running** with the ball.

RUTGERS UNIVERSITY. Rutgers University is located in New Brunswick, New Jersey. They took part in the first intercollegiate **football** game in 1869, and, since then, through 2012, Scarlet Knights' teams have compiled a record of 627–607–42. In addition, they have competed in eight postseason

bowl games, with a record of 5–3. The Scarlet Knights were selected retroactively as national collegiate cochampions in 1869, only because they were one of the only two colleges to play intercollegiate football that year, but they have not won a national championship since. Home games since 1994 have been played at the 52,000-seat Rutgers Stadium (renamed High Point Solutions Stadium in 2011). From 1929 to 1975, Rutgers was a member of the Middle Three Conference, along with Lafayette College and Lehigh University. In 1991, they joined the **Big East Conference**. The school has no current rivalries.

Rutgers' most successful **coaches** have been George Sanford (1913–1923; 56–32–5), Harvey Harman (1938–1941, 1946–1955; 74–44–2), John Bateman (1960–1972; 73–51), and Frank Burns (1973–1983; 78–43–1). There are only three Rutgers' alumni in the **College Football Hall of Fame**. They are **end/fullback** Homer "Pop" Hazel; **center** Alex Kroll; and end **Paul Robeson**, who became better known as an actor and singer. Coaches George Sanford and Harvey Harman and are also enshrined in the Hall.

Through 2012, there have been 76 **National Football League** players and one **American Football League** player who have attended Rutgers, including Darion Barnes, Marco Battaglia, Jay Bellamy, Gary Brackett, Kenny Britt, Deron Cherry, Carl Howard, James Jenkins, Nate Jones, Ray Lucas, Dino Mangiero, Bob Nash, Shaun O'Hara, Bill Pellington, Bill Pickel, Ray Rice, Paul Robeson, L. J. Smith, Tyronne Stowe, and Harry Swayne.

S

SACRAMENTO GOLD MINERS. *See* SAN ANTONIO TEXANS.

SACRAMENTO SURGE. *See* SAN ANTONIO TEXANS.

SAFETY (POSITION). Safety is a position on the defensive team in **football**. He is usually lined up in the defensive backfield as the last man before the **goal line**. There are usually two players at this position, a strong safety who usually plays on the side of the field opposite the **tight end**, and a free safety who plays further back and is the last line of defense.

SAFETY (SCORE). A safety is scored when the offensive team carries the ball into its own **end zone** and is **tackled** there or commits a **penalty** in the end zone. It is usually the result of an aggressive defensive play, although it can be used as a strategic offensive play by a team deliberately downing the ball in their end zone to improve field position, thus the origin of the name. It is worth two points for the defensive team, who then receives possession of the ball via a **free kick** from the opponent's 20-**yard line**. *See also* TOUCHBACK.

SAMOANS AND SOUTH SEA ISLANDERS. The impact that the South Pacific islands of Samoa and neighboring Tonga have had on American **football** is incredible. Some 29 **National Football League (NFL)** players were born in American Samoa, seven in Western Samoa, and 13 in Tonga. In addition, there have been quite a few more second-generation Polynesian players, for example, **Tiaina "Junior" Seau**, Manu Tuiasosopo, and Troy Polamalu, born in Hawaii or the mainland United States. Hawaiian-born Joe Paopao, of Samoan extraction, was a star player and coach in the **Canadian Football League**. One factor for the interest in football among Samoans was the large Mormon influence (nearly 25 percent of Samoans belong to the Church of Latter Day Saints) and the recruiting efforts of Brigham Young University. Another is the culture's traditional love for contact sports. **Rugby** is also a popular sport, but Samoan youth prefer football since it can provide for a much more lucrative profession. *See also* APPENDIX J for a list of foreign-born NFL players.

SAN ANTONIO TEXANS. The San Antonio Texans were a **professional football** team in the **Canadian Football League (CFL)** from 1993 to 1995. The team was originally known as the Sacramento Surge and competed in the **World League of American Football** in 1991 and 1992. When that league disbanded in 1993, the team's owners renamed the team the Sacramento Gold Miners and entered the CFL, as the league had decided to expand and add teams in the United States in 1993. The Gold Miners played at the 21,195-seat Hornet Stadium in Sacramento, California, and had a record of 6–12 as the only U.S.-based team in the CFL. In 1994, the team finished at 9–8–1, and three more non-Canadian teams were added to the league that year. For the 1995 season, the team relocated to San Antonio and played at the 59,000-seat Alamodome. They had a successful year on the field, finishing at 12–6, but the team lost in the first round of the postseason **playoffs**.

Head **coach** of the franchise was Kay Stephenson, a former **National Football League** player and coach. Among the team's top players were **quarterback** David Archer; defensive **back** Malcolm Frank; **running back** Mike Pringle, who was later voted into the **Canadian Football Hall of Fame**; and **cornerback** and kick **returner** Bobby Humphrey.

SAN DIEGO CHARGERS. The San Diego Chargers are a **professional football** team in the American Football Conference (AFC) West Division of the **National Football League (NFL)**. They began in 1960 as a charter member of the **American Football League (AFL)** as the Los Angeles Chargers and played their home games that season at the 93,000-seat **Los Angeles Memorial Coliseum** in Los Angeles, California. In 1961, the Chargers relocated to San Diego after they found that they could not successfully compete with the NFL's Los Angeles Rams. In San Diego, the Chargers played at the 34,000-seat Balboa Stadium from 1961 to 1966, and in the 70,000-seat San Diego Stadium since then. The **stadium** was renamed Jack Murphy Stadium after the passing of San Diego sportswriter Jack Murphy, who was instrumental in getting the city of San Diego to construct the facility. In 1997, the Qualcomm Corporation acquired the naming rights and changed the name to Qualcomm Stadium.

The Chargers were one of the AFL's most successful teams, compiling a regular-season record of 86–48–6. The played in the AFL Championship Game in five of the league's first six years but were only able to win it in 1963. They transferred to the NFL in 1970, when the AFL and NFL merged. In their 43 years in the NFL, they have not done nearly as well and have compiled a record of 313–346–5 in regular-season play and 9–12 in **playoff** competition. In the 12 NFL seasons in which they qualified for the playoffs, they lost in the **Super Bowl** once (1994), the AFC championship three times, the second round or divisional playoffs six times, and the **wild-card playoff** twice.

Sid Gillman, Don Coryell, and Marty Schottenheimer are the three head **coaches** who had the most success at San Diego. Gillman, coach from 1960 to 1969, and again briefly in 1971, led them to five AFL Championship Games. Coryell, coach from 1978 to 1986, had five straight winning seasons and four playoff appearances. And Schottenheimer, coach from 2002 to 2006, led them to a 14–2 regular-season record in 2006, a franchise best. Other San Diego coaches have been Charlie Waller (1969–1970), Harland Svare (1971–1973), Ron Waller (interim 1973), Tommy Prothro (1974–1978), Al Saunders (1986–1988), Dan Henning (1989–1991), Bobby Ross (1992–1996), Kevin Gilbride (1997–1998), June Jones (interim 1998), Mike Riley (1999–2001), and Norv Turner (2007–2012). On 15 January 2013 Mike McCoy was hired as the head coach of the Chargers for the 2013 season.

Chargers' **Pro Football Hall of Fame** players include **quarterback Dan Fouts**, **wide receivers** Lance Alworth and Charlie Joiner, **tight end Kellen Winslow**, offensive **tackle** Ron Mix, and defensive **end** Fred Dean. Other players of note include **running backs** Keith Lincoln, Paul Lowe, and LaDanian Tomlinson; quarterbacks John Hadl and Philip Rivers; wide receivers Wes Chandler and Gary Garrison; tight end Jacque MacKinnon; **kicker** Rolf Benirschke; offensive **linemen** Walt Sweeney, Russ Washington, Ed White, and Doug Wilkerson; defensive linemen Earl Faison, Gary Johnson, Louie Kelcher, and Ernie Ladd; and **linebackers** Chuck Allen, Frank Buncom, and Emil Karas.

SAN FRANCISCO 49ERS. The San Francisco 49ers began as a **professional football** team in the **All-America Football Conference (AAFC)** in 1946. They played their home games at the 59,000-seat Kezar Stadium in San Francisco, California. They were one of the more successful franchises in the AAFC but had the misfortune of being in the same division as the **Cleveland Browns**, who won the league championship in all four years of the league's existence. The 49ers finished second to the Browns in each of those four years and had a total won-lost record of 38–14–2. They played the Browns in the AAFC Championship Game in 1949 but were defeated, 21–7. When the AAFC merged with the **National Football League (NFL)** in 1950, the 49ers were one of the three teams to be added to the NFL.

In the 49ers' 63 years in the NFL from 1950 to 2012, their overall record is 495–413–14 in regular-season games and 28–19 in postseason play. Prior to the National Football League–**American Football League** merger in 1970, the 49ers appeared in only one postseason game in the NFL, a Western Conference tiebreaker, which they lost to the **Detroit Lions** in 1957. From 1970 to 2012, the Niners qualified for the **playoffs** 23 times and had a record of 28–19. They have appeared in six **Super Bowls** and won the first five but were defeated for the first time in 2012. They won in 1981, 1984, 1988, 1989, and 1994. They lost in the conference championships seven times, the divisional playoffs seven times, and the **wild-card playoff** twice. San Francisco's home field was Kezar Stadium through 1970 and has been the 69,000-seat Candlestick Park in San Francisco since then. They are one of the few NFL franchises that have not required that a new facility be built for them.

The two most successful 49ers' head **coaches** have been Bill Walsh and George Seifert. Walsh coached from 1979 to 1988. His teams had a record of 92–59–1, reached the playoffs seven times, and won three Super Bowls. Seifert continued from 1989 to 1996 and reached the playoffs in seven of eight years, missing only in 1991, when the team still won 10 games. His record was 98–30, with two Super Bowl wins. Other head coaches of the 49ers have been Lawrence "Buck" Shaw (1946–1954), Norman "Red" Strader (1955), **Frankie Albert** (1956–1958), Howard "Red" Hickey (1959–1963), Jack Christiansen (1963–1967), Dick Nolan (1968–1975), Monte Clark (1976), Ken Meyer (1977), Pete McCulley (1978), Fred O'Connor (interim 1978), Steve Mariucci (1997–2002), Dennis Erickson (2003–2004), Mike Nolan (2005–2008), Mike Singletary (2008–2010), Jim Tomsula (interim 2010), and Jim Harbaugh (2011–2012).

Pro Football Hall of Famers who have played for San Francisco include **quarterbacks Joe Montana, Y. A. Tittle**, and **Steve Young**; **fullback Joe Perry**; **cornerback** Jimmy Johnson; **running back Hugh McElhenny**; cornerback/**safety** Ronnie Lott; **linebacker** Dave Wilcox; offensive and defensive **tackle Leo Nomellini**; defensive end Fred Dean; defensive **lineman** Chris Doleman; offensive guard Larry Allen; offensive tackle Bob St. Clair, and **wide receiver Jerry Rice**. Other noteworthy players include quarterbacks Frankie Albert and John Brodie; defensive lineman Charlie Krueger; wide receivers Dwight Clark, **Terrell Owens**, and Gene A. Washington; running backs Roger Craig, Frank Gore, Wendell Tyler, and Ricky Watters; wide receiver/**kicker** Gordy Soltau; end Billy Wilson; linebacker Matt Hazeltine; and kickers Tommy Davis and Ray Wersching.

SANDERS, BARRY. B. 16 July 1968, Wichita, Kansas. Although some sources list his middle name as David, Barry Sanders has been quoted as saying he has no middle name. He attended North High School in Wichita, Kansas, and Oklahoma State University. At Oklahoma State, he was used as a backup **running back** to **Thurman Thomas** during his first two years. After Thomas moved on to the **National Football League (NFL)**, Sanders had one of the most outstanding years for a running back in collegiate football history in 1988. In that year, he played in 12 games and carried the ball 373 times for 2,850 yards and 42 **touchdowns**. He averaged 237.5 yards per game and 7.6 yards per carry. He also caught 19 **passes** for 106 yards and two touchdowns. His feats earned him the **Heisman Trophy** that year.

Sanders passed up his senior year in college and was selected by the **Detroit Lions** in the first round of the 1989 NFL **Draft** as the third overall selection. Although short for an NFL player, at just five feet, eight inches tall, he weighed slightly more than 200 pounds and had very strong legs, making him difficult to **tackle**. He played his entire NFL career with the Lions, from 1989 to 1998, and was selected for the **Pro Bowl** each year. Although they reached the **playoffs** in five of his 10 seasons, the Lions lost four times in the **wild-card playoff** and once in the **conference** championship round. Following the 1998 season, Sanders, although still healthy and only 1,457 yards behind **Walter Payton's** NFL career **rushing** record, retired as the Lions' inability to do better began to weigh on him.

In his 10-year NFL career, Sanders played in 153 regular-season games, ran 3,062 times for 15,269 yards and 99 touchdowns, and caught 352 passes for 2,921 yards and 10 touchdowns. In 1989, he was occasionally used as a kick **returner** and returned five **kickoffs** for an average of 23.6 yards per return. In six postseason games, he ran 91 times for 386 yards and one touchdown and caught 21 passes for 111 yards and no touchdowns. He led the league in rushing yardage four times, including 1997, when, with 2,053 yards, he became only the third NFL player (there are now seven) to rush for more than 2,000 yards in one season. Sanders was inducted into the **College Football Hall of Fame** in 2003 and the **Pro Football Hall of Fame** in 2004.

SANDERS, DEION LUWYNN "PRIME TIME," NEON DEION." B. 9 August 1967, Fort Myers, Florida. Deion Sanders is one of the most unique athletes in recent history. He played two professional sports, baseball and **football**; acted on both **offense** and **defense** in football; and played in both the **Super Bowl** and World Series. He attended North Fort Myers High School in North Fort Myers, Florida, and played baseball, football, and basketball there, achieving All-State recognition in all three sports. He continued his education at **Florida State University** from 1985 to 1989 and also played three sports there, replacing basketball with track. During his four years at Florida State, the school's football team had a record of 38–9–1 and played and won a postseason **bowl game** each year.

Sanders was selected by the Kansas City Royals in the sixth round of the 1985 Major League Baseball (MLB) **Draft** but did not sign and remained at Florida State. He was then selected by the New York Yankees in the 30th round in the 1988 MLB Draft and signed with them. He was also selected by the **Atlanta Falcons** in the first round of the 1989 **National Football League (NFL)** Draft as the fifth overall selection.

The six-foot, one-inch, 195-pound Sanders began his NFL career with the Falcons in 1989 and was with them through the 1993 season. He returned **punts** and **kickoffs**, played **cornerback** on defense, and was occasionally used as a **wide receiver** on offense due to his exceptional speed. He was signed by the **San Francisco 49ers** for the 1994 season and played in the 1995 Super Bowl with them, **intercepting** a **pass** in that game and winning the Super Bowl championship. The following season, he signed with the **Dallas Cowboys** for one of the highest-paying contracts for a defensive player in NFL history. The investment paid off, as the Cowboys won the Super Bowl that season and Sanders became one of only a few players to play for two different Super Bowl champions in consecutive seasons. For part of the 1996 season, Sanders played both offense and defense, lining up on offense as a wide receiver and on defense as a cornerback. On 30 September 1996, in a *Monday Night Football* game against the **Philadelphia Eagles**, he caught three passes for 55 yards as a wide receiver and also intercepted one as a defender. Sanders played for the Cowboys through the 1999 season and then signed with the **Washington Redskins** for 2000. He retired from football following that season but made a comeback several years later, playing for the **Baltimore Ravens** in 2004 and 2005.

In his 14-year NFL career, Sanders played in 188 regular-season games. He returned 212 punts for an average of 10.4 yards per punt return and six **touchdowns**, as well as 155 kickoffs for an average of 22.7 yards per kickoff return and three touchdowns, including one of 100 yards and another of 99 yards. He also recorded 53 interceptions and nine touchdowns on interception returns and recovered 19 **fumbles**, including one for a touchdown. As a pass receiver, Sanders caught 60 passes for 784 yards and three touchdowns and ran nine times for a total of minus 14 yards. In 11 postseason games, he ran four times for 39 yards and one touchdown, caught three passes for 95 yards and no touchdowns, returned eight kickoffs for 177 yards and 11 punts for 118 yards, and intercepted five passes for 80 yards.

Sanders played the outfield in MLB from 1989 to 1995 with the New York Yankees, Atlanta Braves, Cincinnati Reds, and San Francisco Giants. He was out of baseball in 1996 but returned to play for the Reds in 1997 and again in 2001. In nine years of MLB, he played in 641 games and batted .263, with 39 home runs and 186 stolen bases. He led the major leagues in triples in 1992, with 14. Although the Braves reached the 1991 World Series, Sanders was playing football and did not compete in the postseason. He played in the 1992 World Series with them and had an excellent series, batting .533 with five stolen bases in four games.

Since retiring from competitive sports, Sanders has worked as a television analyst for NFL games and released several rap albums. During his athletic career, he was known as "Prime Time" and "Neon Deion" and was one of the most flamboyant athletes in history. He was inducted into the **Pro Football Hall of Fame** in 2011 and the **College Football Hall of Fame** in 2012.

SASKATCHEWAN ROUGHRIDERS. The Saskatchewan Roughriders are a team in the **Canadian Football League (CFL)**. They were founded in 1910 as the Regina Rugby Club, changed their name to the Regina Roughriders in 1924, and changed to their present name in 1948. They began play as members of the Western Canada Rugby Football Union and, in 1936, transferred to the newly formed Western Interprovincial Football Union, where they remained until 1958, when the CFL was formed.

The Roughriders are a publicly owned company, with no one individual allowed to own more than 20 voting shares. Although they have played in 18 **Grey Cups**, they have only won three, in 1966, 1989, and 2007. The Roughriders have played home games at the 30,000-seat Taylor Field in Regina, Saskatchewan, since 1936. Prior to 1936, the grounds were known as Park Hughes and did not contain permanent seating. In 2005, naming rights were purchased by the Mosaic Company, and the field is presently known as Mosaic Stadium at Taylor Field.

Among the Roughriders' head **coaches** have been Danny Barrett, Frank Filchock, Fred Grant, John Gregory, Eagle Keys, Don Matthews, Ken Miller, Steve Owen, and John Payne. Roughriders in the **Canadian Football Hall of Fame** include Roger Aldag, Ron Atchison, Bill Baker, Al Benecick, Hugh Campbell, Ken Charlton, Bill Clarke, Ray Elgaard, Eddie James, Bobby Jurasin, Ron Lancaster, Ed McQuarters, Don Narcisse, George Reed, Dave Ridgway, Martin Ruby, Neil "Piffles" Taylor, and Ted Urness.

SAYERS, GALE EUGENE. B. 30 May 1943, Wichita, Kansas. Gale Sayers could have possibly been the greatest **running back** in **football** history had injuries not drastically shortened his career. He was born in Kansas but raised in Nebraska and is a graduate of Omaha Central High School in Omaha, Nebraska, where he played football and was on the track team. As a long jumper on the track team, he set the Nebraska state high school record. He matriculated to the University of Kansas, where he starred as a running back on the **varsity** from 1962 to 1964. In his three years there, Kansas had a record of 17–12–1, and Sayers **rushed** for 2,675 yards, including one game in which he gained 283 yards in only 21 attempts.

Sayers was taken by the **Chicago Bears** in the first round of the 1965 **National Football League (NFL) Draft** as the fourth overall selection, and by the **Kansas City Chiefs** in the 1965 **American Football League** Draft as the fifth overall selection. He chose the Bears and played for them from 1965 to 1971. Sayers had a spectacular rookie season and set an NFL record (since broken) with 22 **touchdowns** for the season and even **passed** for one touchdown in only three pass attempts. He had a 96-yard **kickoff** return and 85-yard **punt** return among them and, on 12 December 1965, scored six touchdowns in one game, equaling the NFL record. This **tied** the NFL record previously set by **Ernie Nevers** and William "Dub" Jones and, through the 2012 season, the feat has not been duplicated since. Sayers was selected as NFL Rookie of the Year.

Sayers had two and a half more excellent seasons, but, midway through the 1968 campaign, he badly damaged his right knee. This effectively finished his career as a premier runner. He returned in 1969 and was able to lead the league in **rushing**, although he no longer had excellent speed. He managed to accomplish this by also leading the league in rushing attempts. Sayers was injured again in 1970 and played in only two games. In 1971, he was again only able to play in two games. In 1972, after a brief attempt at a comeback during the preseason, he retired after realizing he was no longer able to play effectively.

In his relatively brief seven-year NFL career, Sayers played in 68 regular-season games, ran 991 times for 4,956 yards and 39 touchdowns, and caught 112 passes for 1,307 yards and nine touchdowns. He also completed four of 18 passes for one touchdown. As a kick and punt **returner**, he returned 91 kickoffs and 27 punts. He averaged 30.6 yards per kick return and 14.5 yards per punt return and scored two punt return touchdowns and six kickoff return touchdowns, including ones of 103 yards and 96 yards. In three different NFL games Sayers scored three or more touchdowns, one by rushing, one by receiving a pass, and one on a kick return. The Bears did not compete in any **playoff** games during Sayers' time with them.

During his rehabilitation from his initial injury, Sayers was befriended by another Bears' running back, **Brian Piccolo**. Piccolo later developed cancer while with the Bears, and the relationship between the two athletes, one white and one black, became the subject for the popular film *Brian's Song*.

Since retiring from football, Sayers has become the athletic director at Southern Illinois University, owner of a Chicago-area computer supply company, and chairman of the consulting firm Sayers 40. He was inducted into both the **College Football Hall of Fame** and **Pro Football Hall of Fame** in 1977. *See also* FOOTBALL FILMS.

SCHMIDT, JOSEPH PAUL "JOE." B. 19 January 1932, Pittsburgh, Pennsylvania. Joe Schmidt attended Brentwood High School in Pittsburgh and the **University of Pittsburgh**, where he starred as a **linebacker**. Although only six feet tall and 195 pounds, a bit undersized for his position, his tenacity earned him the reputation as a hard-nosed player.

Schmidt was chosen by the **Detroit Lions** in the 1953 **National Football League (NFL) Draft** in the seventh round as the 85th overall selection and remained with the Detroit organization his entire **professional football** career, first as a player and then as a **coach**. With the Lions, he played all three linebacker positions—left, middle, and right—but was primarily used as their middle linebacker. He was a member of the NFL champions in both 1953 and 1957 and played on the losing side in the 1954 NFL Championship Game. In 1955, he recovered eight **fumbles** during the season to set an NFL record (since broken).

After his retirement from active play following the 1965 season caused by a series of injuries, Schmidt was named **assistant coach** of the Lions in 1966. The following year, he became head coach and remained in that job through 1972. In his six-year stint as coach, the team had a record of 43–34–7 and finished second in their division in four of the six years, reaching the **playoffs** only in 1970 but losing their divisional playoff game to the **Dallas Cowboys**. As a perfectionist, Schmidt became frustrated with coaching and, after the 1972 season, retired from football and became a manufacturer's representative in industry.

In his 13-year NFL career, he played in 155 regular-season games, **intercepted** 24 **passes** for two **touchdowns**, and recovered 17 fumbles for one touchdown. In four postseason games, Schmidt had two interceptions. He played in 10 **Pro Bowls** and was inducted into the **Pro Football Hall of Fame** in 1973 and the **College Football Hall of Fame** in 2000.

SCHNEIDER, JOHN GEORGE. *See* NESSER FAMILY.

SCREEN PASS. A screen **pass** is a short pass to a receiver, usually a **back**, who has **blockers** in front of him. It is sometimes used to foil a defensive **blitz** attack.

SEATTLE SEAHAWKS. The Seattle Seahawks have been a **professional football** team in the **National Football League (NFL)** since 1976. They played in the National Football Conference (NFC) West Division in 1976 but were moved to the American Football Conference West Division in 1977 and remained there until 2002, when they returned to the NFC West. Since 2002, they have played home games at a 67,000-seat **stadium** originally known as Seahawks Stadium but later renamed Qwest Field and, in 2011, renamed CenturyLink Field.

In their 37-year history from 1976 to 2012, the Seahawks have compiled a record of 280–300 in regular-season play and 9–12 in postseason **playoff** competition. Their best season was 2005, when they reached the **Super Bowl** but were defeated by the **Pittsburgh Steelers**. In their 10 other playoff years, they were defeated in the NFC championship once (1983), the divisional playoffs six times (1984, 1988, 2006, 2007, 2010, 2012), and the **wild-card playoff** four times (1987, 1999, 2003, 2004). Three of their playoff losses came in games that went into **overtime** (1987, 2003, 2006). In 2010, Seattle became the first team in NFL history to reach the playoffs with a losing record (7–9) in regular-season play and, in an upset, defeated the favored **New Orleans Saints** in the wild-card playoff game but were then defeated by the **Chicago Bears** in the divisional playoff game.

Seattle's **coaches** have been Jack Patera (1976–1982), Mike McCormack (interim 1982), Chuck Knox (1983–1991), Tom Flores (1992–1994), Dennis Erickson (1995–1997), Mike Holmgren (1999–2008), Jim Mora (2009), and Pete Carroll (2010–2012). Their best players have included **Pro Football Hall of Famers wide receiver Steve Largent** and defensive **tackle** Cortez Kennedy. Other of their top players include **running backs** Shaun Alexander, Curt Warner, Chris Warren, and Ricky Watters; **safety** Kenny Easley; **quarterbacks** Matt Hasselbeck, Dave Krieg, **Warren Moon**, and Jim Zorn; wide receivers Brian Blades, Joey Galloway, and Darrell Jackson, defensive **end** Jacob Green; **fullback** Mack Strong; tackle Walter Jones; and **linebacker** Lofa Tatupu.

SEAU, TIAINA BAUL, JR. "JUNIOR." B. 19 January 1969, San Diego, California. D. 2 May 2012, Oceanside, California. Although Junior Seau was born in California, his American **Samoan** parents returned to their native land and he was raised there as a child. The family returned to the West Coast, and he attended Oceanside High School in Oceanside. There, Seau starred on the **football** team and helped lead them to the California state 2A high school championship. He also played on the basketball team and was named player of the year for his section. In track and field, he won the league championship in shot put. Seau attended the **University of Southern California (USC)**, and, after sitting out his freshman year due to scholastic ineligibility, he helped lead the Trojans to the Pacific-10 Conference championship in 1988 and 1989, **Rose Bowl** appearances each of those years, and a two-year record of 19–4–1.

Seau passed up his senior year at USC and chose to enter the 1990 **National Football League (NFL) Draft**, where he was taken in the first round by the **San Diego Chargers** as the fifth overall selection. A six-foot, three-inch, 250-pound **linebacker**, he played with the Chargers from 1990 to 2002 and the **Miami Dolphins** from 2003 to 2005 and concluded his **professional football** career with the **New England Patriots** from 2006 to 2009. Injuries slowed him his last several seasons, and, in his last six seasons, he only played in all 16 regular-season games in one of those years. But in that year, 2007, he helped lead the Patriots to an undefeated 16–0 regular season, two playoff victories, and a game with the **New York Giants** in the **Super Bowl** (which the Patriots unfortunately lost). With the Chargers, Seau had played in the 1995 Super Bowl, also on the losing side.

In his 20-year NFL career, Seau played in 268 regular-season games, **intercepted** 18 **passes**, and recovered 18 **fumbles** for one **touchdown**. In 1999, he caught two passes for eight yards. He played in the **Pro Bowl** each year from 1991 to 2002.

In retirement, Seau owned a restaurant in Mission Valley, California. He also owned a clothing line and was involved with the Junior Seau Foundation, which raises money for programs to support young people. On 2 May 2012, he died from an apparently self-inflicted shotgun wound to the chest.

SENIOR BOWL. The Senior Bowl is an annual postseason all-star game for college seniors who have exhausted their eligibility for **college football**. The first game took place in 1950 at the 36,000-seat Gator Bowl Stadium in Jacksonville, Florida, and all subsequent games have been played in Mobile, Alabama, at the 40,000-seat Ernest F. Ladd Memorial Stadium, renamed Ladd-Peebles Stadium in 1997. The game serves as a tryout for **professional football**, and professional scouts attend the week-long pregame practice, as well as the game. Teams are divided into North and South squads and are **coached** by active **National Football League** coaches.

SHARPE, SHANNON. B. 26 June 1968, Chicago, Illinois. Although born in Chicago, Shannon Sharpe and his older brother, Sterling, were raised in Georgia and attended Glennville High School. While Sterling attended the integrated University of South Carolina, Shannon went to Savannah State College, a historically black school. There, he was named the **conference** player of the year following his sophomore year in 1987.

A six-foot, two-inch, 225-pound **tight end**, Sharpe was not chosen in the 1990 **National Football League (NFL) Draft** until the seventh round. He was taken by the **Denver Broncos** as the 192nd overall selection. Sharpe played with Denver from 1990 to 1999, when injuries limited him to just five games that year. In 2000 and 2001, he was a member of the **Baltimore Ravens** and then returned to Denver to conclude his NFL career in 2002 and 2003. He was a member of the **Super Bowl** winners in Denver in 1998 and 1999 and Baltimore in 2001.

In his 14-year NFL career, Sharpe played in 204 regular-season games, caught 815 **passes** for 10,060 yards and 62 **touchdowns**, and ran only three times for nine yards and no touchdowns. In 18 postseason games, he caught 62 passes for 814 yards and four touchdowns.

Since retiring from active play, Sharpe has worked as a studio analyst covering NFL games. His outspoken nature and lively sense of humor have made him one of the more popular analysts. His brother, Sterling, also had a fine NFL career as a **running back** with the **Green Bay Packers** from 1988 to 1994, but his pro football career was cut short by a neck injury suffered in 1994. He, too, works as a television football analyst. Shannon was inducted into the **Pro Football Hall of Fame** in 2011 and in his enshrinement speech said, "I'm the only pro football player that's in the Hall of Fame, and the second-best player in my own family."

SHOTGUN FORMATION. The shotgun formation is an offensive formation first used during the 1950s and 1960s. In it, the **quarterback** lines up five to seven yards behind the **center** rather than immediately behind him, as in most other formations, and the three other **backs** are spread to become more effective **pass** receivers. It is primarily used for passing plays.

SHOULDER PADS. Shoulder pads are one type of protective equipment worn by **football** players. They were first used as early as the 1890s and throughout the years have become a standard piece of equipment. *See also* FACE MASK; HELMET.

SHREVEPORT PIRATES. The Shreveport Pirates were a **professional football** team in the **Canadian Football League (CFL)** in 1994 and 1995. They played their home games at the 53,000-seat Independence Stadium in Shreveport, Louisiana. Former **Green Bay Packer** star Forrest Gregg was the Pirates' head **coach**. The 1994 team had a record of 3–15 and finished last in the CFL East Division. The Pirates improved slightly to 5–13 in 1995. Among the team's best players were **quarterback** Billy Joe Tolliver, **wide receiver** Charles Thompson, **running back** Martin Patton, kick **returner** Freeman Baysinger; and Swedish-born **kicker** Björn Nittmo. The team was disbanded after the 1995 season.

SHULA, DONALD FRANCIS "DON." B. 4 January 1930, Grand River, Ohio. Although Don Shula played **professional football** for seven seasons in the **National Football League (NFL)**, he is best known for his exceptional **coaching** abilities. He attended Harvey High School in Painesville, Ohio, a small town about 30 miles northeast of Cleveland. Shula then went to John Carroll University, also in the Cleveland area. He played football in both high school and college but was far from being a star.

A five-foot, 11-inch, 190-pound defensive **back**, Shula was taken by the **Cleveland Browns** in the ninth round of the 1951 NFL **Draft** as the 110th selection. He played for the Browns in 1951 and 1952 and was a member of the NFL team that won their division championship and played in the NFL Championship Game both years, albeit in a losing effort. He was traded to the newly formed **Baltimore Colts** for the 1953 season in a 15-player trade, the largest in the NFL to that point. Shula played for the Colts from 1953 to 1956 and concluded his professional playing career with one year with the **Washington Redskins**. In his seven-year NFL playing career, he appeared in 73 regular-season games and had 21 **interceptions** and four **fumble** recoveries. He caught one **pass** for six yards and **rushed** twice for three yards.

Shula then turned to coaching and, for the next 38 years, was employed as a football coach. He began in 1958 as an **assistant coach** at the University of Virginia coaching the defensive backs. In 1959, he moved to the University of Kentucky in the same role. The **Detroit Lions** of the NFL hired him as defensive coordinator in 1960, and he remained in that position through the 1962 season. Although only 33 years old, Shula received his big opportunity and was named head coach of the Baltimore Colts in 1963. He was their coach for seven seasons, winning the NFL championship with them in 1968 but being upset by the **New York Jets** in the **Super Bowl** on 12 January 1969.

In 1970, Shula became coach of the **Miami Dolphins** and remained with them for the next 26 years. During that time, he led them to five Super Bowls (1972, 1973, 1974, 1983, 1985) and Super Bowl championships in 1973 and 1974. The 1972 team is the only team in NFL history to win all of their regular-season and postseason games. Shula retired at the age of 65, following the 1995 season. In 33 years as an NFL head coach, his teams compiled a record of 328–156–6 in the regular season and 19–17 in the postseason. He holds NFL coaching records for most games coached, most total victories, and most consecutive seasons coached.

Shula was inducted into the **Pro Football Hall of Fame** as a coach in 1997 and has also been honored by having both the John Carroll University football **stadium** and an expressway in Miami named for him. Since 2002, an annual **college football** game between Florida Atlantic University and Florida International University has been called the Shula Bowl.

SIDE JUDGE. *See* OFFICIALS.

SIDELINE. The sideline is the side boundary of the **football field**. Once a ball carrier touches it, the play ends. A player not carrying the ball can legally **run out of bounds** and then return to the field of play to **block** or **tackle**.

SIMPSON, ORENTHAL JAMES "O. J.," "THE JUICE." B. 9 July 1947, San Francisco, California. O. J. Simpson has led two lives. In the first, from birth through the early 1990s, he was one of the best and most popular **football** players, a Hollywood actor, and popular star in television commercials. In the second, which began in the early 1990s, he was tried and exonerated for murder, tried and convicted of wrongful death, heavily fined, and tried and convicted of multiple crimes (including robbery). His life since 1994 has been spent in courtrooms and prison.

Simpson was raised in the San Francisco area and attended Galileo High School, where he starred in football. After graduation, he spent two years at City College of San Francisco, where he continued his football exploits. He concluded his education at the **University of Southern California (USC)**, where he led the nation in **rushing** in both 1967 and 1968. During those two years, he led USC to records of 10–1 and 9–1–1, **Rose Bowl** appearances in each year, and the national championship in 1967. In 1968, Simpson won both the **Heisman Trophy** and **Maxwell Award**. He also ran track at USC and was a member of a world-record-breaking relay team in 1967.

Nicknamed "The Juice," the six-foot, two-inch, 210-pound **running back** was selected by the **Buffalo Bills** of the **American Football League (AFL)** as the first overall selection in the combined American Football League–**National Football League (NFL) Draft** in 1969. His professional career started slowly, but, in his fourth year, 1972, he led the NFL in rushing yardage. In 1973, he became the first NFL player to rush for more than 2,000 yards in one season, finishing at 2,003 in 14 games. That record stood until 1984, when **Eric Dickerson** surpassed it with 2,105 yards, albeit in 16 games. Simpson's average of 143.1 yards per game remains the best in that category and has not been topped as of the 2012 season.

On 16 September 1973, Simpson ran for 250 yards in one game, setting another NFL record and tying a long-forgotten professional mark set in the **All-America Football Conference** by Orban "Spec" Sanders in 1947. On 25 November 1976, he bettered his record by rushing for 273 yards, but it only stood for one year before **Walter Payton** surpassed it in 1977. Simpson remains the only NFL player to rush for 250 yards or more in one game twice in a career. After injuries limited his play to just seven games in 1977, he was traded to his hometown **San Francisco 49ers** in 1978. He concluded his pro career with two unspectacular years in San Francisco.

In his 11-year combined AFL–NFL career, Simpson played in 135 regular-season games, ran 2,404 times for 11,236 yards and 61 **touchdowns**, caught

203 **passes** for 2,142 yards and 14 touchdowns, and completed six of 16 passes for 110 yards and one touchdown. He also returned 33 **kickoffs** for an average of 30.0 yards per return and had one 95-yard touchdown as a **returner**. He played in only one postseason game, in 1974, when he ran 15 times for 49 yards and caught three passes for 37 yards and one touchdown. Simpson was inducted into the **College Football Hall of Fame** in 1983 and the **Pro Football Hall of Fame** in 1985.

While a star at Buffalo, Simpson had made several Hollywood films and television shows. After retiring from active play, he continued as an actor and was featured by Hertz rental cars in a series of televised advertisements. He also worked on *Monday Night Football* from 1983 to 1985.

In 1992, Simpson divorced his second wife, Nicole Brown, and his legal troubles began shortly thereafter. On 13 June 1994, Brown and her friend, Ronald Goldman, were found murdered outside her home in Los Angeles. Evidence collected by police led them to suspect Simpson of the crime. He was told to turn himself into the police, and, when he did not, he was spotted riding in a Ford Bronco on a Los Angeles freeway. He became the subject of a low-speed chase by police that was televised nationally. Arrested later that night, he was tried later that year in one of the most publicized trials in U.S. history. Although Simpson was found not guilty of murder on 3 October 1995, he was then tried in a civil court for "wrongful death" and found guilty on 3 February 1997. He was obliged to pay $33.5 million in damages.

Simpson was in and out of court during the next 10 years for various infractions, but, in September 2007, he and several other men allegedly entered a room in a Las Vegas, Nevada, hotel and took sports memorabilia at gunpoint. In October 2008, he and one of his accomplices were found guilty on multiple felony counts, including criminal conspiracy, assault, robbery, and kidnapping, and, in December 2008, he was sentenced to 33 years in prison. As of 2012, he remains incarcerated at the Lovelock Correctional Center in Nevada with the possibility of probation not occurring until 2017.

SINGLE. *See* ROUGE.

SIRAGUSA, ANTHONY "TONY," "GOOSE." B. 14 May 1967, Kenilworth, New Jersey. Tony Siragusa is a graduate of David Brearley High School in Kenilworth, New Jersey. He was the New Jersey state high school wrestling champion and a defensive **lineman**, **punter**, and placekicker on the **football** team. He played football from 1986 to 1989 for the **University of Pittsburgh**. In those four years, Pittsburgh had a record of 28–16–2.

Although six feet, three inches tall and 330 pounds, Siragusa was not **drafted** in the 1990 **National Football League (NFL)** Draft and was signed as a free agent by the **Indianapolis Colts** in 1990. He played defensive **tackle** for them from 1990 to 1996 and was with the **Baltimore Ravens** from 1997 to 2001. He was a member of the 2000 Ravens **Super Bowl** championship team. The 2000 Ravens also set an NFL record for fewest points allowed in a 16-game season, and Siragusa was an integral part of the **defense** that created the record. In his 12-year NFL career, he played in 169 regular-season games and was credited with 22 sacks and 488 tackles.

Since retiring from active play, "Goose," as he is termed by his colleagues, has worked as a football analyst and uses the novel approach of reporting the game from the **sidelines**. He has also appeared in a recurring role in the television series *The Sopranos* and done some other film work as well. In addition, Siragusa is a partner in a restaurant chain. As a result of these activities, he has become much better known to the public than when he played as a virtually anonymous lineman in the NFL.

SIX-MAN FOOTBALL. In some parts of the United States, notably Texas, for much of the 20th century, some high schools with small enrollments played a version of **football** using just six players. There were other variations to the rules. Some schools played an eight-man football version. In modern times, as high schools have been consolidated and enrollments expanded, this variety of the sport has virtually disappeared.

SLOTBACK. Canadian football employs 12 men on a team rather than the 11 used in the American **football** game. The 12th man is known as the slotback and is used as an additional **running back**, **wide receiver**, or **blocker**. The term *slotback* is also occasionally used in the American version to denote a **back** positioned between a wide receiver and offensive **tackle** with similar versatile duties to the Canadian position.

SMITH, CHARLES AARON "BUBBA." B. 28 February 1945, Orange, Texas. D. 3 August 2011, Los Angeles, California. Bubba Smith attended Charlton-Pollard High School in Beaumont, Texas, where he played **football** for his father, Willie Ray Smith Sr., the **coach** of the team and one of the best high school coaches in the area. Although Bubba wanted to attend the **University of Texas**, he could not do so since the school had not yet integrated its sports teams. He enrolled at **Michigan State University** and starred on their teams as a defensive **end**. In his junior and senior years, he helped lead them to a combined record of 19–1–1 in 1965 and 1966 and the national championship each year.

The six-foot, seven-inch, 265-pound Smith (whose weight escalated toward 300 pounds during his professional career) was selected by the **Baltimore Colts** as the first overall selection in the 1967 **National Football**

League (NFL) Draft. He played for the Colts from 1967 to 1971, spent the next two years with the **Oakland Raiders**, and concluded his NFL playing career with the Houston Oilers. With the Colts, he played on the losing side in the 1969 **Super Bowl** and was a member of the Super Bowl champions in 1971. In his nine-year NFL career, Smith appeared in 111 regular-season games and was credited with four **fumble** recoveries. He played in the **Pro Bowl** in 1970 and 1971. His younger brother, Lawrence "Tody" Smith, also a big man, at six feet, five inches tall and 250 pounds, played six years in the NFL and was also a defensive end.

After retiring from football, Bubba became an actor and appeared in more than 40 Hollywood films and television episodes. He had a leading role in the Police Academy series of films. He was inducted into the **College Football Hall of Fame** in 1988. Smith died from acute drug intoxication resulting from an overdose of a weight-loss drug but also had had a history of heart disease.

SMITH, EMMITT JAMES, III. B. 15 May 1969, Pensacola, Florida. **Running back** Emmitt Smith holds **National Football League (NFL)** career records for most **rushing** attempts, most rushing yardage, and most rushing **touchdowns**. He is considered by some to be the greatest runner in NFL history. Smith began his **football** career at Escambia High School in Pensacola, Florida, and, while there, played in 49 games and ran for more than 100 yards in 45 of them, compiling a remarkable total of 8,804 yards rushing with 106 touchdowns. He received a scholarship to the **University of Florida** and continued his football success there. While still a freshman in 1987, he rushed for 224 yards in one game and set an all-time Florida record. After three years at Florida, he had rushed for a total of 3,928 yards and 36 touchdowns. After Florida changed **coaches** in 1990, Smith decided to forgo his senior year and made himself eligible for the NFL **Draft**. He did, however, continue his studies at Florida and eventually received his bachelor's degree several years later.

Smith was chosen in the first round of the 1990 NFL Draft by the **Dallas Cowboys** as the 17th overall selection. He played with the Cowboys for 13 years, before spending two years with the **Arizona Cardinals**. Although only five feet, nine inches tall, he was a strong 210 pounds. Smith helped lead the Cowboys to **Super Bowl** victories in 1993, 1994, and 1996 and was named the Super Bowl Most Valuable Player following the 1994 Super Bowl. That year, he was also voted the NFL Most Valuable Player.

In his 15-year NFL career, Smith played in 226 regular-season games, ran 4,409 times for 18,355 yards and 164 touchdowns, and caught 515 **passes** for 3,224 yards and 11 touchdowns. In 2004, he completed his only pass attempt, which went for a 21-yard touchdown. In 17 postseason games, he ran 349 times for 1,586 yards and 19 touchdowns and caught 46 passes for 342 yards and two touchdowns. Smith also played in eight **Pro Bowls**.

After announcing his retirement from active play following the 2004 season as a member of the Arizona Cardinals, he signed a one-day contract with the Dallas Cowboys and then retired again so that he would retire from **professional football** as a member of the Cowboys, the team with which he spent 13 years in the NFL. Since retiring, Smith has worked as a television studio analyst for NFL games and become involved in real-estate development. He was inducted into the **College Football Hall of Fame** in 2006 and the **Pro Football Hall of Fame** in 2010.

SOCCER. Soccer is a sport known as **football** throughout most of the world, with the exception of the United States, Canada, Australia, and New Zealand. The sport originated in 19th-century England and was originally called association football. It is by far the most widely played team sport in the world. In soccer, touching the ball with the hands and arms is forbidden, and players generally use their feet or head to propel the ball. In the last half of the 20th century, American football teams began hiring soccer players as placekickers, and they changed the style of placekicking so that the side of the foot, rather than the toe, makes contact with the ball. Although the sport is called football throughout the world, it bears less resemblance to American football than does the sport of **rugby**.

SOUTHEASTERN CONFERENCE (SEC). The Southeastern Conference (SEC) is an organization of **major colleges** and universities that compete athletically in the **National Collegiate Athletic Association**. The SEC was established in 1932 and is based in Birmingham, Alabama. As of 2011, the 12 member schools were the **University of Alabama**, the University of Arkansas, **Auburn University**, the **University of Florida**, the **University of Georgia**, the University of Kentucky, **Louisiana State University**, Mississippi State University, the University of Mississippi (also known as Ole Miss), the University of South Carolina, the **University of Tennessee**, and Vanderbilt University. In 2012 **Texas A&M University** and the University of Missouri were added to the SEC, bringing the total number of members to 14.

SOUTHERN CALIFORNIA, UNIVERSITY OF (USC). The University of Southern California (USC) is located in Los Angeles, California. Their **football** program began in 1888 and has been one of the most successful in the country. They have won three times as many **Rose Bowl** games than any other school. Their record in that event is 24–9, and second-place **Michigan** is 8–12. USC has had seven **Heisman Trophy** winners, and the school is tied with the **University of Notre Dame** and **Ohio State University** for that distinction. Their overall record through 2012 is 755–302–53. In addition, the Trojans have competed in 49 postseason **bowl games**, with a record of 31–17 and one win vacated. They have been selected as national collegiate champions 17 times, in 1928, 1929, 1931, 1932, 1933, 1939, 1962, 1967, 1972, 1974, 1976, 1978, 1979, 2002, 2003, 2004, and 2007.

The 92,000-seat **Los Angeles Memorial Coliseum** has been their home field since its opening in 1923. USC football teams have competed in the Pacific Coast Conference (now known as the **Pacific-12 Conference**) of the **National Collegiate Athletic Association (NCAA)** since 1922. They have rivalries with several teams. One is the **University of California, Los Angeles (UCLA)**. The two teams have played most years since 1929, with the winner receiving a trophy known as the "Victory Bell." USC leads UCLA in the series, 44–29–7, with two wins vacated. Another rival is the University of Notre Dame. They have played one another since 1926 (except for three years during World War II). Notre Dame leads that series, 44–34–5, with one win vacated in the game played for the Jeweled Shillelagh. **Stanford University** and the University of California, Berkeley, are also rivals and have a long series of games with USC.

USC has had several successful head **coaches**. Howard Jones led the Trojans to five Rose Bowl victories in his 16 years as coach (1925–1940). His record during that time was 121–36–13. John McKay was coach from 1960 to 1975. His record was 127–40–8. Under McKay, the Trojans went to the Rose Bowl eight times, winning five, and the Liberty Bowl once, which they won. John Robinson was USC coach from 1976 to 1982 and again from 1993 to 1997. In his 12 years there, his record was 104–35–4, with four Rose Bowl victories and a record of 3–1 in other bowl games. From 2001 to 2009, Pete Carroll was the USC coach. His record of 97–19 and 7–2 in bowl games was marred by NCAA accusations of violations and subsequent vacating of Trojan victories.

There are 30 former USC players in the **College Football Hall of Fame**. They are **halfbacks Marcus Allen**, Jon Arnett, Mike Garrett, **Frank Gifford**, Mort Kaer, Erny Pinckert, **O. J. Simpson**, and Charles White; **running backs** Ricky Bell and Anthony Davis; **quarterbacks** Morley Drury and Irvine "Cotton" Warburton; **fullback** Sam Cunningham; **ends** Hal Bedsole, Paul Cleary and Charles Young; **wide receiver** Lynn Swann; **linemen** John Baker, Tay Brown, Brad Budde, John Ferraro, Mike McKeever, Dan McMillan, Marvin Powell, Aaron Rosenberg, Ernie Smith, Harry Smith, and Ron Yary; **safety** Ronnie Lott; and **linebacker** Richard Wood. Head coaches Howard Jones, John McKay, and John Robinson have also been enshrined.

USC has also had other former players who have found successful careers in other fields. Actors John Wayne (then known as Marion Morrison) and Ward Bond were both linemen for the Trojans in the 1920s, as were film directors Aaron Rosenberg and Nate Barragar.

Through 2012, there have been 449 **professional football** players who have attended USC, the second most of all schools. There have been 421 in the **National Football League**, 15 in the **American Football League**, and 13 in the **All-America Football Conference**. They include Marcus Allen, Jon Arnett, Ricky Bell, Joey Browner, Rudy Bukich, **Reggie Bush**, Lyndon Crow, Sam Cunningham, Jack Del Rio, Vince Evans, Mike Garrett, Frank Gifford, Pat Haden, Keyshawn Johnson, Matt Leinart, Ronnie Lott, Rod Martin, Bruce Matthews, Clay Matthews Jr., Tim McDonald, Willie McGinest, Marlin McKeever, Ron Mix, Anthony Muñoz, Carson Palmer, Rodney Peete, Troy Polamalu, Marvin Powell, Mark Sanchez, **Tiaina "Junior" Seau**, O. J. Simpson, Dennis Smith, Lynn Swann, Mosi Tatupu, Willie Wood, and Ron Yary.

SOUTHWEST CONFERENCE. The Southwest Conference was an organization of **major colleges** and universities that competed athletically. It was established in 1914 and was one of the major athletic conferences in **college football**. For much of its existence, the Southwest Conference football champion received an automatic invitation to the **Cotton Bowl** Classic game. During the 1980s, several of the schools were penalized for recruiting violations, and the quality of play in the league suffered. In 1991, the University of Arkansas left to join another conference, and, several years later, most of the other schools did the same. As a result, the conference was disbanded in May 1996. Four schools were conference members for the entire existence of the Southwest Conference. They are Baylor University, Rice Institute (later Rice University), the **University of Texas**, and **Texas A&M University**. Other members were the University of Arkansas (1914–1991), the University of Houston (1971–1996), Oklahoma A&M University (1919–1925), the **University of Oklahoma** (1914–1919), Phillips University (1920), Southern Methodist University (1918–1996), Southwestern University (1914–1916), Texas Christian University (1923–1996), and Texas Tech University (1956–1996).

SPECIAL TEAMS. In modern football, teams use players in kicking situations who may or may not be part of their regular offensive or defensive teams. Teams have different offensive units for **kickoffs**, **punts**, and **field goal** and **conversion** tries, while the defensive team matches them with unique units for kickoff returns, punt returns, and field goal and conversion **blocking** teams.

SPIKE. In recent years, **quarterbacks** who are attempting to conserve time have been allowed to deliberately **pass** the ball directly down to the ground, causing an **incomplete pass** and its consequent stoppage of time. This technique is known as a spike. Although the play results in a loss of **down**, stopping the clock from advancing is usually seen as more advantageous.

SPLIT END. The split end is a **football position** in which the **end** lines up on the **line of scrimmage** several yards from his adjacent offensive **tackle** teammate. The split end's main function is to **run** downfield to catch **passes**. He is usually one of the faster players on the team.

ST. LOUIS CARDINALS. *See* ARIZONA CARDINALS.

ST. LOUIS RAMS. The St. Louis Rams are a **professional football** team in the **National Football League (NFL)**. They began in 1937 as the Cleveland Rams. In 1943, they suspended operations for the season due to World War II. After winning the NFL championship in 1945, they became the first major-league sports franchise to move to the West Coast and played as the Los Angeles Rams from 1946 through the 1994 season. In 1995, they relocated to St. Louis. The Rams have played in the West Division of the National Football Conference since 1970.

In Cleveland, Ohio, their home fields were the 83,000-seat Cleveland Municipal Stadium (1937, 1939–1941, 1945), the 21,000-seat League Park (1937, 1942, 1944–1945), and Shaw Stadium (1938), a small high school field in East Cleveland. When they moved to Los Angeles, the team played at the 93,000-seat **Los Angeles Memorial Coliseum** from 1946 to 1979 and, from 1980 to 1994, at the 69,000-seat Anaheim Stadium in Anaheim, California (about 30 miles southeast of Los Angeles). One of the reasons for the move to Anaheim was that the NFL telecasts were blacked out in the home city when games were not sold out, and, with the huge capacity of Los Angeles Memorial Coliseum, they were seldom sold out, thus minimizing the local television opportunities. When the Rams moved to St. Louis, they played at the 60,000-seat Busch Memorial Stadium for their first four home games, until the 67,000-seat Trans World Dome (since renamed the Edward Jones Dome) was available on 12 November 1995, where they have played since.

The Rams' overall record from 1937 to 2012 is 520–514–21 in regular-season play and 19–24 in **playoff** competition. They won the NFL championship in 1945 and 1951 and lost the NFL Championship Game in 1949, 1950, and 1955. In 1952, they lost a postseason conference tiebreaker. In 1967 and 1969, they lost conference playoff games. Since the **American Football League**–National Football League merger in 1970, the Rams have qualified for the postseason playoffs 19 times. They won the **Super Bowl** in 1999, lost the Super Bowl in 1979 and 2001, lost the conference championship six times, lost the divisional playoffs five times, and lost the **wild-card playoff** five times.

Rams' head **coaches** throughout the years have been Hugo Bezdek (1937–1938), Art Lewis (interim 1938), Earl "Dutch" Clark (1939–1942, 1943), Aldo Donelli (1944), Adam Walsh (1945–1946), Bob Snyder (1947), Clark Shaughnessy (1948–1949), Joe Stydahar (1950–1952), Hampton Pool (1952–1954), Sid Gillman (1955–1959), **Bob Waterfield** (1960–1962), Harland Svare (1962–1965), **George Allen** (1966–1970), Tommy Prothro (1971–1972), Chuck Knox (1973–1977, 1992–1994), Ray Malavasi (1978–1982), John Robinson (1983–1991), Rich Brooks (1995–1996), Dick Vermeil (1997–1999), Mike Martz (2000–2005), Joe Vitt (interim 2005), Scott Linehan (2006–2008), Jim Haslett (interim 2008), Steve Spagnuolo (2009–2011), and Jeff Fisher (2012).

Rams in the **Pro Football Hall of Fame** are **quarterbacks Norm Van Brocklin** and Bob Waterfield; offensive **tackles** Bob Brown and Jackie Slater; **running backs Eric Dickerson**, Marshall Faulk, and **Elroy "Crazylegs" Hirsch**; **end** Tom Fears; defensive ends **Deacon Jones** and Jack Youngblood; **guard** Tom Mack; defensive tackle **Merlin Olsen**; **kicker/linebacker** Les Richter; coach George Allen; and owner **Dan (Farrell) Reeves**. Other noteworthy players for the Rams include quarterbacks Sam Bradford, Jim Everett, Roman Gabriel, Pat Haden, John Hadl, and Kurt Warner; running backs Jon Arnett, Jerome Bettis, Steven Jackson, Lawrence McCutcheon, and Dan Towler; receivers Jim Benton, Isaac Bruce, Henry Ellard, Torry Holt, **Harold Jackson**, and Del Shofner; **cornerback** Ed Meador; linebackers Marlin McKeever, Jack Pardee, and Jim Youngblood; defensive **back** Leroy Irvin; and **punter** Sean Landeta.

STADIUM. Most **football** is played in large arenas, often seating between 50,000 and 100,000 spectators. Most of these facilities are known as stadiums, although some, for example, the **Rose Bowl**, Carrier Dome, **Lambeau Field**, and Candlestick Park, use such names as bowls, domes, fields, or parks. *See also* COWBOYS STADIUM; HARVARD STADIUM; LOS ANGELES MEMORIAL COLISEUM; YALE BOWL.

STAGG, AMOS ALONZO. B. 16 August 1862, West Orange, New Jersey. D. 17 March 1965, Stockton, California. Amos Alonzo Stagg came in on the ground floor of two of America's greatest sports: **football** and basketball. He attended Orange High School, Phillips Exeter Academy, and **Yale University**. He played baseball and football at Yale and was a member of the very first **All-American** team in 1889 as an **end**. From 1885 to 1889, Stagg played on the Yale football teams that had a combined record of 53–2–1 and were national champions in 1886, 1887, and 1888. The 1888 team won all 15 games and outscored their opponents, 694–0.

Stagg entered Yale Divinity School but found that he was not a good speaker and decided to become a physical education instructor. He enrolled at the YMCA Training School at Springfield, Massachusetts, and was there from 1890 to 1892. He was **coach** of the football team, and, while he did not play in James Naismith's very first basketball game, he did play in the first public demonstration of the new sport. In 1892, Stagg was hired by the University of Chicago as associate professor and director of physical culture and athletics. On 16 January 1896, he was the coach of the first intercollegiate basketball game played with five players on each team. (In earlier years, the number of players varied.)

Stagg created a national interscholastic championship basketball tournament, held in Chicago from 1917 to 1931. He remained at Chicago until 1932, when he was retired at the mandatory retirement age. He was on various **Olympic** committees and was involved with coaching the 1924 U.S. Olympic track team. After being forced to retire at the age of 70, he was hired by the College of the Pacific in 1933 to coach their football team and remained there until 1946. After he resigned at the age of 84, Stagg worked as an **assistant coach** to his son at Susquehanna College for the next six years. He then moved to a warmer climate in California and worked another six years as **punting** and kicking coach at Stockton Junior College. He finally retired from coaching at the age of 98. His record as a football head coach was 314–181–35.

In the latter part of his life, Stagg was often referred to as "The Grand Old Man." Although most of the major work in his life was in the sport of football, he was enshrined in the Naismith Memorial Basketball Hall of Fame in 1959, in the category of contributor, for his early promotion of the sport. He had previously been enshrined in the inaugural class of the **College Football Hall of Fame** as both a player and coach in 1951. Stagg died on 17 March 1965, at 102 years of age, in Stockton, California.

STANFORD UNIVERSITY. Stanford University is located in Stanford, California. Their **football** program began in 1891, and, since then, through 2012, Cardinal teams have compiled a record of 586–425–49. In addition, they have competed in 24 postseason **bowl games**, with a record of 11–12–1. They were selected as national collegiate champions in 1926 and 1940. Since 1919, Stanford football teams have competed in the Pacific Coast Conference (currently known as the **Pacific-12 Conference**) of the **National Collegiate**

Athletic Association. Home games since 1921 have been played at Stanford Stadium on the school's campus. Although the **stadium's** seating capacity was once 85,500, in 2005, the original stadium was demolished and a new 50,000-seat stadium bearing the same name was constructed. Stanford's main rival is the **University of California.** The teams have met nearly annually since 1892 in a contest known simply as the "Big Game." Through 2012, the series stands at Stanford 53 victories, California 43 victories, and 10 ties.

Stanford's most notable **coach** was **Glenn "Pop" Warner.** He coached them from 1924 to 1932 and had a record of 71–17–8. Other successful Stanford head coaches include **Walter Camp** (1892, 1894–1895; 11–3–3), Andy Kerr (1922–1923; 11–7), Claude Thornhill (1933–1939; 35–25–7), Chuck Taylor (1951–1957; 40–29–2), John Ralston (1963–1971; 55–36–3), Jack Christiansen (1972–1976; 30–22–3), Bill Walsh (1977–1978, 1992–1994; 34–24–1), Tyrone Willingham (1995–2001; 44–36–1), and Jim Harbaugh (2007–2010; 29–21).

Stanford alumni in the **College Football Hall of Fame** are **quarterbacks Frankie Albert**, John Brodie, **John Elway**, and Jim Plunkett (a **Heisman Trophy** winner); **ends** Chris Burford, Bill McColl, and James Moscrip; **guards** Bill Corbus and Chuck Taylor; **halfbacks** Hugh Gallarneau and Bob Hamilton; **fullbacks** Bobby Grayson and **Ernie Nevers**; **wide receiver** Ken Margerum; **linebacker** Jeff Siemon; and **tackles** Bob Reynolds and Paul Wiggin. Stanford coaches inducted in the Hall are Walter Camp, Andy Kerr, John Ralston, Clark Shaughnessy, Glenn "Pop" Warner, and Fielding "Hurry-Up" Yost.

Through 2012, there have been 210 **professional football** players who have attended Stanford, 202 in the **National Football League**, five in the **American Football League**, and three in the **All-America Football Conference**. They include John Brodie, Pat Donovan, Chris Draft, John Elway, Jason Fisk, Tony Hill, **James Lofton**, John Lynch, Ed McCaffrey, Ernie Nevers, Jim Plunkett, Jeff Siemon, Norm Standlee, Randy Vataha, Gene A. Washington, and Bob Whitfield.

STARR, BRYAN BARTLETT "BART." B. 9 January 1934, Montgomery, Alabama. Bart Starr is best remembered as the **quarterback** of **Vince Lombardi's** great **Green Bay Packers** teams of the 1960s and the winning quarterback of the **National Football League's (NFL)** first two **Super Bowls**. He attended Sidney Lanier High School in Montgomery, Alabama, and quarterbacked them to an undefeated season as a junior. He received a scholarship to the **University of Alabama** and played on their team for four seasons, from 1952 to 1955 (in 1952 the **Southeastern Conference** allowed freshman to play on the **varsity** teams). Starr played sparingly as a freshman but was the starting quarterback and **punter** as a sophomore. Alabama was Southeastern Conference champion that year and played in the 1 January 1954 **Cotton Bowl** game. In that contest, which Alabama lost to Rice University, 28–6, Alabama player Tommy Lewis came off his team's bench to **tackle** Rice **halfback** Dicky Moegle, who was running down the **sideline**.

Starr severely sprained his back prior to his junior year and, consequently, saw little action that season. During his senior year, although fully healed, Alabama's new **coach** preferred not to play his seniors, and Starr again played sparingly. As a result, in the 1956 NFL **Draft**, Starr was not one of the prime prospects and was not selected until the 17th round as the 200th player taken that year. The Green Bay Packers made him their draft choice, and he signed with them.

Starr's **professional football** career began slowly, and he was used as a backup quarterback for his first few seasons. He did not become Green Bay's regular starting quarterback until the fifth game of the 1960 season. From then until his final season with the Packers, in 1971, Starr started as quarterback in nearly every game. He helped lead the Packers to the NFL Championship Game in 1960, which they lost to the **Philadelphia Eagles**. The Packers then won the NFL title in 1961, 1962, 1965, 1966, and 1967. The latter two seasons, the team also won the first two **American Football League**–National Football League Championship Games (later known as the Super Bowl), and Starr was named the game's Most Valuable Player both years.

In his 16-year NFL career, Starr played in 196 regular-season games, completed 1,808 **passes** in 3,149 attempts for 24,718 yards and 152 **touchdowns**, and ran 247 times for 1,308 yards and 15 touchdowns. In 10 postseason games, he completed 130 passes in 213 attempts for 1,753 yards and 15 touchdowns and ran eight times for 26 yards and one touchdown. He played in four **Pro Bowls**.

In 1972, after he retired from active play, Starr remained with the Packers as an **assistant coach**. In 1973 and 1974, he worked as an NFL broadcaster. In 1975, he became the head coach of the Packers. As head coach, his teams were not nearly as successful as when he was a player, and Green Bay's record from 1975 to 1983 was just 52–76–3 in the regular season. They only reached the **playoffs** in 1982 and lost their second playoff game that year. Starr was replaced by former teammate Forrest Gregg as coach of the Packers in 1984. He was inducted into the **Pro Football Hall of Fame** in 1977.

STATUE OF LIBERTY PLAY. The statue of liberty play is seldom seen in modern **football**. It occurs when the **quarterback** goes back to **pass** and raises his arm as if to do so but one of the other offensive players **runs** behind him and takes the ball for a running play.

STAUBACH, ROGER THOMAS. B. 5 February 1942, Cincinnati, Ohio. Roger Staubach was a **Heisman Trophy** winner and Vietnam veteran when he began his **professional football** career at the age of 27. He attended Purcell High School in Cincinnati and spent one year at the New Mexico Military Institute before enrolling at the United States Naval Academy (**Navy**). He played **quarterback** for Navy's **varsity** team from 1962 to 1964. In that time, he helped lead Navy to a record of 17–13–1. His best year was 1963 when Navy had a record of 9–2 and defeated **Army** but lost the national championship to Texas in the **Cotton Bowl**. Staubach won both the Heisman Trophy and **Maxwell Award** for his performance that year.

Since he had spent one year at the New Mexico Military Institute, Staubach was eligible for the professional **draft** following his junior year. He was chosen by the **Dallas Cowboys** in the 10th round of the 1964 **National Football League (NFL)** Draft as the 129th overall selection, and by the **Kansas City Chiefs** in the 1964 **American Football League (AFL)** Draft as the 122nd overall choice, even though both teams knew that he first had to complete a five-year military commitment. After graduating in 1965, Staubach volunteered to serve in Vietnam for one year as part of his military obligation. He spent the remaining time in the United States and, while stateside, was able to play some **football** for various naval teams. After completing his military service, he resigned his commission and signed with the Dallas Cowboys.

Staubach played 11 years with Dallas, from 1969 to 1979. During his first two years, he was the backup quarterback for Craig Morton. The Cowboys reached the **Super Bowl** following the 1970 season, losing to the **Baltimore Colts**, 16–13, but Staubach did not play in the game. The following season, he became the starting quarterback shortly after the season began, and he led Dallas to a Super Bowl championship. In 1972, he suffered a separated shoulder and was only able to play in four games. From 1973 to 1979, Staubach started in nearly every game. He led the Cowboys to the Super Bowl in 1976, 1978, and 1979, but they only won the 1978 game.

On 28 December 1975, in a divisional **playoff** game against the **Minnesota Vikings**, Staubach launched a last-second 50-yard **pass** that was caught for the winning **touchdown** by Cowboys' receiver Drew Pearson. When interviewed after the game, Staubach, a Catholic, said in jest, after I threw the ball I prayed a "**Hail Mary**." Since that time, the phrase "Hail Mary pass" has been used by the media to describe a last-second long pass effort.

In his 11-year NFL career, the Hail Mary quarterback played in 131 regular-season games, completed 1,685 passes in 2,958 attempts for 22,700 yards and 153 touchdowns, and ran 410 times for 2,264 yards and 20 touchdowns. In 19 postseason games, he completed 223 passes in 410 attempts for 2,791 yards and 24 touchdowns and ran 76 times for 432 yards and no touchdowns.

After retiring from the Cowboys, Staubach developed a commercial real estate business, the Staubach Company, and became its chairman and chief executive officer. In 2007, after 30 years, he retired from that enterprise, which now is a multibillion dollar concern with more than 70 offices. In 2006, he became part owner, along with former Cowboy **Troy Aikman**, of a stock car racing team known as Hall of Fame Racing. Staubach was inducted into the **College Football Hall of Fame** in 1981 and the **Pro Football Hall of Fame** in 1985.

STENERUD, JAN. B. 26 November 1942, Fetsund, Norway. From 1954 to 1980, one of the intercollegiate sports administered by the **National Collegiate Athletic Association (NCAA)** was ski jumping. As with other sports, colleges were permitted to offer athletic scholarships for ski jumping, although there were very few in comparison to other NCAA athletic sports. One of those recipients was a Norwegian, Jan Stenerud, who received a ski jumping scholarship from Montana State University in 1964. As a college ski jumper, he won the **conference** championship three times. One of the school's **coaches** saw him kick a **football** and persuaded him to join the football team as a placekicker. Stenerud first attempted to kick the football with his toe, as all **kickers** did at that time, but then, using his **soccer** background, he used the side of his foot and instep. With the Montana State football team, he successfully kicked a 59-yard **field goal** (a college record at the time that has since been broken) and set another field goal record that will probably never be broken, when he attempted a 113-yard field goal. With the ball on Montana State's own four-**yard line**, the coach called on Stenerud to attempt a field goal from three yards deep in his own **end zone**, knowing that Stenerud could kick the ball further than Montana State's **punter** and that the ball would probably reach midfield, which it did.

Stenerud was signed by the **Kansas City Chiefs** of the **American Football League (AFL)** in 1967 and played for them through 1979. He then played four years with the **Green Bay Packers** and two for the **Minnesota Vikings**, concluding his **National Football League (NFL)** career with the 1985 season. With the Chiefs, he was a member of the 1970 **Super Bowl**–winning team.

In his 19-year NFL career, Stenerud played in 263 regular-season games and kicked 373 field goals in 558 attempts and 580 extra points in 601 attempts. He also punted once for 28 yards and played in six **Pro Bowls**. In seven postseason games, he was successful on 15 of 16 extra point attempts and 13 of 21 field goal attempts.

Since retiring from football, Stenerud has worked for a firm that designs sports arenas and **stadiums** and done football commentary work for Scandinavian television. In 1994, he was selected as the placekicker on the NFL

75th Anniversary All-Time Team. He was inducted into the **Pro Football Hall of Fame** in 1991 and, as of 2012, is still the only placekicker who did not play another position enshrined in the Hall.

STRAM, HENRY LOUIS "HANK." B. 3 January 1923, Chicago, Illinois. D. 4 July 2005, Covington, Louisiana. Although born in Chicago, Hank Stram was raised in Gary, Indiana, where he attended Lew Wallace High School. He played both **football** and baseball in high school. After graduation in 1941, he enrolled at **Purdue University**, but his time there was interrupted by World War II. He played football at Purdue in 1942 and again in 1946 and 1947. After graduating from college, he was employed by Purdue as an **assistant coach** of the football team from 1948 to 1955, and head baseball **coach** from 1951 to 1955. He then served as an assistant coach at the **University of Notre Dame**, Southern Methodist University, and the **University of Miami** in Florida.

In 1960, Stram was chosen to be the head coach of the **Dallas Texans** of the new **American Football League (AFL)**. He coached that franchise for 15 years, the first three years in Dallas, and from 1963 to 1974 in Missouri, where they played as the **Kansas City Chiefs**. His final two years as a **National Football League (NFL)** head coach in 1976 and 1977 were spent as the coach of the **New Orleans Saints**. His greatest success with the Texans/Chiefs franchise came when he led them to the AFL championship in 1962, 1966, and 1969, and the **Super Bowl** following the 1969 season. The 1962 championship was memorable in that it was not decided until the second **overtime** period in what was the longest **professional football** game played to that date. In 1967, the Chiefs were the losers in the first Super Bowl (then called the AFL–NFL Championship Game). Stram was named AFL Coach of the Year in 1968.

After his final year coaching the Saints, Stram became a television football commentator. He remained in this capacity for the next 16 years. He succumbed to complications from diabetes in 2005. Stram was inducted into the **Pro Football Hall of Fame** as a coach in 2003.

STRONG, ELMER KENNETH "KEN." B. 21 April 1906, West Haven, Connecticut. D. 5 October 1979, New York, New York. Ken Strong attended West Haven High School and New York University (NYU). He played on the university's **football** team from 1926 to 1928. At that time, NYU had one of the better football teams in the country, compiling a three-year record of 23–4–2, although they have since discontinued their football program.

In 1929, Strong was signed by the Staten Island Stapletons of the **National Football League (NFL)** and played with them from 1929 to 1932. That franchise folded following the 1932 season, and Strong was signed by the **New York Giants**. The six-foot, 205-pound former NYU star played with them from 1933 to 1935 and played in the NFL championship all three years, being a member of the winning team in 1934. In that game, Strong scored 17 points on two **touchdowns**, two extra points, and a **field goal** and helped the Giants defeat the **Chicago Bears** on an icy field, 30–13. He played with the **New York Yankees** in the rival **American Football League** in 1936 and 1937, did not play in 1938, and returned to the Giants in 1939. Strong retired following the 1939 season but was coaxed out of retirement by the Giants to be used primarily as a **kicker**. He played for them for four more seasons, from 1944 to 1947. He played in three more NFL Championship Games, 1939, 1944, and 1946, but the Giants lost all three of those games.

In his 12 years in the NFL, Strong appeared in 131 games. Official statistics are not available for his entire NFL career, but he scored at least 31 touchdowns, 24 **rushing** and seven receiving. He also kicked 38 field goals and 166 extra points. Strong was inducted into the **College Football Hall of Fame** in 1957 and the **Pro Football Hall of Fame** in 1967.

STRONG SAFETY. *See* SAFETY (POSITION).

STRONG SIDE. In designing an offensive play, the strong side is the side of the field that the **tight end** lines up on. It can be either to the left or right of the **quarterback**. It receives its name since there are three down **linemen** (including the tight end) to the side of the **center**. *See also* WEAK SIDE.

STUHLDREYER, HARRY. *See* FOUR HORSEMEN OF NOTRE DAME.

SUDDEN-DEATH. In **professional football playoff** games, if a game is **tied** at the end of 60 minutes, an **overtime** period is played. The game is ended after the first score. This practice is known as sudden-death. In 2010, the **National Football League** modified its overtime rules, and games are now not always played with a sudden-death ending.

SUGAR BOWL. The Sugar Bowl was first played on 1 January 1935, and along with the **Orange Bowl** and **Sun Bowl**, also played on that date, is the second-oldest postseason **college football** game. From 1935 to 1974, the game was played at Tulane Stadium in New Orleans, Louisiana. Since 1976, it has been played at the Louisiana Superdome in New Orleans, with the exception of 2006, when the game was played at the Georgia Dome in Atlanta due to the effects of Hurricane Katrina on the Superdome. In 2000 and 2004, the Sugar Bowl game was designated as the **Bowl Championship Series**

National Championship Game. The **University of Alabama** and **Louisiana State University (LSU)** have each made 13 appearances in the Sugar Bowl, with LSU's eight victories being the most of any team.

SUMMERALL, GEORGE ALLEN "PAT." B. 10 May 1930, Lake City, Florida. D. 16 April 2013. Pat Summerall is probably best known today as a sports announcer, yet he had an outstanding career in **professional football** and helped the **New York Giants** reach the **National Football League (NFL)** Championship Game three times in four seasons from 1958 to 1961. He was a star in four sports at Columbia High School in Lake City, Florida, including baseball, **football**, basketball, and tennis. On the University of Arkansas **varsity** football team from 1949 to 1951, he played **end** on both **offense** and **defense** and was the team's placekicker. His nickname "Pat" was derived from his ability to kick points after touchdowns, also known as PATs. In 1950, Summerall played Minor League Baseball for the St. Louis Cardinals organization Lawton, Oklahoma, farm team in the Western Association, a Class C league. Among his opponents that year was future baseball Hall of Famer Mickey Mantle, who played for the Joplin, Missouri, team and led the league in batting.

Summerall was selected in the fourth round of the 1952 NFL **Draft** by the **Detroit Lions** as the 45th overall choice. He began his professional career with the Lions in 1953 but broke his arm and appeared in only two games. The six-foot, four-inch, 225-pound Summerall was traded to the Chicago Cardinals and played for them from 1954 to 1957. The turning point in his life occurred in 1958, when he was traded to the New York Giants. In the last regular-season game in 1958, the Giants played the **Cleveland Browns**. The Giants needed to defeat the Browns to finish the season in a **tie** for first place with Cleveland. The game was played in a driving snowstorm, and Summerall kicked the game-winning 49-yard **field goal** in the last two minutes of the game to give the Giants a 13–10 victory. The two teams played again the following week in a divisional tiebreaker game, and the Giants again defeated the Browns and played the **Baltimore Colts** the following week in the NFL Championship Game. That game was the first NFL game to go into **overtime** and has since become known as "the Greatest Football Game Ever Played." It became a milestone in the popularity of the sport.

Summerall retired from professional football in 1962 to pursue a career as a sportscaster with CBS. At that time, most television sports announcers were not former professional athletes, and Summerall was one of the first. He also became one of the best and, for more than 45 years, has been at the top of his second profession. One of the best and most versatile announcers who handled football, tennis, golf, and occasionally basketball, his announcing career reached its peak beginning in 1981, when he teamed with **John Madden** to form one of the best football announcing tandems. In his announcing career, Summerall has worked during 16 **Super Bowls**, many more than any other announcer.

In his 10-year NFL career, Summerall played in 109 regular-season games and kicked 100 field goals in 212 attempts and 257 extra points in 265 attempts. His only career **interception** occurred in 1955, when he returned an intercepted **pass** 26 yards for a **touchdown**. He was perfect in three postseason games, making all four extra point attempts and all five field goal attempts. In 1994, Summerall received the Pete Rozelle Award from the **Pro Football Hall of Fame** for his "longtime exceptional contributions to radio and television in professional football."

SUN BELT CONFERENCE. The Sun Belt Conference is an organization of **major colleges** and universities that compete athletically in the **National Collegiate Athletic Association**. It was established in 1976 and is based in New Orleans, Louisiana. As of 2012, the 11 member schools were Arkansas State University, the University of Arkansas at Little Rock, Florida Atlantic University, Florida International University, the University of Louisiana at Lafayette, the University of Louisiana at Monroe, Middle Tennessee State University, the University of North Texas, the University of South Alabama, Troy University, and Western Kentucky University. The University of Arkansas at Little Rock does not field **football** teams.

On 1 July 2013, Florida Atlantic, Florida International, Middle Tennessee and North Texas will leave the conference to join **Conference USA**. Georgia State University, Texas State University, San Marcos, and the University of Texas at Arlington are scheduled to join the Sun Belt Conference in 2013 although the latter school will not play football.

SUN BOWL. Along with the **Orange Bowl** and **Sugar Bowl**, the Sun Bowl is the second-oldest postseason **college football** game. All three games were first played on 1 January 1935. The Sun Bowl game was played at the El Paso High School field from 1935 to 1937. From 1938 to 1962, it was played at Kidd Field in El Paso, and, since 1963, it has been contested at the 50,000-seat Sun Bowl Stadium on the campus of the University of Texas, El Paso (UTEP). Through 1958, it was played on 1 or 2 January, but, since then, it has usually been played in December, most often on 31 December. Texas Tech has made the most appearances, with nine, but won only one of those games. UTEP has won the most games, with five victories.

SUPER BOWL. The Super Bowl game is the championship game of the **National Football League (NFL)**. It has become the most widely watched sports event in the United States and is second only to **soccer's** quadrennial World Cup as the most widely watched single sports event worldwide. The Super Bowl has virtually become a national holiday in the United States, and many **fans** organize parties around the event.

The contest began in 1967, when the newly merged National Football League and **American Football League (AFL)** played a season-ending championship game billed as the AFL–NFL Championship Game on 15 January 1967, at the **Los Angeles Memorial Coliseum**. The 100,000-seat **stadium** was only about two-thirds filled, with a crowd of 61,946 who watched the **Green Bay Packers** of the NFL easily defeat the **Kansas City Chiefs** of the AFL, 35–10.

The winning team members in the Super Bowl are presented with rings, and these are prized more highly than the cash prize awarded to each member of the winning team, which totaled $92,000 in 2012, with $46,000 per man to the losing team. The winners of the first Super Bowl in 1967 received $15,000 per man, and the losers were awarded $7,500 each.

Since the Super Bowl is played in January or February following the football season, it has been referred to using Roman numerals, as the phrase 2011 Super Bowl carries ambiguity as to whether it refers to the game played on 6 February 2011 between the Green Bay Packers and **Pittsburgh Steelers** or the one played following the 2011 season between the **New York Giants** and **New England Patriots**. That game is generally referred to as Super Bowl XLV.

Although many of the early Super Bowl games were unexciting and one sided, in recent years most of them have been closely played, although none, as of 2013, have gone into **overtime**. As of 2013, the Pittsburgh Steelers have won the most Super Bowl games, with six, and are **tied** with the **Dallas Cowboys** for most Super Bowl appearances, with eight each. Only the **Detroit Lions** and the expansion teams the **Cleveland Browns**, **Jacksonville Jaguars**, and **Houston Texans** have yet to play in one. *See also* APPENDIX C (for a list of results).

SWANN, LYNN CURTIS. B. 7 March 1952, Alcoa, Tennessee. Although born in Tennessee, Lynn Swann was raised in California. He attended Junipero Serra High School in San Mateo, California, where he played **football** and basketball and was a long jumper on the track team. He received a scholarship to the **University of Southern California (USC)**. At six feet tall and 180 pounds, he was a **wide receiver** at USC from 1971 to 1973. In 1972, he was a member of the national collegiate championship team that was undefeated in 12 games and victorious in the **Rose Bowl**. In 1973, USC won the

Pacific-10 Conference championship and had a 9–2–1 record but lost in the Rose Bowl.

Swann was chosen in the first round of the 1974 **National Football League (NFL) Draft** by the **Pittsburgh Steelers** as the 21st overall selection. He played with the Steelers from 1974 to 1982. In that time, he played on four **Super Bowl** championship teams, in 1975, 1976, 1979, and 1980, and was chosen as the Most Valuable Player in the 1976 Super Bowl. Swann was known for his acrobatic **pass**-catching ability and graceful running style. He credits some of his gracefulness to the fact that his mother made him take dance lessons from the age of four until his senior year in high school.

In his nine-year NFL career, Swann played in 115 regular-season games, caught 336 passes for 5,462 yards and 51 **touchdowns**, and ran 11 times for 72 yards and one touchdown. He also returned 61 **punts** for an average of 12.1 yards per return and one touchdown. In 16 postseason games, he caught 48 passes for 907 yards and nine touchdowns. Swann also ran three times for 17 yards and returned 12 punts for 92 yards. He played in three **Pro Bowls**.

Since retiring from active play, Swann has been quite busy. He was a sports broadcaster for ABC from 1976 to 2006, and, aside from commenting on football, he worked at six **Olympic Games**, summer and winter, and such other diverse events as the Iditarod Trail Dog Sled Race, horse racing, and diving. From 2002 to 2005, he was chairman of the U.S. President's Council on Physical Fitness and Sports. In 2006, Swann ran for governor of Pennsylvania but was defeated. In 2010, he became part owner of the Pittsburgh entry in the **Arena Football League**, the Pittsburgh Power. He was inducted into the **College Football Hall of Fame** in 1993 and the **Pro Football Hall of Fame** in 2001.

SYRACUSE UNIVERSITY. Syracuse University is located in Syracuse, New York. Their **football** program began in 1889, and, since then, through 2012, Orange teams have compiled a record of 685–488–48. In addition, they have competed in 24 postseason **bowl games**, with a record of 14–9–1. Since 1979, Syracuse football teams have competed in the **Big East Conference** of the **National Collegiate Athletic Association**. Home games since 1980 have been played at the Carrier Dome on the school's campus. The Carrier Dome, the largest domed **stadium** on any college campus, was one of the first domed stadiums in the United States and seats 49,250 for football. Syracuse has no one traditional rival but has played **Penn State University**, Colgate University, **Rutgers University**, West Virginia University, and the **University of Pittsburgh** on a fairly regular basis.

Syracuse's most noted **coach** has been Floyd "Ben" Schwartzwalder. He coached the Orangemen from 1949 to 1973, with a record of 153–91–3, and led them to their only national championship in 1959. In an era with far less postseason bowl games than in the 21st century, his teams played in seven. Other noteworthy coaches have included Frank "Buck" O'Neill (1906–1907, 1913–1915, 1917–1919; 52–19–6), Vic Hanson (1930–1936; 33–21–5), Dick MacPherson (1981–1990; 66–46–4), and Paul Pasqualoni (1991–2004; 107–59–1).

Syracuse alumni in the **College Football Hall of Fame** are **guard/center** Joe "Doc" Alexander; **halfbacks Jim Brown**, Ernie Davis, and Floyd Little; **fullback Larry Csonka**; defensive **tackle** Tim Green; **wide receiver Art Monk**, **end** Vic Hanson; and **quarterback** Don McPherson. Hanson was also a star basketball player and is a member of the Naismith Memorial Basketball Hall of Fame as well. Although Brown, Davis, and Little were all outstanding **running backs** for Syracuse, only Davis was a **Heisman Trophy** winner. Syracuse coaches in the College Football Hall of Fame are brothers Howard and Thomas "Tad" Jones, Dick MacPherson, Clarence "Biggie" Munn, Frank "Buck" O'Neill, and Floyd "Ben" Schwartzwalder. The Jones brothers and Biggie Munn were selected based on their contributions at other schools, as all three only coached at Syracuse briefly.

Through 2012, there have been 230 **professional football** players who have attended Syracuse, 223 in the **National Football League** and seven in the **American Football League**. They include Will Allen, Gary Anderson, Jim Brown, Keith Bulluck, Rob Burnett, Ken Clarke, Larry Csonka, Kirby Dar Dar, Dwight Freeney, **Marvin Harrison**, Daryl Johnston, Tebucky Jones, Carl Karilivacz, Floyd Little, John Mackey, Olindo Mare, **Donovan McNabb**, Art Monk, Rob Moore, Joe Morris, Jim Nance, Jim Ringo, Walt Sweeney, Stan Walters, Otis Wilson, and Craig Wolfley. **Al Davis**, coach and general manager of the **Oakland Raiders**, was also a graduate of Syracuse.

T

T FORMATION. The T formation is one of the oldest offensive formations in **football**. It dates back to the 19th century and, for much of the 20th century, was the most widely used offensive set. In it, the **quarterback** lines up directly behind the **center**, with the **fullback** directly behind him and a **halfback** on each side of the fullback. As the sport has become more complex, many other starting offensive formations have been created, including the **shotgun formation**, wishbone formation, and "I" formation.

TACKLE (PLAY). In **football**, a play ends when some part of the ball carrier's body, other than his hands or feet, touches the ground. The method of bringing him to the ground is known as tackling.

TACKLE (POSITION). The tackle is a **football position**. The offensive tackles line up between the offensive **guards** and **ends**, one on each side of the **center**. Their function is to **block** for the **quarterback** and ball carriers. The defensive tackles line up on the **line of scrimmage** opposite the offensive tackles. Their function is to stop the ball carrier or quarterback by tackling him.

TAGLIABUE, PAUL JOHN. B. 24 November 1940, Jersey City, New Jersey. Paul Tagliabue is a graduate of St. Michael's High School in Union City, New Jersey. The six-foot, five-inch **center**-forward received a basketball scholarship to Georgetown University and was captain of their basketball team during his senior year. He was also president of his senior class and a Rhodes scholarship finalist. In 1962, Tagliabue continued his education at the New York University School of Law, and, after graduation in 1965, he worked for the Washington, D.C., law firm Covington & Burling, one of whose clients was the **National Football League (NFL)**. He helped represent the NFL in the 1986 antitrust lawsuit brought against them by the **United States Football League** and, in 1989, was selected as the league's commissioner, succeeding **Alvin "Pete" Rozelle**. Tagliabue served as NFL commissioner until 1 September 2006. While he was commissioner, the league developed the **World League of American Football**, exposing American

football to Europe, and expanded from 28 to 32 franchises and had several franchise relocations. After retiring from the NFL, he rejoined Covington & Burling. Tagliabue was also appointed to Georgetown University's board of directors in 2008.

TAILBACK. *See* BACK.

TAILGATING. Given the logistics of filling **stadiums** with 50,000 to 100,000 **fans** in a brief period of time, with the consequent parking and traffic delays incurred, fans began arriving at stadiums three or more hours prior to the game. They then began bringing food and entertainment to fill the time. Portable barbecues on the back (or tailgate) of station wagons were used to prepare pregame meals. This practice, known as tailgating, has spread, and, consequently, many fans now spend more time doing this than actually entering the stadium and watching the game.

TAMPA BAY BUCCANEERS. The Tampa Bay Buccaneers are a **professional football** team in the National Football Conference (NFC) South Division of the **National Football League (NFL)**. They entered the NFL as an expansion team in 1976, in the American Football Conference (AFC) West Division, and lost their first 26 games. In 1977, they were transferred to the NFC Central Division and remained there through 2001. Since 2002, they have played in the NFC South Division. Home games from 1976 to 1997 were played at the 71,000-seat Tampa Stadium in Tampa, Florida (also known as Houlihan's Stadium). Since 1998, the Bucs have played their home games at the 65,000-seat Raymond James Stadium, also in Tampa.

The success of the Tampa Bay team has ranged widely in their 36-year existence. In their first year, they were winless in 14 games. In eight other seasons, they won four or fewer games. In seven seasons, the Bucs won 10 or more games, and, in 2002, their best season, they won 12 games in the regular season and three more in the postseason **playoffs**, including the **Super Bowl**. Their overall record for 36 years, from 1976 to 2012, is 229–350–1 in regular-season play and 6–9 in playoff competition. In 10 seasons of postseason play, Tampa Bay won the Super Bowl once, lost in the conference championship twice (1979, 1999), lost in the divisional playoffs twice (1981, 1997), and lost in the first round or **wild-card playoff** round five times (1982, 2000, 2001, 2005, 2007).

Their head coaches have been John McKay (1976–1984), Leeman Bennett (1985–1986), Ray Perkins (1987–1990), Richard Williamson (1990–1991), Sam Wyche (1992–1995), Tony Dungy (1996–2001), Jon Gruden (2002–2008), Raheem Morris (2009–2011), and Greg Schiano (2012). Their only

Pro Football Hall of Famers have been defensive **linemen** Lee Roy Selmon and Warren Sapp, **guard** Randall McDaniel, and **quarterback Steve Young**, although McDaniel and Young played only briefly with the Bucs. Other of Tampa Bay's best players include quarterbacks Trent Dilfer, Brad Johnson, Vinny Testaverde, and Doug Williams; **running backs** Mike Alstott, Ricky Bell, Warrick Dunn, Michael Pittman, and James Wilder; **wide receivers** Mark Carrier, Joey Galloway, and Keyshawn Johnson; offensive **tackle** Paul Gruber; defensive **backs** Ronde Barber and John Lynch; and **linebackers** Derrick Brooks, Hugh Green, and Hardy Nickerson.

TARKENTON, FRANCIS ASBURY "FRAN." B. 3 February 1940, Richmond, Virginia. Fran Tarkenton was one of the most exciting **quarterbacks** in **professional football** history, even if he was not one of the winningest. The son of a Pentecostal minister, Tarkenton attended Athens High School in Athens, Georgia. He played quarterback there and led Athens to the Georgia state high school championship. From 1958 to 1960, he was the quarterback of the **University of Georgia varsity** and, in 1959, led them to a 10–1 record, the **Southeastern Conference** championship, and a victory in the **Orange Bowl**.

Tarkenton was taken by the expansion **Minnesota Vikings** in the 1961 **National Football League (NFL) Draft** in the third round as the 29th overall selection. He was also selected by the Boston Patriots in the fifth round of the **American Football League (AFL)** Draft that year as the 34th overall choice. He chose the Vikings and played for them through 1966. During those six years, he and Vikings' **coach Norm Van Brocklin** often disagreed, as Van Brocklin had been an effective **pocket** quarterback during his 12-year NFL career and Tarkenton preferred to scramble in an attempt to find open receivers. Tarkenton was traded to the **New York Giants** and, from 1967 to 1971, thrilled Giants' **fans** with his scrambling style, although he was unable to lead the Giants to postseason play in any of those five years. Tarkenton was traded back to the Vikings in 1972, and he enjoyed the best years of his professional career during that time, as the Vikings coach was now **Harry "Bud" Grant**, who had a different appreciation of Tarkenton's scrambling style. The quarterback led the Vikings to the **Super Bowl** in 1974, 1975, and 1977, but Minnesota lost all three games. Tarkenton retired after the 1978 season. In 1975, he was named the NFL Most Valuable Player.

In his 18-year NFL career, Tarkenton played in 246 regular-season games, started in 239 of them, and had a won-lost record of 124–109–6. He completed 3,686 **passes** in 6,467 attempts for 47,003 yards and 342 **touchdowns** and ran 675 times for 3,674 yards and 32 touchdowns. In 11 postseason games, he completed 149 passes in 292 attempts for 1,803 yards and 11 touchdowns and ran 25 times for 70 yards and one touchdown. He was selected for the **Pro Bowl** nine times.

At the time of his retirement, Tarkenton was the NFL career leader in several categories, including passes completed, passes attempted, passing yardage, and passing touchdowns, but, since his retirement, NFL teams have changed their style of play, and passes are now much more prolific. Consequently, he no longer holds those records, although he is still among the top 10. In retirement, Tarkenton devoted much of his time to a computer software business he developed called Tarkenton Software. He also worked as an analyst on *Monday Night Football*, cowrote a murder mystery, and authored two self-help motivational books. He was inducted into the **Pro Football Hall of Fame** in 1986 and the **College Football Hall of Fame** in 1987.

TAXI SQUAD. The taxi squad is the name used to designate a group of **professional football** players who are allowed to practice with their team but are not included on their official roster of players. (In 2012, this roster limit was 53 in the **National Football League**, with eight additional players allowed on the taxi squad.) The name originated with **Cleveland Browns'** owner Art McBride, who wanted to keep additional players under contract but was limited by league rules. To get around the limitation, he hired the extra players to work for his taxicab company. The taxi squad is also referred to as the practice team or scout team.

TAYLOR, JAMES CHARLES "JIM." B. 20 September 1935, Baton Rouge, Louisiana. Jim Taylor played basketball and **football** at Baton Rouge High School and **Louisiana State University**. A six-foot, 215-pound **fullback**, he was chosen by the **Green Bay Packers** in the 1957 **National Football League (NFL) Draft** in the second round as the 15th overall selection. He played with Green Bay from 1958 to 1966 and was with them when they were the worst team in the NFL (1958; 1–10–1) and the best team (1961, 1962, 1965, 1966; NFL champions). In five of his nine years with the Packers, Taylor played in the NFL Championship Game, being a member of the losing team in 1960.

His final year in **professional football** was played for the expansion **New Orleans Saints**. Although Taylor was signed to a 10-year contract by New Orleans, he retired after playing just one season for them. During his era, he was one of the premier **running backs** in the NFL and led the league in **rushing** in 1962, with 1,474 yards, the second most in a single season to that date. He likely would have led the league more had he not played at the same time as **Pro Football Hall of Famer Jim Brown**.

In his 10-year NFL career, Taylor played in 132 regular-season games, ran 1,941 times for 8,597 yards and 83 **touchdowns**, and caught 225 **passes** for 1,756 yards and 10 touchdowns. During his rookie season, he was also occasionally used as a kick **returner** and, in seven returns, averaged 26.4 yards per return. In seven postseason games, he ran 146 times for 508 yards and two touchdowns and caught 19 passes for 137 yards and no touchdowns. Taylor was inducted into the Pro Football Hall of Fame in 1976.

TAYLOR, LAWRENCE JULIUS. B. 4 February 1959, Williamsburg, Virginia. Lawrence Taylor was one of the most effective **linebackers** during his **professional football** career and has been called by some the greatest defensive player in **National Football League (NFL)** history. He attended Lafayette High School in Williamsburg, Virginia, and the University of North Carolina. He was a catcher on the baseball team in high school and a defensive **lineman** on the **football** team. At North Carolina, Taylor was converted to linebacker, and it was at that position that he excelled. In 1980, he helped lead the Tarheels to an 11–1 record and the **Atlantic Coast Conference** championship.

Taylor was selected by the **New York Giants** in the 1981 NFL **Draft** in the first round as the second overall pick. He played with the Giants for his entire NFL career, from 1981 to 1993, and helped lead them to **Super Bowl** championships in 1987 and 1991. He was named the NFL Most Valuable Player (MVP) for the 1986 season, only the second time that the award had been won by a defensive player. (In 1971, **Alan Page** was the first defensive player to be selected league MVP.) Taylor was also named the NFL Defensive Player of the Year in 1981, 1982, and 1986, and NFL Rookie of the Year in 1981.

In his 13-year NFL career, Taylor appeared in 184 regular-season games and recorded nine **interceptions** for two **touchdowns** and 132 1/2 sacks. Sacks were not officially recorded in his first season. In 15 postseason games, he scored a touchdown on a 34-yard interception return, recovered a **fumble** for a two-yard gain, and recorded 6 1/2 sacks. He played in 10 **Pro Bowls** in his first 10 seasons. In retirement, Taylor has done some television work, some acting in Hollywood films, and been involved with several business enterprises. He was inducted into the **Pro Football Hall of Fame** in 1999.

TEBOW, TIMOTHY RICHARD "TIM." B. 14 August 1987, Makati City, Philippines. Tim Tebow was born to American parents who were missionaries in the Philippines. He was raised in Florida and homeschooled. He attended Trinity Christian Academy in Jacksonville, Florida, for one year and then transferred to Nease High School in Ponte Vedra Beach, Florida, for the remainder of his high school education. Tebow attended the **University of Florida** from 2006 to 2009 and was a member of the national championship team in 2006, although only a backup **quarterback**.

In 2007, as a sophomore, Tebow became the starting quarterback and led Florida to a record of 9–4. He was awarded the **Heisman Trophy** following that season and became the first sophomore to win that honor. In 2008, he led Florida to a record of 13–1 and the national championship. Tebow concluded his college career with another 13–1 season at Florida, but their one loss occurred in the **Southeastern Conference** championship game. In four years at Florida, Tebow completed 661 **passes** in 985 attempts for 9,286 yards and a 67.1 completion percentage. He also ran for 2,947 yards in 692 carries. He scored 57 **touchdowns rushing** and passed for 88 more. A deeply religious person, he kneels on one knee in silent prayer following a touchdown, and the word *Tebowing* has been coined to describe this practice.

Left-handed and six feet, three inches tall and 235 pounds, Tebow presents a challenge to most **defenses**, as he is a capable runner and passer. He was chosen by the **Denver Broncos** in the first round of the 2010 **National Football League (NFL) Draft** as the 25th overall selection. He began his NFL career as a backup quarterback and started in only three games his first season. In 2011, he was used more frequently and appeared in 14 games, 11 as a starter. On 23 October 2011, Tebow brought the Broncos back from a 15–0 deficit with three minutes to play in the game and led them to an 18–15 **overtime** victory. The following week, he rushed for 117 yards and another Denver win. By season's end, he had led the Broncos to six come-from-behind victories in his 11 starts. In the first game of the **playoffs**, Tebow completed an 80-yard pass on the first play of overtime to give the Broncos yet another sensational victory.

Through the 2011 season, Tebow had played in 24 NFL games in two seasons. He started in 14 games and had a won-lost record of 8–6. He had completed 167 passes in 353 attempts for 2,383 yards and 17 touchdowns. He also carried the ball 165 times for 887 yards and 12 touchdowns. In two postseason games, he completed 19 passes in 47 attempts for 452 yards and two touchdowns and ran 15 times for 63 yards and one touchdown. In March 2012, quarterback **Peyton Manning** was signed by the Denver Broncos, and, as a result, Tebow was traded to the **New York Jets**. With the Jets in 2012, he was used sparingly and although he appeared in 12 games he started only two, completed six of eight passes for 39 yards and no touchdowns, ran 32 times for 102 yards and no touchdowns. After his first two seasons, his professional career had promised to be a rewarding one but after the 2012 season with the Jets it has become questionable.

TENNESSEE, UNIVERSITY OF. The University of Tennessee is located in Knoxville, Tennessee. Their **football** program began in 1891, and, since then, through 2012, Volunteers' teams have compiled a record of 774–330–54. In addition, they have competed in 49 postseason **bowl games**, with a record of 25–24. They have been selected as national collegiate champions seven times, in 1938, 1940, 1950, 1951, 1956, 1967, and 1998. Since 1932, Tennessee football teams have competed in the **Southeastern Conference** of the **National Collegiate Athletic Association**.

Home games have been played at Neyland Stadium (formerly Shields-Watkins Field) in Knoxville since 1921. The **stadium's** seating capacity in 1921 was 3,200 and has been expanded more than a dozen times and now seats more than 102,000. Tennessee's main rival is Kentucky, and the Volunteers hold a 75–24–9 edge over the Wildcats. At one time, the game was played for a barrel of beer and was known as the "Battle for the Barrel," but this practice was discontinued after 1998, when an alcohol-related auto accident killed two Kentucky players.

Tennessee's most successful **coach** has been Robert Neyland. He led them from 1926 to 1934, 1936 to 1940, and 1946 to 1952. As their coach, his record was an exceptional 173–31–12. He was also an officer in the U.S. Army and attained the rank of brigadier general. After his death in 1962, Tennessee's football stadium was renamed in his honor. Other notable head coaches include John "Chief" Bender (1916, 1919–1920; 18–5–4), John Barnhill (1941–1942, 1944–1945; 32–5–2), Bowden Wyatt (1955–1962; 49–29–4), Doug Dickey (1964–1969; 46–15–4), Johnny Majors (1977–1992; 116–82–8), and Phillip Fulmer (1992–2008; 152–52).

Tennessee alumni in the **College Football Hall of Fame** are **tackle** Doug Atkins; **halfbacks** George Cafego, Beattie Feathers, Hank Lauricella, Johnny Majors, and Gene McEver; middle **guard** Steve DeLong; **quarterback** Bobby Dodd; guards Nathan Dougherty, Herman Hickman, John Michels, Ed Molinski, Joe Steffy, and Bob Suffridge; **linebackers** Frank Emanuel and Steve Kiner; **center** Bob Johnson; guard/center Chip Kell; defensive tackle **Reggie White**; and **end** Bowden Wyatt. Wyatt was also inducted as a coach. Other former Tennessee coaches in the Hall are Robert Neyland, Phillip Fulmer and Doug Dickey.

Through 2012, there have been 291 **professional football** players who have attended Tennessee, 279 in the **National Football League**, eight in the **American Football League**, and four in the **All-America Football Conference**. They include Doug Atkins, Bill Bates, Steve DeLong, Charlie Garner, Willie Gault, John Gordy, Albert Haynesworth, Tim Irwin, Steve Kiner, Jamal Lewis, Mike Lucci, **Peyton Manning**, Darris McCord, Terry

McDaniel, brothers Raleigh and Reggie McKenzie, Anthony Miller, Stanley Morgan, Paul Naumoff, Peerless Price, Bert Rechichar, Fuad Reveiz, Jack Reynolds, Donte Stallworth, Mike Stratton, Jack Stroud, Reggie White, and Jason Witten.

TENNESSEE OILERS. *See* TENNESSEE TITANS.

TENNESSEE TITANS. The Tennessee Titans are a **professional football** team in the American Football Conference South Division of the **National Football League (NFL)**. They began play as the Houston Oilers and were a charter member of the **American Football League (AFL)** in 1960. In 10 years in the AFL, they had a record of 70–66–4 in regular-season play. They won the AFL championship in 1960 and 1961, lost the AFL Championship Game in 1962 and 1967, and lost in the division **playoffs** in 1969. They joined the NFL in 1970, when the AFL and NFL merged. In their 43 years of NFL competition, they have an overall regular-season record of 322–340–2 and a record of 12–16 in playoff activity. Their best NFL season was 1999, when they were 13–3 in the regular season and lost in the **Super Bowl**, 23–16, to the **St. Louis Rams**. This has been their only Super Bowl appearance through 2012.

From 1960 to 1964, the Oilers played home games at the 35,000-seat Jeppesen Stadium in Houston, Texas. They used the 50,000-seat Rice Stadium as their home field from 1965 to 1967. The team moved to the 62,000-seat Houston Astrodome in 1968 and remained there through the 1996 season. In 1997, they moved to the state of Tennessee and played at the 62,000-seat Liberty Bowl Memorial Stadium in Memphis in 1997 and the 39,000-seat Vanderbilt Stadium in Nashville in 1998. They played as the Tennessee Oilers those two years. In 1999, the Oilers were renamed the Tennessee Titans and, since then, have played at the 68,000-seat LP Field in Nashville. That **stadium** was known as Adelphia Coliseum from 1999 to 2002, and simply the Coliseum from 2002 to 2006.

The franchise's head **coaches** have been Lou Rymkus (1960–1961), Wally Lemm (interim 1961; 1966–1970), Frank "Pop" Ivy (1962–1963), **Sammy Baugh** (1964), Hugh Taylor (1965), Ed Hughes (1971), Bill Peterson (1972–1973), Sid Gillman (1973–1974), Oail A. "Bum" Phillips (1975–1980), Ed Biles (1981–1983), Chuck Studley (interim 1983), Hugh Campbell (1984–1985), Jerry Glanville (1985–1989), Jack Pardee (1990–1994), Jeff Fisher (1994–2010), and Mike Munchak (2011–2012). Fisher was the most successful, leading the Titans to six playoff seasons and the 1999 Super Bowl.

The Oilers'/Titans' best players include **Pro Football Hall of Famers quarterbacks George Blanda** and **Warren Moon**, defensive tackle Curley

Culp, defensive **end** Elvin Bethea, **running back Earl Campbell, safety** Ken Houston, and offensive **linemen** Bruce Matthews and Mike Munchak. Other top players include quarterbacks Steve McNair and Dan Pastorini; safety/**punter** Jim Norton; running backs Billy Cannon, Eddie George, Chris Johnson, and Charlie Tolar; offensive **guard** Bob Talamini; **wide receivers** Ken Burrough, Charlie Hennigan, Drew Hill, and Derrick Mason; **linebacker** Keith Bulluck; and **kickers** Rob Bironas and Al Del Greco.

TEXAS, UNIVERSITY OF. The University of Texas is located in Austin, Texas. Their **football** program began in 1893, and, since then, through 2012, Longhorns' teams have compiled a record of 840–315–32. In addition, they have competed in 51 postseason **bowl games**, with a record of 27–22–2. They have been selected as national collegiate champions nine times, in 1914, 1941, 1963, 1968, 1969, 1970, 1977, 1981, and 2005. Home games since 1924 have been played at Darrell K. Royal–Texas Memorial Stadium (originally War Memorial Stadium) in Austin. The facility's seating capacity has been enlarged throughout the years and now holds more than 100,000 spectators.

From 1915 to 1995, Texas football teams competed in the **Southwest Conference** of the **National Collegiate Athletic Association**. Since 1996, they have been members of the **Big 12 Conference**. Their main rival is the **University of Oklahoma**. The teams have met in most years since 1900 in a contest known as the "Red River Rivalry." Texas leads the series, 59–43–5.

One of the most remarkable facts about Texas football is that Texas has had 28 head **coaches** from 1893 to 2012, and only two had losing records (and that was by only one game). Those two coaches are Jack Chevigny (1934–1936; 13–14–2) and Harry "Jake" Robinson (1896; 4–5–2). Chevigny later joined the U.S. Marines and was killed in the Battle of Iwo Jima during World War II. A total of 22 of the 28 Texas head coaches had winning percentages of .600 or better. Texas's most noteworthy coach was Darrell Royal. He was their head coach from 1957 to 1976 and compiled a record of 167–47–5. Other exceptional Texas coaches include Dave Allerdice (1911–1915; 28–5), Berry Whitaker (1920–1922; 22–3–1), Dana X. Bible (1937–1946; 63–31–3), Blair Cherry (1947–1950; 32–10–1)), Fred Akers (1977–1986; 86–31–2), and Mack Brown (1998–2012; 150–43).

Texas alumni in the **College Football Hall of Fame** are **quarterback Bobby Layne**; **ends** Hub Bechtol and Mal Kutner; **halfbacks Earl Campbell**, Chris Gilbert, James Saxton, and Harrison Stafford; **safety** Johnnie Johnson; **running back** Roosevelt Leaks; **guard/tackle** Lewis "Bud" McFadin; defensive tackles Doug English and Steve McMichael; **linebacker/** guard Tommy Nobis; guard Harley Sewell; and offensive tackles Jerry

Sisemore and Bud Sprague. Texas head coaches in the Hall are Dana X. Bible and Darrell Royal. **Heisman Trophy** winners were Earl Campbell in 1977 and Ricky Williams in 1998.

Through 2012, there have been 271 **professional football** players who have attended Texas, 255 in the **National Football League**, seven in the **American Football League**, and nine in the **All-America Football Conference**. They include Raul Allegre, Bill Bradley, Earl Campbell, Raymond Clayborn, Phil Dawson, Bobby Dillon, Doug English, Russell Erxleben, Casey Hampton, Priest Holmes, Quentin Jammer, Pete Lammons, **Tom Landry**, Bobby Layne, Colt McCoy, Steve McMichael, Eric Metcalf, Tommy Nobis, George Sauer, Adam Schreiber, Jerry Sisemore, Diron Talbert, Ricky Williams, Bob Young, and Vince Young.

TEXAS A&M UNIVERSITY. Texas A&M University is located in College Station, Texas. Their **football** program began in 1894, and, since then, through 2012, Aggies' teams have compiled a record of 678–433–48. In addition, they have competed in 34 postseason **bowl games**, with a record of 15–19. They have been selected as national collegiate champions three times, in 1919, 1927, and 1939. Since 1927, the Aggies have played home games at Kyle Field, located on their campus with a present-day seating capacity of 83,000.

From 1915 to 1995, Texas A&M football teams competed in the **Southwest Conference** of the **National Collegiate Athletic Association**. From 1996 to 2011, they were members of the **Big 12 Conference**, and, as of 2012, they are members of the **Southeastern Conference**. Their main rival is the **University of Texas**. The teams have met in most years since 1894, and, through 2012, Texas leads the series, 76–37–5.

Among the most successful of Texas A&M's head **coaches** have been Dana X. Bible (1917, 1919–1928; 72–19–9), Homer Norton (1934–1947; 82–53–9), **Paul "Bear" Bryant** (1954–1957; 25–14–2), and R. C. Slocum (1989–2002; 123–47–2). Texas A&M alumni in the **College Football Hall of Fame** include **quarterback** Joel Hunt, defensive **end** Ray Childress, **halfbacks** John David Crow (the **Heisman Trophy** winner in 1957) and Joe Utay, **fullbacks** Jack Pardee and John Kimbrough, **safety** Dave Elmendorf, **tackle** Charlie Krueger, and **guard** Joe Routt. Former A&M head coaches in the Hall include Matty Bell, Dana X. Bible, Paul "Bear" Bryant, Homer Norton, R. C. Slocum, and Gene Stallings. Although Bryant was successful at A&M, he coached there for only four years and was inducted primarily for his work at the **University of Alabama**, where he coached for 25 years.

Through 2012, there have been 253 **professional football** players who have attended Texas A&M, 238 in the **National Football League**, eight in the **American Football League**, and seven in the **All-America Football Conference**. They include Sam Adams, Robert "Rocky" Bernard, Lee Roy Caffey, Ray Childress, Bobby Joe Conrad, DeWitt "Tex" Coulter, John David Crow, Curtis Dickey, Dave Elmendorf, Jerry Fontenot, Tony Franklin (a barefooted **kicker**), Aaron Glenn, Jacob Green, Dante Hall, Lester Hayes, Earnest Jackson, Charlie Krueger, Gary Kubiak, Yale Lary, Shane Lechler, Mark Moseley, Jack Pardee, Martin Ruby, Karl Sweetan, William Thomas, Richmond Webb, and Pat Williams.

THANKSGIVING DAY. At one time, Thanksgiving Day in the United States was known for turkey and **football**. Many traditional high school and college rivalry games were played in the morning or afternoon of Thanksgiving Day. In recent years, however, **professional football** has dominated, with two or three games being played on Thanksgiving, in the afternoon, early evening, and night. As a result, there are now very few high school or college games played on Thanksgiving. Most of the college traditional rivalry games are currently played on the Friday or Saturday following Thanksgiving.

Professional football games have been played on Thanksgiving since 1892, when professional football first began. The **National Football League (NFL)** has played one or more games on Thanksgiving each year since its inception in 1920. Both the **All-America Football Conference** and **American Football League** of the 1960s also played each Thanksgiving. The **Detroit Lions** of the NFL have played a home game on Thanksgiving Day each year since 1945. From 1951 to 1963, their opponent was the **Green Bay Packers**. Since 1966, the **Dallas Cowboys** have hosted a Thanksgiving Day game each year. The NFL has played a third game on Thanksgiving night since 2006.

Thanksgiving Day in Canada is celebrated on the second Monday in October. The **Canadian Football League** has played one or two games on that day each year since 1970.

THEISMANN, JOSEPH ROBERT "JOE." B. 9 September 1949, New Brunswick, New Jersey. Joe Theismann attended South River High School in South River, New Jersey, and played baseball, basketball, and **football**. He received a football scholarship to the **University of Notre Dame** in 1967 and became their starting **quarterback** with three games remaining in the 1968 season, compiling a record of 25–3–2 as a starter through 1970. During his senior year, he **passed** for a Notre Dame record 2,429 yards and 16 **touchdowns**, including 33 completions for 526 yards in a game against the **University of Southern California**, and was the runner-up in the **Heisman Trophy** balloting.

Theismann, a six-foot, 190-pound quarterback, was selected by the **Miami Dolphins** in the fourth round of the 1971 **National Football League (NFL) Draft** as the 99th overall choice but could not come to terms with them and played in the **Canadian Football League** from 1971 to 1973 for the **Toronto Argonauts**. In 1971, he led the Argos to the **Grey Cup**, where they were defeated by the **Calgary Stampeders**. The versatile Theismann was also drafted by the Minnesota Twins of Major League Baseball but did not pursue a baseball career. In 1974, he signed with the **Washington Redskins** of the NFL and led them to a **Super Bowl** championship in 1983. Washington and Theismann played in the Super Bowl the following year but were defeated by the Los Angeles Raiders.

In 12 NFL seasons, all with the Redskins, Theismann played in 167 games, started in 124 of them, and had a 77–47 won-lost record as a starter. He completed 2,044 of 3,602 passes for 25,206 yards and 160 touchdowns and ran 355 times for 1,815 yards and 17 touchdowns. In his first two seasons, he was also used as a **punt returner** and returned 17 punts for an average of 9.5 yards per return. In 1985, he was used as a **punter** when the Redskins' punter, Jeff Hayes, was hurt, but on Theismann's only punt he hit the ball with the side of his foot and the ball only traveled one yard. In nine postseason games, he completed 128 passes in 211 attempts for 1,728 yards and 11 touchdowns, ran 19 times for 95 yards and no touchdowns, and returned four punts for 22 yards. Theismann played in the **Pro Bowl** in 1982 and 1983 and was named the NFL Player of the Year in 1982 and NFL Most Valuable Player in 1983. His playing career ended on a *Monday Night Football* game against the **New York Giants** on 19 November 1985, when his leg was badly broken.

Since retiring from active play, Theismann has worked in television as an analyst and has worked for most of the networks that have broadcast NFL games. He was also briefly involved as a coowner of a **United Football League** team, the Florida Tuskers, and the former Redskin owns a restaurant in Arlington, Virginia. He was elected to the **College Football Hall of Fame** in 2003.

THOMAS, EMMITT EARL. B. 3 June 1943, Angleton, Texas. Emmitt Thomas attended Marshall High School in Angleton, Texas, and Bishop College in Dallas, Texas, a historically black institution that competed in Division III of the **National Collegiate Athletic Association**. Consequently, he had little national publicity and was not **drafted** by the **American Football League (AFL)** or **National Football League (NFL)**. He was signed by the **Kansas City Chiefs** of the AFL in 1966 and played his entire **professional football** career as a **cornerback** with that franchise, moving to the NFL in 1970 when the two leagues merged. Thomas played in the first **Super Bowl**

in 1967, in the Chiefs' loss to the **Green Bay Packers**, and was a member of the Super Bowl champions in 1970, when the Chiefs defeated the **Minnesota Vikings**. In that game, he recorded an **interception**.

In his 13-year combined AFL–NFL career, Thomas appeared in 181 regular-season games and had 58 interceptions for five **touchdowns**. He was also used as a **punt** and **kickoff returner** in his first two seasons and had 11 punt returns for a 5.8-yard average and 29 kickoff returns for a 23.2-yard average. In six postseason games, Thomas had five interceptions for 101 yards and no touchdowns and one punt return for two yards. He played in the AFL All-Star Game in 1968 and four **Pro Bowls**.

After retiring from active play, Thomas worked as head coach at Central Missouri State University from 1979 to 1980 and as an **assistant coach** for several NFL teams since then. In 2007, he was the interim head coach of the **Atlanta Falcons** for three games and had a record of 1–2. In 2008, he was elected to the **Pro Football Hall of Fame**.

THOMAS, THURMAN LEE. B. 16 May 1966, Houston, Texas. Thurman Thomas attended Willowridge High School in Houston, where he starred as a **running back** on their **football** team and received a scholarship to Oklahoma State University. There he played alongside future **College Football Hall of Fame** and **Pro Football Hall of Fame** running back **Barry Sanders**. In four years on the **varsity** football team, Thomas ran for 4,847 yards and 43 **touchdowns**, and the school compiled a 34–13 won-lost record, with two appearances in the Gator Bowl and one in the **Sun Bowl**.

Thomas was selected by the **Buffalo Bills** in the second round of the 1988 **National Football League (NFL) Draft** as the 40th overall selection. He played for the Bills from 1988 to 1999 and then concluded his **professional football** career with one season with the **Miami Dolphins**. In 1991, he was named the NFL Most Valuable Player. He played on the losing side in four consecutive **Super Bowls** from 1991 to 1994 with Buffalo.

In his 13-year NFL career, Thomas played in 182 regular-season games, carried the ball 2,877 times for 12,074 yards and 65 touchdowns, and caught 472 **passes** for 4,458 yards and 23 touchdowns. In 21 postseason games, he ran 339 times for 1,442 yards and 16 touchdowns and caught 76 passes for 672 yards and five touchdowns. He appeared in five **Pro Bowls**. After retiring from active play, Thomas runs a training center for athletes in a Buffalo suburb. He was inducted into the **Pro Football Hall of Fame** in 2007 and the **College Football Hall of Fame** in 2008.

THORPE, JACOBUS FRANCISCUS "JIM." B. 28 May 1888, Prague, Oklahoma. D. 28 March 1953, Lomita, California. In a poll taken in 1950,

Jim Thorpe was voted the greatest athlete of the first half of the 20th century. In a poll taken a half century later, he was voted the greatest athlete of the century, although in the latter 50 years, such figures as Muhammad Ali, Michael Jordan, Wilt Chamberlain, Jack Nicklaus, Arnold Palmer, **Jim Brown**, and Martina Navratilova provided competition for that title.

Thorpe was born of mixed Native American heritage. His father was of Irish American and Sac and Fox Native American ancestry, and his mother was of French American and Pottawatomi Native American ancestry. Thorpe was raised as a Sac and Fox and a Roman Catholic. He was schooled at the Sac and Fox Indian Agency School in Oklahoma and later at the Haskell Indian School in Kansas. When he was 16 years old, he was sent to the **Carlisle Indian Industrial School** in Carlisle, Pennsylvania. He competed in track and field and **football** at Carlisle in 1907 and 1908 and then dropped out of school, returning in 1911. Carlisle was **coached** by **Glenn "Pop" Warner**, and he developed his team to the point where they played **major colleges**. The 1907 team had a record of 10–1 and was 10–2–1 in 1908. In 1911, they were 11–1 and, in 1912, were 12–1–1. Among the teams they defeated in those years were **Harvard University**, **Army**, **Navy**, **Syracuse University**, Brown University, the University of Chicago, and Georgetown University.

In 1912, Thorpe competed in athletics (track and field) in the **Olympic Games** in Stockholm, Sweden, and was the winner of the 10-event decathlon and five-event pentathlon, an event no longer held. When he was presented the gold medals by King Gustav V of Sweden, the king reportedly said, "You, sir, are the greatest athlete in the world." The king, himself, was a formidable athlete who has since been enshrined in the International Tennis Hall of Fame.

In 1913, it was discovered that Thorpe had played Minor League Baseball in 1909 and 1910 in the Eastern Carolina Class D league. The concept of amateurism in that era was that a player was considered to be a professional athlete and ineligible for amateur competition if he ever earned more than a penny for engaging in or coaching sports, or even if he competed in an event in which a known professional competed. Thorpe was ostracized and stripped of his Olympic medals, even though he was unaware that his baseball experience had made him ineligible for Olympic competition. This injustice was finally eradicated in 1982, when the International Olympic Committee reversed their original decision and declared Thorpe official cochampion, along with the runners-up, who had previously been awarded the medals that were taken from Thorpe.

Thorpe became a Major League Baseball player in 1913. He played the outfield for the **New York Giants**, Cincinnati Reds, and Boston Braves through the 1919 season. He had a career batting average of .252 with a high of .327 in 1919 and played for the Giants in the 1917 World Series.

Jim Thorpe, the greatest athlete of the 20th century.
Mike Moran

He also played **professional football** from 1913 to 1928 for a variety of teams. In 1915, Thorpe was signed by the Canton Bulldogs, one of the stronger teams at that time. He was with them through the 1920 season. In that year, the Bulldogs became charter members of the American Professional Football Association (APFA), a league that two years later was renamed the **National Football League (NFL)**. In 1921, Thorpe left the Bulldogs to play for and coach the Cleveland Indians in the APFA.

In 1922, the **Oorang Indians**, an NFL team composed of all Native American players, were formed, with Thorpe as tailback and head coach. That club was disbanded after two seasons, and Thorpe joined the Rock Island Independents in 1924. He played for them that year and part of 1925, when he was traded to the New York Giants. He played for Canton in 1926 and closed his NFL career with one game for the Chicago Cardinals in 1928, at the age of 41.

During Thorpe's professional NFL career, the league was in its infancy and few reliable statistics exist. He appeared in 52 games in eight seasons, ran for at least six **touchdowns**, and kicked at least four **field goals** and three extra points. For the remainder of his life, he had a variety of jobs, mostly manual labor, and even briefly joined the U.S. Merchant Marine in 1945, at the age of 57.

Thorpe was voted the Greatest Athlete of the First Half-Century by the Associated Press in 1950. In 1953, he died of a heart attack at the age of 64, although he had also been suffering from cancer. In 1951, a Hollywood film, *Jim Thorpe: All-American*, was made about his life, starring Burt Lancaster as Thorpe. In 1954, the Pennsylvania towns of Mauch Chunk and East Mauch Chunk merged, purchased Thorpe's remains, erected a monument to him, and were renamed Jim Thorpe, Pennsylvania. Thorpe was inducted into the **College Football Hall of Fame** in 1951 as a charter member and also the **Pro Football Hall of Fame** as a charter member in 1963. *See also* FOOTBALL FILMS.

TIE. For most of **football's** history, a tie (with both teams having the same number of points) was a successful outcome of a game. In 1958, the **National Football League's (NFL)** Championship Game between the **Baltimore Colts** and **New York Giants** ended in a tie. Because the NFL insisted on having only one champion, an additional **sudden-death overtime** period was played. The game was an overwhelming success and helped start **professional football's** enormous popularity with the American public. Subsequent professional **playoff** games employed the overtime method to determine a winner. In 1974, the NFL decided that regular-season games that ended with the score tied would play one sudden-death overtime period, and, if the score was still tied, a tie game would be the result. Playoff games would still be played to a definite conclusion, with additional overtime periods if necessary.

In 1996, the NCAA decided that all games would be played to a conclusion, and tie games would be no longer. Their overtime rules are a bit more complicated, with each team receiving the ball at least once before a conclusion is reached.

TIGHT END. The tight end is a **football position** in which the offensive player lines up on the **line of scrimmage** at the end of the line. His functions are to help **block** the opposition to aid the **quarterback** or ball carrier. Tight ends are also eligible to receive **passes** and will often fake a block and **run** downfield to catch passes. They are usually among the bigger, stronger players on the team, and the television announcers' phrase "Big Tight End" has become a cliché. *See also* DITKA, MICHAEL KELLER, JR. "MIKE"; WINSLOW, KELLEN BOSWELL, SR.

TILLMAN, PATRICK DANIEL, JR. "PAT." B. 6 November 1976, Fremont, California. D. 22 April 2004, Sperah, Afghanistan. Pat Tillman attended Leland High School in San Jose, California, and played on a division championship team. After receiving a scholarship to **Arizona State Univer-**

sity (ASU), the five-foot, 11-inch, 200-pound Tillman played **linebacker** there from 1994 to 1997. In 1996, he helped lead ASU to 11 consecutive victories and a **Rose Bowl** appearance, but they were defeated by **Ohio State University** in that contest.

Tillman was chosen by the **Arizona Cardinals** in the seventh round of the 1998 **National Football League (NFL) Draft** as the 226th overall selection. As a defensive **back**, he played both free **safety** and strong safety with the Cardinals from 1998 to 2001. In his four years in the NFL, he played in 60 regular-season games and had three **pass interceptions** and one **fumble** recovery.

After the 11 September 2001 terrorist attacks, Tillman completed the 2001 NFL season and turned down a reported $3.6 million contract offer from the Cardinals to enlist in the U.S. Army on 31 May 2002, along with his brother, Kevin, a Major League Baseball prospect. After completing Rangers' school in 2003, Pat was sent to Afghanistan. On 22 April 2004, he was killed by friendly fire, although the army first reported that he was killed by an enemy attack. Subsequent investigations by the military and civilian media have yet to disclose the entire story. Tillman was inducted into the **College Football Hall of Fame** in 2010.

TIME-OUT. Although **football** is played for 60 minutes, divided into four 15-minute quarters, the time is not continuous and is stopped for various reasons, for example, a ball carrier going **out of bounds** or an **incomplete pass**. In addition, each team is allowed to call time-out three times in each half to further stop the game clock from advancing. Strategic use of time-outs can often prolong the last two minutes of a game as much as 30 minutes of actual clock time.

TITANS OF NEW YORK. *See* NEW YORK JETS.

TITTLE, YELBERTON ABRAHAM "Y. A." B. 24 October 1926, Marshall, Texas. Y. A. Tittle was named after his father, who had been named for an uncle. His father's name was to be Yelverton, but it was misspelled on the birth certificate, so when his son was born, he, too, was named Yelberton Abraham Tittle Jr. Y. A. (no one except maybe his mother called him Yelberton) played **quarterback** at Marshall High School in Texas. After graduation in 1944, he committed to play **football** for **Louisiana State University (LSU)**. Prior to enrolling there, he was recruited by the **University of Texas** and began there. Once there, he found that **Bobby Layne** had also been recruited as quarterback for Texas. Tittle then reconsidered and entered LSU. Exempt from military service as an asthma sufferer, he played for LSU from

1944 to 1947. During his junior year, he led the Tigers to a 9–1–1 record and was named the most valuable player of the **Cotton Bowl** on 1 January 1947, after playing a 0–0 **tie** against the University of Arkansas in an ice storm.

Tittle was selected by the **Detroit Lions** in the first round of the 1948 **National Football League (NFL) Draft** as the sixth overall pick, but he signed with the **Cleveland Browns** of the **All-America Football Conference (AAFC)**. When the league decided that it needed more competitive balance, he was assigned to the **Baltimore Colts**. He played with the Colts in 1948 and 1949 in the AAFC, and with them in 1950 when they moved to the NFL. After the Colts folded in 1951, Tittle signed with the **San Francisco 49ers**, remaining with them through 1960. In 1961, he was traded to the **New York Giants**, and it was with the Giants that he made his most indelible mark in pro football. Tittle led the Giants to the NFL Championship Game each year from 1961 to 1963, although they lost each year. On 28 October 1962, he tied a league record with seven **touchdown passes** in one game.

Although the prematurely bald Tittle played **professional football** until the age of 38, for much of his career, he appeared to be a generation older. In a game against the **Pittsburgh Steelers** in 1964, he was knocked down and received a concussion and cracked sternum on the play. A photo of him on his knees, helmetless, with blood streaking down his bald head, is one of football's most classic images.

In his 17-year combined AAFC–NFL career, Tittle appeared in 203 regular-season games, completed 2,427 passes in 4,395 attempts for 33,070 yards and 242 touchdowns, and ran 372 times for 1,245 yards and 39 touchdowns. In five postseason games, he completed 70 passes in 157 attempts for 874 yards and four touchdowns and ran six times for minus 12 yards and no touchdowns. Tittle played in seven **Pro Bowls**. After retiring from football, he started his own insurance firm and was inducted into the **Pro Football Hall of Fame** in 1971.

TOLER, BURL ABRON, SR. B. 9 May 1928, Memphis, Tennessee. D. 16 August 2009, Castro Valley, California. Burl Toler attended McClymonds High School in Oakland, California. He attended the City College of San Francisco and played **center** on their **football** team. One of his teammates was **Ollie Matson**, who went on to become a **Pro Football Hall of Fame** player in the **National Football League (NFL)**. Toler then went to the University of San Francisco (USF) and was cocaptain and played **end** and **linebacker** on their team with Matson, Gino Marchetti, and Bob St. Clair, three players who all went on to play in the NFL. The 1951 USF team was undefeated and untied in nine games and also uninvited to a **bowl game**, possibly because most of the bowl games in that era were held in the southern

United States and both Matson and Toler were black. USF discontinued its football program the following year.

Toler was chosen by the **Cleveland Browns** in the ninth round of the 1951 NFL **Draft** as the 105th overall selection, even though he had another year of college eligibility. He was traded to the Chicago Cardinals in July 1952, but the following month he injured his knee in the **College All-Star Game** and, although he went to **training camp**, he was unable to play well and his NFL career ended before he played one game.

Toler decided to become a football **official** and became a head linesman in the NFL in 1965, the first African American to officiate in a major-league sport. The following year, he received a master's degree from USF. He worked as an NFL official until 1989 and was then appointed by the league to be an observer of officials, a job he held for eight years. Toler was also a school teacher and later became the principal of the Benjamin Franklin Middle School in San Francisco. His son, Burl Toler Jr., and grandson, Burl Toler III, played collegiately for the **University of California**, and his grandson has also played in the **Arena Football League**.

TOMLINSON, LADAINIAN TRAMAYNE "L. T." B. 23 June 1979, Rosebud, Texas. Known as L. T. to his **fans** and teammates, LaDainian Tomlinson has established a **professional football** career that will most likely result in his induction into the **Pro Football Hall of Fame** shortly after his retirement from active play. He is a graduate of University High School in Waco, Texas, and was a three-sport star there, playing baseball, basketball, and **football**. He later attended Texas Christian University (TCU). On 20 November 1999, Tomlinson carried the ball 43 times and gained 406 yards **rushing**, an all-time **National Collegiate Athletic Association (NCAA)** Football Bowl Subdivision record. In four years at TCU, he gained 5,263 yards rushing, sixth best in NCAA history. His collegiate football achievements make it likely that he will also be inducted in the **College Football Hall of Fame** once he is eligible.

The five-foot, 10-inch, 220-pound **running back** was chosen by the **San Diego Chargers** in the 2001 **National Football League (NFL) Draft** in the first round as the fifth overall selection. He played with the Chargers from 2001 to 2009 and was then signed by the **New York Jets**. With the Chargers, Tomlinson had several outstanding seasons, although the team only reached the **playoffs** in five of his nine seasons with them. They reached the American Football Conference (AFC) Championship Game in 2007 and the division championship game in 2008 but lost in the first round in their other three playoff appearances. In his first year with the Jets, Tomlinson helped lead them to the AFC Championship Game. In 2006, he set NFL records, with 31

touchdowns for the season (28 rushing touchdowns, another NFL record) and 186 points scored, and was named the league's Most Valuable Player.

In his career, Tomlinson played 11 seasons, appeared in 170 regular-season games, carried the ball 3,174 times for 13,684 yards and 145 touchdowns, caught 624 **passes** for 4,772 yards and 17 touchdowns, and completed eight passes in 12 attempts for 143 yards and seven touchdowns. He appeared in five **Pro Bowls**. In 10 postseason games, he ran 131 times for 468 yards and six touchdowns and caught 25 passes for 176 yards and one touchdown. Tomlinson's 145 career rushing touchdowns is the NFL's second all-time best behind **Emmitt Smith's** 164.

On 18 June 2012, it was announced that Tomlinson would sign a one-day contract with the Chargers and then retire from professional football. Since then, he has worked as a football analyst. He is a worthy candidate for the Pro Football Hall of Fame.

TORONTO ARGONAUTS. The Toronto Argonauts are a team in the **Canadian Football League (CFL)**. They were founded in 1873 and are one of the oldest sports franchises in North America. In 1883, they joined the Ontario Rugby Football Union as charter members. In 1907, they moved to the new Interprovincial Rugby Football Union and remained there until 1958, when the CFL was formed. In their long history, the Argonauts have played in 22 **Grey Cup** games and won 16, more than any other team. Only six of those victories have come since the Argos joined the CFL. Three of their six Grey Cup losses have occurred since 1958. From 1959 to 1988, Toronto played home games at the 33,000-seat Exhibition Stadium in Toronto, Ontario. When the new 50,000-seat domed **stadium**, the Skydome, was built in 1989, they moved there. In 2005, the Skydome was renamed the Rogers Centre.

Among the Argos' head **coaches** have been **Mike "Pinball" Clemons**, Don Matthews, Bob O'Billovich, and Lew Hayman (also general manager of the Toronto Huskies professional basketball team in 1946–1947, the first year of the Basketball Association of America, forerunner of the National Basketball Association). Argos head coaches with **National Football League** ties include Forrest Gregg, John Huard, Scott Milanovich, Steve Owen, Hamp Pool, John Rauch, Bob Shaw, Bill Swiacki, and Willie Wood.

Notable players for the Argonauts include Les Ascott, Mike "Pinball" Clemons, Lionel Conacher (also a National Hockey League [NHL] star), Royal Copeland, Jim Corrigal, Ulysses Curtis, Dan Ferrone, **Doug Flutie**, Terry Greer, Ed Harrington, Conredge Holloway, Joe Krol, Marv Luster, Dave Mann, Paul Masotti, Don Moen, Teddy Morris, Danny Nykoluk, Willie Pless, Jim Rountree, Dick Shatto, Jim Stillwagon, Roy "Red" Storey (later a famed NHL referee), Bill Symons, Ricky Williams, and William Zock.

TOUCH FOOTBALL. Touch **football** is a social version of football with minimal contact and no protective equipment. It can be played by any number of players. The rules and scoring are generally similar to football, except that touching the ball carrier by the opposition (instead of **tackling**) stops the play. Variants of the game include one-hand touch (in which touching is only required with one hand), two-hand touch (where both hands of the defender must contact the ball carrier to stop play), and flag football (in which players carry a handkerchief in their back pocket that must be removed from the ball carrier by the defender to stop play).

TOUCHBACK. A touchback occurs when the offensive team sends the ball into the defensive team's **end zone** by **kickoff** or **punt** and the ball is not returned. It can also occur when the defensive team **intercepts** the ball or recovers a **fumble** in their own end zone. The team receiving the ball is awarded possession at their own 20-**yard line**. **Canadian football** does not have touchbacks. Instead, kickoffs and punts that are not brought out of the end zone result in a single point, called a **rouge**, for the kicking team, with possession going to their opponents on the 35-yard line. In Canadian football, fumbles or interceptions recovered in the end zone result in possession on the 25-yard line for the recovering team. *See also* SAFETY (SCORE).

TOUCHDOWN. A touchdown is the primary scoring play in **football**. Six points are awarded to the team in possession of the ball if they successfully cross their opponent's **goal line**. A try for an additional point or two points is awarded to the scoring team on the following play. *See also* CONVERSION.

TRAINING CAMP. Because of the extreme physical nature of **football**, as well as the need for coordinated team efforts to play the game, most teams set aside a month or two to ensure that their players are in top physical shape and can work well together to carry out their offensive or defensive assignments. A team will generally reserve a facility, known as a training camp, for this purpose. Training camps are also used to trim a team's roster from 90 or 100 prospective players to the league-mandated maximum roster size (53 in the **National Football League** in 2012).

TRIPPI, CHARLES LOUIS "CHARLEY." B. 14 December 1921, Pittston, Pennsylvania. Charley Trippi played **football** at Pittston High School on a team that was undefeated. Although only about 160 pounds at the time, he was offered a scholarship to the **University of Georgia** after a Georgia alumnus who resided in Pittston saw him play but suggested that he first spend one year at a prep school, LaSalle Military Institute in Oakdale,

New York. In Trippi's words, "I gained 10 pounds, because they had a dinner menu that they gave you all you can eat buffet-style food and I ate real good." Trippi then enrolled at Georgia. As a college sophomore during the 1942 season, he, along with **Heisman Trophy** winner Frank Sinkwich, helped lead the football team to a 10–1 record and a trip to the **Rose Bowl**, where they defeated the **University of California, Los Angeles**. Trippi's college career was then interrupted by a stint in the U.S. Air Force. He was chosen by the Chicago Cardinals as the first overall selection in the 1945 **National Football League (NFL) Draft** but returned to school in 1945 and, in 1946, won the **Maxwell Award** as the best **college football** player in the country.

Trippi became the beneficiary of one of **professional football's** bidding wars. The **All-America Football Conference (AAFC)** was just beginning in 1946 and attempted to sign Trippi, but the Cardinals offered him a four-year contract for $100,000 (an enormous sum for that era) and were able to sign him. The investment paid dividends in its first year, as Trippi helped lead the Cardinals to the NFL championship in 1947. The following year, the team again reached the NFL Championship Game but lost, 7–0, to the **Philadelphia Eagles** in a snowstorm in Philadelphia. This was the last time the Cardinals franchise played in the league championship until 2009.

Trippi was also an excellent baseball player. In the summer of 1947, before he played in the NFL, he played for the Atlanta Crackers of the Southern Association and batted .334. Rather than attempt to play both sports, he chose football.

The versatile Trippi played **halfback**, **quarterback**, and defensive **back**, as well as returned **punts** and **kickoffs**. He punted throughout his nine-year NFL career, from 1947 to 1955. He appeared in 99 regular-season games, ran 687 times for 3,506 yards and 23 **touchdowns**, caught 130 **passes** for 1,321 yards and 11 touchdowns, completed 205 passes in 134 attempts for 2,547 yards and 16 touchdowns, punted 196 times for an average of 40.3 yards per punt, returned 63 punts for an average of 13.7 yards per return and two touchdowns, returned 66 kickoffs for an average of 22.1 yards per return with no touchdowns, and **intercepted** four passes for one touchdown. In two postseason games, Trippi ran 20 times for 110 yards and one touchdown, caught one pass for 20 yards and no touchdowns, returned four punts for 113 yards and one touchdown, and did not complete a pass in two attempts.

Trippi is one of only three players in NFL history to have more than 1,000 career yards passing, **rushing**, and receiving. He is one of the few players in league history to score a touchdown in four different ways, rushing, receiving, via a punt return, and by an interception return, in addition to also passing for a touchdown. The **Pro Bowl** only started in 1950, otherwise Trippi would have played in more than just two of them.

After retirement from football, Trippi became a real estate developer in Athens, Georgia, and worked as an assistant football **coach** for the University of Georgia, and also for the Cardinals. He was inducted into the **College Football Hall of Fame** in 1959 and the **Pro Football Hall of Fame** in 1968.

TRIPPING. Tripping is a rules infraction that occurs when a player uses his leg to hinder an opponent's progress. The **penalty** is 15 yards.

TRY. *See* CONVERSION.

TUNNELL, EMLEN LEWIS. B. 29 March 1925, Bryn Mawr, Pennsylvania. D. 22 July 1975, Pleasantville, New York. Emlen Tunnell achieved several distinctions in his brief lifetime. He was the first black player hired by the **New York Giants** and, in 1967, became the first African American inducted into the **Pro Football Hall of Fame**, as well as the first purely defensive player inducted there. In 14 years of **professional football** with the Giants and **Green Bay Packers**, he was an outstanding defensive **back** who was selected for the **Pro Bowl** nine times. Tunnell attended Radnor High School in Radnor, Pennsylvania, and continued his education at the University of Toledo. He played **football** there until a broken vertebrae in his neck halted his participation in that sport. He was able to play on the basketball team and helped lead them to the National Invitation Tournament finals in 1943. He enlisted in the U.S. Coast Guard after being rejected by both the army and navy for medical reasons. Tunnell regained the ability to play football while in the service and was named to the United Press Pacific Coast All-Service Team.

After his discharge from the military in 1946, Tunnell enrolled at the **University of Iowa** upon the recommendation of a former black Iowa player he met while in the service. Tunnell played for Iowa in 1946 and 1947, but, in the spring of 1948, he developed an eye infection and dropped out of school, intending to resume his studies in the fall. While at home, he found a questionnaire sent to him by the New York Giants of the **National Football League (NFL)** and decided to pursue it. He hitchhiked to New York and met with Giants' owner **Tim Mara**, who offered him a tryout. Although undrafted, Tunnell made the team and played with the Giants from 1948 to 1958 as a defensive back and kick **returner**. The six-foot, one-inch, 185-pound former Iowa star played on the Giants' NFL championship team in 1956 and was with them during their memorable **overtime** loss in the 1958 NFL Championship Game.

Following the 1958 season, Tunnell asked to be released by the Giants and was signed by the Green Bay Packers. He played three more seasons in the NFL for the Packers and was on their NFL runner-up team in 1960 and NFL championship team in 1961. As a veteran player, he served as a mentor to the black players on the Giants, and, when he was hired by the Packers, he continued in that role.

In his 14-year NFL career, Tunnell appeared in 167 regular-season games and recorded 79 **interceptions** for four **touchdowns**. He was also used as a **punt** and kick returner and returned 258 punts for an average of 8.6 yards per return, with five punt returns going for touchdowns. He returned 46 **kickoffs** for an average of 26.4 yards per return, with one in 1951 being returned 100 yards for a touchdown. In his first two years with the Giants, Tunnell was also occasionally used as a ball carrier and **pass** receiver, and he **rushed** 17 times for 43 yards and caught five passes for 39 yards. He also completed one of two passes for 23 yards. When he retired from active play, he was the NFL leader in career pass interceptions (and still remains second best), interception return yardage (still fifth best), punt returns (now 15th best), and punt return yardage (now 25th best).

In 1963, Tunnell was hired by the Giants as a scout. Two years later he was working as an **assistant coach** for them. He died of a heart attack at the age of 50 while working at the Giants **training camp** in 1975.

TURNOVER. A turnover occurs when the defensive team gains possession of the ball either through **interception** or **fumble** recovery.

TWO (THREE)-MINUTE WARNING. The two-minute warning is a **time-out** taken by the **officials** in **professional football** to notify both teams that only two minutes remain in the game. The rules of the game are then modified slightly following this time-out. **College football** does not have a similar official timeout. In **Canadian football**, this warning is given with three minutes remaining. Some high school associations use a four-minute warning.

U

UMPIRE. *See* OFFICIALS.

UNIFORM NUMBERS. In 1952, to assist **officials** in making calls, the **National Football League (NFL)** adopted a numbering system for all players. The numbering system was updated in 1973 as follows: 1 to 9 **quarterbacks** and **kickers**; 10 to 19 quarterbacks, receivers, **tight ends**, and kickers; 20 to 49 **running backs** and defensive **backs**; 50 to 59 **centers** and **linebackers**; 60 to 79 defensive and offensive **linemen**; 80 to 89 receivers and tight ends; 90 to 99 defensive linemen and linebackers. Receivers and tight ends can also wear 40 to 49 if all numbers from 80 to 89 are used. Numbers 0 and 00 can no longer be used, although a few players prior to 1973 wore them.

The **National Collegiate Athletic Association** has the following number stipulations: 1 to 49 backs, 50 to 59 snapper (center), 60 to 69 **guard**, 70 to 79 **tackle**, 80 to 99 **end**. No distinction is made between offensive and defensive players. More than one player on a college team may wear the same uniform number, although they may not both play in the game at the same time. (Many college squads have more than 100 players, but the majority of them are reserves who see little game action.) High schools have recommended (but not required) numbering similar to that of colleges.

Unlike other major team sports, since football rosters are much larger, NFL teams are discouraged from retiring the numbers of notable players for fear of running out of available ones.

UNITAS, JOHN CONSTANTINE "JOHNNY." B. 7 May 1933, Pittsburgh, Pennsylvania. D. 11 September 2002, Timonium, Maryland. Johnny Unitas attended St. Justin's High School in Pittsburgh, where he played both **halfback** and **quarterback**. Although he was a starting quarterback as a freshman at the University of Louisville, his four years there were anything but stellar. Louisville's record for that period was 12–23. As a result, Unitas was not chosen until the ninth round of the **National Football League (NFL) Draft** in 1955 as the 102nd overall selection by the **Pittsburgh Steelers**. The six-foot, one-inch, 190-pound Unitas was cut by the Steelers and did not play

professional football in 1955, keeping busy by working in construction and playing semipro football.

In 1956, Unitas tried out for the **Baltimore Colts** and made the team. After Baltimore's starting quarterback, George Shaw, was injured in the fourth game of the season, Unitas got a chance to play. Extremely nervous in his debut, the Colts were defeated, 58–27. Fortunately he recovered and played well the rest of the year. In his last three games in 1956, Unitas threw a **touchdown pass** in each one. For the next 44 games, through 4 December 1960, he threw at least one touchdown pass. This streak of throwing a touchdown pass in 47 consecutive games is one of the NFL's records that appeared likely to never be broken (but **Drew Brees**, with touchdown passes in 54 consecutive games from 18 October 2009 to 25 November 2012, surpassed it).

In 1957, Unitas led the NFL in passing yardage and was named the league's Most Valuable Player by the Newspaper Enterprise Association, one of a series of organizations that selected annual league Most Valuable Players. In 1958, Unitas helped lead the Colts to the NFL Championship Game, which the Colts won in **overtime** in a game sometimes called "the Greatest Football Game Ever Played." The Colts repeated as champions in 1959. In 1964, they lost in the NFL Championship Game but won again in 1968. That year, they played the **New York Jets** in the **Super Bowl** and were defeated by them.

Unitas continued as Colt quarterback through 1972, being named Most Valuable Player again in 1959, 1964, and 1967, and he concluded his professional career with the **San Diego Chargers** in 1973. He completed 2,830 of 5,186 passes for 40,239 yards in 211 games and threw for 290 touchdowns in his 18 years in the NFL. He started in 186 games and had a won-lost record of 118–64–4 in those contests. In nine postseason games, he completed 120 passes in 226 attempts for 1,663 yards and seven touchdowns and ran 21 times for 92 yards and one touchdown.

After retiring from active play, Unitas did some television commentary work. He was inducted into the **Pro Football Hall of Fame** in 1979. He died of a heart attack while working out at a physical therapy center in Timonium, Maryland, on 11 September 2002.

UNITED FOOTBALL LEAGUE (UFL). The United Football League (UFL) was a **professional football** league that began play in 2009. It was a quasi-major league that mainly employed players who had previous **National Football League (NFL)** experience. The UFL fielded four teams in 2009, playing six games each; five teams in 2010, playing eight games each; and four teams in 2011. Games were played on weekday nights during the NFL season. League rules were generally similar to those in the NFL, with a few minor exceptions. Teams were originally in New York City; Orlando,

Florida; Las Vegas, Nevada; and San Francisco, California. In 2010, a team was added in Omaha, Nebraska. The league suspended operations midway through the 2011 season. It resumed in 2012 with four teams but only lasted four weeks before again suspending operations.

UNITED STATES FOOTBALL LEAGUE (USFL). The United States Football League (USFL) was a **professional football** league that played three seasons from 1983 to 1985. Games were scheduled in the spring and summer months so as not to directly compete with the **National Football League (NFL)**. Plans were made for the league to play in the fall of 1986, but they did not come to fruition. The league was able to attract several top-caliber players, and it signed **Heisman Trophy** winner **Herschel Walker** after his junior season of college in opposition to the NFL, whose league rules at that time forbade the signing of a college underclassman. Other USFL players who are now in the **Pro Football Hall of Fame** include **Jim Kelly**, **Reggie White**, **Steve Young**, and Gary Zimmerman. Hall of Fame **coaches** include **George Allen** and Marv Levy. Among the league's innovations, both later adopted by the NFL, were the two-point **conversion** option and the use of instant **replay** by **officials**.

In 1983, there were 12 teams in the USFL. Teams played an 18-game regular-season schedule. The Michigan Panthers defeated the Philadelphia Stars for the league championship. The league expanded to 18 teams in 1984. An 18-game schedule was again played, and the Stars repeated as league champion, this time defeating the Arizona Wranglers. In 1985, only 14 teams remained. They again played an 18-game schedule, and the Stars (relocated to Baltimore) again won the league championship.

Following the 1985 season, the USFL sued the NFL for antitrust violations, claiming that the NFL interfered with the USFL's ability to televise games. Although the USFL technically won the 42-day jury trial, with the statement that the NFL was a "duly adjudicated illegal monopoly," it also stated that the USFL's financial problems were of their own making, and the league was awarded only one dollar in nominal damages. The decision destroyed the league, which had initiated the suit in an attempt to force a merger. The USFL did not play in 1986 and eventually dissolved in 1988. *See also* DAVIS, ALLEN "AL."

UNITED STATES MILITARY ACADEMY. *See* ARMY.

UNITED STATES NAVAL ACADEMY. *See* NAVY.

UNIVERSITY OF ALABAMA. *See* ALABAMA, UNIVERSITY OF.

UNIVERSITY OF CALIFORNIA, BERKELEY. *See* CALIFORNIA, UNIVERSITY OF.

UNIVERSITY OF CALIFORNIA, LOS ANGELES (UCLA). The University of California, Los Angeles, more popularly known as UCLA, began their **football** program in 1919, and, since then, through 2012, Bruins' teams have compiled a record of 543–375–36. In addition, they have competed in 32 postseason **bowl games**, with a record of 14–17–1. They were selected as national collegiate champions only once, in 1954. Since 1928, UCLA football teams have competed in the Pacific Coast Conference (now known as the **Pacific-12 Conference**) of the **National Collegiate Athletic Association**. Since 1982, UCLA has played home games at the 92,542-seat **Rose Bowl** in Pasadena, California, a Los Angeles suburb. Their main rival is the **University of Southern California (USC)**. The teams have met in most years since 1929, with the winner receiving a trophy known as the "Victory Bell." USC leads in the series, 46–29–7.

Terry Donahue (1976–1995; 144–81–8) has been the UCLA **coach** with the most longevity. Other noteworthy UCLA head coaches have been Henry "Red" Sanders (1949–1957; 66–19–1), Tommy Prothro (1965–1970; 41–18–3), Franklin "Pepper" Rogers (1971–1973; 19–12–1), and Dick Vermeil (1974–1975; 15–5–3).

UCLA alumni in the **College Football Hall of Fame** include **quarterbacks Troy Aikman** and Gary Beban (**Heisman Trophy** winner in 1967); **halfbacks** Billy Kilmer and Kenny Washington; **end** Tom Fears; **linemen** Randy Cross, Donn Moomaw, and Al Sparlis; **safety** Kenny Easley; and **linebacker** Jerry Robinson. Head coaches Terry Donahue, Tommy Prothro, and Henry "Red" Sanders have also been inducted. Baseball pioneer Jackie Robinson also played football for UCLA.

Through 2012, there have been 278 **professional football** players who have attended UCLA, 267 in the **National Football League**, seven in the **American Football League**, and four in the **All-America Football Conference**. They include Troy Aikman, Kermit Alexander, Steve Bono, Randy Cross, Dave Dalby, Brad Daluiso, Donnie Edwards, Mel Farr Jr., Mel Farr Sr., Tom Fears, Efren Herrera, Jimmy Johnson, Norm Johnson, Maurice Jones-Drew, Billy Kilmer, Carnell Lake, J. P. Losman, Freeman McNeil, Max Montoya, Ken Norton, Jonathan Ogden, Roman Phifer, Jerry Robinson, Jay Schroeder, Don Shinnick, Woody Strode, Manu Tuiasosopo, Mark Tuinei, Wendell Tyler, Kenny Washington, and **Bob Waterfield**.

UNIVERSITY OF COLORADO. *See* COLORADO, UNIVERSITY OF.

UNIVERSITY OF FLORIDA. *See* FLORIDA, UNIVERSITY OF.

UNSPORTSMANLIKE CONDUCT • 411

UNIVERSITY OF GEORGIA. *See* GEORGIA, UNIVERSITY OF.

UNIVERSITY OF ILLINOIS. *See* ILLINOIS, UNIVERSITY OF.

UNIVERSITY OF IOWA. *See* IOWA, UNIVERSITY OF.

UNIVERSITY OF MIAMI. *See* MIAMI, UNIVERSITY OF.

UNIVERSITY OF MICHIGAN. *See* MICHIGAN, UNIVERSITY OF.

UNIVERSITY OF MINNESOTA. *See* MINNESOTA, UNIVERSITY OF.

UNIVERSITY OF NEBRASKA. *See* NEBRASKA, UNIVERSITY OF.

UNIVERSITY OF NOTRE DAME. *See* NOTRE DAME, UNIVERSITY OF.

UNIVERSITY OF OKLAHOMA. *See* OKLAHOMA, UNIVERSITY OF.

UNIVERSITY OF PENNSYLVANIA. *See* PENNSYLVANIA, UNIVERSITY OF.

UNIVERSITY OF PITTSBURGH. *See* PITTSBURGH, UNIVERSITY OF.

UNIVERSITY OF SOUTHERN CALIFORNIA. *See* SOUTHERN CALIFORNIA, UNIVERSITY OF.

UNIVERSITY OF TENNESSEE. *See* TENNESSEE, UNIVERSITY OF.

UNIVERSITY OF TEXAS. *See* TEXAS, UNIVERSITY OF.

UNIVERSITY OF WASHINGTON. *See* WASHINGTON, UNIVERSITY OF.

UNIVERSITY OF WISCONSIN. *See* WISCONSIN, UNIVERSITY OF.

UNSPORTSMANLIKE CONDUCT. Unsportsmanlike conduct is a type of **penalty** that can be assessed when, in the judgment of the **officials**, an act occurs that is improper but is not a specific rules infraction, as are **offsides** or **holding**. The penalty is 15 yards. It can also result in a player's ejection from the game. In recent years, it has become permissible for excessive celebration by a player following a score to be treated as unsportsmanlike conduct.

UPRIGHTS. *See* GOALPOSTS.

UPSHAW, EUGENE THURMAN, JR. "GENE." B. 15 August 1945, Robstown, Texas. D. 20 August 2008, Lake Tahoe, California. Gene Upshaw attended Robstown High School, where he starred in baseball and also played a little bit of **football** along with his brother, Marvin, who also later became a **professional football** player. In high school, Gene was only five feet, 10 inches tall and 185 pounds and did not impress college **coaches** as a football player. He enrolled at nearby Texas A&I University (the school was renamed Texas A&M University, Kingsville, in 1993). He eventually received a football scholarship there and grew to a height of six feet, five inches and was 285 pounds by his senior year.

Upshaw was **drafted** in the first round, 17th overall, by the **Oakland Raiders** of the **American Football League (AFL)** in the 1967 combined draft of the **National Football League (NFL)** and AFL. He played offensive **guard** with the Raiders from 1967 through 1981, and played in the **Super Bowl** with them in 1968, 1977, and 1981, winning the championship the latter two years.

As an offensive **lineman**, virtually no statistics are published that measure his performance. In his 15 years in the NFL, he played in 217 of a possible 218 regular-season games and recovered three **fumbles**. Sacks, a current statistical measure of offensive line performance, were not officially recorded during Upshaw's professional career. He was selected for seven **Pro Bowls**.

One of Upshaw's most important contributions to football was as a labor leader. As the executive director of the NFL Players Association, he helped acquire a larger share of league revenues for the players. He was inducted into the **Pro Football Hall of Fame** in 1987 and died just three days after being diagnosed with pancreatic cancer in 2008.

V

VAN BROCKLIN, NORMAN MACK "NORM," "THE DUTCHMAN." B. 15 March 1926, Parade, South Dakota. D. 2 May 1983, Social Circle, Georgia. Norm Van Brocklin was raised in California and attended Acalanes High School in Lafayette, California. After graduation from high school, he served in the U.S. Navy from 1943 to 1945, before enrolling at the University of Oregon. He played three years of **college football** at Oregon, forgoing his final year of eligibility to play **professional football**. In 1948, he helped lead Oregon to the cochampionship of the Pacific Coast Conference and an invitation to the **Sugar Bowl**.

Van Brocklin was chosen by the Los Angeles Rams in the fourth round of the **National Football League (NFL) Draft** as the 37th overall selection. The six-foot, one-inch, 190-pound Van Brocklin, known as "the Dutchman" to his teammates, played **quarterback** for the Rams from 1949 to 1957 and also did their **punting**. In 1958, he moved to the **Philadelphia Eagles** and finished his NFL career with three years in Philadelphia. In his 12 years in the NFL, Van Brocklin played in the NFL Championship Game five times, in 1949, 1950, 1951, and 1955 with the Rams, and in 1960 with the Eagles. He was a member of the league champions in 1951 and 1960.

During his career, Van Brocklin appeared in 140 regular-season NFL games and completed 1,553 **passes** in 2,895 attempts for 23,611 yards and 173 **touchdowns**. He also carried the ball 102 times for 11 touchdowns. Doubling as the team's **punter**, he also punted 523 times for a 42.9-yard average. In seven postseason games, Van Brocklin completed 46 passes in 95 attempts for 736 yards and four touchdowns and ran five times for minus 10 yards and no touchdowns. He also punted 17 times for a 40.1-yard average. He was selected for the **Pro Bowl** nine times.

After retiring from active play, Van Brocklin became the first **coach** of the expansion **Minnesota Vikings** in 1961. He coached them from 1961 to 1966. He then served as head coach of the **Atlanta Falcons** from 1968 to 1974. In 84 games coaching the Vikings, his teams had a record of 29–51–4. The Vikings improved in each of his first four years with the team and, in 1964, finished second in the NFL West Division. With the Falcons, Van Brocklin was also able to improve their record each year, and, in 1973, they finished second in the National Football Conference West Division. His overall record with them was 37–49–3.

After the 1974 season, Van Brocklin returned to his pecan farm in Georgia and did some television work and assisted as a coach at **Georgia Tech**. He suffered a brain tumor and died from a stroke in 1983. He was inducted into the **College Football Hall of Fame** in 1966 and the **Pro Football Hall of Fame** in 1971.

VAN BUREN, STEPHEN W. "STEVE." B. 28 December 1920, La Ceiba, Honduras. D. 23 August 2012, Lancaster, Pennsylvania. Steve Van Buren was one of the few professional athletes born in Honduras. Orphaned as a young boy, he was sent to live with relatives in Louisiana. He attended Easton High School in New Orleans, Louisiana, and his **football** prowess there gained him a scholarship to **Louisiana State University**.

Van Buren was selected by the **Philadelphia Eagles** in the first round of the 1944 **National Football League (NFL) Draft** as the fifth overall pick and played for them through the 1951 season. A six-foot, 200-pound **halfback**, he also returned **punts** and kicks. He played in NFL Championship Games in 1947, 1948, and 1949 and was a member of the NFL champions in 1948 and 1949. On 19 December 1948, he scored the Eagles' only **touchdown** in the fourth quarter of the NFL Championship Game, which was played in a blizzard.

In his eight-year NFL career, Van Buren played in 83 regular-season games, carried the ball 1,320 times for 5,860 yards and 69 touchdowns, and caught 45 **passes** for 523 yards and three touchdowns. As a punt and **kickoff returner**, he returned 34 punts for a 13.9-yard average and two touchdowns, as well as 76 kickoffs for a 26.7-yard average and three touchdowns. In four postseason games, he ran 93 times for 365 yards and two touchdowns, caught four passes for 29 yards and one touchdown, and returned one kickoff for 12 yards. Van Buren was inducted into the **Pro Football Hall of Fame** in 1965.

VARSITY. High schools and colleges in the United States and Canada often field more than one team in a sport. Lower-class students in those institutions may play on a freshman or junior varsity team. The main teams fielded by the school are designated varsity teams and are usually comprised of upper-class students in their junior or senior years. In recent years, schools have been permitted to allow freshman students to play on varsity teams, although at one time they were forbidden to do so by the high school and collegiate administrative organizations.

VICK, MICHAEL DWAYNE. B. 26 June 1980, Newport News, Virginia. Michael Vick was a left-handed **quarterback** as a high school freshman at

Homer L. Ferguson High School in Newport News, Virginia. The school closed in 1996 after his freshman year, and he transferred to Warwick High School in Newport News, along with his **coach**, former **National Football League (NFL)** player Tommy Reamon. Vick continued to excel in **football** and accepted a scholarship to **Virginia Tech**. After **redshirting** in 1998, he was Virginia Tech's starting quarterback in 1999. He led them to an 11–0 regular-season record and the **Big East Conference** championship, but they were defeated in the **Sugar Bowl** by **Florida State University** in a contest for the **Bowl Championship Series** national championship. In 2000, Vick led Virginia Tech to an 11–1 record and a victory in the Gator Bowl.

Vick decided to become a professional player and not complete his remaining two years at Virginia Tech. He was the first overall selection in the 2001 NFL **Draft** and was chosen by the **Atlanta Falcons**. The six-foot, 215-pound Vick played for the Falcons from 2001 to 2006. In 2007, he was indicted for being involved with a dogfighting ring and, in August 2007, pled guilty and was sentenced to 21 months in prison.

After he was released from prison, Vick was also released by the Falcons' organization, who did not want him to play for them even though he was still physically capable. He signed with the **Philadelphia Eagles** and has played for them from 2009 to 2012. In 2010, he was named the NFL Comeback Player of the Year after helping lead the Eagles to the National Football Conference East Division championship.

Through 2012, Vick has played in 121 regular-season games in 10 seasons. His **rushing** ability, along with his **passing** ability, has made him exceptional among quarterbacks. He has been the starting quarterback in 101 games, with a 56–44–1 won-lost record in those contests. Vick has completed 1,626 passes for 2,889 yards and 123 **touchdowns**. He has run with the ball 791 times for 5,551 yards and 34 touchdowns. He is, however, quite **fumble** prone and twice has led the NFL in fumbles and has registered a career total of 87. In six postseason games, he has completed 79 of 141 passes for 977 yards and five touchdowns and run 37 times for 271 yards and one touchdown. Vick has been selected for four **Pro Bowls**.

VIRGINIA POLYTECHNIC INSTITUTE AND STATE UNIVERSITY. *See* VIRGINIA TECH.

VIRGINIA TECH. Virginia Polytechnic Institute and State University, popularly known as VPI or Virginia Tech, is located in Blacksburg, Virginia. Their **football** program began in 1892, and, since then, through 2012, Hokies' teams have compiled a record of 687–424–46. In addition, they have competed in 26 postseason **bowl games** (20 in consecutive seasons from

1993 to 2012), with a record of 10–16. They have never been selected as national collegiate champion but came close in 2000, as they were defeated in the **Bowl Championship Series** National Championship Game by **Florida State**, 46–29, in the **Sugar Bowl**, after winning their first 11 games that season. The Hokies have played as an independent and in several different **conferences** throughout their history, most recently in the **Big East Conference** from 1991 to 2003 and the **Atlantic Coast Conference** since 2004. The 66,000-seat Lane Stadium has been their home field since 1965.

Until 1984, Virginia Tech had a rivalry with the Virginia Military Institute, usually playing on **Thanksgiving Day**, but it was discontinued as the two teams' football programs began to become noncompetitive. The University of Virginia and Virginia Tech still play a series that originated in 1895, which Virginia Tech leads, 52–37–5. Since 1995, the Commonwealth Cup has been awarded to the victor.

Virginia Tech's nickname, the Hokies, is a nonsense word derived from a cheer written in 1896 that goes, "Hokie Hokie Hokie Hi; Tech Tech VPI; Solah-rex, Solah-rah; Poly Tech Vir-gin-ia; Ray Rah VPI; Team Team Team." The original school mascot was a turkey called the "Fighting Gobbler."

Virginia Tech's most successful **coach** has been Frank Beamer. He has coached the Hokies since 1987. His record through 2012 is 216–104–2. Other notable coaches include Frank Moseley (1951–1960; 54–42–4); Jerry Claiborne (1961–1970; 61–39–2), and Bill Dooley (1978–1986; 64–37–1). Virginia Tech alumni in the **College Football Hall of Fame** are **halfback** Hunter Carpenter, **end** Carroll Dale, **safety** Frank Loria, and **tackle** Bruce Smith. Coaches Jerry Claiborne and Andy Gustafson are also enshrined there.

Through 2012, there have been 120 **professional football** players who have attended Virginia Tech, 117 in the **National Football League**, two in the **American Football League**, and one in the **All-America Football Conference**. They include Robert Brown, Carroll Dale, Andre' Davis, Antonio Freeman, Shayne Graham, DeAngelo Hall, Mike Johnson, Madison "Buzz" Nutter, George Preas, Pierson Prioleau, Bruce Smith, Nick Sorenson, Don Strock, and **Michael Vick**.

WALKER, EWELL DOAK, JR. "DOAK." B. 1 January 1927, Dallas, Texas. D. 27 September 1998, Steamboat Springs, Colorado. Doak Walker attended Highland Park High School in Dallas, where he and **Bobby Layne** were teammates on the **football** team. The two went their separate ways to college, Layne to the **University of Texas**, and Walker to Southern Methodist University (SMU), but they were reunited in the **National Football League (NFL)** with the **Detroit Lions** from 1950 to 1955.

At SMU, the five-foot, 11-inch, 175-pound Walker played **halfback** and defensive **back** and was also the team's **punter**, placekicker, and kick **returner**. After his freshman year in 1945, he served in the U.S. Army. Returning to school in 1947, he won the **Maxwell Award**, and, as a junior in 1948, he was awarded the **Heisman Trophy**. Walker helped lead SMU to the **Southwest Conference** championship in 1947 and 1948, as well as appearances in the **Cotton Bowl** following those two seasons. He was selected by the **New York Bulldogs** in the first round of the 1949 NFL **Draft** as the third overall selection. He remained at SMU for the 1949 season and signed a professional contract with the Detroit Lions in 1950.

In his six-year NFL career (all with Detroit), Walker played in 67 regular-season games, carried the ball 309 times for 1,520 yards and 12 **touchdowns**, caught 152 **passes** for 2,539 yards and 21 touchdowns, and completed seven of 28 passes for two touchdowns. As a kick and **punt** returner, he returned 18 punts for a 15.8-yard average and one touchdown and 38 **kickoffs** for a 25.5-yard average with no touchdowns. As a placekicker, he scored 49 **field goals** in 87 attempts and 183 extra points in 191 attempts. While Walker served as a punter in three of his six years, he averaged 39.1 yards per punt in 50 punts. He was named to the **Pro Bowl** five times and was a member of the NFL champions in 1952 and 1953 and NFL runners-up in 1954.

After retirement from football, Walker turned down several offers to be a **coach** and instead became involved in real estate development with former Detroit teammate Cloyce Box. His second wife, Gladys "Skeeter" Werner, was a member of the U.S. women's 1956 **Olympic** Alpine ski team. They resided in Steamboat Springs, Colorado, where Walker died from injuries sustained in a skiing accident in 1998. Ironically, his accident occurred on

Mt. Werner, named for Skeeter's brother, Wallace "Buddy" Werner, also an Olympian, who was killed in an avalanche 34 years earlier. Walker was inducted into the **College Football Hall of Fame** in 1959 and the **Pro Football Hall of Fame** in 1986.

WALKER, HERSCHEL JUNIOR. B. 3 March 1962, Wrightsville, Georgia. Herschel Walker attended Johnson County High School in Wrightsville, Georgia, where, as a **running back**, he led the **football** team to the state championship in 1979. At the **University of Georgia** from 1980 to 1982, he won both the **Maxwell Award** and **Heisman Trophy** in 1982. During his three years at Georgia, they had a record of 31–3, were the **Southeastern Conference** champion or cochampion each year, and appeared in the **Sugar Bowl** each year. The undefeated 1980 team was declared the national champion.

After his junior year, the six-foot, one-inch, 225-pound Walker signed a contract with the New Jersey Generals of the new **United States Football League (USFL)**. At that time, both the **National Football League (NFL)** and USFL had rules about signing collegians before their class graduated, but the Generals defied the league, reasoning that the ban would not hold up in court should it be challenged. It did not, and Walker played for the Generals from 1983 until 1985, when the league folded.

Walker was selected in the fifth round of the 1985 NFL **Draft** by the **Dallas Cowboys** as the 114th overall choice and played with them from 1986 to 1989. After three successful seasons with Dallas, he was traded to the **Minnesota Vikings** for five players. He did not do as well with Minnesota and, in 1992, signed with the **Philadelphia Eagles**. After three years with them, he played with the **New York Giants** in 1995 and returned to Dallas for 1996 and 1997.

Although his NFL individual statistics are exceptional, when his NFL statistics are combined with those from the USFL, Walker ranks among the top five all-time **rushing** leaders. In 187 regular-season NFL games in 13 seasons, he carried the ball 1,954 times for 8,225 yards and 61 **touchdowns**. He also caught 512 **passes** for 4,859 yards and 21 touchdowns. Walker was also used as a kick **returner** for much of his NFL career and returned 215 kicks for 5,084 yards and two touchdowns of more than 90 yards each. In five postseason games, he ran 28 times for 132 yards and no touchdowns, caught 10 passes for 60 yards and no touchdowns, and returned eight **kickoffs** for 146 yards. Surprisingly, he appeared in only two **Pro Bowls**, in 1987 and 1988. He also never appeared in the **Super Bowl**.

In 1992, Walker became one of the few black athletes to compete in the Winter **Olympics** when he was selected for the U.S. two-man bobsled team due to his exceptional strength and speed. With Brian Shimer as driver, the team did not win a medal but did finish a commendable seventh of the 46 teams competing. In 2010, Walker extended his versatile athletic career with a victory in a mixed martial arts (MMA) competition. He won his second MMA bout in 2011. He was inducted into the **College Football Hall of Fame** in 1999.

WARD, HINES E., JR. B. 8 March 1976, Seoul, Korea. Although Hines Ward is one of the few Asian-born **National Football League (NFL)** players, he has spent little time in his birth country, moving to the United States when he was just one year old. His father was an African American serviceman stationed in Korea, and his mother was a native Korean. Ward was raised in the Atlanta area and attended Forest Park High School in the Atlanta suburbs. He played **quarterback** in high school and played both quarterback and **wide receiver** at the **University of Georgia**.

Ward had a stellar college career but was only chosen in the third round by the **Pittsburgh Steelers** in the 1998 NFL **Draft** as the 98th overall selection. This may have been due to the fact that an examination disclosed that Ward was missing an anterior cruciate ligament in his left knee as a result of a childhood accident. Ward signed with the Steelers and played wide receiver for them from 1998 to 2011. The six-foot, 205-pound receiver helped lead the Steelers to **Super Bowls** in 2006, 2009, and 2011, with victories in the first two. Ward was named Most Valuable Player of the 2006 Super Bowl.

Through the 2011 season, Ward played 14 seasons in the NFL, all with the Steelers. He caught exactly 1,000 **passes** for 12,083 yards and 85 **touchdowns** in 217 regular-season games. He also **rushed** 57 times for 428 yards and one touchdown and was selected to the **Pro Bowl** four times from 2001 to 2004. In 18 postseason games, he caught 88 passes for 1,181 yards and 10 touchdowns and ran seven times for 31 yards and no touchdowns.

In 2006, he returned to his native land for the first time and established the Hines Ward Helping Hands Foundation to help mixed-race children overcome discrimination in Korea. In 2010, Ward was selected by U.S. president Barack Obama to work on the President's Advisory Commission on Asian Americans and Pacific Islanders. Ward's versatility also helped him to win the 2011 *Dancing with the Stars* competition. On 20 March 2012, after being released by Pittsburgh, he announced his retirement.

WARFIELD, PAUL DRYDEN. B. 28 November 1942, Warren, Ohio. Paul Warfield attended Warren High School in Warren, Ohio, where he starred in **football** and track. He continued participating in both sports at **Ohio State University** and graduated from there in 1964. He was picked by the **Cleveland Browns** in the 1964 **National Football League (NFL) Draft** in the first round as the 11th overall selection. Warfield was also chosen by the **Buffalo Bills** in the fourth round of the 1964 **American Football League** Draft as the 28th overall selection. The six-foot, 190-pound **wide receiver** played with the Browns from 1964 to 1969. He was traded to the **Miami Dolphins** in 1970 and was with them in their glory years, when they reached the **Super Bowl** three times, winning twice, and had an undefeated season, at 17–0, in 1972. In 1975, Warfield, along with Miami backs **Larry Csonka** and Jim Kiick, signed with the Memphis Southmen of the new **World Football League (WFL)**. Unfortunately for them, the WFL folded midway through the 1975 season, and the trio returned to the NFL. Warfield signed with the Browns and concluded his NFL career with them in 1976 and 1977.

In 13 years in the NFL, Warfield played in 157 regular-season games and caught 427 **passes** for 8,565 yards and 85 **touchdowns**. He also recovered a teammate's **fumble** in the **end zone** for an additional touchdown. In 18 post-season games, he caught 58 passes for 1,121 yards and five touchdowns and ran five times for 31 yards and no touchdowns. He was selected for eight **Pro Bowls**, in 1964, 1968, 1969, 1970, 1971, 1972, 1973, and 1974.

In 1977, Warfield received a master's degree from Kent State University. He has worked in radio as a sports broadcaster and held scouting and executive positions with the Browns. He was inducted into the **Pro Football Hall of Fame** in 1983.

WARNER, GLENN SCOBEY "POP." B. 5 April 1871, Springville, New York. D. 7 September 1954, Palo Alto, California. Glenn "Pop" Warner attended **Cornell University** and played **guard** on their **football** team from 1892 to 1894. As one of the oldest players on the team, he was given the nickname "Pop" and, for the rest of his life, was best known as "Pop" Warner. He then spent the next 44 years of his life as a **college football** head **coach** and worked at the **University of Georgia** (1895–1896), Iowa State University (1895–1899), Cornell University (1897–1898, 1904–1906), **Carlisle Indian Industrial School** (1899–1903, 1907–1914), the **University of Pittsburgh** (1915–1923), **Stanford University** (1924–1932), and Temple University (1933–1938). Warner was also an associate coach at San Jose State University in 1939. At some points in his early coaching career, he coached at more than one school during the same season.

Warner's most impactful years were at Carlisle, where he led a small group of Native American students to national prominence on the **football field**; Pittsburgh, where his teams were national champions in 1915, 1916, and 1918; and Stanford, where his teams won the national championship in 1926 and appeared in three **Rose Bowl** games. In his 44 years as a collegiate head football coach, his teams compiled a record of 318–107–32.

Warner was one of football's greatest innovators and is responsible for the **screen pass**, the spiral **punt**, single- and double-wing formations, and shoulder and thigh pads. In 1934, Warner, along with Joe Tomlin, began a youth football program in Philadelphia emphasizing scholarship as well as football. This evolved throughout the years to become the Pop Warner Little Scholars program, which, in the 21st century, has grown to include more than 400,000 boys and girls, ages five to 16, on more than 5,000 teams worldwide.

Warner was a charter member of the **College Football Hall of Fame**, inducted as a coach in 1951. He died of throat cancer in 1954. In 1986, he was selected to the College Football Hall of Fame for his coaching ability and success. In 1997, he was honored on a U.S. commemorative postage stamp, along with **George Halas**, **Paul "Bear" Bryant**, and **Vince Lombardi**.

WASHINGTON, UNIVERSITY OF. The University of Washington is located in Seattle, Washington. Their **football** program began in 1889, and, since then, through 2012, Huskies' teams have compiled a record of 663–407–49. In addition, they have competed in 33 postseason **bowl games**, with a record of 16–16–1. They have been selected as national collegiate champions four times, in 1960, 1984, 1990, and 1991. In 1915, Washington was one of the four charter members of the Pacific Coast Conference (since renamed the **Pacific-12 Conference**). Since 1920 home games have been played at Husky Stadium, which now seats 72,500 and is located on the school's Seattle campus. Their main rival is Washington State University, and their annual game is for the Apple Cup, which, prior to 1962, was known as the Governor's Trophy. The teams have played 104 times from 1900 to 2012, with Washington leading the series, 67–32–6.

Washington's most successful **coach** has been **Robert "Gloomy Gil" Dobie**. He was their coach from 1908 to 1916, and, in that time, the Huskies were undefeated, with three **ties** in 61 games, and had a 39-game winning streak. Other coaches of note include Enoch Bagshaw (1921–1929; 63–22–6); Jimmy Phelan (1930–1941; 65–37–8); Jim Owens (1957–1974; 99–82–6), and Don James (1975–1992; 153–57–2).

Washington alumni in the **College Football Hall of Fame** include **halfbacks** Chuck Carroll, **Hugh McElhenny**, and George Wilson; defensive **tackle** Steve Emtman; **quarterbacks** Don Heinrich and Bob Schloredt; offensive tackles Vic Markov and Paul Schwegler; **guard** Mark Starcevich; and guard/**linebacker** Rick Redman. Head coaches Robert "Gloomy Gil" Dobie, Don James, Jimmy Phelan, and Darrell Royal have also been enshrined there.

Through 2012, there have been 243 **professional football** players who have attended Washington, 237 in the **National Football League**, three in the **American Football League**, and three in the **All-America Football**

Conference. They include Chuck Allen, Mark Brunell, Blair Bush, Rich Camarillo, Chris Chandler, Junior Coffey, Ben Davidson, Corey Dillon, Kevin Gogan, Lee Grosscup, Jeff Jaeger, Terry "Tank" Johnson, Lincoln Kennedy, Olin Kreutz, Mike Lansford, Hugh McElhenny, Lawyer Milloy, **Warren Moon**, and Arnie Weinmeister.

WASHINGTON REDSKINS. The Washington Redskins are a **professional football** team in the **National Football League (NFL)**. They began in 1932 as the Boston Braves. The team played as the Boston Redskins from 1933 to 1936 and then moved to Washington, D.C., in 1937, where they have remained. In Boston, Massachusetts, they played at the 40,000-seat Braves Field in 1932 and the 37,000-seat Fenway Park from 1933 to 1936. They used the 35,000-seat Griffith Stadium in Washington as their home field from 1937 through 1960. The Redskins played at the 56,000-seat District of Columbia Stadium (renamed Robert F. Kennedy Memorial Stadium in 1969) from 1961 to 1996. In 1997, they moved to the 82,000-seat Jack Kent Cooke Stadium (renamed FedEx Field in 1998) located in Lancaster, Maryland.

From 1932 to 2012, the team's overall regular-season record is 562–532–27, and their **playoff** record is 23–18. Prior to the **American Football League**–National Football League merger in 1970, when the current system of postseason playoffs began, the Redskins played six times in the NFL Championship Game, winning in 1937 and 1942 and losing in 1936, 1940, (by the score of 73–0), 1943, and 1945. In 1943, they **tied** with the **New York Giants** for first place in the Eastern Division and won a tiebreaker playoff game to earn the right to play in the league championship game. Since 1970, they have qualified for the postseason playoffs 17 times. The team won the **Super Bowl** three times, 1982, 1987, and 1991, and were defeated in it in 1972 and 1983. They lost the **conference** championship in 1986, lost in the divisional **playoffs** nine times, and lost in the **wild-card playoff** twice, in 2007 and 2012.

The team's head **coaches** have been Lud Wray (1932), William "Lone Star" Dietz (1933–1934), Eddie Casey (1935), Ray Flaherty (1936–1942), Arthur "Dutch" Bergman (1943), Dudley DeGroot (1944–1945), Albert "Turk" Edwards (1946–1948), John Whelchel (1949), Herman Ball (1949–1951), Dick Todd (interim 1951), **Earl "Curly" Lambeau** (1952–1953), Joe Kuharich (1954–1958), Mike Nixon (1959–1960), Bill McPeak (1961–1965), **Otto Graham** (1966–1968), **Vince Lombardi** (1969), Bill Austin (1970), **George Allen** (1971–1977), Jack Pardee (1978–1980), **Joe Gibbs** (1981–1992, 2004–2007), Richie Petitbon (1993), Norv Turner (1994–2000), Terry Robiskie (interim 2000), Marty Schottenheimer (2001), Steve Spurrier (2002–2003), Jim Zorn (2008–2009), and Mike Shanahan (2010–2012).

The Redskins' Hall of Famers include **quarterbacks Sammy Baugh** and **Sonny Jurgensen**; **running backs** Cliff Battles, Bill Dudley, Bobby Mitchell, and John Riggins; **wide receivers Art Monk** and Charley Taylor; **safeties** Ken Houston and Paul Krause; **guard** Russ Grimm; **linebackers** Chris Hanburger, **Sam Huff**, and Dave Robinson; **cornerback** Darrell Green; and **tackle** Albert "Turk" Edwards. Other star players for the franchise include quarterbacks Bill Kilmer, **Eddie LeBaron**, Mark Rypien, **Joe Theismann**, and Doug Williams; running **back** Larry Brown; tackles Dave Butz and Joe Jacoby; **tight end** Jerry Smith; **center** Len Hauss; and defensive **end** Dexter Manley.

WATERFIELD, ROBERT STANTON "BOB." B. 26 July 1920, Elmira, New York. D. 25 March 1983, Los Angeles, California. Although born in Elmira, New York, Bob Waterfield was raised in California and was a graduate of Van Nuys High School in Van Nuys, California. In high school, he met Jane Russell, who went on to become one of Hollywood's leading actresses. The two married in 1943, adopted three children, and remained married for 25 years, until their divorce in 1968. Waterfield attended the **University of California, Los Angeles (UCLA)**, where he starred as their **quarterback** and led them to the **Rose Bowl** in 1943. After enlisting in the U.S. Army in 1943, he was assigned to Officers Candidate School at Fort Benning, Georgia. Shortly after being commissioned as a second lieutenant, he was discharged from the army in the spring of 1944 due to a knee injury and returned to UCLA for the 1944 football season.

Drafted by the Cleveland Rams of the **National Football League (NFL)** in 1944 in the fifth round as the 42nd overall selection, Waterfield began his NFL career in 1945 with the Rams, led them to the NFL championship, and was awarded the Joe F. Carr Trophy as the league's most valuable player. The Rams moved to Los Angeles in 1946, and Waterfield remained with them through 1952. He led the Rams to the NFL Championship Game in 1949, 1950, and 1951, but they were only victorious in 1951.

In his eight-year NFL career, Waterfield appeared in 91 regular-season games, attempted 1,617 **passes** and completed 814 of them for 11,849 yards and 97 **touchdowns**, and ran with the ball 75 times for 13 touchdowns. As a **kicker**, he scored 60 **field goals** in 100 attempts and made 315 of 336 extra points. In addition, he **punted** 315 times for an average of 42.4 yards per **punt** and had an NFL record punt of 88 yards and another of 86 yards. His record of 88 yards, set in 1948, was not surpassed until 1965. Waterfield was also selected for the NFL's first two **Pro Bowls** in 1950 and 1951.

Waterfield **coached** the Rams from 1960 to 1962 but was not suited for coaching and only compiled a record of 9–24–1 in two and a half seasons.

He was inducted into the **Pro Football Hall of Fame** in 1965 and died of respiratory failure following a lengthy illness in 1983.

WEAK SIDE. In designing an offensive play, the weak side is the opposite side of the field from where the **tight end** is positioned. It can be either to the left or right of the **quarterback**. It receives its name since there are only two down **linemen** to the side of the **center**. *See also* STRONG SIDE.

WEATHER. Football is a game played regardless of the weather. Early season and preseason games played in August and September can often be played in temperatures exceeding 90 degrees. Late-season games in December and January are often played in temperatures below 20 degrees and have occasionally been played in below-zero weather. Likewise, precipitation, be it rain, snow, or sleet, rarely causes a football game to be postponed, and strong winds only alter the game's strategy.

Some notable **professional football** games played in extreme weather conditions include the following:

- 9 December 1934 **National Football League (NFL)** Championship Game, **New York Giants** 30, **Chicago Bears** 13 at New York. Freezing rain caused a slippery field. The Giants changed footwear to sneakers in the second half and scored 27 points in the fourth quarter.
- 19 December 1948 NFL Championship Game, **Philadelphia Eagles** 7, Chicago Cardinals 0 at Philadelphia. The game was played under blizzard conditions. The only score came after a **fumble** recovery in the fourth quarter.
- 30 December 1956 NFL Championship Game, New York Giants 47, Chicago Bears 7 at New York. In a game reminiscent of the 1934 NFL Championship Game, the Giants again wore sneakers and easily won on an icy field.
- 1–2 December 1962 **Canadian Football League Grey Cup** championship game, **Winnipeg Blue Bombers** 28, **Hamilton Tiger-Cats** 27 at Toronto. Heavy fog rolled in during the second quarter. Visibility became so limited that the referee suspended play midway through the fourth quarter, and the game was concluded the following day.
- 31 December 1967 NFL Championship Game, **Green Bay Packers** 21, **Dallas Cowboys** 17 at Green Bay. The game was played in 15 degrees below zero weather, with strong winds making the windchill factor nearly 40 degrees below zero. The referee's whistle froze, players suffered frostbite, and one spectator died from exposure. The game has become known as the **Ice Bowl**.
- 4 January 1976 NFL American Football Conference Championship Game, **Pittsburgh Steelers** 16, **Oakland Raiders** 10 at Pittsburgh. A

hard-hitting game played in weather in the teens and a windchill factor of minus 12 caused eight lost fumbles and five **pass interceptions**.

16 December 1979   **Tampa Bay Buccaneers** 3, **Kansas City Chiefs** 0 at Tampa. The game was played in heavy rain and fog.

4 January 1981   Oakland Raiders 14, **Cleveland Browns** 12 at Cleveland. The game was played in arctic conditions and a temperature of one degree above zero.

10 January 1982   **Cincinnati Bengals** 27, **San Diego Chargers** 7 at Cincinnati. During possibly the coldest game in NFL history, with a temperature of 9 degrees below zero and a windchill factor of minus 59, the San Diego **quarterback**, **Dan Fouts**, had icicles form on his beard during the contest.

12 December 1982   **New England Patriots** 3, **Miami Dolphins** 0 at Foxboro, Massachusetts. A heavy snow kept falling during the game, obliterating the **yard lines**. Late in the fourth quarter, a section of the field was cleared by a snowplow, allowing Patriots' placekicker John Smith to kick a game-winning 33-yard **field goal**.

1 December 1985   Green Bay Packers 21, Tampa Bay Buccaneers 0 at Green Bay. Twelve inches of snow fell before the game and another four inches during the game. Fewer than 20,000 **fans** showed up at the 55,000-seat **stadium**.

31 December 1988   Chicago Bears 20, Philadelphia Eagles 12 at Chicago. In a division **playoff** game nicknamed the "Fog Bowl," a heavy fog occurred midway through the second quarter and lasted for the remainder of the game. Despite the poor conditions, Eagles quarterback Randall Cunningham was able to pass for 407 yards, but the Eagles could not score a **touchdown**. Both quarterbacks were intercepted three times each. Fans and announcers were unable to see most of the action on the field, and even the players were unable to see the **sidelines** and **first-down** markers.

15 January 1994   **Buffalo Bills** 29, Los Angeles Raiders 23 at Buffalo. In the division playoff game, the temperature at game time was three degrees above zero, but the wind caused a windchill factor that reached 32 degrees below zero during the game.

19 January 2002   New England Patriots 16, Oakland Raiders 13 at Foxboro, Massachusetts. A heavy snowstorm took place as New England and Oakland met in the division playoff. Adam Vinatieri kicked a 45-yard field goal with 27 seconds left to **tie** the game and another one of 23 yards to win the game in **overtime**. A **Tom Brady**–attempted pass with less than two minutes to go was initially ruled a fumble but was overturned upon viewing the instant **replay** and considered an **incomplete pass**.

26 November 2007   Pittsburgh Steelers 3, Miami Dolphins 0 at Pittsburgh. In a Monday night game initially delayed 25 minutes by lightning

and played in a driving rain on an extremely muddy field, neither team was able to score until there were only 17 seconds left in the game. A 24-yard field goal ended the league's lowest-scoring game since 1993.

16 December 2007   Cleveland Browns 8, Buffalo Bills 0 at Cleveland. In a game played in heavy snow and wind gusts of up to 40 miles per hour, neither team was able to score a touchdown. Cleveland **kicker** Phil Dawson scored two field goals by aiming his kicks outside the uprights and having the wind blow the ball between them. Bills **coach** Dick Jauron, who had been in the league since 1973, said it was the worst weather he had experienced for a football game in his lifetime.

12 January 2008   Green Bay Packers 42, **Seattle Seahawks** 20 at Green Bay. In a game played in a snowstorm that ended with Green Bay's quarterback throwing snowballs at his **wide receiver** on the sidelines, the Packers easily won the NFC division playoff game and advanced to the NFC Championship Game.

20 January 2008   New York Giants 23, Green Bay Packers 20 at Green Bay. The National Football Conference Championship Game began with a temperature of minus 7 degrees and a windchill factor of minus 27 degrees. The game unmercifully went into overtime before it ended on a 47-yard field goal. This was the second consecutive week that the Packers played a playoff game in extreme weather conditions.

25 September 2011   **Carolina Panthers** 16, **Jacksonville Jaguars** 10 at Charlotte, North Carolina. In a game played in a torrential downpour, Maurice Jones-Drew still was able to **rush** for 122 yards in a losing cause.

In recent years, with the increase in domed stadiums, extreme weather plays a much lesser role in the outcome of a football game.

WESTERN ATHLETIC CONFERENCE (WAC). The Western Athletic Conference is an organization of **major colleges** and universities that compete athletically in the **National Collegiate Athletic Association**. It was established in 1962 and is based in Greenwood Village, Colorado. As of 2011, the eight member schools were California State University, Fresno; the University of Hawai'i at Manoa; the University of Idaho; Louisiana Tech University; the University of Nevada, Reno; New Mexico State University; San Jose State University; and Utah State University. Major changes to conference affiliations began in 2012 and the 10-school WAC lineup for that year included the University of Denver, Seattle University, the University of Texas at Arlington, the University of Texas at San Antonio and the Texas State University, San Marcos, in addition to Idaho, Louisiana Tech, New Mexico State, San Jose State, and Utah State.

On 1 July 2013, seven of these 10 schools will leave the WAC and another school will leave on 1 July 2014. Six schools will join the WAC in 2013 but none of them compete in Division I-AA football. As a result of these moves, the WAC will drop football as a conference sport beginning with the 2013–2014 season.

WHITE, REGINALD HOWARD "REGGIE," "THE MINISTER OF DEFENSE." B. 19 December 1961, Chattanooga, Tennessee. D. 26 December 2004, Cornelius, North Carolina. Reggie White played **football** at the Howard School of Academics and Technology in Chattanooga, Tennessee, and then attended the **University of Tennessee**. A six-foot, five-inch, 300-pound defensive **end**, he had a stellar career at Tennessee and helped lead them to a record of 28–18–1 and three bowl appearances from 1980 to 1983. He signed with the Memphis Showboats of the **United States Football League** in 1984 and played two seasons with them. He was then **drafted** in the first round as the fourth overall selection by the **Philadelphia Eagles** in the 1984 **National Football League (NFL)** Supplemental Draft.

White joined the Eagles in 1985 and was with them through 1992. From 1993 to 1998, he played for the **Green Bay Packers**. He retired in 1999 but came back for a final season in 2000 with the **Carolina Panthers**. In his NFL career as a defensive end and defensive **tackle**, he appeared in 232 regular-season games. White is credited with three **interceptions**; 20 **fumble** recoveries, with two being for **touchdowns**; and 198 sacks, which was an NFL career sack record when White retired but has since been surpassed. He played in 13 **Pro Bowls** (all but his first and last year) during his 15 years in the NFL. He played in the **Super Bowl** twice with Green Bay, winning the 1996 NFL championship and losing to the **Denver Broncos** the following year. An ordained minister, he was nicknamed "The Minister of **Defense**." White died at the age of 43 from a heart attack and was inducted into the **College Football Hall of Fame** in 2002 and the **Pro Football Hall of Fame** in 2006.

WIDE RECEIVER. Wide receiver is a **football position** also known as a flanker. He usually lines up to the left or right of the rest of the team, and his primary function is to **run** downfield to catch a **pass**. The wide receiver is usually one of the fastest players on the team. *See also* SPLIT END.

WILD-CARD PLAYOFF. From 1970 to 1977, the **National Football League's (NFL)** regular season consisted of 14 games per team, with three rounds of postseason **playoffs**. In the first round, the three division champions, plus the team with the next best record, competed in division playoff games in each **conference**. Those winners advanced to the conference championship game, and the conference champions met in the **Super Bowl**.

In the 1978 season, the NFL decided to expand the regular season to 16 games and modified the playoff system to include five teams from each conference. The two teams in each conference that were not division winners met in a "wild-card" playoff game, with the winner advancing to the division playoffs the following week. This proved successful and, in 1990, the league added two more teams to the playoff system. The two division winners in each conference receive a bye in the first round, and the remaining teams play in the wild-card round. It is conceivable for a team to finish with the fifth-best record in their conference but, by winning three playoff games, reach the Super Bowl. Through the 2012 season, there have been 11 wild-card teams that reached the Super Bowl, and seven have won it.

WILSON, RALPH C., JR. B. 17 October 1918, Columbus, Ohio. Ralph Wilson was raised in Michigan and is a graduate of the University of Virginia and the **University of Michigan** Law School. He began his professional career in the insurance business and then founded Ralph Wilson Industries, in which he acquired interests in several diverse firms. He was also a minority owner of the **Detroit Lions** of the **National Football League (NFL)**. In 1959, Wilson became owner of the **Buffalo Bills** and was one of the founders of the new **American Football League (AFL)**. As one of the more influential and prosperous owners in the AFL, he helped initiate the merger with the NFL. He remains the Bills' owner through the 2012 season. In 1998, Buffalo's **stadium** was renamed Ralph Wilson Stadium. One of Wilson's many other interests is thoroughbred horse racing, and he has had entries in such major stakes events as the Breeders' Cup and Kentucky Derby. He was inducted into the **Pro Football Hall of Fame** as a contributor in 2009.

WINNIPEG BLUE BOMBERS. The Winnipeg Blue Bombers are a team in the **Canadian Football League (CFL)**. They were founded in 1930 as the Winnipeg Football Club. During the 1930s, a sportswriter referred to them as the Blue Bombers of **Canadian football**, in reference to the heavyweight boxer Joe Louis, who was known as the "Brown Bomber." The name stuck, and they have since been known as the Winnipeg Blue Bombers.

In 1936, the team became a charter member of the Western Interprovincial Football Union (WIFU). While in the WIFU, the Blue Bombers reached the **Grey Cup** 10 times but won only twice. In 1958, the WIFU joined with the Interprovincial Rugby Football Union to form the CFL. Since then, the Blue Bombers have won the Grey Cup seven times and were runners-up six times.

From 1935 to 1952, the Blue Bombers played home games at the 7,800-seat Osborne Stadium in Winnipeg, Manitoba. Since 1953, they have played at the 29,500-seat Winnipeg Stadium (renamed Canad Inns Stadium in

2001). A new **stadium** in Winnipeg is scheduled to open in 2013 and will be the Blue Bombers' new home. The Blue Bombers remain one of the few community-owned major-league sports franchises in North America.

Among the Blue Bombers' head **coaches** have been several with ties to the **National Football League (NFL)**, including George Trafton (coach 1951–1953; NFL player 1920–1932, member of the **Pro Football Hall of Fame**), Allie Sherman (coach 1954–1956; NFL player and coach 1943, 1969), and **Harry "Bud" Grant** (coach 1957–1966; NFL player and coach 1951, 1985). **Canadian Football Hall of Famer** Cal Murphy (coach 1983–1986, 1993–1996) has also been one of Winnipeg's more notable head coaches.

Winnipeg's top players include the following members of their 75th anniversary team: Greg Battle, Dieter Brock, Bob Cameron, Tom Casey, Tom Clements, Herb Gray, Fritz Hanson, Rick House, Jack Jacobs, Gerry James, Trevor Kennard, Leo Lewis, James Murphy, Ken Ploen, Joe Poplawski, Willard Reaves, Frank Rigney, Charles Roberts, Milt Stegall, and Chris Walby.

WINSLOW, KELLEN BOSWELL, SR. B. 5 November 1957, St. Louis, Missouri. Kellen Winslow is regarded by many observers as the greatest **pass** catcher to play **tight end** in **football** history. He is a graduate of East St. Louis High School in East St. Louis, Illinois, where he only first began playing football in his senior year. His outstanding ability won him a football scholarship to the University of Missouri, where he played from 1975 to 1978.

Winslow was **drafted** by the **San Diego Chargers** of the **National Football League (NFL)** in the first round as the 13th overall selection. The six-foot, five-inch, 235-pound tight end played with the Chargers from 1979 to 1987, when a series of injuries to his knees and ankle ended his career. In nine years of **professional football**, all with the Chargers, Winslow played in 109 regular-season games and caught 541 passes for 6,741 yards and 45 **touchdowns**. In six postseason games, he caught 28 passes for 380 yards and four touchdowns. He led the NFL in **receptions** in both 1980 and 1981, an unusual feat for a tight end. He was selected for the **Pro Bowl** five times.

Winslow has worked as the athletic director of Central State University since 2008. His son, Kellen Winslow Jr., also a tight end, played in the NFL with the **Cleveland Browns, Tampa Bay Buccaneers**, and **New England Patriots** from 2004 to 2012. Kellen Sr. was inducted into the **Pro Football Hall of Fame** in 1995 and the **College Football Hall of Fame** in 2002.

WISCONSIN, UNIVERSITY OF. The University of Wisconsin is located in Madison, Wisconsin. Their **football** program began in 1889, and, since then, through 2012, Badgers' teams have compiled a record of 633–464–53. In addition, they have competed in 24 postseason **bowl games**, with a record of 11–13. They were selected as national collegiate champions only once, in 1942. Wisconsin was a charter member of the **Big Ten Conference** in 1896 and still plays in that **conference**. Home games are played at the 80,000-seat Camp Randall Stadium on Wisconsin's campus in Madison. Their rivalry with the **University of Minnesota** has seen 121 games since 1890. Since 1948, the winner of their annual game has been awarded the Paul Bunyan's Axe trophy. Wisconsin has a 38–25–3 record in those trophy games, while overall Minnesota leads the series, 59–55–8.

Barry Alvarez, who **coached** Wisconsin from 1990 to 2005, has been their coach with the most longevity. His record of 118–74–4 is one of the better records as well. Philip King, coach from 1896 to 1902, has compiled the best record, at 66–11–1, although coach Bret Bielema (2006–2012) threatened that mark. Through 2012, Bielema compiled a record of 68–24 but then left to be the head coach at the University of Arkansas.

Wisconsin alumni in the **College Football Hall of Fame** include **fullbacks** Alan Ameche, Marlin "Pat" Harder, and Pat O'Dea; **tackles** Marty Below and Bob Butler; **halfback Elroy "Crazylegs" Hirsch**; and **ends** Pat Richter and Dave Schreiner. Coaches Barry Alvarez and George Little are also among those enshrined. Alan Ameche in 1954 and Ron Dayne in 1999 were **Heisman Trophy** winners. Hall of Fame coach **Bob Zuppke** was also a Wisconsin alumnus but did not play football there and was inducted based on his coaching prowess at the **University of Illinois**.

Through 2012, there have been 277 **professional football** players who have attended Wisconsin, 266 in the **National Football League**, eight in the **American Football League**, and three in the **All-America Football Conference**. They include Alan Ameche, Jim Bakken, Ken Bowman, Chris Chambers, Jeff Dellenbach, Lee Evans, Charles "Buckets" Goldenberg, Paul Gruber, Dale Hackbart, Marlin "Pat" Harder, Arnie Herber, Elroy "Crazylegs" Hirsch, **Earl "Curly" Lambeau**, Nate Odomes, Pat Richter, Ron Smith, Al Toon, Dan Turk, Ron Vander Kelen, Troy Vincent, and Mike Webster.

WOMEN IN FOOTBALL. For most of its nearly 150-year history, American **football** has been a sport played by males. Women have been relegated to being spectators and/or **cheerleaders**. In Cleveland, Ohio, in 1965, a promoter began billing exhibitions of women playing full-contact football as the "Women's Professional Football League," although he had only two teams to begin with. That league eventually expanded to eight teams but received scant **fan** support. In 1974, the National Women's Football League was created in California and survived until the mid-1980s, with a spinoff league, the Western States Women's Professional Football League, also operating briefly. In 1999, another Women's Professional Football League was created. That league lasted until 2007.

The Independent Women's Football League (IWFL) began play in 2001. The IWFL, a loose connection of women's football teams, had 41 teams affiliated with it in 2012. The Women's Football Alliance, also in existence in 2012, has 60 teams. The Women's Spring Football League featured 18 teams in 2012. Although these organizations provide the opportunity for women to play football, there has yet to be an appreciable amount of fan support, television coverage, or monetary profit gained by any of them.

The **International Federation of American Football** began including a women's division, and, from 26 June to 3 July 2010, in Stockholm, Sweden, a six-team international competition was held for women's football teams. The United States, Canada, Germany, Austria, Finland, and Sweden entered, and the United States won handily, outscoring their opposition, 201–0, in three games.

Patricia "Pat" Barzi Palinkas became the first woman to play **professional football** in a men's league when she played for the Orlando Panthers in the minor-league Atlantic Coast Football League. She was the placekick **holder** for her husband, Steve Palinkas, in a preseason game against the Bridgeport Jets on 15 August 1970. But her football career was short lived (only two preseason games), as Steve Palinkas became injured and was cut from the team prior to the start of the regular season.

Elizabeth "Liz" Heaston was the first female to score in a **college football** game when she kicked two extra points for Willamette University against Linfield College on 18 October 1997 in a **National Association of Intercollegiate Athletics** game. Those were the only points she scored, as she only played one other game for the school. In 2001, Ashley Martin became the first female to score in a **National Collegiate Athletic Association (NCAA)** football game when she kicked three extra points for Jacksonville State University in a 72–10 defeat of Cumberland University. And Katharine "Katie" Hnida played college football as a placekicker for the University of New Mexico in 2003. She became the first female to score a point in a NCAA Division I-A game when she kicked two extra points in a 72–8 victory over Texas State University on 30 August 2003. In 2010, she signed with the Fort Wayne Firehawks of the Continental Indoor Football League.

There have also been several female team owners in the **National Football League**, as a result of inheriting ownership following their husbands' passing. Violet Bidwill Wolfner was the first when she became the owner of the Chicago Cardinals in 1947, following the death of her husband, Charles Bidwill. Georgia Frontiere became a 70 percent owner of the Los Angeles Rams in 1979 after her husband, Carroll Rosenbloom, drowned. And Virginia Halas McCaskey, daughter of **George Halas**, inherited an 80 percent share in the ownership of the **Chicago Bears**. In 2009, the tennis champion Williams sisters, Venus and Serena, each purchased a small share in the ownership of the **Miami Dolphins** and became limited partners.

WORLD FOOTBALL LEAGUE (WFL). The World Football League (WFL) was a **professional football** league in existence in 1974 and 1975. It attempted to be a major league and had teams in major markets, although the caliber of play was slightly below that of the **National Football League (NFL)**. The WFL was created by Gary Davidson, a sports innovator who had previously created competitive leagues in both basketball (the American Basketball Association) and ice hockey (the World Hockey Association).

The league began play on 10 July 1974, with five games scheduled. In its first season, each of the 12 teams were scheduled to play 20 games each, with all counting in the league standings and no preseason games. The 12 teams were divided into three divisions. The Eastern Division had the Florida Blazers (based in Orlando), New York Stars (who moved to Charlotte midway during the season, played one game as the Charlotte Stars, and then were renamed the Charlotte Hornets), Philadelphia Bell, and Jacksonville Sharks. The Central Division had the Memphis Southmen, Birmingham Americans, Chicago Fire, and Detroit Wheels. The Western Division had the Southern California Sun (based in Anaheim), the Hawaiians (who played their games in Honolulu), Portland Storm, and Houston Texans (who moved to Shreveport, Louisiana, midway during the season and were renamed the Shreveport Steamer). As the season went on, financial problems plagued several teams, and the Sharks folded after 14 games. The Wheels also fell off after 14 games.

A series of postseason **playoffs** were held among the top two teams in the three divisions, with the Birmingham Americans defeating the Florida Blazers, 22–21, on 5 December 1974, in the final playoff game, dubbed the World Bowl. Although the Charlotte Hornets were eligible to compete in the playoffs, they withdrew because they were financially unable to travel to Orlando for their scheduled game and were replaced by the third-place team, Philadelphia.

The WFL continued in 1975, with 11 teams in two divisions. They still scheduled 20 games, but the first two were designated as preseason games and did not count in the league standings. Most of the teams had gained new ownership and either renamed the name or relocated the team. The Birmingham Americans became the Birmingham Vulcans, the Chicago Fire became the Chicago Winds, the Florida Blazers folded and were replaced by the San Antonio Wings, the Jacksonville Sharks became the Jacksonville Express, the Portland Storm became the Portland Thunder, and the Detroit Wheels did not return. Chicago dropped out after only five games, and the league's financial difficulties caused its termination two-thirds of the way through the regular season and it ceased operations on 23 October 1975. The Birmingham Vulcans, with a 9–3 record, were declared league champions.

In its brief lifetime, the WFL made a significant mark in professional football history. Several of the league's many innovations were later adopted by the NFL. **Kickoffs** were taken from the 30-**yard line** instead of the 40-yard line. **Goalposts** were moved to the back of the **end zone** instead of on the **goal line**. Some **penalties** were reduced to 10 yards instead of 15. Missed **field goals** were returned to the **line of scrimmage** instead of the 20-yard line. And bump-and-**run pass** coverage was prohibited once the receiver was more than three yards downfield. Several rule differences that have not yet been placed into the NFL rulebook but have been part of the Canadian game include that no **fair catch** was allowed on **punts**, backs were allowed to be in forward motion prior to the snap of the ball, and receivers only needed to have one foot in bounds for a catch to be legal. Two innovations that have not been adopted by either the CFL or NFL are that **overtime** was a 15-minute non-**sudden-death** period and **touchdowns** were worth seven points and an "action point" try occurred following a touchdown. The ball was placed on the five-yard line and had to be run or passed over the goal line for an additional point.

The WFL employed quite a few well-known former NFL players. The Memphis Southmen signed three **Miami Dolphin** stars from their **Super Bowl**–winning teams, including **Larry Csonka**, **Paul Warfield**, and Jim Kiick. The New York Stars signed **New York Jets** Super Bowl players Gerry Philbin and John Elliott. And after retiring from the **Cleveland Browns**, **Leroy Kelly** played one season for the Chicago Fire.

WORLD LEAGUE OF AMERICAN FOOTBALL (WLAF). The World League of American Football (WLAF) was an experiment by the **National Football League (NFL)** to introduce the sport of American **football** to countries outside the United States. It began in 1991 with 10 teams, three in Europe (London, England; Barcelona, Spain; and Frankfurt, Germany), one in Canada (Montreal), and six in the United States (New York/New Jersey, Orlando, Raleigh-Durham, Birmingham, San Antonio, and Sacramento). A 10-game season was played during the spring months, and the season culminated with the World Bowl, won by London over Barcelona. The league's second season saw the Raleigh-Durham franchise relocate to Columbus, Ohio. Sacramento defeated Orlando in World Bowl II.

The WLAF did not draw well, especially in the United States, and it suspended play for two seasons. The league resumed play in 1995 as a strictly European league, with teams in Amsterdam, the Netherlands; Edinburgh, Scotland; and Dusseldorf, Germany (which competed as the Rhein Fire) added to the other three European teams. In 1998, the league was renamed the NFL Europe (later changed to NFL Europa in 2007).

NFL Europe lasted through the 2007 season but only was popular in Germany. London dropped out after 1997 and was replaced by a team in Berlin, Germany. Barcelona dropped out after 2003 and was replaced by a team in Cologne. And Edinburgh dropped out after 2004 and was replaced by a team in Hamburg. By the 2007 season, five of the six teams in the league were based there.

The league employed several experimental rules. Included among them was four points awarded for a **field goal** taken from 50 yards or longer, a 10-minute **overtime** period in which each team had at least one possession in the case of a game ending in a **tie**, and the requirement that at least one player born outside the United States participate in every other **down** for each team.

Each season ended with the championship being decided in the World Bowl, and, by the time the league dissolved following the 2007 season, there had been 15 World Bowl games played. Following the demise of NFL Europa, the NFL began the practice of playing an annual regular-season NFL game in Europe. *See also* APPENDIX H (for a list of World Bowl champions).

WRESTLERS. *See* PROFESSIONAL FOOTBALL PLAYERS WHO WERE PROFESSIONAL WRESTLERS.

X'S AND O'S. When **coaches** design plays, they often use the symbols "x" and "o" to designate the positioning of their players. The symbol "x" is used to mark the defensive players, and "o" is used for the offensive players. The phrase "x's and o's" refers to a coach's ability to design effective plays.

XFL. The XFL (its initials did not stand for anything) was an attempt at a **professional football** league that lasted only one season, 2001. It was created by professional wrestling promoter Vince McMahon Jr. and was marketed as a league in which roughness was acceptable. Among the rule differences from **National Football League (NFL)** games were the elimination of **fair catches** on **punts** (similar to **Canadian Football League [CFL]** rules); allowing one **back** to be in forward motion prior to the snap (also similar to the CFL); requiring the point after touchdown to be a **run** or **pass** play; and, the most novel innovation, the use of the opening scramble. Rather than a **coin toss** to determine initial ball possession, one player from each team lined up at the 30-**yard line**; the ball was placed at midfield, and when the referee blew his whistle, the two players raced to gain possession of the ball.

Despite the innovations and a television contract with NBC, the XFL did not succeed. One reason was that due to the league's association with professional wrestling, **fans** were skeptical that the results of games were pre-scripted, although that was never proven to be the case.

The XFL began play on 3 February 2001 and managed to complete a 10-game schedule for all eight of its teams. It played a championship game on 21 April 2001, won by the Los Angeles Xtreme over the San Francisco Demons, 38–6. Many of the league's players continued their professional football careers in the NFL, including the XFL's most valuable player, **quarterback** Tommy Maddox.

YALE BOWL. The 61,446-seat Yale Bowl, about one mile west of the campus of **Yale University** in New Haven, Connecticut, is one of the oldest **football stadiums** in the United States. It was completed in 1914, and, since then, has hosted Yale University football games. It was the first bowl-shaped stadium in the United States, and its design was mimicked by the **Rose Bowl** in Pasadena, California, the **Los Angeles Memorial Coliseum**, and Michigan Stadium. In 1973 and 1974, it was also the home of the **New York Giants** of the **National Football League** while their regular home field, Yankee Stadium, was being renovated. In 1987, the Yale Bowl was declared a National Historic Landmark.

YALE UNIVERSITY. Yale University is located in New Haven, Connecticut. Their **football** program began in 1872, and, since then, through 2012, Bulldogs' teams have compiled a record of 872–354–55. Yale is second only to the **University of Michigan** in the highest total of **college football** victories. The Bulldogs traditionally do not compete in postseason **bowl games** and have been selected as national collegiate champions 27 times (although all but one were prior to 1910), second only to **Princeton University's** 28. Yale was named champion in 1872, 1874, 1876, 1877, 1879, 1880, 1881, 1882, 1883, 1884, 1886, 1887, 1888, 1891, 1892, 1893, 1894, 1895, 1897, 1900, 1901, 1902, 1905, 1906, 1907, 1909, and 1927. **Yale Bowl**, opened in 1914 and presently seating more than 64,000 spectators, is their home field. Since 1955, Yale football teams (also known as the Elis after the school's founder, Elihu Yale) have competed in the **Ivy League** of the **National Collegiate Athletic Association**. Their main rival is **Harvard University**. The teams have met nearly annually since 1875 in a contest known simply as "The Game." Through 2012, Yale leads in the series, 65–56–8.

Walter Camp, known as the "Father of American Football," was their first **coach** from 1888 to 1892. (In prior years the team did not have a coach, as was the practice in that era.) During those five years, Yale had a record of 67–2. Carmen Cozza had the most longevity as a Yale head coach. He led the Bulldogs from 1965 to 1996 and had a record of 179–119–5.

There are 24 Yale alumni in the **College Football Hall of Fame**. Most are 19th-century or early 20th-century players, including Albie Booth, Gordon "Skim" Brown, Ted Coy, **William "Pudge" Heffelfinger**, "Silent" Frank Hinkey, James Hogan, and **Amos Alonzo Stagg**. Yale coaches in the Hall are Walter Camp, Carmen Cozza, Howard Jones, Thomas "Tad" Jones, and John Reed Kilpatrick. In 1936 and 1937, Yale's Larry Kelley and Clint Frank each won the **Heisman Trophy**.

Through 2012, there have been 28 **National Football League** players who have attended Yale. They include Brian Dowling, Pat Eilers, Gary Fencik, Chris Hetherington, Calvin Hill (father of professional basketball player Grant Hill), Kenny Hill, Dick Jauron, Chuck Mercein, Mike Pyle, Jeff Rohrer, and John Spagnola. Alex Kroll played the 1962 season for the Titans in the **American Football League**.

YARD LINE. To aid both **officials** and players, each of the 100 yards of the **football field** is marked in a white substance, most commonly lime. The markings are referred to as yard lines.

YEPREMIAN, GARABED SARKIS "GARO." B. 2 June 1944, Larnaca, Cyprus. Although only five feet, eight inches tall and 175 pounds, Garo Yepremian made a name for himself in the **National Football League (NFL)**. It was widely reported that the first **football** game he ever saw in person was the one in which he played to begin his 14-year NFL career. After recently immigrating to the United States with his brother Krikor, he saw some football on television. Convinced that he could placekick, he and his brother attempted to get a tryout to prove to an NFL team that he could do so. They managed to convince the **Detroit Lions**, and, in 1966, Garo became the team's placekicker.

In only his fourth NFL game, Yepremian set an NFL record by kicking six **field goals** in one game. The record lasted less than one year, as Jim Bakken kicked seven in one game the following year. After serving in the U.S. Army in 1968, Yepremian was not re-signed for 1969 and did not play that year. In 1970, the **Miami Dolphins** signed him, and he played for them for nine seasons. The Dolphins reached the **Super Bowl** in 1972, 1973, and 1974, winning in 1973 to cap an undefeated 17–0 season and repeating in 1974.

Yepremian is best remembered for two incidents. On 25 December 1971, his game-winning field goal after seven minutes and 40 seconds in the second **overtime** in the NFL divisional **playoffs** gave the Dolphins the victory over the **Kansas City Chiefs** in the NFL's longest game. In the Super Bowl against the **Washington Redskins** the following season, Yepremian had a field goal attempt **blocked** but caught the ball when it bounced back to him.

He then attempted to **pass** the ball, but the ball slipped and went straight up into the air, where it was **intercepted** by a Redskin, who then ran for a **touchdown**. Fortunately for Yepremian, the Dolphins held on and won, 14–7.

In his 14-year NFL career, Yepremian played in 177 regular-season games and kicked 210 field goals in 313 attempts and 444 **conversions** in 464 attempts. In 12 postseason games, he was successful on 28 of 29 extra points and 12 of 20 field goals. He was selected for the **Pro Bowl** in 1973 and 1978. In retirement, he has worked as a motivational speaker and heads the Garo Yepremian Foundation for Brain Tumor Research.

YOUNG, CLAUDE HENRY K. "BUDDY." B. 5 January 1926, Chicago, Illinois. D. 4 September 1983, Terrell, Texas. At only five feet, four inches tall, Buddy Young was one of the shortest players to play in the **National Football League (NFL)** but was one of the fastest. At 175 pounds, he was strong and stocky. He began high school at Englewood High School in Chicago, but the **football coach** there thought he was too small to play football and refused to let him play on the team. Young switched schools to Wendell Phillips High School and starred there. His daily four-mile **run** to high school helped keep him in top condition. He received a scholarship to the **University of Illinois** and, during his freshman year in 1944, **rushed** for 8.9 yards per carry, second in the nation, and **tied Harold "Red" Grange's** Illinois record of 13 **touchdowns** in one season.

Young was also an exceptional track sprinter in college. He won the **National Collegiate Athletic Association** 100- and 220-yard dashes and tied the world record in the 45- and 60-yard dashes. Following the 1944 season, he was **drafted** by the U.S. Navy and spent 1945 at the naval base in Fleet City, California, where he played on their football team. In the service championship game, he scored three touchdowns, two on **kickoff** returns of 88 and 94 yards, and the Fleet City team completed an undefeated season.

After being discharged in 1946, Young returned to Illinois and helped lead them to an 8–2 record, the **Big Ten Conference** championship, and a **Rose Bowl** victory over the **University of California, Los Angeles**. In 1947, he was signed by the **New York Yankees** of the **All-America Football Conference (AAFC)**. He played with them in the AAFC from 1947 to 1949 as a **running back**, defensive **back**, and kick **returner**. The Yankees disbanded after the 1949 season, but several of their players, including Young, were signed by the **New York Yanks** of the NFL in 1950. After the Yanks' franchise folded after the 1951 season, they were replaced by the **Dallas Texans** in 1952. That team became the **Baltimore Colts** in 1953. Young remained with that franchise during their changes and retired after the 1955 season with the Colts.

In 105 regular-season AAFC and NFL games in nine seasons, Young carried the ball 597 times for 2,727 yards and 17 touchdowns. He also caught 179 **passes** for 2,711 yards and 21 touchdowns. As a kick and **punt** returner, he returned 125 kickoffs for 3,465 yards and four touchdowns of more than 90 yards each, including an NFL record (since broken) 104-yard return in 1953. As a punt returner, he returned 67 punts for 698 yards and two touchdowns. He played in the **Pro Bowl** in 1954.

After retiring from active play, Young worked in the NFL office as administrative assistant to the commissioner and later became the NFL director of player relations. He was inducted into the **College Football Hall of Fame** in 1968. He died in an automobile accident in 1983 at the age of 57.

YOUNG, JON STEVEN "STEVE." B. 11 October 1961, Salt Lake City, Utah. Although Steve Young was born in Utah and is a direct descendent of Mormon pioneer Brigham Young, he spent his high school years in Greenwich, Connecticut, where he attended Greenwich High School and starred in baseball, **football**, and basketball. He selected football and went to Brigham Young University (BYU). He played for the Cougars from 1981 to 1983 and helped lead the team to three consecutive **Western Athletic Conference** championships, three appearances in the Holiday Bowl, and an overall record of 30–7. A six-foot, two-inch, 215-pound left-handed **quarterback**, Young's **college football** career climaxed with an outstanding senior year in 1983, when he led the country in total **offense** at 4,346 yards (3,802 **passing**, 306 pass completions, 33 **touchdowns**, and a pass completion percentage of 71.3 percent).

Young signed a $40 million contract with the Los Angeles Express of the new **United States Football League (USFL)** in 1984. This was the largest contract ever offered to a **professional football** player at that time. But the team and the league folded after two years. In 1984, the **National Football League (NFL)** held a supplemental **draft** of those players under contract in leagues like the USFL and **Canadian Football League**, and the **Tampa Bay Buccaneers** chose Young as the first player selected in that draft. Since the USFL played in the spring and summer, after the league folded in 1985, Young was able to play part of the 1985 season in the NFL for Tampa Bay.

Young did not do particularly well for the Bucs in 1985 and 1986, and he was traded to the **San Francisco 49ers** in April 1987 to be a backup quarterback for **Joe Montana**. From 1987 to 1990, he did well as a backup and had a record of 7–3 in the 10 games he started in those four years. After Montana was hurt in 1991, Young became the regular starter, but then he hurt his knee and was only able to play in 11 of the team's 16 games. From 1992 to 1998, Young started in nearly all the 49ers games. In 1999, he suffered the seventh concussion of his career and was advised to retire.

Young was a member of three **Super Bowl** champions, in 1989, 1990, and 1995, although he only played briefly in 1990 and did not play at all in 1989. In the 1995 game, he was named the Super Bowl Most Valuable Player. In his 15-year NFL career, he played in 169 regular-season games, started in 143 of those games, and had a won-lost record of 94–49. Young completed 2,667 passes for 33,124 yards and 232 touchdowns in 4,149 pass attempts for a 64.3 completion percentage. He also ran 722 times for 4,239 yards and 43 touchdowns. In 20 postseason games, he completed 292 passes in 471 attempts for 3,326 yards and 20 touchdowns and ran 96 times for 594 yards and eight touchdowns. He was named the NFL Most Valuable Player in 1992 and 1994 and was selected for the **Pro Bowl** seven times from 1992 to 1998.

Young earned a law degree from BYU in 1994 and, since retiring from football, has been a managing director of a private equity investment firm. He spoke at the 2000 Republican National Convention and has done television football analysis work. He has also appeared in a Hollywood feature film and several episodes of various television series. Young was inducted into the **College Football Hall of Fame** in 2001 and the **Pro Football Hall of Fame** in 2005.

Z

ZUPPKE, ROBERT CARL "BOB." B. 2 July 1879, Berlin, Germany. D. 22 December 1957, Champaign, Illinois. No dictionary is complete without an entry under "Z." Although there have been several outstanding **professional football** players that would fall in this section, like Gary Zimmerman, seven-time **Pro Bowler** and **Pro Football Hall of Fame** inductee who played offensive **tackle** for 12 years in the **National Football League (NFL)** for Minnesota and Denver, or Jim Zorn, a left-handed NFL **quarterback** who played 11 years in the league mostly with the **Seattle Seahawks**, the one person with a surname beginning with Z that did the most for the sport of **football** is Bob Zuppke.

Zuppke was born in Germany and immigrated with his family to Milwaukee, Wisconsin, when he was just two years old. After graduating from high school in Milwaukee, he attended the Milwaukee Normal School for two years and then transferred to the **University of Wisconsin**. He participated in sports, but his short, slight build did not allow him to be a good football player, although he did excel in basketball.

After his college graduation in 1905, Zuppke worked as a commercial artist for a year and, in 1906, began teaching high school and doubling as the football **coach** at a high school in Muskegon, Michigan. He transferred to Oak Park and River Forest High School in 1910 and was there for three years as a history teacher and coach. After leading the school to state **high school football** championships in 1911 and 1912, he was hired by the **University of Illinois** in 1913 to be their football coach. Zuppke remained at Illinois through 1941 and, in 29 years as their head coach, compiled a record of 131–81–12. Illinois was the national collegiate football champion in 1914, 1919, 1923, and 1927, and the 1914, 1915, 1923, and 1927 teams were undefeated. One of his players from 1923 to 1925 was **halfback Harold "Red" Grange**, possibly the most famous football player of that decade.

Zuppke was also a writer who wrote syndicated newspaper columns during the 1930s and a painter who had a one-man art show in 1937 in Chicago. He was inducted into the **College Football Hall of Fame** in 1951 as a charter member. *See also* FLEA FLICKER.

Appendix A
Pro Football Hall of Fame Inductees

Player	Year Inducted
Herb Adderley	1981
Troy Aikman	2006
Larry Allen	2013
Marcus Allen	2003
Lance Alworth	1978
Doug Atkins	1982
Morris "Red" Badgro	1981
Lem Barney	1992
Cliff Battles	1968
Sammy Baugh	1963
Chuck Bednarik	1967
Bobby Bell	1983
Raymond Berry	1973
Elvin Bethea	2003
Fred Biletnikoff	1988
George Blanda	1981
Mel Blount	1989
Terry Bradshaw	1989
Bob "Boomer" Brown	2004
Jim Brown	1971
Roosevelt Brown	1975
Willie Brown	1984
Junious "Buck" Buchanan	1990
Nick Buoniconti	2001
Dick Butkus	1979
Jack Butler	2012
Earl Campbell	1991
Tony Canadeo	1974
Harry Carson	2006
Cris Carter	2013
Dave Casper	2002
Jack Christiansen	1970

Player	Year Inducted
Earl "Dutch" Clark	1963
George Connor	1975
Lou Creekmur	1996
Larry Csonka	1987
Curley Culp	2013
Willie Davis	1981
Dermontti Dawson	2012
Len Dawson	1987
Fred Dean	2008
Joe DeLamielleure	2003
Richard Dent	2011
Eric Dickerson	1999
Dan Dierdorf	1996
Mike Ditka	1988
Chris Doleman	2012
Art Donovan	1968
Tony Dorsett	1994
John "Paddy" Driscoll	1965
Bill Dudley	1966
Albert "Turk" Edwards	1969
Carl Eller	2004
John Elway	2004
Marshall Faulk	2011
Tom Fears	1970
Len Ford	1976
Dan Fortmann	1965
Dan Fouts	1993
Benny Friedman	2005
Frank Gatski	1985
Bill George	1974
Frank Gifford	1977
Otto Graham	1965
Harold "Red" Grange	1963
Darrell Green	2008
Joe Greene	1987
Forrest Gregg	1977
Bob Griese	1990
Russ Grimm	2010
Lou Groza	1974
Joe Guyon	1966
Jack Ham	1988

Player	Year Inducted
Dan Hampton	2002
Chris Hanburger	2011
John Hannah	1991
Franco Harris	1990
Bob Hayes	2009
Mike Haynes	1997
Ed Healey	1964
Mel Hein	1963
Ted Hendricks	1990
Wilbur "Pete" Henry	1963
Arnie Herber	1966
Bill Hewitt	1971
Gene Hickerson	2007
Clarke Hinkle	1964
Elroy "Crazylegs" Hirsch	1968
Paul Hornung	1986
Ken Houston	1986
Robert "Cal" Hubbard	1963
Sam Huff	1982
Don Hutson	1963
Michael Irvin	2007
Rickey Jackson	2010
Jimmy Johnson	1994
John Henry Johnson	1987
Charlie Joiner	1996
Deacon Jones	1980
Stan Jones	1991
Henry Jordan	1995
Christian "Sonny" Jurgensen	1983
Jim Kelly	2002
Leroy Kelly	1994
Cortez Kennedy	2012
Walt Kiesling	1966
Frank "Bruiser" Kinard	1971
Paul Krause	1998
Jack Lambert	1990
Dick "Night Train" Lane	1974
Jim Langer	1987
Willie Lanier	1986
Steve Largent	1995
Yale Lary	1979

Player	Year Inducted
Dante Lavelli	1975
Bobby Layne	1967
Dick LeBeau	2010
Alphonse "Tuffy" Leemans	1978
Bob Lilly	1980
Floyd Little	2010
Larry Little	1993
James Lofton	2003
Howie Long	2000
Ronnie Lott	2000
Sid Luckman	1965
William Roy "Link" Lyman	1964
Tom Mack	1999
John Mackey	1992
Gino Marchetti	1972
Dan Marino	2005
Curtis Martin	2012
Ollie Matson	1972
Bruce Matthews	2007
Don Maynard	1987
George McAfee	1966
Mike McCormack	1984
Randall McDaniel	2009
Tommy McDonald	1998
Hugh McElhenny	1970
John "Blood" McNally	1963
Mike Michalske	1964
Wayne Millner	1968
Bobby Mitchell	1983
Ron Mix	1979
Art Monk	2008
Joe Montana	2000
Warren Moon	2006
Lenny Moore	1975
Marion Motley	1968
Mike Munchak	2001
Anthony Muñoz	1998
George Musso	1982
Bronko Nagurski	1963
Joe Namath	1985
Ernie Nevers	1963

Player	Year Inducted
Ozzie Newsome	1999
Ray Nitschke	1978
Leo Nomellini	1969
Jonathan Ogden	2013
Merlin Olsen	1982
Jim Otto	1980
Alan Page	1988
Clarence "Ace" Parker	1972
Jim Parker	1973
Walter Payton	1993
Joe Perry	1969
Pete Pihos	1970
Fritz Pollard	2005
John Randle	2010
Mel Renfro	1996
Jerry Rice	2010
Les Richter	2011
John Riggins	1992
Jim Ringo	1981
Willie Roaf	2012
Dave Robinson	2013
Andy Robustelli	1971
Barry Sanders	2004
Charlie Sanders	2007
Deion Sanders	2011
Warren Sapp	2013
Gale Sayers	1977
Joe Schmidt	1973
Lee Roy Selmon	1995
Shannon Sharpe	2011
Billy Shaw	1999
Art Shell	1989
O. J. Simpson	1985
Mike Singletary	1998
Jackie Slater	2001
Bruce Smith	2009
Emmitt Smith	2010
Jackie Smith	1994
Bob St. Clair	1990
John Stallworth	2002
Bart Starr	1977

Player	Year Inducted
Roger Staubach	1985
Ernie Stautner	1969
Jan Stenerud	1991
Dwight Stephenson	1998
Ken Strong	1967
Joe Stydahar	1967
Lynn Swann	2001
Fran Tarkenton	1986
Charley Taylor	1984
Jim Taylor	1976
Lawrence Taylor	1999
Derrick Thomas	2009
Emmitt Thomas	2008
Thurman Thomas	2007
Jim Thorpe	1963
Andre Tippett	2008
Y. A. Tittle	1971
George Trafton	1964
Charley Trippi	1968
Emlen Tunnell	1967
Clyde "Bulldog" Turner	1966
Johnny Unitas	1979
Gene Upshaw	1987
Norm Van Brocklin	1971
Steve Van Buren	1965
Doak Walker	1986
Paul Warfield	1983
Bob Waterfield	1965
Mike Webster	1997
Roger Wehrli	2007
Arnie Weinmeister	1984
Randy White	1994
Reggie White	2006
Dave Wilcox	2000
Bill Willis	1977
Larry Wilson	1978
Kellen Winslow	1995
Alex Wojciechowicz	1968
Willie Wood	1989
Rod Woodson	2009
Rayfield Wright	2006

Player	Year Inducted
Ron Yary	2001
Steve Young	2005
Jack Youngblood	2001
Gary Zimmerman	2008

COACHES

Coach	Year Inducted
George Allen	2002
Paul Brown	1967
Guy Chamberlin	1965
Jimmy Conzelman	1964
Weeb Ewbank	1978
Ray Flaherty	1976
Joe Gibbs	1996
Sid Gillman	1983
Harry "Bud" Grant	1994
George Halas	1963
Earl "Curly" Lambeau	1962
Tom Landry	1990
Marv Levy	2001
Vince Lombardi	1971
John Madden	2006
Earl "Greasy" Neale	1969
Chuck Noll	1993
Steve Owen	1966
Bill Parcells	2013
Don Shula	1997
Hank Stram	2003
Bill Walsh	1993

CONTRIBUTORS

Contributor	Year Inducted
DeBenneville "Bert" Bell	1963
Charles Bidwell	1967
Joe Carr	1963
Al Davis	1992
Jim Finks	1995

Contributor	Year Inducted
Lamar Hunt	1972
Tim Mara	1963
Wellington Mara	1997
George Preston Marshall	1963
Hugh "Shorty" Ray	1966
Dan Reeves	1967
Art Rooney	1964
Dan Rooney	2000
Alvin "Pete" Rozelle	1985
Ed Sabol	2011
Texas "Tex" Schramm	1991
Ralph Wilson	2009

Appendix B
Canadian Football Hall of Fame Inductees

Player	Year Inducted
Jack Abendschan	2012
Junior Ah You	1997
Roger Aldag	2002
Damon Allen	2012
Ron Atchison	1978
Byron Bailey	1975
Bill Baker	1994
John Barrow	1976
Danny Bass	2000
Harry Batstone	1963
Greg Battle	2007
Ormond Beach	1963
Al Benecick	1996
Paul Bennett	2002
John Bonk	2008
Ab Box	1965
Joe Breen	1963
Johnny Bright	1970
Dieter Brock	1995
Tom Brown	1984
Less Browne	2002
Willie Burden	2001
Bob Cameron	2010
Jerry Campbell	1996
Tom Casey	1964
Ken Charlton	1992
Bill Clarke	1996
Tom Clements	1994
Mike "Pinball" Clemons	2008
Tommy Joe Coffey	1977
Lionel Conacher	1963
Rod Connop	2005

Player	Year Inducted
Royal Copeland	1988
Jim Corrigall	1990
Grover Covington	2000
Ernie Cox	1963
Ross Craig	1964
Carl Cronin	1967
Dave Cutler	1998
Wes Cutler	1968
Peter Dalla Riva	1993
Rocky DiPietro	1997
George Dixon	1974
Matt Dunigan	2006
Ray Elgaard	2002
Abe Eliowitz	1969
Eddie Emerson	1963
Ron Estay	2003
Sam Etcheverry	1969
Terry Evenshen	1984
Bernie Faloney	1974
Alfred "Cap" Fear	1967
Dave Fennell	1990
Johnny Ferraro	1966
Norm Fieldgate	1979
Willie Fleming	1982
Darren Flutie	2007
Doug Flutie	2008
Chris Flynn	2011
Bill Frank	2001
Tony Gabriel	1984
Gene Gaines	1994
Hugh Gall	1963
Ed George	2005
Tony Golab	1964
Tommy Grant	1995
Herb Gray	1983
Dean Griffing	1965
Tracy Ham	2010
Fritz Hanson	1963
Dickie Harris	1998
Wayne Harris	1976
Herm Harrison	1993

Player	Year Inducted
John Helton	1985
Garney Henley	1979
Larry Highbaugh	2004
Tom Hinton	1991
Conredge Holloway	1998
Dick Huffman	1987
Bob Isbister	1965
Russ Jackson	1973
Jack Jacobs	1963
Eddie James	1963
Gerry James	1981
Alondra Johnson	2009
Harvey "Tyrone" Jones	2012
Bobby Jurasin	2006
Greg Kabat	1996
Joe Kapp	1984
Jerry Keeling	1989
Brian Kelly	1991
Ellison Kelly	1992
Danny Kepley	1996
Joe Krol	1963
Norman Kwong	1969
Ron Lancaster	1982
Eric LaPointe	2012
A. Smirle Lawson	1963
Frank "Pep" Leadlay	1963
Les Lear	1974
Ken Lehmann	2011
Leo Lewis	1973
Earl Lunsford	1983
Marv Luster	1990
Don Luzzi	1985
Chester McCance	1976
Frank McGill	1965
George McGowan	2003
Danny McManus	2011
Ed McQuarters	1988
Rollie Miles	1980
Jim Mills	2009
Percival Molson	1963
Joe Montford	2011

Player	Year Inducted
Warren Moon	2001
Frank Morris	1983
Teddy Morris	1964
Angelo Mosca	1987
James Murphy	2000
Don Nacisse	2010
Roger Nelson	1985
Ray Nettles	2005
Peter Neumann	1979
John "Red" O'Quinn	1981
Tony Pajaczkowski	1988
Jackie Parker	1971
James Parker	2001
Lui Passaglia	2004
Hal Patterson	1971
Elfrid Payton	2010
Gordon Perry	1970
Norm Perry	1963
Rudy Phillips	2009
Allen Pitts	2006
Willie Pless	2005
Ken Ploen	1975
Joe Poplawski	1998
Mike Pringle	2008
Sylvester "Silver" Quilty	1968
Dave Raimey	2000
Russ Rebholz	1963
George Reed	1979
Ted Reeve	1963
Dave Ridgway	2003
Frank Rigney	1984
Larry Robinson	1998
Rocco Romano	2007
Paul Rowe	1964
Martin Ruby	1974
Jeff Russel	1963
Tom Scott	1998
Vince Scott	1982
Dick Shatto	1975
Ben Simpson	1963
Bob Simpson	1976

Player	Year Inducted
Dave Sprague	1963
Milt Stegall	2010
Art Stevenson	1969
Ron Stewart	1977
Hugh "Bummer" Stirling	1966
Don Sutherlin	1992
Bill Symons	1997
Dave Thelen	1989
Brian Timmis	1963
Robert "Buddy" Tinsley	1982
Andy Tommy	1989
Herb Trawick	1975
Joe Tubman	1968
Whit Tucker	1995
Ted Urness	1989
Kate Vaughan	1978
Terry Vaughn	2011
Pierre Vercheval	2007
Virgil Wagner	1980
Chris Walby	2003
Glen Weir	2009
Hawley "Huck" Welch	1964
Tom Wilkinson	1987
Henry "Gizmo" Williams	2006
Al Wilson	1997
Harvey Wylie	1980
Dan Yochum	2004
Jim Young	1991
Ben Zambiasi	2004
Bill Zock	1984

BUILDERS

Player	Year Inducted
Bob Ackles	2002
Tony Anselmo	2009
Len Back	1971
R. Harold Bailey	1965
Harold Ballard	1987
Donald Barker	1999

Player	Year Inducted
Sam Berger	1993
David Braley	2012
Tom Brook	1975
D. Wes Brown	1963
Hugh Campbell	2000
Arthur Chipman	1969
Frank Clair	1981
Peter Connellan	2012
Ralph Cooper	1992
Bruce Coulter	1997
Hec Crighton	1985
Andrew Currie	1974
Gord Currie	2005
Bernie Custis	1998
Andrew Davies	1969
John DeGruchy	1963
Paul Dojack	1978
Eck Duggan	1981
Seppi DuMoulin	1963
Sidney Forster	2001
William Foulds	1963
Gino Fracas	2011
Greg Fulton	1995
Jake Gaudaur	1984
Frank Gibson	1996
Harry "Bud" Grant	1983
Albert Grey, 4th Earl Grey	1963
Harry Griffith	1966
Sydney Halter	1966
Frank Hannibal	1963
Lew Hayman	1975
Ed Henick	2003
Billy Hughes	1974
Eagle Keys	1990
Norm Kimball	1991
Tuffy Knight	2007
Bob Kramer	1987
Moe Lieberman	1973
Dave Matthews	2011
Harry McBrien	1978
Jimmy McCaffery	1967

Player	Year Inducted
Dave McCann	1966
Donald McNaughton	1994
Don McPherson	1983
Johnny Metras	1980
Ken Montgomery	1970
Cal Murphy	2004
Jack Newton	1964
Joe Pistilli	2010
Ken Preston	1990
Al Ritchie	1963
Mike Rodden	1964
Joe Ryan	1968
Ralph Sazio	1988
Frank Shaughnessy	1963
Tom Shepherd	2008
William T. H. "Hap" Shouldice	1977
Jimmie Simpson	1985
Karl Slocomb	1989
Victor Spencer	2006
Harry Spring	1976
Annis Stukus	1974
Neil "Piffles" Taylor	1963
Frank Tindall	1984
Clair Warner	1965
Bert Warwick	1964
Seymour Wilson	1984

Appendix C
Super Bowl Champions

Date	Winner, League	Loser, League	Score
15 January 1967	Green Bay Packers, NFL	Kansas City Chiefs, AFL	35–10
14 January 1968	Green Bay Packers, NFL	Oakland Raiders, AFL	33–14
12 January 1969	New York Jets, AFL	Baltimore Colts, NFL	16–7
11 January 1970	Kansas City Chiefs, AFL	Minnesota Vikings, NFL	23–7
17 January 1971	Baltimore Colts, AFC	Dallas Cowboys, NFC	16–13
16 January 1972	Dallas Cowboys, NFC	Miami Dolphins, AFC	24–3
14 January 1973	Miami Dolphins, AFC	Washington Redskins, NFC	14–7
13 January 1974	Miami Dolphins, AFC	Minnesota Vikings, NFC	24–7
12 January 1975	Pittsburgh Steelers, AFC	Minnesota Vikings, NFC	16–6
18 January 1976	Pittsburgh Steelers, AFC	Dallas Cowboys, NFC	21–17
9 January 1977	Oakland Raiders, AFC	Minnesota Vikings, NFC	32–14
15 January 1978	Dallas Cowboys, NFC	Denver Broncos, AFC	27–10
21 January 1979	Pittsburgh Steelers, AFC	Dallas Cowboys, NFC	35–31
20 January 1980	Pittsburgh Steelers, AFC	Los Angeles Rams, NFC	31–19
25 January 1981	Oakland Raiders, AFC	Philadelphia Eagles, NFC	27–10
24 January 1982	San Francisco 49ers, NFC	Cincinnati Bengals, AFC	26–21

Date	Winner, League	Loser, League	Score
30 January 1983	Washington Redskins, NFC	Miami Dolphins, AFC	27–17
22 January 1984	Los Angeles Raiders, AFC	Washington Redskins, NFC	38–9
20 January 1985	San Francisco 49ers, NFC	Miami Dolphins, AFC	38–16
26 January 1986	Chicago Bears, NFC	New England Patriots, AFC	46–10
25 January 1987	New York Giants, NFC	Denver Broncos, AFC	39–20
31 January 1988	Washington Redskins, NFC	Denver Broncos, AFC	42–10
22 January 1989	San Francisco 49ers, NFC	Cincinnati Bengals, AFC	20–16
28 January 1990	San Francisco 49ers, NFC	Denver Broncos, AFC	55–10
27 January 1991	New York Giants, NFC	Buffalo Bills, AFC	20–19
26 January 1992	Washington Redskins, NFC	Buffalo Bills, AFC	37–24
31 January 1993	Dallas Cowboys, NFC	Buffalo Bills, AFC	52–17
30 January 1994	Dallas Cowboys, NFC	Buffalo Bills, AFC	30–13
29 January 1995	San Francisco 49ers, NFC	San Diego Chargers, AFC	49–26
28 January 1996	Dallas Cowboys, NFC	Pittsburgh Steelers, AFC	27–17
26 January 1997	Green Bay Packers, NFC	New England Patriots, AFC	35–21
25 January 1998	Denver Broncos, AFC	Green Bay Packers, NFC	31–24
31 January 1999	Denver Broncos, AFC	Atlanta Falcons, NFC	34–19
30 January 2000	St. Louis Rams, NFC	Tennessee Titans, AFC	23–16
28 January 2001	Baltimore Ravens, AFC	New York Giants, NFC	34–7
3 February 2002	New England Patriots, AFC	St. Louis Rams, NFC	20–17

Date	Winner, League	Loser, League	Score
26 January 2003	Tampa Bay Buccaneers, NFC	Oakland Raiders, AFC	48–21
1 February 2004	New England Patriots, AFC	Carolina Panthers, NFC	32–29
6 February 2005	New England Patriots, AFC	Philadelphia Eagles, NFC	24–21
5 February 2006	Pittsburgh Steelers, AFC	Seattle Seahawks, NFC	21–10
4 February 2007	Indianapolis Colts, AFC	Chicago Bears, NFC	29–17
3 February 2008	New York Giants, NFC	New England Patriots, AFC	17–14
1 February 2009	Pittsburgh Steelers, AFC	Arizona Cardinals, NFC	27–23
7 February 2010	New Orleans Saints, NFC	Indianapolis Colts, AFC	31–17
6 February 2011	Green Bay Packers, NFC	Pittsburgh Steelers, AFC	31–25
5 February 2012	New York Giants, NFC	New England Patriots, AFC	21–17
3 February 2013	Baltimore Ravens, AFC	San Francisco 49ers, NFC	34–31

SUMMARY

League/Conference/Team	Won–Lost
National Football League	2–2
American Football League	2–2
National Football Conference	23–20
American Football Conference	20–23
Pittsburgh Steelers	6–2
San Francisco 49ers	5–1
Dallas Cowboys	5–3
Green Bay Packers	4–1
New York Giants	4–1
Los Angeles/Oakland Raiders	3–2
Washington Redskins	3–2
New England Patriots	3–4
Baltimore Ravens	2–0

League/Conference/Team	Won–Lost
Baltimore/Indianapolis Colts	2–2
Miami Dolphins	2–3
Denver Broncos	2–4
New Orleans Saints	1–0
New York Jets	1–0
Tampa Bay Buccaneers	1–0
Chicago Bears	1–1
Kansas City Chiefs	1–1
Los Angeles/St. Louis Rams	1–2
Arizona Cardinals	0–1
Atlanta Falcons	0–1
Carolina Panthers	0–1
San Diego Chargers	0–1
Seattle Seahawks	0–1
Tennessee Titans	0–1
Cincinnati Bengals	0–2
Philadelphia Eagles	0–2
Buffalo Bills	0–4
Minnesota Vikings	0–4
Cleveland Browns	0–0
Detroit Lions	0–0
Houston Texans	0–0
Jacksonville Jaguars	0–0

Appendix D
National Football League Champions

Season	League Champion	Won–Lost–Tied
1920	Akron Pros	8–0–3
1921	Chicago Staleys	9–1–1
1922	Canton Bulldogs	10–0–2
1923	Canton Bulldogs	11–0–1
1924	Cleveland Bulldogs	7–1–1
1925	Chicago Cardinals	11–2–1
1926	Frankford Yellow Jackets	14–1–2
1927	New York Giants	11–1–1
1928	Providence Steam Roller	8–1–2
1929	Green Bay Packers	12–0–1
1930	Green Bay Packers	10–3–1
1931	Green Bay Packers	12–2–0
1932	Chicago Bears	7–1–6

Season	Winner, Conference	Loser, Conference	Score
1933	Chicago Bears, West	New York Giants, East	23–21
1934	New York Giants, East	Chicago Bears, West	30–13
1935	Detroit Lions, West	New York Giants, East	26–7
1936	Green Bay Packers, West	Boston Redskins, East	21–6
1937	Washington Redskins, East	Chicago Bears, West	28–21
1938	New York Giants, East	Green Bay Packers, West	23–17
1939	Green Bay Packers, West	New York Giants, East	27–0
1940	Chicago Bears, West	Washington Redskins, East	73–0
1941	Chicago Bears, West	New York Giants, East	37–9
1942	Washington Redskins, East	Chicago Bears, West	14–6
1943	Chicago Bears, West	Washington Redskins, East	41–21
1944	Green Bay Packers, West	New York Giants, East	14–7
1945	Cleveland Rams, West	Washington Redskins, East	15–14
1946	Chicago Bears, West	New York Giants, East	24–14
1947	Chicago Cardinals, West	Philadelphia Eagles, East	28–21
1948	Philadelphia Eagles, East	Chicago Cardinals, West	7–0
1949	Philadelphia Eagles, East	Los Angeles Rams, West	14–0

Season	Winner, Conference	Loser, Conference	Score
1950	Cleveland Browns, East	Los Angeles Rams, West	30–28
1951	Los Angeles Rams, West	Cleveland Browns, East	24–17
1952	Detroit Lions, West	Cleveland Browns, East	17–7
1953	Detroit Lions, West	Cleveland Browns, East	17–16
1954	Cleveland Browns, East	Detroit Lions, West	56–10
1955	Cleveland Browns, East	Los Angeles Rams, West	38–14
1956	New York Giants, East	Chicago Bears, West	47–7
1957	Detroit Lions, West	Cleveland Browns, East	59–14
1958*	Baltimore Colts, West	New York Giants, East	23–17
1959	Baltimore Colts, West	New York Giants, East	31–16
1960	Philadelphia Eagles, East	Green Bay Packers, West	17–13
1961	Green Bay Packers, West	New York Giants, East	37–0
1962	Green Bay Packers, West	New York Giants, East	16–7
1963	Chicago Bears, West	New York Giants, East	14–10
1964	Cleveland Browns, East	Baltimore Colts, West	27–0
1965	Green Bay Packers, West	Cleveland Browns, East	23–12
1966	Green Bay Packers, West	Dallas Cowboys, East	34–27
1967	Green Bay Packers, West	Dallas Cowboys, East	21–17
1968	Baltimore Colts, West	Cleveland Browns, East	34–0
1969	Minnesota Vikings, West	Cleveland Browns, East	27–7

* Indicates that the game was decided in overtime.

NOTES

1. The league was known as the American Professional Football Association in 1920–1921.
2. From 1920 to 1932, no championship playoffs were held.
3. From 1933 to 1965, a championship game was played between the winners of the Eastern Conference and Western Conference.
4. From 1966 to 1969, an overall professional championship game was played between the National Football League and American Football League champions. This game later became known as the Super Bowl.

Appendix E
American Football League Champions

Season	Winner	Loser	Score
1960	Houston Oilers	Los Angeles Chargers	24–16
1961	Houston Oilers	San Diego Chargers	10–3
1962*	Dallas Texans	Houston Oilers	20–17
1963	San Diego Chargers	Boston Patriots	51–10
1964	Buffalo Bills	San Diego Chargers	20–7
1965	Buffalo Bills	San Diego Chargers	23–0
1966	Kansas City Chiefs	Buffalo Bills	31–7
1967	Oakland Raiders	Houston Oilers	40–7
1968	New York Jets	Oakland Raiders	27–23
1969	Kansas City Chiefs	Oakland Raiders	17–7

* Indicates that the game was decided in double overtime.

SUMMARY

Team	Won–Lost
Dallas Texans/Kansas City Chiefs	3–0
Buffalo Bills	2–1
Houston Oilers	2–2
New York Jets	1–0
Oakland Raiders	1–2
Los Angeles/San Diego Chargers	1–4
Boston Patriots	0–1
Cincinnati Bengals	0–0
Denver Broncos	0–0
Miami Dolphins	0–0

Appendix F
All-America Football Conference Champions

Season	Winner, Conference	Loser, Conference	Score
1946	Cleveland Browns, West	New York Yankees, East	14–9
1947	Cleveland Browns, West	New York Yankees, East	14–3
1948	Cleveland Browns, West	Buffalo Bills, East	49–7
1949	Cleveland Browns	San Francisco 49ers	21–7

SUMMARY

Team	Won–Lost
Cleveland Browns	4–0
Buffalo Bills	0–1
San Francisco 49ers	0–1
New York Yankees	0–2
Baltimore Colts	0–0
Brooklyn Dodgers	0–0
Brooklyn New York Yankees	0–0
Chicago Rockets/Hornets	0–0
Los Angeles Dons	0–0
Miami Seahawks	0–0

Appendix G
Grey Cup Champions

Year	Winner	Loser	Score
1909	U. Toronto Varsity Blues	Toronto Parkdale Canoe Club	26–6
1910	U. Toronto Varsity Blues	Hamilton Tigers	16–7
1911	U. Toronto Varsity Blues	Toronto Argonauts	14–7
1912	Hamilton Alerts	Toronto Argonauts	11–4
1913	Hamilton Alerts	Toronto Parkdale Canoe Club	44–2
1914	Toronto Argonauts	U. Toronto Varsity Blues	14–2
1915	Hamilton Tigers	Toronto Rowing Association	13–7
1916–1919	no game played		
1920	U. Toronto Varsity Blues	Toronto Argonauts	16–3
1921	Toronto Argonauts	Edmonton Eskimos	23–0
1922	Queen's University	Edmonton Elks	13–1
1923	Queen's University	Regina Rugby Club	54–0
1924	Queen's University	Toronto Balmy Beach	11–2
1925	Ottawa Senators	Winnipeg Tammany Tigers	24–1
1926	Ottawa Senators	U. Toronto Varsity Blues	10–7
1927	Toronto Balmy Beach	Hamilton Tigers	9–6
1928	Hamilton Tigers	Regina Roughriders	30–0
1929	Hamilton Tigers	Regina Roughriders	14–3
1930	Toronto Balmy Beach	Regina Roughriders	11–6
1931	Mont. AAA Winged Wheelers	Regina Roughriders	22–0
1932	Hamilton Tigers	Regina Roughriders	25–6
1933	Toronto Argonauts	Sarnia Imperials	4–3
1934	Sarnia Imperials	Regina Roughriders	20–12
1935	Winnipeg 'Pegs	Hamilton Tigers	18–12
1936	Sarnia Imperials	Ottawa Rough Riders	26–20

Year	Winner	Loser	Score
1937	Toronto Argonauts	Winnipeg Blue Bombers	4–3
1938	Toronto Argonauts	Winnipeg Blue Bombers	30–7
1939	Winnipeg Blue Bombers	Ottawa Rough Riders	8–7
1940*	Ottawa Rough Riders	Toronto Balmy Beach	8–2
			12–5
1941	Winnipeg Blue Bombers	Ottawa Rough Riders	18–16
1942	Toronto RCAF Hurricanes	Winnipeg RCAF Bombers	8–5
1943	Hamilton Flying Wildcats	Winnipeg RCAF Bombers	23–14
1944	Montreal HMCS Donnacona	Hamilton Flying Wildcats	7–6
1945	Toronto Argonauts	Winnipeg Blue Bombers	35–0
1946	Toronto Argonauts	Winnipeg Blue Bombers	28–6
1947	Toronto Argonauts	Winnipeg Blue Bombers	10–9
1948	Calgary Stampeders	Ottawa Rough Riders	12–7
1949	Montreal Alouettes	Calgary Stampeders	28–15
1950	Toronto Argonauts	Winnipeg Blue Bombers	13–0
1951	Ottawa Rough Riders	Saskatchewan Roughriders	21–14
1952	Toronto Argonauts	Edmonton Eskimos	21–11
1953	Hamilton Tiger-Cats	Winnipeg Blue Bombers	12–6
1954	Edmonton Eskimos	Montreal Alouettes	26–25
1955	Edmonton Eskimos	Montreal Alouettes	34–19
1956	Edmonton Eskimos	Montreal Alouettes	50–27
1957	Hamilton Tiger-Cats	Winnipeg Blue Bombers	32–7
1958	Winnipeg Blue Bombers	Hamilton Tiger-Cats	35–28
1959	Winnipeg Blue Bombers	Hamilton Tiger-Cats	21–7
1960	Ottawa Rough Riders	Edmonton Eskimos	16–6
1961***	Winnipeg Blue Bombers	Hamilton Tiger-Cats	21–14
1962**	Winnipeg Blue Bombers	Hamilton Tiger-Cats	28–27
1963	Hamilton Tiger-Cats	BC Lions	21–10
1964	BC Lions	Hamilton Tiger-Cats	34–24
1965	Hamilton Tiger-Cats	Winnipeg Blue Bombers	22–16
1966	Saskatchewan Roughriders	Ottawa Rough Riders	29–14
1967	Hamilton Tiger-Cats	Saskatchewan Roughriders	24–1
1968	Ottawa Rough Riders	Calgary Stampeders	24–21
1969	Ottawa Rough Riders	Saskatchewan Roughriders	29–11

Year	Winner	Loser	Score
1970	Montreal Alouettes	Calgary Stampeders	23–10
1971	Calgary Stampeders	Toronto Argonauts	14–11
1972	Hamilton Tiger-Cats	Saskatchewan Roughriders	13–10
1973	Ottawa Rough Riders	Edmonton Eskimos	22–18
1974	Montreal Alouettes	Edmonton Eskimos	20–7
1975	Edmonton Eskimos	Montreal Alouettes	9–8
1976	Ottawa Rough Riders	Saskatchewan Roughriders	23–20
1977	Montreal Alouettes	Edmonton Eskimos	41–6
1978	Edmonton Eskimos	Montreal Alouettes	20–13
1979	Edmonton Eskimos	Montreal Alouettes	17–9
1980	Edmonton Eskimos	Hamilton Tiger-Cats	48–10
1981	Edmonton Eskimos	Ottawa Rough Riders	26–23
1982	Edmonton Eskimos	Toronto Argonauts	32–15
1983	Toronto Argonauts	BC Lions	18–17
1984	Winnipeg Blue Bombers	Hamilton Tiger-Cats	47–17
1985	BC Lions	Hamilton Tiger-Cats	37–24
1986	Hamilton Tiger-Cats	Edmonton Eskimos	39–15
1987	Edmonton Eskimos	Toronto Argonauts	38–36
1988	Winnipeg Blue Bombers	BC Lions	22–21
1989	Saskatchewan Roughriders	Hamilton Tiger-Cats	43–40
1990	Winnipeg Blue Bombers	Edmonton Eskimos	50–11
1991	Toronto Argonauts	Calgary Stampeders	36–21
1992	Calgary Stampeders	Winnipeg Blue Bombers	24–10
1993	Edmonton Eskimos	Winnipeg Blue Bombers	33–23
1994	BC Lions	Baltimore Stallions	26–23
1995	Baltimore Stallions	Calgary Stampeders	37–20
1996	Toronto Argonauts	Edmonton Eskimos	43–37
1997	Toronto Argonauts	Saskatchewan Roughriders	47–23
1998	Calgary Stampeders	Hamilton Tiger-Cats	26–24
1999	Hamilton Tiger-Cats	Calgary Stampeders	32–21
2000	BC Lions	Montreal Alouettes	28–26
2001	Calgary Stampeders	Winnipeg Blue Bombers	27–19
2002	Montreal Alouettes	Edmonton Eskimos	25–16
2003	Edmonton Eskimos	Montreal Alouettes	34–22
2004	Toronto Argonauts	BC Lions	27–19
2005****	Edmonton Eskimos	Montreal Alouettes	38–35
2006	BC Lions	Montreal Alouettes	25–14

Year	Winner	Loser	Score
2007	Saskatchewan Roughriders	Winnipeg Blue Bombers	23–19
2008	Calgary Stampeders	Montreal Alouettes	22–14
2009	Montreal Alouettes	Saskatchewan Roughriders	28–27
2010	Montreal Alouettes	Saskatchewan Roughriders	21–18
2011	BC Lions	Winnipeg Blue Bombers	34–23
2012	Toronto Argonauts	Calgary Stampeders	35–22

* Indicates that a two-game series was played.
** Indicates that the game was called due to fog and continued on the next day.
*** Indicates that the game was decided in overtime.
**** Indicates that the game was decided in double overtime.

SUMMARY

Team	Won–Lost
Toronto Argonauts	16–6
Edmonton Eskimos	13–10
Winnipeg Blue Bombers	9–14
Hamilton Tiger-Cats	8–10
Ottawa Rough Riders	7–6
Montreal Alouettes	7–11
BC Lions	6–4
Calgary Stampeders	6–7
U. Toronto Varsity Blues	4–2
Hamilton Tigers	4–3
Queen's University	3–0
Saskatchewan Roughriders	3–8
Hamilton Alerts	2–0
Ottawa Senators	2–0
Sarnia Imperials	2–1
Toronto Balmy Beach	2–2
Montreal AAA Winged Wheelers	1–0
Montreal HMCS Donnacona	1–0
Toronto RCAF Hurricanes	1–0
Winnipeg 'Pegs	1–0
Baltimore Stallions	1–1
Hamilton Flying Wildcats	1–1
Edmonton Elks	0–1

Team	Won–Lost
Regina Rugby Club	0–1
Toronto Rowing Association	0–1
Winnipeg Tammany Tigers	0–1
Toronto Parkdale Canoe Club	0–2
Winnipeg RCAF Bombers	0–2
Regina Roughriders	0–6

Appendix H
World Bowl Champions

Season	Winner	Loser	Score
1991	London Monarchs	Barcelona Dragons	21–0
1992	Sacramento Surge	Orlando Thunder	21–17
1993	not played		
1994	not played		
1995	Frankfurt Galaxy	Amsterdam Admirals	26–22
1996	Scottish Claymores	Frankfurt Galaxy	32–27
1997	Barcelona Dragons	Rhein Fire	38–24
1998	Rhein Fire	Frankfurt Galaxy	34–10
1999	Frankfurt Galaxy	Barcelona Dragons	38–24
2000	Rhein Fire	Scottish Claymores	13–10
2001	Berlin Thunder	Barcelona Dragons	24–17
2002	Berlin Thunder	Rhein Fire	26–20
2003	Frankfurt Galaxy	Rhein Fire	35–16
2004	Berlin Thunder	Frankfurt Galaxy	30–24
2005	Amsterdam Admirals	Berlin Thunder	27–21
2006	Frankfurt Galaxy	Amsterdam Admirals	22–7
2007	Hamburg Sea Devils	Frankfurt Galaxy	37–28

SUMMARY

Team	Won–Lost
Frankfurt Galaxy	4–4
Berlin Thunder	3–1
Rhein Fire	2–3
London Monarchs	1–0
Sacramento Surge	1–0
Hamburg Sea Devils	1–0
Scottish Claymores	1–1
Amsterdam Admirals	1–2
Barcelona Dragons	1–3
Orlando Thunder	0–1

Appendix I
International National Football League Games

PRESEASON EXHIBITIONS: THE NATIONAL FOOTBALL LEAGUE VERSUS THE CANADIAN FOOTBALL LEAGUE

Date	Winner	Loser	Score	Site
12 August 1950	New York Giants	Ottawa	27–6	Ottawa, CAN
11 August 1951	New York Giants	Ottawa	41–18	Ottawa, CAN
5 August 1959	Chicago Cardinals	Toronto	55–26	Toronto, CAN
3 August 1960	Pittsburgh	Toronto	43–16	Toronto, CAN
2 August 1961	St. Louis	Toronto	36–7	Toronto, CAN
5 August 1961	Chicago	Montreal	34–16	Montreal, CAN
8 August 1961	Hamilton	Buffalo	38–21	Hamilton, CAN

PRESEASON NATIONAL FOOTBALL LEAGUE GAMES

Date	Winner	Loser	Score	Site
15 August 1960	Chicago	New York Giants	16–7	Toronto, CAN
25 August 1969	Detroit	Boston	22–9	Montreal, CAN
11 September 1969	Pittsburgh	New York Giants	17–13	Montreal, CAN
16 August 1976	St. Louis	San Diego Chargers	20–10	Tokyo, JPN
5 August 1978	New Orleans	Philadelphia	14–7	Mexico City, MEX
6 August 1983	Minnesota	St. Louis	28–10	London, ENG
3 August 1986	Chicago	Dallas	17–6	London, ENG
9 August 1987	Los Angeles Rams	Denver	28–27	London, ENG

Date	Winner	Loser	Score	Site
31 July 1988	Miami	San Francisco	27–21	London, ENG
15 August 1988	Minnesota	Chicago	28–21	Gothenburg, SWE
18 August 1988	New York Jets	Cleveland	11–7	Montreal, CAN
5 August 1989	Los Angeles Rams	San Francisco	16–13	Tokyo, JPN
6 August 1989	Philadelphia	Cleveland	17–13	London, ENG
4 August 1990	Denver	Seattle	10–7	Tokyo, JPN
5 August 1990	New Orleans	Los Angeles Raiders	17–10	London, ENG
9 August 1990	Pittsburgh	New England	30–14	Montreal, CAN
11 August 1990	Los Angeles Rams	Kansas City	19–3	W. Berlin, GER
28 July 1991	Buffalo	Philadelphia	17–13	London, ENG
3 August 1991	San Francisco	Chicago	21–7	Berlin, GER
3 August 1991	Miami	Los Angeles Raiders	19–17	Tokyo, JPN
1 August 1992	Houston	Dallas	34–23	Tokyo, JPN
15 August 1992	Miami	Denver	31–27	Berlin, GER
16 August 1992	San Francisco	Washington	17–15	London, ENG
31 July 1993	New Orleans	Philadelphia	28–16	Tokyo, JPN
1 August 1993	San Francisco	Pittsburgh	21–14	Barcelona, ESP
7 August 1993	Minnesota	Buffalo	20–6	Berlin, GER
8 August 1993	Dallas	Detroit	13–13	London, ENG
14 August 1993	Cleveland	New England	12–9	Toronto, CAN
31 July 1994	Los Angeles Raiders	Denver	25–22	Barcelona, ESP
6 August 1994	Minnesota	Kansas City	17–9	Tokyo, JPN
13 August 1994	New York Giants	San Diego	28–20	Berlin, GER
15 August 1994	Houston	Dallas	6–0	Mexico City, MEX

Date	Winner	Loser	Score	Site
5 August 1995	Denver	San Francisco	24–10	Tokyo, JPN
12 August 1995	Buffalo	Dallas	9–7	Toronto, CAN
27 July 1996	San Diego	Pittsburgh	20–10	Tokyo, JPN
5 August 1996	Kansas City	Dallas	32–6	Monterrey, MEX
27 July 1997	Pittsburgh	Chicago	30–17	Dublin, IRL
4 August 1997	Miami	Denver	38–19	Mexico City, MEX
16 August 1997	Green Bay	Buffalo	35–3	Toronto, CAN
1 August 1998	Green Bay	Kansas City	27–24	Tokyo, JPN
15 August 1998	San Francisco	Seattle	24–21	Vancouver, CAN
17 August 1998	New England	Dallas	21–3	Mexico City, MEX
7 August 1999	Denver	San Diego	20–17	Sydney, AUS
5 August 2000	Atlanta	Dallas	20–9	Tokyo, JPN
19 August 2000	Indianapolis	Pittsburgh	24–23	Mexico City, MEX
27 August 2001	Dallas	Oakland	21–6	Mexico City, MEX
3 August 2002	Washington	San Francisco	38–7	Osaka, JPN
2 August 2003	Tampa Bay	New York Jets	30–14	Tokyo, JPN
6 August 2005	Atlanta	Indianapolis	27–21	Tokyo, JPN
14 August 2008	Buffalo	Pittsburgh	24–21	Toronto, CAN
19 August 2010	Buffalo	Indianapolis	34–21	Toronto, CAN

REGULAR-SEASON NATIONAL FOOTBALL LEAGUE GAMES

Date	Winner	Loser	Score	Site
2 October 2005	Arizona	San Francisco	31–14	Mexico City, MEX
28 October 2007	New York Giants	Miami	13–10	London, ENG
26 October 2008	New Orleans	San Diego	37–32	London, ENG

Date	Winner	Loser	Score	Site
7 December 2008	Miami	Buffalo	16–3	Toronto, CAN
25 October 2009	New England	Tampa Bay	35–7	London, ENG
3 December 2009	New York Jets	Buffalo	19–13	Toronto, CAN
31 October 2010	San Francisco	Denver	24–16	London, ENG
7 November 2010	Chicago	Buffalo	22–19	Toronto, CAN
23 October 2011	Chicago	Tampa Bay	24–18	London, ENG
30 October 2011	Washington	Buffalo	23–0	Toronto, CAN
28 October 2012	New England	St. Louis	45–7	London, ENG
16 December 2012	Seattle	Buffalo	50–17	Toronto, CAN

NOTES

1. The NFL–CFL games from 1950 to 1961 were played using CFL rules for the first half and NFL rules for the second half.
2. The preseason games from 1986 through 2005 were called the American Bowl.

Appendix J
Foreign-Born National Football League Players

AMERICAN SAMOA

George Achica
Jonathan Fanene
Wilson Faumuina
Toniu Fonoti
Mekeli Ieremia
Junior Ioane
Mike Iupati
Reagan Mauia
Al Noga
Niko Noga
Pete Noga
Lonnie Palelei
Anton Palepoi
Ropati Pitoitua
Gabe Reid
Spencer Reid
Pio Sagapolutele
Joe Salave'a
Lauvale Sape
Don Sasa
Junior Siavii
Isaac Sopoaga
Maa Tanuvasa
Mosi Tatupu
Daniel Te'o-Nesheim
Jack Thompson
Mao Tosi
Navy Tuiasosopo
Tuufuli Uperesa

ARGENTINA

Bob Breitenstein
Bill Gramatica
Martin Gramatica

ARMENIA

Mike Gulian

AUSTRALIA

Darren Bennett
Chris Bryan
Ben Graham
Mat McBriar
Colin Ridgway
Saverio Rocca
Colin Scotts

AUSTRIA

Toni Fritsch
Andy Gross
Milo Gwosden
Toni Linhart
Peter Rajkovich
Ray Wersching

BAHAMAS

Jocelyn Borgella
Devard Darling
Ed Smith

BARBADOS

Robert Bailey
Roger Farmer
Elvis Joseph
Sam Seale

BELGIUM

George Jakowenko
Terry Ray

BELIZE

Bill Gutteron

BERMUDA

Ron Davenport
Ken Hartley
Rocky Thompson

BRAZIL

Tim Mazzetti

BULGARIA

Boni Petcoff

CAMEROON

Adrian Awasom
Moise Fokou
Mathias Nkwenti
Roman Oben

CANADA

O. J. Atogwe
Ian Beckles
Brian Belway
Mitch Berger
Doug Brown
Jim Bryant
Gene Ceppetelli
Gordy Ceresino
Randy Chevrier
Steve Christie
Colin Cole
Bill Crawford
Justin Cross
Hector Cyre
Jean-Phillipe Darche
Clifton Dawson
Dean Dorsey
Paul Duhart
Daniel Federkeil
Brian Forde
Brian Fryer
Roy Gerela
Sam Giguere
Howard Glenn
Rick Goltz
Cory Greenwood
Hal Griggs
Cece Hare
Ray Hare

Bill Hitchcock
Bill Howell
Tommy Hughitt
Hank Ilesic
Teyo Johnson
Nick Kaczur
Tommy Kane
Alain Kashama
Jerry Kauric
Allan Kennedy
Michael Kostiuk
Joe Krol
Art Kuehn
Mike Labinjo
L. P. Ladouceur
Buck MacDonald
Corey Mace
Tony Mandarich
Rueben Mayes
Russ McLeod
Rob Meier
Jim Mills
Mark Montreuil
Steve Morley
Eddie Murray
Bronko Nagurski
Tom Nutten
Charlie O'Rourke
Jesse Palmer
Russ Peterson
Gary Pettigrew
Ed Philion
Harry Robertson
Brett Romberg
Bill Rooney
Joe Rooney
Ed Ryan
Jon Ryan
Mark Rypien
Davis Sanchez

O. J. Santiago
Mike Schad
Chris Schultz
Dave Sparenberg
Jeff Spek
Wayne Stewart
Frank Stojack
Cecil Sturgeon
Lyle Sturgeon
Shaun Suisham
Ryan Thelwell
Tim Tindale
Mike Vanderjagt
Fred Vant Hull
Joe Watt
Arnie Weinmeister
Lloyd Wickett
Ted Williams
Tyrone R. Williams
Klaus Wilmsmeyer
Joe Wilson
Glen Young
Jim Young

COLOMBIA

Jairo Penaranda
Fuad Reveiz

CONGO

Wilkie Moody

CROATIA

Momcilo Gavric
George Perpich

CUBA

Joe Lamas
Lou Molinet
Ralph Ortega
Luis Sharpe

CYPRUS

Garo Yepremian

CZECHOSLOVAKIA

Alex Gorgal
Al Hust
Jerry Krysl
Mirro Roder
Will Svitek

DENMARK

Morten Andersen
Bud Jorgensen
Wagner Jorgensen
Hans Nielsen

EL SALVADOR

Jose Cortez

ENGLAND

Vince Abbott
Ken Clark
Harry Collins
Mike Dawson
John Dibb
Mike Estep
Domonique Foxworth
Owen Gill
Larry Green
Bobby Howfield
Ian Howfield
Rhys Lloyd
Mick Luckhurst
Pat Morrison
Vince Newsome
Wayne Radloff
Mike Reed
Maury Segal
Rick Sharp
Tim Shaw
John Smith
Galand Thaxton
Osi Umenyiora
Mike Walker

ESTONIA

Michael Roos

FRANCE

Jethro Franklin
Charles Romes
Pat Saindon
Richard Tardits

GERMANY

Mark Adickes
John Alt
Zenon Andrusyshyn
Frank Aschenbrenner

Darnell Autry
Robert Awalt
Terry Billups
Willie Blade
Dorian Boose
Ken Brown
Bruce Collie
Dick Dobeleit
John Engelberger
Jerome Felton
James FitzPatrick
Ron George
Brandon Gibson
Domenik Hixon
Mike Jenkins
John Jurkovic
Terry Kinard
Jeff Knapple
Markus Koch
Chris Kolodziejski
Karl Kremser
Mike Kullman
Doug Legursky
D. D. Lewis
Nick Lowery
Marvin Marshall
Tony Mayberry
Anthony McDowell
Dan McMillen
Gerald McNeil
Ray Mickens
Dwayne Missouri
Ralf Mojsiejenko
Kyle Moore
Horst Muhlmann
Jamar Nesbit
John Nesser
Phil Nesser
Jeff Nixon
Joel Patten
Hank Piro
Kavika Pittman

Alan Reid
Ed Reynolds
Tony Richardson
Constantin Ritzmann
Gerhard Schwedes
Mike Sellers
Siddeeq Shabazz
Arnie Simkus
William Sims
Gary Smith
Ernie Stautner
Joel Steed
Fred Steinfort
Tony Stewart
Joe Szczecko
Jamaar Taylor
Tony Vinson
Sebastian Vollmer
Uwe von Schamann
Gary Walker
David Whitehurst
Reggie Williams

GHANA

Ebenezer Ekuban
Phil Yeboah-Kodie

GREECE

Chris Farasopoulos
Angelo Loukas
John Maskas
Gust Zarnas

GUAM

Troy Andrew

GUATEMALA

Ted Hendricks
John Hendy

GUYANA

Lance Schulters

HAITI

Gosder Cherilus
Vlad Ducasse
Junior Galette
Ricot Joseph

HONDURAS

Ebert Van Buren
Steve Van Buren

HUNGARY

Charlie Gogolak
Pete Gogolak
Steve Mike-Mayer

IRAN

Shahriar Pourdanesh

IRELAND

France Fitzgerald
Birdie Maher
Brian McGrath
Tom McLaughlin
Bob Nash
Con O'Brien
Neil O'Donoghue
Paddy Quinn
John Sinnott
Adrian Young

ITALY

Bruno Banducci
Ping Bodie
Jack Bonadies
Mac Cara
Enio Conti
Frank Gaziano
Pete Gorgone
David Knight
Massimo Manca
Nick Mike-Mayer
Leo Nomellini
Kerry Porter
Joe Santone
Joe Savoldi
Ralph Sazio
Rocky Segretta
Ralph Vince
Sandro Vitiello
Elnardo Webster

IVORY COAST

Amos Zereoue

JAMAICA

Dwight Anderson
Atari Bigby
Craig Bingham

Dwight Bingham
Mark A. Campbell
Patrick Chung
Oniel Cousins
Rohan Davey
Dahrran Diedrick
Omar Easy
Andrew Greene
Morlon Greenwood
Kwame Harris
Lloyd Harrison
Jovan Haye
Chris Hewitt
Sean Jones
Andre King
Vaughn Martin
Ryan McBean
Devon McDonald
Ricardo McDonald
Damion McIntosh
Kevin McLeod
Devon Mitchell
Chris Samuels
Donovan Small
Khreem Smith
Omar Smith
Floyd Wedderburn
Fearon Wright

JAPAN

John Arnold
Rick Berns
Guy Bingham
Anthony Brown
Dan Clark
John Hagy
John Jackson
J. C. Pearson
Matt Russell
Marcus Thomas

LATVIA

Vilnis Ezerins

LEBANON

Hicham El-Mashtoub
Jimmy Jemail

LIBERIA

Jehuu Caulcrick
Tamba Hali
Bhawoh Jue
Thomas Tapeh
Mansfield Wrotto
Ashton Youboty

LIBYA

Tony Cherry

LITHUANIA

Bill Lajousky
Arunas Vasys

MARSHALL ISLANDS

Todd Lyght

MEXICO

Sergio Albert
Raul Allegre
Rolando Cantu

Frank Corral
Dave Etherly
Efren Herrera
Jose Portilla
Aldo Richins
Rafael Septien
Joaquin Zendejas
Luis Zendejas
Max Zendejas
Tony Zendejas

NETHERLANDS

Jim Asmus
Romeo Bandison
Case deBruijn
Harald Hasselbach

NEW ZEALAND

Johan Asiata
David Dixon
Riki Ellison

NIGERIA

Victor Adeyanju
Obed Ariri
Patrick Chukwurah
Adimchinobe Echemandu
Patrick Egu
Isaiah Ekejiuba
Mohammed Elewonibi
Samkon Gado
Israel Idonije
Israel Ifeanyi
Donald Igwebuike
Tony Okanlawon
Amobi Okoye

Christian Okoye
Willie Oshodin
Iheanyi Uwaezuoke

NORWAY

Halvor Hagen
Bill Irgens
Leif Larsen
Mike Mock
Jan Stenerud

PANAMA

Alvin Powell

PANAMA CANAL ZONE

Leo Barker
Jim Schuber

PARAGUAY

Benny Ricardo

PHILIPPINES

Sanjay Beach
Mike Corgan
Steve Haworth
Fred Jones
Tim Tebow

POLAND

Dutch Connor
Jack Grossman

Sebastian Janikowski
Jason Maniecki
Chester Marcol
Rich Szaro

PUERTO RICO

Ken Amato
Tony Holloway

ROMANIA

George Gross
Zoltan Mesko
Red Seidelson

RUSSIA

John Barsha
Morris Glassman
Al Greene
Ace Gutowsky
Max Padlow

SAUDI ARABIA

Jordan Kent

SCOTLAND

Tom Birney
Graham Gano
Chick Lang
Arthur Matsu
Andrew Peterson
Ian Sunter

Lawrence Tynes
Alex Waits

SIERRA LEONE

B. J. Tucker
Madieu Williams

SOUTH AFRICA

Gary Anderson
Jerome Pathon

SOUTH KOREA

John Lee
Kyle Love
Hines Ward

SPAIN

Kelly Rodriguez
Ray Rowe

ST. KITTS

Erasmus James

SWEDEN

Chris Gartner
Stone Hallquist
Ove Johansson
Pike Johnson
Ola Kimrin

Goran Lingmerth
Bjorn Nittmo
Curly Oden

SYRIA

Heinie Jawish

TAIWAN

Tony Daykin
David J. Jones

THAILAND

Tony Brown

TONGA

Tuineau Alipate
Spencer Folau
Lakei Heimuli
Steve Kaufusi
Ma'ake Kemoeatu
Deuce Lutui
Siupeli Malamala
Tim Manoa
Stan Mataele
Viliami Maumau
Alfred Pupunu
Vai Sikahema
Peter Tuipulotu

TRINIDAD

Kerry Carter
Anthony Herrera
Sankar Montoute
Curvin Richards

TURKEY

Tunch Ilkin

UGANDA

Mathias Kiwanuka
Kato Serwanga
Wasswa Serwanga

UKRAINE

Art Dorfman
Buckets Goldenberg
Igor Olshansky

VENEZUELA

Alan Pringle
Pat Ragusa

VIETNAM

Dat Nguyen

VIRGIN ISLANDS

Joe Aska
Ivan Caesar
Quentin Coryatt
Mike Evans
Jeff Faulkner
Abdul Hodge

Linval Joseph
Hanik Milligan
Renaldo Turnbull
Andre Wadsworth

WALES

Jon Norris
Allan Watson

WESTERN SAMOA

Ricky Andrews
Richard Brown
Ta'ase Faumui
Al Lolotai

Malaefou MacKenzie
Frank Manumaleuga
Jesse Sapolu

YUGOSLAVIA

Novo Bojovic
Joe Cerne
Filip Filipovic
Visco Grgich
Joe Kodba

ZAIRE

Tim Biakabutuka
Muadianvita Kazadi

Appendix K
Bowl Championship Series National Champions

Year	Winner	Loser	Score
4 January 1999	Tennessee	Florida State	23–16
4 January 2000	Florida State	Virginia Tech	46–29
3 January 2001	Oklahoma	Florida State	13–2
3 January 2002	Miami (FL)	Nebraska	37–14
3 January 2003	Ohio State	Miami (FL)	31–24
4 January 2004	Louisiana State	Oklahoma	21–14
4 January 2005	Southern California	Oklahoma	55–19
4 January 2006	Texas	Southern California	41–38
8 January 2007	Florida	Ohio State	41–14
7 January 2008	Louisiana State	Ohio State	31–24
8 January 2009	Florida	Oklahoma	24–14
7 January 2010	Alabama	Texas	37–21
10 January 2011	Auburn	Oregon	22–19
9 January 2012	Alabama	Louisiana State	21–0
7 January 2013	Alabama	Notre Dame	42–14

SUMMARY

Team	Won–Lost
Alabama	3–0
Florida	2–0
Louisiana State	2–1
Auburn	1–0
Tennessee	1–0
Miami (FL)	1–1
Southern California	1–1
Texas	1–1
Florida State	1–2
Ohio State	1–2
Oklahoma	1–3

Team	Won–Lost
Nebraska	0–1
Oregon	0–1
Virginia Tech	0–1
Notre Dame	0–1

Appendix L
College Champions

Although collegiate football has been played in the United States since 1869, it is one of the few sports that do not have an official champion for major colleges. The National Collegiate Athletic Association, formed in 1906, governs the sport but does not name a champion. Various news media organizations have selected annual champions but often disagree. The following list identifies the schools that have had the most recognition as national champion.

Year	School
1869	Princeton, Rutgers
1870	Princeton
1871	no games played
1872	Princeton, Yale
1873	Princeton
1874	Harvard, Princeton, Yale
1875	Columbia, Harvard, Princeton
1876	Yale
1877	Princeton, Yale
1878	Princeton
1879	Princeton, Yale
1880	Princeton, Yale
1881	Princeton, Yale
1882	Yale
1883	Yale
1884	Princeton, Yale
1885	Princeton
1886	Princeton, Yale
1887	Yale
1888	Yale
1889	Princeton
1890	Harvard
1891	Yale
1892	Yale
1893	Princeton, Yale

Year	School
1894	Pennsylvania, Princeton, Yale
1895	Pennsylvania, Yale
1896	Lafayette, Princeton
1897	Pennsylvania, Yale
1898	Harvard, Princeton
1899	Harvard, Princeton
1900	Yale
1901	Harvard, Michigan, Yale
1902	Michigan, Yale
1903	Michigan, Princeton
1904	Michigan, Minnesota, Pennsylvania
1905	Chicago, Yale
1906	Princeton, Yale
1907	Yale
1908	Harvard, Louisiana State, Pennsylvania
1909	Yale
1910	Harvard, Pittsburgh
1911	Penn State, Princeton
1912	Harvard, Penn State
1913	Auburn, Chicago, Harvard
1914	Army, Illinois, Texas
1915	Cornell, Oklahoma, Pittsburgh
1916	Army, Pittsburgh
1917	Georgia Tech
1918	Michigan, Pittsburgh
1919	Centre, Harvard, Illinois, Notre Dame, Texas A&M
1920	California, Harvard, Notre Dame, Princeton
1921	California, Cornell, Iowa, Lafayette, Washington & Jefferson
1922	California, Cornell, Princeton
1923	California, Cornell, Illinois, Michigan
1924	Notre Dame, Pennsylvania
1925	Alabama, Dartmouth, Michigan
1926	Alabama, Lafayette, Michigan, Navy, Stanford
1927	Georgia, Illinois, Notre Dame, Texas A&M, Yale
1928	Detroit, Georgia Tech, Southern California
1929	Notre Dame, Pittsburgh, Southern California
1930	Alabama, Notre Dame
1931	Pittsburgh, Purdue, Southern California
1932	Colgate, Michigan, Southern California
1933	Michigan, Ohio State, Princeton, Southern California
1934	Alabama, Minnesota

Year	School
1935	Louisiana State, Minnesota, Princeton, Southern Methodist, Texas Christian
1936	Louisiana State, Minnesota, Pittsburgh
1937	California, Pittsburgh
1938	Notre Dame, Tennessee, Texas Christian
1939	Cornell, Southern California, Texas A&M
1940	Minnesota, Stanford, Tennessee
1941	Alabama, Minnesota, Texas
1942	Georgia, Ohio State, Wisconsin
1943	Notre Dame
1944	Army, Ohio State
1945	Alabama, Army
1946	Army, Georgia, Notre Dame
1947	Michigan, Notre Dame
1948	Michigan
1949	Notre Dame, Oklahoma
1950	Kentucky, Oklahoma, Princeton, Tennessee
1951	Georgia Tech, Illinois, Maryland, Michigan State, Tennessee
1952	Georgia Tech, Michigan State
1953	Maryland, Notre Dame, Oklahoma
1954	Ohio State, UCLA
1955	Michigan State, Oklahoma
1956	Georgia Tech, Iowa, Oklahoma, Tennessee
1957	Auburn, Michigan State, Ohio State, Oklahoma
1958	Iowa, Louisiana State
1959	Mississippi, Syracuse
1960	Iowa, Minnesota, Mississippi, Missouri, Washington
1961	Alabama, Ohio State
1962	Louisiana State, Mississippi, Southern California
1963	Texas
1964	Alabama, Arkansas, Michigan, Notre Dame
1965	Alabama, Michigan State
1966	Alabama, Michigan State, Notre Dame
1967	Notre Dame, Oklahoma, Southern California, Tennessee
1968	Georgia, Ohio State, Texas
1969	Ohio State, Penn State, Texas
1970	Arizona State, Nebraska, Notre Dame, Ohio State, Texas
1971	Nebraska
1972	Southern California
1973	Alabama, Michigan, Notre Dame, Ohio State, Oklahoma
1974	Ohio State, Oklahoma, Southern California

Year	School
1975	Alabama, Arizona State, Ohio State, Oklahoma
1976	Pittsburgh, Southern California
1977	Alabama, Arkansas, Notre Dame, Texas
1978	Alabama, Oklahoma, Southern California
1979	Alabama, Southern California
1980	Florida State, Georgia, Nebraska, Oklahoma, Pittsburgh
1981	Clemson, Nebraska, Penn State, Pittsburgh, Southern Methodist, Texas
1982	Nebraska, Penn State, Southern Methodist
1983	Auburn, Miami, Nebraska
1984	Brigham Young, Florida, Nebraska, Washington
1985	Florida, Michigan, Oklahoma
1986	Miami, Oklahoma, Penn State
1987	Florida State, Miami
1988	Miami, Notre Dame
1989	Miami, Notre Dame
1990	Colorado, Georgia Tech, Miami, Washington
1991	Miami, Washington
1992	Alabama, Florida State
1993	Auburn, Florida State, Nebraska, Notre Dame
1994	Florida State, Nebraska, Penn State
1995	Nebraska
1996	Florida, Florida State
1997	Michigan, Nebraska
1998	Tennessee
1999	Florida State
2000	Miami, Oklahoma
2001	Miami
2002	Ohio State, Southern California
2003	Louisiana State, Oklahoma, Southern California
2004	Southern California
2005	Texas
2006	Florida, Boise State
2007	Louisiana State, Missouri, Southern California
2008	Florida, Utah
2009	Alabama
2010	Auburn, Oregon, Texas Christian
2011	Alabama
2012	Alabama

SUMMARY BY SCHOOL

Alabama (19): 1925, 1926, 1930, 1934, 1941, 1945, 1961, 1964, 1965, 1966, 1973, 1975, 1977, 1978, 1979, 1992, 2009, 2011, 2012
Arizona State (2): 1970, 1975
Arkansas (2): 1964, 1977
Army (5): 1914, 1916, 1944, 1945, 1946
Auburn (5): 1913, 1957, 1983, 1993, 2010
Boise State (1): 2006
Brigham Young (1): 1984
California (5): 1920, 1921, 1922, 1923, 1937
Centre (1): 1919
Chicago (2): 1905, 1913
Clemson (1): 1981
Colgate (1): 1932
Colorado (1): 1990
Columbia (1): 1875
Cornell (5): 1915, 1921, 1922, 1923, 1939
Dartmouth (1): 1925
Detroit (1): 1928
Florida (5): 1984, 1985, 1996, 2006, 2008
Florida State (7): 1980, 1987, 1992, 1993, 1994, 1996, 1999
Georgia (5): 1927, 1942, 1946, 1968, 1980
Georgia Tech (6): 1917, 1928, 1951, 1952, 1956, 1990
Harvard (12): 1874, 1875, 1890, 1898, 1899, 1901, 1908, 1910, 1912, 1913, 1919, 1920
Illinois (5): 1914, 1919, 1923, 1927, 1951
Iowa (4): 1921, 1956, 1958, 1960
Kentucky (1): 1950
Lafayette (3): 1896, 1921, 1926
Louisiana State (7): 1908, 1935, 1936, 1958, 1962, 2003, 2007
Maryland (2): 1951, 1953
Miami (9): 1983, 1986, 1987, 1988, 1989, 1990, 1991, 2000, 2001
Michigan (16): 1901, 1902, 1903, 1904, 1918, 1923, 1925, 1926, 1932, 1933, 1947, 1948, 1964, 1973, 1985, 1997
Michigan State (6): 1951, 1952, 1955, 1957, 1965, 1966
Minnesota (7): 1904, 1934, 1935, 1936, 1940, 1941, 1960
Mississippi (3): 1959, 1960, 1962
Missouri (2): 1960, 2007
Navy (1): 1926
Nebraska (11): 1970, 1971, 1980, 1981, 1982, 1983, 1984, 1993, 1994, 1995, 1997

Notre Dame (21): 1919, 1920, 1924, 1927, 1929, 1930, 1938, 1943, 1946, 1947, 1949, 1953, 1964, 1966, 1967, 1970, 1973, 1977, 1988, 1989, 1993

Ohio State (13): 1933, 1942, 1944, 1954, 1957, 1961, 1968, 1969, 1970, 1973, 1974, 1975, 2002

Oklahoma (17): 1915, 1949, 1950, 1953, 1955, 1956, 1957, 1967, 1973, 1974, 1975, 1978, 1980, 1985, 1986, 2000, 2003

Oregon (1): 2010

Penn State (7): 1911, 1912, 1969, 1981, 1982, 1986, 1994

Pennsylvania (6): 1894, 1895, 1897, 1904, 1908, 1924

Pittsburgh (11): 1910, 1915, 1916, 1918, 1929, 1931, 1936, 1937, 1976, 1980, 1981

Princeton (28): 1869, 1870, 1872, 1973, 1874, 1875, 1877, 1878, 1879, 1880, 1881, 1884, 1885, 1886, 1889, 1893, 1894, 1896, 1898, 1899, 1903, 1906, 1911, 1920, 1922, 1933, 1935, 1950

Purdue (1): 1931

Rutgers (1): 1869

Southern California (17): 1928, 1929, 1931, 1932, 1933, 1939, 1962, 1967, 1972, 1974, 1976, 1978, 1979, 2002, 2003, 2004, 2007

Southern Methodist (3): 1935, 1981, 1982

Stanford (2): 1926, 1940

Syracuse (1): 1959

Tennessee (7): 1938, 1940, 1950, 1951, 1956, 1967, 1998

Texas (9): 1914, 1941, 1963, 1968, 1969, 1970, 1977, 1981, 2005

Texas A&M (3): 1919, 1927, 1939

Texas Christian (3): 1935, 1938, 2010

UCLA (1): 1954

Utah (1): 2008

Washington (4): 1960, 1984, 1990, 1991

Washington & Jefferson (1): 1921

Wisconsin (1): 1942

Yale (27): 1872, 1874, 1876, 1877, 1879, 1880, 1881, 1882, 1883, 1884, 1886, 1887, 1888, 1891, 1892, 1893, 1894, 1895, 1897, 1900, 1901, 1902, 1905, 1906, 1907, 1909, 1927

SUMMARY BY NUMBER OF APPEARANCES

28 Princeton
27 Yale
21 Notre Dame
19 Alabama

17	Oklahoma, Southern California
16	Michigan
13	Ohio State
12	Harvard
11	Nebraska, Pittsburgh
9	Miami, Texas
7	Florida State, Louisiana State, Minnesota, Penn State, Tennessee
6	Georgia Tech, Michigan State, Pennsylvania
5	Army, Auburn, California, Cornell, Florida, Georgia, Illinois
4	Iowa, Washington
3	Lafayette, Mississippi, Southern Methodist, Texas A&M, Texas Christian
2	Arizona State, Arkansas, Chicago, Maryland, Missouri, Stanford
1	Boise State, Brigham Young, Centre, Clemson, Colgate, Colorado, Columbia, Dartmouth, Detroit, Kentucky, Navy, Oregon, Purdue, Rutgers, Syracuse, UCLA, Utah, Washington & Jefferson, Wisconsin

Appendix M
Rose Bowl Champions

Year	Winner	Loser	Score
1 January 1902	Michigan	Stanford	49–0
1 January 1916	Washington State	Brown	14–0
1 January 1917	Oregon	Pennsylvania	14–0
1 January 1918	Mare Island (Marines)	Camp Lewis (Army)	19–7
1 January 1919	Great Lakes (Navy)	Mare Island (Marines)	17–0
1 January 1920	Harvard	Oregon	7–6
1 January 1921	California	Ohio State	28–0
2 January 1922*	California	Washington & Jefferson	0–0
1 January 1923	Southern California	Penn State	14–3
1 January 1924*	Washington	Navy	14–14
1 January 1925	Notre Dame	Stanford	27–10
1 January 1926	Alabama	Washington	20–19
1 January 1927*	Alabama	Stanford	7–7
2 January 1928	Stanford	Pittsburgh	7–6
1 January 1929	Georgia Tech	California	8–7
1 January 1930	Southern California	Pittsburgh	47–14
1 January 1931	Alabama	Washington State	24–0
1 January 1932	Southern California	Tulane	21–12
2 January 1933	Southern California	Pittsburgh	35–0
1 January 1934	Columbia	Stanford	7–0
1 January 1935	Alabama	Stanford	29–13
1 January 1936	Stanford	Southern Methodist	7–0
1 January 1937	Pittsburgh	Washington	21–0
1 January 1938	California	Alabama	13–0
2 January 1939	Southern California	Duke	7–3
1 January 1940	Southern California	Tennessee	14–0
1 January 1941	Stanford	Nebraska	21–13
1 January 1942	Oregon State	Duke	20–16
1 January 1943	Georgia	UCLA	9–0
1 January 1944	Southern California	Washington	29–0
1 January 1945	Southern California	Tennessee	25–0
1 January 1946	Alabama	Southern California	34–14

Year	Winner	Loser	Score
1 January 1947	Illinois	UCLA	45–14
1 January 1948	Michigan	Southern California	49–0
1 January 1949	Northwestern	California	20–14
2 January 1950	Ohio State	California	17–14
1 January 1951	Michigan	California	14–6
1 January 1952	Illinois	Stanford	40–7
1 January 1953	Southern California	Wisconsin	7–0
1 January 1954	Michigan State	UCLA	28–20
1 January 1955	Ohio State	Southern California	20–7
2 January 1956	Michigan State	UCLA	17–14
1 January 1957	Iowa	Oregon State	35–19
1 January 1958	Ohio State	Oregon	10–7
1 January 1959	Iowa	California	38–12
1 January 1960	Washington	Wisconsin	44–8
2 January 1961	Washington	Minnesota	17–7
1 January 1962	Minnesota	UCLA	21–3
1 January 1963	Southern California	Wisconsin	42–37
1 January 1964	Illinois	Washington	17–7
1 January 1965	Michigan	Oregon State	34–7
1 January 1966	UCLA	Michigan State	14–12
2 January 1967	Purdue	Southern California	14–13
1 January 1968	Southern California	Indiana	14–3
1 January 1969	Ohio State	Southern California	27–16
1 January 1970	Southern California	Michigan	10–3
1 January 1971	Stanford	Ohio State	27–17
1 January 1972	Stanford	Michigan	13–12
1 January 1973	Southern California	Ohio State	42–17
1 January 1974	Ohio State	Southern California	42–21
1 January 1975	Southern California	Ohio State	18–17
1 January 1976	UCLA	Ohio State	23–10
1 January 1977	Southern California	Michigan	14–6
2 January 1978	Washington	Michigan	27–20
1 January 1979	Southern California	Michigan	17–10
1 January 1980	Southern California	Ohio State	17–16
1 January 1981	Michigan	Washington	23–6
1 January 1982	Washington	Iowa	28–0
1 January 1983	UCLA	Michigan	24–14
2 January 1984	UCLA	Illinois	45–9
1 January 1985	Southern California	Ohio State	20–17
1 January 1986	UCLA	Iowa	45–28
1 January 1987	Arizona State	Michigan	22–15

Year	Winner	Loser	Score
1 January 1988	Michigan State	Southern California	20–17
2 January 1989	Michigan	Southern California	22–14
1 January 1990	Southern California	Michigan	17–10
1 January 1991	Washington	Iowa	46–34
1 January 1992	Washington	Michigan	34–14
1 January 1993	Michigan	Washington	38–31
1 January 1994	Wisconsin	UCLA	21–16
2 January 1995	Penn State	Oregon	38–20
1 January 1996	Southern California	Northwestern	41–32
1 January 1997	Ohio State	Arizona State	20–17
1 January 1998	Michigan	Washington State	21–16
1 January 1999	Wisconsin	UCLA	38–31
1 January 2000	Wisconsin	Stanford	17–9
1 January 2001	Washington	Purdue	34–24
3 January 2002	Miami (FL)	Nebraska	37–14
1 January 2003	Oklahoma	Washington State	34–14
1 January 2004	Southern California	Michigan	28–14
1 January 2005	Texas	Michigan	38–37
4 January 2006	Texas	Southern California	41–38
1 January 2007	Southern California	Michigan	32–18
1 January 2008	Southern California	Illinois	49–17
1 January 2009	Southern California	Penn State	38–24
1 January 2010	Ohio State	Oregon	26–17
1 January 2011	Texas Christian	Wisconsin	21–19
2 January 2012	Oregon	Wisconsin	45–38
1 January 2013	Stanford	Wisconsin	20–14

* Indicates a tie game.

NOTES

1. The 1942 game was played in Durham, North Carolina, due to World War II.
2. The 2002 and 2006 games were designated as the BCS National Championship Game.

SUMMARY

Team	Won–Lost–Tied
Southern California	24–9
Michigan	8–12

Team	Won–Lost–Tied
Washington	7–6–1
Ohio State	7–7
Stanford	6–6–1
UCLA	5–7
Alabama	4–1–1
Michigan State	3–1
Illinois	3–2
Wisconsin	3–6
Texas	2–0
Iowa	2–3
Oregon	2–4
California	2–5–1
Columbia	1–0
Georgia	1–0
Georgia Tech	1–0
Great Lakes (Navy)	1–0
Harvard	1–0
Miami (FL)	1–0
Notre Dame	1–0
Oklahoma	1–0
Texas Christian	1–0
Arizona State	1–1
Mare Island (Marines)	1–1
Minnesota	1–1
Northwestern	1–1
Purdue	1–1
Oregon State	1–2
Penn State	1–2
Pittsburgh	1–3
Washington State	1–3
Navy	0–0–1
Washington & Jefferson	0–0–1
Brown	0–1
Camp Lewis (Army)	0–1
Indiana	0–1
Pennsylvania	0–1
Southern Methodist	0–1
Tulane	0–1
Duke	0–2
Nebraska	0–2
Tennessee	0–2

Appendix N
Heisman Trophy Winners

Year	Winner	School	Position
1935	Jay Berwanger	Chicago	halfback
1936	Larry Kelley	Yale	end
1937	Clint Frank	Yale	halfback
1938	Davey O'Brien	Texas Christian	quarterback
1939	Nile Kinnick	Iowa	halfback
1940	Tom Harmon	Michigan	halfback
1941	Bruce Smith	Minnesota	halfback
1942	Frank Sinkwich	Georgia	halfback
1943	Angelo Bertelli	Notre Dame	quarterback
1944	Les Horvath	Ohio State	quarterback/halfback
1945	Felix "Doc" Blanchard	Army	fullback
1946	Glenn Davis	Army	halfback
1947	Johnny Lujack	Notre Dame	quarterback
1948	Doak Walker	Southern Methodist	halfback
1949	Leon Hart	Notre Dame	end
1950	Vic Janowicz	Ohio State	halfback/punter
1951	Dick Kazmeier	Princeton	halfback
1952	Billy Vessels	Oklahoma	halfback
1953	Johnny Lattner	Notre Dame	halfback
1954	Alan Ameche	Wisconsin	fullback
1955	Howard Cassady	Ohio State	halfback
1956	Paul Hornung	Notre Dame	quarterback
1957	John David Crow	Texas A&M	halfback
1958	Pete Dawkins	Army	halfback
1959	Billy Cannon	Louisiana State	halfback
1960	Joe Bellino	Navy	halfback
1961	Ernie Davis	Syracuse	halfback/linebacker
1962	Terry Baker	Oregon State	quarterback
1963	Roger Staubach	Navy	quarterback
1964	John Huarte	Notre Dame	quarterback
1965	Mike Garrett	Southern California	halfback
1966	Steve Spurrier	Florida	quarterback

Year	Winner	School	Position
1967	Gary Beban	UCLA	quarterback
1968	O. J. Simpson	Southern California	halfback
1969	Steve Owens	Oklahoma	fullback
1970	Jim Plunkett	Stanford	quarterback
1971	Pat Sullivan	Auburn	quarterback
1972	Johnny Rodgers	Nebraska	running back
1973	John Cappelletti	Penn State	running back
1974	Archie Griffin	Ohio State	running back
1975	Archie Griffin	Ohio State	running back
1976	Tony Dorsett	Pittsburgh	running back
1977	Earl Campbell	Texas	running back
1978	Billy Sims	Oklahoma	running back
1979	Charles White	Southern California	running back
1980	George Rogers	South Carolina	running back
1981	Marcus Allen	Southern California	running back
1982	Herschel Walker	Georgia	running back
1983	Mike Rozier	Nebraska	running back
1984	Doug Flutie	Boston College	quarterback
1985	Vincent "Bo" Jackson	Auburn	running back
1986	Vinny Testaverde	Miami (FL)	quarterback
1987	Tim Brown	Notre Dame	wide receiver
1988	Barry Sanders	Oklahoma State	running back
1989	Andre Ware	Houston	quarterback
1990	Ty Detmer	Brigham Young	quarterback
1991	Desmond Howard	Michigan	wide receiver
1992	Gino Torretta	Miami (FL)	quarterback
1993	Charlie Ward	Florida State	quarterback
1994	Rashaan Salaam	Colorado	running back
1995	Eddie George	Ohio State	running back
1996	Danny Wuerffel	Florida	quarterback
1997	Charles Woodson	Michigan	cornerback/punt returner
1998	Ricky Williams	Texas	running back
1999	Ron Dayne	Wisconsin	running back
2000	Chris Weinke	Florida State	quarterback
2001	Eric Crouch	Nebraska	quarterback
2002	Carson Palmer	Southern California	quarterback
2003	Jason White	Oklahoma	quarterback
2004	Matt Leinart	Southern California	quarterback
2005*	Reggie Bush	Southern California	running back
2006	Troy Smith	Ohio State	quarterback

Year	Winner	School	Position
2007	Tim Tebow	Florida	quarterback
2008	Sam Bradford	Oklahoma	quarterback
2009	Mark Ingram	Alabama	running back
2010	Cam Newton	Auburn	quarterback
2011	Robert Griffin III	Baylor	quarterback
2012	Johnny Manziel	Texas A&M	quarterback

* Indicates that the award was vacated in June 2010, when the NCAA ruled that Bush had received improper gifts while at Southern California.

SUMMARY BY SCHOOL

7	Notre Dame, Ohio State, Southern California
5	Oklahoma
3	Army, Auburn, Florida, Michigan, Nebraska
2	Florida State, Georgia, Miami (FL), Navy, Texas, Texas A&M, Wisconsin, Yale
1	Alabama, Baylor, Boston College, Brigham Young, Chicago, Colorado, Houston, Iowa, Louisiana State, Minnesota, Oregon State, Penn State, Pittsburgh, Princeton, South Carolina, Southern Methodist, Stanford, Syracuse, Texas Christian, UCLA

Appendix O
National Collegiate Athletic Association Football Bowl Subdivision

In 2012 conferences began making substantial re-alignments. The information shown below is as of the 2012 football season.

Conference	Abbreviation	Number of Schools Playing Football
Atlantic Coast	ACC	12
Big East	—	8
Big Ten	—	12
Big 12	—	10
Conference USA	Conf. USA	12
Mid-American	Mid-Amer.	13
Mountain West	Mtn. West	10
Pacific-12	Pac-12	12
Southeastern	SEC	14
Sun Belt	—	10
Western Athletic	WAC	8
Independent	—	4

School	Nickname	Location	Conference
Akron	Zips	Akron, OH	Mid-Amer.
Alabama	Crimson Tide	Tuscaloosa, AL	SEC
Alabama, Birmingham	Blazers	Birmingham, AL	Conf. USA
Arizona	Wildcats	Tucson, AZ	Pac-12
Arizona State	Sun Devils	Tempe, AZ	Pac-12
Arkansas	Razorbacks	Fayetteville, AR	SEC
Arkansas State	Red Wolves	Jonesboro, AR	Sun Belt
Auburn	Tigers	Auburn, AL	SEC
Ball State	Cardinals	Muncie, IN	Mid-Amer.
Baylor	Bears	Waco, TX	Big 12

School	Nickname	Location	Conference
Boise State	Broncos	Boise, ID	Mtn. West
Boston College	Eagles	Chestnut Hill, MA	ACC
Bowling Green State	Falcons	Bowling Green, OH	Mid-Amer.
Brigham Young	Cougars	Provo, UT	Independent
California	Golden Bears	Berkeley, CA	Pac-12
California State, Fresno	Bulldogs	Fresno, CA	Mtn. West
Central Florida	Knights	Orlando, FL	Conf. USA
Central Michigan	Chippewas	Mount Pleasant, MI	Mid-Amer.
Cincinnati	Bearcats	Cincinnati, OH	Big East
Clemson	Tigers	Clemson, SC	ACC
Colorado	Buffaloes	Boulder, CO	Pac-12
Colorado State	Rams	Fort Collins, CO	Mtn. West
Connecticut	Huskies	Storrs, CT	Big East
Duke	Blue Devils	Durham, NC	ACC
East Carolina	Pirates	Greenville, NC	Conf. USA
Eastern Michigan	Eagles	Ypsilanti, MI	Mid-Amer.
Florida	Gators	Gainesville, FL	SEC
Florida Atlantic	Owls	Boca Raton, FL	Sun Belt
Florida International	Golden Panthers	Miami, FL	Sun Belt
Florida State	Seminoles	Tallahassee, FL	ACC
Georgia	Bulldogs	Athens, GA	SEC
Georgia Tech	Yellow Jackets	Atlanta, GA	ACC
Hawai'i	Warriors	Honolulu, HI	Mtn. West
Houston	Cougars	Houston, TX	Conf. USA
Idaho	Vandals	Moscow, ID	WAC
Illinois	Fighting Illini	Champaign/Urbana, IL	Big Ten
Indiana	Hoosiers	Bloomington, IN	Big Ten
Iowa	Hawkeyes	Iowa City, IA	Big Ten
Iowa State	Cyclones	Ames, IA	Big 12
Kansas	Jayhawks	Lawrence, KS	Big 12
Kansas State	Wildcats	Manhattan, KS	Big 12
Kent State	Golden Flashes	Kent, OH	Mid-Amer.
Kentucky	Wildcats	Lexington, KY	SEC

School	Nickname	Location	Conference
Louisiana, Lafayette	Ragin' Cajuns	Lafayette, LA	Sun Belt
Louisiana, Monroe	Warhawks	Monroe, LA	Sun Belt
Louisiana State	Tigers	Baton Rouge, LA	SEC
Louisiana Tech	Bulldogs	Ruston, LA	WAC
Louisville	Cardinals	Louisville, KY	Big East
Marshall	Thundering Herd	Huntington, WV	Conf. USA
Maryland	Terrapins	College Park, MD	Big Ten
Massachusetts	Minutemen	Amherst, MA	Mid-Amer.
Memphis	Tigers	Memphis, TN	Conf. USA
Miami, University of	Hurricanes	Coral Gables, FL	ACC
Miami University	RedHawks	Oxford, OH	Mid-Amer.
Michigan	Wolverines	Ann Arbor, MI	Big Ten
Michigan State	Spartans	East Lansing, MI	Big Ten
Middle Tennessee State	Blue Raiders	Murfreesboro, TN	Sun Belt
Minnesota	Golden Gophers	Minneapolis, MN	Big Ten
Mississippi	Rebels	Oxford, MS	SEC
Mississippi State	Bulldogs	Starkville, MS	SEC
Missouri	Tigers	Columbia, MO	SEC
Nebraska	Cornhuskers	Lincoln, NE	Big Ten
Nevada, Las Vegas	Rebels	Las Vegas, NV	Mtn. West
Nevada, Reno	Wolf Pack	Reno, NV	Mtn. West
New Mexico	Lobos	Albuquerque, NM	Mtn. West
New Mexico State	Aggies	Las Cruces, NM	WAC
North Carolina	Tar Heels	Chapel Hill, NC	ACC
North Carolina State	Wolfpack	Raleigh, NC	ACC
North Texas	Mean Green	Denton, TX	Sun Belt
Northern Illinois	Huskies	DeKalb, IL	Mid-Amer.
Northwestern	Wildcats	Evanston, IL	Big Ten

School	Nickname	Location	Conference
Notre Dame	Fighting Irish	Notre Dame, IN	Independent
Ohio	Bobcats	Athens, OH	Mid-Amer.
Ohio State	Buckeyes	Columbus, OH	Big Ten
Oklahoma	Sooners	Norman, OK	Big 12
Oklahoma State	Cowboys	Stillwater, OK	Big 12
Oregon	Ducks	Eugene, OR	Pac-12
Oregon State	Beavers	Corvallis, OR	Pac-12
Penn State	Nittany Lions	University Park, PA	Big Ten
Pittsburgh	Panthers	Pittsburgh, PA	Big East
Purdue	Boilermakers	West Lafayette, IN	Big Ten
Rice	Owls	Houston, TX	Conf. USA
Rutgers	Scarlet Knights	New Brunswick, NJ	Big East
San Diego State	Aztecs	San Diego, CA	Mtn. West
San Jose State	Spartans	San Jose, CA	WAC
South Alabama	Jaguars	Mobile, AL	Sun Belt
South Carolina	Gamecocks	Columbia, SC	SEC
South Florida	Bulls	Tampa, FL	Big East
Southern California	Trojans	Los Angeles, CA	Pac-12
Southern Methodist	Mustangs	University Park, TX	Conf. USA
Southern Mississippi	Golden Eagles	Hattiesburg, MS	Conf. USA
Stanford	Cardinal	Stanford, CA	Pac-12
SUNY, Buffalo	Bulls	Buffalo, NY	Mid-Amer.
Syracuse	Orange	Syracuse, NY	Big East
Temple	Owls	Philadelphia, PA	Big East
Tennessee	Volunteers	Knoxville, TN	SEC
Texas	Longhorns	Austin, TX	Big 12
Texas, El Paso	Miners	El Paso, TX	Conf. USA
Texas, San Antonio	Roadrunners	San Antonio, TX	WAC
Texas A&M	Aggies	College Station, TX	SEC

School	Nickname	Location	Conference
Texas Christian	Horned Frogs	Fort Worth, TX	Big 12
Texas State	Bobcats	San Marco, TX	WAC
Texas Tech	Red Raiders	Lubbock, TX	Big 12
Toledo	Rockets	Toledo, OH	Mid-Amer.
Troy	Trojans	Troy, AL	Sun Belt
Tulane	Green Wave	New Orleans, LA	Conf. USA
Tulsa	Golden Hurricane	Tulsa, OK	Conf. USA
UCLA	Bruins	Los Angeles, CA	Pac-12
U.S. Air Force Academy	Falcons	Colorado Springs, CO	Mtn. West
U.S. Military Academy	Black Knights	West Point, NY	Independent
U.S. Naval Academy	Midshipmen	Annapolis, MD	Independent
Utah	Utes	Salt Lake City, UT	Pac-12
Utah State	Aggies	Logan, UT	WAC
Vanderbilt	Commodores	Nashville, TN	SEC
Virginia	Cavaliers	Charlottesville, VA	ACC
Virginia Tech	Hokies	Blacksburg, VA	ACC
Wake Forest	Deacons	Winston-Salem, NC	ACC
Washington	Huskies	Seattle, WA	Pac-12
Washington State	Cougars	Pullman, WA	Pac-12
West Virginia	Mountaineers	Morgantown, WV	Big 12
Western Kentucky	Hilltoppers	Bowling Green, KY	Sun Belt
Western Michigan	Broncos	Kalamazoo, MI	Mid-Amer.
Wisconsin	Badgers	Madison, WI	Big Ten
Wyoming	Cowboys	Laramie, WY	Mtn. West

Appendix P
Football Films

Title, Year	Genre	Rating
Ace Ventura: Pet Detective (1994)	comedy	6.7
Air Bud: Golden Retriever (1998)	comedy, family	4.0
All the Right Moves (1983)	drama	5.7
The All-American (1953)	drama	5.8
Angels in the End Zone (1997)	comedy, family	4.6
Any Given Sunday (1999)	drama	6.7
*Australian Rules** (2002)	drama	6.9
The Bear (1984)	biography	5.9
The Best of Times (1986)	comedy, drama	5.6
Big Fan (2009)	comedy	6.9
Black Sunday (1977)	action, thriller	6.7
The Blind Side (2009)	biography, drama	7.6
Brian's Song (1971)	biography, drama	7.6
Brian's Song (2001)	biography, drama	6.6
Brown of Harvard (1911)	silent, drama	—
Brown of Harvard (1918)	silent, drama	—
Brown of Harvard (1926)	silent, drama	7.8
*The Club** (1980)	comedy	6.6
Code Breakers (2005)	drama	6.1
College Coach (1933)	drama	6.0
The Comebacks (2007)	comedy	3.9
Crazylegs (1953)	biography, drama	7.3
Damn Good Dog (2004)	documentary	6.8
Division III: Football's Finest (2011)	comedy	5.3
The Drop Kick (1927)	silent, drama	7.1
Easy Living (1949)	drama	6.3
Everybody's All-American (1988)	drama	6.1
The Express (2008)	biography, drama	7.1
Facing the Giants (2006)	drama	6.0
The Fanatics, aka *Fumbleheads* (1997)	comedy	4.4
Father Was a Fullback (1949)	comedy	6.6
Field of Vision (2011)	drama	5.2

Title, Year	Genre	Rating
The 5th Quarter (2010)	biography, drama	5.0
Fighting Back: The Rocky Bleier Story (1980)	biography, drama	6.6
The Forward Pass (1929)	drama	5.0
Friday Night Lights (2004)	drama	7.1
The Freshman (1925)	silent, comedy	7.6
Full Ride (2002)	comedy	5.2
The Galloping Ghost (1931)	serial, drama	6.3
The Game Plan (2007)	comedy	6.1
Game Time: Tackling the Past (2011)	drama	3.9
The Garbage Picking Field Goal Kicking Philadelphia Phenomenon (1998)	comedy	4.5
The Gladiator (1938)	comedy	6.2
Go Tigers (2001)	documentary	7.5
Grambling's White Tiger (1981)	drama	5.8
The Great MacArthy* (1975)	comedy	4.4
Gridiron Gang (2006)	drama	6.8
Gus (1976)	comedy, family	5.6
Halfback of Notre Dame (1996)	drama	5.7
Heaven Can Wait (1978)	comedy	6.8
Hometown Legend (2002)	drama	5.2
Horsefeathers (1932)	comedy	7.7
Jerry Maguire (1996)	comedy	7.2
Jim Thorpe: All-American (1951)	biography, drama	6.8
Johnny Be Good (1988)	comedy	4.1
The Junction Boys (2002)	drama	6.0
Knute Rockne: All-American (1940)	biography, drama	6.7
The Last Boy Scout (1991)	comedy	6.8
Leatherheads (2008)	comedy	6.0
Little Giants (1994)	comedy	5.8
Lombardi (2010)	documentary	8.1
The Longest Yard (1974)	comedy	7.1
The Longest Yard (2005)	comedy	6.2
The Longshots (2008)	biography, comedy	4.3
Lucas (1986)	comedy	6.6
Maker of Men (1931)	drama	5.6
The Man Who Lost Himself, aka *The Stranger I Married*** (2005)	biography, drama	5.8
The Marinovich Project (2011)	documentary	7.0
Marshall University: Ashes to Glory (2000)	documentary	—
Monday Night Mayhem (2002)	drama	6.7
Navy Blue and Gold (1937)	drama	6.7

Title, Year	Genre	Rating
Necessary Roughness (1991)	comedy	5.6
North Dallas Forty (1979)	comedy	6.9
Paper Lion (1968)	comedy	6.1
Pigskin Parade (1936)	musical	6.3
Pony Excess (2010)	documentary	7.6
Possums (1998)	comedy	5.2
The Program (1993)	drama	6.1
Quarterback Princess (1983)	drama	5.9
Radio (2003)	drama	6.8
Reggie's Prayer (1996)	drama	6.0
Remember the Titans (2000)	biography, drama	7.5
The Replacements (2000)	comedy	6.3
Rise and Walk: The Dennis Byrd Story (1994)	biography, drama	5.7
Roll Tide/War Eagle (2011)	documentary	6.9
Rudy (1993)	biography, drama	7.4
A Saintly Switch (1999)	comedy	5.7
Salute (1929)	drama	6.0
School Ties (1996)	drama	6.7
Second String (2002)	comedy	5.6
Semi-Tough (1977)	comedy	5.8
The Slaughter Rule (2002)	drama	6.0
That's My Boy (1951)	comedy	6.1
They Call Me Sirr (2001)	biography, drama	5.4
Touchback (2011)	drama	6.0
Trouble Along the Way (1953)	comedy	6.7
Two for the Money (2005)	drama	6.1
Two-Minute Warning (1976)	drama, thriller	5.9
The U (2009)	documentary	8.4
Undefeated (2011)	documentary	6.0
Uppercut, aka *Lo Chiamavano Bulldozer* (1978)	comedy	6.4
Varsity Blues (1999)	comedy	6.1
The Waterboy (1998)	comedy	5.8
We Are Marshall (2006)	drama	7.0
Weapons of Mass Distraction (1997)	comedy	6.1
Wildcats (1986)	comedy	5.6

Source: Internet Movie Database (www.imdb.com).
* Indicates that the film is about Australian rules football.
** Indicates that the film is about Canadian football.

Bibliography

CONTENTS

I. Introduction	524
II. Reference	525
A. Encyclopedias	525
1. College	525
2. Professional: National Football League	525
3. Professional: Canadian Football League	526
4. Professional: World Football League	526
B. Annuals and Yearbooks	526
C. Statistical Analysis	526
D. Media Guides	527
E. Miscellaneous Promotional Guides	527
III. History	527
A. General	527
B. High School	528
C. College	528
1. General	528
2. Specific Schools and Leagues	528
3. Specific Games and Rivalries	530
4. Bowl Games	530
D. Professional	530
1. General	530
2. Specific Teams	532
3. Specific Games	534
E. Women	534
IV. Biography	534
A. Collections	534
B. Single Individual	535
1. Players	535
2. Coaches	547
3. Others	550
V. Instructional	552
A. Rules and Officiating	552
B. Coaching	552

C. Playing	552
1. General	552
2. Specialized	553
D. Six-Man Football	553
E. Touch Football	553
F. Watching Football	553
1. General	553
2. Watching for Women	553
G. Other	553
VI. Other Books	554
A. Anthology	554
B. Fiction	554
C. Humor	554
D. Miscellaneous	555
E. International	555
1. Dutch	555
2. French	555
3. German	555
4. Italian	556
5. Spanish	556
6. British	556
VII. Periodicals	556
VIII. Programs	557
IX. Websites	557

I. INTRODUCTION

The game of American football has been the most popular American sport since the last half of the 20th century. As such, there are many books written on the sport, ranging from historical, biographical, and instructional to social commentary. There are several useful encyclopedias as well, although with the advent of the Internet, current encyclopedias have become scarce since the most up-to-date statistical information can be found online. Some of the juvenile books are especially useful for a newcomer to the sport, youngster or adult, since the basics of the game are clearly described.

As with all sports, many books are biographies usually written in the first person with an established author as coauthor. Biographies exist for virtually every top modern-day player, but there are not nearly as many for pre-1960 players. There are often several juvenile biographies for recent active players, but not necessarily adult ones. Surprisingly, there are quite a few biographies of players who were not among the best players in the league. Among the best in this category are *Instant Replay*, by Jerry Kramer, with Dick Schaap; *When Pride Still Mattered: A Life of Vince Lombardi*, by David Maraniss; and any of John Madden and Dave Anderson's books. Writer George Plimpton offers up several books on his attempt to play professional football. *Paper Lion* is a classic, and his two sequels, *Mad Ducks and Bears* and *One More July*, are also entertaining.

Individual professional team histories are readily available, and many colleges also have one or more books dedicated to their football history. Two of the best historical books are Robert W. Peterson's *Pigskin: The Early Years of Pro Football* and Matthew Algeo's *Last Team Standing*, a book about how World War II brought about the merging of the Philadelphia Eagles and Pittsburgh Steelers to form the Steagles. Sally Jenkins's book about the Carlisle Indian Industrial School, *The Real All-Americans*, is one of the best about college football.

Instructional books are available, although not nearly as many as can be found for such individual sports as tennis, golf, or bowling. In addition, there is not nearly as much football fiction as there is baseball or boxing fiction, but those works that do exist have achieved near-classic status amongst sports fans. These include former pro player Pete Gent's *North Dallas Forty* and Dan Jenkins's *Semi-Tough*. Both have been made into feature films. *The Fireside Book of Football*, edited by Richard Whittingham, is an excellent anthology that includes many short pieces written by the best sportswriters, among them many former players.

Football websites of interest include the ones for the major professional leagues, the National Football League and Canadian Football League. The National Collegiate Athletic Association has an extensive one; the collegiate conferences each have their own; and virtually every college that fields a football team has a website devoted to their team, as well as their team's history. There are also several websites that contain extensive team and individual player statistical history, and the three major football Halls of Fame also have useful sites. The Pro Football Hall of Fame Research Center, located in Canton, Ohio, has a huge collection that can be consulted by appointment. The following bibliography provides a comprehensive selection of football resources.

II. REFERENCE

A. Encyclopedias

1. College

MacCambridge, Michael, ed. *ESPN College Football Encyclopedia*. New York: Hyperion, 2005.

2. Professional: National Football League

Bennett, Tom, and National Football League Properties. *The NFL's Official Encyclopedic History of Professional Football*. New York: Macmillan, 1977.
Carroll, Bob, John Thorn, and Michael Gershman. *Total Football: The Official Encyclopedia of the National Football League*. New York: HarperCollins, 1997.
Claasen, Harold, ed. *Ronald Encyclopedia of Football*. New York: Ronald, 1960.

Palmer, Pete, Ken Pullis, Sean Lahman, Tod Maher, Matthew Silverman, and Gary Gillette. *ESPN Pro Football Encyclopedia*, 2nd ed. New York: Sterling, 2007.

Treat, Roger. *The Encyclopedia of Football*. New York: A. S. Barnes, 1952–1979 (16 editions).

3. Professional: Canadian Football League

Maher, Tod, and Bob Gill. *The Canadian Pro Football Encyclopedia*. Lexington, Ky.: Maher Sports Media, 2011.

4. Professional: World Football League

Maher, Tod, and Mark Speck. *World Football League Encyclopedia*. Haworth, N.J.: St. Johann, 2006.

B. Annuals and Yearbooks

Bock, Hal, and Ben Olan. *Football Stars of 1973*. New York: Pyramid, 1973.

Buffalo Bills Official 1999 Team Yearbook. Playa del Rey, Calif.: CWC Sports, 1999.

Canadian Football League Facts, Figures, and Records, 2006 Edition. Toronto: Canadian Football League, 2006.

Football Register. St. Louis, Mo.: Sporting News, 1966–2006.

Gifford, Frank. *NFL–AFL Football Guide, 1968*. New York: New American Library, 1968.

Hutchens, A. R., ed. *Official NCAA Football Guide*. New York: A. S. Barnes, 1949.

Lattimore, Reuben, ed. *Street & Smith's Guide to Pro Football 1994*. New York: Ballantine, 1994.

Official 1981 National Football League Record Manual. New York: NFL Properties, 1981.

Okeson, Walter R., ed. *Official NCAA Football Guide*. New York: A. S. Barnes, 1941.

Preller, James. *National Football League Team Tracker, 2004–05*. New York: Scholastic, 2004. (juvenile)

Rathet, Mike. *Official 1967 American Football League Guide*. St. Louis, Mo.: Sporting News, 1967.

Weiss, Don, et al. *Official National Football League Record Book, 1970 Edition*. New York: Rutledge, 1970.

C. Statistical Analysis

Creamer, Richard, et al. *Pro Football Revealed, 1994: The 100-Yard War*. Skokie, Ill.: STATS, 1994.

Ignatin, George, and Allen Barra. *Football by the Numbers, 1987*. New York: Prentice-Hall, 1987.

Lahman, Sean. *The Pro Football Historical Abstract*. Guilford, Conn.: Lyons, 2008.
Massillon Society. *Inside Football, 1983*. New York: Fawcett Columbine, 1983.

D. Media Guides

Most NFL teams and many college teams have published annual media guides. In recent years, they have been available online, and print versions have become rare.

E. Miscellaneous Promotional Guides

Many businesses have issued brief annual professional and college football guides that contain that season's schedule and a few miscellaneous facts. They are of interest to the collector but seldom contain information that cannot be found elsewhere. The following list is a small sample of them.

1948 Grantland Rice Cities Service Football Guide
1959 Marlboro Football Guide
1966 Johns Manville Pro Football TV Roster Round-Up
1967 Schrafft's Football Facts
1967 This Is NFL Football: Giants' Edition
1971–72 Pro Football Hall of Fame Appointment Calendar
1972 La-Z-Boy Football Guide
1980 Exxon NFL, College Football Handbook
1983 Kessler Football Handbook
1986 Old Spice Presents 50 Years of NFL Excitement
1991 Lite Beer Football Handbook

III. HISTORY

A. General

Amdur, Neil. *The Fifth Down: Democracy and the Football Revolution*. New York: Coward, McCann & Geoghegan, 1971.
Baker, L. H. *Football: Facts and Figures*. New York: Farrar & Rinehart, 1945.
Brondifield, Jerry. *100 Years of Football*. New York: Scholastic, 1969. (juvenile)
Conner, Floyd. *Football's Most Wanted*. Washington, D.C.: Potomac, 2000.
Falk, Gerhard. *Football and American Identity*. Binghamton, N.Y.: Haworth, 2005.
Goodman, Murray, and Leonard Lewin. *My Greatest Day in Football*. New York: Bantam, 1949.
Gutman, Bill. *Pro Football's Record Breakers*. New York: Archway, 1987.
Hill, Dean. *Football Thru the Years*. New York: Gridiron, 1940.
Leckie, Robert. *The Story of Football*. New York: Random House, 1965.
Lorimer, Larry, and John Devaney. *The Football Book*. New York: Random House, 1977.

Newcombe, Jack. *The Game of Football*. Champaign, Ill.: Garrard, 1967. (juvenile)
Stern, Bill. *Bill Stern's Favorite Football Stories*. New York: Pocket, 1948.
Underwood, John. *The Death of an American Game: The Crisis in Football*. New York: Little, Brown, 1979.

B. High School

Bissinger, H. G. *Friday Night Lights: A Town, a Team, and a Dream*. Cambridge, Mass.: DaCapo, 2000.
Frolund, Vic. *Down Memory Lane with Rayen and South*. New York: William Frederick, 1961.

C. College

1. General

Baker, L. H. *Football: Facts and Figures*. New York: Farrar & Rinehart, 1945.
Benagh, Jim. *Making It to #1: How College Football and Basketball Teams Get There*. New York: Dodd, Mead, 1976.
Camp, Walter. *American Football*. Whitefish, Mont.: Kessinger, 2010. Reprint of 1891 original.
Danzig, Allison. *The History of American Football: Its Great Teams, Players, and Coaches*. Englewood Cliffs, N.J.: Prentice-Hall, 1956.
———. *Oh, How They Played the Game*. New York: Macmillan, 1971.
Durant, John, and Les Etter. *Highlights of College Football*. New York: Hastings House, 1970.
Edwards, William H. *Football Days*. New York: Moffat, Yard, 1916.
Jenkins, Dan. *Saturday's America*. Boston: Little, Brown, 1970.
Kaye, Ivan N. *Good Clean Violence: A History of College Football*. Philadelphia: Lippincott, 1973.
Larson, Melissa. *The Pictorial History of College Football*. Greenwich, Conn.: Brompton, 1989.
Marx, Jeffrey. *Season of Life*. New York: Simon & Schuster, 2003.

2. Specific Schools and Leagues

a. Alabama

Bolton, Clyde. *The Crimson Tide: A Story of Alabama Football*. Huntsville, Ala.: Strode, 1972.

b. Carlisle

Anderson, Lars. *Carlisle vs. Army: Jim Thorpe, Dwight Eisenhower, Pop Warner, and the Forgotten Story of Football's Greatest Battle*. New York: Random House, 2007.
Jenkins, Sally. *The Real All-Americans*. New York: Doubleday, 2007.

c. Cornell

Mintz, Ben, ed. *Cornell Football, 1949–1976: From Home Game Programs*. Ithaca, N.Y.: Cornell Alumni Association, 1976.

d. Florida State

Alexander, Caroline. *Battle's End: A Seminole Football Team Revisited*. New York: Alfred A. Knopf, 1995.

Jones, James P. *FSU One Time! A History of Seminole Football*. Tallahassee, Fla.: Sentry, 1973.

e. Grambling

Bahrenburg, Bruce. *My Little Brother's Coming Tomorrow*. New York: G. P. Putnam's Sons, 1971.

f. Harvard

Smith, Ronald A., ed. *Big-Time Football at Harvard, 1905: The Diary of Coach Bill Reid*. Urbana: University of Illinois Press, 1994.

g. Ivy League

McCallum, John. *Ivy League Football since 1872*. New York: Stein and Day, 1977.

h. Marshall

Nolte, Rick, Dave Wellman, Tim Stephens, and Mickey Johnson. *The Marshall Story: College Football's Greatest Comeback*. Macon, Ga.: Henchard, 2006.

i. Notre Dame

Holtz, Lou, with John Heisler. *The Fighting Spirit: A Championship Season at Notre Dame*. New York: Simon & Schuster, 1989.

Jeffers, Jeff. *Rally! The 12 Greatest Notre Dame Football Comebacks*. South Bend, Ind.: Icarus, 1981.

Pagna, Tom, with Bob Best. *Notre Dame's Era of Ara*. Huntsville, Ala.: Strode, 1976.

Prister, Tim. *The New Gold Standard: Charlie Weis and Notre Dame's Rise to Glory*. New York: Hyperion, 2006.

Singular, Stephen. *Notre Dame's Greatest Coaches*. New York: Pocket, 1993.

j. Ohio State

Vare, Robert. *Buckeye: A Study of Coach Woody Hayes and the Ohio State Football Machine*. New York: Harper's Magazine Press, 1974.

k. Penn State

Denlinger, Ken. *For the Glory: College Football Dreams and Realities Inside Paterno's Program*. New York: St. Martin's, 1994.

Riley, Ridge. *Road to Number One: A Personal Chronicle of Penn State Football*. Garden City, N.Y.: Doubleday, 1977.

l. San Diego State

Barone, Steve. *Aztec Uprising*. San Diego, Calif.: Joyce, 1975.

m. Texas A&M

Dent, Jim. *The Junction Boys: How Ten Days in Hell with Bear Bryant Forged a Championship Team*. New York: St. Martin's, 1999.

n. Virginia Tech

Beamer, Frank, with Chris Colston. *Turn Up the Wick*. Birmingham, Ala.: Epic Sports, 2000.

Schlambach, Mark. *What It Means to Be a Hokie: Frank Beamer and Virginia Tech's Greatest Players*. Chicago: Triumph, 2006.

3. Specific Games and Rivalries

Bergin, Thomas G. *The Game: The Harvard–Yale Football Rivalry, 1875–1983*. New Haven, Conn.: Yale, 1984.

Clary, Jack. *An American Classic: Army vs. Navy, the First 100 Games*. Syracuse: Signature, 2000.

Feinstein, John. *A Civil War: Army vs. Navy, a Year Inside College Football's Purest Rivalry*. New York: Little, Brown, 1996.

Paul, Jim. *"You Dropped It, You Pick It Up!"* Baton Rouge, La.: Ed's Publishing, 1983.

4. Bowl Games

Bell, Joseph N. *Bowl Game Thrills*. New York: Julian Messner, 1966.

DiMarco, Anthony C. *The Big Bowl Football Guide*. New York: G. P. Putnam's Sons, 1976.

Hamlin, Rick. *Tournament of Roses: A 100-Year Celebration*. New York: McGraw-Hill, 1988.

O'Brien, Emmett J. *History of College Bowls [sic] Games*. Bloomington, Ind.: Author House, 2005.

D. Professional

1. General

a. American Football League

Miller, Jeff. *Going Long: The Wild Ten-Year Saga of the Renegade American Football League in the Words of Those Who Lived It*. New York: Contemporary, 2003.

Orr, Jack. *We Came of Age: A Picture History of the American Football League*. New York: Lion, 1969.

b. Canadian Football League

O'Brien, Steve. *The Canadian Football League: The Phoenix of Professional Sports Leagues*. Raleigh, N.C.: Lulu, 2005.

c. Minor League: Atlantic Coast Football League

Acton, Jay. *The Forgettables*. New York: Thomas Y. Crowell, 1973.

d. National Football League

Barber, Tiki, and Ronde Barber, with Paul Mantell. *Kickoff!* New York: Scholastic, 2007. (juvenile)
Bass, Tom. *National Football League between the Lines Reader*. New York: Scholastic, 2005. (juvenile)
Brenner, Richard J. *Football's Super Six*. Huntington, N.Y.: East End, 2005. (juvenile)
Brondfield, Jerry. *All-Pro Football Stars '79*. New York: Scholastic, 1979. (juvenile)
Clary, Jack. *Pro Football's Great Moments*. New York: Bonanza, 1982.
Cohen, Richard M., Jordan A. Deutsch, Roland T. Johnson, and David S. Neft. *The Scrapbook History of Pro Football*. New York: Bobbs-Merrill, 1976.
Diles, David L. *Twelfth Man in the Huddle*. Waco, Tex.: Word, 1976.
Fatsis, Stefan. *A Few Seconds of Panic*. New York: Penguin, 2008.
Freeman, Mike. *Bloody Sunday: Inside the Dazzling Rough-and-Tumble World of the NFL*. New York: HarperCollins, 2003.
Hand, Jack. *Great Running Backs of the NFL*. New York: Random House, 1966.
———. *Heroes of the NFL*. New York: Random House, 1965.
Herskowitz, Mickey. *The Quarterbacks: The Uncensored Truth about the Men in the Pocket*. New York: William Morrow, 1990.
Hollander, Zander. *More Strange but True Football Stories*. New York: Random House, 1973.
———. *Strange but True Football Stories*. New York: Random House, 1967.
Holtz, Lou. *Winning Every Day: The Game Plan for Success*. New York: HarperCollins, 1998.
Izenberg, Jerry. *No Medals for Trying: A Week in the Life of a Pro Football Team*. New York: Macmillan, 1990.
Klosinski, Emil. *Pro Football in the Days of Rockne*. New York: Carlton, 1970.
MacCambridge, Michael. *America's Game: The Epic Story of How Pro Football Captured a Nation*. New York: Random House, 2004.
Maule, Tex. *The Players*. New York: New American, 1967.
———. *The Pro Season*. Garden City, N.Y.: Doubleday, 1970.
Oates, Bob, Jr., ed. *The First Fifty Years*. New York: Simon & Schuster, 1969.
O'Brien, Jim. *Lambert: The Man in the Middle and Other Outstanding Linebackers*. Pittsburgh: James P. O'Brien, 2004.
Peterson, Robert W. *Pigskin: The Early Years of Pro Football*. New York: Oxford, 1997.
Phillips, Louis, and Arnie Markoe. *Football Records, Stars, Feats, and Facts*. New York: Harcourt Brace Jovanovich, 1979.

Plimpton, George. *Mad Ducks and Bears*. New York: Lyons & Burford, 1973.
———. *Paper Lion*. New York: Harper & Row, 1965.
———, with Bill Curry. *One More July*. New York: Harper & Row, 1977.
Polzer, Tim. *Quarterback Power*. New York: Scholastic, 2004. (juvenile)
Richter, Ed. *The Making of a Pro Quarterback*. New York: Grosset & Dunlap, 1966.
Rosenthal, Harold. *Fifty Faces of Football*. New York: Atheneum, 1981.
Smith, Don R. *The Official Pro Football Hall of Fame Book of Superstars*. New York: Simon & Schuster, 1990. (juvenile)
Smith, Robert. *Illustrated History of Pro Football*. New York: Grosset & Dunlap, 1970.
Sullivan, George. *The Gamemakers: Pro Football's Great Quarterbacks from Baugh to Namath*. New York: G. P. Putnam's Sons, 1971.
Wismer, Harry. *The Public Calls It Sport*. Englewood Cliffs, N.J.: Prentice-Hall, 1965.
Zimmerman, Paul. *The New Thinking Man's Guide to Pro Football*. New York: Simon & Schuster, 1984.
———. *A Thinking Man's Guide to Pro Football*. New York: Warner, 1971.

e. NFL Europe
Anderson, Lars. *The Proving Ground: A Season on the Fringe in NFL Europe*. New York: St. Martin's, 2001.

f. United States Football League
Byrne, Jim. *One Dollar League: Rise and Fall of the United States Football League*. Upper Saddle River, N.J.: Prentice-Hall, 1987.

2. Specific Teams

a. Chicago Bears
Freedman, Lew. *Chicago Bears: The Complete Illustrated History*. Minneapolis, Minn.: Voyageur, 2008.

b. Chicago Cardinals
Ziemba, Joe. *When Football Was Football: The Chicago Cardinals and the Birth of the NFL*. Chicago: Triumph, 1999.

c. Dallas Cowboys
Sugar, Bert Randolph, ed. *I Hate the Dallas Cowboys: And Who Elected Them America's Team, Anyway?* New York: St. Martin's Griffin, 1997.

d. Denver Broncos
Martin, Russell. *The Color Orange: A Super Bowl Season with the Denver Broncos*. New York: Henry Holt, 1987.

e. Green Bay Packers
Lombardi, Vince, with W. C. Heinz. *Run to Daylight*. Englewood Cliffs, N.J.: Prentice-Hall, 1963.
Wolfe, Rich. *For Packers Fans Only!* Burbank, Calif.: Lone Wolfe Press, 2004.

f. Los Angeles Rams
Rambeck, Richard. *Los Angeles Rams*. Mankato, Minn.: Creative Education, 1991. (juvenile)

g. Montreal Alouettes
Bacon, Dick. *Sam Berger's Alouettes*. Saint-Lambert, Quebec, Canada: Les Éditions Héritage, 1978.

h. New England Patriots
Cafardo, Nick. *The Impossible Team: The Worst to First Patriots' Super Bowl Season*. Chicago: Triumph, 2002.

i. New York Giants
Burt, Jim, with Hank Gola. *Hard Nose: The Story of the 1986 Giants*. New York: Harcourt Brace Jovanovich, 1987.
Terzian, Jim. *New York Giants*. New York: Macmillan, 1973.
Zipay, Steve. *"Then Bavaro Said to Simms . . ."* Chicago: Triumph, 2009.

j. New York Jets
Curran, Bob. *The Violence Game*. New York: Macmillan, 1966.
Sahadi, Lou. *The Long Pass*. New York: World, 1969.

k. Philadelphia Eagles
Longman, Jere. *If Football's a Religion, Why Don't We Have a Prayer?* New York: HarperCollins, 2005.

l. Phil-Pitt Steagles
Algeo, Matthew. *Last Team Standing*. Philadelphia: DaCapo, 2006.

m. San Diego Chargers
Rambeck, Richard. *San Diego Chargers*. Mankato, Minn.: Creative Education, 1991. (juvenile)

n. San Francisco 49ers
Newhouse, Dave. *The Million Dollar Backfield: The San Francisco 49ers in the 1950s*. Berkeley, Calif.: Frog, 2000.

o. Seattle Seahawks
Rambeck, Richard. *Seattle Seahawks*. Mankato, Minn.: Creative Education, 1991. (juvenile)

3. Specific Games

a. NFL Championship Games

Gifford, Frank, with Peter Richmond. *The Glory Game: How the 1958 NFL Championship Changed Football Forever*. New York: HarperCollins, 2008.

Gruver, Ed. *The Ice Bowl*. Ithaca, N.Y.: McBooks, 1998.

Izenberg, Jerry. *Championship: The NFL Title Games plus Super Bowl*. New York: Scholastic, 1970.

b. Super Bowl

Brenner, Richard J. *The Complete Super Bowl Story: Games I–XXVIII*. Syosset, N.Y.: East End, 1994.

Didinger, Ray, Kevin Lamb, Mickey Herskowitz, Phil Musick, and Bill McGrane. *The Super Bowl: Celebrating a Quarter-Century of America's Greatest Game*. New York: Simon & Schuster, 1990.

Hanks, Stephen. *The Game That Changed Pro Football*. New York: Carol, 1989.

Koppett, Leonard, ed. *The New York Times at the Super Bowl*. New York: Quadrangle, 1974.

Ralbovsky, Marty. *Super Bowl: Of Men, Myths, and Moments*. New York: Hawthorn, 1971.

E. Women

Hnida, Katie. *Still Kicking: My Journey as the First Woman to Play Division I College Football*. New York: Scribner, 2006.

IV. BIOGRAPHY

A. Collections

Anderson, Dave. *Great Pass Receivers of the NFL*. New York: Random House, 1966.

———. *Great Quarterbacks of the NFL*. New York: Random House, 1965.

Clary, Jack. *The Game-Makers: Winning Philosophies of Eight NFL Coaches*. Chicago: Follett, 1976.

Cope, Myron. *The Game That Was*. New York: World, 1970.

Duroska, Lud, ed. *Great Pro Quarterbacks*. New York: Grosset & Dunlap, 1972.

Green, Tim. *The Road to the NFL*. New York: Scholastic, 2003. (juvenile)

Gutman, Bill. *Gridiron Greats: Campbell, Zorn, Swann, Grogan*. New York: Grosset & Dunlap, 1979.

Layden, Joe. *National Football League Megastars, 2006*. New York: Scholastic, 2006. (juvenile)

Newhouse, Dave. *Heismen: After the Glory*. St. Louis: Sporting News, 1985.

Oshins, Louis R. *Famous Names in Football*. Garden City, N.Y.: Blue Ribbon, 1949. (juvenile)

Porter, David L., ed. *Biographical Dictionary of American Sports: Football*. New York: Greenwood, 1987.
Pratt, John Lowell. *Pro, Pro, Pro*. New York: Franklin Watts, 1963.
Whittingham, Richard. *Sunday's Heroes: NFL Legends Talk about the Times of Their Lives*. Chicago: Triumph, 2003.
———. *What a Game They Played*. New York: Harper & Row, 1984.

B. Single Individual

1. Players

a. Troy Aikman
Aikman, Troy. *Aikman: Mind, Body, and Soul*. Chicago: Triumph, 1999.

b. Shaun Alexander
Alexander, Shaun, with Cecil Murphey. *Touchdown Alexander: My Story of Faith, Football, and Pursuing the Dream*. Eugene, Ore.: Harvest House, 2007.

c. Marcus Allen
Allen, Marcus, with Carlton Stowers. *Marcus: The Autobiography of Marcus Allen*. New York: St. Martin's, 1997.

d. Ronde and Tiki Barber
Barber, Tiki, and Ronde Barner, with Robert Burleigh. *Teammates*. New York: Simon & Schuster, 2006. (juvenile)
Brenner, Richard J. *Tiki Barber–Ronde Barber*. Huntington, N.Y.: East End, 2006. (juvenile)

e. Sammy Baugh
Canning, Whitt. *Sammy Baugh: Best There Ever Was*. Indianapolis, Ind.: Masters, 1997.

f. Chuck Bednarik
Safarowic, Ken, and Eli Kowalski. *Concrete Charlie: An Oral History of Philadelphia's Greatest Football Legend, Chuck Bednarik*. Philadelphia: Sports Challenge Network, 2009.

g. Tom Beer
Beer, Tom, with George Kimball. *Sunday's Fools: Stomped, Tromped, Kicked, and Chewed in the NFL*. Boston: Houghton Mifflin, 1974.

h. George Blanda
Twombly, Wells. *Blanda, Alive and Kicking: The Exclusive Authorized Biography*. Los Angeles, Calif.: Nash, 1972.

i. Mel Blount
Blount, Mel, with Cynthia Sterling. *The Cross Burns Brightly*. Grand Rapids, Mich.: Zondervan, 1993.

j. Terry Bradshaw
Bradshaw, Terry, with David Fisher. *Keep It Simple*. New York: Atria, 2002.
Bradshaw, Terry, with Buddy Martin. *Looking Deep*. New York: Berkley, 1991.

k. Tom Brady
Pierce, Charles P. *Moving the Chains: Tom Brady and the Pursuit of Everything*. New York: Farrar, Straus and Giroux, 2006.

l. Drew Brees
Brees, Drew, with Chris Fabry. *Coming Back Stronger: Unleashing the Hidden Power of Adversity*. Carol Stream, Ill.: Tyndale House, 2010.

m. John Brodie
Brodie, John, with James D. Houston. *Open Field*. New York: Bantam, 1975.

n. Jim Brown
Brown, Jim, with Myron Cope. *Off My Chest*. Garden City, N.Y.: Doubleday, 1964.
Freeman, Mike. *Jim Brown: The Fierce Life of an American Hero*. New York: HarperCollins, 2007.

o. Larry Brown
Brown, Larry, and William Gildea. *I'll Always Get Up*. New York: Simon & Schuster, 1973.

p. Brandon Burlsworth
Kinley, Jeff. *Through the Eyes of a Champion: The Brandon Burlsworth Story*. Green Forest, Ark.: New Leaf, 2001.

q. Dick Butkus
Butkus, Dick. *Butkus: Flesh and Blood*. New York: Doubleday, 1997.

r. Dennis Byrd
Byrd, Dennis, with Michael D'Orso. *Rise and Walk: The Trial and Triumph of Dennis Byrd*. New York: HarperCollins, 1993.

s. Earl Campbell
Campbell, Earl, and John Ruane. *The Earl Campbell Story: A Football Great's Battle with Panic Disorder*. Toronto, Ontario, Canada: ECW Press, 1999.

t. Gino Cappelletti
Baker, Jim. *A View from the Booth: Gil Santos and Gino Cappelletti: 25 Years of Broadcasting the New England Patriots.* Cambridge, Mass.: Rounder, 2008.

u. John Cappelletti
McNeely, Jerry, and Richard E. Peck. *Something for Joey.* New York: Bantam, 1983.

v. Mike "Pinball" Clemons
Clemons, Michael Pinball. *All Heart: My Story.* New York: HarperCollins, 1999.

w. Charlie Conerly
Conerly, Charlie, with Tom Meany. *The Forward Pass.* New York: E. P. Dutton, 1960.

x. Larry Csonka
Csonka, Larry, Jim Kiick, and Dave Anderson. *Always on the Run.* New York: Bantam, 1974.

y. Len Dawson
Dawson, Len, and Lou Sahadi. *Len Dawson: Pressure Quarterback.* New York: Cowles, 1970.

z. Eric Dickerson
Dickerson, Eric, and Steve Delsohn. *On the Run.* New York: Contemporary, 1986.

aa. Mike Ditka
Ditka, Mike, with Don Pierson. *Ditka: An Autobiography.* New York: Bonus, 1987.

ab. Conrad Dobler
Dobler, Conrad. *Pride and Perseverance: A Story of Courage, Hope, and Redemption.* Chicago: Triumph, 2009.

ac. Marty Domres
Domres, Marty, and Robert Smith. *Bump and Run: The Days and Nights of a Rookie Quarterback.* New York: Bantam, 1971.

ad. Art Donovan
Donovan, Arthur J., and Bob Drury. *Fatso: When Men Were Really Men.* New York: W. Morrow, 1987.

ae. Tony Dorsett
Dorsett, Tony, and Harvey Frommer. *Running Tough.* New York: Berkley, 1991.

af. Warrick Dunn
Dunn, Warrick, and Don Yaeger. *Running for My Life: My Journey in the Game of Football and Beyond*. New York: HarperCollins, 2008.

ag. Joe Ehrmann
Marx, Jeffrey. *Season of Life*. New York: Simon & Schuster, 2003.

ah. John Elway
Latimer, Clay. *John Elway: Armed and Dangerous*. Lanham, Md.: Taylor Trade, 1998.

ai. Kevin Everett
Carchidi, Sam. *Standing Tall: The Kevin Everett Story*. Chicago: Triumph, 2008.

aj. Brett Favre
Favre, Brett, with Chris Havel. *Favre: For the Record*. Jackson, Tenn.: Main Street, 1998.

ak. Doug Flutie
Thomsen, Ian. *Flutie!* Chester, Conn.: Globe Pequot, 1985.

al. Frank Gifford
Gifford, Frank, and Harry Waters. *The Whole Ten Yards*. New York: Random House, 1993.

am. George Gipp
Cavanaugh, Jack. *The Gipper: George Gipp, Knute Rockne, and the Rise of Notre Dame Football*. New York: Skyhorse, 2010.

an. Pete Gogolak
Gogolak, Pete. *Nothing to Kick About: The Autobiography of a Modern Immigrant*. New York: Dodd, Mead, 1973.

ao. Tony Gonzalez
Sandler, Michael. *Tony Gonzalez: Football Heroes Making a Difference*. New York: Bearport, 2010. (juvenile)

ap. Otto Graham
Graham, Duey. *OttoMatic: The Remarkable Story of Otto Graham*. Wayne, Mich.: Immortal Investments, 2004.

aq. Red Grange
Schoor, Gene. *Red Grange: Football's Greatest Halfback*. New York: Julian Messner, 1962.

ar. Roosevelt Grier
Grier, Roosevelt, with Dennis Baker. *Rosey, an Autobiography: The Gentle Giant*. Tulsa, Okla.: Harrison House, 1986.

as. Bob and Brian Griese
Griese, Bob, and Brian Griese. *Undefeated: How Father and Son Triumphed Over Unbelievable Odds Both On and Off the Field*. Nashville, Tenn.: Thomas Nelson, 2008.

at. Archie Griffin
Griffin, Archie, with Dave Diles. *Archie: The Archie Griffin Story*. New York: Doubleday, 1977.

au. Lou Groza
Groza, Lou, with Mark Hodermarsky. *The Toe: The Lou Groza Story*. Cleveland, Ohio: Gray, 2003.

av. Cliff Harris
Harris, Cliff. *Captain Crash and the Dallas Cowboys*. Champaign, Ill.: Sports Publishing, 2006.

aw. Franco Harris
Kowet, Don. *Franco Harris*. New York: Coward, McCann & Geoghegen, 1977.

ax. Alex Hawkins
Hawkins, Alex. *Then Came Brain Damage: Life (?) after Pro Football*. Atlanta, Ga.: Longstreet, 1991.

ay. Bob Hayes
Hayes, Bob, with Robert Pack. *Run, Bullet, Run: The Rise, Fall, and Recovery of Bob Hayes*. New York: Harper & Row, 1992.

az. Devin Hester
Young, Jeff C. *Devin Hester*. Broomall, Pa.: Mason Crest, 2007. (juvenile)

ba. Paul Hornung
Hornung, Paul, and William Reed. *Golden Boy*. New York: Simon & Schuster, 2004.
Hornung, Paul, as told to Al Silverman. *Football and the Single Man*. Garden City, N.Y.: Doubleday, 1965.

bb. Sam Huff
Huff, Sam, with Leonard Shapiro. *Tough Stuff: The Man in the Middle*. New York: St. Martin's, 1988.

bc. Michael Irvin
Rosenblatt, Richard. *Michael Irvin.* New York: Chelsea House, 1997. (juvenile)

bd. Keyshawn Johnson
Johnson, Keyshawn, with Shelley Smith. *Just Give Me the Damn Ball! The Fast Times and Hard Knocks of an NFL Rookie.* New York: Warner, 1997.

be. Deacon Jones
Klawitter, John, and Deacon Jones. *Headslap: The Life and Times of Deacon Jones.* Amherst, N.Y.: Prometheus, 1996.
Libby, Bill. *Life in the Pit: The Deacon Jones Story.* New York: Doubleday, 1970.

bf. Alex Karras
Karras, Alex, and Herb Gluck. *Even Big Guys Cry.* New York: Holt, Rinehart and Winston, 1977.

bg. David Kopay
Kopay, David, and Perry Deane Young. *The David Kopay Story: An Extraordinary Self-Revelation.* New York: Arbor House, 1977.

bh. Jerry Kramer
Kramer, Jerry, with Dick Schaap. *Distant Replay.* New York: G. P. Putnam's Sons, 1985.
——. *Instant Replay.* New York: New American, 1968.
——. *Jerry Kramer's Farewell to Football.* New York: Bantam, 1970.

bi. Dick "Night Train" Lane
Burns, Mike. *Night Train Lane: The Life of NFL Hall of Famer Richard "Night Train" Lane.* Austin, Tex.: Eakin, 2001.

bj. Elmer Layden
Layden, Elmer, with Ed Snyder. *It Was a Different Game.* Englewood Cliffs, N.J.: Prentice-Hall, 1969.

bk. Bobby Layne
St. John, Bob. *Heart of a Lion: The Wild and Woolly Life of Bobby Layne.* Dallas, Tex.: Taylor, 1991.

bl. Bob Lilly
Lilly, Bob, with Kristine Setting Clark. *A Cowboy's Life.* Chicago: Triumph, 2008.

bm. Ronnie Lott
Lott, Ronnie, and Jill Lieber. *Total Impact: Straight Talk from Football's Hardest Hitter.* New York: Simon & Schuster, 1998.

bn. Sid Luckman
Luckman, Sid. *Luckman at Quarterback: Football as a Sport and a Career*. Chicago: Ziff-Davis, 1949.

bo. Archie, Eli, and Peyton Manning
Nagle, Jeanne. *Archie, Peyton, and Eli Manning: Football's Royal Family*. New York: Rosen Central, 2010. (juvenile)

bp. Dan Marino
Marino, Dan. *Dan Marino: My Life in Football*. Chicago: Triumph, 2007.

bq. Jim McMahon
McMahon, Jim, with Bob Verdi. *McMahon!* New York: Warner, 1986.

br. Donovan McNabb
Robinson, Tom. *Donovan McNabb: Leader On and Off the Field*. Berkeley Heights, N.J.: Enslow, 2009. (juvenile)

bs. John "Blood" McNally
Gullickson, Denis J. *Vagabond Halfback: The Life and Times of Johnny Blood McNally*. Boulder, Colo.: Trails, 2006.

bt. Dave Meggysey
Meggyesy, Dave. *Out of Their League*. New York: Ramparts, 1971.

bu. Joe Montana
Brenner, Richard J. *Joe Montana and Jerry Rice*. New York: East End, 1990. (juvenile)

bv. Warren Moon
Moon, Warren, with Don Yaeger. *Never Give Up on Your Dream: My Journey*. Philadelphia, Pa.: DaCapo, 2009.

bw. Lenny Moore
Moore, Lenny, with Jeffrey Jay Ellish. *All Things Being Equal: The Autobiography of Lenny Moore*. Champaign, Ill.: Sports Publishing, 2006.

bx. Eugene "Mercury" Morris
Morris, Eugene "Mercury," and Steve Fiffer. *Against the Grain*. New York: McGraw-Hill, 1988.

by. Randy Moss
Bernstein, Ross. *Randy Moss: Star Wide Receiver*. Berkeley Heights, N.J.: Enslow, 2007. (juvenile)

bz. Bronko Nagurski
Dent, Jim. *Monster of the Midway: Bronko Nagurski, the 1943 Chicago Bears, and the Greatest Comeback Ever*. New York: St. Martin's Griffin, 2004.

ca. Joe Namath
Bortstein, Larry. *The Joe Namath Story*. New York: Grosset & Dunlap, 1973.
Kriegel, Mark. *Namath: A Biography*. New York: Penguin, 2004.
Lipman, David. *Joe Namath: A Football Legend*. New York: G. P. Putnam's Sons, 1968.
Namath, Joe Willie, with Dick Schaap. *I Can't Wait Until Tomorrow . . . 'Cause I Get Better Looking Every Day*. New York: Random House, 1969.

cb. Ernie Nevers
Frederick, Chuck. *Leatherheads of the North: The True Story of Ernie Nevers and the Duluth Eskimos*. Duluth, Minn.: X-Communication, 2007.

cc. Ray Nitschke
Nitschke, Ray, and Robert Wells. *Mean on Sunday: The Autobiography of Ray Nitschke*. Garden City, N.Y.: Doubleday, 1973.

cd. Chad Ochocinco
Ochocinco, Chad, and Jason Cole. *Ocho Cinco: What Football and Life Have Thrown My Way*. New York: Crown Archetype, 2009.

ce. Michael Oher
Lewis, Michael. *Blind Side: The Evolution of a Game*. New York: W. W. Norton, 2009.

cf. Chip Oliver
Oliver, Chip, edited by Ron Rapoport. *High for the Game*. New York: William Morrow, 1971.

cg. Jim Otto
Otto, Jim. *Jim Otto: The Pain of Glory*. Urbana, Ill.: Sagamore, 2000.

ch. Terrell Owens
Owens, Terrell, and Stephen Singular. *Catch This! Going Deep with the NFL's Sharpest Weapon*. New York: Simon & Schuster, 2004.

ci. Alan Page
McGrane, Bill. *All Rise: The Remarkable Journey of Alan Page*. Chicago: Triumph, 2010.

cj. Vito "Babe" Parilli
Burdette, Dick. *Kentucky Babe: The Babe Parilli Story*. Charleston, S.C.: CreateSpace, 2011.

ck. Bernie Parrish
Parish, Bernie. *They Call It a Game*. New York: New American, 1971.

cl. Dan Pastorini
Pastorini, Dan. *Taking Flak: My Life in the Fast Lane*. Bloomington, Ind.: AuthorHouse, 2011.

cm. Walter Payton
Pearlman, Jeff. *Sweetness: The Enigmatic Life of Walter Payton*. New York: Gotham, 2011.

cn. Preston Pearson
Pearson, Preston. *Hearing the Noise: My Life in the NFL*. New York: William Morrow, 1987.

co. William "Refrigerator" Perry
Roberts, Andre. *William Perry: The Refrigerator*. Chicago: Children's, 1986. (juvenile)

cp. Brian Piccolo
Blinn, William. *Brian's Song*. New York: Bantam, 1972. Screenplay.
Morris, Jeannie. *Brian Piccolo: A Short Season*. New York: Rand McNally, 1972.

cq. Jim Plunkett
Gutman, Bill. *Jim Plunkett*. New York: Grosset & Dunlap, 1973.

cr. Fritz Pollard
Carroll, John M. *Fritz Pollard: Pioneer in Racial Advancement*. Chicago: University of Illinois Press, 1992.

cs. Ahmad Rashad
Rashad, Ahmad, with Peter Bodo. *Rashad*. New York: Signet, 1989.

ct. Jerry Rice
Brenner, Richard J. *Joe Montana and Jerry Rice*. New York: East End, 1990. (juvenile)
Rice, Jerry, with Brian Curtis. *Go Long! My Journey beyond the Game and the Fame*. New York: Ballantine, 2007.

cu. Simeon Rice
Rice, Simeon with Mark Stewart. *Rush to Judgment: The Simeon Rice Story*. Guilford, Conn.: Lyons, 2004.

cv. Paul Robeson
Robeson, Paul. *Here I Stand*. Boston: Beacon, 1998. Reissue of 1958 original.
Robeson, Paul, Jr. *The Undiscovered Paul Robeson: An Artist's Journey, 1898–1939*. Hoboken, N.J.: Wiley, 2001.
———. *The Undiscovered Paul Robeson: Quest for Freedom, 1939–1976*. Hoboken, N.J.: Wiley, 2010.

cw. Aaron Rodgers
Reischel, Rob. *Aaron Rodgers: Leader of the Pack*. Chicago: Triumph, 2011.

cx. Ben Roethlisberger
Heits, Rudolph T. *Ben Roethlisberger*. Broomall, Pa.: Mason Crest, 2009. (juvenile)

cy. Don Rogers
Harvey, Sean D. *One Moment Changes Everything: The All-America Tragedy of Don Rogers*. Champaign, Ill.: Sports Publishing, 2007.

cz. Bill Romanowski
Romanoski, Bill, with Adam Schefter and Phil Towle. *Romo: My Life on the Edge: Living Dreams and Slaying Dragons*. New York: William Morrow, 2005.

da. Johnny Sample
Sample, Johnny, with Fred J. Hamilton and Sonny Schwartz. *Confessions of a Dirty Ballplayer*. New York: Dell, 1970.

db. Barry Sanders
Ellenport, Craig. *Head to Head Football: Barry Sanders/Emmitt Smith*. New York: Bantam, 1995. Double book. (juvenile)
Sanders, Barry, with Mark E. McCormick. *Barry Sanders: Now You See Him: His Story in His Own Words*. Covington, Ky.: Clerisy, 2005.

dc. Deion Sanders
Sanders, Deion. *Power, Money, and Sex*. Nashville, Tenn.: Thomas Nelson, 1999.

dd. Gale Sayers
Sayers, Gale, and Fred Mitchell. *Sayers: My Life and Times*. Chicago: Triumph, 2007.
Sayers, Gale, with Al Silverman. *I Am Third*. New York: Viking, 1970.

de. Tiaina "Junior" Seau
Stewart, Mark. *Junior Seau*. Chicago: Children's, 1999. (juvenile)

df. Phil Simms
Simms, Phil, and Phil McConkey, with Dick Schaap. *Simms to McConkey: Blood, Sweat, and Gatorade*. New York: Crown, 1987.

dg. Orenthal "O. J." Simpson
Bugliosi, Vincent. *Outrage: The Five Reasons Why O. J. Simpson Got Away with Murder*. New York: W. W. Norton, 2008.
Dear, William C. *O. J. Is Innocent and I Can Prove It*. New York: Skyhorse, 2012.
Simpson, O. J. *I Want to Tell You*. Boston: Little, Brown, 1995.
Simpson, O. J., with Pete Axthelm. *O. J.: The Education of a Rich Rookie*. New York: Macmillan, 1970.

dh. Tony Siragusa
Siragusa, Tony. *Goose: The Outrageous Life and Times of a Football Guy*. New York: Crown Archetype, 2012.

di. Fred Smerlas
Smerlas, Fred, and Vic Carucci. *By a Nose: The Off-Center Life of Football's Funniest Lineman*. New York: Simon & Schuster, 1990.

dj. Charles "Bubba" Smith
Smith, Bubba. *Kill, Bubba, Kill!* New York: Simon & Schuster, 1983.

dk. Emmitt Smith
Ellenport, Craig. *Head to Head Football: Barry Sanders/Emmitt Smith*. New York: Bantam, 1995. Double book. (juvenile)

dl. Ken Stabler
Stabler, Ken, and Berry Stainback. *Snake*. New York: Berkley, 1986.

dm. Bart Starr
Starr, Bart, and Murray Olderman. *Starr: My Life in Football*. New York: William Morrow, 1987.

dn. Roger Staubach
Staubach, Roger, with Frank Luska. *Time Enough to Win: Roger Staubach*. Waco, Tex.: Word, 1980.

do. Michael Strahan
Strahan, Michael, with Jay Glazer. *Inside the Helmet: Life as a Sunday Afternoon Warrior*. New York: Gotham, 2007.

dp. George "Pat" Summerall
Summerall, Pat. *Summerall: On and Off the Air*. Nashville, Tenn.: Thomas Nelson, 2008.

dq. Adam Taliaferro
Brown, Scott, and Sam Carchidi. *Miracle in the Making: The Adam Taliaferro Story*. Chicago: Triumph, 2001.

dr. Fran Tarkenton
Klobuchar, Jim and Fran Tarkenton. *Tarkenton*. Harper & Row, 1976.

Tarkenton, Fran, as told to Brock Yates. *Broken Patterns: The Education of a Quarterback*. New York: Simon & Schuster, 1971.

ds. Jim Taylor
Taylor, Jim, and Kristine Setting Clark. *The Fire Within*. Chicago: Triumph, 2010.

dt. Lawrence Taylor
Taylor, Lawrence, with Steve Serby. *L. T.: Over the Edge: Tackling Quarterbacks, Drugs, and a World beyond Football*. New York: Harper Torch, 2004.

du. Tim Tebow
Tebow, Tim, with Nathan Whitaker. *Through My Eyes*. New York: Harper, 2011.

dv. Thurman Thomas
Savage, Jim. *Thurman Thomas: Star Running Back*. Berkeley Heights, N.J.: Enslow, 1994. (juvenile)

dw. Jim Thorpe
Buford, Kate. *Native American Son: The Life and Sporting Legend of Jim Thorpe*. New York: Alfred A. Knopf, 2010.

dx. Pat Tillman
Krakauer, Jon. *Where Men Win Glory: The Odyssey of Pat Tillman*. New York: Doubleday, 2009.

dy. Y. A. Tittle
Tittle, Y. A., as told to Don Smith. *Y. A. Tittle: I Pass!* New York: Franklin Watts, 1964.

dz. LaDainian Tomlinson
Tomlinson, Loreane, with Patti M. Britton and Ginger Kolbaba. *L. T. and Me: What Raising a Champion Taught Me about Life, Faith, and Listening to Your Dreams*. Carol Stream, Ill.: Tyndale House, 2009.

ea. Emlen Tunnell
Tunnell, Emlen, with William Gleason. *Footsteps of a Giant*. New York: Doubleday, 1966.

eb. John Unitas
Callahan, Tom. *Johnny U: The Life and Times of John Unitas*. New York: Three Rivers, 2006.

Unitas, John, and Ed Fitzgerald. *Pro Quarterback: My Own Story*. New York: Simon & Schuster, 1965.

Unitas, John, with Harold Rosenthal. *Playing Pro Football to Win*. New York: New American, 1971.

ec. Doak Walker
Bracken, Dorothy Kendall. *Doak Walker: Three-Time All-American*. Austin, Tex.: Steck, 1950.

ed. Herschel Walker
Walker, Herschel, with Gary Brozek and Charlene Maxfield. *Breaking Free: My Life with Dissociative Identity Disorder*. New York: Touchstone, 2008.

ee. Reggie White
White, Reggie. *Reggie White in the Trenches: The Autobiography*. Nashville, Tenn.: Thomas Nelson, 2004.

ef. John Williams
Williams, John, and Birgit Erika Nardell. *Bittersweet: A Look Inside the NFL: The Autobiography of John McKay Williams*. New York: Vantage, 1985.

eg. Steve Wright
Wright, Steve, with William Gildea and Kenneth Turan. *I'd Rather Be Wright*. New York: Grosset & Dunlap, 1975.

eh. Garo Yepremian
Sears, Norman. *I Keek a Touchdown*. Berkeley, Calif.: Garnel, 1997.

ei. Steve Young
Christopher, Matt, and Glenn Stout. *In the Huddle with . . . Steve Young*. New York: Little, Brown, 1996. (juvenile)

ej. Jack Youngblood
Youngblood, Jack, and Joel Engel. *Blood*. New York: McGraw-Hill, 1988.

2. Coaches

a. George Allen
Gildea, William, and Kenneth Turan. *The Future Is Now*. New York: Dell, 1973.

b. Bill Belichick
Halberstam, David. *The Education of a Coach*. New York: Hyperion, 2005.

c. Paul Brown
Cantor, George. *Paul Brown: The Man Who Invented Modern Football*. Chicago: Triumph, 2008.

d. Paul "Bear" Bryant
Herskowitz, Mickey. *The Legend of Bear Bryant*. New York: McGraw-Hill, 1987.
Staff of the Birmingham News. *Remembering Bear*. Indianapolis, Ind.: News and Features, 1983.

e. Tom Cahill
White, Gordon S., Jr., and Mervin D. Hyman. *Coach Tom Cahill: A Man for the Corps*. London: Macmillan, 1969.

f. Gilmour Dobie
Borland, Lynn. *Gilmour Dobie: Pursuit of Perfection*. Charleston, S.C.: Tribute, 2010.

g. Tony Dungy
Dungy, Tony, with Nathan Whitaker. *Quiet Strength: The Principles, Practices, and Priorities of a Winning Life*. Carol Stream, Ill.: Tyndale House, 2007.

h. Jerome Evans
Jordan, Pat. *Black Coach*. New York: Dodd, Mead, 1971.

i. Wilbur "Weeb" Ewbank
Ewbank, Weeb, as told to Neil Roiter. *Goal to Go: The Greatest Football Games I Have Coached*. New York: Hawthorn, 1972.

j. Joe Gibbs
Gibbs, Joe, with Jerry Jenkins. *Joe Gibbs: Fourth and One*. Nashville, Tenn.: Thomas Nelson, 1992.

k. Harry "Bud" Grant
McGrane, Bill. *Bud: The Other Side of the Glacier*. New York: HarperCollins, 1986.

l. George Halas
Davis, Jeff. *Papa Bear: The Life and Legacy of George Halas*. New York: McGraw-Hill, 2006.

m. Woody Hayes
Lombardo, John. *A Fire to Win: The Life and Times of Woody Hayes*. New York: St. Martin's Griffin, 2006.

n. Mike Holovak
Holovak, Mike, and Bill McSweeny. *Violence Every Sunday: The Story of a Professional Football Coach.* New York: Coward, McCann & Geoghegan, 1967.

o. Jimmy Johnson
Johnson, Jimmy, as told to Ed Hinton. *Turning the Thing Around: Pulling America's Team Out of the Dumps and Myself Out of the Doghouse.* New York: Hyperion, 1993.

p. Earl "Curly" Lambeau
Zimmerman, David. *Lambeau: The Man Behind the Mystique.* Hales Corners, Wisc.: Eagle, 2003.

q. Tom Landry
Landry, Tom, with Gregg Lewis. *Landry: An Autobiography.* New York: Harper, 1991.
St. John, Bob. *The Man Inside . . . Landry.* New York: Word, 1979.

r. Frank Leahy
Twombly, Wells. *Shake Down the Thunder! The Official Biography of Notre Dame's Frank Leahy.* Chilton, Pa.: Radnor, 1974.

s. Vince Lombardi
Dowling, Tom. *Coach: A Season with Lombardi.* New York: W. W. Norton, 1970.
Maraniss, David. *When Pride Still Mattered: A Life of Vince Lombardi.* New York: Simon & Schuster, 1999.

t. John Madden
Madden, John, with Dave Anderson. *All Madden: Hey, I'm Talking Pro Football.* New York: HarperCollins, 1996.
——. *Hey, Wait a Minute (I Wrote a Book!).* New York: Villard, 1984.
——. *One Knee Equals Two Feet (and Everything Else You Need to Know about Football).* New York: Villard, 1986.
——. *One Size Doesn't Fit All (and Other Thoughts from the Road).* New York: Villard, 1988.

u. Bill Parcells
Parcells, Bill, with Will McDonough. *The Final Season: My Last Year as Head Coach in the NFL.* New York: William Morrow, 2000.

v. Joe Paterno
Paterno, Joe, with Bernard Asbell. *Paterno: By the Book.* New York: Random House, 1989.

w. Dan Reeves
Reeves, Dan, with Dick Connor. *Reeves: An Autobiography*. Chicago: Bonus, 1988.

x. Eddie Robinson
Robinson, Eddie, with Richard Lapchick. *Never Before, Never Again: The Autobiography of Eddie Robinson*. New York: Thomas Dunne, 1999.

y. Knute Rockne
Brondfield, Jerry. *Rockne: The Coach, the Man, the Legend*. New York: Random House, 1976.

Rockne, Bonnie Stiles. *The Autobiography of Knute K. Rockne*. Indianapolis, Ind.: Bobbs-Merrill, 1931.

Stuhldreher, Harry A. *Knute Rockne: Man Builder*. New York: Grosset & Dunlap, 1931.

z. Don Shula
Shula, Don, with Lou Sahadi. *The Winning Edge*. New York: E. P. Dutton, 1973.

aa. Amos Alonzo Stagg
Lucia, Ellis. *Mr. Football: Amos Alonzo Stagg*. New York: A. S. Barnes, 1970.

ab. Hank Stram
Stram, Hank, with Lou Sahadi. *They're Playing My Game*. Chicago: Triumph, 2006.

ac. Barry Switzer
Switzer, Barry, with Bud Shrake. *Bootlegger's Boy*. New York: William Morrow, 1990.

ad. Charlie Weis
Weis, Charlie, and Vic Carucci. *No Excuses: One Man's Incredible Rise through the NFL to Head Coach of Notre Dame*. New York: HarperCollins, 2006.

ae. Bob Zuppke
Brichford, Maynard. *Bob Zuppke: The Life and Football Legacy of the Illinois Coach*. Jefferson, N.C.: McFarland, 2009.

3. Others

a. Bert Bell
Lyons, Robert. *On Any Given Sunday: A Life of Bert Bell*. Philadelphia, Pa.: Temple University Press, 2009.

b. Walter Camp
Powel, Harford. *Walter Camp: The Father of American Football*. Redwood Valley, Calif.: Borah, 2007.

c. Joe Carr

Willis, Chris. *The Man Who Built the National Football League: Joe F. Carr*. Lanham, Md.: Scarecrow Press, 2010.

d. Howard Cosell

Cosell, Howard. *Like It Is*. Chicago: Playboy, 1974.

Cosell, Howard, with Peter Bonventre. *I Never Played the Game*. New York: William Morrow, 1985.

e. Al Davis

Ribowsky, Mark. *Slick: The Silver and Black Life of Al Davis*. New York: Macmillan, 1991.

f. Gerald Ford

Brinkley, Douglas. *Gerald R. Ford*. New York: Times Books, 2007.

Ford, Gerald R. *A Time to Heal: The Autobiography of Gerald R. Ford*. New York: Harper & Row, 1979.

g. Joe Foss

Foss, Joe, with Donna Wild Foss. *A Proud American: The Autobiography of Joe Foss*. Pacifica, Calif.: Pacifica Military History, 2002.

h. Lamar Hunt

Sweet, David A. F. *Lamar Hunt: The Gentle Giant Who Revolutionized Professional Sports*. Chicago: Triumph, 2010.

i. Tim and Wellington Mara

DeVito, Carlo. *Wellington: The Maras, the Giants, and the City of New York*. Chicago: Triumph, 2006.

j. Grantland Rice

Rice, Grantland. *The Tumult and the Shouting: My Life in Sport*. New York: A. S. Barnes, 1954.

k. Art Rooney

Rooney, Art, Jr. *Ruanaidh: The Story of Art Rooney and His Clan*. Pittsburgh, Pa.: Self-published, 2008.

Ruck, Rob, Maggie Jones Patterson, and Michael P. Weber. *Rooney: A Sporting Life*. Lincoln, Nebr.: Bison, 2011.

l. Dan Rooney

Rooney, Dan, as told to Andrew E. Masich and David F. Halaas. *Dan Rooney: My 75 Years with the Pittsburgh Steelers and the NFL*. New York: DaCapo, 2007.

m. Alvin "Pete" Rozelle

Davis, Jeff. *Rozelle: Czar of the NFL.* New York: McGraw-Hill, 2007.

n. Norm Schachter

Schachter, Norm. *Close Calls: Confessions of a NFL Referee.* New York: William Morrow, 1981.

o. Jim Tunney

Tunney, Jim, and Glenn Dickey. *Impartial Judgment: The "Dean of NFL Referees" Calls Pro Football as He Sees It.* New York: F. Watts, 1988.

V. INSTRUCTIONAL

A. Rules and Officiating

Markbreit, Jerry. *The Armchair Referee.* Garden City, N.Y.: Doubleday, 1973.
Schiffer, Don, and Lud Duroska. *Football Rules in Pictures.* New York: Grosset & Dunlap, 1976.
Upson, Larry, ed. *2002–2003 Official Rules of the NFL.* Chicago: Triumph, 2002.

B. Coaching

Shanahan, Mike, with Adam Schefter. *Think Like a Champion.* New York: Harper, 1999.

C. Playing

1. General

Bible, Dana X. *Championship Football: A Guide for the Player, Coach, and Fan.* New York: Prentice-Hall, 1947.
DeLuca, Sam. *The Junior Football Playbook.* Middle Village, N.Y.: Jonathan David, 1973. (juvenile)
Dodd, Robert "Bobby" L. *Bobby Dodd on Football.* New York: Prentice-Hall, 1954.
Flynn, George L. *Vince Lombardi on Football.* Greenwich, Conn.: New York Graphic Society, 1973. Two-volume boxed set.
Masin, Herman L. *How to Star in Football.* New York: Scholastic, 1966. (juvenile)
Nisenson, Sam. *A Handy Illustrated Guide to Football.* New York: Permabooks, 1949.
Pickens, Richard. *How to Punt, Pass, and Kick.* New York: Random House, 1965. (juvenile)
Sherman, Allie. *Allie Sherman's Book of Football.* Garden City, N.Y.: Doubleday, 1963.
Smith, Don. *Backfield in Motion.* New York: Galahad, 1973.

Warner, Glenn Scobey. *A Course in Football for Players and Coaches*. Whitefish, Mont.: Kessinger, 2009. Reprint of 1912 original.

2. Specialized

Anderson, Ken, with Jack Clary. *The Art of Quarterbacking*. New York: Linden, 1984.
Gogolak, Pete, and Ray Siegener, eds. *Kicking the Football Soccer Style*. New York: Macmillan, 1972.
Guy, Ray, and Rick Sang. *Football Kicking and Punting*. Champaign, Ill.: Human Kinetics, 2009.
Starr, Bart, and Ralph Lewis. *How to Pass, Kick, Run, Block*. New York: North American Phillips, 1965.
Van Brocklin, Norm. *Norm Van Brocklin's Football Book: Passing, Punting, Quarterbacking*. New York: Ronald, 1961.
Wilkinson, Bud. *Sports Illustrated Football: Defense*. Philadelphia, Pa.: J. P. Lippincott, 1973.

D. Six-Man Football

Duncan, Ray O. *Six-Man Football*. New York: A. S. Barnes, 1940.

E. Touch Football

Marciani, Louis M. *Touch and Flag Football: A Guide for Players and Officials*. New York: A. S. Barnes, 1976.

F. Watching Football

1. General

Rote, Kyle, and Ray Siegener. *Pro Football for the Fan: How to Watch the Game the Way the Pros Do*. Garden City, N.Y.: Doubleday, 1964.

2. Watching for Women

Caron, Sandra L., and J. Michael Hodgson. *Tackling Football: A Woman's Guide to Understanding the College Game*. Orono: Maine College, 2011.
Peete, Holly Robinson, with Daniel Paisner. *Get Your Own Damn Beer, I'm Watching the Game*. Emmaus, Pa.: Rodale, 2005.

G. Other

Creedman, Michael. *The NFL All-Pro Workout*. New York: St. Martin's, 1987.

VI. OTHER BOOKS

A. Anthology

Fitzgerald, Ed. *Kick-Off!* New York: Bantam, 1948.
Grange, Harold "Red". *My Favorite Football Stories.* New York: A. S. Barnes, 1955.
Noe, Eric, ed. *The Greatest Football Stories Ever Told: Twenty Tales of Gridiron Glory.* Guilford, Conn.: Lyons, 2003.
Whittingham, Richard, ed. *The Fireside Book of Pro Football.* New York: Simon & Schuster, 1989.

B. Fiction

Brooks, Jonathan. *Jimmy Makes the Varsity.* New York: Grosset & Dunlap, 1938. (juvenile)
Christopher, Matt. *Long-Arm Quarterback.* New York: Little, Brown, 1999. (juvenile)
Dygard, Thomas J. *Game Plan.* New York: Puffin, 1993. (juvenile)
Franks, Owen, and Arnold S. Hirsch. *Gotcha, Gipper!* Southfield, Mich.: 4-D, 1974.
Furman, Josh, ed. *Gridiron Stories.* New York: Pocket, 1970.
Garis, Howard R. *Dick Hamilton's Football Team or A Young Millionaire on the Gridiron.* Cleveland, Ohio: Goldsmith, 1912. (juvenile)
Gent, Peter. *North Dallas after Forty.* New York: Villard, 1989.
——. *North Dallas Forty.* New York: William Morrow, 1973.
Jenkins, Dan. *Fast Copy.* New York: Simon & Schuster, 1988.
——. *Rude Behavior.* New York: Doubleday, 1998.
——. *Semi-Tough.* New York: New American, 1972.
Lupica, Mike. *Bump and Run.* New York: G. P. Putnam's Sons, 2000.
——. *Red Zone.* New York: G. P. Putnam's Sons, 2003.
Olson, Gene. *Fullback Fury.* New York: Dell, 1964.
Owen, Frank, ed. *Teen-Age Football Stories.* New York: Grosset & Dunlap, 1948. (juvenile)
Sainsbury, Noel, Jr., Ros Hackney, and Charles Lawton. *Stirring Football Stories: Three Complete Stories.* New York: Cupples & Leon, 1934. (juvenile)
Scholz, Jackson. *Goal to Go.* New York: William Morrow, 1945. (juvenile)
Sherman, Harold M. *Interference and Other Football Stories.* Chicago: Goldsmith, 1932. (juvenile)
Tunis, John R. *All-American.* New York: Harcourt, Brace & World, 1942. (juvenile)

C. Humor

Masin, Herman L. *For Laughing Out Loud.* New York: Scholastic, 1954.
Ward, Gene, and Dick Hyman. *Football Wit and Humor.* New York: Grosset & Dunlap, 1970.

D. Miscellaneous

Berkow, Ira. *The Minority Quarterback: And Other Lives in Sports*. Chicago: Ivan R. Dee, 2002.

Hawkes, Robert. *Playbook! Football #2: You Are the Quarterback, You Call the Shots*. Boston: Little, Brown, 1991. (juvenile)

Hollander, Zander, and Paul Zimmerman. *Football Lingo*. New York: W. W. Norton, 1967.

Hoppel, Joe, ed. *The Sporting News Football Trivia Book*. St. Louis, Mo.: Sporting News, 1985.

Jenkins, Sally. *Men Will Be Boys*. New York: Doubleday, 1996.

Mazer, Bill, and Stan Fischler. *The Amazin' Bill Mazer's Football Trivia Book*. New York: Warner, 1981.

Pellowski, Michael J. *The Little Giant Book of Football Facts*. New York: Sterling, 2005. (juvenile)

Rockwell, Bart. *World's Strangest Football Stories*. Mahwah, N.J.: Watermill, 1993.

Rosenthal, Harold. *505 Football Questions Your Friends Can't Answer*. New York: Walker, 1980.

E. International

In searching for international books, the phrase *American football* must be used, as the word *football* alone will retrieve the many books written on soccer, known throughout the world as football. The Libreria dello Sport s.r.l., Via Carducci, 9, 20123 Milano has an extensive inventory of books, both in Italian and English. The website www.livresquebecois.com provides a source for books written in French. The website www.awesomebooks.com is a good source for books written in the United Kingdom.

1. Dutch

van Damme, Mike. *Amsterdam Admirals, 1995–2007*. Amsterdam, Netherlands: Carrera, 2008.

2. French

Lemay, Daniel. *Montreal Football: Un Siècle et des Poussières*. Montreal, Quebec, Canada: Editions la Presse, 2006.

Turbis, Pierre. *La Grande Histoire des Alouettes de Montréal*. Montreal, Quebec, Canada: L'Homme, 2007.

Vinet, Alain. *Avec le Rouge et Or*. Sainte-Foy, Quebec, Canada: Laval, 2009.

3. German

Hupke, Frank. *PR Konzeption für die Dublin Dragons: American Football Club*. Munich, Germany: GRIN Verlag, 2007.

Kalwa, Jurgen. *Faszination American Football*. Munich, Germany: Copress Sport, 1995.
Knitter, Wolfram, Marcus Rosenstein, and Eberhard Bowy. *American Football: Vom Kick-off zum Touchdown*. Berlin, Germany: Wolfgang Weinmann, 2006.
Korber, Holger. *Edition American Football 3: Erfolgreiche Offense—Strategie und Taktik des Angriffs im Modernen Football*. Berlin, Germany: Huddle, 2009.

4. Italian

Batella, Fausto. *Football in Italy—I Primi Passi*. Montefiascone, Viterbo, Italy: Studio Batella, 2003.
———. *Football Italo Americano*. Montefiascone, Viterbo, Italy: Studio Batella, 1992.
———. *Gladiatori Migranti-Dall'Italia Alla National*. Montefiascone, Viterbo, Italy: Studio Batella, 2005.
———. *Jack Kerouac: Halfback: Il protagonista del beat generation e il gioco del football*. Montefiascone, Viterbo, Italy: Studio Batella, 2010.
———. *Rapido Jack*. Montefiascone, Viterbo, Italy: Studio Batella, 2002.
———. *Spaghetti Football—Il Campo di Vince*. Montefiascone, Viterbo, Italy: Studio Batella, 2002.
Exley, Frederick. *Appunti di un Tifoso*. Padua, Veneto, Italy: Alet Edizioni, 2005.
Grisham, John. *Il Professionista*. Milan, Italy: Mondadori, 2009.

5. Spanish

Crossingham, John. *Futbol Americano en Accion*. New York: Crabtree, 2005. (juvenile)
Perez Gimenez, Diego. *Futbol Americano para Todos*. College Station, Tex.: Virtualbookworm.com Publishing, 2008.

6. British

Horne, Nicky. *The Complete American Football Book*. London: Robson, 1986.
Kelner, Simon. *The Puffin Book of American Football*. London: Puffin, 1988.
Morrison, Ian. *American Football Fact Book*. London: Guinness, 1992.
Phillips, Radcliffe R. *British American Football Official Rule Book*. London: Virgin Books, 1987.

VII. PERIODICALS

Blue and Gold Illustrated (Notre Dame). Durham, N.C.: Coman Publishing. (20 issues annually)

Cavalier Corner (University of Virginia). Durham, N.C.: Coman Publishing. (Six issues annually)
Football Digest (1973–2005). Evanston, Ill.: Century Publishing.
Gridiron Strategies. North Palm Beach, Fla.: AFM Media. (six issues annually)
Inside the Auburn Tigers. Auburn, Ala.: Auburn University Press. (12 issues annually)
NFL Magazine (only four issues published 2011–2012). New York: Dauphin Media Group.
Pro Football Weekly. Riverwoods, Ill: Hub Arkush. (30 issues annually)
Sooners Illustrated (University of Oklahoma). Scout Publishing. (10 issues annually)
The Wolfpacker (University of North Carolina). Durham, N.C.: Coman Publishing. (Six issues annually)
The Wolverine (University of Michigan). Durham, N.C.: Coman Publishing. (11 issues annually)

VIII. PROGRAMS

College and professional football game programs often provide much useful information.

IX. WEBSITES

www.profootballresearchers.org (Professional Football Researchers Association)
www.pro-football-reference.com (professional football records)
www.secsportsfan.com/college-football-association.html (Intercollegiate Football Researchers Association)
www.collegefootball.org (College Football Hall of Fame)
www.cfbdatawarehouse.com (college football records)
www.fightsongs.com (college fight songs)
www.nfl.com (National Football League)
www.profootballhof.com (Pro Football Hall of Fame)
www.cfhof.ca (Canadian Football Hall of Fame)
www.cfl.ca (Canadian Football League)
www.arenafootball.com (Arena Football League)
www.ncaafootball.com (National Collegiate Athletic Association)

In addition, many professional football players maintain their own websites with varying amounts of information and insight.

About the Author

John Grasso was born in New York, New York, and raised in Whitestone, New York. Educated as an accountant, he spent most of his working life in data processing. Grasso moved to Guilford, New York, in 1980. He has written on boxing, basketball, and tennis and traveled extensively, visiting more than 40 countries and attending eight Olympic Games with his wife, Dorothy, and his two children, Steven and Laurel.

A sports historian, Grasso has been the treasurer of the International Society of Olympic Historians since 2004, and he is a member of the Association for Professional Basketball Research, the North American Society for Sport History, and the Professional Football Researchers Association. He founded the International Boxing Research Organization in 1982.

Grasso's published work on boxing includes *505 Boxing Questions Your Friends Can't Answer*, with Bert R. Sugar; *The 100 Greatest Boxers of All Time*, with Bert R. Sugar; *The Olympic Games Boxing Record Book*; and *1984 Ring Record Book and Boxing Encyclopedia*, for which he served as the Olympic editor. He also contributed boxing essays to the *Biographical Dictionary of American Sports* and *American National Biography*, as well as several columns to *Ring* magazine and *Boxing and Wrestling* magazine.

Grasso has also written about basketball in such books as *Historical Dictionary of Basketball* and has written two monographs, *The Absurd "Official" Statistics of the 1954–55 NBA Season*, and *Olympic Games Basketball Records*. Along with Robert Bradley, he authored a section on early professional basketball in *Total Basketball*, and he has contributed to several editions of *Harvey Pollack's NBA Statistical Yearbook*, as well as to Robert Bradley's *Compendium of Professional Basketball, 2nd edition*. He is also the author of *Historical Dictionary of Tennis*, also in Scarecrow Press's Historical Dictionaries of Sports series.